THE HARMONY OF SYMBOLS

The Windmill Hill causewayed enclosure, Wiltshire

By

Alasdair Whittle, Joshua Pollard and Caroline Grigson

With contributions by

Janet Ambers, Don Brothwell, Joanna Brück, Caroline Cartwright, Andrew David,
Andrew Fairbairn, Mark Fishpool, Michael Hamilton, Rupert Housley, Richard Macphail,
David McOmish, Amanda Rouse, Stephen Rowland, Michael Walker, Michael Wysocki
and Lesley Zienkiewicz

Cardiff Studies in Archaeology

Oxbow Books
1999

Published by
Oxbow Books, Park End Place, Oxford OX1 1HN

ISBN 1 900188 89 9

This book is available direct from
Oxbow Books, Park End Place, Oxford OX1 1HN
(Phone: 01865–241249; Fax: 01865–794449)

and

The David Brown Book Company
PO Box 511, Oakville, CT 06779, USA
(Phone: 860–945–9329; Fax: 860–945–9468)

or from our website

www.oxbowbooks.com

This report has been published with the support of The National Trust, English Heritage, The Wiltshire Archaeological and Natural History Society, The Marc Fitch Fund, University of Wales College, Newport, and Cardiff University.

*Cover: Windmill Hill from the air from the north-west.
Photo: © Crown copyright. NMR 15403/22.*

*Printed in Great Britain at
The Short Run Press, Exeter*

for Isobel Smith

'There are some heights in Wessex, shaped as if by a kindly hand,
for thinking, dreaming, dying on ....'
Thomas Hardy, *Wessex Heights* (1896)

'I am quite convinced that the excavation of Windmill Hill will throw a flood of light upon the
neolithic period; in fact it will almost mark the beginning of our knowledge of this period.'
O.G.S. Crawford, letter to H. St
George Gray, November 13, 1924

'What giants ?' said Sancho Panza.
'Those that you see there,' replied his master, 'those with the long arms, some of which are as
much as two leagues in length.'
'But look your Grace, those are not giants but windmills, and what appear to be arms are their
wings which, when whirled in the breeze, cause the millstone to go.'
'It is plain to be seen,' said Don Quixote, 'that you have had little experience in this matter of
adventures.'
Cervantes, *The Ingenious Gentleman, Don Quixote de la Mancha*

Contents

Addresses of Authors

AMBERS, CARTWRIGHT:
Department of Scientific Research,
The British Museum,
London WC1B 3DG

BROTHWELL, ROWLAND:
Department of Archaeology,
University of York,
King's Manor,
York YO1 2EP

BRÜCK:
Department of Archaeology,
University College,
Belfield,
Dublin 4

DAVID:
Ancient Monuments Laboratory,
The English Heritage Archaeology Centre,
Fort Cumberland,
Fort Cumberland Road,
Eastney,
Portsmouth, PO4 9LD

FAIRBAIRN, GRIGSON, MACPHAIL:
Institute of Archaeology,
University College London,
31–34 Gordon Square,
London WC1H OPY

FISHPOOL, WHITTLE, WYSOCKI, ZIENKIEWICZ:
School of History and Archaeology,
Cardiff University,
Cardiff CF1 3XU

HAMILTON, POLLARD:
Department of Humanities and Science,
University of Wales College, Newport,
Caerleon Campus,
PO Box 179,
Newport NP18 3YG

HOUSLEY:
Department of Archaeology,
University of Glasgow,
10 The Square,
Glasgow G12 8QQ

McOMISH:
Royal Commission
on the Historical Monuments of England,
Brooklands,
24 Brooklands Avenue,
Cambridge CB2 2BU

ROUSE:
School of Engineering,
Cardiff University,
Cardiff CF2 1XH

WALKER:
Department of Geography,
University of Wales Lampeter,
Lampeter,
Ceredigion SA48 7ED

Acknowledgements

Alasdair Whittle

As ever with a project of this size and duration, the list of debts incurred is long. Consent to excavate was granted by the Secretary of State for the Environment, through the good offices of English Heritage; I am especially grateful to Brian Davison for his guidance. Access to the site was granted by the owner, The National Trust; I am especially grateful to David Thackray for his advice, to Simon Evans, then area warden, for his practical help, and to the tenant farmer Robin Butler, for his forbearance. The 1988 fieldwork was supported by grants from The British Academy, The Society of Antiquaries, The Wiltshire Archaeological and Natural History Society, The Prehistoric Society, and Cardiff University. Radiocarbon dates were undertaken by The British Museum and the Oxford Accelerator Unit. Gill and Robin Swanton gave magnificent support at base camp. I am very grateful to all the Cardiff students and other volunteers who did the hard work, and to Jim Bonnor for his organisation. Subsequent research and then preparations for publication in the Alexander Keiller Museum, Avebury, were facilitated by Stanley Jenkins of English Heritage and especially later by Ros Cleal and Clare Conybeare; thanks are due also to Melanie Pomeroy. I am very grateful to Richard Bradley, Barry Cunliffe, Ian Kinnes and John Evans for support and encouragement; to Julian Richards and Niall Sharples for advice in advance of excavation; to Melanie Pomeroy, Nick Barton, Dave Field, Martyn Barber and Duncan Coe for help with illustrations and maps; to Lesley Zienkiewicz and especially Rick Schulting and Amanda Rouse for invaluable help with editing; and to Chris Evans, Francis Pryor and Niels Andersen for information about their own excavations at similar enclosures. Martyn Barber, Richard Bradley, Ros Cleal, Mark Edmonds, John Evans, Frances Healy, Ian Hodder and Rick Schulting gave constructive criticism of earlier drafts. The drawings were done by Howard Mason. Finally, this research would not have been possible without the cooperation and hard work of all the colleagues involved. It is perhaps invidious to single any one out, but special tribute must be paid to Caroline Grigson for her persistence and to Joshua Pollard for his ground-breaking work on the Keiller archive and for his considerable contribution to bringing the report together.

Finally, all involved would like to pay tribute to Isobel Smith, as a link between us and the 1920s research, and for the inspiration provided to us all by her classic book *Windmill Hill and Avebury*, which this report supplements and complements.

Archive

The finds and archive of the 1988 excavations have been deposited in the Alexander Keiller Museum, Avebury, to join the existing Keiller archive already housed there.

Radiocarbon Dates

Radiocarbon dates are normally given in the text in calibrated form as ranges at one standard deviation, using the OxCal programme v2.18 (Bronk Ramsey 1995). Original determinations, where stated, are given in years BP. For further details see chapter 5.

Chronological Terminology

In the text that follows, we use both 'Earlier Neolithic' and 'Early Neolithic' to denote the period *c.* 4000–3000 BC, and both 'Later Neolithic' and 'Late Neolithic' to denote the period *c.* 3000–2000 BC, according to the preferences of individual authors.

Summary

The Earlier Neolithic enclosure on Windmill Hill, north Wiltshire, consists of three circuits of causewayed, interrupted or segmented ditches (the outer one accompanied by a bank), which encompass an area of over 8 ha. The site was first investigated by Kendall and was then the scene of the first major investigation of a causewayed enclosure in Britain, carried out in the 1920s by Alexander Keiller. This work was later published by Isobel Smith, supplemented by her own excavations at the site in 1957–58 (Smith 1965a). The enclosure was also chosen as the eponymous site for his Windmill Hill culture by Piggott (1954).

This report presents the results of excavations in 1988 at the site, together with reassessments of the investigations by Keiller and Smith. The 1988 research was carried out as part of a wider research investigation into the Neolithic sequence and environment of the area, and into the context in which Neolithic monuments were built, used and abandoned.

Detailed results are set out by category and theme, chapter by chapter. Most chapters include specific reference to and reassessment of the earlier investigations, notably chapter 3 on the detail of the Keiller excavations, chapter 11 on the animal bone, and chapter 13 on pottery. An extensive range of environmental evidence is presented in chapters 6–10 and 12, covering soils, land snails, plant remains, charcoals, pollen and amphibian and small mammal remains.

The enclosure belonged to the period which succeeds the earliest stages of the Neolithic, and dates to the middle of the fourth millennium BC (in calibrated radiocarbon chronology). It was constructed in a world of woodland, in which some shrines and ossuaries had already been built, marking out the area as special. People herded animals, especially cattle, in and through woodland, and in the probable mosaic of short-lived and small-scale clearances cultivated some cereals. The idea of such a construction, quite new in southern Britain and monumental in the sense that the outer ditch had a maximum diameter of 360 m, could have come from memory of a distant Neolithic past in Europe. It is possible, but unproven, that the outer circuit was added after the middle and inner circuits.

The hill chosen for the construction of the enclosure was probably already a special place, marked by a history of occupation, burial and perhaps feasting. It was a prominent location, widely visible, although the enclosure itself may not have been easy to see from any distance, not least for the woodland surrounding it. Construction of the enclosure must have involved many people, and its size allows many people at a time to have been present. Imported pottery and stone axes suggest that some people came from far afield. It is unlikely that anyone lived permanently at the site, and the people who used the enclosure may have ranged, at varying temporal and spatial scales, over a wide area.

The ditches of the enclosure contained considerable deposits of animal bone, some human bone, pottery and lithics. The character of these is fully described and discussed. The nature of these deposits, dominated by animal bone, suggests that the use of the site could be characterised by a repeated series of small-scale events; though a considerable audience could have gathered around even a single ditch segment. It is unclear therefore how many people would have gathered for any one event, how decisions were taken as to what was appropriate to deposit and where, and whether every event of deposition was of equal significance. The monument could be seen as the preserve of preeminent groups in society, but it may also have fostered a very wide participation: the harmony of symbols of the title of the report. It is not easy to discern individual actors, but by comparison with other monuments and occupations it is possible that issues of gender role between men and women were played out in the layout and use of the enclosure. In total, the enclosure could be seen by the end of the primary phase of repeated use to have a map-like character, with differing deposits emphasising different circuits and parts of circuits. In the outer circuit, the principal concern could have been with nature or the natural surroundings, with the dead, ancestors and the past, with animals in their own right and in relationship with people, and perhaps with the unsocialised or not fully socialised; in the middle and inner circuits, the focus may have been on domesticity, socialisation, and the sphere of the living including their use of animals in meals, feasts and rituals.

The enclosure, once built, may have had an immediacy of significance or an importance which was taken for granted. It must also have held many wider meanings. Its layout symbolised both inclusion and exclusion, and perhaps themes such as the relationship between culture and nature, or between people and their surroundings. Its idea drew on memory of the past, however imperfect, and the enclosure may itself have been a metaphor for time. A very wide range of concerns and activities is expressed and presented through the deposits made at the site, including subsistence, eating and drinking, perhaps feasting, alliance and exchange, and death, as well as perhaps gender roles as already noted. The consumption of meat, apart from other foods, was clearly important. Some bone assemblages appear to derive from entire or semi-entire individuals, deposited complete with ligaments and flesh, but animal remains were normally deposited as groups, spreads or scatters of bone derived from different parts of the body of different species, presumably discarded without flesh; detailed criteria are presented for the different kinds of history which can be seen in the various deposits. The possible storage and likely selection behind many deposits also drew on the past. Eating animals necessitates killing them, and the symbolic importance of sacrifice, for example as a route to the divine, or as a means of capturing fertility and vitality, can be considered. Animal bone may also have been treated in ways parallel to human bone.

The later history of the enclosure is also considered, principally in the Later Neolithic and Early Bronze Age. Renewed occupation or activity may have reaffirmed the memory of the place as special.

Résumé

(traduit par Christian Jeunesse)

L'enceinte Néolithique ancien de Windmill Hill (north Wiltshire) se compose de trois systèmes de fossés interrompus ou segmentés (le fossé externe est accompagné par une levée) qui englobent une aire de plus de 8 ha. Les premières recherches sur ce site sont l'oeuvre de Kendall; plus tard, dans les années vingt, une grande opération, la première de cette ampleur sur un site fossoyé, a été menée par Alexander Keiller. Ce travail a été publié par Isobel Smith, en même temps que les résultats de ses propres fouilles conduites en 1957–58 (Smith 1965a). L'enceinte a également été choisie comme site éponyme de la culture de Windmill Hill par Piggott (1954).

Dans ce travail, nous présentons le résultat des fouilles menées en 1988 en même temps qu'une révision des recherches de Keiller et Smith. Les recherches de 1988 s'inscrivent dans un programme plus vaste consacré à la séquence néolithique et à l'environnement de la région dont l'un des objectifs a été de comprendre dans quel contexte les monuments néolithiques ont été construits, utilisés et abandonnés.

Les résultats détaillés sont exposés par thèmes et par catégories, chapitre après chapitre. La plupart des chapitres reprennent les résultats des fouilles antérieures, en particulier les chapitres 3 (détail de la fouille de Keiller), 11 (ossements animaux) et 13 (céramique). Un large éventail de données concernant l'environnement est présenté dans les chapitres 6–10 et 12 (pédologie, escargots terrestres, restes botaniques, charbons de bois, pollen, amphibiens et petits mammifères).

L'enceinte appartient à la période qui suit le Néolithique le plus ancien et date du milieu du quatrième millénaire av. J.-Ch. Elle a été aménagée dans une zone boisée dans laquelle on avait déjà installé des sépultures et des ossuaires qui donnaient un statut particulier au lieu. Les habitants de la région élevaient du bétail (particulièrement le boeuf) dans la forêt et cultivaient des céréales dans des clairières de défrichement peu étendues et de courte durée de vie. L'idée d'une telle construction monumentale (le fossé externe présente un diamètre maximal de 360 m), assez nouvelle dans le sud de l'Angleterre, pourrait provenir du souvenir d'un Néolithique continental plus ancien. Sans qu'il soit possible de le prouver, il se pourrait que le fossé externe ait été rajouté après les deux autres.

La colline choisie pour la construction de l'enceinte avait probablement une signification particulière liée à une utilisation déjà ancienne comme habitat, lieu de sépulture et, éventuellement, de cérémonies. C'était un endroit remarquable, visible de loin, ce qui n'était probablement pas le cas de l'enceinte elle-même à cause, entre autres, du caractère boisé des environs. Sa construction a du impliquer un grand nombre de personnes et sa taille permettait le rassemblement simultané de très nombreuses personnes. Des poteries et des haches en pierre importées suggèrent que certains visiteurs venaient de régions lointaines. Il est peu probable que quiconque ai vécu en permanence sur le site dont les utilisateurs devaient habiter dans les environs, sur des aires de taille variable suivant les époques.

Les fossés ont livré des dépôts très importants d'ossements animaux, quelques os humains, de la poterie et de l'outillage lithique. Tous ces ensembles font l'objet d'une description et d'un commentaire détaillés. La nature de ces dépôts dominés par les ossement animaux suggère que l'utilisation du site pourrait être caractérisée par une série répétée d'événements d'échelle restreinte, et cela bien qu'une foule importante ai pu se rassembler même autour d'un unique segment de fossé. Le nombre de personnes qui se réunissait pour un événement est difficile à déterminer, tout comme la manière dont était décidé ce qui devait être déposé et à quel endroit. On ne sait pas davantage si les cérémonies de dépôt avaient toutes la même signification. Le monument était peut-être réservé à un groupe prééminent dans la société, mais on ne peut exclure une participation beaucoup plus large, comme le suggère le titre de ce travail. Il n'est pas facile de discerner des acteurs individuels; cependant, par comparaison avec d'autres monuments, on peut imaginer que les relations entre les genres (hommes et femmes) ont du jouer un rôle aussi bien dans l'aménagement que dans l'utilisation du monument. A la fin de la phase primaire d'utilisation répétée, l'enceinte devait avoir l'allure d'une carte, avec différents dépôt mettant l'accent sur les différents fossés ou segments de fossés. Au niveau du fossé externe, l'accent a sans doute été mis sur la nature ou l'environnement naturel, les morts, les ancêtres et le passé, avec les animaux en tant que tels et dans leur relation avec les humains, ainsi que, peut-être, avec les individus non socialisés ou incomplètement socialisés. Le fossé central et le fossé interne étaient probablement associés plutôt au domestique, à la socialisation et à la sphère des vivants avec, entre autres, une insistance sur leur manière d'utiliser les animaux dans des repas, des fêtes et des rituels.

Une fois construite, l'enceinte a probablement eu tout

de suite une grande signification. Elle possédait probablement bien d'autres dimensions. Son aménagement symbolisait à la fois l'exclusion et l'inclusion, et, vraisemblablement, des thèmes comme la relation entre la culture et la nature, ou encore entre le groupe et ses voisins. Son idée évoquait la mémoire du passé, même imparfaitement, et l'enceinte elle-même a peut être fonctionné comme une métaphore du temps. Un éventail très large de préoccupations et d'activités est exprimée et présentée à travers les ensembles déposés sur le site, la subsistance, le fait de boire et de manger, peut-être de faire la fête, l'alliance, l'échange et la mort ainsi que, comme nous l'avons déjà noté, les rôles de chacun des genres. Il est clair que la consommation de viande était importante. Quelques-uns des assemblages osseux semblent dériver d'animaux entiers ou de moitiés d'animaux déposés complets avec la chair et les ligaments, mais les restes animaux étaient ordinairement déposés sous la forme de groupes ou d'épandages d'ossements probablement rejetés alors qu'il ne portait plus de chair. Des critères détaillés sont présentés pour les différentes sortes de scénarios qui peuvent se cacher derrière les différents types de dépôts osseux. Les activités de conservation et, éventuellement, de sélection que l'on croit percevoir dans nombre de ces dépôts faisait également resurgir le passé. Pour manger des animaux, il est nécessaire de les tuer, et l'importance symbolique du sacrifice comme moyen d'accéder au divin, ou comme un moyen d'acquérir fertilité et vitalité, peut également être envisagée. Les os d'animaux ont également pu recevoir des traitements analogues à ceux des os humains.

L'histoire plus récente de l'enceinte est également présentée, en particulier pour ce qui est des occupations néolithique plus tardives et du Bronze ancien. Des occupations ou des activités nouvelles ont pu réaffirmer le caractère particulier de la mémoire attachée à l'endroit.

Zusammenfassung
(übersetzt von Helga van den Boom)

Das Erdwerk des Frühneolithikums auf dem Windmill Hill (Nord-Wiltshire) besteht aus drei Kreisgräben vom Typ 'causewayed', d. h. aus segmentierten bzw. unterbrochenen Gräben; am Innenrand des äusseren verläuft ein Wall. Die ganze Anlage nimmt eine Fläche von ca. acht Hektar ein. Der Platz wurde zuerst durch Kendall untersucht; später, in den 20er Jahren, fand hier unter der Leitung von A. Keiller die erste grössere Untersuchung einer 'causewayed enclosure' in Grossbritannien statt. Diese Ausgrabung wurde von Isobel Smith veröffentlicht, ergänzt durch die Ergebnisse ihrer eigenen Ausgrabungen in den Jahren 1957–58. Das Erdwerk wurde auch namengebend für S. Piggotts (1954) 'Windmill Hill Kultur'.

Die vorliegende Studie präsentiert die Ergebnisse der Ausgrabungen im Jahr 1988, zusammen mit Nachuntersuchungen der Forschungen von Keiller und Smith. Die Untersuchung von 1988 wurde durchgeführt im Zuge einer breiter angelegten Erforschung der chronologischen Abfolge und der Umwelt der Region im Neolithikum sowie des Kontextes, in welchem die neolithischen Monumente gebaut, genutzt und aufgegeben wurden.

Die Ergebnisse werden in Kapiteln nach Fundgattungen und Fragestellungen detailliert abgehandelt. Die meisten Kapitel enthalten Verweise auf die früheren Untersuchungen und ihre Neubewertung, insbesondere Kapitel 3 auf die Details der Ausgrabungen Keillers, Kapitel 11 auf die Tierknochen, und Kapitel 13 auf die Keramik. Ein breites Spektrum von Umweltbefunden wird in den Kapiteln 6–10 und 12 vorgestellt. Es umfasst Böden, Schnecken, Pflanzenreste, Holzkohle, Pollen sowie Amphibien und kleine Säuger.

Das Erdwerk gehört in die Periode, die auf die frühesten Stufen des Neolithikums folgt, und datiert (kalibriert) in die Mitte des 4. Jahrtausends. Es wurde in einer waldigen Umgebung errichtet, in welcher Opferplätze und grössere Ansammlungen menschlicher Knochen, sog. 'ossuaries', bereits bestanden haben, die die Besonderheit der Gegend hervorhoben. Die Menschen betrieben an den Waldrändern und unter Nutzung des Waldes Viehzucht, insbesondere von Rindern. In begrenztem Umfang kultivierten sie auch Getreide in einem Mosaik von kurzlebigen und kleinräumigen Rodungen. Die Idee zu einer solchen Konstruktion, die ein *novum* im Süden Grossbritanniens war, und wegen ihrer Abmessungen – der äussere Graben hat einen grössten Durchmesser von 360 m – als monumental angesprochen werden kann, könnte von einer Erinnerung an eine weit zurückliegende Vergangenheit in Europa herrühren. Es ist wahrscheinlich, wenn auch nicht bewiesen, dass der äussere Graben später als der innere und der mittlere ausgehoben wurde.

Die Geländeerhebung, die für die Errichtung des Erdwerks gewählt wurde, war vermutlich schon durch die vorangegangene Siedlungsgeschichte, die Bestattungen und vielleicht auch Feste, die hier stattfanden, ein besonderer Platz. Es war zweifellos eine prominente, von weither sichtbare Lage, obwohl das Erdwerk selbst, vielleicht wegen der umgebenden Wälder, wahrscheinlich nicht leicht zu erkennen war. Der Bau des Erdwerks erforderte eine grössere Anzahl von Menschen, und seine Abmessungen erlaubten vielen, sich dort zur selben Zeit aufzuhalten. Importierte Keramik und Steinäxte lassen vermuten, dass auch Ortsfremde unter ihnen waren. Es ist unwahrscheinlich, dass innerhalb des Erdwerks jemand dauerhaft lebte. Genutzt wurde es wahrscheinlich von Gruppen, die als Hirten in einem zeitlich und räumlich unterschiedlichen Ausmass die Gegend durchstreift haben.

Die Gräben des Erdwerks enthalten grössere Mengen von Tierknochen, einige Menschenknochen, Keramik und bearbeitete Steine. Ihre Beschaffenheit wurde ausführlich beschrieben und diskutiert. Die Art der Deponierungen, bei denen Tierknochen dominieren, legt nahe, dass der Platz für wiederholte Folgen eher kleinräumiger Zusammenkünfte genutzt wurde, wenngleich prinzipiell eine beträchtliche Anzahl von Teilnehmern sich sogar um ein einzelnes Grabensegment versammeln konnte. Es ist daher völlig offen, wieviele Menschen sich für ein einzelnes Treffen versammelt haben, wie Entscheidungen getroffen wurden, was jeweils als zur Deponierung geeignet erachtet wurde und an welcher Stelle zu deponieren war, und ferner, ob jede Deponierung denselben Rang hatte. Das Monument könnte als eine Hinterlassenschaft herausragender gesellschaftlicher Gruppen angesehen werden, es mag aber genauso eine sehr breit angelegte Teilnahme begünstigt haben, in einer 'Harmonie von Symbolen' sozusagen wie sie der Titel der vorliegenden Studie nahelegt.

Es ist nicht einfach, einzelne Agierende zu unterscheiden, aber durch den Vergleich mit anderen Monumenten und Nutzungen ist es möglich, dass im Entwurf und der Nutzung des Erdwerks Geschlechterrollen dargestellt waren. Insgesamt könnte die Anlage am Ende der Hauptphase wiederholter Nutzung einen Landkartencharakter besessen haben, worin unterschiedliche Deponierungen die verschiedenen Kreise und Kreisabschnitte betonten. Der Hauptbezug beim äusseren Kreis könnte die Beziehung zur Natur und zur natürlichen Umgebung gewesen sein, auch zu den Toten, den Vorfahren und der Vergangenheit überhaupt wie auch zu den Tieren und ihres Verhältnisses zu den Menschen. Denkbar ist hier auch ein Bezug auf Menschen, die nicht oder noch nicht in die Gesellschaft integriert waren. Der Schwerpunkt beim mittleren und inneren Kreis könnte auf Domestikation, Sozialisation und auf der Sphäre der Lebenden gelegen haben, einschliesslich der Nutzung von Tieren in Mahlzeiten, Festen und Ritualen.

Das Erdwerk, einmal errichtet, dürfte seine Bedeutung und Wichtigkeit unmittelbar verkörpert und vermittelt haben. Es ist anzunehmen, dass es noch weitere, umfassendere Bedeutungen hatte. Die Anlage symbolisiert sowohl Einbeziehung wie Ausschluss, und vielleicht auch Aspekte wie die Beziehung zwischen Kultur und Natur, in anderen Worten zwischen den Menschen und ihrer Umwelt. Seine Idee beschwor die Erinnerung an die Vergangenheit, und das Erdwerk selbst mag eine Metapher für die Zeit gewesen sein.

Eine breite Skala von Bezügen und Tätigkeiten ist durch die Deponierungen ausgedrückt und vergegenständlicht, die auf dem Platz vorgenommen wurden, einschliesslich der Subsistenzaktivitäten, dem Essen und Trinken, vielleicht auch den Festlichkeiten, den Bündnissen und dem Austausch, dem Tod wie auch den schon genannten Geschlechterrollen. Das Verzehren von Fleisch, abgesehen von anderen Speisen, wär sicher sehr bedeutsam. Manche der Ansammlungen scheinen von ganzen oder halben Individuen zu stammen, die komplett im Verband deponiert worden waren. Zumeist wurden aber Tierreste in Gruppen oder als Streuungen von Knochen von verschiedenen Körperteilen und von verschiedenen Tierarten abgelegt. Es werden Kriterien für die verschiedenen Enstehungsarten benannt, wie sie sich an den unterschiedlich zusammengesetzten Depots ablesen lassen. Die mögliche Aufbewahrung und wahrscheinlich auch Selektion hinter vielen der Depots mag ebenfalls einen Bezug zur Vergangenheit enthalten haben. Das Verspeisen von Tieren setzt deren Tötung voraus und damit die symbolische Bedeutung des Opfers, z. B. als Zugang und Weg zum Göttlichen, oder auch als ein Mittel, Fruchtbarkeit und Lebenskraft einzufangen.

Die spatere Geschichte des Erdwerks wird ebenfalls berücksichtigt, insbesondere das späte Neolithikum und die frühe Bronzezeit. Eine erneute Inbesitznahme oder Aktivität mögen die Erinnerung an die Bedeutung des Platzes bestärkt haben.

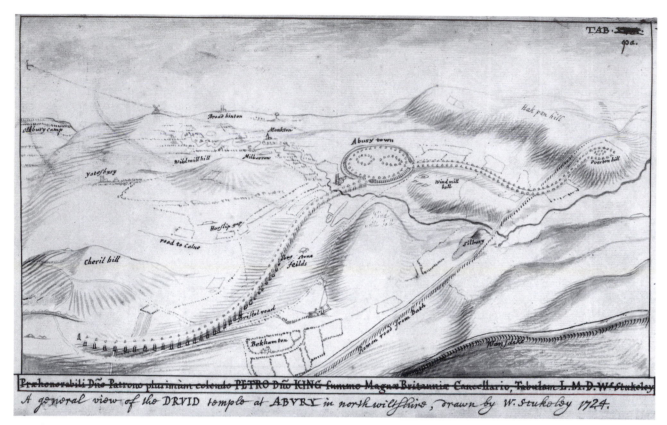

Fig. 1. A schematic Stukeley sketch of the Avebury complex, including Windmill Hill (Bodleian Library MS. Top. Gen. b.53, 31av).

Fig. 2. An idealised Stukeley version of Avebury, with a more realistic version of Windmill Hill in the background (Bodleian Library MS. Eng. Misc. b.65, 31).

1

History of Research and the 1988 Excavations

Alasdair Whittle

'A circular trench exceeding old': early records

Windmill Hill came quietly into the archaeological record. Silbury Hill was referred to in Camden's sixteenth-century *Britannia*, and Aubrey came across Avebury in the mid-seventeenth century. Windmill Hill first appears (figs 1–2) in the many sketches of the district by Stukeley from 1719–23 (Piggott 1985; Ucko *et al.* 1991), and there are later descriptions by him of 'a very delicate hill ... The turf as soft as velvet...' 'Tis encompassed with a circular trench exceeding old' (Stukeley 1743). Stukeley noted 15 round barrows on and below the hill, of which he opened one. By the early nineteenth century, Colt Hoare (1819, 95–96) reported that ploughing since Stukeley's day 'has committed sad havock with this hill, deprived it of its verdant turf, and levelled very considerably its sepulchral mounds, and earthen bank of enclosure. I have no doubt but that in remote times, this was one of the simple and primitive circles of the Britons, resembling those which I have mentioned in South Wiltshire, as placed on high ground'. Smith suggests that the ploughing began at the site during Colt Hoare's lifetime, pointing to the Napoleonic Wars as a possible context for opening up new areas of downland (Smith 1959).

There is no certain record of any barrow excavation by Colt Hoare and Cunnington at Windmill Hill, though there is a later report of such (A.C. Smith 1885, 88–90). Dean Merewether opened three barrows below the hill in 1849 when avoiding visitors to the tunnel into Silbury Hill. Merewether (1851, 93) mentioned the earthwork briefly: 'The apex of Windmill Hill is surrounded by a slight and single foss, in diameter – for it is almost an exact circle – about 150 yards'.

Late in the nineteenth century, A.C. Smith (1885, 88–90) judged that 'in all probability this was a British camp'. He referred to a single ditch and bank, which 'though in places indistinct, may be traced on the land when fallow, all round the south and east of the hill, and partly on the north; and is prolonged nearly up to the plantation on the extreme west of the hill'. Without specifically committing himself on the age of the site, he drew on the views of contemporaries like Evans to suggest a date for the Stone Period of 3000–4000 years ago. In the early twentieth century, Mrs Cunnington adjudged 'the old hill camp' at Knap Hill, now recognised as another causewayed enclosure not far away from Windmill Hill, as 'of very great antiquity', and concluded about finds on the bottom of its ditch that 'it is quite likely that they are Neolithic' (Cunnington 1912, 56–57). There is no record that she took any interest in Windmill Hill.

Kendall, Crawford and Keiller

This was the slow background to the rapid changes of the 1920s, when the efforts of Kendall, Crawford and Keiller established the date, extent and significance of the site. This story is well known (Smith 1965a; Malone 1989; Barber *et al.* 1999; Murray 1999) but needs brief, selective rehearsal again in order to put the work reported on here into context. More detail specifically relevant to the development of Keiller's excavations is given in chapter 3.

From the early part of the century several people began collecting struck flint from the field surfaces of the area. (The only lithic implements from the area referred to by Evans (1872) had been from barrow excavations.) Among these was the rector of Winterbourne Bassett, H.G.O. Kendall, who collected on the slopes of Windmill Hill itself (Kendall 1914; 1919; 1922). He became interested in the enclosure itself and in 1922–23 dug sections across what is now recognised as the outer ditch (in the segment just to the south of Outer Ditch I; Smith 1965a, 1), recovering Neolithic pottery. Sketches of sections survive in his notebooks in Avebury Museum (along with cures for indigestion and lists of parishioners to visit). His work was visited by O.G.S. Crawford, newly appointed archaeological officer of the Ordnance Survey and responsible

Fig. 3. Alexander Keiller on Windmill Hill (photo: Alexander Keiller Museum, Avebury).

Fig. 4. (Left to right) W.E.V. Young, Harold St George Gray and Alexander Keiller on Windmill Hill (photo: Alexander Keiller Museum, Avebury).

for encouraging so much activity in the field at this time (Crawford 1955). During a visit in early 1923 Crawford confirmed what Kendall had already recognised: the existence of the middle ditch; and during sandwiches on top of one of the barrows Kendall spotted the inner ditch (Crawford 1953, 133).

When a wireless station was threatened on the hill in 1923, Kendall contacted Crawford. Crawford in turn contacted among others Alexander Keiller, then in search of an archaeological outlet for his considerable energies and financial resources. Part of the site was eventually purchased by Keiller in 1924. As Crawford put it, 'The scheme was eventually dropped, not on grounds of amenity or archaeology, but because the RAF objected to high masts near their aerodromes on Salisbury Plain. But I wanted to be sure that such a threat should never occur again, and I persuaded Mr Keiller to buy the hill' (Crawford 1953, 134). Keiller was keen to excavate a site whose age and significance had been recognised by Crawford. As he was inexperienced, it was necessary for an assistant to be engaged to satisfy other archaeologists (in a 1925 letter Keiller wrote that 'Goddard and the Cunningtons regard Wiltshire as their special preserve'; the Keiller correspondence and diaries are held in the Avebury museum), and Crawford was instrumental in securing the services of Harold St. George Gray, first trained by Pitt Rivers (Bowden 1991) and who had already undertaken excavations at Avebury itself (Gray 1935). Curiously, Crawford makes very little of his fundamental contribution in his auto-biography (Crawford 1955), though his account is fuller in his slightly earlier book on field archaeology (Crawford 1953). The excavations began before it was realised that the site was already scheduled.

Isobel Smith has set out in detail the history of (and surviving sources for) Keiller's excavations of 1925–29 (Smith 1965a, 2–3), and some further details are given in chapter 3 (figs 3–6). Gray was in charge of methods and recording until the middle of the 1927 season. His diary (in Avebury museum) for May 26, 1927 laconically records 'My last morning at Windmill Hill ... I left the ground finally at 11.45 am. Left Avebury 12.45 to catch 1.15 train at Swindon in Mrs Keiller's Lancia'. This was preceded by considerable frustration on Keiller's part. To judge by letters to Crawford in 1925, Keiller had been impatient with Gray's standards from the outset. By 1926, a letter from Keiller complained that 'this is just the sort of muddle in recording which has cost my wife and myself hours of useless vain endeavour in the museum ever since the first lot of finds came up from Taunton' (Gray's base). After Gray's departure, Keiller caused re-excavation of the ditch segments dug in 1925. Keiller was determined on high standards. A letter in late 1926 referred to 'the unedifying behaviour of certain visitors last year, who were in the habit of jumping into the cuttings and stamping about in them, and even grubbing about with trowels and forks. This particularly applied to Passmore...'. (A.D. Passmore, who lived near Swindon, was an avid flint collector in the region.)

The excavations continued until 1929, when the record-ing was probably at its best. In 1926–27 the intention declared by letter to Crawford was to excavate the entire site ('and any adjacent ground which might tend to throw light upon that site'), apart from a control sample for future generations, and to publish reports on every three years' work at three-year intervals beginning in 1928 (Crawford 1927). In July 1929, on the last day of the excavations,

Fig. 5. The excavation team in 1928. Front row (left to right): W.E.V. Young; Veronica Keiller; Alexander Keiller; ?Kay Duncan (photo: Alexander Keiller Museum, Avebury).

Keiller had a bad accident driving his Bugatti in Savernake Forest. In a letter to Gray he wrote, 'we were climbing this hill at a reasonable speed, but not by any manner of means, I consider, an excessive one, viz. some 84 miles an hour, when my back axle broke and, the car turning round and rising into the air, we hurtled ourselves on the angular portion of the bridge'. In a letter in 1930 he reported that he had been prevented from working for several months, and for this and perhaps other reasons, the work at Windmill Hill was not resumed.

A letter to Gray in 1932 excused the delay in publication as 'originally due to reasons outside my control, and more recently to the fact that work in the museum has brought to light much further data'. Keiller did prepare extensive lists of finds, layer charts and so on; and specialist reports were considered (for example by Professor D.M.S. Watson on the animal bones). Letters to the Clarendon Press by Keiller in 1931 discuss publication of one volume on the 1925–28 seasons, and of another on the 1929 season ('The second volume I would suggest should contain nothing except the superb 1929 report, which is as complete as a report from Windmill Hill could ever possibly be'). Another letter in 1932 accepts proofs of a new format, and there are a few pages of proofs surviving in the Avebury museum which relate to the 1925–27 seasons. The letter continues, 'As for new reports, we have not got them finished yet, but it has not been for want of work...'. It remains unclear whether any single report was actually completed, because the proofs may only be of a sample section to test a larger format. Only a summary account of the site actually appeared in print (Keiller 1934).

From 1934 Keiller was active at Avebury. (His young

Fig. 6. Alexander Keiller in his Citroën half-track outside The Red Lion, Avebury (photo: Alexander Keiller Museum, Avebury).

assistant, Stuart Piggott, had joined him in 1933, having got to know him through the private museum of Windmill Hill material at Keiller's home in London (Piggott 1983).) In 1937 Keiller achieved full ownership of Windmill Hill, and had all the excavated ditches dug out again, as well as the ditch of the Picket Barrow, the bell barrow within the middle ditch (Winterbourne Monkton 1). Much activity centred around restoration of the archaeological remains and their presentation to the public. This involved re-excavating those ditches previously dug, as well as returfing the mound and ditches of the bell and bowl barrows

(Winterbourne Monkton 1 and 2) and the enclosure ditches. The original edge of the outer ditch was restored in the area where it had been cut into by the adjacent chalk quarry. Keiller also had rabbit-proof fencing erected around the site and converted the arable fields on the south side to pasture. The entire site was then opened up to the public.

According to the diary of W.E.V. Young (Keiller's foreman, who later became custodian of the Avebury Museum), by 1948 Keiller's third wife, Doris Emerson Chapman, was considering a general account of Windmill Hill and Avebury, but within a few months Keiller had denied her and others access to the archive. Some of the archive had gone by the time it came to be worked on by Isobel Smith after Keiller's death (Smith 1965a, 3), but the circumstances of these losses remain unexplained. Windmill Hill was later used as the type site for the southern British primary Neolithic culture by Piggott (1954), whose book included the first published sections of the enclosure ditches.

Keiller died in 1955; Windmill Hill had been acquired by The National Trust in 1943. Isobel Smith was commissioned by Mrs Gabrielle Keiller, Keiller's widow, to prepare a publication on his work at both Windmill Hill and Avebury. She carried out limited excavations on Windmill Hill in 1957–58, to check details of stratigraphy (pl. 4). Her ensuing account of Windmill Hill has long been a classic of its kind (Smith 1965a). The intention of the present report is to complement this rather than to replace it.

The fieldwork of 1957–58 was followed in 1959–60 by the refilling of the ditches. All the open ditch segments from earlier excavation were filled with soil and rubble brought from elsewhere, and then sown with grass. Shallow depressions were deliberately left in order to mark the location of these segments and to show the intervening causeways. The remains of these renovations retain a fresh and distinctive profile, and today are the most clearly visible elements of the surviving Neolithic enclosures on Windmill Hill (see McOmish, below).

The 1988 excavations

The 1988 season was part of a wider programme of investigation, from 1987 to 1993, into the Neolithic sequence and context of the area (see Whittle 1993; 1994; 1997a; Whittle *et al.* 1993; forthcoming; Evans *et al.* 1993). The area is a promising one in which to investigate many aspects of the Neolithic period, but the fame of the area has somewhat run ahead of our detailed knowledge of it. Since Keiller's day, there had been further notable fieldwork, for example at West Kennet, Horslip, South Street and Beckhampton long barrows (Piggott 1962a; Ashbee *et al.* 1979; see also Barker 1985), Knap Hill causewayed enclosure (Connah 1965), an occupation at Cherhill (Evans and Smith 1983) and pits under round

barrows at Roughridge and Hemp Knoll (WANHM 1965, 132–33; Robertson-Mackay 1980). Much of this work was episodic, but environmental investigations both on the surrounding downland and in the upper Kennet valley itself provided stronger continuity of research (Evans 1972; Evans *et al.* 1985; 1988; 1993; Ashbee *et al.* 1979). The strategy of the overall project was to sample a number of sites, rather than explore a single site in more detail. Other sites investigated in the project, Easton Down long barrow to the south-west, Millbarrow chambered tomb to the north of Windmill Hill, and the West Kennet palisade enclosures (with Silbury Hill) have already been published (Whittle 1993; 1994; 1997a; Whittle *et al.* 1993). The basic aims have been in each case to obtain radiocarbon dates and fuller environmental evidence, with the hope of establishing a more secure local sequence and a fuller sense of environmental variation through time and across the region. As part of the same project, research in 1993 on the slopes of Windmill Hill outside the causewayed enclosure was based on surface survey, test pits and very limited excavation of Earlier and Later Neolithic pits; results will be published separately (Whittle *et al.* forthcoming) but are discussed briefly in chapter 17.

At Windmill Hill itself, there were only three radiocarbon dates available before 1988, all on charcoal: one from the upper fill of the outer ditch (OD V); one, a bulked sample, from the primary fills of three segments of the outer and middle ditches (OD IV and V, and MD XII); and one from the old land surface below the outer bank (Outer Bank VI) (Smith 1965a, 11 and 28). Some pollen analysis had been possible of samples collected in 1957–58 from the buried soil under the outer bank, and there was unsystematic molluscan analysis of samples from the same context and the adjoining Outer Ditch V (Smith 1965a, chapter 3). Detailed molluscan analysis was later undertaken of a small portion of buried soil under the outer bank (Evans 1972). In both aspects there was clearly considerable scope for more precise results.

The excavations of 1988 were also undertaken in the general hope of recovering a range of other information relevant to the use of the site. In particular, studies by Caroline Grigson of the animal bone retained from the Keiller excavations had indicated both variation in the spatial occurrence of different species and skeletal parts, and very uneven recovery in, and retention after, the Keiller excavations. Independent study by Thomas (1991) had similar implications. There was also a general hope that fresh excavation would make further sense of the information from the Keiller excavations. The account given by Smith (1965a) is very general, and there is little sense of variation across the site. The 1988 excavations were also conducted at a time when notions of 'structured deposition' were being debated (see Richards and Thomas 1984; Edmonds 1993), and recording was designed to capture in detail the patterning of deposits in the ditches. Because the site is scheduled, however, the 1988 excavations were necessarily on a small scale. Seven cuttings (counting Trench B and BB as separate: see chapter 4) were dug in 1988, but generated a considerable amount of evidence.

It is evident from recent excavations at other causewayed enclosures that very large-scale investigations are needed for better understanding of this kind of monument (e.g. Mercer 1980; Dixon 1988; Pryor 1988b; C. Evans 1988b; Hodder 1992). At the time of excavation in 1988, it is fair to say that it was not anticipated how much could be done with the surviving Keiller archive on Windmill Hill. Keiller's work, despite the imperfections of recording and recovery, and the subsequent losses from the archive, was far in advance of its time in the extent of examination achieved. It is to the great credit of Joshua Pollard (Pollard 1993a) and other colleagues who report here that so much understanding of spatial variation within the site has been recovered.

The structure and scope of this report

This report first describes the site and presents in more detail results from the individual ditch segments excavated by Keiller. The 1988 excavations are then described. Where possible and appropriate, the specialist reports re-evaluate material from the Keiller excavations, but this is an incomplete task. More detailed consideration needs to be given to the flint assemblage; and it will be desirable to analyse samples of pottery scientifically (see Cleal 1992c, 303; as this report goes to press, an initial programme of lipid analysis is being started by Richard Evershed). This is work for the future. The primary focus here is on achievable results from the site, which lead to new interpretations of the enclosure. The final discussion is deliberately confined to such interpretation of meanings at Windmill Hill itself. It is another task for the future to relate the enclosure to a wider Neolithic world.

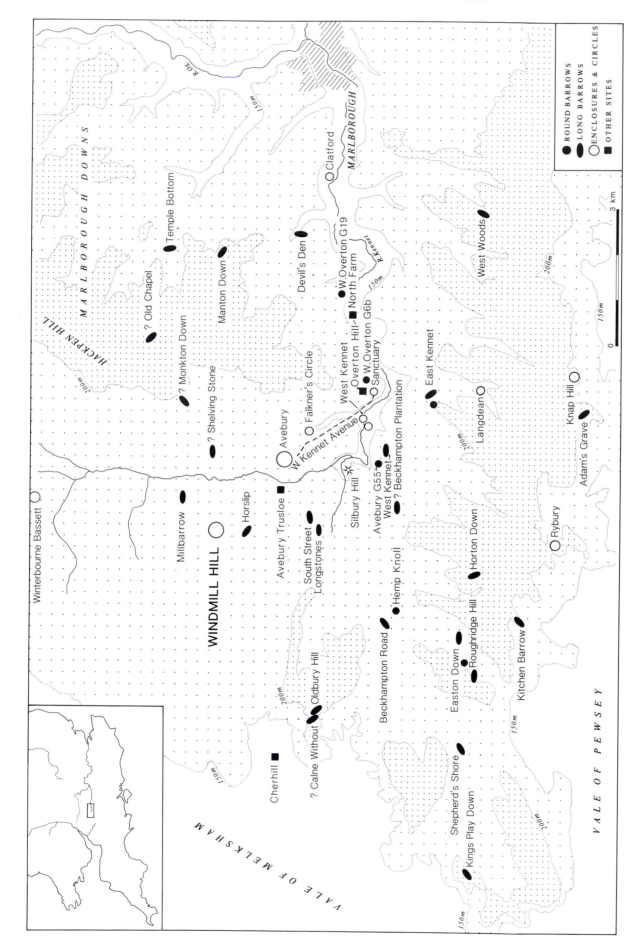

Fig. 7. General location map of Windmill Hill with selected surrounding monuments (various sources).

2

The Layout of the Enclosure: Earthwork and Geophysical Survey

Andrew David, David McOmish and Alasdair Whittle

The setting (Alasdair Whittle)

Windmill Hill lies on the chalk downland of north Wilt-shire (figs 7–10; pls 1–3). It is a low, broad hill (over 190 m OD) which rises some 35–40 m above two small branches of the upper Kennet valley. Geologically, it is an outlying block of Middle Chalk above surrounds of Lower Chalk. The hill commands views in all directions (figs 11–12). To the north, there is an undulating plateau of Lower Chalk, while to the east, south and west there is higher downland above the upper Kennet valley. On a wider scale, the chalk downland is scarped to the north, west and south at its junction with lower lying vales, while to the east the Kennet continues to be flanked by chalk hills.

The site is thus near the centre of a definable region in terms of topography and geology, but whether that corresponded with a region or territory in human terms during the Neolithic period should be an open question from the outset. The enclosure belongs to a cluster of Earlier Neolithic monuments on the chalk downland surrounding the upper Kennet valley (figs 7–9). Overlooking the Vale of Pewsey are two other enclosures, at Knap Hill and Rybury (Connah 1965; Smith 1971). Another, much larger, causewayed enclosure lies at Crofton in the Vale of Pewsey (Lobb 1995), but its size and position might suggest a date other than in the Earlier Neolithic (RCHME *pers. comm.*) (fig. 13). Over twenty long barrows lie within 10 km of Windmill Hill (Barker 1985) (figs 7–9). Some precede the enclosure, like the Horslip or Windmill Hill long barrow to the south (Ashbee *et al.* 1979), while others appear to be roughly contemporary with it, like Millbarrow to the north-east (Whittle 1993; Whittle 1994). Numbers of flint scatters (Holgate 1988) and some occupations, as at Cherhill to the west (Evans and Smith 1983), are known within the immediate area, but more systematic search is needed and over a wider area. One zone within the area which could still yield new features, because the Neolithic surface is buried, is the valley bottom (Evans *et al.* 1993). The relationship of the enclosure to its wider setting is discussed in chapter 17.

According to Smith the 'windmill' place name derives from the positioning of such a structure on one of the round barrows on the hilltop, possibly Winterbourne Monkton 1 (Smith 1965a, xxvii).

Principal features of the site (fig. 14, and pl. 3) (Alasdair Whittle)

Excavations have shown the presence of a number of pre-enclosure features, including pits, postholes and a grave, in the area of the east side of the inner circuit of the enclosure and under the bank within the outer ditch circuit on the east side of the site. Pits between these two areas might also be part of a pre-enclosure phase.

The outer circuit consists of ditch segments of varying length with a bank inside. One notable feature is the way the circuit leaves the hilltop on the west side to run below the scarp of the hill, which is occupied there by the middle circuit. The area enclosed by the middle circuit slopes so that the principal outlook is to the north and west. The circuit consists of ditch segments of variable length. It appears to consist of stretches of longer and shorter segments, the latter in some cases almost pit-like. The inner circuit, of similar outlook to the middle one, also consists of ditch segments of variable length. One notable feature is the slight indentation to the north-west, which finds parallels elsewhere in southern England (C. Evans 1988a). The site encloses over 8 ha, and the maximum diameter across the outer circuit is 360 m. It is therefore the largest causewayed enclosure with surviving earth-works in the British Isles. Only one other Neolithic enclosure, that at the now levelled site of Crofton, is larger, covering an area of 28 ha (Lobb 1995).

To the east of the outer circuit there is a small, square ditched enclosure of probable Neolithic date (Smith 1965a). Within the causewayed enclosure are two upstanding and at least two ploughed down round barrows; others lie outside to the north-east, east and south. The slopes to the south of the enclosure have yielded many thousands of

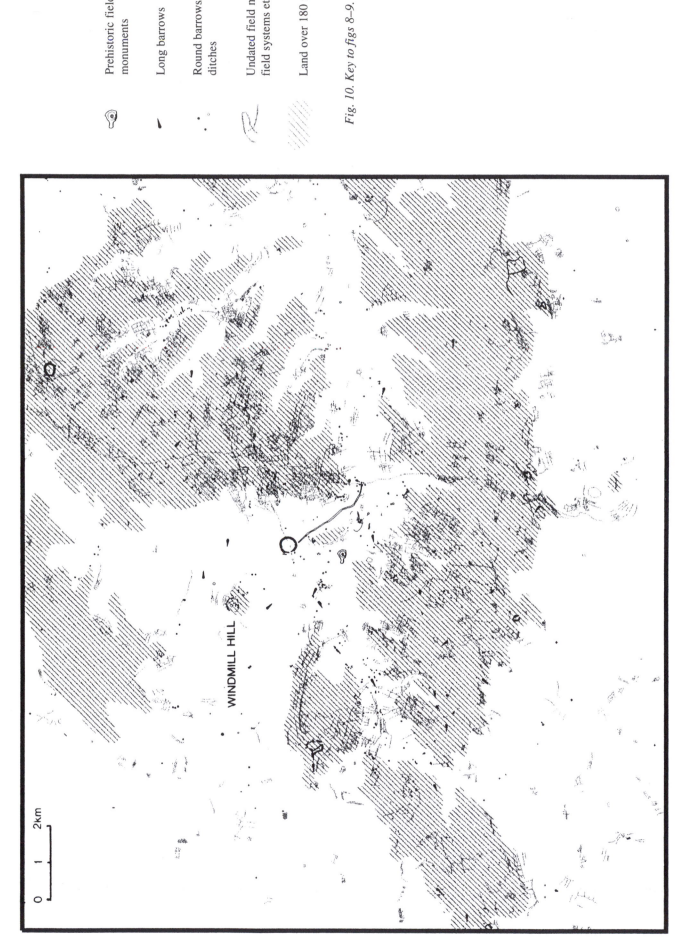

Prehistoric field
monuments

Long barrows

Round barrows/ring
ditches

Undated field monuments,
field systems etc.

Land over 180 m A.O.D.

Fig. 10. Key to figs 8–9.

WINDMILL HILL

2km

1

0

Fig. 8. Windmill Hill in relation to other monuments, finds and surviving or visible field systems (source: county SMR).

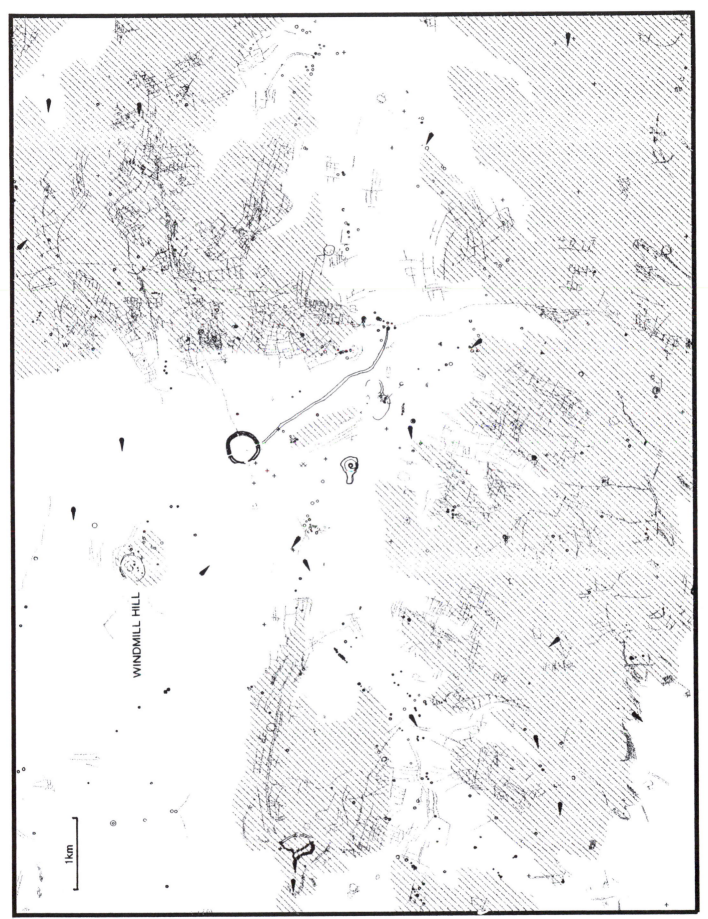

WINDMILL HILL

1km

Fig. 9. Windmill Hill in relation to other monuments, finds and surviving or visible field systems (source: county SMR).

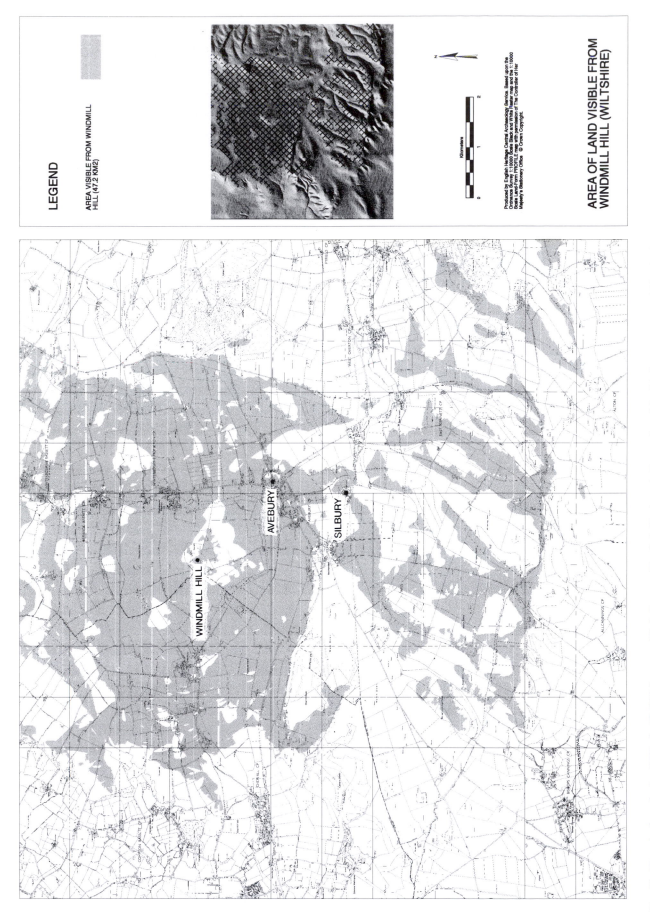

Fig. 11. Viewshed analysis of Windmill Hill (source: Nick Burton, English Heritage). Reproduced by kind permission of The Ordnance Survey. © Crown copyright (NC-99-253).

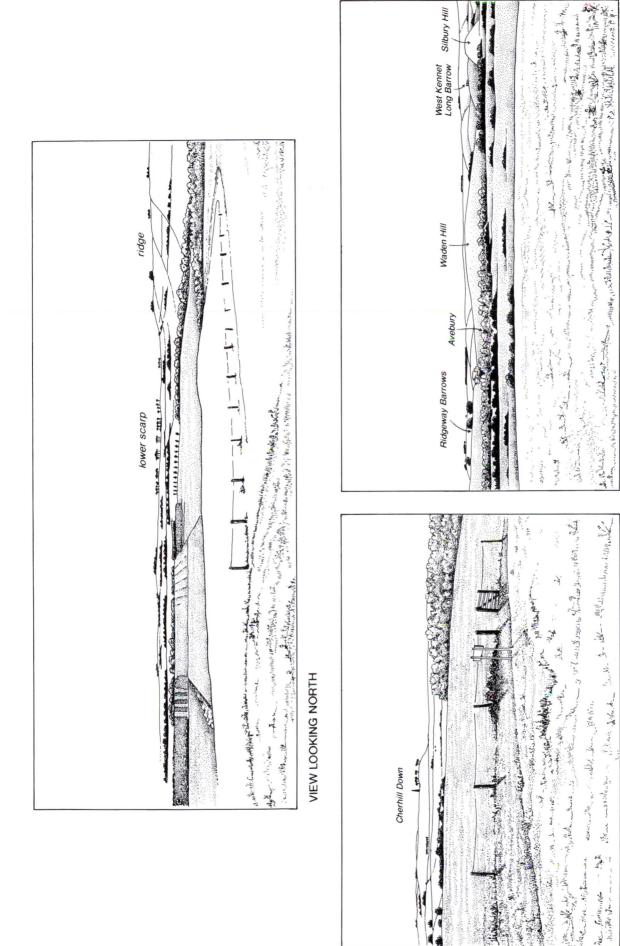

ridge

lower scarp

VIEW LOOKING NORTH

Ridgeway Barrows

Avebury

Waden Hill

West Kennet
Long Barrow

Silbury Hill

VIEW LOOKING SOUTH

Cherhill Down

VIEW LOOKING SOUTH WEST

Fig. 12. Modern views from Windmill Hill (adapted from the CBA Avebury World Heritage Site Landscape Assessment on behalf of English Heritage).

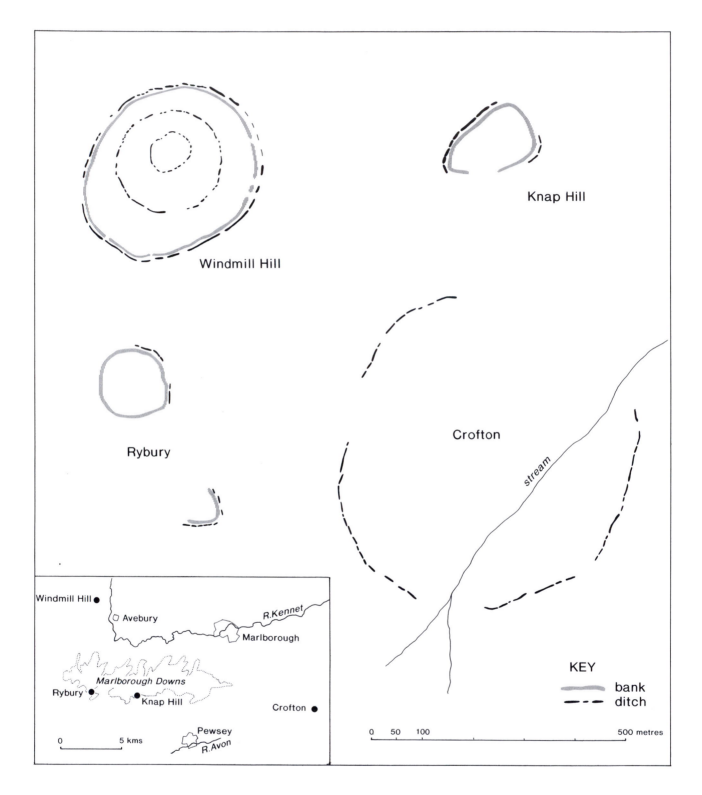

*Fig. 13. Outline plans of Windmill Hill, Knap Hill, Rybury and Crofton
(source: RCHME, with modifications for Windmill Hill).*

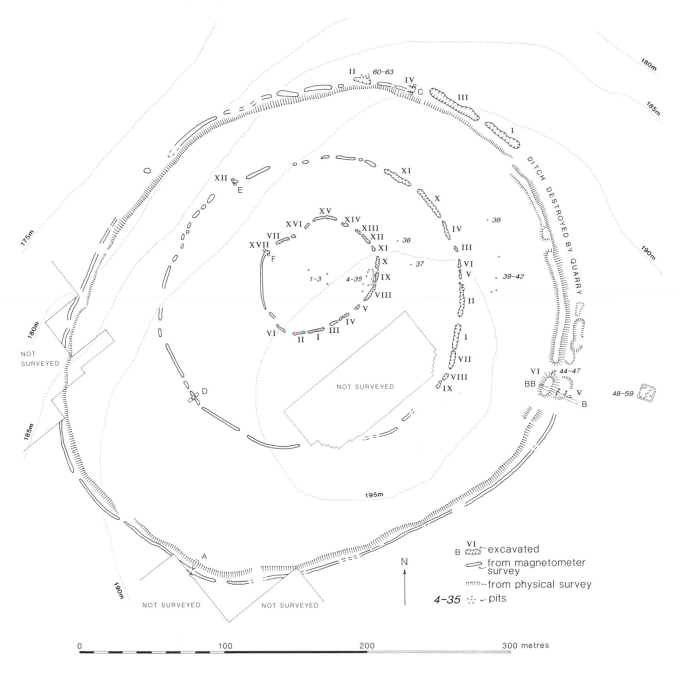

Fig. 14. Summary plan of Windmill Hill, based on the existing plan and the new topographic and geophysical surveys, showing also the Keiller ditch segment numbers, the Smith cuttings, and the 1988 trenches (BB and A–F).

struck flints (Smith 1965a). These were the focus of a season of survey and sample excavation in 1993; a report will appear separately (Whittle *et al.* forthcoming). Present indications are that some but not many Earlier Neolithic pits lie in this area, and that the greater part of the lithic assemblage may be of Later rather than Earlier Neolithic date.

Better preservation is to be found across roughly the northern half of the enclosure and to its north. Land use to the south of the Avebury-Winterbourne Monkton parish boundary running across the site was more intensive, from at least the eighteenth century into the twentieth century.

There is also evidence, presented below, for medieval ridge-and-furrow in this zone, and virtually all the cuttings (thus over the enclosure as a whole) show a Romano-British ploughsoil as the tertiary fill (*sensu* Evans 1990).

Much of this was already recognised before 1988 (Smith 1965a), but as part of the research reported here two new surveys were made, topographical and geophysical, to check details of the enclosure, to look for further features within it, and to examine its immediate surrounds. The earthwork survey is presented before the sub-surface geophysical survey.

A new earthwork survey *(fig. 15)*
(David McOmish)

This survey recorded the three partially concentric circuits of the causewayed enclosure; ten round barrows, including a previously undiscovered example; traces of a field system; hollow-ways; and a post-medieval boundary bank.

Survey method

The ground survey was carried out using a Wild TC 2000 Total Station theodolite. Individual survey stations were established as a ring traverse around the enclosure and field system. Data were computed using Mathshop survey software linked to a Calcomp plotter. Detailed measurements were then added to the framework by taped off-sets. The survey was carried out by D. S. McOmish and C. R. Lewis. (Comments on the text were kindly provided by David Field, Mark Corney and Chris Dunn. The plan was drawn by Deborah Cunliffe.)

The causewayed enclosure
(SU 086714; NMR No. SU 07 SE 22; former county number: Wilts 101; new English Heritage national RSM number: 21717)

Outer circuit. The outer enclosure, 8.45 ha in area, measures a maximum 360 m in diameter on its longest, north-east/south-west axis. On close inspection the outer enclosure is polygonal in shape, and appears to have been constructed in a series of short straight sections, which vary from 50 m to 120 m in length.

The enclosure is now most clearly defined at the north-east, in the area of Keiller's reconstruction. Here a substantial bank is accompanied by an external ditch. The bank, in its present form, appears to be a continuous feature, surviving to a height of 0.7 m and 5 m across; it has an undulating profile. It is unclear whether or not the peaks and troughs are original features, but this seems unlikely in view of the renovation and reconstruction. Although frequent interruptions occur along its course, there are no convincing entrance gaps through the bank. The possible east-facing double entrance break (fig. 15, A), is not a wholly original feature. The southernmost of the two breaks may be an original feature but it has clearly been widened since the bank terminals on either side of the gap are sharply truncated. Additionally, there are traces of a slight bank 0.3 m high, crossing the 10 m wide gap to the north; this appears to be the vestige of an earlier continuous bank underneath.

Slight traces of the bank survive on the south-eastern side of the hill, in an area that has been severely damaged by ploughing. The bank has been reduced to a height of only 0.1 m above internal ground level and is 10 m wide. Elsewhere the enclosure is marked by a continuous, outward facing lynchet or terrace which varies between 0.2 m and 2.3 m in height. The more substantial dimensions are recorded on the north-eastern side, to the north of the parish boundary, where the enclosure spills over the edge of the natural escarpment; lesser dimensions are recorded along the plough-damaged south and western sectors.

An external ditch survives intermittently around much of the northern part of the enclosure. Quarrying has destroyed a short stretch, 120 m long, to the north of the Winterbourne Monkton 3 round barrow. North of the reservoir, in an area excavated and subsequently restored by Keiller, the ditch survives as a continuous hollow 4 m wide. Along its base there are numerous interruptions defining deeper pockets of ditch 2–10 m in length, surviving to a depth of 0.3 m. Elsewhere, where excavation has not taken place, the ditch is represented by a series of elongated depressions, 4 m wide, 2–14 m in length and up to 0.5 m deep. In places, especially on the north-west, the causewayed ditch is accompanied by an external lynchet, measuring 0.3 m in height. This is either the remains of an outer, though now much damaged, bank, or more likely, given the presence of a field system in this area, the remains of a slight negative lynchet.

Middle circuit. The middle circuit is almost circular in plan and measures 220 m in diameter; it encloses an area of 3.32 ha. It is of a much slighter construction than the outer enclosure and survives to its greatest height north of the parish boundary, particularly on the east, where it has been excavated and subsequently restored by Keiller. This is visible now as a shallow trench, 1.5–3 m wide and up to 0.2 m deep. There are frequent interruptions along its course, caused by deeper ditch or pit segments, which are 0.5 m deep at most. Beyond the areas excavated, principally on the north and north-west, the original course of the enclosure survives as a series of irregular elongated pit or ditch segments up to 4 m wide and 0.3 m deep. In places, these are flanked internally by a slight lynchet, 0.3 m in height, which may be the last traces of a now destroyed internal bank. South of the parish boundary the enclosure circuit seems to survive only intermittently as a slight outward facing lynchet 0.2 m high.

One possible entrance into the enclosure was recorded during the survey. This faces north and consists of a gap, 16 m across, between ditch or pit segments (fig. 15, B).

Inner circuit. The enclosure does not occupy the highest point on the hilltop, with the centre of the inner enclosure lying some distance to the north of the summit. The inner enclosure is sub-circular in plan with a slight indentation on the north-western side and encloses an area of 0.52 ha. It is the slightest of the three enclosures and is the one which has been most extensively excavated. At least 75 percent of the ditch circuit has been excavated, together with the eastern half of the interior. Only the short section of ditch forming the western side of the enclosure appears undisturbed.

Overall the ditch consists of a discontinuous hollow, 2 m wide, which survives to a depth of 0.2 m. Within its bottom there are numerous deeper segments which tend to be narrower and measure 1–1.5 m wide and up to 0.4 m in depth. Occasional causeways are evident; they vary in

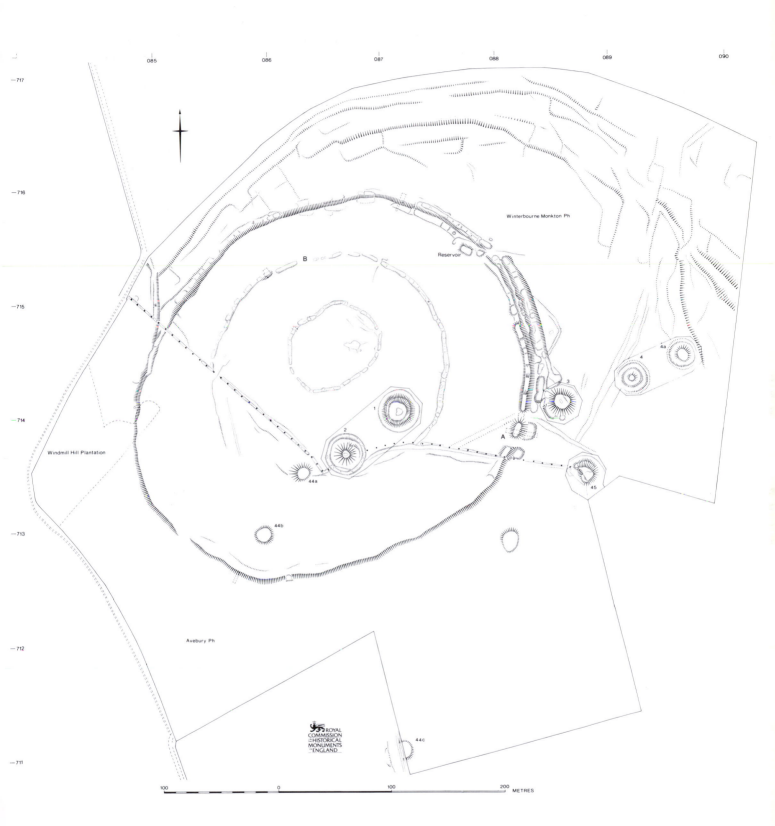

Fig. 15. Topographic survey by RCHME in 1988 of the enclosure and its immediate surroundings.
© crown copyright RCHME.

width from 1–3 m. It is not clear whether those visible in the eastern half of the enclosure are original features or the result of the excavations.

Round barrows

A total of ten round barrows were recorded during the survey. All but one of these, that at SU 08817129, have been previously recorded and the nomenclature used here will follow that established by Grinsell in the *Victoria County History of Wiltshire* (Grinsell 1957).

The barrow group includes bowl, bell, saucer and possible disc variants, arranged in a dispersed linear fashion. The largest examples, Winterbourne Monkton 1 and 2, occupy the highest point of the hill and are very conspicuous landscape features. The others, placed on false-crests on the gentle east-facing slope overlooking the Winterbourne valley, are also prominent features when viewed from below. Three of the barrows, Winterbourne Monkton 2 and 3, and Avebury 44a, clearly impinge upon the middle and outer circuits of the enclosure. The barrows are listed and described in the appendix below.

Field system

Slight remains of a field system are present on much of the steep, north-facing slope to the north of the outer Neolithic enclosure within Winterbourne Monkton parish. Numerous north-facing lynchets, now spread, generally follow the contour of the hill with the most substantial surviving to a height of 2 m. Transverse field boundaries at right angles to these are visible as a series of very slight scarps, 0.1 m high. These define small rectangular fields which range in area from 0.1–0.8 ha. The overall morphology of this field system suggests that it is of prehistoric or Roman origin. It is likely that similar fields also extended across the south-facing slopes of the hill in Avebury parish, but have been destroyed by ploughing. Ridge-and-furrow cultivation of medieval or post-medieval date is visible on aerial photographs, and perhaps on the geophysical plots, though it was not included in the earthwork survey, over much of the southern part of the hilltop and this has been truncated by a series of parallel modern drainage features (again not surveyed). There is no sign of further enclosure circuits.

Other features

A hollowed trackway approaches the site from the north-west and impinges upon the outer circuit of the enclosure. This holloway is in turn bisected by the boundary bank which separates the parishes of Winterbourne Monkton and Avebury. This survives as a low bank 1–2 m wide and up to 0.3 m in height, with a slight and intermittent ditch 1.5 m wide and 0.2 m deep on the northern side. Another slightly hollowed track approaches the site from the east and enters the enclosure through the gap in the outer circuit to the south of round barrow Winterbourne Monkton 3.

Discussion

The most striking feature of the multiple enclosure complex at Windmill Hill relates to its topographical positioning. All three enclosures are centred some distance (over 40 m) to the north of the hill summit, and the middle and outer circuits spill dramatically over the well-defined northern edge of the chalk ridge. Indeed, it is possible that these enclosures are sited on a false crest perhaps to provide, or afford, a prospect to or from the lower-lying areas to the north and north-west. False-crest siting is a common feature in the positioning of, for instance, many burial mounds including Neolithic long mounds, and is usually regarded as a deliberate attempt to maximise the visual impact of the burial mound placing it at a point where it appears, from the valley bottom, to be on the horizon (Dunn 1988, 36). Thus, when seen from a lower altitude, the feature becomes conspicuous, as the whole of its profile is outlined against the sky. This implies that the contemporary landscape was relatively open and allowed this form of related visibility, an argument which may or may not be applicable in the case of the enclosures at Windmill Hill. Nonetheless, the enclosures here dominate the skyline when seen from the north, east and west and it seems reasonable to conjecture that, at the very least, defence or fear of attack were not over-riding considerations in the planning and construction of the enclosure boundaries.

The circuit of each enclosure has a slightly different morphology, although this may, of course, relate to the effects of subsequent land-use, damage and excavation. It is clear, however, that moving from the interior outwards, the enclosure boundaries become more substantial, with the outer circuit being the most monumental. There are no banks or ramparts associated with the inner and middle circuits, for instance, and it is unclear whether or not banks originally accompanied all of the ditch segments. Smith has suggested that the asymmetrical silting of the inner and middle ditches does point to the existence of internal banks (1965a, 5); this is debated below (Chapters 4 and 7).

Although the monument on first impression appears to have been causewayed, and the magnetometer survey indicates gaps in the outer ditch, earthwork survey suggests that the outer enclosure bank may in fact have been continuous. It is unfortunate that the best preserved sections of the bank are those that have been reconstructed by Keiller, so a definitive statement as to their original condition is difficult. It may be interesting to note that a recent RCHME survey of the causewayed enclosure at Whitesheet Hill, Wiltshire, has shown there to be a slight but continuous bank underneath the interrupted rampart (RCHME forthcoming). Continuously ditched and banked Neolithic enclosures are known elsewhere in southern England, being recorded, for instance, at Court Hill and Bury Hill, West Sussex (Bedwin 1984).

The enclosure complex at a later stage formed the focus for an extensive group of round barrows. Ten burial mounds were surveyed and these are arranged in a dispersed linear alignment, on a roughly east-west axis. Geophysical survey (see below) indicates the presence of one or two ring ditches which may be the remnants of other barrows. As has been stated, at least three of the barrows impinge upon the enclosure circuits, and this general association between Neolithic enclosures and round barrow cemeteries is a commonly repeated one (Barber *et al.* 1999; cf. Woodward and Woodward 1996). At Whitesheet Hill, for example, several barrows are located in the vicinity of the enclosure and one of these, Kilmington 4 (Grinsell 1957, 179), overlies the ditch of the causewayed enclosure.

The effect of the later episodes of ploughing on the hilltop undoubtedly contributes to the slight nature of the earlier remains. It is difficult to date the origin of this field system with any precision, but the tertiary ploughsoil of Romano-British date in the ditches may be noted. That this episode of ploughing was long-lived is suggested by the substantial size of the associated field boundaries. They themselves appear to have been over-ploughed, probably in recent times, since much of the survey area retained slight traces of ridge-and-furrow.

Appendix: round barrows on Windmill Hill

Winterbourne Monkton parish

No. 1; SU 087097140; NMR No. SU07SE 21. Bowl barrow c. 34 m in diameter surviving to a height of 1.8 m and surrounded by a ditch 5 m wide and up to 0.4 m deep. A partial break or ledge c. 0.5 m from the markedly flat-topped summit suggests that the mound profile is not original and has seen some alteration. It is possible that this is the site of the mill mentioned by Smith (1965a, xxvii).

No. 2; SU 08667137; NMR No. SU07SE 21. Bell barrow c. 22 m in diameter and c. 3 m high; it is separated from the enclosing ditch by a berm, 4 m wide. The ditch, which varies between 2–5 m in width, is up to 1 m deep and is interrupted by numerous shallow causeways. It appears to impinge upon the line of the middle circuit of the Neolithic enclosure and is further overlain by the Winterbourne Monkton-Avebury parish boundary bank.

No. 3; SU 08857141; NMR No. SU07SE 16. Bowl barrow c. 25 m in diameter, 2 m high is partially enclosed by an interrupted ditch, in places, 4 m wide and up to 0.8 m deep. This barrow overlies the ditch of the outer circuit of the enclosure.

No. 4; SU 08917144; NMR No. SU07SE 16. Grinsell records this as a saucer barrow (1957, 224). Survey suggests, however, that it may be a small disc barrow. It consists of a low mound 10 m in diameter, standing to a height of 1 m, placed on a circular platform 18 m wide. This is enclosed by a continuous ditch 5 m wide and 0.6 m deep with an external bank 2 m wide and 0.3 m in height above ground level.

No. 4a; SU 08957146; NMR No. SU07SE 16. Saucer barrow consisting of a low spread oval mound 15 m long (maximum). The surrounding ditch is 6 m wide and up to 0.3 m deep with traces of an external bank, 2 m wide and 0.2 m high, surrounding it on all but the north-western side.

Avebury parish

No. 44a; SU 08637135; NMR No. SU07SE 21. Bowl barrow reduced by ploughing to a low sub-circular mound, 20 m in diameter, standing to a height of 0.5 m. The associated ring ditch shown by the magnetometer survey lies within the line of the middle ditch.

No. 44b; SU 08607130; NMR No. SU07SE 21. Bowl barrow severely damaged by ploughing; it survives as a low sub-circular mound, 17 m in diameter, and 0.3 m high.

No. 44c; SU 08717110. Bowl barrow reduced by ploughing and bisected by a modern fence line. Only the eastern half survives as a semi-circular mound 18 m wide and up to 0.3 m high.

No. 45; SU 08877135; NMR No. SU07SE 16. Bowl barrow, now sub-rectangular in shape with a maximum diameter of 23 m. The mound, where best preserved, stands to a height of 2 m and is enclosed by a ditch which varies from 1.5–3 m in width and 0.3 m in depth. The parish boundary bank has encroached upon the western half of the site.

SU 08817129. Bowl barrow (?) recorded for the first time. Oval in plan with a maximum length of 22 m. It has been reduced by ploughing to a height of 0.2 m.

Geophysical survey *(figs 16–18) (Andrew David)*

Introduction

Non-destructive site investigation has a long history at Windmill Hill. Early this century the site had originally been identified by observation on the ground of faint earthworks and also by the presence of worked flints in the topsoil (Kendall 1914). When Keiller later came to investigate the hilltop (1925–29) he not only employed aerial photography but also made extensive use of a probe, the first results of which he excitedly reported to Harold St George Gray in a letter dated 5th May 1925: '...we spent our time, since the weather was too bad to survey, in probing for further pits with a long, sharp, skewer-like device, which I had designed and had made in London. The result was quite remarkable and far surpassed thumping (bosing: Atkinson 1953) in certainty and accuracy' (ms at Alexander Keiller Museum, Avebury). Probing was the simple but very effective method that later allowed much of the unexcavated detail of the outer and middle circuits to be plotted (Smith 1965a, fig. 3).

Since these early days several other methods of archaeological prospecting have been developed and are now a commonplace in site exploration (A. Clark 1996). Amongst the most successful of these geophysical techniques are resistivity and magnetometer survey. It was the latter that was used at Windmill Hill, in conjunction with the topographic survey described above, and partly in advance of the subsequent excavations. It was hoped that such survey, by covering the entire enclosure, would not only confirm and perhaps amplify the earlier evidence for sub-surface features but might also locate other features in areas not previously examined.

Magnetometer survey was chosen, not only because of the relative speed with which it can be conducted, but

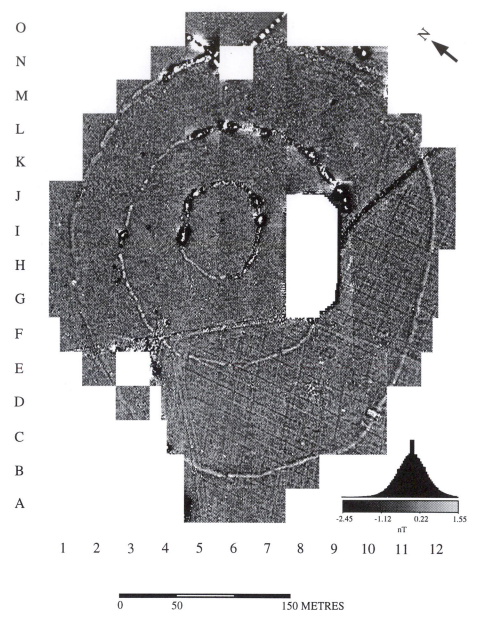

Fig. 16. Greyscale plot of magnetometer survey.

because of its well proven ability to locate features cut into chalk, especially when these are associated with previous occupation. Newly developed and very sensitive magnetometers had recently become available alongside much improved data treatment procedures. Resistivity survey, whilst benefiting from similar advances, and despite its effectiveness elsewhere in the Avebury area (Ucko *et al.* 1991), is nevertheless a more time-consuming method and is vulnerable to seasonal variation in soil moisture. For these reasons, and on account of the nature of the features to be expected on Windmill Hill, it was not attempted there and full reliance was placed instead on magnetic survey.

Method

Altogether, some 10.6 ha were surveyed, covering most of

the area encompassed by the causewayed enclosure ditches (see fig. 16). The fenced area containing the two upstanding barrows on the hill summit was not surveyed, however, nor were other small areas near the edges of the enclosure where modern magnetic interference was excessive. A grid of 30 m squares was established over the remaining area and surveyed with a Geoscan FM36 fluxgate gradiometer. The instrument was carried along successive 30 m traverses, 1.0 m apart, with readings logged every 25 cm. The data thus accumulated was periodically downloaded on to a portable computer and the entire dataset was subsequently processed at the Ancient Monuments Laboratory (AML). The fieldwork was conducted at intervals between 1988 and 1993.

In addition, samples of topsoil were extracted at 10m intervals along two of the grid axes (7/8 and H/I) crossing

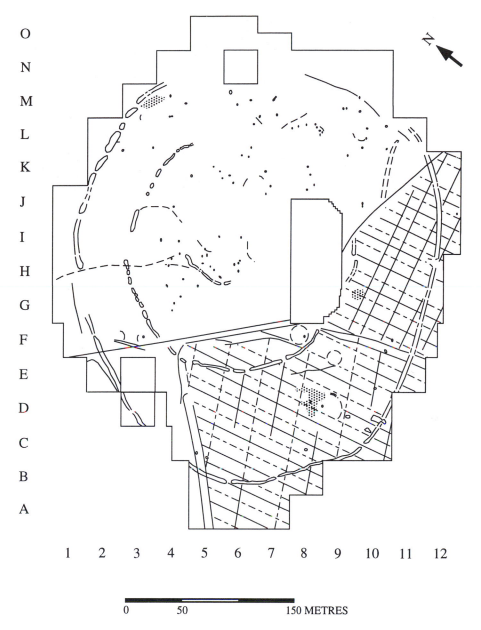

Fig. 17. Interpretation of magnetometer survey. Anomalies identified as pits and ditches are outlined; interrupted or dashed lines indicate more weakly defined or tentative features; areas of shading indicate areas of localised magnetic disturbance of possible archaeological significance; the lattice of straight lines in the southern part of the survey area indicates more recent agricultural features.

the hilltop at right angles to each other. These samples were later measured for magnetic susceptibility (MS) to provide supporting information for the interpretation of the magnetometer survey.

Full details of all the technical procedures used, as well as the complete data archive, are available for consultation at the AML.

Results

The magnetic information is illustrated here (figs 16 and 18) as a greyscale plot which depicts the raw data following the removal of responses to spurious items of ferrous litter. Positive magnetic anomalies are represented as white or pale in tone, whilst negative anomalies are darker. An interpretation of this plot is shown in fig. 17.

The ditch circuits

Excepting the anomalies generated by recent intrusions, the magnetic response over the hilltop is extremely weak, with variations mostly confined within a range of less than 3 nanotesla (nT). Within this narrow range it is nevertheless possible to identify a number of significant features, in particular the ditch circuits themselves. Most of the inner ditch has been excavated and the response to ferrous

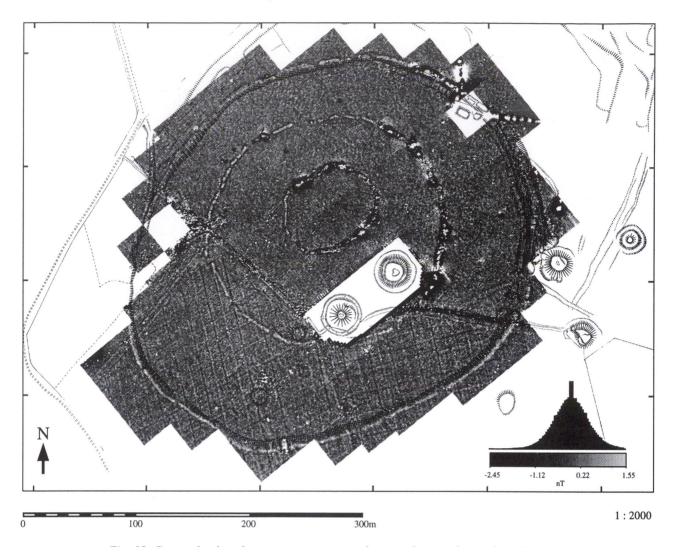

N

0   100   200   300m

1 : 2000

Fig. 18. Greyscale plot of magnetometer survey data overlain on the earthwork survey.

debris in the backfill is clear. The unexcavated portion, to the west, can now be shown to run an approximately straight course between Keiller's trenches XVII and VI (grid square 5H). An obvious causeway has been located about l0 m to the west of Inner Ditch Trench VI, coincident with that observed by the topographic survey. Further northwards along the unexcavated circuit the magnetic evidence suggests that causeways, if present, are likely to be very narrow or highly degraded. Whilst the magnetic evidence is thus suggestive of an uncharacteristically long segment here, the conflicting results of probing (Smith 1965a, fig. 3) indicate that this portion of the ditch circuit is broken by three causeways. Topographic survey indicates that there is perhaps one causeway (fig. 15).

The middle enclosure ditch is fully depicted for the first time, and in particular the survey data confirm the previously inferred south-western portion of its circuit. However, the actual course of the ditch here lies up to some 15 m to the north-east of the conjectural route (Smith 1965a, fig. 3), lending the middle circuit a more nearly circular outline than had been thought earlier. Detailed

plots of grid square 6E allowed for the accurate positioning of Trench D in 1988.

As expected, the middle ditch is interrupted by causeways although only the wider of these can be distinguished with confidence. Very narrow or degraded causeways, especially where these are numerous and closely spaced, are difficult to single out from the magnetic data alone. It nevertheless seems clear that both the magnetic survey and the topographic survey are in general agreement and have detected more detail than probing. It was already acknowledged that the probe could miss the narrowest causeways (Smith 1965a, 5). The concordance between the results of probing and magnetometer survey is generally very good, as seen for instance in the circuit between Middle Ditch Trenches XII and XI. Thus, whilst obvious causeways have been indicated on the unprobed part of the circuit, to the south-west, it is possible that minor gaps or vestigial causeways are too small to be resolved. This same caution applies to the inner circuit as well.

The outer circuit has been detected as a series of broader, more robust, and apparently less disconnected series of linear anomalies. The alignment is particularly distinct for the 420 m or so along its southern portion between grid squares 5B and 12K. Despite the clarity of this section it is again difficult to be certain of identifying causeways. Many of the gaps indicated on the interpretation plan must be admitted to be conjectural. That indicated in grid square 12H, for instance, has no equivalent break in the bank at this point. Indeed there is only one instance in this part of the outer circuit, in grid square 7B, where an apparent causeway is matched by a break in the bank as defined by the topographic survey. Elsewhere, the congruence between causeways and gaps in the bank, if present, may have been obscured by the possible subsequent development of the bank as a lynchet (for discussion of the topography of the outer circuit, see this chapter above).

The situation is slightly clearer to the north where both magnetic data and probing clearly indicate causeways south-west of Outer Ditch Trench II (grid squares 3M, 2L and 2K). Tracing the circuit further around (anti-clockwise) between grid squares 1J and 2E, below the brow of the hill, the definition of the anomaly fades away almost beyond recognition. There is also some discrepancy with the results of probing in this area since the magnetic data indicate quite firmly that there is no gap in the ditch in grid square 1I. Where the magnetic signal is at its most indistinct, south of grid line I/H, topographic survey is suggestive of the presence of many short ditch segments, as in the adjacent sector of the middle circuit. Further around, in grid square 3D, the magnetic data picks up the outer ditch again and a causeway has been located there. The remainder of the circuit, between Outer Ditch Trenches II and V, has not been detected owing to previous excavation, quarrying and other modern activities.

All three ditch circuits, then, have been detected more or less clearly and on the whole do not diverge significantly from expectations. Apart from confirming this basic outline it was hoped that magnetometer survey would, in addition, provide clues as to the presence of any other features within or adjacent to the enclosures which might throw further light on the Neolithic use of the hilltop. Keiller had of course located a cluster of pits (1–35) near the centre of the site, as well as other isolated pits, and a square enclosure eastward of the outer ditch. Causewayed enclosures elsewhere have been shown to contain a variety of internal features.

Internal features

Examination of the plot in fig. 16 immediately makes it clear that very few, if any, very major internal features that could reasonably be associated with the causewayed enclosure are present. Excepting certain later and more modern features (see below) the hilltop appears to be without convincing evidence for major surviving features. Unfortunately, this is not to say that significant features do *not* exist particularly where these may be small and/or shallow or where their fill is non-magnetic (backfilled chalk, for instance). Post-holes, stake-holes, graves, small and shallow pits or gullies will probably have remained undetected. Fig. 17 very cautiously indicates the position of small and slight anomalies that might indicate the presence of features such as pits. However, most of these are so indeterminate and close to the threshold of background magnetic 'noise' (particularly within the inner and middle circuits), that this interpretation must be highly tentative. Stray iron objects in the soil can also produce confusing anomalies at times although it has been possible to recognise and discount most of these. It is questionable as to whether or not the survey would have detected the central pit cluster (Keiller's pits 1–35), or the square enclosure and its associated pits. All that it is possible to say with some confidence is that larger features of over a metre in diameter, and with a filling at least as magnetic as that within the ditch circuits, are unlikely to have been missed.

With this last statement in mind there are a small number of such anomalies which might be pits comparable to some of those already known to have existed on the hilltop (e.g. Keiller's pits 36, 37, 63, 41, 42). At least four of the latter (36, 37, 41, 42) may have been contemporary with the primary occupation and had fillings similar to those of the enclosure ditches, pits 41 and 42 in particular containing refuse and hearth sweepings (Smith 1965a, 29). The positioning of the latter appears random, roughly intermediate between the inner and middle (36, 37) and middle and outer ditches (41, 42). The few magnetic anomalies which may be responses to similar features are widely and sparsely scattered but with an apparent tendency to be located away from the core of the site, nearer its periphery, for instance in grid squares 5C, 8C, 9D, 6M, 7M and perhaps at the intersection of 2L, 3L, 2K and 3K.

Apart from these suggestive individual anomalies there are slight indications that elsewhere there may be clusters of pits, although nowhere can these be reliably distinguished from more recent magnetic activity. Promising areas include that on the inner edge of the outer circuit in grid squares 3M and 4M (significantly close to Keiller's late Neolithic-'Beaker' pits 60–63), and in the general area to the south and south-east of the two summit barrows (e.g. in grid square 10H).

Apart from such anomalies, which – if genuine – may or may not be pits, there are other anomalies which more certainly represent prehistoric activity on the hill. More obvious are the ring ditches of two former barrows, the approximate positions of which were already known (Smith 1965a, fig. 3), and which have been partially detected in grid squares 8F and 8D-9D exactly where topographic survey has also located their remnant mounds (see above). The southernmost of the two has a diameter of nearly 30 m and may therefore have been comparable in stature to those that survive to the north-east. A third and smaller ring ditch, previously unrecorded, with a diameter of approximately 15 m, has been detected at the junction of grid squares 9E and 9F. Each of these three ring ditches is associated with slight magnetic 'noise' which may indicate some interference with them in the past.

A small number of extremely weakly defined linear anomalies, perhaps insubstantial ditches or gullies, have been cautiously indicated by dashed lines on fig. 17. These are again at the limit of detectability and their validity and archaeological significance must remain uncertain.

Recent features

Now that all the apparently prehistoric aspects of the magnetometer data have been discussed it remains briefly to draw attention to the geophysical evidence for more recent activity. This category includes the curious and roughly rectangular-shaped anomaly, with dimensions of some 12 m by 5 m, that lies across the outer ditch alignment in grid square 10D. Topographic survey (fig. 15) reveals that this coincides with a gap in the bank and a slight depression. Whilst the date of this feature is therefore uncertain and it has no obvious analogue to this author's knowledge, there is a temptation to suggest that it is a modern intrusion, perhaps an unrecorded excavation. The presence there of burnt material in some form also seems probable.

The most distinct amongst the anomalies located by the survey are those that are perhaps least relevant to the interpretation of the site: these include the alignments of ferrous disturbance that distinguish the positions of former fences, particularly those that once defined the parish boundary. Another previous fence alignment, although much less pronounced, runs south-eastwards from its junction with the parish boundary at grid square 8F. These field boundaries were all extant at the time of the Keiller excavations and the parish boundary remains as a distinct earthwork. Keiller's excavations themselves have left a substantial magnetic signature, as it was clearly his practice to backfill the emptied ditches with miscellaneous ferrous litter as well as soil. The site of the open area excavation within the inner circuit is 'clean', however, and indistinguishable from non-excavated areas. Other modern interference has been caused by two pipes leading downhill from the water tank, the effects of the quarrying at the north-eastern perimeter of the enclosure, and at the site of a former temporary agricultural building in and around grid square 3E. Items of iron litter are thinly distributed over the rest of the hilltop but tend to concentrate nearer the more major intrusions.

Of rather more interest but nonetheless 'modern' in origin is the magnetic evidence for trackways and former cultivation. Two hollow-ways are visible as faint positive magnetic anomalies: one approaching the outer ditch at an oblique angle, seen in grid square 2E and also as a topographic feature (and in Smith 1965a, fig. 3), and the other between the middle and outer circuits north of the former boundary fence, in grid squares 11L, 10K and 10J, but invisible as a topographic feature. It nevertheless appears to be an extension of a hollowed trackway, detected by the earthwork survey, which approaches the enclosure from the east, apparently entering it through a

gap in the bank in grid square 11L. A third trackway approaches the site from the south-west and has been detected as a dual alignment running between grid squares 5A and 4E. Although invisible at the surface this is probably a heavily rutted farm track, now erased from the surface, servicing the former building referred to above.

The evidence for cultivation is very distinctive and is markedly restricted to that part of the hillside south of the parish boundary. The two former fields are each criss-crossed by alternating positive and negative magnetic anomalies; both fields are traversed by a series of negative alignments spaced at 25 m intervals. In the northerly field these are crossed by an orthogonal series of similar anomalies, spaced about 30 m apart, giving a rectangular lattice with units of approximately 30 m by 25 m. An identical lattice of positive anomalies is offset halfway between both sets of negative lines, giving a unit of roughly 15 m by 12 m. The southerly field has a similar but skewed pattern of alignments; such a pattern is too widely spaced, too rigidly geometric, and the individual anomalies too narrow, to support its interpretation entirely as ridge-and-furrow cultivation (cf. Ucko *et al.* 1991, pl. 63). Aerial photography of the hilltop in 1929 (Smith 1965a, pl. I), as well as surface observation (see above), does nevertheless reveal a more convincing appearance of ridge-and-furrow congruent with one direction of the magnetic pattern. It therefore seems probable that both medieval and more recent patterns (perhaps related to drainage operations) are superimposed.

Conclusions

The magnetometer survey, taken together with the detailed new topographic survey, has usefully refined our knowledge of the disposition and survival of archaeological features on Windmill Hill. Both lines of evidence, topographic and magnetic, have relied upon the recogition of more or less subtle patterns in essentially very subdued datasets. This is especially true of the magnetic data in which the range of contrasts is extremely slight, despite a high average topsoil magnetic susceptibility (75.5×10^{-8} SI/Kg: based on measurements from 95 samples). This generally high level of magnetic susceptibility lends some support to the impression noted above that the magnetic survey is unlikely to have missed any large earth-filled features. However, small and poorly contrasted features will not have been detectable.

It is interesting to note that individual magnetic susceptibility values from the two sample transects (see above) reveal a wide range of variation (range: max. 134.5 $\times 10^{-8}$ SI/Kg, min. 20.1×10^{-8} SI/Kg), and that such variation appears to be systematic in places. For instance, there are consistently above-average values in the south-western part of the hilltop where the sample transect crosses between the inner and outer ditch circuits. Although such variations are more likely to reflect the historic use of the landscape rather than any prehistoric signature, it would nonetheless be of interest at some future date to obtain a comprehensive coverage of magnetic susceptibility values from the entire hilltop in order to explore this issue further.

This aside, and given the extremely slight level of magnetic response to the gradiometer on Windmill Hill, it is remarkable that much has been detected at all, let alone in the detail that has been achieved.

3

The Keiller Excavations

Joshua Pollard

Keiller as a field archaeologist

Because the work at Windmill Hill and Avebury never saw publication during his lifetime, or under his name, Keiller's position as a field archaeologist has largely been neglected in accounts of British archaeology between the wars. He was a figure that spanned two archaeological traditions, that of the late nineteenth-century legacy of Pitt Rivers, and the emerging professionalism and functionalism of the inter-war years (C. Evans 1989). Keiller came to Windmill Hill as a novice excavator with grand intentions and an appetite to learn (figs 19–20; and see also figs 3–6). The five seasons of work on the enclosure chart his early development as a field archaeologist, initially guided by Harold St. George Gray, and then gradually gaining enough personal confidence and expertise (not to mention frustration with Gray) to take on the direction of the excavation himself. Unlike Gray, whose lack of self-critical approach can be seen in the continued use throughout his career of the same excavation methods that he learnt as assistant to Pitt Rivers (Bowden 1991, 164), Keiller's fascination with precision and an openness to new techniques (also seen with his work on aerial photography and stone implement petrology (Piggott 1965)) resulted in continual improvement and standardisation in digging and recording.

Inevitably, Keiller's methodology owed much to that of Gray (and by extension Pitt Rivers), including the use of a spit-digging technique (see fig. 27), the recording of finds according to level, and the rather minimal use of vertical sections. His improvements to this came in the employment of more systematic excavation strategies and recording methods (the abundant use of photography and high precision survey, for example), alongside a keen eye for detail and trench discipline. On a visit to the site in 1929, the orderly layout of the Windmill Hill trenches impressed the young Stuart Piggott, who during 1928 and 1930 worked as a volunteer with the Curwens at The Trundle. Piggott's laying out of a trench at The Trundle in the 'Keiller manner', rectilinear with neatly cut and stacked turf, prompted

Reginald Smith to remark 'very marmaladish' (Piggott 1983, 30).

Whilst in the field technically superior to many of his contemporaries, Keiller appears to have been uncomfortable when it came to interpretation and synthesis. The surviving notebooks and correspondence relating to Windmill Hill give remarkably little insight into Keiller's thoughts on the function of the enclosure, activities within it, or of its relationship to contemporary sites in the region. Windmill Hill generated considerable excitement largely due to the then unparalleled stratified assemblages of pottery, lithics and faunal remains recovered from the ditches, which were instrumental in the creation of a sequence for the British Neolithic. But an account presented to the First International Congress of Prehistoric and Protohistoric Sciences details finds but little else (Keiller 1934). In line with contemporary opinion, it may have been tacitly accepted that the enclosure represented an occupation site, with habitation taking place within the ditches (C. Evans 1988a). Keiller must certainly have been

Fig. 19. Alexander Keiller weighing finds (photo: Alexander Keiller Museum, Avebury).

Fig. 20. Excavation scene, possibly of the Middle Ditch; ? Keiller and Gray on the spoilheap,
Young in the foreground (photo: Alexander Keiller Museum, Avebury).

aware of current thinking given his wide-ranging contacts within the British archaeological establishment (there are numerous letters to and from key players such as Crawford, Childe and Sir Charles Peers in the Keiller archive in Avebury Museum). Much of the interpretative direction and academic context for Keiller's later excavations, at Avebury, Lanhill (Keiller and Piggott 1938) and the Badshot long barrow (Keiller and Piggott 1939), was probably provided by his brilliant assistant Stuart Piggott, who worked with the Morven Institute from 1933 until the outbreak of war.

Excavation strategy at Windmill Hill

Kendall's excavations were limited to one small section of the outer ditch south-east of OD I (Smith 1965a, 1). Keiller's work began in 1925 with the examination of selected parts of the outer, middle and inner circuits; the last two newly discovered (fig. 14). The initial season included the sectioning of three large ditch segments (OD I, MD I and II), the partial excavation of five medium-sized ditches (MD IV, ID I, II, III and IV), and the total excavation of three smaller (MD III, ID V and VI). The 1926 season was more ambitious, targeting two large segments, OD II and ID VII, for complete excavation. 1927 involved the excavation of remaining sections of the ditch on the south side of the inner circuit first dug in 1925 (ID IV to II), and the completion of a stretch of the middle circuit from MD IV to II. By this stage a policy appears to have been formulated to work around the ditch circuits systematically, beginning with the eastern half of the enclosure. 1928 saw the excavation of one segment of the inner ditch (ID VIII), one of the outer (the remainder of OD I), and four consecutive sections of the middle (MD I to IX). The pace of work increased in 1929 with the total excavation of a substantial outer ditch segment (OD III), two large middle ditch segments (X and XI) and eight of

the inner ditch (ID IX to XVI), along with the stripping of a large part of the interior of the inner enclosure on its eastern side (Smith 1965a, pl. 1). By this stage the policy was one of working systematically around the circuits in an anti-clockwise manner, a strategy later adopted for the excavations in the interior of Avebury (Smith 1965a, 188–91). In total, 145 m of inner, 144 m of middle, and 85 m of the outer circuit were excavated. In addition, several isolated Neolithic pits were located by bowsing and dug during the 1925–27 seasons, and a square earthwork enclosure 40 m to the east of OD V was discovered and totally excavated during 1928 (Smith 1965a, 30–33). The stripping of the large area within the interior of the inner circuit in 1929 probably represented a systematic approach to the discovery of pits, following the chance encounter of several during the excavation of ID VIII to X.

The recording of Keiller

Kendall had made very schematic notes and sketches of his cuttings, some of which survive. These are not very informative. Gray kept a site diary and site notebooks throughout the 1925–27 seasons (held with the archive in Avebury Museum). The latter concentrate on finds of artefacts, but say little on the whole about animal bone finds or deposits, nor much about stratigraphy, which is referred to as self-evident from sections. The few surviving sections are schematic, and at the very small scale of 5 feet to 1 inch. After Gray's departure, the rate of recovery of finds improved, and re-excavated segments yielded finds missed earlier. (In the re-excavation in 1937 of ID VII, in excess of 200 sherds, 440 flint flakes and 60 flint tools were found in the backfill, along with animal bones and several pieces of worked chalk and sarsen.) After 1925 attention was paid increasingly to animal bone deposits, though descriptions in the site notebooks remain general-ised. Photos show some bone groups re-assembled on the surface (for example from layer 5 of MD VII), as well as *in situ*. The ditches were now dug in pre-determined horizontal spits (surface-0.8, 0.8–1.4, 1.4–2.3, 2.3–3.5 feet, and so on).

During the 1928 and 1929 seasons, the method was refined, principally by the removal of the ditch fill in uniform spits one foot deep and the recording of the stratigraphy and major finds groups within each spit on a series of 'layer charts'. Longer lengths of ditch were dug as a series of consecutive segments (e.g. ID XV, MD X and XI, and OD I and III). Vertical sections were photographed and levelled. Contour plans of the emptied ditch segments were then produced at a scale of 10 feet to 1 inch. There is some formal description of stratigraphy in the site notebooks, but often the details are only implied or referred to obliquely. Especially in the secondary fill, material from several different layers might have been included in a single spit, particularly where the fill was asymmetrical. From 1928–29 there is a small series of levelled sections (not previously drawn up) for ID XV, MD X, and OD I and III. Recording was perhaps at its best in 1929, for which the majority of the field notebooks survive, along with several sections and contour plans. Significant finds and associated groups of material were frequently three-dimensionally recorded. Apart from this, the most systematic surviving records, completed after the excavations, are the finds catalogues. Ditch contour plans and photographs constitute the remaining part of the archive (Smith 1965a, 3). A large part of the archive, including all Keiller's layer charts, a number of the site notebooks, several of the finds catalogues and specialist reports, along with page proofs of unpublished monograph reports, disappeared in the late 1940s.

Despite the deficiencies of recording during the excavations and the losses suffered since, it is clear that more detail can be added to Smith's excellent general description of the results of Keiller's work (Smith 1965a). In particular, it is possible to appreciate variation in the spatial occurrence of both stratigraphic features and finds deposits. To this in fact reasonably detailed record can be added the results from the 1957–58 excavations, designed to enable and facilitate publication of Keiller's work, and from those of 1988. This chapter sets out what can be added to Smith's account of Keiller's work, concentrating principally on the ditches.

Ditch infill processes and terminology

In both this chapter and the following discussion of the 1988 ditch cuttings, the question of ditch infill is considered principally with reference to natural processes (Evans 1990; Case and Whittle 1982, 7–8; Bell *et al.* 1996). *Primary fill* of chalk rubble, fine chalk, turves and humic lenses is formed by rapid weathering of the ditch sides. The timescale is likely to be rapid, usually within the span of a human generation (Bell 1990; Bell *et al.* 1996). *Secondary fill* is formed after initial stability of the ditch sides has been achieved, and accumulates in the form of much less chalky, more humic material, which is gradually washed or eroded into the ditch or forms *in situ* under a litter of vegetation. The timescale may be considerable, and may be measurable in some cases in centuries. Eventually further stabilisation may be achieved, and *a soil* may form across the *upper secondary fill*. Further, *tertiary fill* may be formed by cultivation, and there may be a further soil. On a level surface, the pattern of filling in cross-section may be expected to be symmetrical. Slope may produce some asymmetry of fill, more coming from the uphill side, and transposing the centre of silting in the ditch to the downhill side. The presence of a bank may also produce asymmetry, through natural collapse if close enough to the ditch. Bank and other material can also be thrown into the ditch nonconformably with the natural process of infill, and such deliberate slighting will be referred to as backfilling (Smith 1965a; Smith 1971). Recutting may also interfere with the natural process of infill (Smith 1971). At its most severe, the whole fill accumulated to date may be scoured out; in other cases, there can be partial truncation of already naturally accumulated layers. Recutting and backfilling can occur together.

Finds of bone, flint, pottery and other materials occurred throughout the filling of all ditch segments, frequently in localised concentrations. Surviving detail of these concentrations is varied, and where they cannot be precisely characterised they are referred to in the text simply as 'deposits'. Where detailed written and/or visual records of individual finds deposits exist, the terms 'scatter', 'spread' and 'group' are occasionally employed; definitions of which are given in Chapter 4 in relation to the fully recorded deposits encountered during the 1988 excavations. Interpretation of the deposits is given in Chapter 17.

THE DITCHES

Each of Keiller's segments (fig. 21) is described separately, followed by a summary table of finds, based on the surviving notebooks and catalogues. By no means all material was kept, and quantities and descriptions or classifications have in many cases to be taken as given; it is not now possible to check, for example, every struck flake. Animal bone is referred to here in general terms; chapter 11 provides an important discussion of the surviving corpus of bone material, but much was not kept.

In the tables, the following abbreviations are used. For worked bone, P = pin or awl; for antler, C = comb, W = worked piece, F = fragment; for chalk, B = ball, C = cup, I = incised or perforated piece, M = miscellaneous shaped piece, P = phallus, PE = perforated pendant; for sarsen, P = pounder, Q = quern, R = rubbing stone F = miscellaneous fragment. Details of imported stone and human bone are added as appropriate. Depth is in feet and inches. OD = Outer Ditch; MD = Middle Ditch; ID = Inner Ditch.

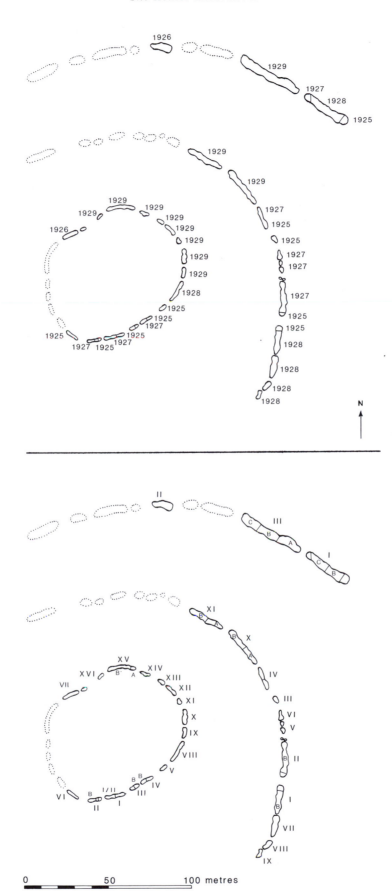

Fig. 21. Outline plan of the Keiller excavations, showing year of excavation and ditch segment numbers.

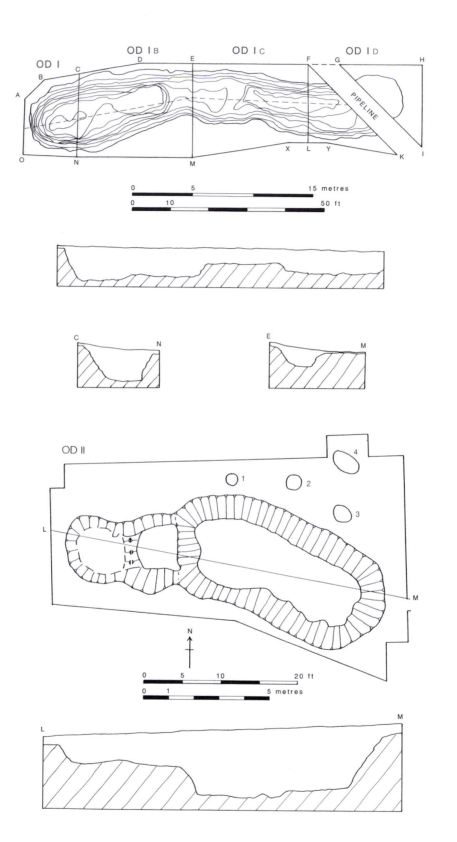

Fig. 22. Plans and profiles of OD I and OD II.

Outer Ditch II (fig. 22–24; table 1)

Fully excavated 1926. 12.8 m long, maximum depth 2.9 m. The segment is irregular in plan and profile. Its western part consists of two small intersecting portions, joining a more massive sub-rectangular pit in the eastern part. The limited comments on silting in Gray's notebooks provide little information.

Animal bone and sarsen came from the base of the ditch. A very dark lens of silt, with burnt material and ash, was found within chalk rubble at the west end of the deeper eastern portion of the segment, in layer 5. This contained a 'fair number' of animal bones.

Four small oval and circular pits (60–3) were excavated immediately to the north of the segment, beyond its outer edge (Smith 1965a, 29–30). Sherds of Beaker and Early Bronze Age worked flint came from two of these.

Table 1: Finds by layer and depth in Outer Ditch II.

Layer	1	2	3	4	5	6	7
Depth	top-8"	8"-1,4	1,4-2,3	2,3-3,5	3,5-6	6-8	8-base
Flint							
Tools	99	62	51	13	12	2	9
Flakes	-	-	-	-	-	-	-
Cores	-	-	-	-	-	-	-
Pottery (sherds)							
WH	17	20	25	64	302	20	8
LN	42	30	38	8	-	-	-
Beaker/EBA	107	105	111	15	-	-	- .
RB	45	30	3	2	-	-	-
Worked bone	M	-	-	P	-	-	-
Chalk	-	B	-	-	-	-	-
Stone	1	2	5	-	-	-	-
Sarsen	2P	P,M	P	R,F	-	P	-
Human bone	-	-	-	1	-	-	-

Stone, layer 1: polishing stone of silicified sandstone; layer 2: piece of Lower Greensand,
piece of ferruginous grit; layer 3: fragment Grp Xa stone, 2 pieces ferruginous sandstone, 'honing
stone' of micaceous sandstone, piece of Lower Greensand. Human bone, layer 4: adult ?rt tibia.

Fig. 23. View of OD II as excavated, from the west (photo: Alexander Keiller Museum, Avebury).

Fig. 24. View of OD II during excavation, from the east (Keiller with back to camera, Gray facing camera in middle-ground) (photo: Alexander Keiller Museum, Avebury).

Outer Ditch III *(figs 25–29; tables 2–4)*

Fully excavated 1929, as three units, south (A), middle (B), and north (C). 42.4 m long, maximum depth over 2.4 m (Smith 1965a, pl. IIIc). The segment is bipartite, with an internal ridge approximately in the centre of the ditch. Leading away from this, shallower parts give way to deeper terminals. The north-west terminal is deeper; the south-east terminal has a curious, small extension, which is suggestive of an earlier feature cut through by the ditch.

The recording of the silting is somewhat confusing. There are separate layer lists for B and C, which being based on spits do not take sufficient notice of stratigraphic succession. Layer charts were used by Piggott to reconstruct sections for A, B and C (of which he published A and C (Piggott 1954, fig. 4)). Levelled sections, not previously drawn up, also exist. These suggest that primary rubble and silt (perhaps partially cleared out in the outer part of B) were succeeded by secondary, more humic silting, which in turn was followed by dumping or bank collapse, from the inner side, of more chalk rubble (figs 27–8). There was a little further humic silting in C, and then a substantial amount of what the notebooks describe as a 'very hard white silt', which was presumably dumped in some way.

Table 2: Finds by layer and depth in Outer Ditch IIIA.

Layer	1	2	3	4	5	6	7	8	9	refill
Depth	top-1'	1-2	2-3	3-4	4-5	5-6	6-7	7-8	8-9	
Flint										
Tools	28	23	7	8	6	2	-	-	-	-
Flakes	1076	534	92	79	55	13	-	-	36	-
Cores	80	30	6	-	11	2	-	-	22	-
Pottery (sherds)										
WH	↑	65	22	76	57	10	4	-	-	↑
LN	'	4	-	-	-	-	-	-	-	'
	146									5
Beaker/EBA	'	42	-	-	-	-	-	-	-	'
RB	↓	-	-	-	-	-	-	-	-	↓
Worked bone	-	-	M,P	-	-	-	-	-	-	-
Chalk	-	-	-	M	-	-	B,P	-	-	-
Stone	-	2	4	1	1	-	-	-	-	-
Sarsen	P	2R,F	Q,F	3Q,2R,2P	2P,F	-	-	-	-	-

Stone, layer 2: part of dolerite macehead, complete Grp IIa axe; layer 3: 4 fragments of Grp I axe; layer 4: flake of micaceous quartzite; layer 5: piece of Stonesfield slate.

Table 3: Finds by layer and depth in Outer Ditch IIIB.

Layer	1	2	3	4	5	6	7	8	9	refill
Depth	top-1'	1-2	2-3	3-4	4-5	5-6	6-7	7-8	8-9	
Flint										
Tools	57	5	8	3	1	-	-	-	-	-
Flakes	1043	113	48	42	15	4	2	-	-	-
Cores	75	1	7	-	2	1	-	-	-	-
Pottery (sherds)										
WH	↑	↑	12	17	28	3	1	-	-	↑
LN	'	'	-	-	-	-	-	-	-	'
	184	5								3
Beaker/EBA	'	'	-	-	-	-	-	-	-	'
RB	↓	↓	-	-	-	-	-	-	-	↓
Worked bone	-	P	-	-	-	-	-	-	-	-
Chalk	-	-	-	-	M	-	I	-	-	-
Sarsen	R,F	R	-	Q	-	-	-	-	-	-
Human bone	-	-	-	-	1	-	-	-	-	-

Human bone, layer 5: child skeleton on base of ditch.

Table 4: Finds by layer and depth in Outer Ditch IIIC.

Layer	1	2	3	4	5	6	7	8	9	refill
Depth	top-1'	1-2	2-3	3-4	4-5	5-6	6-7	7-8	8-9	
Flint										
Tools	89	10	4	10	6	6	1	1	1	-
Flakes	2016	191	68	41	45	35	12	10	5	-
Cores	144	25	16	3	6	11	1	1	1	-
Pottery (sherds)										
WH	↑	23	↑	14	17	28	34	10	15	↑
LN	'	12	'	-	-	-	-	-	-	'
	305		22							8
Beaker/EBA	'	1	'	-	-	-	-	-	-	'
RB	↓	-	↓	-	-	-	-	-	-	↓
Worked bone	-	M	P	-	-	-	-	-	-	-
Antler	-	1	1	-	-	C	-	1	-	-
Chalk	-	-	-	-	-	-	-	I	-	-
Stone	-	1	-	-	-	-	-	-	-	-
Sarsen	4P,F	P	-	-	-	-	3P	-	-	-
Human bone	1	-	1	-	2	3	1	-	-	-

Stone, layer 2: piece of Stonesfield slate.
Human bone, layer 1: adult tooth; layer 3: adult female femur; layer 5: adult tooth, humerus; layer 6: humerus fragments, occipital and parietal fragments of young adult, occipital fragment of adult ?male; layer 7: cervical vertebra.

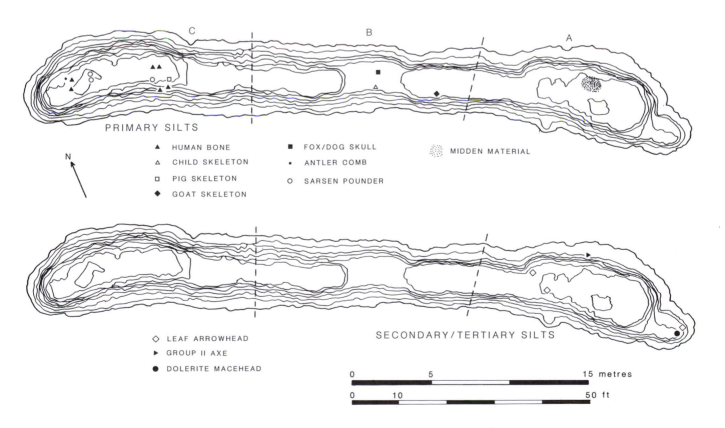

Fig. 25. Finds distributions in OD III.

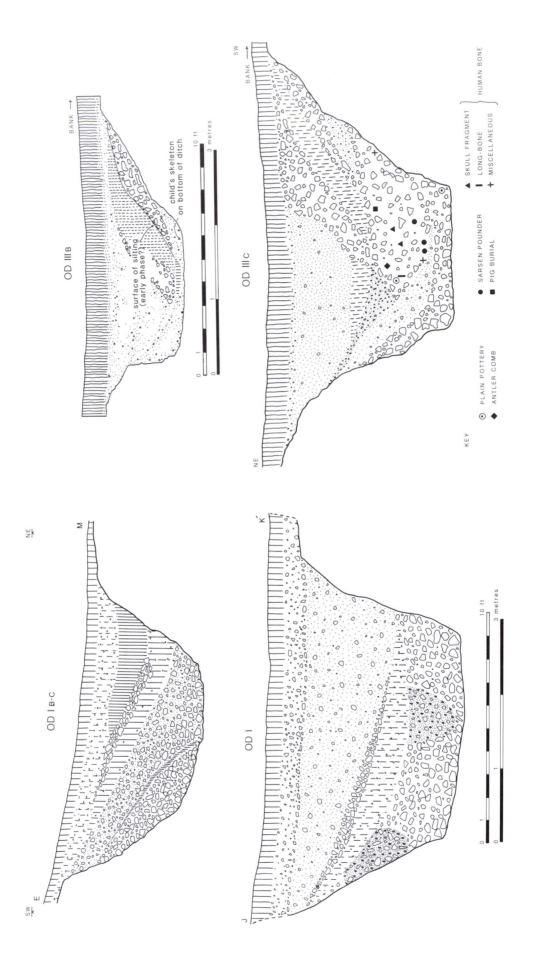

Fig. 26. Sections of OD I and OD III. OD I sections reconstructed from level measurements; OD III sections after Piggott.

Fig. 27. View of OD IIIA during excavation, from the south-east, after removal of spit 1. Note chalkier fill on inner (left) side (photo: Alexander Keiller Museum, Avebury).

Fig. 28. Section of OD III B–C. Left is inside (photo: Alexander Keiller Museum, Avebury).

In the centre of the segment at the base of the ditch and near its inner side there was a crouched inhumation, of a 2–3 year old child (fig. 29). There were seven other occurrences of human bone (limb and skull fragments from a minimum of three individuals), mainly in the lower levels and mainly in C. There was a complete pig skeleton in layer 5 in C, an antler fragment in layer 8 and an ox tibia in layer 9.

In the secondary fill of B there was one human bone. A complete sheep/goat skeleton occurred in layer 3 in the eastern half of B, covered by chalk rubble and silt. Several fragments of human bone occurred in the primary fill above and below the pig burial, and the skeleton of the young child (Smith 1965a, 136) lay directly on the base of the centre of the ditch within 5 m of the goat. Also from layer 3, the packed chalk noted above, which the notebooks also refer to as a 'chalk floor', there were considerable quantities of sherds and flints (and more from layers 2 and 1), as well as two stone axes and half a macehead.

Fig. 29. Excavation of child skeleton in OD IIIB. Inside of the ditch is to the left.
The excavator may be Veronica Keiller (photo: Alexander Keiller Museum, Avebury).

Outer Ditch I *(figs 22, 26 and 30–32; tables 5–7)*

Part of south terminal (OD I) excavated 1925, and re-excavated 1928; remainder (OD IB and C), apart from north end, excavated 1928; north end (OD ID) excavated 1937. 29.6 m long, maximum depth 2.6 m. The segment is tripartite. On either side of a shallower central portion there are deeper terminal parts, deeper and broader to the south. A pipeline cuts the north terminal.

Although there is little information on silting in the remaining notebooks, sections survive, across the south end by Gray, and across the middle of the ditch. Both show a markedly asymmetrical fill (cf. Smith 1965a, pl. VIb), with large amounts of primary chalk rubble on the inner side, followed by fine secondary silt, and succeeded by further chalk rubble. This is suggestive of backfilling or bank collapse.

Gray recorded bones and 'roundabout, a mass of charcoal' at 8 ft in OD I.

Few of Keiller's notebooks for this segment survive. There are records of finds from layer 6 in the southern terminal area of OD IB: two entire, articulated cattle forelegs (with more bones in layer 7 below), along with an ox

Table 5: Finds by layer and depth in Outer Ditch I.

Layer	1	2	3	4	5	6		
Depth	top-8"	8"-1,4	1,4-2,3	2,3-3,5	3,5-6	6-base	?	re-exc
Flint								
Tools	1	3	-	-	1	2	4	23
Flakes	-	-	-	-	-	-	-	198
Cores	-	-	-	-	-	-	-	22
Pottery (sherds)								
WH	-	-	-	-	-	12	19	↑
LN	-	-	-	12	-	-	1	'
								30
Beaker/EBA	-	-	-	-	-	-	24	'
RB	-	-	-	-	-	-	9	↓
Chalk	-	-	-	-	-	2I	-	-
Stone	-	-	-	-	-	-	-	4
Sarsen	-	-	-	-	-	P	-	P,2F,Q

Stone, re-excav: 3 pieces Lower Greensand, piece Corallian sandstone.

Table 6: Finds by layer and depth in Outer Ditch IB.

Layer	1	2	3	4	5	6	7	8
Depth	top-1	1-2	2-3	3-4	4-5	5-6	6-7	7-8
Flint								
Tools	41	20	4	16	4	12	3	3
Flakes	965	292	85	111	29	23	33	16
Cores	93	23	2	8	8	4	4	4
Pottery (sherds)								
WH	↑	↑	↑	36	20	37	36	44
LN	'	'	'	-	-	-	-	-
	101	51	18					
Beaker/EBA	'	'	'	-	-	-	-	-
RB	↓	↓	↓	-	-	-	-	-
Antler	-	-	-	-	-	2	-	-
Chalk	B	-	-	-	-	-	-	M
Sarsen	-	-	-	R	-	R,Q	-	-

Table 7: Finds by layer and depth in Outer Ditch IC.

Layer	1	2	3	4	5	6	7
Depth	top-1	1-2	2-3	3-4	4-5	5-6	6-7
Flint							
Tools	97	10	25	11	8	1	-
Flakes	1581	182	231	117	121	14	7
Cores	152	10	11	14	9	1	1
Pottery (sherds)							
WH	↑	↑	↑	43	54	10	5
LN	'	'	'	-	-	-	-
	247	34	40				
Beaker/EBA	'	'	'	-	-	-	-
RB	↓	↓	↓	-	-	-	-
Antler	-	-	-	C	-	-	-
Chalk	C	-	C	-	I	-	-
Stone	1	1	-	-	-	-	-
Sarsen	2P,M	P,M	-	-	-	6	-

Stone, layer 1: smoothed piece of Lower Greensand; layer 2: shaped piece of glauconite sandstone.

Fig. 30. OD I in 1928 during re-excavation of the 1925 cutting (photo: Alexander Keiller Museum, Avebury).

Fig. 31. OD IB during excavation, from the south-east (photo: Alexander Keiller Museum, Avebury).

femur and the broken remains of two antlers, and a complete quern in direct association with a rubbing stone.

Among the other finds, four retouched flint flakes were found closely associated with 10 flakes and 13 cores in layer 3 of OD IC 'near the north-east corner'.

Middle Ditch XI *(figs 33–35; tables 8–9)*

Fully excavated 1929 as two halves, south (A) and north (B). 23.5 m long, maximum depth 1.5 m. The segment is formed by three intersecting portions, the longest to the south, the deepest in the middle; the northern portion appears to deepen adjacent to the causeway.

The silting is normal, including what appears to be a soil above the secondary fill (in the terms of Evans 1990); some asymmetry in the primary chalk rubble in the middle portion could suggest limited backfilling. Deposits of burnt material (listed in the notebooks as 'hearths') occur above the secondary fill, in the northern half of the segment only. The sections produced from Keiller's layer charts suggest that this material could have been in the fill of pits cut into the silting below, as far down as the top of the primary fill.

The southern half (A) produced comparatively little material. Part of an ox skull and two cattle horncores were found on the base of the ditch towards the middle of the ditch. In the primary fill there were sarsen pounders and other fragments, and an adult human femur occurred in the primary fill at the southern terminal.

The northern half (B) was richer. The upper primary and the secondary fill incorporated several deposits. On or just above the base in the north terminal pit were a polished flint axe fragment, two fragments of human jaw, and two groups of dog bone; one of these was associated with the

Fig. 32. Section of OD IC, from the south-east. Left is inside (photo: Alexander Keiller Museum, Avebury).

Table 8: Finds by layer and depth in Middle Ditch XIA.

Layer	1	2	3	4	5	re-fill
Depth	top-1'	1-2	2-3	3-4	4-5	
Flint						
Tools	34	52	31	10	9	-
Flakes	1605	1351	735	189	96	-
Cores	82	72	40	22	5	-
Pottery (sherds)						
WH	↑	507	161	↑	-	-
LN	'	-	-	'	-	-
	295			37		
Beaker/EBA	'	-	-	'	-	-
RB	↓	-	-	↓	-	-
Antler	-	-	2	3	-	-
Stone	-	1	-	-	-	-
Sarsen	-	F	2P,2R,Q	-	-	-
Human bone	-	-	-	-	-	4

Stone, layer 2: possible axe fragment, Grp VIII.
Human bone, layer 5: juvenile occipital fragment; child skull fragment; 2 pieces of jaw.

Table 9: Finds by layer and depth in Middle Ditch XIB.

Layer	1	2	3	4	5	re-fill
Depth	top-1'	1-2	2-3	3-4	4-5	
Flint						
Tools	44	52	12	4	2	-
Flakes	1844	934	225	23	18	-
Cores	75	51	28	10	-	-
Pottery (sherds)						
WH	< 246 >		64	25	11	↑
LN	< 9 >		-	-	-	'
						16
Beaker/EBA	< 4 >		-	-	-	'
RB	< 1 >		-	-	-	↓
Worked bone	-	-	P	P	-	-
Antler	-	-	-	F	-	-
Chalk	-	B	B	-	-	-
Stone	1	3	-	-	-	-
Sarsen	-	P,R	3P,3R	-	-	-
Human bone	-	-	1	1	-	-

Stone, layer 1: axe fragment; layer 2: cutting edge of tuff axe; 2 pieces of calcareous grit; piece of micaceous sandstone.
Human bone, layer 3: juvenile upper jaw fragment; layer 4: adult femur.

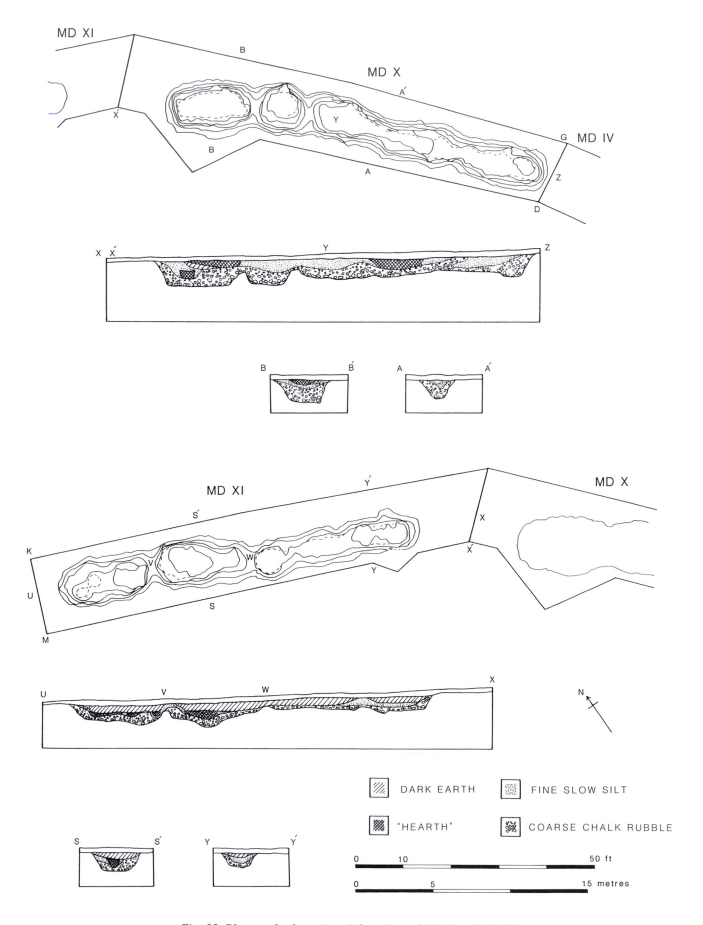

Fig. 33. Plans and schematic axial sections of MD X and MD XI.

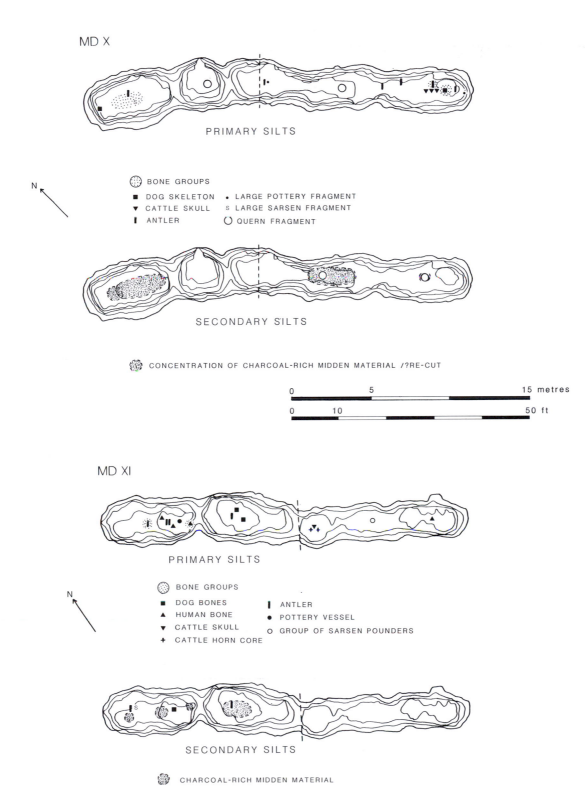

MD X

PRIMARY SILTS

BONE GROUPS

■ DOG SKELETON   • LARGE POTTERY FRAGMENT

▼ CATTLE SKULL   s LARGE SARSEN FRAGMENT

❚ ANTLER   ○ QUERN FRAGMENT

N

SECONDARY SILTS

CONCENTRATION OF CHARCOAL-RICH MIDDEN MATERIAL /?RE-CUT

0   5   15 metres

0   10   50 ft

MD XI

PRIMARY SILTS

BONE GROUPS

■ DOG BONES   ❚ ANTLER

▲ HUMAN BONE   • POTTERY VESSEL

▼ CATTLE SKULL   ○ GROUP OF SARSEN POUNDERS

+ CATTLE HORN CORE

N

SECONDARY SILTS

CHARCOAL-RICH MIDDEN MATERIAL

s SARSEN POUNDER

Fig. 34. Finds distributions in MD X and MD xI.

Fig. 35. MD XIB under excavation, probably at the north-west end, from the south.
This is probably a view of the primary fill at the level of pottery above human remains
(photo: Alexander Keiller Museum, Avebury).

feet and tail bones of a cat, perhaps from a pelt. On the slope of the south edge of the north terminal pit there were a human infant skull, and fox and pig bones. Slightly above, a pot was inverted over the area of human remains. In layer 4b there were three cattle horncores and limb bones, and in layer 4a two large pieces of antler and some cattle bone.

articulated vertebral column from layer 5b of MD XB, associated with a quantity of cattle bones and a number of worked flints. Further above, still in chalk rubble, was a large piece of sarsen, and a charcoal-rich area with hazel charcoal and carbonised shells, and some cattle bone, in layers 3b–4.

The middle portion appears to have been largely devoid of finds.

Middle Ditch X *(figs 33–34, 36; tables 10–11)*

Fully excavated 1929 as two halves, south (A) and north (B). 24.7 m long, maximum depth 1.7 m. The segment consists of three parts, the longest (and least regular) to the south, with a slight terminal pit. The other two portions are more regular and deeper (Smith 1965a, pl. IIIb). There is much primary chalk rubble, spread unevenly across the segment, especially at the north end. Quantity and asymmetry suggest some backfilling. Secondary chalky silt follows, with lenses of chalk rubble at the south end suggestive of further backfilling. Burnt material (charcoal, sarsen, and bone) recorded from upper levels in the northern half, and from above the primary fill in the southern half, could be from pits cut into the fill of the ditch.

In the northern portion, a young dog skeleton (probably articulated) and an ox horn core were found against the terminal at its base; low in the primary fill above the terminal was a 'great quantity' of cattle bone including articulated vertebrae, a skull, three horncores of different sizes, a scapula, a pelvis fragment, and limb/feet bones; there was also a sheep/goat skull. Photographs show an

Fig. 36. View of bone deposit in layer 5b of MD XB
(photo: Alexander Keiller Museum, Avebury).

Table 10: Finds by layer and depth in Middle Ditch XA.

Layer	1	2	3	4	5	6	re-fill
Depth	top-1'	1-2	2-3	3-4	4-5	5-6	
Flint							
Tools	51	43	15	-	4	-	-
Flakes	1789	1127	411	60	13	-	-
Cores	92	62	5	6	2	-	-
Pottery (sherds)							
WH	↑	↑	270	138	31	-	9
LN	'	'	-	-	-	-	-
	152	213					
Beaker/EBA	'	'	-	-	-	-	-
RB	↓	↓	-	-	-	-	-
Antler	-	-	3	-	2	-	-
Chalk	-	-	B	-	-	-	-
Stone	-	1	1	-	-	-	-
Sarsen	2R	3P,Q	2R	Q,R	R	-	-
Human bone	-	1	-	-	-	-	-

Stone, layer 2: limestone fragment; layer 3: quartzite fragment.
Human bone, layer 2: adult rt maxilla.

Table 11: Finds by layer and depth in Middle Ditch XB.

Layer	1	2	3	4	5	6	re-fill
Depth	top-1'	1-2	2-3	3-4	4-5	5-6	
Flint							
Tools	45	31	28	2	3	3	1
Flakes	1408	610	301	80	25	25	-
Cores	111	32	32	9	6	2	-
Pottery (sherds)							
WH	↑	↑	298	46	102	25	7
LN	'	'	-	-	-	-	-
	113	86					
Beaker/EBA	'	'	-	-	-	-	-
RB	↓	↓	-	-	-	-	-
Worked bone	M	-	P	-	-	-	-
Antler	-	-	1	-	-	-	-
Stone	-	-	1	-	-	-	-
Sarsen	Q,F,R,P	3P,2F	Q	Q	R	-	-
Human bone	-	-	1	-	-	-	-

Stone, layer 3: chert piece.
Human bone, layer 3: ?adult lft femur.

In the primary fill of the southern portion, there were finds of a large quern fragment, an antler pick and rake and a sherd, and sherds from a single vessel against the southern terminal. Within chalk rubble at the southern end (layers 3b–4), there were a dog skeleton, cattle bones (some slightly charred) including several limb/feet bones, a pelvis, a sacrum, and a jaw, sherds, two large pieces of sarsen and two of flint, flint waste, and five iron pyrites. Immediately to the north at the same level there were three cattle skulls and two horncores. More or less above in layer 3a, there were a very large ox horncore, an antler, other bones (possibly deer), and sherds. A little to the north in layer 2b, there were an ox mandible, sherds, a greensand quern fragment and a sarsen rubbing stone. Also in layer 2b (position uncertain) there was a substantial spread of material, including some animal bone, sherds, flint flakes, sarsen chips, a sarsen quern fragment, charcoal and burnt earth. Just above and to the west, in layer 2a, a leaf arrowhead was found beside a decomposed horn core.

Middle Ditch IV *(fig. 37; tables 12–13)*

Southern half excavated 1925 (MD IV), re-excavated 1927; north half excavated 1927 (MD IVB). 14.6 m long, maximum depth 1.4 m. The segment cuts a small pit on its inner side. Gray describes 'burnt mould' (in association with small quantities of burnt animal bone and sherds) in the middle of MD IV, from 3 ft down to the base; this could suggest either a recut or successive dumps of hearth material. Otherwise, there is no information on silting.

A letter from Keiller to Childe (6.3.28) refers to a complete ox skeleton from the basal two layers of MD IV, but there is no further surviving reference to this in the field notes. In layer 3 of MD IVB there was a concentration of animal bone, sherds, flint (including a knife, seven serrated flakes, five worked flakes, 43 flakes of which 10 were burnt, and three cores) and sarsen, in a matrix of dark soil. Above this in layer 2, there was a large number of sarsen pieces.

Middle Ditch III *(fig. 37; table 14)*

Fully excavated 1925, re-excavated 1927. 4.9 m long, maximum depth 1.2 m. The notebooks record that the segment was regularly cut, with steep ends. Gray notes that large chalk rubble was present 'at a comparatively high level', which is suggestive of partial backfilling.

Many sherds came from near the base. The notebooks record that animal bone, particularly cattle, was plentiful in the secondary fill. At a depth of 3 ft there was a large area of black soil mixed with chalk rubble, associated with bone (some burnt), five sherds and possibly a young human upper jaw. The relationship of the other jaw fragments is unclear.

Table 12: Finds by layer and depth in Middle Ditch IV.

| Layer | 1 | 2 | 3 | 4 | | |
Depth	top-8"	8"-1,4	1,4-2,3	2,3-3,5	?	re-excav
Flint						
Tools	9	13	4	3	3	18
Flakes	-	-	-	-	-	1045
Cores	-	-	-	-	-	41
Pottery (sherds)						
WH	<	87	>	170	-	94
Beaker/EBA	-	-	-	-	-	1
RB	<	9	>	2	-	14
Stone	-	-	-	-	-	1
Sarsen	-	-	-	-	P	-

Stone, re-excav: flake of Grp VI axe.

Table 13: Finds by layer and depth in Middle Ditch IVB.

| Layer | 1 | 2 | 3 | 4 | 5 | refill |
Depth	top-8"	8-1,4	1,4-2,3	2,3-3,5	3,5-base	
Flint						
Tools	21	16	13	-	-	-
Flakes	514	350	183	30	8	-
Cores	28	27	34	2	1	-
Pottery (sherds)						
WH	71	79	153	68	36	27
LN	2	16	4	-	-	-
Beaker/EBA	-	-	-	-	-	-
RB	36	17	1	-	-	8
Stone	1	-	-	-	-	-
Sarsen	-	-	-	Q,P	-	-

Stone, layer 1: chip of Grp VII, probably from axe.

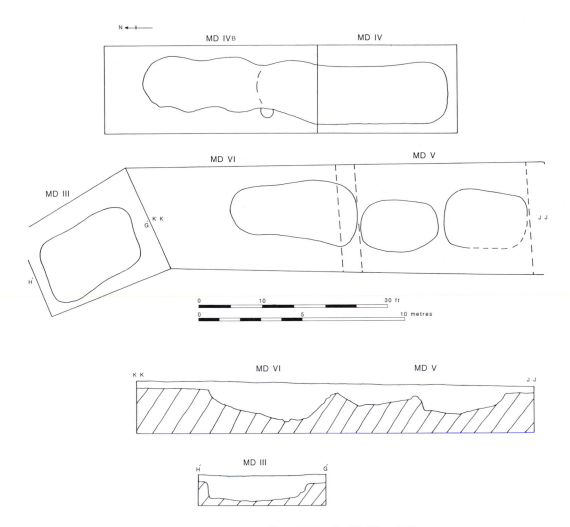

Fig. 37. Plan and profiles of MD IV, III, VI and V.

Table 14: Finds by layer and depth in Middle Ditch III.

Layer	1		2	3		
Depth	0-2'		2-3,5	3,5-base	re-excav	?
Flint						
Tools	1		1	6	29	8
Flakes	-		-		517	-
Cores	-		-	-	20	-
Pottery (sherds)						
WH	<	86	>	126	46	-
Beaker/EBA	<	5	>	-	-	-
RB	<	4	>	-	5	-
Worked bone	-		-	-	P	-
Chalk	-		-	-	B	B,M
Sarsen	-		-	-	Q,R	-
Human bone	-		2	-	1	-

Human bone, c.3': upper and lower jaw of one juvenile; re-excav: juvenile upper jaw.

Middle Ditch VI *(figs 37–38 and 40; table 15)*

Fully excavated 1927. 6.1 m long, maximum depth 1.8 m. The base deepens and widens to the south. Gray records that the lower part of layer 1, all of layer 2, and the upper half of layer 3 were composed of chalk rubble (suggestive of backfilling); below this, the silting is described as normal.

This 'productive' segment had much animal bone. There was a red deer skull in layer 4 in the centre of the ditch. Many other bones (principally cattle) came from the same layer, and a chalk ball and an incised chalk piece in association with an antler tine.

In layer 5 (primary fill) there was an ox skull (precise location not recorded), and a large portion of pot towards the southern terminal. Two lots of articulated cattle bone were found on the base of the ditch. At the north end, part of a vertebral column rested on part of a mandible, with scapulae on either side (Smith 1965a, pl. Vc). Against the outer side of the ditch and to the south of the first group, there was a vertebral column. A little above the base, there were a skull and horncores from a young sheep/goat, and a large number of cattle bones, including ribs, a burnt humerus and two scapulae. The notebook emphasises that 'no animal bone was found on the bottom of the ditch at the deepest part', in the southern terminal.

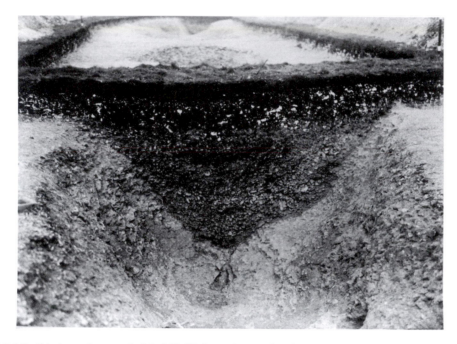

Fig. 38. A Middle Ditch section, probably MD VI from the north (photo: Alexander Keiller Museum, Avebury).

Table 15: Finds by layer and depth in Middle Ditch VI.

Layer	1	2	3	4	5	refill	re-excav
Depth	top-8"	8"-1,4	1,4-2,3	2,3-3,5	3,5-base		
Flint							
Tools	39	6	8	10	8	-	-
Flakes	1073	251	116	310	102	-	-
Cores	63	21	9	46	6	-	-
Pottery (sherds)							
WH	↑	↑	↑	256	104	↑	↑
LN	'	'	'	-	-	'	'
	40	40	48			1	87
Beaker/EBA	'	'	'	-	-	'	'
RB	↓	↓	↓	-	-	↓	↓
Worked bone	-	-	M	P	-	-	-
Antler	-	-	-	3	-	-	-
Chalk	-	B	-	B,M	-	-	-
Stone	2	-	3	-	-	-	-
Sarsen	R,F,2P	P	P,R	-	P	-	-

Stone, layer 1: core made from Grp VIII axe, piece of Lower Greensand; layer 3: 3 pieces of limestone.

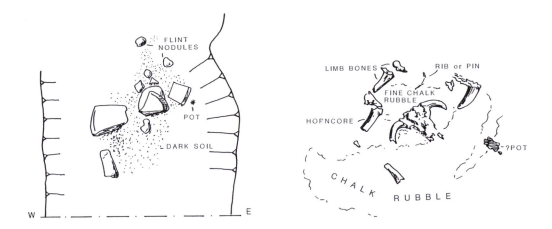

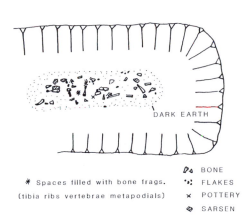

Fig. 39. Finds groups in top left: *MD IB, layer 3, sarsen group;* top right: *MD IB, layer 4b, south terminal; and* left: *MD IX, layer 3b.*

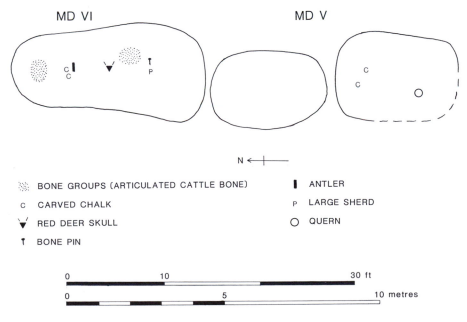

Fig. 40. Finds distributions in MD VI and MD V.

Table 16: Finds by layer and depth in Middle Ditch V.

Layer Depth	1 top-8"	2 8"-1,4	3 1,4-2,3	4 2,3-3,5	5 3,5-base	refill
Flint						
Tools	39	11	16	10	3	-
Flakes	1300	523	389	189	10	-
Cores	50	26	22	12	1	-
Pottery (sherds)						
WH	↑ 67	↑ 52	311	83	2	↑ 3
LN	↓	↓	-	-	-	↓
Antler	-	-	-	C	-	-
Chalk	-	2M	-	B	M	-
Stone	2	-	-	-	-	-
Sarsen	2R	R,Q,F	3Q,F,2P	Q,R	-	-

Stone, layer 1: 2 pieces Lower Greensand.

Middle Ditch V *(figs 37 and 40; table 16)*

Two separate segments, fully excavated 1927. North segment 3.7 m long, maximum depth 1 m; south segment 4 m long, maximum depth 1.2 m. In both, the deepest part was in the northern portion. The notebooks contain no information on silting, though photographs show an asymmetric primary fill of pure chalk, succeeded by more humic upper silts with a large admixture of chalk (Smith 1965a, pl. VIc).

Some at least of the recorded artefacts appear to be from the southern segment, but it is not clear whether this holds good for all the finds. There is minimal information on animal bone; two only were retained from layers 3 and 4, an antler fragment and part of an ox femur. There was also an antler comb in layer 4.

Middle Ditch II *(figs 41–42; tables 17–18)*

South terminal (MD II) excavated 1925, re-excavated 1927. Remainder (MD IIB) and two pits at north end excavated 1927. 19.8 m long, maximum depth 2.1 m. The segment is tripartite. An oval pit forms the northern end; its weathered end connects with the rest of the segment. The southern portion consists of two intersecting, shallow pits.

Two schematic sections by Gray show a markedly asymmetrical fill, with particularly large quantities of primary chalk rubble deriving from the inner side, and filling almost half the ditch at the north end. This is suggestive of backfilling. Secondary fill of chalky silt overlies this.

Table 17: Finds by layer and depth in Middle Ditch II.

Layer Depth	1 top-8"	2 8"-1,4	3 1,4-2,3	4 2,3-4	re-excav
Flint					
Tools	1	1	8	6	17
Flakes	-	-	-	-	260
Cores	-	-	-	-	18
Pottery (sherds)					
WH	<	54	>	28	45
LN	<	3	>	-	1
Beaker/EBA	<	6	>	-	2
RB	-	-	-	-	6
Worked bone	-	-	-	P	-
Sarsen	-	-	-	2Q	-
Human bone	-	-	-	1	-

Human bone, layer 4: rt ?male femur.

Table 18: Finds by layer and depth in Middle Ditch IIB.

Layer	1	2	3	4	5	6	refill
Depth	top-8"	8"-1,4	1,4-2,3	2,3-3,5	3,5-5	5-base	
Flint							
Tools	56	97	19	55	45	9	-
Flakes	1020	1307	411	428	306	40	-
Cores	34	70	12	22	7	5	-
Pottery (sherds)							
WH	110	279	331	419	321	43	45
LN	13	61	167	5	1	-	6
Beaker/EBA	17	61	4	-	-	-	-
RB	17	17	3	-	-	-	-
Worked bone	-	-	-	2P	2P	-	-
Antler	-	-	-	M	-	C	-
Chalk	-	-	-	2I	I,B	-	-
Stone	6	1	-	-	1	-	-
Sarsen	-	3Q,3R,F	P,F,2R	3P,2Q,R	P,3R,F	-	-
Human bone	-	1	-	-	-	-	-

Stone, layer 1: piece Lower Greensand, 5 pieces ferruginous grit; layer 2:
piece Lower Greensand; layer 5: piece Lower Greensand.
Human bone, layer 2: adult parietal bone.

The segment produced a wide range of material. Sherds from 15 Ebbsfleet vessels came from MD IIB (Smith 1965a, 73–74). There was a notable quantity of bone pins.

Layer 4 of MD IIB produced two substantial groups of associated finds. Because of confusion in the notebooks and finds catalogues over nomenclature of the two main areas of the segment, the location of these finds groups is uncertain.

One group contained a small ox jaw, a sheep/goat jaw, sherds, part of a polished flint axe (according to the finds catalogue conjoining with another fragment from layer 1), four flint flakes, and charcoal; below were a fragment of cattle radius, part of a pig jaw, a worked antler shaft, and a flint pot boiler. The other group included a bone awl, 10 sherds, a piece of sarsen, eight worked flakes, three serrated flakes and three other flakes; most of the flint was burnt. A bone pin occurred below this group on the base of the ditch.

The finds catalogues refer to a third group of associated material, in layer 5, comprising 17 sherds, a scraper, core, worked flakes and two other flakes. Several pieces of sarsen were found together in layer 4 at the 'S. end of the cutting'.

Middle Ditch I (*figs 39, 41–46; tables 19–20*)

North terminal (MD I) excavated 1925; remainder (MD IB) excavated 1928. 17.1 m long, maximum depth 1.7 m. The ditch sides are near-vertical and appear largely unweathered. The segment widens and deepens towards the north end. The segment is tripartite, with a north terminal pit, a south terminal pit, and a central portion.

A schematic section by Gray shows chalk rubble filling more than half of the ditch, which is suggestive of partial backfilling in the north part at least. Consistent with this, the 1928 notebooks record layer 3b in MD IB as particularly 'rubbly' at the north end.

Charcoal-rich bone deposits were present as high as layer 2 in MD IB. Keiller speculated that 'food was roasted on sarsens laid on a charcoal hearth ... and that the flesh was then cut from the bones with flakes knocked from cores on the spot and then thrown away'.

Layer 3 produced many dog and cattle bones, associated with burnt sarsens. In layer 3b, three charcoal-rich bone deposits were recorded in the southern part of the central portion. That to the north contained burnt bones and four burnt flakes. Another comprised cattle bone and sherds mixed with charcoal. A third, to the south, virtually on the base of the ditch, had numerous cattle bones, dog bones, a piece of antler, flakes and lumps of burnt sarsen. The northern and central of these deposits continued into layer 4a, and rested on the ditch base. The northern consisted of large pieces of charcoal, unburnt bone, small sherds, a piece of burnt flint and two pieces of burnt sarsen. Merging with this, the central group contained a number of cattle bones, a core and 10 flakes. In layer 4b there were some bones, sherds, flint and charcoal ('very large pieces ... were thick here like the remains of a good wood-fire').

At the extreme south end of the ditch, near the base of the terminal pit, there were two cattle skulls and other bones, with a sherd and flakes beneath them. One of the skulls was placed centrally, facing the terminal, fragments of the other being arranged around it.

At the extreme north end of MD IB and close to the base of the ditch there were three sarsen quern fragments close together.

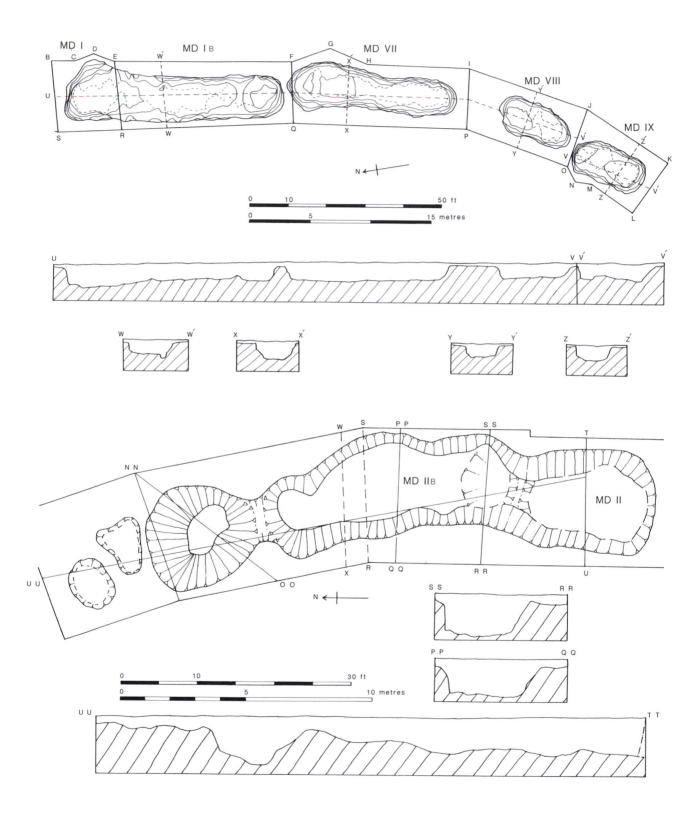

Fig. 41. Plans and profiles of MD I, MD VII, MD VIII, MD IX and MD II.

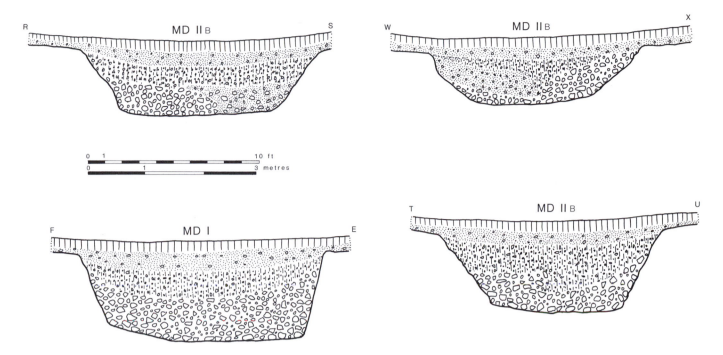

Fig. 42. Sections of MD IIB and MD I, after Gray.

Table 19: Finds by layer and depth in Middle Ditch I.

Layer	refill	re-excav	1-4	5
Depth			top-3,5	3,5-base
Flint				
Tools	1	21	-	-
Flakes	-	-	-	-
Cores	-	-	-	-
Pottery (sherds)				
WH	-	↑	47	116
LN	-	'	5	-
		40		
Beaker/EBA	-	'	-	-
RB	-	↓	3	-
Chalk	-	B	-	4B
Stone	-	1	-	-
Sarsen	2P,3R	P,2Q,2R,F	2R,Q	R,P
Human bone	1	-	-	-

Stone, re-excav: piece Lower Greensand.
Human bone, refill: 2 molars.

Joshua Pollard

Table 20: Finds by layer and depth in Middle Ditch IB.

Layer	1	2	3	4	5
Depth	top-1'	1-2	2-3	3-4	4-5
Flint					
Tools	42	31	8	8	-
Flakes	2192	685	309	150	-
Cores	87	48	31	12	-
Pottery (sherds)					
WH	↑	↑	108	222	39
LN	'	'	-	-	-
	179	83			
Beaker/EBA	'	'	-	-	-
RB	↓	↓	-	-	-
Worked bone	-	-	-	P	-
Antler	-	-	1	1	-
Stone	-	-	1	-	-
Sarsen	R,2F	2P,2R,2F	Q,2R,P,F	3Q,P,F	3Q,F
Human bone	-	-	-	1	-

Stone, layer 3: fragment Grp XIII axe.
Human bone, layer 4: rt male femur.

*Fig. 43. Excavating the south end of MD IB, layer 3b. Bone deposits are described in the text
(photo: Alexander Keiller Museum, Avebury).*

Fig. 44. Sarsen group in MD IB (see also fig. 39) (photo: Alexander Keiller Museum, Avebury).

Fig. 45. Cattle skull, horncores and fragments from MD IB, layer 4b, south end (photo: Alexander Keiller Museum, Avebury).

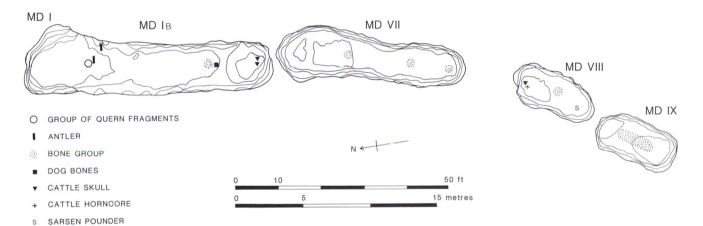

Fig. 46. Finds distributions in MD I, MD VII, MD VIII and MD IX.

Middle Ditch VII *(figs 38, 41 and 46–48; table 21)*

Fully excavated 1928 as a single unit. 13.1 m long, maximum depth 1.5 m. The segment widens and deepens to the north end. There is no information on silting.

Near the base of the ditch were articulated cattle limb bones, a bone deposit (details unknown) and a large sherd from the north terminal. There was a group of bones in layer 4a at the south terminal, including closely set long bones in dark earth. It is probably from this group that various conjoined flakes, a core, two knives, two retouched flakes and a serrated flake, were recovered.

In layer 3 a bone deposit was associated with flakes, seven cores, a knife, a scraper and other tools. Photographs show abundant bone and sherds, placed around and over a patch of charcoal or dark soil. There were the trunk and upper fore-limbs of one animal, from which the head had been severed and placed at the base of the spinal column. Layer 3b contained the skull, articulated vertebrae, ribs, scapulae and upper fore-limbs of a cow; the skull was found at the rear of the animal (fig. 48).

There was a 'hearth' with sarsens in layer 2b.

Middle Ditch VIII *(fig. 41 and 46; table 22)*

Fully excavated in 1928 as a single unit. 6.1 m long, maximum depth 1 m. The segment widens and deepens towards the north end. There is no information on silting; a large number of Peterborough sherds came from layer 2.

A bone deposit is recorded from the centre of this segment close to the base in layer 4, containing cattle and

Table 21: Finds by layer and depth in Middle Ditch VII.

Layer	1	2	3	4	5
Depth	top-1	1-2	2-3	3-4	4-5
Flint					
Tools	26	33	15	42	10
Flakes	1340	782	354	556	366
Cores	154	59	31	74	28
Pottery (sherds)					
WH	↑	79	266	464	217
LN	'	6	-	-	-
	130				
Beaker/EBA	'	13	-	-	-
RB	↓	-	-	-	-
Worked bone	P	-	-	P	-
Chalk	-	-	-	-	I
Sarsen	Q,R,F	2P,2F	R,F	2R,2Q,3R,F	2R

Table 22: Finds by layer and depth in Middle Ditch VIII.

Layer	1	2	3	4
Depth	top-1'	1-2	2-3	3-4
Flint				
Tools	17	10	12	6
Flakes	475	276	166	41
Cores	52	8	29	10
Pottery (sherds)				
WH	↑	↑	136	34
LN	'	'	-	-
	67	206		
Beaker/EBA	'	'	-	-
RB	↓	↓	-	-
Antler	-	-	-	2C
Chalk	I	B	-	-
Stone	1	-	-	-
Sarsen	-	Q,F	P,F	2R
Human bone	-	1	1	1

Stone, layer 1: fragment of Lower Greensand.
Human bone, layer 2: fragment of lft fibula.

Fig. 47. MD VII, layer 3, from the south, showing bone deposit (photo: Alexander Keiller Museum, Avebury).

pig bone, sherds, a flint core and a sarsen rubbing stone. Also close to the base at the north terminal there was an ox skull, associated with a scraper and retouched flake, in layer 4a.

Middle Ditch IX *(figs 39, 41 and 46; table 23)*

Fully excavated 1928 as a single unit. 6.1 m long, maximum depth 1.4. Shallower in the centre, the segment deepens at both ends, particularly the northern. Its sides are near-vertical.

There are photographs and a detailed plan (the only one of its kind surviving) of a large deposit of bone in the centre of the ditch in layer 3b. Largely of cattle, most parts of the skeleton are present; a single cow may be represented.

Photographs also show the articulated vertebral column of an animal on or near the base of the ditch against one of the causeways, along with ribs, scapulae and pelvis. These must be the dog remains from layer 4 which have survived with the retained bone.

Fig. 48. Cattle bone deposit in MD VII, layer 3b (photo: Alexander Keiller Museum, Avebury).

Table 23: Finds by layer and depth in Middle Ditch IX.

Layer	1	2	3	layer 3 hearth	4
Depth	top-1'	1-2	2-3		3-4
Flint					
Tools	11	8	21	4	2
Flakes	438	287	286	52	279
Cores	48	16	25	5	26
Pottery (sherds)					
WH	↑	↑	80	42	103
LN	'	'	-	-	-
	43	40			
Beaker/EBA	'	'	-	-	-
RB	↓	↓	-	-	-
Chalk	-	-	I	-	-
Sarsen	-	P,2Q	2F,P,R	R	R

Inner Ditch VII *(figs 49–52; table 24)*

Fully excavated 1926, re-excavated 1937. West segment 11.3 m long, maximum depth 1.5 m; east segment 4 m long, maximum depth 1.4 m. Although excavated and recorded as one unit, ID VII comprises two separate segments. The western segment consisted of an elongated ditch with expanded western terminal. Its base was flat, but with some slight depressions, and a terminal pit may have existed at the eastern end. Two schematic sections by Gray show primary chalk rubble followed by a very humic secondary silt, in part (especially in layer 4) charcoal-rich. This could represent substantial backfilling with midden material. The eastern segment is regularly cut, and slightly shallower; there is no information on its silting.

With the exception of worked bone, there were many finds. Large quantities of animal bone (mainly cattle) are recorded from the east terminal of the west segment around and below 2.5 ft, in 'black mould'. Charcoal was present with the bone. Gray suggested that 'the ditch was probably lived in'.

Inner Ditch XVI *(figs 49 and 53–54; table 25)*

Fully excavated 1929. 6.4 m long, maximum depth 1.3 m. The segment is slightly deeper at the eastern end. There is little information on silting, though the upper layers were described in Keiller's notebooks as 'very earthy' and layer 4 was 'clean rubble', probably implying natural silting throughout.

Most of layer 2b was very earthy, with a charcoal-rich bone deposit running down the centre of the segment. This included cattle, pig, sheep/goat, a fragment of antler and

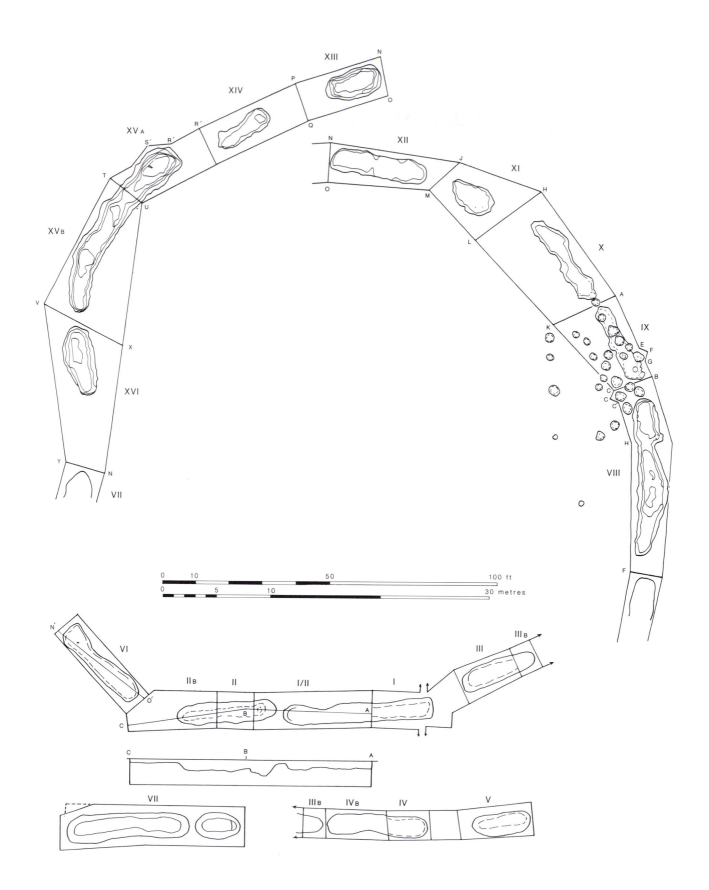

Fig. 49. Plans and profiles of the inner ditch segments excavated by Keiller.

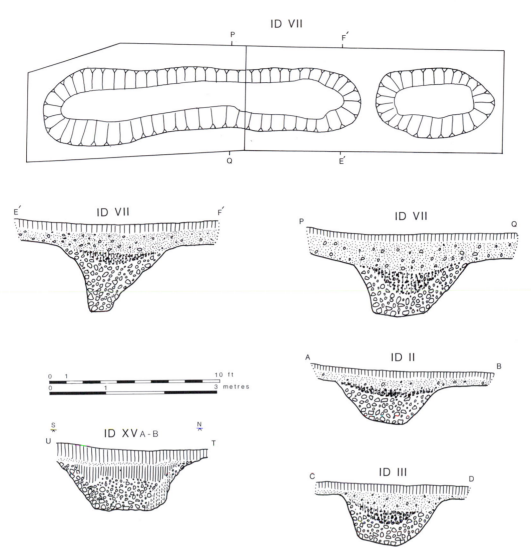

Fig. 50. Plan of ID VII (after Gray), and sections (reconstructed from level measurements) of ID VII, ID II, ID III and ID XV.

Table 24: Finds by layer and depth in Inner Ditch VII.

Layer	1	2	3	4	5	re-fill	re-excav
Depth	top-8"	8-1,4	1,4-2,3	2,3-3,5	3,5-base		
Flint							
Tools	31	13	15	13	-	-	65
Flakes	-	-	-	-	-	-	441
Cores	3	2	2	8	1	1	1
Pottery (sherds)							
WH	152	300	265	803	14	36	↑
LN	1	5	3	-	-	1	'
							216
Beaker/EBA	3	2	-	3	-	-	'
RB	18	9	2	-	-	-	↓
Antler	-	-	-	-	-	-	CF
Chalk	-	-	I,P	-	-	-	I,2C
Stone	-	3	-	-	-	-	-
Sarsen	-	2P,2R,2M	M	3P,2R	P	-	3Q,R
Human bone	-	-	1	-	-	-	-

Stone, layer 3: Grp VII macehead fragment; Grp VI axe blade (joins with butt in ID XVI, layer 1); hammerstone of 'ferruginated grit' from Bunter Beds.
Human bone, layer 3: adult rt lower second premolar.

Fig. 51. View of ID VII, as excavated, from the north-east. Keiller is in the ditch (probably using a cine camera), Gray to right at top, and ? Veronica Keiller to left (photo: Alexander Keiller Museum, Avebury).

Table 25: Finds by layer and depth in Inner Ditch XVI.

Layer	1	2	3	4	5
Depth	top-1'	1-2	2-3	3-4	4-5
Flint					
Tools	26	24	14	3	1
Flakes	709	478	164	?	?
Cores	45	28	6	?	1
Pottery (sherds)					
WH	↑	↑	97	51	1
LN	'	'	-	-	-
	67	89			
Beaker/EBA	'	'	-	-	-
RB	↓	↓	-	-	-
Antler	-	F	-	-	-
Chalk	-	B	-	-	-
Stone	3	1	-	-	-

Stone, layer 1: butt of Grp VI axe (joins with blade in ID VII, layer 3); fragment of Grp Xa; fragment of silicified sandstone; layer 2: chip from axe of tuff.

substantial amounts of pottery (fig. 54 and see Smith 1965a, pl. Vb).

There were two substantial groups of bone in layer 3a, 'which practically filled the ditch'. One, at the south-west end, immediately adjacent to the widest causeway of the inner circuit, was dominated by cattle bone including a skull, with sheep/goat horncores also present. An ox pelvis, femur, tibia and astragalus were articulated and unbroken (Smith 1965a, pl. Vb). The field notebook states that at least two cattle of different age and size were represented. The second bone group (presumably in most of the rest of the segment) was more mixed in terms of species. Two

articulated cattle radii and ulnae occurred along with some vertebrae. There was also a large piece of pottery.

Very little material seems to have come from the lower fill.

Inner Ditch XV *(figs 49–50 and 53; tables 26–27)*

Fully excavated 1929, as two halves, east (A) and west (B). 16.8 m long, maximum depth 1.8 m. Mostly shallow and narrow, the segment widens and deepens in its eastern third to form a substantial terminal pit.

Fig. 52. Section of ID VII, looking north-east (photo: Alexander Keiller Museum, Avebury).

Table 26: Finds by layer and depth in Inner Ditch XVA.

Layer	1	2	3	4	re-fill
Depth	top-1'	1-2	2-3	3-4	
Flint					
Tools	13	10	2	-	-
Flakes	347	481	39	2	-
Cores	35	48	8	3	-
Pottery (sherds)					
WH	↑	↑	21	-	↑
LN	'	'	-	-	'
	32	67	-	-	8
Beaker/EBA	'	'	-	-	'
RB	↓	↓	-	-	↓
Chalk	-	-	-	-	I
Sarsen	-	2P	-	-	-

Table 27: Finds by layer and depth in Inner Ditch XVB.

Layer	1	2	3	4	re-fill
Depth	top-1'	1-2	2-3	3-4	
Flint					
Tools	21	42	6	1	1
Flakes	542	648	63	-	-
Cores	40	62	15	2	-
Pottery (sherds)					
WH	↑	↑	42	20	↑
LN	'	'	-	-	'
	41	161	-	-	19
Beaker/EBA	'	'	-	-	'
RB	↓	↓	-	-	↓
Worked bone	-	P	-	-	P
Antler	-	-	-	C	-
Sarsen	-	M	-	-	-

Joshua Pollard

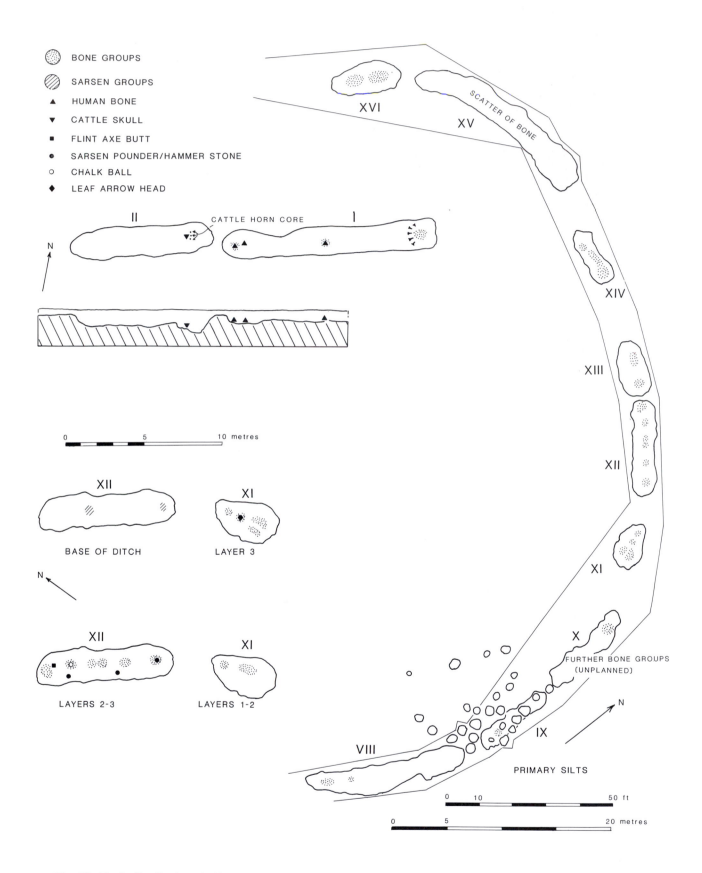

Fig. 53. Finds distributions in ID II, ID I, ID XVI, ID XV, ID XIV, ID XIII, ID XII, ID XI, ID X, ID IX and ID VIII.

Fig. 54. Bone deposit in ID XVI, layer 2
(photo: Alexander Keiller Museum, Avebury).

The layer books record layer 4 as chalk rubble, and layers 2 and 1 as mostly 'ordinary' or 'normal'. Layer 3 in B was very rubbly, and in A partly rubble, but black earth at the north-west end and on the outer side; layer 2 in B was 'on the rubbly side with less soft earth than usual'. The shallowness of the segment and the section suggest backfilling.

Layers 2–3a contained a scatter of bones running across both cuttings. Cattle, sheep/goat, and pig are recorded. The cattle bone included an astragalus 'of preposterous size', presumably of *Bos primigenius*, and the sheep/goat bone a horncore. Several of the bones from layer 2a in A were burnt. Patches of 'black earth' occurred in layers 2 and 3 of A. Several flakes struck from the same core were recorded in layer 2 in B, though there is no indication that these occurred in a group.

Inner Ditch XIV *(figs 49, 53 and 55–57; table 28)*

Fully excavated 1929. 5.5 m long, maximum depth 0.9 m. Shallow and rather irregular, the segment deepens at its east end to form a terminal pit. There is no information on silting.

There were five distinct groups of bone ('an immense amount of bones') down the length of the ditch, appearing in great abundance in layer 2, and continuing in smaller quantities into layer 3, just above the base of the ditch. There are no detailed lists in the field notebook. There were also charcoal, carbonised nuts, sarsen fragments, worked flints and dog faeces.

At the base of the ditch at the west end there was a worked antler (part of a beam and tine with groove and splinter working) and a complete sarsen quern 1.2 m to its east; there was also another quern fragment.

Table 28: Finds by layer and depth in Inner Ditch XIV.

Layer	1	2	3	re-fill
Depth	top-1'	1-2	2-3	
Flint				
Tools	14	10	3	8
Flakes	478	310	13	-
Cores	23	23	-	-
Pottery (sherds)				
WH	↑	↑	4	↑
LN	'	'	-	'
	45	63		3
Beaker/EBA	'	'	-	'
RB	↓	↓	-	↓
Antler	-	-	W	-
Chalk	-	B	-	I
Stone	1	1	-	-
Sarsen	P	3P	2Q	-

Stone, layer 1: possible axe fragment, Grp Xa; layer 2: piece of silicious rock from Portland Beds

Fig. 55. Quern and antler in situ *in ID XIV, on the base of the ditch, from the east (photo: Alexander Keiller Museum, Avebury).*

Fig. 56. Bone deposits in ID XIV, layer 2, from the south-east
(photo: Alexander Keiller Museum, Avebury).

Fig. 57. Bone deposits in ID XIV, layer 2, from the east
(photo: Alexander Keiller Museum, Avebury).

Inner Ditch XIII *(figs 49, 53 and 58; table 29)*

Fully excavated 1929. 5.2 m long, maximum depth 1.3 m. Separated from ID XII by a very narrow causeway; flat base.

The notebooks comment on an unusual quantity of chalk rubble in layer 4, and on a very compact lens of chalk rubble against the eastern side in layers 2 and 3, possibly the result of backfilling.

Three major groups of bone are recorded (in dark, charcoal-rich soil, 'black like soot'), in layers 2, 3 and 4 (almost to the base). Those in 2 and 3 lay superimposed at the north-west end of the ditch. That in 2 was accompanied by pottery and sarsen; the rest of the layer 'was not noteworthy' and 'very dull'. That in 3 was associated with pottery and flint. Cattle bone appears to have been dominant in both, and in both cases several animals were represented. In layer 2 the cattle bone included 12 limb/feet bones, two scapulae, three pelvis fragments, and vertebrae, teeth and ribs; and there were 'various' sheep/goat and pig bones. In layer 3 the cattle bone included over 20 limb/feet bones, three pelvis fragments, part of a mandible, seven vertebrae, two scapulae, and 16 ribs. There were also animal bones from the compact lens of chalk rubble against the inner ditch edge. The layer 4 bone deposit was concentrated at the south-east end, though bone was also scattered in quantity throughout the layer. Several of the bones (which are not listed in detail) were burnt. There were sherds (including a perforated lug) and sarsen. The notebook comments that dog faeces were present 'as usual'.

Fig. 58. Bone deposit in ID XIII, layer 3 (photo: Alexander Keiller Museum, Avebury).

Table 29: Finds by layer and depth in Inner Ditch XIII.

Layer	1	2	3	4	re-fill
Depth	top-1'	1-2	2-3	3-4	
Flint					
Tools	34	11	12	6	1
Flakes	1233	83	191	47	-
Cores	33	16	11	4	-
Pottery (sherds)					
WH	↑	↑	86	17	↑
LN	'	'	-	-	'
	66	20			4
Beaker/EBA	'	'	-	-	'
RB	↓	↓	-	-	↓
Stone	-	-	1	-	-
Sarsen	-	P	P	P	-

Stone, layer 3: piece of Stonesfield slate.

Inner Ditch XII *(figs 49, 53 and 59–60; table 30)*

Fully excavated 1929. 8.5 m long, maximum depth 0.7 m. The elongated shallow segment is formed by two intersecting parts of roughly equal length; flat base, with slight ridge at intersection. There is no information on silting, though the segment is very shallow, and to judge from the quantity of bone deposited within them the primary fills probably accumulated rapidly.

Extensive groups of bone occurred in layers 2 and 3; the notebook comments that those in layer 2 'must create a record' (Smith 1965a, pl. Va). There were five distinct bone groups in each layer, occurring in similar positions. Either these represent the same groups, of some thickness, or they are the result of two separate phases of deposition. There were also other scattered bones.

Only vague details are available for the layer 2 groups. The first had cattle (ribs, limb bones, scapula) and sheep/goat (skull). The second was 'simply' a mixture of cattle and sheep/goat bones. The third was described as the most interesting, because of quantities of associated flint, pottery and sarsen. The bone included an ox skull, placed upright on the top of the group according to surviving photographs. A portion of a pot looked as though 'it had been standing upright when a large bit of chalk was thrown or had fallen in', as several broken sherds were superimposed. The other two groups are recorded as similar, the fourth including cattle ribs and a scapula, and sarsen artefacts.

Fig. 59. Bone deposits in ID XII, layer 2, from the outside (photo: Alexander Keiller Museum, Avebury).

Fig. 60. Sarsen groups on the base of ID XII, from the north-west (photo: Alexander Keiller Museum, Avebury).

Table 30: Finds by layer and depth in Inner Ditch XII.

Layer	1	2	3	re-fill
Depth	top–1'	1–2	2–3	
Flint				
Tools	106	27	19	-
Flakes	2310	504	110	-
Cores	62	28	6	-
Pottery (sherds)				
WH	↑	↑	61	-
LN	'	'	-	-
	104	105		
Beaker/EBA	'	'	-	-
RB	↓	↓	-	-
Worked bone	P	-	-	-
Antler	-	2F	-	-
Chalk	-	-	B	-
Sarsen	-	3P,F	P	-

Uniquely, detailed records survive of the composition of the five bone groups in layer 3 of ID XII. These consist of field identifications, probably made by Professor D.M.S. Watson during the course of the excavation, which list the skeletal elements present according to species and bone group. 380 identified bones are listed, a remarkable quantity from a single layer of a segment 8.5 m long. Cattle bone comprised over 70 percent of the assemblage, with pig representing 14.2 percent and sheep/goat 2.6 percent; unidentified medium-sized animals (probably pig and sheep/goat) form 11.6 percent. Cattle bones from more than one animal were present in groups 1, 2 and 3. Meat-bearing bones from the trunk and upper limbs account for over 73 percent of the assemblage. A wide range of skeletal parts is represented, and more than one individual of a particular species was present.

Group 1 in layer 3 had approximately a dozen cattle limb and feet bones, a scapula, vertebrae, ribs, a horncore and pelvis fragments; six limb and feet bones of pig, with a scapula and pelvis fragments; and of sheep/goat, fragments of a tibia, a scapula, and a pelvis. Group 2 contained approximately 14 cattle limb and feet bones, two scapulae, five vertebrae, 24 rib fragments, three pelvis fragments, a sacrum and a tooth (somewhat disconcertingly, the field notebook adds 'etc. etc.'); and three pig mandible fragments, two pelvis fragments, 11 vertebrae, and three limb bones. Group '3a' contained about 21 cattle limb and feet bones (some 'gnawed by dog'), three pelvis fragments, a scapula, seven vertebrae, a horncore, and over 30 rib fragments; a pig jaw and radius; a sheep/goat horncore and tibia; and of pig or goat, a femur, pelvis, ulna and 15 vertebrae. Group '3b' contained an ox horncore, six limb/feet bones, four ribs, and four teeth; and two pig limb bones, a scapula and three vertebrae. Group '3c' contained an ox horncore, skull fragments, a scapula, a vertebra, a humerus, two foot bones, and 13 ribs; a pig pelvis and two humeri; a sheep/goat humerus; and two ribs and two vertebrae of pig or sheep/goat. Group 4 had an ox femur, a vertebra, and 12 rib fragments; and a pig jaw, two humerus fragments, and three vertebrae. Group 5 had an ox horncore, eight limb/feet bones, two scapula, three pelvis fragments, 15 vertebrae, and over 30 rib fragments; and a pig mandible, two pelvis fragments, and two limb bones.

Small amounts of dog faeces were present in each group of layer 3. A chalk ball was included in group 2, and a small hammerstone in group 5. Two groups of sarsen occurred on the base of the ditch, at the south end and close to the medial ridge.

Inner Ditch XI *(figs 49, 53 and 61–63; table 31)*

Fully excavated 1929. 4 m long, maximum depth 0.7 m. Pear-shaped with gently sloping sides and a level base. There is no information on silting.

Fig. 61. Bone groups 1–4 in layer 3 of ID XI, from the south (photo: Alexander Keiller Museum, Avebury).

Fig. 62. Bone groups 2–4 in layer 3 of ID XI, at the south end (photo: Alexander Keiller Museum, Avebury).

Fig. 63. Detail of bone groups 3 and 4 in layer 3, ID XI (photo: Alexander Keiller Museum, Avebury).

A remarkable quantity of worked flint came from layer 1, corresponding with a high density within the interior of the inner circuit.

There was a deposit of bone in layer 1 on the east side, and another (a 'clutter') in layer 2 at the north end.

Four well defined groups of bone were found in layer 3. Group 1 consisted mainly of cattle bone (approximately 60 pieces included a horncore, two pelvises, a scapula and a jaw), associated with sarsen, 48 flakes, three cores, a hammerstone, a scraper and three serrated flakes, and six large sherds. Group 2 comprised around 40 pieces of bone, together with sarsen, four sherds and other fragments, a stone axe flake, 60 flint flakes, two cores, one retouched flake, three serrated flakes and an arrowhead. Charcoal was plentiful. Group 3 included 27 pieces of bone, a sarsen and a serrated flake. Group 4 comprised 76 bones, many burnt (including two almost complete cattle mandibles, a piece of pig jaw and an ox pelvis), with 52 flint flakes, a lump of flint, sarsen and some sherds. The notebook describes the group as a mass of burnt earth and charcoal, with bone and other finds intermixed.

Inner Ditch X (figs 49 and 53; table 32)

Fully excavated 1929. 8.8 m long, maximum depth 0.7 m. This segment was very irregular and shallow, narrowing towards the centre (suggestive of two intersecting parts). At the south end traces of three pits were found in the sides of the ditch. These were probably part of the pre-enclosure pit group which is cut by ID VIII and ID IX (nos 4–6 in Smith 1965a), a pit belonging to which lies in the causeway between ID X and ID IX (no. 16 in Smith 1965a).

The notebooks record that the ditch was exceptionally free of chalk rubble, but primary chalk rubble was found in layer 3.

Table 31: Finds by layer and depth in Inner Ditch XI.

Layer	1	2	3	3 bone dump	re-fill
Depth	top-1'	1-2	2-3		
Flint					
Tools	85	54	24	2	1
Flakes	2140	628	305	-	-
Cores	74	40	17	-	-
Pottery (sherds)					
WH	↑	79	73	17	-
LN	'	-	-	-	-
	98				
Beaker/EBA	'	-	-	-	-
RB	↓	-	-	-	-
Worked bone	-	P	-	-	-
Stone	-	-	2	-	-
Sarsen	-	-	-	P	-
Human bone	-	-	1	-	-

Stone, layer 3: 2 flakes from Grp VI axes.
Human bone, layer 3: lft fibula.

Table 32: Finds by layer and depth in Inner Ditch X.

Layer	1	2	3	re-fill
Depth	top-1'	1-2	2-3	
Flint				
Tools	13	18	4	-
Flakes	1618	378	55	-
Cores	101	40	9	-
Pottery (sherds)				
WH	↑	↑	39	↑
LN	'	'	-	'
	104	91		6
Beaker/EBA	'	'	-	'
RB	↓	↓	-	↓
Sarsen	-	P,2R,F	Q,R	-

Table 33: Finds by layer and depth in Inner Ditch IX.

Layer	1	2	3	re-fill
Depth	top-1'	1-2	2-base	
Flint				
Tools	29	27	-	2
Flakes	977	241	-	-
Cores	54	20	-	-
Pottery (sherds)				
WH	↑	47	4	12
LN	'	-	-	-
	109			
Beaker/EBA	'	-	-	-
RB	↓	-	-	-
Antler	-	2F	-	-
Chalk	-	I	-	I
Stone	1	1	-	-
Sarsen	-	2F	R	-

Concentrated groups of bone were noted in layers 2 and 3. There is little detail for layer 2. A group of bone was recorded from the north end in layer 3, with cattle bone (including a jaw), flint flakes and sarsen. Dog faeces occurred in the centre of the ditch in layer 3.

Inner Ditch IX *(figs 49 and 53; table 33)*

Fully excavated 1929. 7.3 m long, maximum depth 0.6 m. The segment cuts eight small pits (nos 7–14 in Smith 1965a). There is no information on silting.

A group of bones is recorded in layers 2a-b towards the southern end of the ditch. This included cattle and sheep/goat bones, with quantities of sarsen, sherds, and a number of tiny flint flakes. Two vertebrae were articulated.

Two large pieces of antler occurred close to the base of the ditch at the north end.

Inner Ditch VIII *(figs 49, 53 and 64; table 34)*

Fully excavated 1928. 14.3 m long, maximum depth 1.2 m. The segment comprises two intersecting parts. The shorter northern part forms a terminal pit, while the greatest depth occurs in the centre of the southern portion. A shallow pit is cut by the northern part (no. 15 in Smith 1965a). There is no information on silting.

The quantities of sherds, chalk and sarsen were notable.

A group of bones was found in layer 2, near the southwest terminal. There is no information on the bone present; sherds, sarsens, 25 flint flakes, three serrated flakes and

Fig. 64. Bone and other material in layer 2 of ID VIII (photo: Alexander Keiller Museum, Avebury).

Table 34: Finds by layer and depth in Inner Ditch VIII.

Layer	1	2	3	4
Depth	top-1'	1-2	2-3	3-4
Flint				
Tools	53	80	23	4
Flakes	1670	707	108	18
Cores	140	75	21	3
Pottery (sherds)				
WH	↑	↑	80	12
LN	'	'	-	-
	258	261		
Beaker/EBA	'	'	-	-
RB	↓	↓	-	-
Worked bone	-	-	P	-
Chalk	B	C,I,M,B	B	-
Sarsen	P,R,F	5F,P,R	3P,R,F	Q

two worked flakes were associated. A bone group was also found in layer 3 on the base of the segment, comprising cattle and pig bone, along with sherds, a sarsen pounder, 20 flint flakes and an arrowhead. 1.2 m to the north-east and almost on the base, was a sarsen pounder with cattle horncores on three sides. Close by, on the base of the ditch (in layer 4), was a very large piece of sarsen quern.

Inner Ditch V (*fig. 49; table 35*)

Fully excavated 1925, re-excavated 1927. 5.2 m long, maximum depth 1.3 m. No contour plan exists. There is little information on silting. Gray noted that 'chalk rubble began to appear at 2.5 ft', suggesting natural silting, and recorded a large amount of animal bone, particularly at the base of the 'mould' or secondary silting.

Inner Ditch IV (*fig. 49; tables 36–37*)

East half (ID IV) excavated 1925, west half 1927 (ID IVB). 9.1 m long, maximum depth 1 m. There is a slight kink just to the west of centre, perhaps formed by two intersecting parts. The eastern terminal was recorded by Gray as 'nicely rounded'. There is no information on silting.

Gray recorded a large quantity of pottery throughout the fill. A 'cache' of 11 serrated flakes was found in layer 2 in IVB. The chalk objects, from apparently similar depth, are noteworthy. The primary fill of IVB (the base of layer 3 and the top of layer 4) produced a mass of charcoal-rich earth with animal bone, much pottery and sarsen. Among the bones were pig mandibles, cattle horncores, and many other cattle bones.

Table 35: Finds by layer and depth in Inner Ditch V.

Depth	1'	2'	2,2	2,3	3,5-base	re-excav
Flint						
Tools	2	4	3	2	2	-
Flakes	-	-	-	-	-	633
Cores	-	-	-	-	-	30
Pottery (sherds)						
WH	11	1	4	2	44	89
LN	-	1	-	-	2	-
RB	-	-	-	-	-	9
Antler	-	C	-	-	-	-
Stone	-	-	-	-	-	1
Sarsen	-	-	-	-	-	R,Q,F

Stone, re-excavation: piece of Lower Greensand.

Table 36: Finds by layer and depth in Inner Ditch IV.

Depth	8"	1'	1,2	1,3-2,5	2,2	?	re-excav
Flint							
Tools	1	1	1	1	1	4	22
Flakes	-	-	-	-	-	-	175
Cores	-	-	-	-	-	-	12
Pottery (sherds)							
WH	<	112	>	19	-	-	25
RB	<	9	>	-	-	-	7
Worked bone	-	-	-	-	-	-	P
Chalk	-	-	-	I,PE	-	-	-
Sarsen	-	-	-	-	-	2R	-

Table 37: Finds by layer and depth in Inner Ditch IVB.

Layer	1	2	3	4
Depth	top-8"	8"-1,4	1,4-2,3	2,3-base
Flint				
Tools	4	54	11	2
Flakes	-	901	305	16
Cores	-	16	12	1
Pottery (sherds)				
WH	-	172	248	13
LN	-	2	-	-
Beaker/EBA	-	1	-	-
RB	-	13	-	-
Chalk	-	B	-	-
Sarsen	-	Q,F	-	-

Table 38: Finds by layer and depth in Inner Ditch III.

Depth	under turf	1,5	?	re-excav
Flint				
Tools	2	1	4	13
Flakes	-	-	-	408
Cores	-	-	-	26
Pottery (sherds)				
WH	<	132	>	40
LN	-	1	-	-
Beaker/EBA	-	1	-	-
RB	<	9	>	6
Sarsen	-	-	-	3F,R

Inner Ditch III *(figs 49–50; tables 38–39)*

Western two thirds (ID III) excavated 1925, re-excavated 1927; eastern third excavated 1927 (ID IIIB). 7 m long, maximum depth 1 m (Smith 1965a, pl. IIIa). A schematic section by Gray shows enough primary chalk rubble to hint at limited interference or backfilling, followed by secondary fill.

Gray's very limited notes record a large quantity of animal bone (cattle and some pig), mostly at the top of the primary chalk rubble.

Table 39: Finds by layer and depth in Inner Ditch IIIB.

Layer	1	2	3
Depth	top-8"	8"-1,4	1,4-2,3
Flint			
Tools	1	9	3
Flakes	-	303	-
Cores	-	5	1
Pottery (sherds)			
WH	-	51	20
RB	-	1	-

Inner Ditch I *(figs 49 and 53; tables 40–41)*

East half excavated 1925 (ID I), re-excavated 1927; west half excavated 1927, along with east terminal of ID II (ID I/II). 13.7 m long, maximum depth 0.9 m (Smith 1965a, pl. IIIa). A profile of ID I/II shows a slight terminal pit at the west end; the notebook refers to a 'decided hollow' at the east end, probably a more substantial terminal pit. There is no information on silting.

Gray's notes for ID I mention much pottery and animal bone (mostly cattle, and some pig and sheep/goat). Small pieces of sarsen were plentiful (contrary to the impression given by the finds catalogue).

From layer 3 in ID I (in 1927), close to the centre of the ditch and almost on its base, were a human infant cranium, a human temporal bone, two scapulae (one of pig, the other from a large ungulate, probably red deer), unidentified fragments of long bones, and a burnt flake. In the west terminal, in an area about 1 m in diameter, there were a human humerus and ulna, a pig frontal orbit, an ox vertebra, a sheep/goat astragalus, a sherd, two flint flakes, other burnt flakes and a large piece of sarsen.

Inner Ditch II *(figs 49–50 and 53; tables 41–43)*

Central portion (ID II) excavated 1925, re-excavated 1927; west end (ID IIB) and east end (ID I/II) excavated 1927. 9.1 m long, maximum depth 1.5 m. A profile by Gray

Table 40: Finds by layer and depth in Inner Ditch I.

Depth	1'-1,5	1,5-base	w end,1'-base	w end,2,1	re-excav
Flint					
Tools	-	-	-	-	20
Flakes	-	-	-	-	434
Cores	-	-	-	-	15
Pottery (sherds)					
WH	11	15	25	9	29
LN	-	-	-	1	1
Beaker/EBA	1	-	-	-	-
RB	4	-	3	-	4
Chalk	-	-	-	-	M
Sarsen	-	-	-	-	Q,4F

Table 41: Finds by layer and depth in Inner Ditch I/II.

Layer	1	2	3	4	re-fill
Depth	top-8"	8"-1,4	1,4-2,3	2,3-base	
Flint					
Tools	9	24	8	-	-
Flakes	206	369	222	27	3
Cores	3	33	24	3	-
Pottery (sherds)					
WH	25	96	168	21	17
LN	-	1	-	-	-
Beaker/EBA	-	4	-	-	-
RB	7	24	-	-	2
Chalk	-	-	B	-	-
Sarsen	-	-	2Q,R	-	-
Human bone	-	-	4	-	-

Human bone, layer 3: fragmentary child skull; temporal bone; adult lft ulna; adult humerus fragment.

Table 42: Finds by layer and depth in Inner Ditch II.

Depth	1,3	?	re-excav
Flint			
Tools	2	2	9
Flakes	-	-	90
Cores	-	-	19
Pottery (sherds)			
WH	< 77 >		28
LN	< 5 >		-
Beaker/EBA	< 1 >		-
RB	-	4	3
Stone	-	-	3
Sarsen	-	R	3P,2F

Stone, re-excavation: 3 pieces Lower Greensand

Table 43: Finds by layer and depth in Inner Ditch IIB.

Layer	1	2	3	4
Depth	top-8"	8"-1,4	1,4-2,3	2,3-base
Flint				
Tools	9	7	5	3
Flakes	177	274	84	1
Cores	3	5	9	1
Pottery (sherds)				
WH	13	28	81	-
RB	-	3	-	-
Sarsen	-	R	F	-

three cattle horncores along with two horncores and part of the skull of another animal.

Inner Ditch VI *(fig. 49; table 44)*

Fully excavated 1925, re-excavated 1928. 9.1 m long, maximum depth 1 m. Gray noted a considerable rise in the level of the ditch base towards the northern terminal. The deeper south end might be a terminal pit. There is no information on silting, and very little material is recorded.

shows a pronounced terminal pit at the east end; the rest is flat-based. A schematic section by Gray shows an unusual depth of primary chalk rubble, which may suggest back-filling, but archive film shows Keiller explaining the stratigraphy of ID II, in which there appears to have been rather little primary chalk rubble.

In the east terminal of ID II in layers 3 and 4, there were

Table 44: Finds by layer and depth in Inner Ditch VI.

Depth	1'	1,3	3	3,5	3,8	4	re-fill	re-excav
Flint								
Tools	6	1	1	1	2	4	-	15
Flakes	-	-	-	-	-	-	-	302
Cores	-	-	-	-	-	-	1	30
Pottery (sherds)								
WH	-	71	<	58	>	-		↑
LN	-	2	-	-	-	-	-	'
								87
Beaker/EBA	-	-	-	-	-	-	-	'
RB	-	3	-	-	-	-	-	↓

FEATURES OTHER THAN THE DITCHES

The remaining part of Keiller's excavations is described in chapter 2 of Smith (1965a). Approximately half of the interior within the inner circuit was stripped in 1929, some 1800 square metres; pits were found in the area of ID X, VIII and especially IX (fig. 66). During 1925–27 scattered pits were located by probing in the other half of the inner interior, and between the inner and middle circuits, and the middle and outer (see fig. 14). All of these were fully excavated, though surviving details of stratigraphy are sparse. A small square ditched enclosure of probable Earlier Neolithic date was excavated to the east of the outer circuit (fig. 14). There is little to add to Smith's account, particularly in relation to the pits, but it has been possible to use the archive to investigate the density and nature of struck flint from the excavated portions of the interior within the inner ditch circuit. These may indicate the former existence of middens in this area.

No bone and very little prehistoric pottery survived on the chalk surface of the inner interior, but around 14,000 struck flints were recovered. The method of excavation, which involved clearing the area in a series of 20 foot wide strips, with finds recorded according to each such trench, has enabled reconstruction of relative densities (fig. 65). The presence of Earlier Neolithic types and the virtual absence of Later Neolithic forms (for example, no barbed and tanged arrowheads, and only three transverse ones) suggest that most of the worked flint is broadly contemporary with the primary activity at the enclosure. The distribution of worked flint was uneven. Low densities were found in the central area and adjacent to ID III, IV and XIV, in contrast to high concentrations around the periphery, particularly on the east side adjacent to ID IX-XI, ID XIII and XV. Gaps in the distribution occur adjacent to ID XIV, and between ID IV and V, corresponding to major breaks in the enclosure circuit.

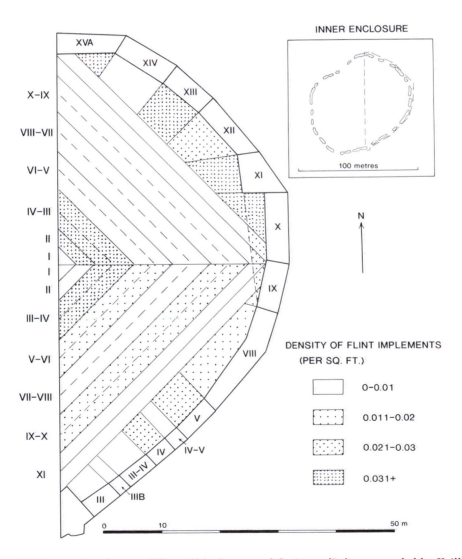

Fig. 65. The relative density of flint within the area of the inner ditch as recorded by Keiller.

Fig. 66. Pits adjacent to ID IX, from the south. Spoilheaps from MD XI and X are visible in the background (photo: Alexander Keiller Museum, Avebury).

THE 1957–58 EXCAVATIONS

These are described in Smith (1965a) (see also pl. 4). The four ditch cuttings V, VI, XII and XVI, will be referred to in the descriptions of Trenches B, C, E and F of 1988, and the two bank/old land surface cuttings, V and VI, in the description of Trench BB of 1988. General information on the context of finds from Smith's excavations are given in tables 45–51. These are summaries of the finds catalogues held in Avebury Museum. As with the Keiller material, it has not been possible to check many of the identifications, though it is assumed that these are reliable.

Table 45: Finds by layer from the 1957–58 excavations, Outer Ditch IV.

Layer	1	2	3	4	5
Flint					
Tools	-	24	3	1	-
Cores	-	3	-	-	-
Pottery (sherds)					
WH	-	4	1	3	7
LN	-	2	3	-	-
Beaker/EBA	-	-	2	-	-
RB	-	1	-	-	-
Chalk	-	-	-	B	-
Sarsen	-	-	R	-	Q

Table 46: Finds by layer from the 1957–58 excavations, Outer Ditch V.

Layer	1	2	3	4	5	6
Flint						
Tools	-	53	45	7	6	2
Cores	-	5	6	-	2	-
Pottery (sherds)						
WH	-	-	↑	3	9+	12
LN	-	-	37	-	-	-
Beaker/EBA	-	1	↓	-	-	-
RB	-	1	-	-	-	-
Worked bone	-	-	P	-	-	-
Chalk	-	-	2M	M	M	-
Stone	-	6	-	1	-	-
Sarsen	-	-	-	-	Q,R	-
Human bone	-	-	-	1	1	-

Stone, layer 2: 3 pieces Old Red Sandstone, 2 pieces oolitic limestone, 1 quartz pebble; layer 4: quartzite pebble
Human bone, layer 4: infant skeleton; layer 5: frontal bone

Table 47: Finds by layer from the 1957–58 excavations, Middle Ditch XII.

Layer	1	2	3	4	5
Flint					
Tools	-	26	8	6	-
Cores	-	7	1	1	-
Pottery (sherds)					
WH	-	↑	1	6	14
LN	-		-	-	-
		90			
Beaker/EBA	-		-	-	-
RB	-	↓	-	-	-
Antler	-	-	-	W	-
Chalk	-	-	-	I	I
Stone	-	2	-	-	-
Sarsen	-	-	P	2P,Q	2R
Human bone	-	-	-	-	1

Stone, layer 2: piece of Old Red Sandstone, piece of Trias Sandstone
Human bone, layer 5:fragments of lower skull

Table 48: Finds by layer from the 1957–58 excavations, Inner Ditch XVII.

Layer	1	2	3	4	5
Flint					
Tools	-	31	34	14	-
Cores	-	1	4	1	-
Pottery (sherds)					
WH	-	↑	21+	11	4
LN	-		-	-	-
		21+			
Beaker/EBA	-		-	-	-
RB	-	↓	-	-	-
Worked bone	-	W	-	-	-
Stone	-	1	1	-	-
Human bone	-	-	1	-	-

Stone, layer 2: piece of Old Red Sandstone; layer 3: piece of Trias
Sandstone. Human bone, layer 3: fragment of frontal bone

Table 49: Finds by layer from the 1957–58 excavations, Outer Bank IV.

Layer	Topsoil	Bank	OLS
Flint			
Tools	10	5	59
Cores	7	3	8
Pottery			
WH	15 sherds from 12 vessels found under bank		
Stone	1	1	-
Sarsen	<	2Q,3F	>

Stone, Topsoil: fragment of sandstone; Bank: Old Red Sandstone pebble

Table 50: Finds by layer from the 1957–58 excavations, Outer Bank V.

Layer	Topsoil	Bank	OLS
Flint			
Tools	14	3	14
Cores	5	-	-
Pottery (sherds)			
WH	-	2	16+

Table 51: Finds by layer from the 1957–58 excavations, Outer Bank VI.

Layer	Topsoil	Bank	OLS	Hearth
Flint				
Tools	15	5	8	2
Cores	2	-	1	1
Pottery (sherds)				
WH	-	8	14+	4+
Stone	2	-	-	-
Sarsen	<	3P	>	-

Stone, Topsoil: fragment of Old Red Sandstone macehead or whetstone, Trias sandstone rubber fragment

4

The 1988 Excavations

Alasdair Whittle, Caroline Grigson and Joshua Pollard

Introduction

Five cuttings were laid out immediately adjacent to selected cuttings of 1957–58 (Trenches B and BB, C, E and F), and two new cuttings were dug (Trenches A and D) (fig. 14). Trench F was 1 m wide, and the others 2 m wide. In the case of Trenches B, C, E and F, the earlier cutting was emptied first of its backfill and the sections recorded before excavation. Depths are given from the modern surface.

Further details of finds are given in subsequent chapters, including animal bone in chapter 11 and pottery in chapter 13.

THE OLD LAND SURFACE UNDER THE OUTER BANK

Trench BB

Trench BB was laid out as a continuation of Trench B, immediately adjacent to Outer Bank V. Under the bank there was an old land surface with artefacts and bone on and in it. The old land surface sealed a subsoil hollow, and was cut by a pit, postholes and a grave. The buried soil was very disturbed. The bank has a primary phase, a low mound, followed by obliquely dumped tip lines of chalky material. Description here includes features from the 1958 cutting.

Subsoil hollow: tree hole or localised solution hole

In the middle of the south section of Outer Bank V from 1958 a feature cutting into the chalk subsoil was sealed by the old land surface or pre-bank soil, which was labelled as a natural solution hole (Smith 1965a, 6 and fig. 4). This feature, 712, was seen to extend irregularly right across Trench BB (figs 67–68, pl. 7). It is at maximum 40 cm deep, with light grey brown soil and small to medium chalk fragments. It contained fragments of bone including

cattle vertebrae, ribs and a distal metatarsal. Micromorphological analysis is detailed below (chapter 6); its sparse Mollusca and the possibility of mixing or contamination make it impossible to assign a specific date (chapter 7). It may be considered as either a tree hollow or, as the micromorphology suggests, a localised solution hole around tree or shrub roots.

Old land surface or pre-bank soil

The old land surface extended under the whole area of the bank, petering out only at the very front and back of the bank (figs 69–71, pls 5–9). It consisted of a slightly undulating but basically flat surface, 705 (also labelled 747 under the primary bank close to the ditch), which was the top of a dark soil, 741, about 8–10 cm thick, though locally a little thicker. This contained abundant small chalk clasts throughout, and John Evans has observed (*pers. comm.*) that this is much more stony than any other Neolithic buried soil profile so far observed in the area. 741 overlay 742, chalky rubble about 10 to 15 cm thick above solid Middle Chalk; since the chalk was in places crumbly, this measurement was variable. In the western part of the trench the top of the rubble horizon was coarser than elsewhere and was distinguished as 749.

Careful search was made in both plan and section for cultivation marks, but without result. A calibrated age range of 3380–3100 BC was obtained from an ox humerus on 705 (OxA-2405), and calibrated age ranges of 3780–3740, 3710–3620 or 3570–3530 BC from an ox vertebra on 747 (OxA-2406); full details of radiocarbon dates are given in chapter 5. (A radiocarbon date of 3775–3755 or 3705–3695 (BM-73) was obtained from charcoal lying on the old surface below Outer Bank V (Smith 1965a, 28).) There is no stratigraphic reason to suspect that the sample for OxA-2405 was in any way intrusive. (Questions of sequence are further discussed in chapters 5 and 17.)

As in 1957–58 (Smith 1965a, 28), no actual turfline was observed at the top of the buried thin chalk soil, though

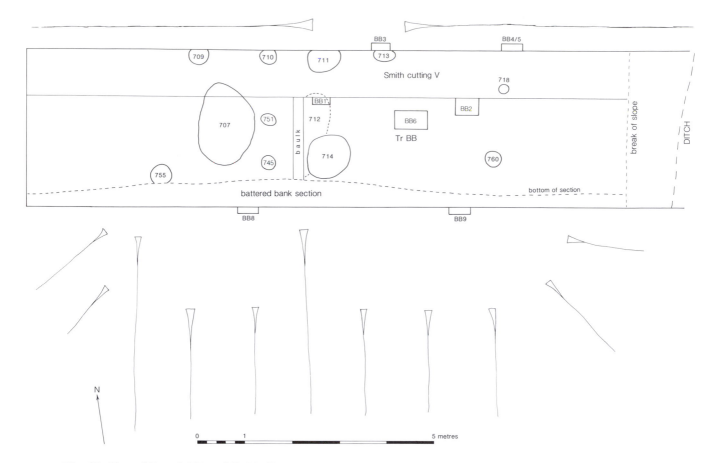

Fig. 67. Plan of Trench BB and Smith Cutting V across the outer bank. BB1 etc: environmental sampling points.

Fig. 68. Context 712 below the pre-bank soil in Trench BB.

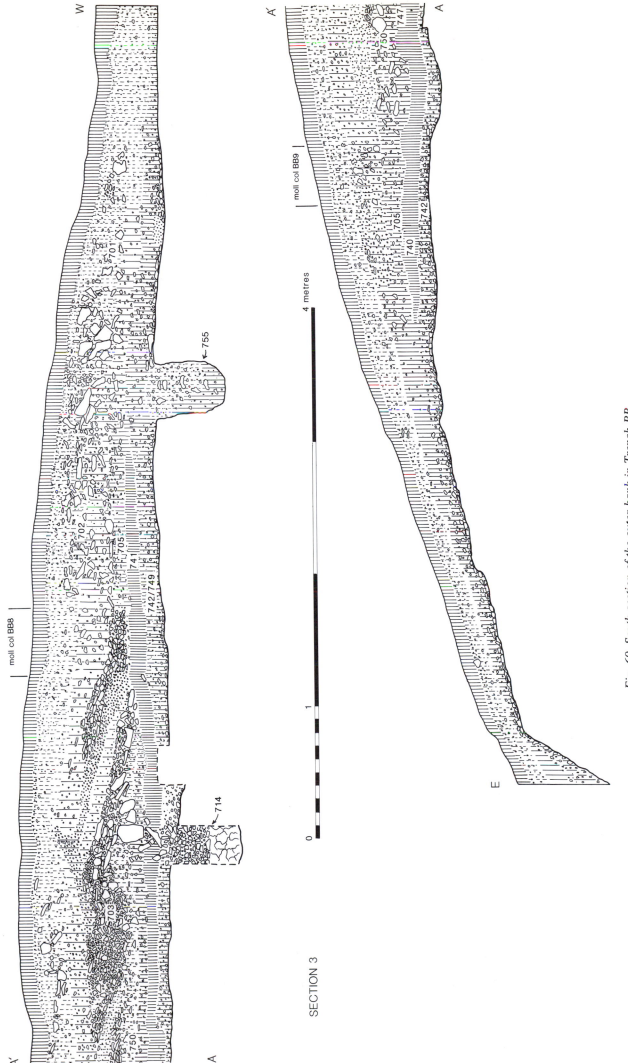

SECTION 3

4 metres

Fig. 69. South section of the outer bank in Trench BB.

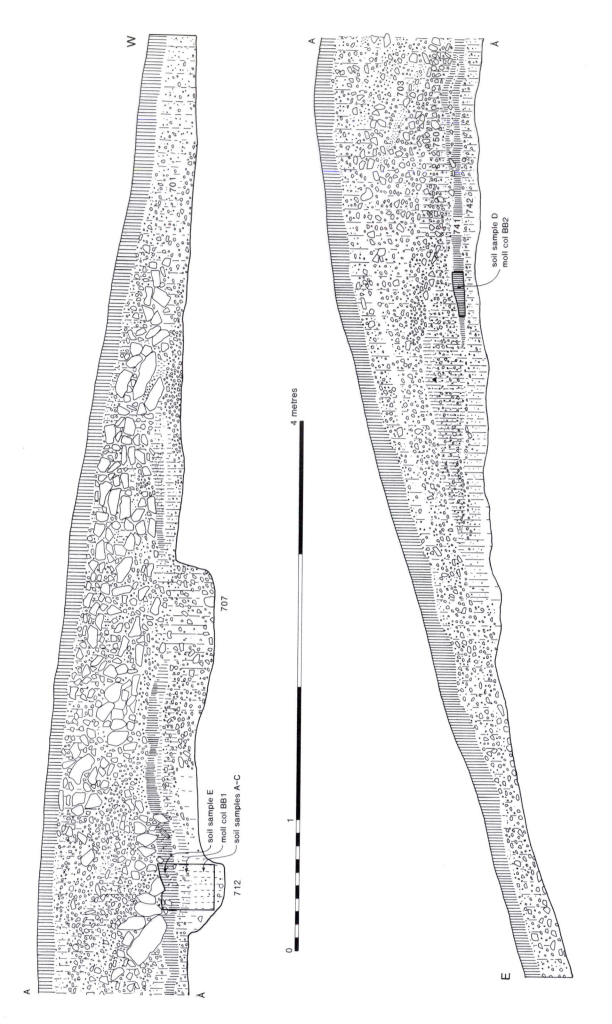

W

701

707

712

soil sample E
moll col BB1
soil samples A–C

A

A

703

750

741

742

soil sample D
moll col BB2

E

4 metres

1

0

Fig. 70. Section of the outer bank in Trench BB at its interface with Smith Cutting V.

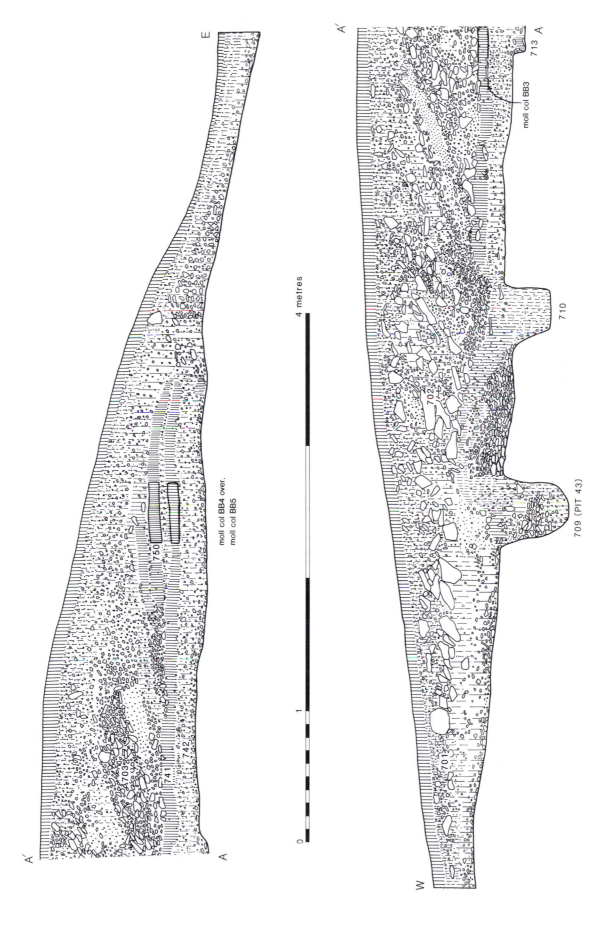

Fig. 71. North section of the outer bank in Smith Cutting V.

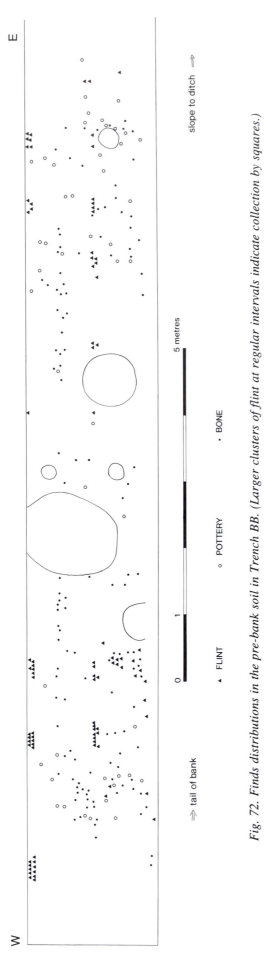

Fig. 72. Finds distributions in the pre-bank soil in Trench BB. (Larger clusters of flint at regular intervals indicate collection by squares.)

▲ FLINT   ○ POTTERY   • BONE

there was a little worm-sorting in 741. Micromorpho-logical analysis (chapter 6) also suggests that the humic uppermost horizon of this rendzina has been lost. The area had seen some burning and dumping, but of low intensity, and there had subsequently been a short period of earth-worm mixing. Molluscan analysis (chapter 6) may indicate that the setting was one of scrub or open woodland, but other scenarios are possible, including grassland among woodland. The molluscan analysis highlights the disturbed (because so chalky) nature of the soil, with only a brief period of stability and worm-sorting at the end of the sequence before bank construction.

Animal bone, antler, flint waste and pottery sherds were found on and in the buried soil (fig. 72); the quantity of finds declined markedly in the lower rubble horizon. Sherds (from simple-rimmed vessels, with lugs and simple pin-prick decoration) were small and extremely abraded. Animal bone was dominated by cattle, with pig and sheep/goat also present. Much of the bone was fragmentary and scattered; a broad range of body parts was found. There were also four finds of human bone on this surface: two teeth, a skull fragment and a tibia shaft fragment. Flecks of charcoal were found throughout the buried soil (and confirmed in micromorphological analysis), and there was one pronounced concentration, 743, to the east of pit 714. Identifiable fragments were dominated by oak, with hazel, hawthorn, birch and yew also present (detailed in chapter 9).

In the eastern part of the trench, between the pit 714 and the primary bank 750 (described below), the soil-line was doubled. This was seen most clearly in section, at the interface between Outer Bank V and Trench BB (Smith 1965a, fig. 4), but could also be detected with some difficulty in the north section of Outer Bank V (fig. 71; and pl. 8); in the south section of Trench BB the two features had more or less merged again into one (fig. 69). The upper soil-line (746 in Trench BB, 763 in Outer Bank V) could be seen as a secondary feature connected with or developed over the primary bank 750. Among the bone fragments in 746 were six large pieces of large mammal rib, probably of cattle.

Postholes *(fig. 73)*
760 was a neatly cut posthole, on the line of the primary bank, 750, and first seen at its base; it was probably cut from the level of the old ground surface rather than sealed by it. Its fill shows a postpipe. On the same line but seen in the chalk subsoil in the adjacent Outer Bank V, the posthole 718 was less regular and its truncated fill did not show a postpipe, although finer fill overlay coarser.

Other neatly cut postholes were 711, in Outer Bank V, 755, 710 and 709, and the smaller 751 and 745. 711 and 710 were formerly considered to be animal burrows (Smith 1965a, 6), but this is over-cautious, since their profiles are regular and their plans reasonably so. The fill of 711 may only be 1958 backfill. There is a postpipe in the fill of 755, but this was not discernible in 710, 751 or 745. Neither

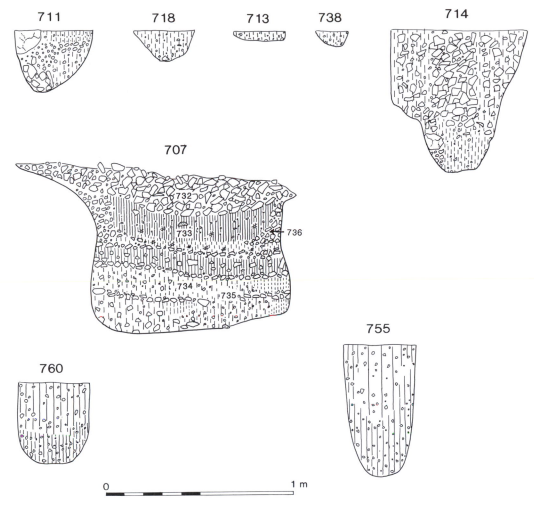

711 718 713 738 714

707

732
733
736
734
735

760

755

0   1 m

Fig. 73. Sections of postholes, pit and grave in Trench BB.

751 nor 745 were detected on the surface of the buried soil. 709 is published as Pit 43 from 1958 (Smith 1965a, 6 and 25). Its profile and core of dark humic soil suggest a posthole far more than a pit, but what appears to be a secondary fill of artefacts and bone should be noted (Smith 1965a, 25).

Smaller and less regular postholes were 757, 753, and 713. 713 in Outer Bank V was probably not seen in 1958. Its truncated chalky fill contained charcoal flecks. 753 was seen on the surface of the buried soil and the very shallow 757 within it.

Pit, 714 *(fig. 73)*
This was visible on the old land surface. Its fill largely consisted of chalk rubble (727), with smaller rubble and dark soil at the base (729, 728), and more brown soil at the top mixed with flint and animal bone (726), including substantial pieces of an ox mandible and humerus shaft. This suggests deliberate filling.

Grave, 707 *(figs 73–76; pl. 6)*
Like 714, the grave 707 appeared first as a chalk rubble-filled depression after the rest of the bank had been

excavated from the old land surface. In the case of 707 this coincided with the presence in the 1958 section of what had been described as an ancient badger hole (Smith 1965a, 6, and fig. 4). The chalk rubble proved merely to be the remnants of the overlying bank. The pit was oval, about 1.7 m long by 1.1 m broad, and cut about 75 cm into the chalk.

Its fill was dark soil, 733, with chalk banding, 736, and charcoal flecking, underlain by more dark soil, 734, containing a few fragments of bones of cattle and sheep/goats, with further chalk rubble banding and a limited area of lighter soil and small chalk rubble at the base of the pit, 735. Animal bone, including a pig's scapula and two fragmentary bones, was deposited in the centre of the pit in 733. There were a few flints and a few small sherds of plain pottery, including a very weathered rim. A sherd of plain pottery had been found in the feature in Outer Bank V.

On the base of the pit, with minimal grey chalk silt underneath it, the contracted skeleton of an adult man was found, lying on its right side, and orientated north-east/south-west. The skeleton was largely complete and mostly articulated; detailed analysis is given in chapter 16. The

Fig. 74. The pre-bank grave in Trench BB.

sternum, manubrium, right clavicle and scapula had collapsed, as well as much of the rib cage. The right tibia, fibula and patella (the lower right leg and knee) were lying across the left arm. The bones of the lower left arm were scattered, but those of the hands and feet were intact, the latter lying closely together. The left femur lay straight but ended at the same position as the right foot. At the time of uncovering the skull was intact (only 10 cm from the 1958 section) but exposure led to partial inwards collapse of already cracked portions. A calibrated age range of 3640–3490 or 3420–3380 BC was obtained from a rib of the skeleton (OxA-2403), and a calibrated age range of 3610–3580 or 3520–3340 BC from a pig scapula in the fill, 733, above the burial (OxA-2404).

With the skeleton was a single flint flake, and at the same level there were several thousand amphibian bones, chiefly of frogs and toads, some small rodent bones and some pig's teeth all probably from the same mandible of a one-year old animal. Detailed analysis is given below (chapter 12). It is possible that this deposit represents an episode during which the grave was kept open. This is discussed further below.

The bank *(figs 69–71; pls 5, 7 and 9)*
As recorded in 1958, there was a primary bank, 750, on the outer part of the bank facing the ditch (Smith 1965a, 6, and fig. 4). This consisted of at least two and possibly three layers (763–5) of soil and chalk rubble, laid on the old land surface to form a gentle and regular mound. The layers were most easily distinguished in the north section of Outer Bank V. The topmost layer, 763, was much less distinct than the other two but appears to meet and overlie the old land surface, 705. At the interface of Outer Bank V and Trench B it was much harder to distinguish layering

within 750, but the double soil-line behind it has been described above. 750 was also distinguishable in the south section of Trench B. Smith too noted the presence of an inner primary bank (1965a, 6, and fig. 4) between 712 and 707. This feature was not repeated in the south section of Trench B, and was not seen in plan in the excavation of the base of the bank and the top of the old land surface. A similar heave can be seen in the north section of Outer Bank V between 709 and 710, but this is further back towards the interior.

The bank proper was constructed by a series of tips of chalk and chalky soil. In sequence from the primary bank towards the interior were two broad zones, 703 and 702. 703 consisted of successive layers of very loose, quite angular chalk rubble on average 5 cm in diameter, with interleaved harder and denser stripes of grey puddled chalk or grey chalky silt with small chalk inclusions. These were variable. Three are visible in the interface between Outer Bank V and Trench B, including one marking the divide between 702 and 703, two in the north section of Outer Bank V and one in the south section of Trench B. In the latter section the forward part of 703 consisted of smaller chalk material with brown soil. At the interface of Outer Bank V and Trench B some large pitched chalk blocks were present on the top of the old land surface on the line of 712 and 714. 702 consisted of larger chalk blocks, also quite angular, of average size 10 by 15 by 5 cm. There were some larger pieces, especially at the back of the bank, and in particular in one location just behind 707 three blocks (706) up to 60 by 50 cm were stacked against each other. The surrounding matrix was loose grey chalky silt and smaller chalk rubble, the soil component becoming browner towards the back of the bank. The talus of the bank, 701, consisted of brown soil mixed with chalk rubble

Fig. 75. The skeleton in the pre-bank grave in Trench BB.

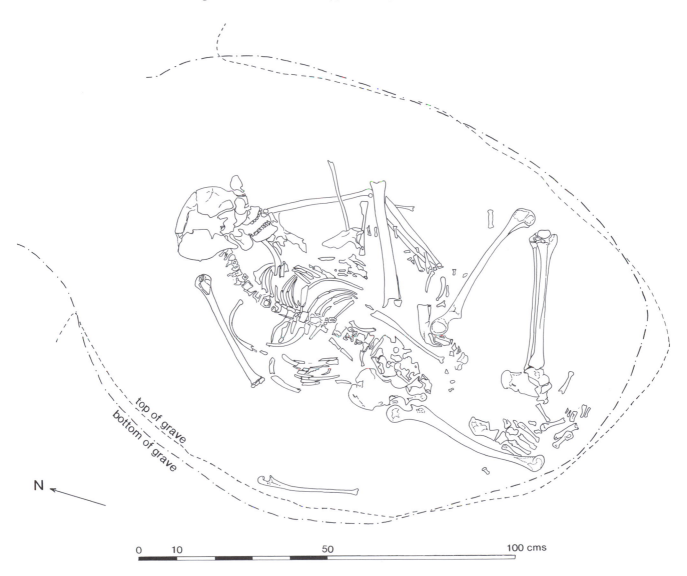

top of grave
bottom of grave

N

0 10   50   100 cms

Fig. 76. Plan of the pre-bank grave, Trench BB.

about 5 cm in diameter, again quite angular. Careful search was made of this part of the bank to see whether secondary material, such as might be expected from ditch scourings, had been deposited, but none was distinguished.

Much animal bone was found incorporated into the bank, predominantly of cattle, with some pig, one of sheep/goat and one red deer antler fragment, as well as a few sherds of plain pottery and a few flint flakes, matching the character of finds in 1958. This material was presumably derived from the surrounding old land surface. Rather more flakes and bone fragments were found at the rear tail of the bank, as well as sherds including Ebbsfleet pottery, a collared vessel of Early Bronze Age style, a probable late Bronze Age sherd and a Romano-British sherd.

THE OUTER DITCH

Trench B *(fig. 77 and pls 9–14)*

Trench B was laid out immediately adjacent to Outer Ditch V. The south edge of the new section was some 3 m from the end of the ditch segment. As excavated here, the ditch was 7.6 m wide and 2.2 m deep. Its outer side showed two slight scallops in the combined cuttings. The inner side of the ditch was a little more regular, and widened a little towards the terminal. Both ditch edges were weathered. The base of the ditch was very slightly concave, and deepened slightly towards the terminal.

Primary fill

The first layer of the primary fill was a thin deposit of fine grey chalk silt, 232. This was only 1–2 cm thick, with charcoal flecks, and was seen only immediately next to the south section and in a molluscan sample column in the south section. Overlying this was basal chalk rubble, 228, composed of small to medium, angular chalk fragments. Within 228 near the outer side of the ditch were two separate small grey chalk silt lenses, 230 and 231, which were localised and not visible in the section. 228 was overlain by 210, small more rounded chalk fragments. Between it and 228 on the inner side of the ditch lay another grey to dark silt lens, 233, again localised in the area of the south section. The uppermost part of 210 on the inner side of the ditch was truncated by an animal burrow. A similar disconformity on the outer side may be explained in the same way, though no burrow was directly observed. A less chalky continuation of 210 up the outer side of the ditch, 209, was more visible in the south section of Outer Ditch V than in the south section of Trench B (Smith 1965a, fig. 4). These primary deposits were little more than 25 cm thick in the centre of the ditch, and 50 cm in the angles.

Animal bone was recorded in groups, probably deliberately placed, on the base of the ditch in the lowest part of 228, between 228 and 210 (context 229), and on top of 210 (context 227). Details of 229, 227, 228 and 210 are given below. Calibrated age ranges of 3630–3500 or 3420–3380

BC were obtained from an ox tibia in 229 (BM-2669). A few weathered sherds of plain pottery, from several vessels, were found in 228, 229 and 210, in small quantities of. In 228 and largely in 229 there was a larger portion of a single plain vessel, P516, with some weathered rim and body sherds. There was a sarsen quern fragment in 229 and a small weathered Ebbsfleet sherd in 227.

Detail of primary bone deposits

The terminology used here for the bone deposits – variously as groups, spreads and scatters – is based upon morphological characteristics, and should not in the first instance be taken to indicate particular modes of deposition (more detailed discussion of which is given in chapters 11 and 17). Groups may be characterised as tight concentrations of bone, spreads as loosely defined concentrations, and scatters as dispersed, low-density deposits; though it should be recognised that a range of formats are present and the distinctions between groups, spreads and scatters are somewhat subjective. In the figures, not every bone is plotted, but those visible at the chosen stage of planning.

229 (fig. 78). Evenly distributed scatter of bone associated with pottery, flint and stone. Observed to run along the longitudinal axis of the ditch, with a maximum width of c. 2 m. May be seen to be composed of two parallel linear scatters, one predominantly of bone (though with a large piece of worked stone), the other (largely restricted to the NW side) with pottery and flint.

The species present include cattle (18 bones), pig (a rib and a tentatively identified vertebra) and sheep/goat (two scapulae, including one from a goat), along with nine unidentified bone fragments. The cattle bones are from the trunk, limbs and feet, with some loose teeth. With the exception of two phalanges from the same foot of an ox, the bone must have been disarticulated before deposition in the ditch, and indeed must have been left around long enough for three of the cattle bones and the sheep/goat scapula to have been gnawed by dogs. There is an irregular distribution of bone fragment size, together with a high mean size and low variability. Nearly 70 percent of the bones can be identified. There were numerous cutmarks on the neck of the pig's rib.

The scatter was associated with a substantial portion of a plain bowl, P516, several pieces of worked flint (both debitage and implements), and a large fragment of sarsen quern. No human bone was present.

The scatter would appear to be the product of one or two depositional events. The disarticulated state of the animal bone and the fragmentary character of the pottery could argue against the material being deposited 'fresh' (i.e. as primary refuse). The scatter follows the axis of the ditch along its centre, an alignment also taken by many of the long pieces of animal bone. This could result from either deliberate arrangement or gravitational alignment as pieces rolled down the ditch sides. However, if due to the latter mechanism then the distribution of bone would be expected to lie to the sides of the ditch rather than its centre.

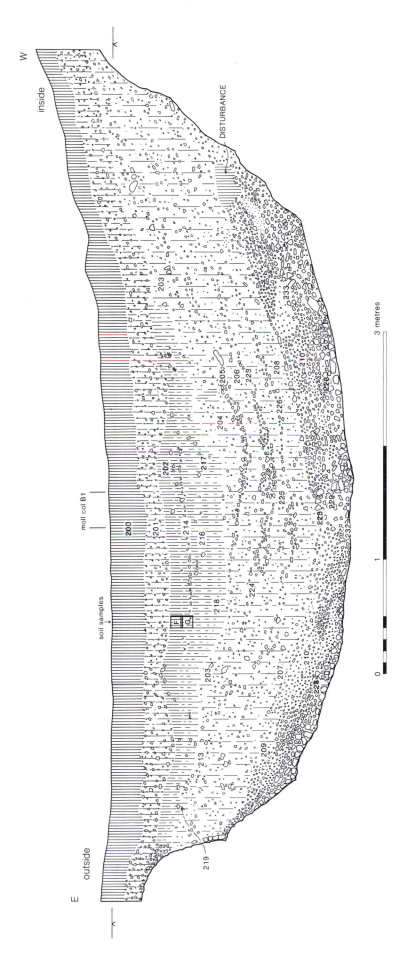

Fig. 77. South section of the outer ditch in Trench B.

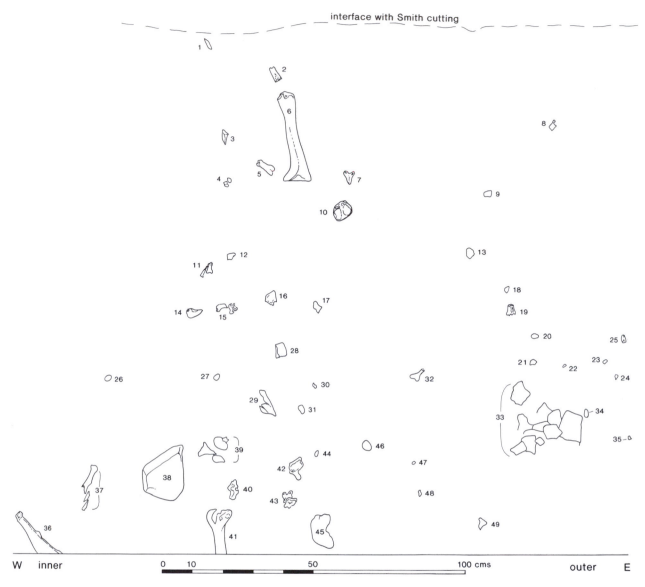

Fig. 78. Bone deposit 229. (Note that in this and subsequent plans of bone deposits not all bones are planned.) The only substantial bones in 229 are all of cattle: the shaft of an tibia, a long strip of scapula spine and a distal radius. A pair of ox proximal phalanges from the same foot is close to the tibia. 229 has a high proportion of identified bones, particularly cattle footbones. The other very fragmentary bones include a pig's rib and two distal fragments of sheep/goat scapulae, one of which is probably from a goat. The key for this and related following figures is given in the appendix at the end of the chapter.

227 (fig. 79 and pl. 13). A scatter of bone of moderate density, with antler, pottery and some flint. Observed to run at a slightly oblique angle to the length of the ditch, with a width of 0.6–1 m. Localised concentrations of bone occurred within the main spread, including a collection of ribs within the centre of the excavated portion. As with 229, the axis of many of the longbones followed that of the ditch.

The species present are cattle (38 bones, including 10 large mammal rib fragments), pig (seven bones), sheep/goat (two bones), red deer (15 fragments of what was probably a single antler) and dog (six footbones), along with 15 fragments of medium-size mammal rib and 96 unidentified bone fragments. Most of the cattle bones are vertebrae and ribs, with small numbers from other parts of the body. The pig bones are from the trunk and limbs.

With the exception of the dog foot bones, which are probably all from the same animal, the bone must have been left around long enough for at least three of the ox bones to have been gnawed by dogs. The regular distribution of the sizes of the bone fragments and the preponderance of small fragments would define this as bone 'waste', though there is a high variability of fragment size and a moderately high proportion of identifiable and matching bones. The presence of four burnt bone fragments suggests that the bones have a varied depositional history. The ox longbones appear to have been chopped horizontally across the shafts and there are cutmarks on one of the large mammal ribs.

A small worn Ebbsfleet sherd, a plain sherd and flint (flakes only) were present with the bone.

The deposit was similar in its general character to that from 229, in as much as it comprised a mixed linear spread confined to the centre of the ditch and following its general axis.

228. A spread of bone over 3 m wide with a specific concentration towards its the centre. Situated more towards the outer edge than the centre of the ditch. Associated with worked flint.

The species present are cattle (34 bones), pig (five), sheep/goat (eight), red deer (five) and roe deer (one tentatively identified tibia fragment), along with two fragments of medium-sized mammal and 92 unidentified bone fragments. There is a fairly even representation of cattle, pig and sheep/goat body parts. In addition to antler, limb and foot bones of red deer are present. The bone appears to have been disarticulated at the time of deposition in the ditch.

Two of the ox bones and the tibia of a red deer have been gnawed, and the tibia has been reduced to a cylinder, a typical result of carnivore activity, indicating that at least some of the bones were lying around long enough to be worked over by dogs. Some of the bones appear to have suffered from decay, probably before deposition, a red

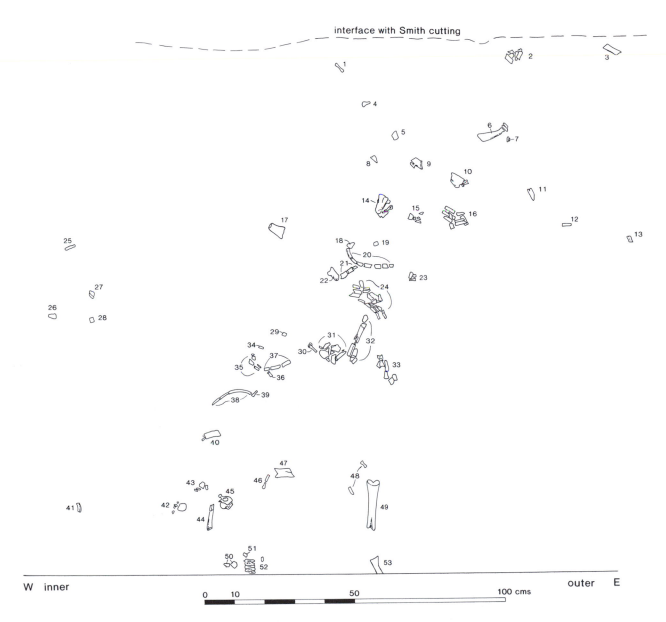

Fig. 79. Bone deposit 227. Although much of the bone is very fragmentary, there is a high proportion of identified bones, which include many ox vertebrae and large mammal rib fragments, probably derived from the same animal. A second group consists of dog footbones with medium mammal rib (perhaps from the same dog). 227 also contains two fragments of the same pig ulna divided by an ancient break and a group of antler fragments which are probably all from the same bone. There were also many unplanned bones.

deer antler being particularly weathered. None of the bones could be articulated, nor are there any paired elements, so apart from three fragments which appear to be from the same ox femur, there is no evidence for any of the bones coming from the same individual. Although there is a smooth distribution of fragment size, both mean fragment size and variability are quite high, and a moderate proportion of the bones can be identified.

Several pieces of flint debitage (including a high proportion of cores) and implements were associated with the bone. There were small weathered sherds.

The general character of the bone deposit echoes that of 229 and 227, but with a lower mean fragment size and a smoother pattern of distribution. However, the composition of the bone assemblage differs, in that it incorporates a wider variety of species with an emphasis upon a different range of body parts.

210. A spread over 4 m wide of bone running along the axis of the ditch, with a specific concentration towards the middle. Associated with flint waste and a few sherds.

The species present are cattle (16 bones including three large mammal rib fragments), pig (eight small bones, all probably from the same neonatal piglet), sheep/goat (five, including a distal scapula definitely identified as sheep), red deer (one antler fragment), bird (three) and 13 unidentified bone fragments. There is a wide range of body parts. Four of the ox foot and ankle bones appear to be of the same animal, as do a femur and tibia of a very young lamb or kid.

210 has an uneven distribution of bone fragment size, accompanied by high mean size, high variability, and a high proportion of identifiable and matching bones. A certain amount of animal bone was entering the ditch at this point as fresh material, rather than being curated from secondary sources.

Secondary fill
In the secondary fill, fine grey chalk silt layers, the upper ones progressively less grey, were interspersed with thin layers of chalk fragments. 207 on the outer side of the ditch and 208 on the inner consisted of fine grey chalk silt, with generally small, relatively sparse chalk fragments. Above lay 226 in the centre and inner side of the ditch, with a more noticeable concentration of small, quite rounded chalk fragments in a matrix of fine chalk silt. 225, another chalk silt layer, with one Ebbsfleet sherd, was overlain by the chalk layers 224 (on the outer side of the ditch) and 223 (on the inner), these slightly thicker than 226. Above, 206, silt with chalk fragments (defined as 213 at the outermost side of the ditch), was overlain by 205, chalk fragments, mostly rounded but with some more angular pieces. 205 was most easily defined in the centre of the ditch, where some chalk fragments on the inner side were over 10 cm long. As below, the run of chalk was harder to trace in the inner and outer parts of the ditch fill. Above 205 in the centre and inner side of the ditch came 204, another silty layer, distinguishable from 203 above it by the slightly browner colour of the latter. In both plan and section 204 appears

to have been truncated a little on the inner side of the ditch by 203. The two sections drawn, on the south sides respectively of Outer Ditch V and Trench B, do not present exactly the same picture, as the layers slope a little downwards from the south, terminal end of the ditch. The top of 203 was a little truncated or cut by features above. Numerous fragments of animal bone were scattered through 203–205, 207, 208 and 223–227; the species represented were cattle, pig, sheep/goat, dog, red deer (antler), roe deer (bone and antler), polecat and amphibian. A little burnt bone was found at the base of 225 in the centre of the ditch. There was a human ulna fragment in 206, and two human bone fragments in 203. The edge of a polished flint axe was found on the inner side of the fill in 204/206. There were weathered plain sherds as high as 203.

Detail of secondary bone deposits
207. A low density scatter of bone with several flint flakes extending over an area of c. 1.3 m on the outer side of the ditch.

The species present are cattle (six bones, including two large mammal rib fragments), and red deer (four decayed fragments of antler), along with five fragments of medium-size mammal rib and 22 unidentified bone fragments. The cattle bone includes pieces of skull, rib, a vertebra and complete metacarpal.

Although the mean fragment size in 207 is low, it includes some larger fragments, resulting in an uneven pattern of fragment size distribution. It also has a fairly high percentage of identifiable bones. This low density scatter contrasts strongly with that in 210 of the upper primary silts.

208. A low density scatter of bone, with several flint flakes, extending over an area of more than 2.0 m on the inner side of the ditch.

The species present are cattle (seven bones including two large mammal rib fragments), pig (a tooth, a vertebra and a fibula), sheep/goat (one metapodial fragment) and red deer (one tentatively identified vertebra fragment), along with 12 unidentified bone fragments. As with 207, the cattle bones include parts of skull, trunk, and feet, in addition to a tibia. The bone appears to have been disarticulated at the time of deposition in the ditch and some has been gnawed.

This is similar in character to 207.

Upper secondary fill
In the upper secondary fill there was a series of very dark deposits and features. Four shallow features, 219–222, were cut into the top of 203; only 219 shows in section (figs 77 and 200; see also pl. 12). These were rather irregular patches of looser material with little chalk in them. 220 is probably an animal burrow, and the others possibly so, but 219, on the line of the south section, contained a significant concentration of finds. 219 had Beaker sherds and a Food Vessel sherd, cattle and pig bones and a roe deer antler. Two larger scoops, 234 and

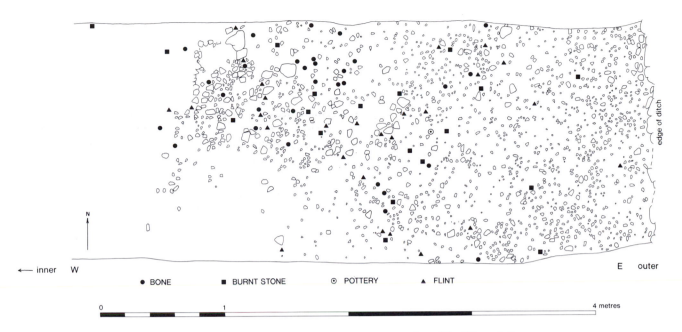

←— inner   W   E   outer

● BONE   ■ BURNT STONE   ⊙ POTTERY   ▲ FLINT

0   1   4 metres

Fig. 80. Plan of surface 214 in the upper secondary fill of Trench B.

235, were also cut into the top of 203. Their fill, 216, was a dark soil with small to very small chalk fragments. At the base of 234 and 235, 217 and 218, on the inner and outer sides respectively, were runs of small to medium chalk fragments, separating the deposits above from 203.

Over 216 was a definable chalk surface, 214, very probably deliberately laid, with large numbers of medium to large chalk fragments, as well as animal bone and other finds (fig. 80). Micromorphology (chapter 6) indicates a moderately rapid sequence. Animal remains in 214, 216 and 217 include bones of cattle, pigs, sheep/goats, dog, polecat and roe deer, as well as red deer antler. 211–212 were thin layers immediately above 214. There were some Beaker and Early Bronze Age sherds in 216 and on 214. There were also some flint waste pieces, a few tools, a barbed and tanged arrowhead from 216 and a petit tranchet derivative on 214, and a fragment of a stone shafthole macehead from 216.

On top of the secondary fill was 202, a very dark to black soil layer with some medium chalk fragments and many small chalk fragments. Micromorphology (chapter 6) suggests an increasingly decalcified deposit, perhaps forming as the result of gentle erosion inwards. This had substantial numbers of animal bone fragments and some more complete pieces. There were bones of cattle, pig, sheep/goat and red deer; ?otter, fox, and roe deer were also present. Many of the cattle bones were pieces of skull and teeth. There were some fragments of human bone. There were some sherds of Beaker and rather more sherds of Early Bronze Age pottery. The pot sequence may suggest gradual accumulation or formation of the deposit, akin to the formation of a soil, but the sherds in 202 are the least abraded of all those in the upper secondary fill of Trench B and could indicate much more rapid dumping or

redeposition (Joanna Brück, below, chapter 17). The issue remains open, and is discussed further in chapter 17.

Analysis of molluscan samples from a complete profile is presented below (chapter 7). The primary and lower secondary fills were absolutely dominated by woodland fauna, with a gradual opening up of woodland in the upper secondary fill, but without the establishment of pure grassland. The uppermost part of the upper secondary fill, above 214, suggests a more rapid trend to open country.

Tertiary fill
The tertiary fill, 201, was a very dark to black soil with very many small rounded chalk fragments. There were many small fragments of bone amongst which those of cattle and sheep/goats were the most numerous. Sherds too were numerous, some Neolithic but mostly Romano-British. There was some flint waste. 201 was sealed by the modern turf and dark topsoil. Moles were active in this, and there had been mole disturbance in 201 and 202.

Discussion
Primary weathering of the chalk sides of the ditch, with only limited silting in of soil or turves was followed by weathering of topsoil and surrounds, including the bank on the inner edge of the ditch. The pattern of the chalk runs (226, 223–224, 205) suggests a bank with a stable profile. The change in colour from grey to brown may reflect an increasing humic content. There is limited truncation of 204 by 203. Above Later Neolithic occupation or activity, there was soil formation. The processes by which the upper secondary fill accumulated are complicated, and are discussed further in chapter 17. The tertiary fill was formed by Romano-British ploughing.

Bone deposits, principally mixed spreads and scatters

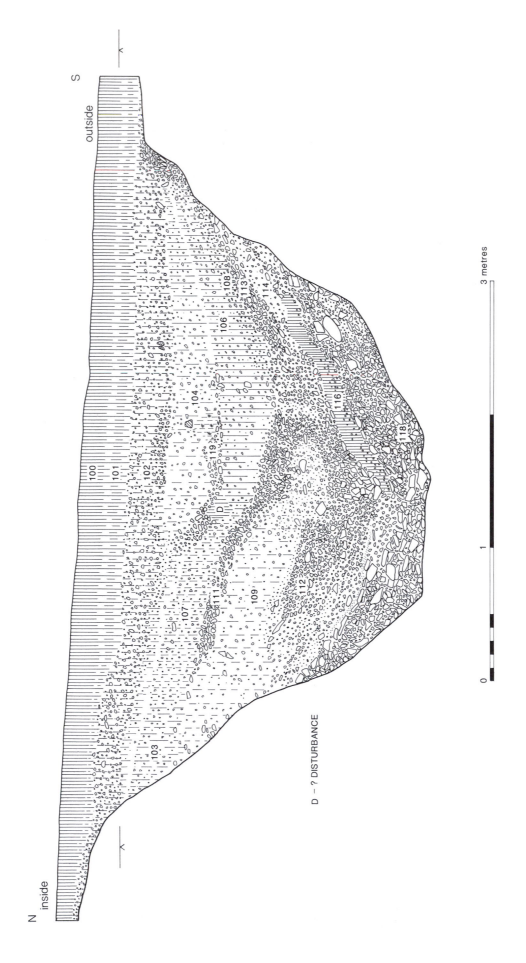

Fig. 81. East section of the outer ditch in Trench A. (Note that the opposite section was sampled for molluscan analysis.)

of disarticulated bone (the exception being 210), were entering the ditch from an early stage, as witnessed by 229. These are largely a feature of the primary and lower secondary silts, several being spread along the length of the ditch.

The adjacent bank seems to have had little effect on the fill. There seemed to be very little primary chalk rubble, in contrast to the primary fill of other cuttings. The actual chalk fragments were also small. The ditch could have been scoured out on one or more occasions. The top of the primary rubble on the outer side may also have been truncated (at the interface of 210 and 209), an impression which is even stronger in the north section of Outer Ditch V. Against the idea of scouring are the substantial width of the ditch (approximately 5 m at the base), the gentle slope of the sides, especially the inner side, and the relatively small size of the weathering ramps on either side of the ditch. In the case of the inner side, the loss of chalk may be fairly closely defined, because of the survival under the bank of the old land surface.

Trench A *(fig. 81 and pls 15–16)*

Trench A was placed across the previously unexcavated southern part of the outer circuit. Remains of the bank can be seen on its inside, and the cutting was probably close to a terminal. The ditch was 5.4 m wide by 2.6 m deep on the east section line, and 5 m wide by 2.4 m deep on the west section line. The inner side of the ditch was steeper than the outer, but with a slight step in its upper part. The base of the ditch was more or less flat, with a very slight narrowing of the base area from east to west.

Primary fill

The primary fill consisted of fresh angular chalk rubble, 118. In the east section it was interleaved with a dark silt lens coming from the outside of the ditch, 116. This was overlain by a fine grey chalk silt layer on the outer side and centre of the ditch, 114, and at the interface of 118 and 112 on the inner side. Over this were layers of smaller chalk rubble, 112 from the inside of the ditch and 113 from the outside. 112 had one very weathered rim sherd from a plain vessel. It contained a few bone fragments including an astragalus which may have come from the same ankle as the articulating ankle bones in 117 (below). It also seems to have been the pair of another astragalus (that is from the same individual ox) in the bone group in the secondary layer above (115, below), which itself articulates with a calcaneum in 115 *and* with a distal tibia in 117, suggesting a single episode of deposition of the bones in these features.

Primary bone deposit 117

An exceptional deposit, 117, in the top of 112 consisted of the cranium of a young child (probably between three and four years old) nested within an intact frontlet of an ox, against which were placed the spine of an ox scapula and a distal tibia (fig. 82 and pl. 15). There were multiple cutmarks on the frontal part of the frontlet, suggesting that the skin had been removed prior to deposition (figs 160A and B). Within 0.8 m of this group was a small number of cattle bones, including a group from the same ankle and a right and a left horncore, which were almost entire; both derive from old cows, but do not exactly match each other, so they probably derive from two different individuals

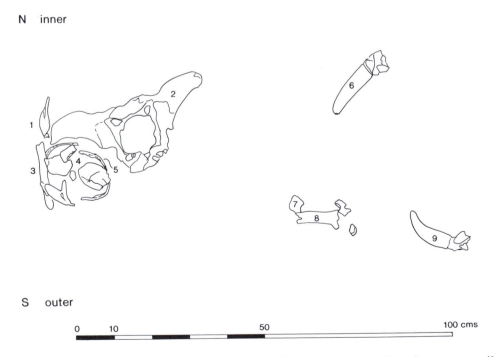

N inner

S outer

0 10 50 100 cms

Fig. 82. Bone deposit 117. The cranium of a young child nested within an ox frontlet. Adjacent, a small collection of cattle bones from the same ankle and two horncores (not a pair).

(fig. 159). There was also a piece of flint waste. Calibrated age ranges of 3640–3500 or 3410–3380 BC were obtained from the child cranium (OxA-2399).

From the detail of composition and position, this is evidently a placed group (suggested in part by the irregular distribution of the sizes of the bone fragments and the presence of many large fragments), and perhaps a single act of deposition (though note the connections between 112 and 115).

Secondary fill

On the inner side of the ditch the primary rubble was overlain by a compact asymmetrical layer of grey puddled chalk and small rounded chalk fragments, 109. This was overlain by a very white compact lens of small chalk fragments, a little more angular, 111. This was more pronounced in the east than in the west section. In the top of 111 next to and extending into the west section there was a bone group, 115, consisting of interleaved cattle ribs, a dorsal vertebra, and the ankle bones mentioned above. On the outer side of the ditch there was a thin layer, 108, of light brown soil mixed with small to medium sized sub-angular chalk fragments. There were several sherds in 111, 115, 106 and 108, the majority from the latter two contexts. The majority of the comparatively unweathered sherds came from one vessel. Over 108 lay a dark brown humic lens, 106. Within this near the east section was one concentration, 105, of darker charcoal-flecked soil with numbers of unworked sarsen fragments. Another localised patch of darker soil, charcoal-flecked and with fragments of burnt bone, 110, lay next to and in the west section. Towards the inner edge of the ditch the layer became markedly lighter in colour though only a little chalkier, 107, and at the inner edge of the ditch had changed further to a greyish compacted chalky wash with some rounded small chalk fragments and occasional larger fragments, 103, which merged with 109 beneath it. Separating 106 from the layer above, 104, was a small lens, 119, of rounded small chalk fragments in a matrix of grey silt. This was again more pronounced in the east than in the west section. It appeared to come from the inner side of the ditch, since it tailed off towards the outer side, but it did not extend to the inner edge. 104 was a brown humic layer, though drying to greyer and lighter hue, and with variable content of rounded and small chalk fragments. It lay in the centre to outer part of the ditch. Its top was truncated by 102 above, and there was some mole or rabbit burrowing, which also extended down into 106. There were scatters of bone in the secondary fill, especially in 106, 104 and 103; these consisted of the usual domestic-ated species and rarer finds of red deer, wild pig, aurochs or wild cattle (*Bos primigenius*) and dog. Sherds of Grooved Ware and Early Bronze Age pottery were found in 106 and 104 (and in 102 above, presumably derived), and there were Beaker sherds from 104 and 102.

Analysis of molluscan samples from the secondary fill (chapter 7) shows the dominance of woodland species.

Detail of secondary bone deposits

115. Sherds of plain pottery including a rim were found in association with a small bone deposit extending into the west section of the trench and comprising six unidentified fragments and six cattle bones: three interleaved proximal ribs, probably discarded together when still attached to one another by ligaments, if not meat; a dorsal vertebra; and a calcaneum and astragalus, which articulate not only with one another, but also with a distal tibia in 117. The astragalus is a pair with another in 112. This suggests a connection between 115 (secondary fill) and 112 and 117 (both primary). 115 is perhaps part of a larger spread extending beyond the western end of the trench.

106. A general scatter of bone, associated with sherds of Grooved Ware and Early Bronze Age pottery, as well as plain Earlier Neolithic sherds, along with 27 flint flakes and a serrated flake.

The species present are cattle (13 bones) and pig (eight), along with two medium-size mammal rib frag-ments and 88 unidentified bone fragments. The cattle bone includes teeth, fragments of vertebrae and foot bones. The pig assemblage, with the exception of a tooth, consists entirely of leg and ankle bones.

Mean bone fragment size in 106 is low, but quite variable, with a low proportion of identifiable bones.

Limited mole or rabbit burrowing was recorded in 106, and this may have caused disturbance to the bone scatter. The scatter consists of cattle and pig bone only, but this may simply reflect the small size of the assemblage. The high percentage of unidentifiable bone hints at severe post-depositional attrition.

104. A general scatter of bone, associated with Grooved Ware and Early Bronze Age sherds. Worked flint was plentiful and includes several cores, over 70 flakes and a range of implements.

The species present are cattle (18 bones, including five large mammal rib fragments), pig (one skull fragment and two shafts of tibiae), sheep/goat (two tibiae) dog (an atlas and a tooth) and red deer (three antler fragments and a patella), along with 84 unidentified bone fragments. The cattle remains include teeth and skull fragments, and leg and ankle bones, probably disarticulated when deposited in the ditch.

The pattern of fragmentation in 104 is similar to that in 106 (above), although with less variability in fragment size.

A wider range of species is present within 104 than in 106, including dog and red deer. As in 106, there is a high percentage of unidentifiable bone. The high proportion of loose teeth suggests a fair degree of post-depositional damage.

103. A general scatter of bone, associated with several flint flakes and a knife.

The species present are cattle (eight bones, including a femur of aurochs, *Bos primigenius*), pig (six, including a lower third molar from a possible wild pig) and dog (a metapodial), along with 42 unidentified bone fragments. The domestic cattle bones are from feet, wrist and ankle, with a single vertebra. The domestic pig bones are two metacarpals, two teeth and a mandible fragment. The bone appears to have been disarticulated at the time of deposition in the ditch.

Low bone fragment size is coupled with low variability, a smooth pattern of distribution and a low proportion of identified bones.

As with the bone assemblages from 104 and 106, there is a high percentage of unidentified fragments. The possible occurrence of wild cattle and pig (otherwise rare on the site) is notable.

Tertiary fill

The tertiary fill consisted of two plough layers. 102 was a light brown soil with many small rounded chalk fragments, in slightly higher density towards the inner side of the ditch. This layer did not extend beyond the edges of the ditch. It contained much fragmented bone, particularly of ox and pig, some flint waste, and sherds including Romano-British ware. 101 above was a fine light grey soil with scattered small chalk fragments, deepest over the centre of the ditch but continuing over the chalk surface at either side of the ditch.

Discussion

The cutting may be across a part of the outer ditch near a terminal. A bank probably stood on the inner side of the ditch. The primary fill is natural. Almost as much comes from the outside as from the inside. 116 and 114, and the 118/112 interface, represent episodes of turf collapse and topsoil weathering. The bone spread 117 (with 112 and 115) is a placed deposit, which may obviously extend further, especially towards the west. With the exception of 117, and in contrast to the situation in Trench B, bone deposits were more a feature of the secondary than primary fills. Generally, the frequency of deposition seems to have been low.

The secondary fill is largely natural but consists chiefly of weathered bank material, 109, since this comes in so asymmetrically from the inside. 111 appears to be a dumped layer, unless it can represent localised bank collapse; the placed bone dump, 115, at its top is more consistent with the former possibility. The rest of the secondary fill is also largely natural, representing the slow humic infill of the ditch over its displaced centre of silting, and interrupted only by depositions of charcoal-flecked soil (105, 110) and a localised dump of chalk, 119. There were plain sherds with the bone group 115. 104 may be an incipient soil; it contained Later Neolithic and Early Bronze Age sherds. The top of the secondary fill is truncated by Romano-British ploughing, which left further bank material over the ditch. The effect of medieval cultivation, seen as ridge-and-furrow to the north of the cutting, is unclear. 101 is presumably the result of this or modern ploughing.

Trench C *(fig. 83 and pls 17–19)*

Trench C was adjacent to Outer Ditch IV, close to the terminal of a segment. The ditch was 4.3 m wide by 2 m deep in the Outer Ditch IV/Trench C interface, and 4.7 m wide by 2.3 m deep in the east section of Trench C. The inner side of the ditch was steeper than the outer. The outer side and base were stepped.

Primary fill

The primary fill consisted of a series of layers of chalk rubble with interleaved fine chalk silt lenses. More fill came from the higher inner side of the ditch, but the same processes seem to be represented on the outer side of the ditch. The lowest layer was 324, angular chalk rubble and dark soil, with 323 in the inner angle of the ditch base in the east section, a lens of grey silt with few small chalk fragments. From the inner side to the centre this was overlain by 315, a thick layer of loose very angular chalk fragments, some of considerable size which created small voids underneath. On the inner edge of the ditch this continued upwards as 312, with a greater admixture of grey silt and chalk fragments of variable size. The outer tail of 315 in the east section merged with 322, a small dark brown lens projecting no more than 50 cm into the cutting. On the outer side of the ditch was a thin layer of chalk rubble in a grey silt matrix, 314, with both small and large chalk fragments. Above 315 lay the asymmetrical light grey to light brown silt lens 311. This had a low density of small rounded chalk fragments. This lens was more pronounced in the east section. On the inner side of the ditch it merged into 308, mixed small and larger chalk fragments and grey silt. Above lay further chalk and silt lenses, of varied lateral distribution. The Outer Ditch IV/ Trench C interface shows 310, small chalk rubble overlain by 309, grey silt and chalk overlain in turn by 306, chalk rubble extending up on the inner side of the ditch into 307, mixed chalk and silt. This layering was far less pronounced in the east section, which shows 310, and 309 and 306 telescoped together. On the outer side of the ditch there was a concentration of larger pieces of chalk, presumably brought there by gravity, at the meeting of 322, 314, 311, 310 and 306. Beyond this 313 overlay 314, a light grey silt with chalk fragments of mixed sizes, but in the east section, this was underlain by 319, a brown silt lens with some small chalk fragments, not dissimilar to 311, but localised and oval in plan. Scattered animal bone (dominated by cattle) was found in these layers, along with weathered sherds of plain pottery. There was a substantial fragment of a sarsen rubber right on the ditch base.

Detail of primary bone deposits

319. A localised spread of animal bone, 1.5 m across; without discernible pattern, situated close to the northern edge of the ditch. Associated with a small collection of flint debitage (including an axe fragment reworked as a core) and a scraper, and sherds including P540 and P592.

The species present are cattle (10 bones, including three

Fig. 83. East section of the outer ditch in Trench C.

large mammal rib fragments), sheep/goat (seven), along with two medium-size mammal rib fragments and 15 unidentified bone fragments. The cattle and sheep/goat bones derive from the trunk, legs, feet and skull, and include a goat scapula and a sheep metacarpal and radius. The bone may have been disarticulated when deposited in the ditch. It is possible that some of the bone in 319 stems from the same source as the bone in the upper secondary layer 317, as a left lower 4th premolar of an ox in 319 is a pair of (i.e. from the same animal as) a right lower 4th premolar in 317.

The representation of body parts is broadly comparable to those from primary contexts in Trench B (e.g. 229, 227). The distribution of the sizes of the bone fragments is irregular and there are some large fragments. Perhaps a single depositional event, the scatter contains a high proportion of identified bones.

308. A localised concentration of bone and flint, without any particular pattern, situated on the inner edge of the ditch.

The species present are cattle (15 bones, including one large mammal rib fragment), pig (three), sheep/goat (a calcaneum) and cat (a metapodial), along with 39 unidentified bone fragments. Most of the cattle bones derive from the trunk, with fragments of skull, legs and feet. The pig bones also show a varied representation of body parts. The cat metapodial seems to belong to the same foot as two cat metapodials in context 307, a nearby locus uncertainly identified as primary. The bone appears to have been disarticulated at the time of deposition in the ditch. A large mammal rib, almost certainly ox, has cutmarks on the inner side of the neck, suggesting removal of the tenderloin.

308 is comparable in character to 319, though with a wider range of species present. Although there is a preponderance of small unidentified fragments, the distribution of the sizes of the bones is irregular. The occurrence of cat bone is notable.

Secondary fill

The secondary fill begins with 320 in the outer part of the ditch and 305 in the inner part. Both seem to have formed at the same time. 320 was a brown-grey triangular shaped silt lens with relatively few small rounded chalk fragments. It contained a large concentrated bone group, 321, next to the east section. This consisted of the partial remains of at least three cattle, a small, young animal, a small adult, and a large young animal. Other animals might also be represented. Most parts of the body are present, though no one individual is near complete. A few bones of sheep/goat were also present. From 321, calibrated age ranges of 3650–3500 or 3420–3380 BC were obtained from an ox astragalus (OxA-2401), and calibrated ranges of 3610–3580 or 3520–3350 BC from an ox humerus (OxA-2402). It is not possible to say whether either of these bones belonged to the cattle skeletons mentioned above as both were used in the dating process before detailed faunal analysis.

The inner edge of 320 merged with 305, a thick, strongly asymmetrical layer of compact grey chalky silt and scattered small and medium rounded chalk fragments. Above lay 304, a brown triangular humic lens with scattered chalk fragments in it similar to those in 320. Vertically this merged very gradually with 320, but in section a more pronounced shallow V could be seen, showing the colour change. Above this lay 303, a crescent-shaped lens of grey brown humic material, with a low density of chalk fragments. A wide range of animal species was represented in these layers, including cat, ?fox and red deer in very small quantities.

Constituting an incipient soil over the secondary fill was 316, thicker towards the outside of the ditch, of fine humic material and dark brown to very dark brown in colour. It had been disturbed by moles. It contained a placed bone spread, 317, at its base and many scattered bone fragments in its upper part (of cattle and sheep/goat), particularly towards the outside of the ditch. 317 consisted of bones of cattle (some of which seem to have been from the same individual), pigs, and several vertebrae from the same dog. Calibrated age ranges of 3040–2960 or 2940–2880 or 2800–2780 BC were obtained from an ox scapula in 317 (BM-2673). There were Beaker and Early Bronze Age sherds in 316 and 317.

Analysis of molluscan samples from the secondary fill (chapter 7) shows the dominance of woodland species.

Detail of secondary bone deposits

321 (fig. 84 and pl. 17). A very compact and tightly defined group of bone, 0.6 by 0.6 m in extent, predominantly of cattle. A core and a flaked flint block were found with the bone.

The species present are cattle (69 bones, including one large-mammal rib fragment), and sheep/goat (two), along with two fragments of medium-sized mammal rib and 32 unidentified bone fragments. A wide range of cattle body parts is present, with a predominance of bones of the trunk. Amongst the bones are articulating groups of vertebrae, foot and leg bones. The cattle bones derive from at least three animals, two young and one adult.

This is an unusual group, whose compact nature and lack of signs of gnawing could indicate that it was in a bag or wrapped in a hide. The high variability, uneven distribution and fairly high mean fragment size, together with an identification rate of 60 percent, as well as the presence of many articulated bones from a few individuals, suggest that the material was deposited 'fresh', almost certainly with meat and ligaments still in place. The cutmarks on a nearly complete ox tibia and astragalus were probably produced in skinning. The small quantity of sheep/goat and medium-sized mammal bone may be token or incidental inclusions. There are no immediate parallels for such a deposit amongst the bone groups excavated in 1988.

317 (fig. 85 and pl. 18). A linear spread of bone (1.4 m wide) running along the axis of the ditch. Pottery and worked flint (both debitage and implements) were also

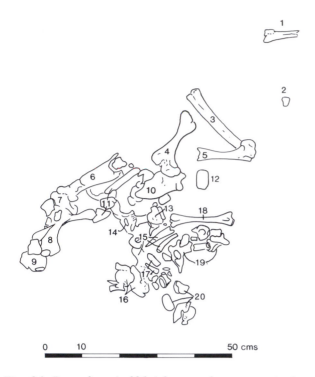

Fig. 84. Bone deposit 321 (close to the east section), a compact deposit of cattle bones, comprising most parts of the skeleton. Many of the pieces can be rejoined or articulated, so it is likely that most are from the same individual animal. Many of the numerous unplanned bones from the same context may also derive from this skeleton. There is one sheep/goat astragalus amongst the bones that have been planned.

present, the latter concentrated within the NE part of the spread.

The species present are cattle (37 bones, including one which may be of an aurochs and three large mammal rib fragments), pig (one tooth) and dog (three), along with 18 unidentified bone fragments. A wide range of body parts is represented amongst the cattle bone, including teeth and fragments of skull, trunk, limb and foot bones. The dog bones are an articulated string of neck vertebrae from the same animal. There were many cattle vertebrae in 317, which may have been in articulation at the time of deposition, although subsequently disturbed, which might derive from the same individual ox as that in secondary context 321, immediately below. Some of the ox longbones appear to have been broken in half.

The deposit has an even higher mean bone fragment size and higher variability than 321, a markedly uneven distribution of fragment size, a similarly high identification rate and many matching bones.

The spread may be seen as comparable in character to those in the primary fills of Trench B. The material may have been drawn from a range of sources, both primary (seen with the presence of 'fresh' animal bone) and secondary (the flint and abraded pottery). The spread may

have undergone limited post-depositional disturbance, and a few of the bones, including the scapula thought to be of an aurochs, have been gnawed. Articulating dog and cattle vertebrae were found in close proximity, but separated horizontally and vertically by up to 0.4 m. Animal burrowing might be a cause.

Tertiary fill

316 was truncated by 302, a light brown tertiary ploughsoil with a high concentration of small rounded chalk fragments. This did not continue beyond the edges of the ditch. There another layer could be distinguished, 301, of similar colour but with larger chalk fragments. 302 contained a great many unidentified fragments of animal bone, with bones of cattle and pigs, a few of sheep/goat, and one each of red and roe deer, as well as flint waste and Romano-British sherds. There was one flint barbed and tanged arrowhead. Over 302 and 301 was the modern turf and topsoil 300.

Discussion

The cutting was near the terminal of a ditch which was backed by an internal bank. The bank is suggested both by the section of the 1958 cutting (Smith 1965a, 5 and fig. 5, A-B) and by the asymmetrical pattern of weathered layers in the ditch such as 305. Yet this need not have been a substantial bank. The pattern of primary silting is already asymmetrical, and the remnants of bank suggested by Smith in Outer Bank IV are far less than those still visible in other bank segments both to the east and west of this particular location.

The primary fill was natural. The greater alternation of chalk and silt, compared with the outer ditch in Trench A, may be to do with the northerly aspect of the ditch here. The secondary fill (320, 305, 304, 303) is largely natural. 305 seems to derive largely from the inside, and presumably comes from the bank. In the displaced centre of silting there was an accumulation of weathered silt and *in situ* formation of humic material. A few deposits of bone occur high in the primary fill and continue into the secondary. The bone group 321 is a deliberately placed deposit in 320. 316 is an incipient soil and contains another placed deposit, 317. Beaker and Early Bronze Age pottery from 316 was presumably later than the age of deposit 317, as indicated by radiocarbon dating.

There were plain sherds in the primary fill, but very little pottery was found in the secondary or tertiary fill. The arrowhead in 302 may be derived from 316, which suggests that the ditch had the same sort of chronology as in Trench A and Trench B. The radiocarbon dates also show an interval between the very beginning of the secondary fill and the formation of soil at its top.

It is noticeable that 302 did not extend beyond the edges of the ditch. The change there to 301 implies that the original surface on either side of the ditch was originally higher.

N outer

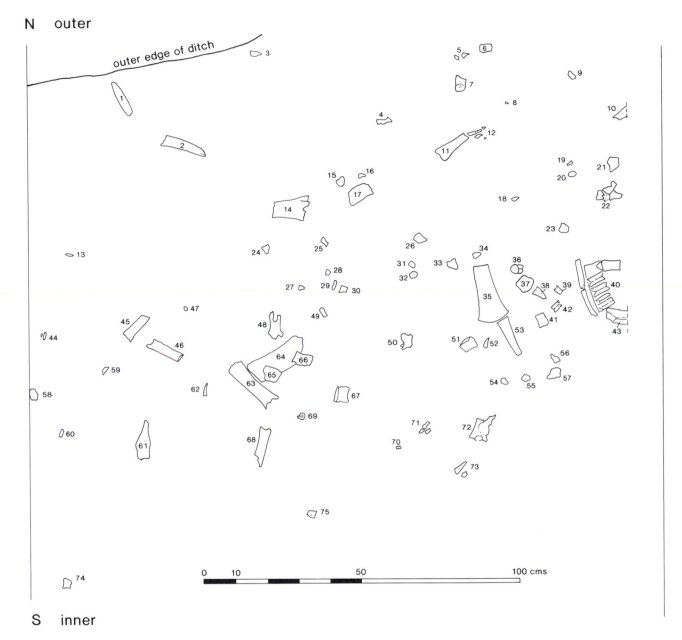

S inner

Fig. 85. Bone deposit 317, consisting of cattle bones in which vertebrae, possibly from the same animal, and other ox bones predominate. A dog's axis and cervical vertebra III were in articulation. An ox distal scapula was from a very large animal, possibly a wild ox. The only bone of other species was a single pig's incisor.

THE MIDDLE DITCH

Trench D *(fig. 86 and pls 20–23)*

The position of Trench D was chosen after magnetometer survey (chapter 2). The cutting was across a segment terminal, created by a submerged causeway. There was no indication of an inner bank, though the cutting extended for over 2 m inside the ditch.

The ditch was 3.4 m wide by 1.5 m deep, on the line of the north-west section. It narrowed to a boat-shaped point on the south-east section. The inner side of the ditch was steep, and overhanging as it curved to the terminal. The

outer side was steep but stepped at the base. The upper parts of the ditch on both sides were weathered, but the chalk surface on either side was more or less flat. The ditch base was concave, rising from the north-west-section towards the terminal, where the depth was only 1.4 m. The top of the submerged causeway was 75 cm below the modern surface.

Primary fill
The primary fill of the ditch consisted of angular chalk rubble of all sizes, 416, in the bottom half of the ditch and coming from both sides. Within 416 on the inside of the

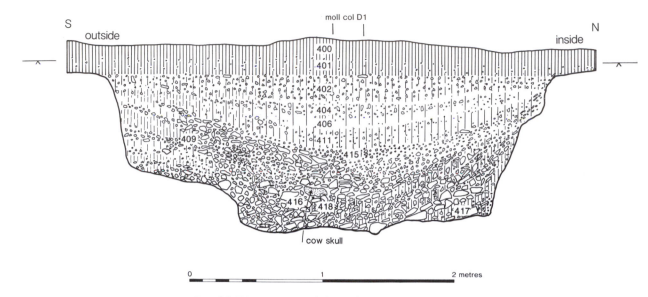

Fig. 86. West section of the middle ditch in Trench D.

ditch towards its base was an area of larger chalk blocks, dark soil and charcoal flecks, 417. The top of the primary fill had a higher humic content and smaller chalk rubble, 415 in the middle of the ditch and 409 on the outer side. Within 416 there was part of a skull which seems to have come from the same cow as the skull fragments found in 414 (below). In the middle of 416 and seen in the section were the remains of a butchered ox skull from an older animal of unknown sex. Between this skull and the ditch base there was a bone spread 418, with animal bone and a piece of antler, dark soil, charcoal flecks and weathered plain pottery. There were scatters of bone in 416 and 415, including the remains of a sheep's skull, and further weathered plain and decorated sherds in 416. A calibrated age range of 3620–3570 or 3530–3340 BC was obtained from an ox tibia in 418 (BM-2670).

418 was a mixture of cattle, pig and red deer bone. There were three cattle tibias together, and one tibia, astragalus, calcaneum and proximal metatarsal could be from an articulated leg. Other cattle bone included long bones, pelvis fragments and pieces of a skull of a cow from an older animal than the skull mentioned above; other fragments which appear to be from the same cow skull were found in secondary deposits (411 and 414) directly above 418, suggesting that these originate from a single episode of deposition. Perhaps at least some of the bone in the primary levels has moved downwards, having originally been deposited in the secondary levels. It is possible that other ox bones in these deposits come from the same individual as above.

Detail of primary bone deposits

416. A general scatter of bone within the centre of which was a discrete spread of cattle, sheep and pig bone, with a large ox skull fragment from the centre of the ditch. Several flint flakes and sherds, including P608, P610 and P608, were associated with the bone.

The species present are cattle (19 bones, including 5 large-mammal rib fragments), pig (a tooth, radius and pelvis), sheep (two complete male horncores), and sheep/goat (a tooth and an astragalus), along with 20 unidentified bone fragments. The cattle bones include teeth, skull fragments and bones of the forelimb and feet. There are no cattle vertebrae. Two sets of ulnae and proximal radii can be articulated; one of these sets has been gnawed, presumably by a dog, and gnawing has reduced the pig's radius to a shaft cylinder.

Amongst the bones from 416 there is an uneven distribution of fragment size, high mean fragment size, and over 50 percent can be identified. However, the morphology of the scatter suggests the presence of at least two separate (though inter-related) deposits, the first a general scatter and the second a more discrete, mixed group of bone. The ox skull fragment may represent a further separate deposit. A bias towards cranial fragments (both cattle and sheep/goat) is evident, and some of the cattle bone appears to have entered the ditch in an articulated state. The implication is of bone selection and the rapid entry, following butchery, of some of this material into the ditch.

418. A small spread (over 0.7 by 0.5 m) of bone, with charcoal flecks and pottery. Patterning was not immediately discernible, though three cattle tibiae were found together. Pottery sherds were also found. The spread was contained within a dark soil.

All the bones in 418 were identified. The species present are cattle (10 bones), pig (a femur and tibia) and red deer (one antler fragment). The cattle bones include several skull fragments, with limb, ankle and footbones also present. There are no bones from the trunk. Some of the cattle bones could be from the same ankle and may have been deposited whilst still articulated. The antler fragment consists of the base, with its rosette and the brow tine; the beam appears to have been cut off above the brow tine. At least some of the bones have been gnawed. Cutmarks on the anterior face of the ox astragalus and the proximal end of a metatarsal are suggestive of skinning.

There were too few bones in 418 for an analysis of fragment size, but there is an absence of unidentified fragments.

The spread was probably a single deposit. It bears a number of points of similarity with 416, particularly in the bias towards large fragments of cattle skull and the presence of articulated cattle bone. Fragments of bone from 418, 411 and 414 may be from the same ox skull, implying either a degree of disturbance, or (lacking positive evidence for the former) a common source for some of the material present within different contexts in the primary silts.

415. A very small, dispersed scatter of bone, covering c. 1.5 m. There were a few struck flakes, a bevelled flake, two cores and a worked block, and sherds including P611.

The species present are cattle (two ankle bones and a vertebral centrum) and pig (a gnawed radius), along with five unidentified bone fragments.

There were too few bones for an analysis of fragment size.

Little comment can be offered on this small deposit, which might mark the edge of a larger spread or scatter.

Seondary fill

The secondary fill begins with 411, a dark brown humic layer but with an admixture of small to medium chalk fragments, some rounded, some quite fresh, as well as a few cattle bones and some ribs of pigs or sheep/goats. In 411 there was a little weathered pottery with plain and decorated rims. 411 contained two successive bone deposits in the centre of the ditch, 414 below 413.

414 was an interleaved bundle of medium-sized mammal (probably sheep/goat) rib fragments with other sheep/goat bones underneath and beside it. The bones had dark soil around them, but rested directly on chalk. There were also some ox bones, including fragments of the same young cow's skull as that found in 416 (see above), and some sheep/goat bones. There were some sherds, including one thought to be from a vessel also represented in 417 below. Separated only by a small amount of chalk and earth above was another concentrated bone group, 413, with smaller bones and sherds of plain pottery. 413 included several ox vertebrae and ribs, two skull fragments (possibly from the same skull as one of those mentioned for 411, 414, 416 and 418), and leg bones. There were also various sheep/goat bones and ribs that were probably sheep/goat. Calibrated age ranges were obtained from an ox scapula in 414, of 3630–3560 or 3540–3370 BC (OxA-2397), and from an ox calcaneum in 413, of 3620–3570 or 3540–3370 BC (OxA-2398).

Above 411 lay dark brown humic silts with occasional chalk fragments, 408, 406 and 404 (labelled 405 closer to the causeway). Both 406 and 404 contained charcoal flecks and sherds of plain and decorated pottery; sherds of Early Bronze Age pottery also occurred in 404, but could be

intrusive. 404 contained a scatter of cattle bones, including two teeth and a huge proximal phalanx of an aurochs. Within 406 there were two successive scatters of bone, nos 4085–6 and 4110–9, and 4082–4 and 4087–4092. These included many unidentifiable fragments, but also cattle ribs, and a sheep humerus in the latter group.

Analysis of molluscan samples from the secondary fill (chapter 7) shows a mixed fauna, with woodland species in decline but open-country ones not especially abundant.

Detail of secondary bone deposits

414 (fig. 87 and pl. 20). A distinct spread of bone, 1.0 by over 0.7 m in extent, positioned within the centre of the ditch. The spread includes a discrete interleaved bundle of rib fragments, probably derived from two ribs. Sherds (including one thought to be from a vessel represented in

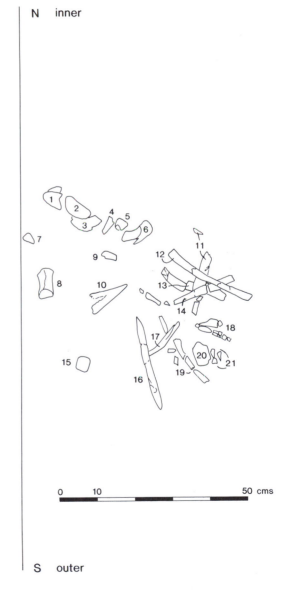

Fig. 87. Bone deposit 414. A distinct spread of bone, including an interleaved bundle of medium-sized mammal ribs, along with other sheep/goat and cattle bone.

417 lower in the ditch) and flint debitage were present with the bone.

The species present are cattle (13 bones) and sheep/goat (six), along with 21 fragments of medium-sized mammal rib, probably derived from no more than two ribs, and 30 unidentified bone fragments. The cattle bone includes several skull fragments (amongst which are two horncore bases), and vertebrae and scapulae. The sheep/goat bone are teeth, two limb bones and a vertebra. The bone appears to have been disarticulated at the time of deposition in the ditch.

There is a slightly uneven distribution of bone fragment size and a moderate mean size, with about 40 percent of bones identified. The ox skull fragment and the rib bundle in the centre of the ditch could suggest deliberate arrangement.

The compact nature of the rib bundle suggests that this component may have been discarded in a block, held together by ligaments or flesh, or may even have been tied or contained in a bag. The emphasis on cattle skull fragments is also notable, and echoes the composition of earlier deposits in the same ditch (i.e. 416 and 418). The possibility of a single source for the cattle skull fragments from this context and 411 and 418 has been noted above (cf. 418).

413 (fig. 88 and pl. 21). A concentrated group of bone, 0.5 by 0.5m in extent, positioned within the centre of the ditch above 414 but separated from it by a small lens of earth and chalk rubble. Plain sherds, flint and pieces of haematite occurred around the edge of the bone concentration, principally on the north side. Unfortunately, the bone has been badly crushed and degraded since deposition.

The species present are cattle (28 bones, including a calcaneum of aurochs and nine large-mammal rib fragments), sheep/goat (three), along with 12 fragments of medium-sized mammal rib (as in 414) and 154 unidentified bone fragments. Almost all the cattle bones are vertebrae and ribs, with a few pieces from the skull, limbs and feet. Almost all the bone appears to have been disarticulated at the time of its incorporation in the ditch, though a bundle of cattle dorsal vertebrae may have been deposited in an articulated state, perhaps held together by ligaments and flesh.

The bone shows a smooth distribution of fragment size, low mean size and a low percentage of identified bones. To some extent the deposit mimics 414 in its format and content. Though badly decayed, it appears to have comprised a central bundle of medium-sized mammal ribs and cattle vertebrae, with other bone and pieces of pottery and flint distributed around the edges.

406. Two small, and probably successive, scatters of bone, with charcoal flecks, sherds and flint debitage and implements, including an axe fragment.

The species present are cattle (14 bones, with many small fragments of large mammal rib, probably derived from only a few ribs), pig (a dorsal vertebra) and sheep/goat (a humerus and two mandible fragments), along with five fragments of medium-sized mammal rib and 46 unidentified bone fragments. Cattle bone includes teeth and bones from the leg and trunk, although vertebrae (apart from a sacral fragment) are notably absent. The bone appears to have been disarticulated at the time of deposition in the ditch. One of the ox phalanges is markedly weathered and another has been etched by rootlets.

406 differs from 413 in a higher mean bone fragment size, due to a small proportion of small fragments. It represents one or two depositional events located within the same general area as the earlier bone groups and scatters. Bone here was highly fragmented through post-depositional compaction and attrition.

404. A small scatter of bone and flint. There were 30 pieces of flint debitage and two retouched pieces, as well as sherds (including P617).

The species present are cattle (a tooth and a pelvic fragment), aurochs (a huge proximal phalanx and three large teeth from the same mandible) and pig (a tooth), along with 17 unidentified bone fragments.

The distribution of bone fragment size is uneven, and the deposit may have undergone a fair degree of post-depositional attrition. The occurrence of aurochs (*Bos primigenius*) should be noted, since it is otherwise rare at Windmill Hill (though present at a lower level in this ditch, in 413).

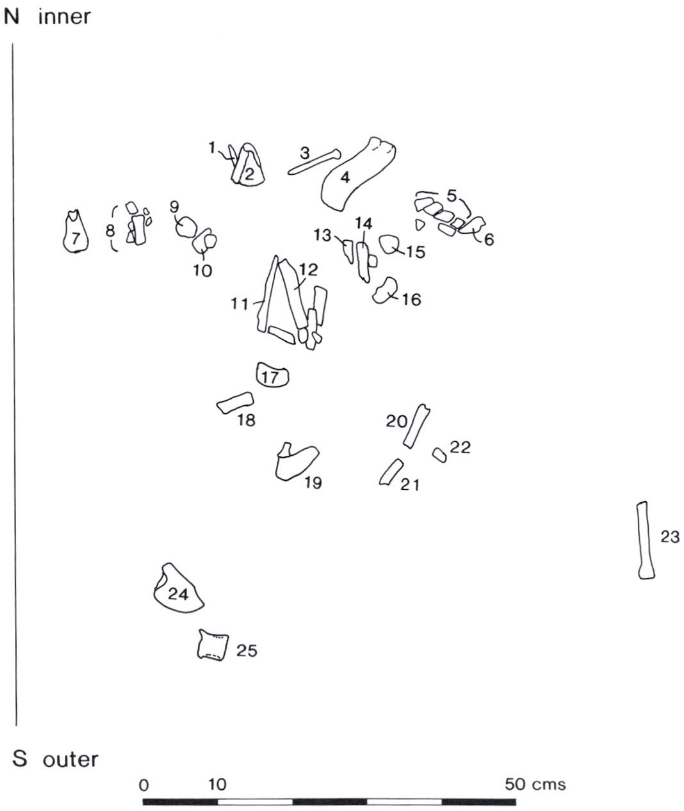

Fig. 88. Bone deposit 413, consisting of cattle bones around the remains of at least four different ox vertebrae, possibly from the same animal, with two fragments of sheep/goat bone and a very large ox calcaneum, probably from an aurochs.

Tertiary fill

Over the top of the ditch was 402, a loose brown soil with dense small rounded chalk fragments. Over this and extending over the edges of the ditch lay 401, a grey soil with very fine chalk fragments, beneath the modern turf and topsoil 400.

Discussion

The primary and secondary filling were formed largely by natural processes. The angular rubble of 416 can be seen as the product of weathering of the sides of the ditch. The quantities of material imply that the surface of the chalk must originally have been higher. It is possible that 417 represents an episode of dumping, but its large chalk blocks may be derived fom the originally overhanging inner side of the ditch. In the secondary fill, 411 may be dumped in part, and 406 and 404 may be an incipient soil. The radiocarbon dates for 414 and 413 suggest the possibility of older material being dumped. In the tertiary fill, a modern ploughsoil overlies an earlier one. Though there was no good dating evidence from 402, it is presumably Romano-British as in other cuttings. There is no clear sign from either the primary or secondary fill, nor from the plough soils above, of the presence of a bank. No formal bank need have accompanied the ditch here, unless it was set so far back from the ditch that its decay was not represented at all in the filling of the ditch.

There were frequent bone deposits, entering the ditch from an early stage and continuing through the primary and into the secondary fill. A number included fragments of cattle skull and bone that may have entered the ditch in an articulated state; such similarities suggest that several of the deposits are interrelated.

Trench E *(fig. 89 and pls 24–28)*

Trench E was laid out adjacent to Middle Ditch XII, close to the segment terminal. The ditch was about 3.2 to 3.3 m wide (on the south section of Middle Ditch XII this was 2.8 m) by 1.6 to 1.7 m deep. The ditch curved a little uphill towards the terminal. The chalk surface on either side of the ditch was regular but sloping, and higher on the inner than on the outer side. The ditch sides were steep and regular. The base was more or less flat but there was a step of uncut chalk near the south section on the inner side of Middle Ditch XII, and the base rose a little towards the north section of Trench E, towards the ditch terminal.

Primary fill

The primary fill consisted of angular chalk rubble with interleaved fine chalk silt lenses. 514 was angular chalk rubble on the inner side of the ditch which merged with 515 on the outer side; both filled the angles of the ditch and met in the centre, where there was a concentration of larger chalk blocks. 514 had one sherd. On the inner side of the ditch there were further runs of chalk 512, 510 and 506 interleaved with grey silt lenses 513, 511, and 509, though 513 did not extend far into the cutting from the Trench B/Middle Ditch XII interface. 510 had rim sherds of two plain vessels. On the inner side, 516 could represent a small episode of dumping. On the outer side 515 was overlain by 508. This was a dark brown humic lens, with sub-angular chalk rubble in parts. This was overlain by 507, a continuation of loose dark brown soil with more rounded chalk fragments. Running down from the outer edge to merge with 509 and 506 was 505, a lens of compact small to medium fairly fresh chalk fragments, which seemed to be somewhat humped or ridged when seen in

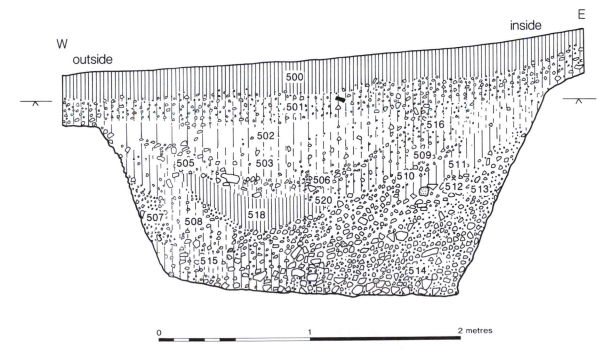

Fig. 89. North section of the middle ditch in Trench E.

plan, even though this feature hardly appears in section. In the north section 518 was a dark scoop or hollow cut into the top of 508/507 and 510/512, extending in plan for about 50 cm into the cutting. Its fill was a very dark brown compact soil with small rounded chalk fragments. Part of 510, 519/520, had slumped over the inner edge of 518, presumably after its filling. Apart from 520, 518 was overlain by the tail of 505/506. Seen in section on the Middle Ditch/Trench E interface and extending into Trench E for about 75 cm was another shallow oval scoop or hollow 504, cut into the top of 505/506. It had a fill of loose dark brown soil.

In the primary fill there were deposits of bone and other material. In 515 just above the base of the ditch 527 consisted of bone fragments, mostly from pigs and sheep/goats, and there were sherds of plain pottery. In 527, calibrated age ranges of 3630–3560 or 3540–3370 BC (OxA-2395) were obtained from a pig humerus, and of 3610–3580 or 3520–3370 BC (OxA-2396) from a pig scapula. In the base of 510, where 512 and 514 also merge, there was a small concentration of bone, 524, in a matrix of dark soil with some flecks of charcoal and a few fragments of burnt chalk, overlain by more burnt chalk and sherds of plain pottery. The bone, nearly all cattle, included a rib and scapula set at right angles to each other and a horncore positioned more or less vertically; the other body parts included skull and rib fragments, vertebrae, and limb and foot bones.

In the top part of 510 there was a larger and more concentrated spread of bone, 523. Sherds of plain pottery were also included. The bone was mostly cattle, with pig and sheep/goat. In the lower part of 508 there was a significant spread of animal bone, 525, together with fresh sherds of plain pottery, the largest assemblage from the

primary fill in Trench E, one or two pieces of burnt chalk and abundant flecks of charcoal. As well as larger bone and sherds there were several small fragments of both. The lowest part of the bone spread rested on 515. 525 contained cattle, pig and sheep/goat bones, which included a horncore positively identified as goat and another as sheep, plus some other sheep bones. A wide range of body parts is represented. A calibrated age range of 3370–3300 or 3240–3100 BC (BM-2671) was obtained from an ox humerus in 525.

518 had little in its fill, except at its base where there were two bones of cattle, small flint flakes, and fresh sherds. 504 contained a small concentration of large animal bones, mainly of cattle and sheep/goat, with one dog and one pig bone, along with sherds of plain pottery and several flint flakes. In the centre of the ditch where 505, 506 and 509 merge, and overlying 518, was another small concentration of bone, 522, extending from the north edge of 504 to the section line beside 518. This contained mainly cattle bones, with 11 of pig and 12 of sheep/goat.

Detail of primary bone deposits

527. A broad but low-density spread of bone, contained within a dark soil (fig. 90). Several sherds of pottery were present in the centre of the scatter; a few flint flakes and a bevelled flake were also recovered.

The species present are cattle (a patella and a cervical vertebra), pig (five), sheep/goat (five, including a definite sheep's humerus), along with six fragments of medium-size mammal rib and 27 unidentified bone fragments. The pig bones are all from the limbs and those of sheep/goat are from limbs and trunk. A pig's patella is very eroded.

There is a low mean bone fragment size (which may be at least partly due to the predominance of pig and sheep/

Fig. 90. View of bone deposit 527 in Trench E.

goat), coupled with high variability, a slightly uneven distribution of fragment size and a moderate proportion of identified bone. The spread is notable for the high proportion of pig and sheep/goat compared with cattle.

524. A small, tightly defined, bone group in a matrix of dark soil and charcoal. An ox horncore was found sticking out vertically from the soil. To the west of this (so on the outer side of the ditch) was a neat bundle of bones and a few sherds; there were three flint flakes.

The species present are cattle (13 bones, including two large-mammal rib fragments), pig (a humerus) and sheep/goat (a phalanx), along with one fragment of medium-size mammal rib and four unidentified bone fragments. A wide range of cattle elements is present, including a tooth and parts of the skull, trunk, foreleg and feet. Cutmarks on the anterior, proximal face of an ox metatarsal and on the nasal bone suggest skinning.

With its high mean fragment size, uneven distribution of size and high proportion of identified fragments, this bone group would appear to represent a single depositional event. The tightly defined nature of the group, along with the unusual vertical positioning of the ox horncore, could suggest deposition within some kind of container (a bag perhaps), dumping within a matrix of soil, or intentional arrangement. Compositionally, it is distinct from 527 in terms of species representation and the lesser degree of bone fragmentation.

523 (fig. 91 and pl. 26). A concentrated linear spread (0.2–0.4m wide) of bone running across the width of the ditch. Pottery sherds and pieces of worked flint were found mixed in with the bone. Scapulae and ribs within the spread were found to lie at an oblique angle to the ditch sides.

The species present are cattle (17 bones, including four large-mammal rib fragments), pig (a tooth, atlas and radius) and sheep/goat (a humerus), along with one fragment of medium-size mammal rib and six unidentified bone fragments. The ox bone assemblage is dominated by elements from the trunk and legs. Cutmarks on the proximal radius of an ox and the pubic symphysis of an ox pelvis indicate dismemberment or defleshing or both.

523 has a very high mean bone fragment size, a very jagged pattern of distribution of fragment size and a low proportion of unidentified fragments. The manner in which the spread ran down the side of the ditch is unusual amongst the bone spreads from the site, and might imply that the material was thrown in from the ditch side. This said, it does not show the 'fanning out' that would characterise dispersal through being casually thrown. It is different in composition and character to the bone spread in 527, and to some extent the group in 524.

525 (figs 92–93 and pl. 27). A dense spread of animal bone, associated with sherds, flint debitage and burnt chalk, located centrally within the ditch. Planned at two levels: the upper comprising a tightly formed bone group around a metre square in extent; the lower being a more dispersed spread running along the centre of the ditch.

The species present are cattle (40 bones, including four large-mammal rib fragments), pig (12) and sheep/goat (11), along with 21 unidentified bone fragments. All species are represented by a wide range of body parts. In the case of cattle, there is a preponderance of vertebrae and pelvic fragments. The sheep/goat bones include three limb bones definitely identified as sheep and some basal fragments of decayed horncore, one of a goat and three probably of sheep. The deposit comprised a mixture of articulated and disarticulated bone. Two small groups of articulated bone were noted: the first at the base of the spread, consisting of elements of an ox wrist; the second comprising a string of cattle vertebrae. Cutmarks on the upper surface of a pig's rib suggest skinning and others on the inner surface of an ox scapula probably dismemberment. The set of lumbar vertebrae of an ox had been split horizontally through the centra.

With its high mean bone fragment size, uneven distribution of fragment size and 70 percent identified fragments, 525 probably represents a single depositional event. In plan the deposit can be seen to consist of one, or possibly two contiguous dumps of large cattle bone, within a general scatter of other bone. Structure exists within the deposit, in that pig and sheep/goat bones are distributed around the periphery of the main group of cattle bone. The presence of articulated groups suggests that the cattle bone at least was entering the ditch soon after butchery. Other components might have been drawn from secondary sources. The structure and scale of the deposit, and its position within the centre of the ditch, would argue for placing rather than casual discard or piecemeal accumulation.

518. A small, dispersed scatter of bone, pottery and flint, both debitage and implements (pl. 25).

The species present are cattle (a large piece of pelvis, a fragment of dorsal vertebra and a large-mammal rib fragment) and pig (a tibia), along with two fragments of medium-size mammal rib and 16 unidentified. Most of the bone is in a fragmentary condition. The ox pelvis has cutmarks on the ilium blade suggestive of dismemberment or defleshing.

The bone in 518 consists of a majority of small fragments, plus a few quite large ones, resulting in high variability. The bone assemblage may, given its position against the section, mark the periphery of a larger scatter.

522 (fig. 94). A small concentration of bone, worked flint and sarsen within the centre of the ditch fills. Planned as a general spread of material, 0.8 by over 1.5 m in extent, which continues into the baulk at the northern end of the trench.

The species present are cattle (44 bones, including 13 fragments of large-mammal rib), pig (11), sheep/goat (12) and dog (a metapodial), along with four fragments of medium-size mammal rib and 76 unidentified bone fragments. All regions of the body of cattle and pigs are represented, with very few loose teeth. Sheep/goat bones

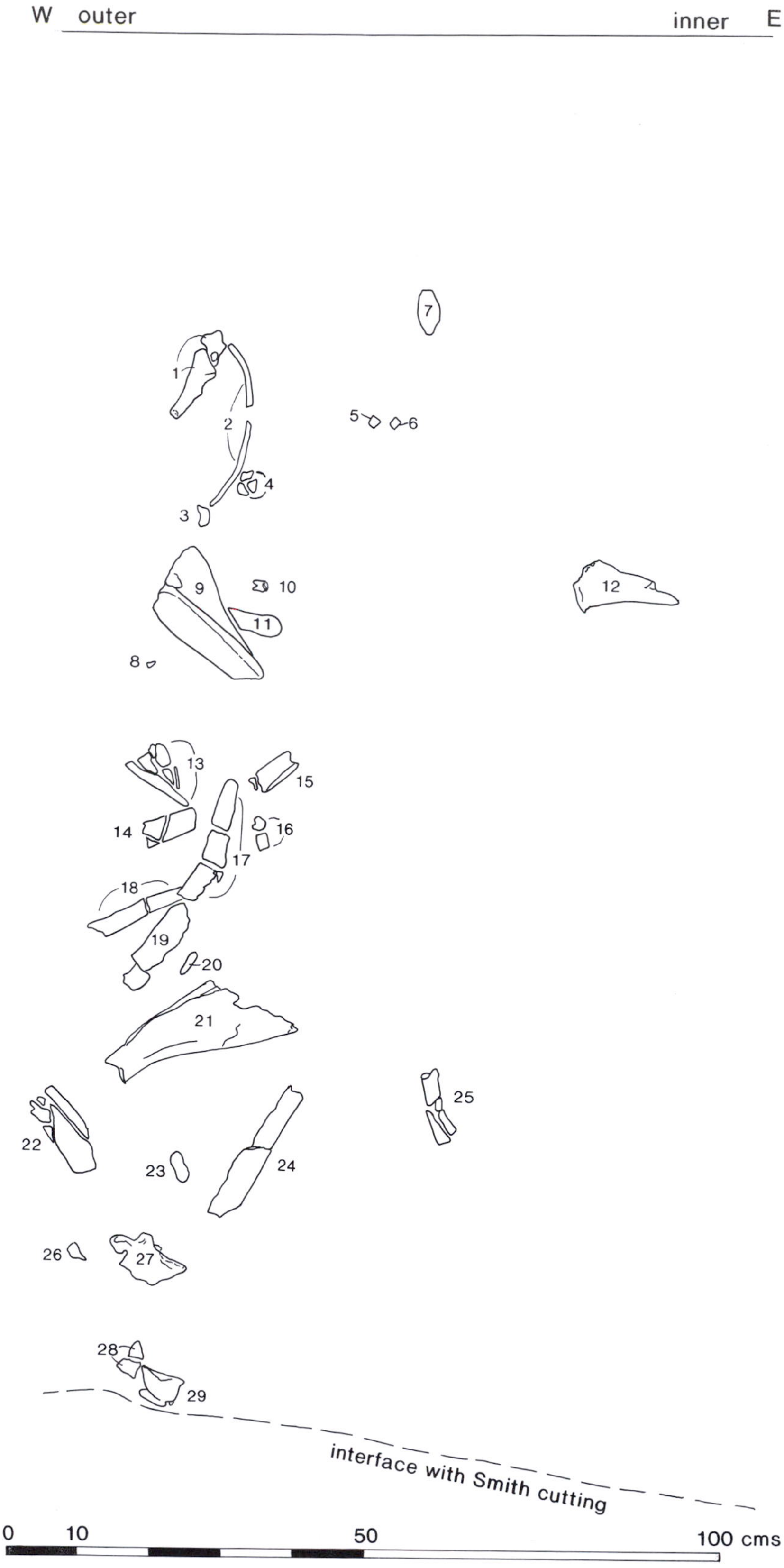

W   outer   inner   E

Fig. 91. Bone deposit 523, consisting of cattle bones, with a high proportion of large fragments of most parts of the body. There were also several pig bones and a nearly complete sheep/goat humerus.

W   outer   inner   E

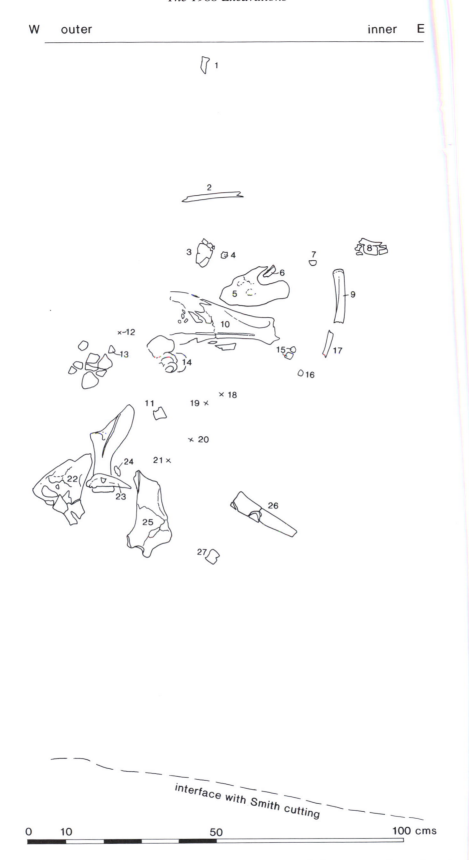

Fig. 92. Bone deposit 525, consisting of quite large fragments of ox bone, with the remains of two sheep horncores and some pig limb bones. In addition there were in 525 some substantial pieces of bone which were not planned, many of which are cattle trunk bones, including lumbar and sacral vertebrae which articulate, with a set of articulated cattle wrist bones, another sheep horncore and several pig bones. The similarities between the bones at the base of 525 and those in the rest of 525, whether planned or unplanned, suggest that the distinction between them may be artificial.

W outer   inner E

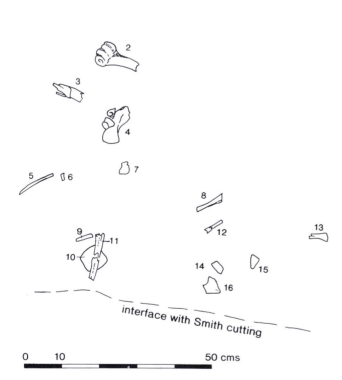

interface with Smith cutting

0   10   50 cms

Fig. 93. Bone deposit 525 at its base, consisting of fragmentary ox bone, with some pig skull fragments and a goat horncore. The ox lunate articulates with the wrist bones in the unmapped part of 525, which suggests that it was part of the same depositional episode (see below).

are from the limbs and feet. The bone appears to have been disarticulated at the time of deposition in the ditch. A few of the bones have been gnawed, including an ox scapula by a rodent. A pig's pelvis had both cutmarks and signs of carnivore gnawing. There were also cutmarks on an ox pelvis and the proximal end of a large-mammal rib fragment.

522 has a fairly high mean bone fragment size, a fairly smooth pattern of fragment size distribution and a moderately high proportion of identified fragments. It was probably a single deposit. Its central position within the rather shallow concavity of the ditch fills at this point argues against the combined effects of casual discard and gravity as mechanisms for its accumulation and position. The material was mixed together without obvious structure, and contains a higher quantity of flint, pottery and sarsen than is usual for this ditch. The material may have been gathered from several sources.

Secondary fill
The secondary fill consisted of two layers of dark humic silt with some rounded chalk fragments. 503 was a loose grey brown soil with scattered chalk fragments. There were flecks of charcoal throughout the layer. 502 was a slightly more compact brown soil with more dense, small chalk fragments. There were few finds in 502 but at the base of 503, resting on 505 in the area between 504 and 518, there was a small spread of bone, sherds and flint. There were some substantial pieces of cattle bone, including some that may have been of aurochs, as well as scattered bones of cattle, pig, and sheep/goat, one or two with small concentrations of darker brown soil around them, and there were sherds of plain Windmill Hill pottery; some body sherds appeared to be from vessels whose sherds occurred lower in the ditch in 525. One Early Bronze Age sherd occurred in 503, and there were Grooved Ware sherds and one Early Bronze Age sherd in 502.

Detail of secondary bone deposits
503. A small spread of bone associated with pottery, flint flakes and a scraper.

The species present are cattle (18 bones, including one possible aurochs radius fragment and three large-mammal rib fragments), pig (a tooth and a vertebra), sheep/goat (a calcaneum, a metatarsal and a tibia), and red deer (an astragalus), along with three fragments of medium-size mammal rib fragments and 22 unidentified bone fragments. Amongst the cattle bone are parts of trunk, limbs (scapulae are well represented) and feet; skull fragments are absent. An ox scapula has cutmarks on the anterior face of the articulation suggesting dismemberment. Another distal ox scapula was very weathered.

There is a high mean bone fragment size and a low-lying, jagged pattern of fragment size distribution, as well as a high proportion of identified fragments. The spread was associated with apparently token selections of flint and pottery. The material may have been drawn from a secondary source.

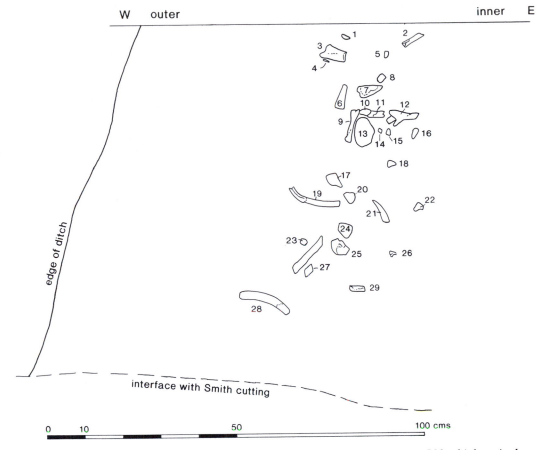

Fig. 94. Bone deposit 522. A spread of bones, mainly of cattle, with a pig's ulna in 510 which articulates with an unplanned radius in the same locus.

Tertiary fill

The top of the primary fill and the edge of the secondary fill on the inner side of the ditch were quite intensively disturbed by animal activity. They were also truncated by 501, a light brown ploughsoil with dense small rounded chalk fragments. This did not extend beyond the edges of the ditch. It contained numerous small bone fragments, flint waste and abraded Late Neolithic, Early Bronze Age and Romano-British sherds.

Discussion

The primary and secondary fills are largely the result of natural processes. The chalk surface must originally have been higher. Making allowance for the slope, as much infill came from the outer side as from the inner. The chalk rubble diminishes in size a little upwards through the fill, and there are silt lenses derived from the falling in of turves or the washing in of topsoil. These features together suggest that the primary fill was not instantaneous, as is also indicated by the deliberate placing of several bone spreads (these probably entering the ditch in short succession). There is an interval between the dates from 527 and 525. But only the scoops 504 and 518, and possibly dumping of at least some of 505 and 516, can be seen as definite interference with the natural accumulation of fill in the ditch. Given that the chalk surface was originally higher,

there is no clear sign in the primary silting of the existence of an inner bank. Neither the secondary fill nor the ploughsoil truncating it show any sign of the existence of an inner bank. Since the ploughsoil is restricted to the area of the ditch, it shows that the surface at the date of its formation was still higher than the modern surface.

THE INNER DITCH

Trench F *(fig. 95 and pls 29–32)*

Trench F was adjacent to Inner Ditch XVII. The inner ditch was here (close to the terminal segment) about 3 m broad by 1.75 m deep. The sides of the ditch were slightly scooped, and just before the terminal began to curve in towards it. The sides of the ditch were fairly regular; the inner side was less steep than the outer. The narrow base was more or less flat. The tops of the ditch sides were little weathered.

Primary fill

The primary fill consisted of angular chalk rubble on both sides of the ditch, 612. This had a greater admixture of fine chalk silt and smaller less angular chalk rubble in its upper parts near the sides, 610 on the inner side and 611

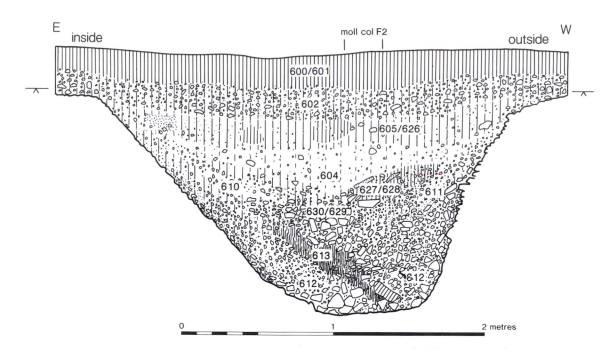

Fig. 95. South section of the inner ditch in Trench F.

on the outer. Large chalk blocks were concentrated in the centre of the ditch towards the top of 612. Interleaved with 612 and derived from the inner side of the ditch was 613, a lens of very dark brown silt. In the south section 613 extended right to the base of the ditch and included four large unworked fragments of sarsen. In the rest of the cutting it ended above the base of the ditch. The primary fill was virtually sterile of finds. A calibrated age range of 3610–3580 or 3520–3360 BC (OxA-2394) was obtained from the only bone in 613, an ox vertebra. There were two sherds of plain pot from 610.

Secondary fill
The secondary fill consisted mostly of dark humic layers. 604 was a grey fine silt with occasional small chalk fragments. Above it was a darker layer, rather varied in composition, some parts being chalkier than others, and also somewhat disturbed by moles (605/626). There was a little scattered bone in 605/626, but the notable feature of the secondary silting was a series of four bone deposits in the lower part of 604. In the base of 604 there was a concentrated bone group 629, with large animal bones and some fresh sherds of plain pottery, in a matrix of dark soil with abundant charcoal flecks. Immediately adjacent to it was 630, another compact group of substantial animal bone and some sherds. This again had some dark soil and charcoal flecks, but was chiefly incorporated in a small heap of loose small rounded chalk fragments. The relationship of 629 and 630 was unclear. 630 had been placed on the surface of 610, and 629 was placed at the base of 604 on top of the primary chalk rubble. 629 may precede 630, or the two may have been deposited essentially at the same time. Directly above 629 came 627/628, with bones, sherds and two broken antler combs in a matrix of dark soil and

charcoal flecks. A calibrated age range of 3040–2920 BC (BM-2672) was obtained from an ox vertebra in 629.

Cattle bones were predominant in both 629 and 630, with a few bones of pig and sheep/goat. 630 also contained part of an immature human femur inserted into the shaft of an ox humerus. Most of the bones in 627/628 were too fragmentary to identify, but cattle, pig, sheep/goat and dog were all represented. There were two coprolites.

Analysis of molluscan samples from the secondary fill (chapter 7) shows a mixed fauna, with woodland species in decline but open-country ones not especially abundant.

Detail of secondary bone deposits
629 (fig. 96 and pl. 29). A loosely structured, but concentrated, group of large bone in a matrix of dark, charcoal-rich soil. It was confined to the centre of the ditch, and extended across the full metre width of the cutting. A localised scatter of sherds was present on the west side, and flint debitage was also present.

The species present are cattle (16 bones), pig (three), sheep/goat (five) and dog (two), along with eight unidentified bone fragments. The cattle bone shows a bias towards forelimb bones and scapulae, with foot, ankle and wrist elements being absent. The pig and sheep/goat assemblages show a similar, if less well marked, pattern of representation. Dog bones comprise a humerus and ulna. The bone appears to have been disarticulated at the time of deposition in the ditch.

629 has a very high mean bone fragment size and a low-lying, jagged pattern of fragment size distribution. 70 percent of the fragments can be identified. Its central position within the ditch suggests it was placed rather than casually dumped from the side. Apparently forming a single deposit, the mixture of large bone and pottery within

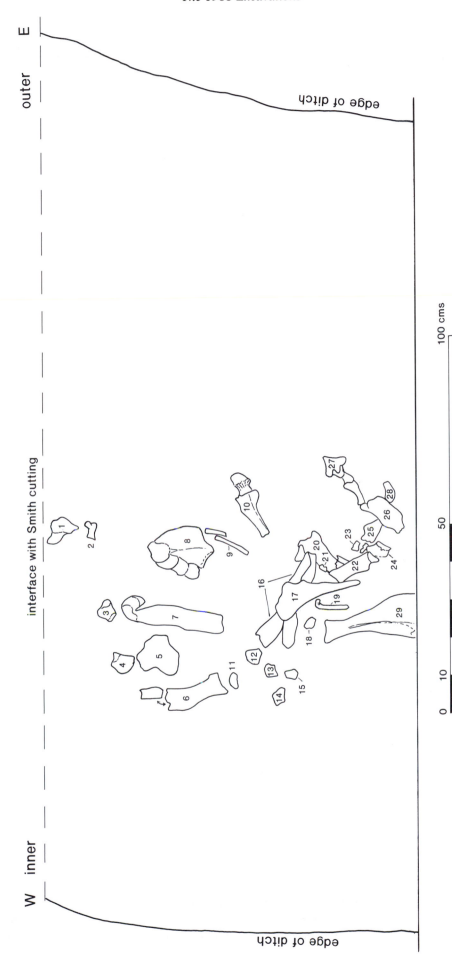

Fig. 96. Bone deposit 629, consisting principally of cattle bones, many of which are piled on top of each other; they include substantial proportions of two distal humeri, two proximal radii and a scapula. There are sheep/goat, pig and dog bones.

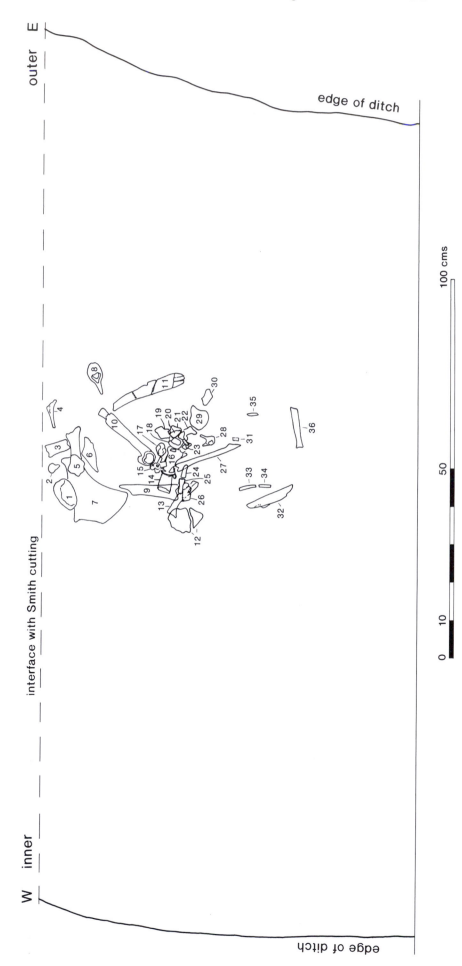

Fig. 97. Bone deposit 630. Deeply embedded in a pile of ox bone fragments, probably all from the same ox skull. This deposit also contained a proximal metatarsal almost in articulation with its ankle bones and a sheep/goat tibia; close to this group are large pieces of a cow's pelvis. A human femur was inserted inside the shaft of an ox humerus.

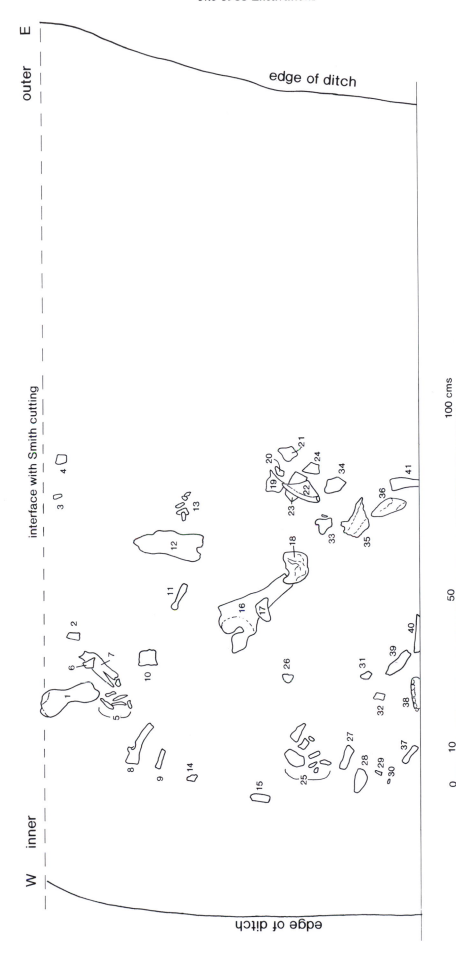

Fig. 98. Bone deposit 627/628. A dense spread of cattle bone, with some sheep/goat and pig bones. The most conspicuous bones are three large pieces of the same ox pelvis with cutmarks.

a dark charcoal-rich soil might accord with the material having been collected from a midden source. The 'token' representation of dog bones is repeated in 630.

630 (fig. 97 and pl. 30). A compact (0.5 by 0.7 m) group of large bones, associated with pottery and worked flint (a flake and retouched pieces), in a dark, charcoal-rich soil. Situated immediately to the east of 629. Located centrally within the ditch. There were two components to the group: the lower comprising a tightly defined collection of cattle vertebrae and skull fragments; the upper, a more general collection of mixed bone.

The species present are cattle (18 bones, including three large-mammal rib fragments), pig (four), sheep/goat (seven), dog (two) and human (one), along with two fragments of medium-sized mammal and 55 unidentified bone fragments. Cattle bone includes parts of the skull, trunk, legs and feet, with a slight bias towards the skull. Pig and sheep/goat bone shows a more partial representation, being restricted to elements from the trunk and legs. The dog bones are radius and ulna, possibly from the same forelimb. Most of the bone appears to have been disarticulated at the time of deposition, though a group of cattle ankle bones can be articulated with the proximal end of a metatarsal.

630 has a moderately high mean bone fragment size, a fairly smooth pattern of fragment size distribution and a fairly low proportion of identified fragments. The tightly defined nature of the group, and its central position within the ditch, suggest it was placed. There is a strong sense of arrangement, seen with the neat bundle of cattle bones in the lower part of the group, and the clearly intentional insertion of a part of the shaft of an immature human femur into the marrow cavity of the shaft of an ox humerus. The group is similar in composition to 629, which it probably post-dates: note, for instance, the matrix of dark, charcoal-rich soil, the presence of much large bone, and the occurrence of dog leg bones in both.

627/628 (fig. 98 and pl. 31). A spread of bone fragments, sherds, worked flint and two bone combs in a matrix of dark, charcoal-flecked soil, situated directly above 629. The worked flint associated with the bone included several flakes and retouched and utilised pieces. Pieces of coprolite were also present. The feature was recorded in the field as two contexts but may better represent one series of depositions.

The species present are cattle (seven bones, including four large-mammal rib fragments), pig (seven), sheep/goat (four) and fox or dog (one), with 11 unidentified bone fragments. Cattle are represented by a radius and pelvic fragments; pig by an atlas and parts of skull and leg; sheep/goat by leg bones, a mandible and a proximal phalanx; and fox or dog by a skull fragment. A few of the bones have been gnawed and there are deep cutmarks on the ox pelvic fragment. There is a very high mean bone fragment size, a low-lying, jagged pattern of fragment size distribution, and over 60 percent of fragments can be identified. 292 small bone fragments were retrieved from sieving and flotation of the soil matrix after excavation and might perhaps indicate the ultimate derivation of the assemblage from an occupation surface.

Tertiary fill

The top of 605/626 was truncated by a brown, very chalky tertiary ploughsoil, 602, with many small fragments of bone and some small sherds of pottery, including Beaker, Early Bronze Age and Romano-British wares. 602 appears again to be restricted to the area of the ditch. Above this was modern turf and topsoil, 600 and 601.

Discussion

Both primary and secondary fills can be seen as the result of natural processes. The rather disturbed 605/626 could be an incipient soil. There is no clear sign of the existence of an inner bank. The original chalk surface is likely to have been higher than the modern one. Plain Windmill Hill pottery was in use throughout the filling of the ditch. The primary fill may have accumulated rapidly, though the radiocarbon dates and the possible incipient soil above the secondary fill suggest slower accumulation subsequently. The interval between the two radiocarbon dates is perhaps surprising. Bone deposition was not a feature of the primary fills, but several deposits of large bone entered the ditch in close succession during the formation of the lower secondary silts. After the deposition of the bone groups and spreads at the base of the secondary silt, there seems to have been little activity.

APPENDIX

KEY TO FIGS 78–79, 82, 84, 85, 87, 88, 91–94 and 96–98

Fig. 78. *Bone deposit 229.*

1	23202 unidentified fragment
2	23201 ox, proximal phalanx, lacking epiphysis
3	23203 unidentified fragment
4	23208 ox, sesamoids
5	23207 ox, proximal phalanx, lacking epiphysis
6	23200 ox, tibia shaft fragment
7	23205 ox, distal phalanx
8	23204 flint
9	23209 pottery
10	23206 ox, navicular
11	23228 sheep/goat, goat?, scapula, distal
12	23227 pottery
13	23210 flint
14	23231 ox, patella
15	23230 ox, lunate
15	23230 unidentified fragment
16	23226 unidentified fragment
17	23225 pottery
18	23211 pottery
19	23212 ox, upper 2nd molar
20	23213 unidentified fragment
21	23214 pottery
22	23217 unidentified fragment
23	23215 unidentified fragment
24	23218 pottery
25	23216 pottery
26	23245 flint
27	23233 pottery
28	23232 flint
29	23236 unidentified fragment
29	23236 sheep/goat, scapula, distal
30	23234 ox, axis fragment
31	23235 ox, proximal phalanx, proximal fragment
32	23220 ox, cervical vertebra, articular fragment
33	23250 pottery
34	23248 flint
35	23219 pottery
36	23370 ox, scapula, spine fragment
37	23244 pig, rib I, proximal end
38	23243 sarsen quern
39	23241 unidentified fragments
40	23242 ox, lumbar vertebra VI
41	23196 ox, radius, distal
42	23239 pig?, dorsal vertebra, centrum fragment
43	23238 ox, sacrum fragment
44	23237 unidentified fragment

Fig. 79. *Bone deposit 227.*

1	23097 unidentified fragment
2	23086 red deer, many fragments probably all from same antler
3	23087 unidentified fragments ?of same rib
4	23095 ox?, cervical vertebra, fragment of articular surface
5	23094 large mammal rib section
6	23073 pig, scapula, distal
7	23085 fragments of ?same unidentified bone

8	23096 unidentified fragment
9	23091 ox, cervical vertebra, fragment of articular surface
10	23090 large mammal rib fragments
11	23084 red deer, antler tine
12	23083 unidentified fragment
13	23088 flint
14	23093 ox?, dorsal vertebra section of dorsal spine
14	23093 ox, lumbar vertebra centrum
15	23092 unidentified fragments
16	23089 large mammal fragments of same rib
17	23098 ox, radius proximal shaft
18	23072 pottery (Ebbsfleet)
19	23082 unidentified fragment
20	23081 medium mammal rib fragments
21	23099 medium mammal rib fragments
22	23100 ox, proximal phalanx complete
23	23080 unidentified fragment
24	23101 ox, scapula, distal fragment
25	23124 unidentified fragment
26	23123 flint
27	23121 unidentified fragment
28	23122 flint
29	23104 ox?, lumbar vertebra centrum fragment
30	23103 dog, metatarsal distal half
31	23102 unidentified fragment
32	23074 unidentified fragment
33	23079 ox, dorsal vertebra damaged
34	23105 unidentified fragment
35	23108 pig, cervical vertebra IV
36	23107 dog, proximal phalanx complete
37	23106 medium mammal rib fragments
37	23106 several unidentified fragments
38	23109 medium mammal rib fragments
39	23110 ox, tibia shaft fragment
40	23111 pig, ulna proximal shaft
41	23120 flint
42	23119 unidentified fragments
43	23118 sheep/goat, scapula spine fragment
43	23118 unidentified fragments
44	23116 large mammal rib section
45	23114 ox, dorsal vertebra
46	23113 dog, metatarsal complete
46	23113 unidentified fragment
46	23113 medium mammal rib fragments
47	23112 ox, radius shaft cylinder
48	23078 dog, proximal phalanx complete
49	23077 unidentified longbone fragment
50	23117 unidentified fragment
51	23115 medium mammal rib fragments
52	23075 ox, upper molars 1–3
53	23076 unidentified longbone fragment

Fig. 82. *Bone deposit 117.*

1	1711 ox, scapula, spine
2	1709 ox, skull, frontlet
3	1717 ox, tibia, distal
4	1710, human, child cranium

5	1719 ox, patella
6	1707 ox, skull, horncore and base
7	1713 flint
8	1712, ox, navicular and cuneiform
9	1708 ox, skull, horncore and base

Fig. 84. Bone deposit 321.

1	10453 ox, lunate
1	10453 large mammal rib fragment
2	10448 pottery
3	10451 ox, 2 sesamoids
3	10451 ox, tibia, proximal fragment, same bone as 4
3	10451 unidentified fragment
3	10451 large mammal rib fragment
4	10452 ox, humerus, distal
4	10452 ox, tibia, nearly complete, same bone as 3
5	10450 ox, humerus, shaft and distal
6	10459 unidentified fragments
7	10458 ox, skull, fragment
7	10458 ox, 3 dorsal vertebrae
7	10458 unidentified fragment
8	10457 ox, astragalus
8	10457 ox, middle phalanx
8	10457 ox, radius, distal epiphysis
8	10457 unidentified fragment
9	10449 flint
10	10456 ox, pelvis, ischium fragment
10	10456 ox, proximal sesamoid
10	10456 large mammal rib fragment
11	10460 ox, femur, distal lateral condyle
11	10460 ox, femur, distal lateral condyle
12	10454 ox, metatarsal, distal epiphyses
13	10461 ox, sacral vertebra I
13	10461 sheep/goat, astragalus
14	10462 ox, middle phalanx, epiphysis
14	10462 ox, dorsal vertebra, less dorsal spine
14	10462 ox, dorsal vertebra, dorsal spine fragment
14	10462 large mammal rib fragment
14	10462 large mammal rib fragment
15	10463 ox, dorsal vertebrae, fragments
16	10469 ox, femur, fragment of distal epiphysis
17	10465 ox, dorsal vertebrae, fragments
17	10465 unidentified fragment
17	10465 large mammal rib fragment
18	10455 ox, metatarsal, less epiphysis
19	10464 ox, navicular
19	10464 ox, middle phalanx, less epiphysis
19	10464 ox, sternebrae
19	10464 ox, cervical vertebrae fragments
20	10466 ox, patella
20	10466 ox, distal phalanx
20	10466 ox, tibia, distal epiphysis
20	10466 ox, tibia, fragment of proximal epiphysis
20	10466 ox, cervical vertebra IV

Fig. 85. Bone deposit 317.

1	3895 large mammal rib section
2	3896 large mammal rib section
3	3978 flint
4	3977 flint
5	3976 unidentified fragment
5	3976 unidentified fragment

6	3975 flint
7	3900 ox, dorsal vertebra, spine fragment
8	3974 unidentified fragment
9	3899 unidentified fragment
10	3903 bone, not recovered from section
11	3953 ox, femur, shaft section
12	3898 unidentified fragment
13	3958 unidentified fragment
14	3904 ox, scapula, blade fragment
15	3897 unidentified fragment
16	3920 unidentified tooth
17	3952 ox, mandible, molar row, same jaw as 29, 40 and 43
18	3872 flint
19	3901 unidentified fragment
20	3973 ox, atlas, anterior fragment, same bone as 21
21	3902 ox, atlas, posterior fragment, same bone as 20
22	3954 ox, radius, distal fragment
22	3954 ox, dorsal vertebra X, fragment
22	3954 ox, dorsal vertebra XII, fragment
23	3925 flint
24	3959 dog, atlas, fragment
25	3905 unidentified fragments
26	3965 flint
27	3960 unidentified fragment
28	3962 unidentified fragment
29	3918 ox, lower lst molar, same jaw as 40 and 43
29	3918 ox, tooth fragment
30	3919 flint
31	3921 flint
32	3964 flint
33	3966 flint
34	3967 flint
35	3929 ox, radius, proximal
36	3926 ox, radius, distal epiphysis
37	3927 ox, navicular
38	3930 ox, dorsal vertebra X, fragment
39	3931 ox, upper premolar
40	3952 ox, mandible, molar row, same jaw as 17, 29 and 43
41	3938 ox, dorsal vertebra XI, fragment
42	3932 ox, lower 4th premolar
43	3939 ox, mandible, coronoid and condyle, same jaw as 17, 29 and 40
44	3957 unidentified fragments
45	3951 ox, radius, proximal shaft
46	3907 ox, metatarsal, proximal half
47	3906 pottery
48	3913 dog, axis
48	3913 dog, cervical vertebra III
49	3961 unidentified fragments
50	3963 ox, cervical vertebra V fragment
51	3922 ox, astragalus
52	3923 pig, lower incisor
53	3928 ox, metatarsal, proximal half
54	3971 ox, dorsal vertebra, fragment of articular surface
55	3934 flint
56	3933 unidentified fragment
57	3935 flint
58	3908 pottery
59	3956 unidentified fragment
60	3955 flint
61	3950 ox, scapula, distal
62	3909 ox, incisor

63   3910 ox, metacarpal, shaft
64   3915 ox, aurochs?, scapula, distal
65   3911 ox, cervical vertebra V fragment
66   3912 ox, lumbar vertebra II, centrum
67   3917 ox, skull, jugal fragment
68   3916 unidentified longbone fragment
69   3914 snail shell
70   3968 ox, proximal phalanx, proximal
71   3970 large mammal rib fragments
72   3924 ox, lumbar vertebra I
73   3969 unidentified fragment
74   3937 flint
75   3936 large mammal rib section

Fig. 87. Bone deposit 414.
1   4224 ox, mandible, fragment
2   4226 pottery
3   4227 ox, scapula, blade
4   4228 sheep/goat, tibia, distal
5   4229 sheep/goat, cervical vertebra IV
6   4230 ox, skull, orbital rim
7   4223 unidentified fragment
8   4225 medium mammal fragment
9   4231 pottery
10 4232 ox, scapula, spine
11 4244 medium mammal rib
12 4242 medium mammal rib
13 4243 medium mammal rib
14 4245 medium mammal rib
15 4233 ox, cervial vertebra IV, centrum
16 4234 medium mammal rib
17 4235 medium mammal rib
18 4246 ox, dorsal vertebra V, fragment
19 4236 medium mammal rib
20 4238 flint
21 239 pottery

Fig. 88. Bone deposit 413.
1   4176 fragments of same unidentified bone
2   4177 sheep/goat, pelvis, acetabulum
3   4178 sheep/goat, ulna, proximal shaft
4   4179 ox, aurochs? Calcaneum
5   4180 pottery
6   4181 unidentified fragment
7   4173 ox, patella
8   4174 ox, skull, 2 orbital rim fragments
8   4174 unidentified fragments
9   4175 ox, cervical vertebra fragments
10 4193 fragments of same unidentified bone
11 4194 ox, dorsal vertebra, base of spine
12 4188 ox, dorsal vertebra, fragments
13 4192 unidentified fragment
14 4190 unidentified fragments
14 4190 large mammal rib fragment
14 4190 medium mammal rib fragments
15 4186 unidentified fragment
16 4189 large mammal rib fragment
16 4189 large mammal rib fragment
17 4187 ox, axis, odontoid
18 4185 medium mammal rib fragment
19 4184 unidentified fragment
20 4182 medium mammal rib fragment

21 4183 unidentified fragments
21 4183 medium mammal rib fragment
22 4191 flint
23 4198 ox, metatarsal, proximal
24 4172 ox, radius, distal
25 4171 ox, lumbar vertebra, centrum fragment

Fig. 91. Bone deposit 523.
1   12095 ox, dorsal vertebra, arch fragment
1   12095 ox, ulna, proximal fragment
2   12098 medium mammal rib, sections
3   12101 flint
4   12102 ox, scapula, distal fragment
5   12099 pottery
6   12075 flint
7   12097 unidentified fragment
8   12103 ox?, deciduous incisor
9   12094 ox, scapula, blade fragment
10 12087 pig, upper 2nd molar
11 12100 ox, radius, distal
12 12090 ox, radius, proximal
13 12092 ox, pelvis, ilium fragment
14 12091 large mammal rib, section
15 12093 unidentified fragments
16 12107 pig, atlas
17 and 19 12077 large mammal rib, section
18 12079 unidentified fragment
20 12084 flint
21 12078 ox, scapula, distal half
22 12083 large mammal rib, section
23 12082 ox, navicular, fragment
24 12080 large mammal rib, section
25 12096 pig, radius, shaft
26 12086 unidentified fragment
27 12081 ox, lumbar vertebra, less spine
27 12081 ox, pelvis, pubic fragment
28 12104 unidentified fragment
29 12085 ox, tibia, shaft fragment
29 12085 unidentified fragments

Fig. 92. Bone deposit 525.
1   12249 ox, lumbar vertebra, spine
2   12248 sheep/goat, tibia, shaft
3   12210 pottery
4   12230 pig, metapodial, epiphysis fragment
5   12229 ox, pelvis, acetabulum
6   12231 unidentified fragment
7   12246 unidentified fragments
8   12240 sheep, horncore, base
9   12237 pig, tibia, distal shaft
10 12216 ox, scapula
11 12244 unidentified fragment
12 12219 unidentified fragment
13 12218 unidentified fragment
14 12214 ox, cervical vertebra VI
15 12238 pottery
16 12239 unidentified fragment
17 12236 pig, humerus
18 12213 pottery
19 12217 unidentified fragment
20 12228 pottery
21 12228 pottery

22	12222 ox, mandible fragment, with M3 and M2
23	12225 ox, ulna, less proximal end
24	12247 ox, lower molar
25	12221 ox, pelvis, ischium
26	12235 large mammal rib fragment
27	12245 sheep, horncore, basal fragments
27	12245 ox?, fragment of ?pelvis

Fig. 93. Bone deposit 525 at its base.

1	12283 ox, scapula, damaged
2	12278 ox, humerus, distal half
3	12290 pig, skull, cheektooth row
4	12291 ox, pelvis, ilium
5	12300 large mammal rib fragments
6	12302 unidentified fragment
7	12301 ox, lunate
8	12294 pig, dorsal vertebra
9	12305 pig, skull, premaxilla with incisors
10	12304 pottery
11	12299 large mammal rib fragments
12	12295 sheep, tibia, distal half
13	12303 pig, mandible, anterior
14	12298 goat, horncore base
15	(no number) flint
16	12297 ox, lumbar vertebra

Fig. 94. Bone deposit 522.

1	5939 flint
2	5928 large mammal rib, proximal fragment
3	5926 ox, ulna, articulation
4	5926 unidentified fragment
5	5935 pottery
6	5923 pig, radius, shaft cylinder
7	5974 ox, humerus, distal
8	5936 flint
9	5906 ox, tibia, proximal epiphysis
10	5908 pottery
11	5924 unidentified fragment
12	5943 large mammal rib, section
13	5929 sarsen
14	5968 flint
15	5937 unidentified fragment
16	5927 unidentified fragment
17	5904 ox, radius, distal
18	5967 flint
19	5965 large mammal rib, proximal fragment
20	5938 flint
21	5948 pig, ulna, less distal end
22	5949 ox, lumbar vertebra, centrum fragment
23	5966 pottery
24	5919 sarsen
25	5920 ox, tibia
26	5957 pig, metapodial, less epiphysis
27	5934 sheep/goat, scapula, blade fragment
28	5922 large mammal rib, section

Fig. 96. Bone deposit 629.

1	6384 ox, lumbar vertebra, damaged
2	6385 sheep/goat, lumbar vertebra
3	6370 ox, pelvis, acetabulum
4	6369 ox, tibia, proximal
5	6368 ox, tibia, proximal

6	6383 ox, scapula, distal
6	6383 ox, scapula, fragment
7	6389 ox, humerus, distal
8	6371 ox, humerus, distal
8	6371 unidentified fragment
9	6372 dog?, shaft fragment of ?ulna
10	6373 ox, dorsal vertebra, centrum
10	6373 ox, dorsal vertebra, spine
11	6367 pottery
12	6366 pottery
13	6365 pottery
14	6364 pottery
15	6363 pottery
16	6380 ox, radio-ulna, proximal
17	6379 ox, ulna, proximal half
18	6362 pottery
19	6361 dog, humerus, distal half
20	6387 ox, dorsal vertebra, arch and spine
21	6388 pottery
22	6386 unidentified fragment
23	6382 unidentified fragment
24	6328 sarsen
25	6381 pig, scapula, distal fragments
25	6381 unidentified fragment
26	6375 ox, pelvis, ischium fragment
27	6374 ox, radius, proximal
27	6374 ox, ulna
28	6376 unidentified fragment
29	6360 ox, scapula, distal half
29	6360 unidentified fragment

Fig. 97. Bone deposit 630.

1	6411 flint
2	6413 flint
3	6412 large mammal rib section
4	6414 pig, cervical vertebra VII, spine
5	6417 flint
6	6418 ox, pelvis, ischium fragment
7	6416 ox, pelvis, acetabulum and ilium
8	6415 ox, dorsal vertebra, less spine
9	6419 ox, metatarsal, proximal
10	6422 ox, humerus, distal, with human femur
11	6423 large mammal rib section
12	6421 pottery
13	6439 goat, scapula, distal
14	6442 ox, lumbar vertebra, centrum
15	6443 pig, dorsal vertebra, less spine
16	6445 ox, lumbar vertebra, less spine
17	6444 ox, skull, temporal fragments
18	6446 ox, skull, petrous fragment
18	6446 unidentified fragments
19	6424 ox, skull, fragment
20	6425 ox, skull, fragment
20	6425 ox, skull, temporal fragments
20	6425 unidentified fragment
21	6421 pottery
22	6448 ox, skull, basioccipital
23	6426 ox, skull, petrous fragment
24	6441 unidentified fragment
25	6440 unidentified fragment
26	6420 ox, navicular
26	6420 ox, posterior cuneiform

27   6428 sheep/goat, tibia, less proximal end
28   6449 ox, skull, condyle
28   6449 ox, skull, horncore base
29   6435 flint
30   6427 unidentified fragment
31   6436 flint
32   6431 ox, femur, shaft fragment
33   6438 dog, radius, shaft cylinder
34   6437 sheep/goat, humerus, proximal shaft
35   6429 medium mammal rib section
36   6430 sheep/goat, radius, shaft cylinder

Fig. 98. Bone deposit 627/628.
1   6340 ox, pelvis, ischium fragment
2   6311 unidentified fragment
3   6312 sheep/goat, proximal phalanx, distal
4   6314 pottery
5   6309 large mammal rib fragments
6   6310 pig, skull, zygomatic process
7   6341 pig, scapula, distal half
8   6308 pig, ulna, less distal
9   6339 sheep/goat, femur, shaft
10   6315 sarsen
11   6342 ox, pelvis, ilium blade fragment
12   6343 ox, pelvis, ischium fragment
13   6313 unidentified fragment
14   6307 dog/fox, skull, alveolar fragment

15   6338 large mammal rib section
16   6344 ox, pelvis, acetabulum
17   6316 unidentified fragment
18   6317 ox, radius, distal epiphysis
19   6352 pottery
20   6353 sarsen
21   5351 pottery
22   6318 unidentified fragment
23   6354 pottery
24   6350 pottery
25   6301 large mammal rib fragments
26   6302 pig, atlas, fragment
27   6303 unidentified fragment
28   6304 unidentified fragment
29   6305 unidentified fragment
30   6306 unidentified fragment
31   6337 unidentified fragment
32   6336 unidentified fragment
33   6345 pig, atlas, fragment
34   6349 pottery
35   6346 pig, skull, toothrow
36   6347 unidentified fragment
37   6335 sheep/goat, tibia, shaft
38   6320 bone, not recovered from section
39   6334 large mammal rib fragments
40   6319 bone, not recovered from section
41   6348 sheep/goat, mandible, diastema and part toothrow

5

Radiocarbon Dating

Janet Ambers and Rupert Housley

Introduction

Seventeen radiocarbon determinations were made on faunal material from the 1988 season. Five were produced at the Department of Scientific Research of the British Museum, using radiometric decay counting, while the remaining twelve were measured at the Oxford University Radiocarbon Accelerator Unit, using accelerator mass spectrometry (AMS). Stratigraphic and sample details are given in table 52 and fig. 99 (and see chapter 4), together with those for one previous measurement, BM-73 (discussed more fully below).

Physical and chemical pretreatment

To produce a reliable age estimate, all radiocarbon samples require thorough pretreatment to remove intrusive carbon. The techniques employed may have a bearing on the results obtained and an appropriate chemical treatment has to be selected, taking account of both the nature of the sample material itself, and of the site conditions under which that sample has been preserved. In the case of the Windmill Hill samples, the pretreatment techniques detailed below were used.

British Museum

Only samples of reasonably well preserved bone were selected for analysis. These were treated with dilute acid to extract 'collagen' (here defined as the acid insoluble fraction of bone rather than the true biochemical definition). In all cases the extracted material formed a pseudomorph of the original, indicating good chemical survival, and an implicit absence of intrusive materials in the collagen structure (Long *et al.* 1989). Only this extracted collagen was used for dating.

Oxford

Chemical pretreatment consisted of the extraction of the protein 'collagen' from the bones followed by purification by means of gelatinisation and ion exchange using the techniques of Law and Hedges (1989; Hedges *et al.* 1989). Only ion-exchanged gelatin was dated.

Sample preparation and isotopic measurement

British Museum

After pretreatment the cleaned samples were chemically converted to benzene and analysed by conventional liquid scintillation counting using the cocktail and configuration described in Ambers *et al.* 1989. The $\delta^{13}C$ value was obtained by conventional mass spectrometric measurement of a small subsample of CO_2. Samples of dendrochronologically dated wood, obtained with the kind assistance of Professors Pilcher and Baillie of the Queen's University, Belfast, were counted simultaneously with the samples, and in all cases gave results in agreement with the published high-precision radiocarbon results produced for wood of the same age, used to construct the calibration curves used here (Stuiver and Pearson 1986). Errors quoted are the counting error for the sample combined with an estimate of the errors contributed by the modern and background samples. This estimate includes both counting and non-counting errors, the latter being computed from differences in the overall count-rates observed among the individual backgrounds and moderns.

Oxford

After chemical pretreatment, the dried ion-exchanged gelatin was combusted to carbon dioxide. This was done by first wrapping the dried product in tin-foil before flash combustion in a stream of pure oxygen inside a commercially available CHN analyser (Hedges *et al.* 1992). The $\delta^{13}C$ values of the bone gelatin were measured by removing a small aliquot of gas and introducing it into a stable isotope mass spectrometer linked to the CHN analyser. The remaining carbon dioxide was collected in ampoules ready for injection into the gas-source in the

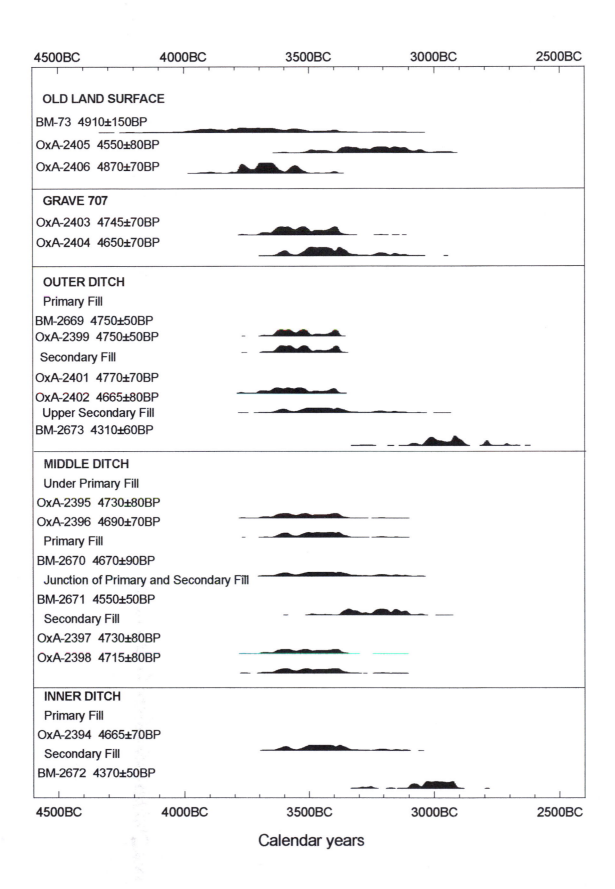

Fig. 99. Calibrated calendar age ranges for the Windmill Hill radiocarbon results, shown as full probability distributions.

accelerator. On average between 1 and 2 mg of carbon was needed. The radiocarbon ages were measured by means of the $^{14}C/^{13}C$ ratio (rather than the more commonly used $^{14}C/^{12}C$ ratio) by comparison with the modern standard. The measured ratios are based on weighted averages from several targets (in the case of standards) and single runs (for the archaeological samples). A correction has been made for the known addition of about 0.5% modern ^{14}C contamination during the sample preparation process. For a full discussion of operational details, see Bronk and Hedges, 1989; 1990; Hedges *et al.* 1989; 1990. The uncertainties, quoted as one standard deviation, are estimates of the total error in the system including the sample chemistry. This includes the statistical precision from the number of ^{14}C nuclei detected, the reproducibility of the mass-spectrometric measurements between different targets and the uncertainty in the estimate of the contamination background. This background level is taken to be $0.5 \pm 0.3\%$ of the oxalic standard and is obtained from measurement of ^{14}C free material.

Both laboratories used the NBS Oxalic II standard (Stuiver 1983) and both quote results in uncalibrated radiocarbon years BP, in the form recommended by Stuiver and Polach 1977, corrected for isotopic fractionation by measured $\delta^{13}C$.

Radiocarbon results must always be calibrated before interpretation, to correct for natural variations in ^{14}C production (for a fuller explanation of this effect see Bowman 1990). Calibrated age ranges for the Windmill Hill data set are given in table 52, and depicted graphically in fig. 99. These were generated using OxCal v2.18 (Bronk Ramsey 1995), and the calibration curve of Pearson *et al.* 1986.

Validity of measurement and quality assurance

There are several important criteria to be considered when assessing the quality of a suite of radiocarbon ages. The measurement accuracy and precision ultimately depend on strict laboratory procedures. The methods used in this case are described above, and can be shown to fulfil this requirement. As part of measurement procedures, both BM and OxA laboratories maintain strict quality assurance procedures, and the results of a series of interlaboratory comparisons, notably the IAEA and TIRI exercises (Rozanski *et al.* 1992; Gulliksen and Scott 1995) indicate no offsets either between the two laboratories or from the median values determined by these exercises. However, the archaeological value of an otherwise accurate result also depends on the strength of the relationship between the age of the sample and the age of the context it is being used to date. The result of a radiocarbon analysis can only relate to the time at which the sample measured stopped exchanging carbon with the atmosphere, and not directly to any other event. In this case, all of the samples analysed were of bone, removing the possibility of 'old' dates occurring due to the use of long-lived materials (such as

the heartwood of long-lived trees); with bone the event being dated is the death of the particular animal involved. However, as in all radiocarbon interpretation, it is still necessary to take into account both stratigraphic consistency and the question of residuality.

Results and discussion

The new dates offer better chronological precision and far greater reliability than the two previous radiocarbon determinations (BM-73: 4910 ± 150 BP from the old land surface; and BM-74: 4530 ± 150 BP, which must be completely disregarded, as it is on a bulked sample of material from several different ditch circuits (Barker and Mackey 1961); it is therefore not included in any of the figures. In general, both the radiometric and the AMS determinations form a very coherent group. There is good agreement both within each laboratory series, and between the two series. This is evidenced by results for samples taken from similar contexts. For example, within the Oxford series, OxA-2403 and OxA-2404, both from grave 707, but taken from different burials (of human and pig, respectively) give results which are statistically indistinguishable, as do OxA-2397 and OxA-2398, for two separate bones from the secondary fill of the middle ditch. Coherence of the Oxford with the British Museum series is indicated by complementary determinations from the primary and lowest secondary filling of the outer ditch (BM-2669 from Trench B should be, and is, coeval with OxA-2401 and OxA-2402 from Trench C). In addition, on inspection of the calibrated age plots, with the exception of the secondary fill of the middle ditch in Trench D, where residuality may have affected OxA-2397 and OxA-2398 (see below for discussion), disturbance, whether through intrusion of younger bones or residuality of older material, does not seem to have been a major problem. For the outer and inner ditches the results for the fills follow the expected pattern, with samples from secondary and tertiary fills being clearly later than those from the primary fills, at the 68 percent confidence level. These figures indicate a period in the order of one or two centuries between the primary silting, and the final fill of these ditches. For the middle ditch, the picture is less clear. Looking at the calibrated results for these figures, there is no obvious distinction between the results for the primary and secondary fills, although BM-2670, from the junction of the two, may give some indication of appreciable elapsed time. The fact that the secondary fill samples give mean results marginally greater than the primary sample may suggest that the secondary material could have been re-used or dumped, or alternatively that the fill process was rapid. In radiocarbon terms all that can be said with certainty is that there is no significant age difference between BM-2670, OxA-2397 and OxA-2398.

If we now look at the sequence of development of the site on the basis of the radiocarbon determinations, there are indications of at least three, and perhaps four, broad

Table 52: Radiocarbon dates.

Lab Ref	Context	Material	Radiocarbon result (BP)	Possible calibrated age ranges (calendar years BC)	
				68% probability	95% probability
BM-73	Old land surface, under bank	charcoal	4910 ± 150	3775 to 3755 or 3705 to 3695	3780 to 3740 or 3710 to 3690 or 3660 to 3640
OxA-2405	Old land surface, under outer bank, Trench BB	*Bos* sp	4550 ± 80	3380 to 3100	3550 to 2900
OxA-2406	Old land surface, under outer bank, Trench BB	*Bos* sp	4870 ± 70	3780 to 3740 or 3710 to 3620 or 3570 to 3530	3900 to 3350
OxA-2403	Grave (707) cut into old land surface, Trench BB	human	4745 ± 70	3640 to 3490 or 3420 to 3380	3690 to 3370
OxA-2404	Grave (707) cut into old land surface, Trench BB	*Sus* sp	4650 ± 70	3610 to 3580 or 3520 to 3340	3650 to 3100
BM-2669	Outer ditch, primary fill, Trench B	*Bos* sp	4740 ± 50	3630 to 3500 or 3420 to 3380	3640 to 3370
OxA-2401	Outer ditch, secondary fill, Trench C	*Bos* sp	4770 ± 70	3650 to 3500 or 3420 to 3380	3700 to 3370
OxA-2402	Outer ditch, secondary fill, Trench C	*Bos* sp	4665 ± 80	3610 to 3580 or 3520 to 3350	3650 to 3100
OxA-2399	Outer ditch, primary fill, Trench A	human child's skull	4750 ± 50	3640 to 3500 or 3410 to 3380	3650 to 3370
BM-2673	Outer ditch, upper secondary fill, Trench C	*Bos* sp	4310 ± 60	3040 to 2960 or 2940 to 2880 or 2800 to 2780	3100 to 2700
OxA-2395	Middle ditch, under primary fill, Trench E	*Sus* sp	4730 ± 80	3630 to 3560 or 3540 to 3370	3700 to 3350
OxA-2396	Middle ditch, under primary fill, Trench E	*Sus* sp	4690 ± 70	3610 to 3580 or 3520 to 3370	3650 to 3330 or 3220 to 3190
BM-2670	Middle ditch, primary fill, Trench D	*Bos* sp	4670 ± 90	3620 to 3570 or 3530 to 3340	3700 to 3100
BM-2671	Middle ditch, junction of primary & secondary fills, Trench E	*Bos* sp	4550 ± 50	3370 to 3300 or 3240 to 3100	3500 to 3470 or 3380 to 3090 or 3070 to 3040
OxA-2397	Middle ditch, secondary fill, Trench D	*Bos* sp	4730 ± 80	3630 to 3560 or 3540 to 3370	3700 to 3350
OxA-2398	Middle ditch, secondary fill, Trench D	*Bos* sp	4715 ± 80	3620 to 3570 or 3540 to 3370	3700 to 3340
OxA-2394	Inner ditch, primary fill, Trench F	*Bos* sp	4665 ± 70	3610 to 3580 or 3520 to 3360	3640 to 3320 or 3240 to 3180 or 3160 to 3130
BM-2672	Inner ditch, secondary fill, Trench F	*Bos* sp	4370 ± 50	3040 to 2920	3300 to 3240 or 3110 to 2900

chronological phases (all such possibilities are discussed further in chapter 17, where a slightly different reading is mooted). The first is represented by two of the three dates from the old land surface (OxA-2406 and BM-73 – one of the two original dates). These would suggest that there was human activity on Windmill Hill prior to the cutting of the ditch circuits. This phase of activity occurred sometime in the first half of the fourth millennium BC.

The second phase is represented by the majority of the results from the site (OxA-2394, from the primary fill of the inner circuit; OxA-2395 to -2398 and BM-2670, from the primary and dumped secondary fills of the middle ditch; and OxA-2399, OxA-2401, OxA-2402 and BM-2669, from the primary and lowest secondary fill of the outer ditch). Taking place in the middle of the fourth millennium BC, this second phase of human activity saw the construction of the enclosure. At approximately the same time as the ditch circuits were dug, the burial cut into the old land surface (represented by OxA-2403 and -2404) was interred. The fact that all the samples from the primary fill of the three ditches are, in radiocarbon terms, contemporaneous, would suggest the enclosure was laid out as one, or at least that the three ditch layout developed very quickly.

The third and fourth phases are more nebulous. Dating to the latter half of the fourth millennium BC, samples from the third phase include *Bos* bones from the old land surface under the outer bank (OxA-2405) and from the junction of the primary and secondary fill of the middle ditch (BM-2671). Whilst the position of the latter sample supports the post-construction dating, the determination on the land surface *Bos* could be explained by assuming that the sample came to be under the outer bank through later burial; this, however, is not in accord with the observed stratigraphy and composition of the outer bank in Trench BB. A different kind of explanation is offered in chapter 17.

The fourth phase differs little from the third since it too is represented by the continued burial of *Bos* bones, in this case dated by BM-2672 and BM-2673, in secondary contexts. This phase can be placed at the end of the fourth millennium or the beginning of the third millennium BC. The stratigraphic position of BM-2673 in upper secondary fill would support the late dating, but that of BM-2672 in lower secondary fill hardly, and whether these two figures are enough to justify the differentiation of a fourth phase is debatable. Although later than OxA-2405 and BM-2671, it may be better to see the third and fourth radiocarbon phases as simply one period, when continuing human use of the monument led to the incorporation of faunal remains in the upper fills of the ditch circuits.

6

Soils

Richard Macphail

Introduction

The soil investigation at Windmill Hill has been carried out in the context of numerous Neolithic buried soil studies on English Chalklands. Macphail (1987) listed 15 Neolithic sites where buried soils had been identified (e.g. Cornwall 1966; Evans 1972; Ashbee *et al.* 1979). In these, environmental studies had focused upon landsnail analysis as the major discipline for the reconstruction of the Neolithic landscape, although rare instances of buried decalcified soils had permitted soil pollen studies (Dimbleby and Evans 1974). Macphail (1987) also listed another 13 Bronze Age and Iron Age sites where buried soils had been identified. The most commonly occurring type of buried soils are rendzinas (B. Avery 1990), with several instances of brown soils, namely brown earths. Argillic brown earths have also occasionally been recorded. Although archaeological soil studies were at an early stage of development, the field descriptions of Evans (1972; 1975) and the pioneering soil micromorphological studies by Cornwall (1958) have provided us with an extremely useful database. This includes the Cornwall thin section collection, housed at the Institute of Archaeology, University College, London. A review of Cornwall's Neolithic Chalkland soil thin sections was produced for the Hazleton North long barrow archive (Macphail 1986).

Since that time, more systematic soil investigations have been carried out on buried chalkland soils. For instance, at Maiden Castle, attempts were made to correlate the site's landuse history, as interpreted from the soil data, with that from archaeological phasing and molluscan zones (Evans 1991, fig. 197). More recently, multidisciplinary investigations of chalky colluvium in general and the nearby barrow sites of Millbarrow and Easton Down in particular, have shown that the results from the independent disciplines of land snail analysis and pedology can be very close indeed (Whittle *et al.* 1993; Whittle 1994; Allen 1994). The latter included both buried soil studies and ditchfill investigations. For example, when soil microfabric analysis of ditchfill layers identified mature and stabilised soil horizons, land snail analysis pointed towards scrub regeneration in and around these ditches (Whittle *et al.* 1993; Whittle 1994). Moreover, soil results from the locally situated Overton Down Experimental Earthwork have clarified, for example, the different taphonomic conditions prevalent under an overburden of both decalcified turf and a chalk bank (Crowther *et al.* 1996; Macphail and Cruise 1996). Such extant studies help to provide accurate data for the reconstruction of past chalkland landscapes and landuse.

Materials and methods

Seven undisturbed soil thin section samples were taken from Trench B:

1: beneath the outer bank, from a subsoil hollow in the buried soil (thin sections A, B, C; context 712), and from two areas of the shallow buried soil (thin section D, context 705; thin section E, context 741/705); and 2: from the outer ditch deposits (thin section F, context 202; thin section G, context 214).

Samples were air dried, impregnated with crystic resin and manufactured into large format (6 by 7.5 cm) thin sections (at Aberdeen University) following the guidelines of Murphy (1986). Thin sections were described according to Bullock *et al.* (1985) and interpreted employing Babel (1975), Bal (1982) and Courty *et al.* (1989). Reference thin sections of chalk downland soils, including modern topsoils and buried soils at the Overton Down Experimental Earthwork have also been utilised in this study. In addition, experimentally cultivated calcareous colluvium, pastures and house floors from Butser Ancient Farm have been under study since sampling in 1986 (Gebhardt 1990; 1992) and 1990 (e.g. Macphail and Goldberg 1995; Cruise and Macphail forthcoming).

Complementary bulk soil samples of thin section

samples A, B, C, D and E (table 53, xA–xD) were analysed for pH, calcium carbonate content, organic carbon and magnetic susceptibility (e.g. Avery and Bascomb 1974) by Dr Stephen Carter, with grain size analysis also being carried out on samples xA, xD and xE.

Results and discussion

Data from the bulk soil samples are presented in tables 53–54, whereas soil micromorphological descriptions are presented in the appendix.

Subsoil hollow *(thin sections A, B and C)*
This subsoil feature, up to 40 cm deep beneath the excavated surface is very dominantly calcareous with dominant amounts of coarse chalk fragments, a strongly bioturbated (earthworm-worked) fine chalk soil that is partially cemented by recalcification, and only small amounts of silt-size quartz (see also table 53, xA–xC). Towards the surface, increased numbers of mollusc shell fragments and biogenic calcite including earthworm/slug granules (e.g. Becze-Deák *et al.* 1997) may testify to additional biological activity. Equally, increasing (but still only in small quantities) amounts of charred organic matter may indicate the influence of probable low intensity coeval anthropogenic activity (note also the increased magnetic susceptibility; table 53, sample xA; Allen 1988, fig. 6.3). The present character of the soil is that of a grey rendzina (Avery 1990), but the more humic topsoil of a typical (humic) rendzina may well have been lost by erosion/truncation some time before bank construction and soil burial.

Although grain size analysis was not carried out on insoluble residues the high amounts of silt to very fine sand-size material may indicate a loessic component (see

also samples xD and xE; Hodgson *et al.* 1967). Within the subsoil feature no patches of decalcified sandy loam/sandy silt loam were noted, although such material occurs in the ditch fill (see below). It can therefore be suggested that a preserved decalcified soil cover was not present in the area of the ground surface exposed by Trench B, because it is likely that this material would have been worked into the subsoil feature. It appears that the feature may not be one of those tree-throw features that commonly dates to the Atlantic period, but instead is a weathered hollow in the chalk parent material formed by the localised solution around tree/shrub roots (cf. Balksbury Camp tree hollow, Hampshire: Macphail and Goldberg 1990; Macphail 1995). The scarcity of recovered molluscs may reflect this (see chapter 7).

The shallow buried soil *(thin sections D and E)*
The 10–13 cm thick buried soil which was examined from two locations only some metres apart, has a uniform original character. The soil appears to have been a stony, markedly calcareous rendzina. Although strong biological activity is in evidence it is not a typical stone-free, earthworm-sorted rendzina (cf. long-term grassland rendzinas: Carter 1990; Crowther *et al.* 1996). In addition, its poorly humic characteristics indicate that its very uppermost humic (Ah1) horizon has been lost. After 32 years, the buried rendzina at Overton Down (Crowther *et al.* 1996) had appeared to have lost up to 50 percent of its organic carbon with only some 7.6 percent organic carbon remaining, while the bAh at Windmill Hill has now only 1.9 percent organic carbon present (table 53, xD). In addition, the soil sampled by thin section D has been affected by a last phase of midden-like dumps (2.1 percent organic carbon) and earthworm mixing. Previous to this last event, on-site domestic activity here

Table 53: Soil chemistry.

Number	Thin Section	Sample	pH (H₂O)	Percent CaCO₃	Percent Organic Carbon	Magnetic Susceptibility (Si¹⁰⁻⁸ Kg.)
xA	A	bA (5cm depth)	7.8	60.8	0.02?	22.4
xB	B	bB (15 cm depth)	7.9	68.2	0.56	8.2
xC	C	bB2 (30 cm depth)	7.9	40.2	0.44	5.2
xD	D	bAh (midden)	7.7	52.6	2.1	35.8
xE	E	bAh	7.6	46.0	1.9	26.3

Table 54: Grain size.

Sample Number	Thin Section	Clay	FZ	MZ	CZ	Silt	VFS	FS	MS	CS	VCS	Sand	Texture
xA	A	15	22	11	11	44	23	7	4	4	3	40	Sandy silt loam
xD (midden)	D	16	22	13	7	42	25	7	5	4	4	45	Sandy silt loam
xE	E	13	20	9	6	35	32	9	4	3	4	52	Sandy loam

NB: clay <2µm, FZ <6µm, MZ<20µm, CZ<50µm, VFS <100µm, FS<200µm, MS<600µm, CS<1000µm, VCS<2000µm.

does not seem to have been intense, but the area as a whole must have been affected by some burning as indicated by the presence of stone-size chalk, fine charcoal and occasional burned soil, burning possibly being associated with landuse management. The magnetic susceptibility shows moderate enhancement despite being diluted by large amounts of chalky soil, but very much less than recorded in places at Easton Down (MS reported in Crowther *et al.* 1996), where burned soil fragments were in evidence (Macphail 1993). A number of Neolithic sites in Cornwall (Carn Brea) and Brittany (*tumuli*) also have soil evidence of having been managed by fire, with corroborative pollen and charcoal data of this at some of the Breton sites (Macphail 1990; Gebhardt 1993).

Textural pedo-features (see Cornwall's thin section, below) as formed by experimental agriculture in calcareous colluvium at Butser (Gebhardt 1992; Macphail, personal observation) have not been found at this specific location at Windmill Hill. Still, these cultivated colluvial soils at Butser are not stone-free, as at Windmill Hill. Further, although research into the Butser cultivated rendzinas (Little Butser Hill) is still at an early stage, these soils are again very stony. This stoniness at Windmill Hill implies two things: first, that the soil was disturbed, and secondly, that there was insufficient time before burial to permit a stone-free earthworm-worked soil horizon to form. Observations of abandoned fields at Butser Ancient Farm, sampled in 1990, show that a noticeable stone-free biologicaly worked horizon starts to form within the first few months after abandonment (Gebhardt and Macphail, personal observations). Therefore on balance, it may be suggested that disturbance, possibly through cultivation, occurred up and until soon before the dumping of burned domestic soil waste (see below) and the construction of the bank. At Easton Down, where several lines of evidence indicated that there had been agricultural activity, the rendzinas were similarly stony (Whittle *et al.* 1993).

Some time prior to bank construction, dumping of a midden-like soil (there were no phytolith indications of cereal processing) from a possible hearth area took place, as indicated by the presence of wood charcoal, burned bone, burned mollusc shell, burned soil inclusions and possible fine bone residues/scat. The blackened nature of the burned soil (see enhanced magnetic susceptibility, table 53, sample xD) and the brownish character of the burned mollusc shell is more indicative of low temperature *ad hoc* camp fires on the soil surface, than a higher temperature 'industrial' one or one used in crop processing or related activities (Courty *et al.* 1989, 107–11). Crop processing waste, rich in cereal spikelet hairs and phytoliths, and high temperature fused ash (melted silica from phytoliths), as found at the Early Iron Age occupation sites of Maiden Castle and Potterne, Wiltshire, are apparently absent (Macphail 1991; 1996). In this sense, the 'midden' soil at Windmill Hill is more comparable to the Neolithic 'midden' soil at Hazleton, Gloucestershire, which was similarly rich

in bone and charcoal (Saville 1990). At Hazleton this midden-like soil was totally mixed into the natural soil. Macphail's (1990) interpretation of this, from the structural and textural features present, was that soil homogenisation had occurred through 'preferred' cultivation of this humic and 'fertile' midden material. At Windmill Hill no textural indicators of soil disturbance that could relate to cultivation were observed, but on the other hand the midden deposit was again very stony. At any rate it seems likely that human activities locally immediately prior to outer bank construction led to the dumping of burned soil and refuse. Possibly this could have occurred at the same time as the pits and grave were constructed during this more intensive use of the area.

From observation of the Experimental Earthwork at Overton Down we can now suggest that it is likely that at Windmill Hill the extant earthworm population continued to be active after burial by the bank, mixing the chalky bank with the buried soil, for at least a short time (Crowther *et al.* 1996; Macphail and Cruise 1996).

Cornwall's thin section

Dr Ian Cornwall studied a soil thin section (*c.* 2.5 by 1.5 cm in size) from the 1957–8 excavation, and described (unpublished notes) the buried soil as a A/C horizon developed on chalk. Although the sample cannot be accurately located now, it is likely to have come from the bank-buried soil only some metres away from this present soil study. An examination of the thin section (held in the collection of the Institute of Archaeology, UCL) found an almost totally calcitic microfabric, but with dusty void infills and inclusion of fine amorphous and charred organic matter. At least one possible bone fragment was also present. In comparison to the buried soils of Trench BB, the whole of the Ah horizon of Cornwall's rendzina appears to be totally missing or transformed, and there is no evidence of the biological working which is so typical of the soils in Trench BB. In contrast, Cornwall's sample is of a possibly truncated rendzina, which had been greatly disturbed (textural features of dusty calcitic infills) by intense on-site activity (trampling/tillage) up to the time of burial. Textural features of a similar appearance, have been observed in thin sections from the base of the plough zone of some of the Butser experimental fields (Macphail, personal observation). Thus, the Cornwall sample differs in character from the biologically active stony soils in Trench BB. Both, however, show evidence of disturbance.

Clearance on its own is unlikely to have produced the stony soils of samples D and E, while Cornwall's thin section sample has features indicative of intensive physical mixing. It is therefore in order to suggest that while some areas were used domestically (camp fires and so on), the soil micromorphological and field evidence (stoniness) imply that other disturbance, such as a ploughing phase, took place at this site.

Outer ditch, upper secondary fill (*thin sections F and G*)
Some layering persists in the upper ditch fill despite the
activities of earthworms. At the base of 214 (thin section
G) a charcoal-free highly calcareous soil layer is buried by
increasingly decalcified and anthropogenic debris-rich soil
layers upwards into context 202 (thin section F). In sample
G, occasional bone waste and a rare example of an
enigmatic, ultraviolet light autofluorescent nodule are
present. Examples of similar nodules studied at Potterne
have proved to be formed of calcium phosphate (micro-
probe) and were termed 'pale nodules' (Macphail 1996).
In that study they were tentatively associated with similar
features that have been collected from ancient cess pits.

The lack of full homogenisation by earthworms of these
layers indicates a moderately rapid sequence of fills, each
forming a distinctive layer. The origin of the decalcified
silt loam is difficult to identify, because little evidence of
this occurred in the buried *in situ* soils (samples D and E).
In addition, much of the soil in these fills is extremely
humic and contains more abundant fine charcoal than
found in the bank buried soils generally.

Three hypotheses can be considered.

1.   At Overton Down, humic decalcified turf soil from
     the edges of the ditch became included as rounded
     soil clasts in the primary fills, forming fine laminae,
     but there is no evidence of this phenomenon at
     Windmill Hill (Macphail and Cruise 1996).
2.   Another possibility is that the upper secondary fills
     relate to the erosion of a localised patch of soil where
     brown rendzinas or brown earths may have formed in
     deeper areas of loess, which were still extant in the
     Neolithic. Loessic silts, for example, formed major
     horizons in ditchfills at Millbarrow but here silty
     argillic brown earths still formed a thick soil cover in
     the Neolithic (Macphail 1994).
3.   Alternatively, these fills may have a more direct
     anthropogenic origin, in that the 'scoops' they infill
     could have been occupation surfaces. Certainly the
     soil does not retain textural features found in some
     multi-period (Copper Age, Bronze Age and Iron Age)
     Italian montane Castellaro sites (e.g. Uscio: Courty *et
     al.* 1989, figs. 7.4 and 17.3; Macphail 1990), where a
     series of superimposed *in situ* trampled mud floors
     are believed to be present. On the other hand, analysis
     of a beaten floor from two locations at the Pimperne
     House at the Butser Ancient Farm showed that textural
     features had not formed here. Instead, those soil floors
     were compact and contained organic fragments and
     burned materials, with an underlying biologically
     open microfabric (Reynolds 1979; Macphail 1996;
     Cruise and Macphail forthcoming). These soil floors
     formed over an approximately 14–year period, but at
     the New Demonstration Area, field observation by
     Macphail in 1994 in the newly constructed Pimperne
     House indicated that such a beaten floor could form in
     months. This is not the place to discuss the hypo-
     thetical differences between floors in protected (con-

tinuously roofed) environments compared to those
that may have undergone exposure to the elements,
because in any case the highly comminuted nature of ·
the abundant charred organic matter and inclusion of
burned materials in samples F and G would be consistent both with ancient mud floors (e.g. Uscio) and
the floor at the Pimperne House. In this last hypothesis, the decalcified loam may well have been
locally imported for the construction of floors, the
within-ditch location being a moderately sheltered and
preferred site (cf. Goldberg and Whitbread 1993).

Conclusions

As the number of soil samples from Windmill Hill is
restricted, the contribution of pedological data to the
understanding of the site must be seen as a minor component. Nevertheless this investigation has been greatly
aided by the large number of relevant studies of archaeological chalk soils in the published literature. The buried
soils at the sampled locations all appear to have been
disturbed in some way, and at Cornwall's site the chalky
parent material appears to have been exposed and disturbed. The use of fire to manage the landscape also seems
likely, contributing to the 'charcoal bank' suggested in
chapter 8. The presence of cereal-type pollen grains at
Cornwall's sampling point where the soil is so deeply
disturbed is also noteworthy (Dimbleby 1965, 36–37; but
see also chapter 10 here), although cereal material from
animal dung and cereal processing waste could be as
possible here as cereal pollen deriving directly from on-site
cultivation. The stony disturbed soils of samples D and E
can also be interpreted as resulting from a ploughing phase.
To summarise, the buried soils at Windmill Hill thus show
that they were affected by three events whilst people were
present: first, general earthworm mixing; then disturbance
that induced stoniness across the site; and finally a short-
lived pre-burial phase of surface soil sorting by biological
activity. The exact cause of the stoniness remains enigmatic.

The type of microscopic inclusions present and the
occurrence of a number of fine charcoal-rich microfabrics
indicate instances of moderately intensive occupation. This
led to the presence of soils containing burned soil, burned
landsnail fragments, burned bone, charcoal and bone waste
and/or possible scat. Charcoal and bone was also found in
Cornwall's thin section. In Trench B, earthworm activity
mixed dark charcoal-rich soils with the local rendzinas,
possibly indicating that human activities were intermittent.

In the ditch, human activity produced charcoal-rich soil
fills, and these could have originated either as an enigmatic
loessic soil fill, or been purposely imported to form a series
of floors. In the last case, the partial reworking of the soil
layers could possibly argue for re-use of a site, with new
soil being added on some occasions. The importation of
fresh soil on to hut floors which were 'dirty' with charred
organic matter was a likely explanation for stratigraphic
sequences at Uscio (Macphail 1990).

Most of the microscopic signatures of intensive occupation, such as fused cereal ash and phytolith-rich microfabrics, calcitic/ashed herbivore coprolite residues (stabling?) or soils stained or cemented by phosphate, and which appear at such sites as Potterne and Chisenbury (on Chalk), in Wiltshire, but are of Later Bronze Age to Early Iron Age in date, are apparently absent at Windmill Hill. The only exception, is the single example of 'pale nodule' found in sample G. Its exact origin is unknown, but its likely calcium phosphate composition is suggestive of a cesspit-like origin.

In conclusion, the soil evidence from Trench B suggests a different kind of landuse compared to Easton Down, where arable and domestic activity appears to have been dominant and intensive on one part of the site. Rather, it appears that although some areas may have been cultivated, others underwent intermittent domestic occupation forming Hazleton-like middens at times. There is also the possibility that later some ditch locations may have been regularly chosen for habitation.

Acknowledgements
The author wishes to thank Dr Stephen Carter for carrying out soil analyses and Dr FitzPatrick at Aberdeen University for thin section manufacture.

APPENDIX

SOIL MICROMORPHOLOGICAL DESCRIPTIONS AND DETAILED INTERPRETATIONS

(PPL = plane polarised light; XPL = crossed polarised light; OIL = oblique incident light.)

Subsoil hollow (712)

Thin section A: 1.5–9 cm, bA(h) horizon
Structure weakly developed fine prisms of coalescing fine aggregates, with spongy microfabric. *Porosity* 30%, very dominant very coarse vughs. *Mineral* Coarse:Fine limit is 10μm; C:F, 50:50. *Coarse* dominant small stone size to sand size chalk fragments, common very small stone size to silt size biogenic (mainly mollusc and fossil material, some possible arionid granules and earthworm crystals) aragonite and calcite; few silt-size quartz *Fine* very slightly brownish grey, lightly speckled (PPL), very high birefringence (XPL), very slightly brownish grey (OIL). *Organic Coarse* rare fine charcoal. *Fine* rare charred and many amorphous organic matter, with thin amorphous plasma. *Groundmass* close porphyric, crystallitic b-fabric. *Pedofeatures Textural* rare colloidal micritic chalk coatings. *Depletion* possible weak calcitic depletion causing spongy fabric. *Fabric* strongly homogenous; many passage features. *Excrements* total biological fabric, with many mammilated excrements of earthworms.

Thin section B: 11.5–21 cm, bB horizon
Structure fine subangular blocky becoming very coarse subangular blocky. *Porosity* 25–30%, frequent moderately accomodated curved planes, medium to coarse vughs and fine channels. *Mineral Coarse* as A, but very coarse chalk fragments a little more dominant and *Fine* a little less brown. *Organic Coarse* as A *Fine* occasional charred and amorphous organic matter. *Groundmass* as A. *Pedofeatures Depletion* decalcification of some chalk fragments. *Fabric* and *Excrements* as A.

Thin section C: 26–35 cm, bB2 horizon
Structure weakly massive with fine to coarse subangular blocky. *Porosity* as A. *Mineral Coarse* as B, but more dominant subrounded stone size chalk fragments. *Fine* grey, cloudy (PPL), very high birefringence, whitish grey (OIL). *Organic Coarse* rare fine charcoal. *Fine* rare charred and amorphous organic matter. *Groundmass* as B. *Pedofeatures* as A and B, with channel infillings of fine calcite earthworm gut crystals.

Interpretation of thin sections A, B and C
The supposed tree hollow contains only small amounts of non-calcareous silt-size (quartz) mineral material. The soil is totally dominated by calcareous chalky soil and biogenic calcite material (fossils, mollusc shell and slug/earthworm granules). Quartz silt and clay, which are found elsewhere on the site, do not appear to be present. This may either indicate that these decalcified superficial materials were eroded off, exposing the chalk substrate before the hollow began to develop or that any superficial soil cover and occupation soil was lost late in the history of the site. As the soil contains very little charcoal, and is only weakly humic at the surface, the latter interpretation may be more accurate. In any case the microfabric may suggest that the hollow relates more to *in situ* weathering of the chalk (see depletion features) by tree/shrub roots, than through a hollow formed by tree toppling/windthrow, as there appears to be no microfabric evidence of mixing. The feature therefore appears to be the bottom of an *in situ* weathered tree hollow.

Buried soil

Thin section D: Ah/occupation
Structure fine subangular blocky. *Porosity* very dominant packing voids and poorly accomodated fissures; few fine vughs and channels. *Mineral* C:F, 60:40. *Coarse* common large stone size to sand size subrounded chalk fragments. Common mainly biogenic sand to silt size calcite and aragonite (fossils, arionid/earthworm granules, mollusc shell, sometimes burned); frequent mainly fine to silt size quartz; very few very fine sand-size bone. *Fine* three fine fabrics. a) dominant (calcareous humic soil) darkish brown, finely dusty (PPL), high birefringence, pale brown (OIL); b) frequent (burned calcareous humic soil) black to blackish brown, dotted (PPL), patchy high birefringence, heavily dotted blackish brown; c) few (chalky soil) dark greyish, finely dotted (PPL), high birefringence, weakly brownish grey with few black specks; d) very few (brown clay) darkish yellow brown (PPL), moderate birefringence, bright yellowish brown

(OIL). *Organic Coarse* many charcoal fragments. *Fine* a) many amorphous organic matter; b) very abundant charred organic matter, c) many charred and amorphous organic matter; d) rare organic matter. *Groundmass* a) close porphyric, crystallitic b-fabric; b) ditto; c) open porphyric, crystallitic b-fabric; d) open porphyric, strrial b-fabric. *Pedofeatures Fabric* strongly heterogeneous (four soil materials), many passage features showing juxtaposed fabrics. *Excrements* moderately total biological fabric, with occasional arionid/earthworm granules, and abundant earthworm excrements.

Interpretation

The thin soil over the chalk substrate appears to have undergone mixing, with charcoal and burned mollusc shell-rich soil from the overlying rampart deposit/midden dump, caused by post depositional earthworm activity. The chalky soil containing fine charcoal may have been similarly introduced. The main *in situ* buried soil is a moderately humic brown calcareous earth. It is a more humic version of the soil found at the tree hollow. The faunally introduced charcoal-rich soil has come from a rather intensive occupation area, where burning and trampling have caused fine charcoal to become mixed into the humic calcareous soil.

It seems likely that the buried soil is like the lower Ah horizon of a rendzina, possibly developed after erosion of any decalcified clay soil (see fabric d). A charcoal-rich 'topsoil' formed by occupation may have been eroded, but it seems more likely that here little occupation took place as little charcoal is present. Elsewhere, however, occupation formed calcareous soils containing charcoal and burned mollusc shell, so some contemporary soils must have been rendzinas.

Thin section E: 74–83 cm, bAh/B horizon
Structure fine to coarse subangular blocky. *Porosity* Ah: 40%, common poorly accomodated packing planes, common open vughs, coarse channels. B; 30%. *Mineral* Ah: C:F, 60:40. *Coarse* common stone to sand size chalk fragments, dominant mainly fine sand size calcite and aragonite (fossil and mollusc) fragments, with few quartz. *Fine* a) dominant (humic calcareous) greyish brown, dusty (PPL), high birefringence, pale greyish brown (OIL); b) common (calcareous) greyish, dusty (PPL), very high birefringence, white (OIL). B: *Coarse* C:F, 70:30, dominant chalk fragments; as Ah. *Fine* as Ah, increasing fabric b). *Organic Coarse* rare charcoal, root fragments. *Fine* a) many to abundant amorphous organic matter; b) rare to occasional amorphous organic matter. *Groundmass* close porphyric, crystallitic b-fabric. *Pedofeatures Fabric* moderately homogeneous because of earthworms bringing in different material from lower down; many passage and curved infills of coarse channels. *Excrements* total biological fabric with abundant mammilated excrements of earthworms.

Interpretation

Probably only the lower part of the Ah horizon of a rendzina is preserved alongside the underlying B/C horizon. Only rare charcoal is present. Either a much more charcoal and humus rich upper layer has been eroded off, or after erosion of any decalcified cover, the soil had only a rather short time to develop naturally, without too much human activity on this particular area of the site.

Outer ditch, upper secondary fill
Thin section G: 67–75 cm, ditchfill (214)
Structure weakly prismatic with subangular blocky, spongy microfabric. *Porosity* 40%, dominant open vughs, common very poorly accomodated packing planes/voids. *Mineral* C:F, 60:40. *Coarse* common small stone size chalk fragments, dominant very coarse sand to silt size calcite and aragonite (mollusc [some burned], arionid/earthworm granules, fossil), frequent quartz. Large fragment of low temperature pot?, a heterogeneous dark brown silty clay material. Single occurrence of an ultra violet light autofluorescent nodule some 800 µm in size, with few silt size quartz and calcite inclusions, very few fine charcoal and probable iron-replaced amorphous organic matter; colourless (PPL) and non-birefringent. Rare fine sand size fragments of brown-stained bone and very pale brown ultra violet light autofluorescent bone waste/scat. *Fine* a) lower layers of greyish brown, lightly speckled (PPL), high birefringence, pale yellowish brown OIL); b) upper layers of darkish brown, speckled (PPL), moderate birefringence, yellowish brown with many black specks (OIL). Very few blackened burned soil. *Organic Coarse* occasional to many charcoal. *Fine* a) many amorphous and charred organic matter; b) abundant amorphous and charred organic matter. *Groundmass* close porphyric, weakly crystallitic (a) to crystallitic (b) b-fabric. *Pedofeatures Textural* rare organic stained fine soil infills and coatings. *Depletion* weak decalcification of chalk. *Fabric* layering, but moderately homogenised generally. *Excrements* total biological fabric with many mammilated excrements.

Thin section F: 55–62 cm, ditchfill (202)
Structure fine subangular blocky. *Porosity* very dominant poorly accomodated packing planes/voids, common open vughs. *Mineral* C:F, 65:35. *Coarse* few small stone and sand size chalk; common stone size to silt size calcite and aragonite fragments; common to dominant silt size quartz. *Organic Coarse* rare charcoal. *Fine* dark (decalcified brown silty clay loam) yellowish brown, dusty (PPL), low birefringence, yellowish brown (OIL); very few patches of calcareous soil (fine fabric a of G) and mixed poorly calcareous soil (blackish brown (PPL), poorly birefringent and greyish brown (XPL)). *Organic Coarse* occasional charcoal. *Fine* many amorphous and some charred organic matter. *Groundmass* close porphyric, speckled b-fabric, rare crystallitic b-fabric. *Pedofeatures Fabric* very slightly heterogeneous; strong homogenisation and coarse channel infills. *Excrements* total biological fabric, with mammilated excrements.

Interpretation

Biological mixing and homogenisation by mainly earthworms, has affected these ditch infill layers. Nevertheless infill can be seen to have been by mainly decalcified and poorly calcareous soils, containing variously high amounts of fine charcoal and burned mollusc, and chalky soil containing little organic matter. In sample G, the presence of pot fragments, rare fine bone and a possible phosphate nodule, are all further indications of anthropogenic inputs.

7

Land Mollusca

Mark Fishpool

Introduction

Molluscan analysis was first undertaken in the wider region at the causewayed enclosure of Knap Hill, where shade-loving species dominated the fauna from the buried soil (Sparks 1965). Molluscan analysis was previously undertaken at Windmill Hill by John Evans, from a profile through the buried soil under the outer bank close to Smith's Outer Bank V (1972, 242–48). In the buried soil, noted as stony, shade-loving species dominated the fauna, and an environment of open woodland was mooted. However, other considerations suggested that de-turfing prior to bank construction after clearance and occupation could in fact have been possible. Other analyses of Earlier Neolithic situations were made, of buried soils at West Kennet long barrow (Evans 1972) and Beckhampton Road, South Street and Horslip or Windmill Hill long barrows (Evans 1972; Ashbee *et al*. 1979), and of ditch profiles at South Street (Evans 1972; Ashbee *et al*. 1979). Subsequently, other analyses were made from the deposits of the Kennet valley itself (Evans *et al*. 1993), and at Easton Down long barrow and Millbarrow chambered tomb as part of the research project to which the present report belongs (Whittle *et al*. 1993; Whittle 1994).

At Windmill Hill, the excavations of 1988 provided the opportunity both to put the site better into its local context and to examine the possibility of variation across the site. The buried soil in Trench BB, the outer ditch in Trenches B, C and A, the middle ditch in Trenches D and E, and the inner ditch in Trench F, were all sampled (figs 100–105; tables 55–57). Further details are given in Fishpool (1992); not all counts are presented here. This report has been edited with the help of John Evans.

The buried soil beneath the outer bank in Trench BB *(figs 100–101; table 55)*

The buried soil was sampled at eight places (figs 67 and 69–71). The species were ordered in the histograms (figs 100–101) largely on the basis of similar responses in the sequences; behaviour in the upper samples of each sequence was particularly taken into account. Species of low abundance were grouped on the basis of ecology (especially the woodland species plotted to the right of *Pupilla muscorum*).

The top samples in each sequence, including 7–8 cm in 6 which was a relatively stone-free horizon, were compared using the Sorenson Index of Similarity modified to include species abundance (Southwood 1978):

C = 2jN/(aN+bN)
where aN = total individuals in sample a
bN = total individuals in sample b
jN = the sum of the lesser values for species
common to a and b.

The results are presented as a dendrogram (fig. 100) in which the pairs of assemblages with the highest similarity are joined, then continuing the process until all are joined. This is the basis for the ordering of the profiles (fig. 100).

Shannon and Brillouin diversity indexes were calculated (Magurran 1988).

The fauna as a whole is quite diverse. Obligate open-country species like *Vallonia excentrica*, *Helicella itala*, *Vertigo pygmaea* and *Pupilla muscorum*, occur throughout the profiles, even in the subsoil hollows, but they are never especially abundant. At the same time the faunas are quite rich in woodland species, and although none of these is utterly confined to woodland the presence of so many species together is unusual for open-country. The main species, in effect, are catholic ones; the high abundance of *Trichia hispida* is unusual for Neolithic faunas in the area. There are few relative abundance changes in any of the profiles (fig. 101) (see below for details).

The subsoil hollows, BB1 7–35 cm and BB8 8–19 cm, had sparse faunas by comparison with the main part of the soil (figs 100–101). They are not different from the upper parts of the sequences and there is no ecological succession from base to top. Woodland faunas might be expected on the basis of other subsoil hollows under Neolithic soils, but there are many other possibilities, such as contamination from late-glacial deposits or downward movement through worm holes, or even an early Holocene fauna that is actually *in situ*. There are so few snails that further speculation is pointless.

The soil itself was very stony throughout except for a thin and often indistinct less stony horizon at the very surface in some profiles (fig. 100). In fact the soil was *much* more stony than any other Neolithic profile seen in the area, and this in itself probably implies disturbance to some depth. Even so, the graded stratification of species in some profiles, especially 1, 3 and 6, indicates that disturbance was less severe in these than elsewhere.

In terms of their surface faunas, the soil profiles fall into three groups (figs 100–101), and these groups are reflected in the profiles as a whole.

Group A

Profiles 1, 3 and the top part of 6 have gradients of increasing shell abundance, and 3 and 6 gradients of decreasing stones. 3 and 6 in particular show very clear indications of an actual soil surface in the huge increase in several species. The abundance of shells, their marked increase by comparison with the underlying assemblages, and the less stony zone at the top in 3 and 6 show that the increase took place *after* any disturbance of the soil and immediately before the bank was built, with the shells being incorporated by worms.

As for trends in the lower part of the soils, that is below the surface one or two centimetres, in view of the overall stoniness of the soils these cannot be due to a reflection of surface changes by downward movement in a worm-sorted profile, unless, however, that took place in a previously worm-sorted soil which was subsequently turbated.

In other words there could be two superimposed molluscan sequences. First, there was a worm-sorted zone right through the profile with a graded sequence of shell abundance. Next, there was disturbance of the soil creating a very rubbly profile, but in which some of the earlier shell stratification was preserved. Finally, there was stability and further worm-sorting, but this time only in the top one or two centimetres because before this action could go deeper the soil was buried by the bank.

There are some relative abundance changes: an increase in *Discus rotundatus*, *Vitrina pellucida* and *Oxychilus cellarius* which suggests a rubbly surface perhaps under scrub; and a decrease in *Carychium tridentatum* and *Vallonia excentrica*, which suggests a trend away from grassland although this is not seen in other open-country species, especially *Helicella itala*. These are consistent trends which occur in all three profiles.

Group B

Profile 8 is different from all the others in the abundance of woodland species. However, this may not be very significant since most other species, especially the open-country ones, are equally of high abundance, and this feature is not apparent in the percentage diagram. There is a decrease towards the surface in practically all species, although some of the trends seen in the profiles 1, 3 and 6 (top) also occur.

Group C

Profiles 2, 4, 5, 6 (bottom) and 9 appear to have more woodland species (fig. 100) though this is not a trend indicated in the percentage diagram (fig. 101). However, the generally higher diversity indexes in these assemblages can be noted, a feature which is largely due to the more even representation of species. The real difference is that there are more *Vallonia excentrica* and *Carychium tridentatum* and less *Discus rotundatus*, *Vitrina pellucida* and *Oxychilus cellarius* than in the other groups (except 8 which is marginal in this respect). So these five species, both in their behaviour in profiles 1, 3 and 6 (top) and in the contrast between these three profiles and those of 2, 4, 5, 6 (bottom) and 9 might provide the key to the environmental situation. *V. excentrica* and *C. tridentatum* often occur together in lightly grazed or ungrazed grassland, with the latter being inhibited or deterred by heavy grazing. The other three can occur in grassland, especially *Vitrina pellucida*, but *D. rotundatus* and *O. cellarius* are more common in scrub amongst moss, twigs and stones on the ground, or in woodland under logs and stones, and *V. pellucida* can be very common in the former.

In comparing the profiles, it has to be kept in mind that they may not be contemporary, although their relatively uniform thickness suggests they probably are. However, the uppermost parts of some of the profiles may have been eroded, dug away, or just mixed in with the part further down (just one or two centimetres would make a difference, considering the sharpness of the changes in, for example, profiles 3 and 6 (top)); or, in sampling, the lowest part of the bank may have been incorporated so that what is classified as soil surface is actually bank material and could have come from anywhere.

However, there is no doubt that the profiles are *broadly* contemporary, in which case the spatial difference implies that disturbance was very localised and did not involve ploughing or arding, or if it did that there were large gaps between the furrows where the soil was undisturbed; there is nothing here like the fine stratification at South Street (Evans in Ashbee *et al.* 1979). This is not like the situation at Easton Down where there were clear trends across the site (Rouse and Evans in Whittle *et al.* 1993). Profiles 2 and 6 in Trench BB were less than a metre apart yet quite different from top to bottom (even if the top sample of 2, which in view of its stoniness may in fact be bank material, were ignored and replaced with the top sample of 6, it would give a quite different profile from 6).

The extreme rubbliness of the soil is unusual (cf. Evans 1972, 246). Nothing else like it has been encountered in the region; simply sampling the soil was much harder than at, for example, South Street or West Kennet long barrows. Under scrub, especially, chalk soils tend to be more stony

Fig. 101. M

Vertigo pusilla
Vertigo substriata
Vertigo pygmaea
Abida secale
Pupilla muscorum
Acanthinula aculeata
Ena obscura
Ena montana
Punctum pygmaeum
Vitrea spp.
Nesovitrea hammonis
Aegopinella pura
Aegopinella nitidula
Oxychilus alliarius
Euconulus fulvus
Cochlodina laminata
Balea perversa
Helicigona lapicida

lluscan histograms for pre-bank soil locations; percentages.

Table 55: Pre-bank soil, molluscan analysis results.

+ = non-apical fragment, wp = well preserved, pp = poorly preserved. Sample weight 1 kg, except BB3 3-4 cm, 0.879 kg, and 4-5 cm, 0.597 kg.

	BB1									BB2				BB3						BB4		
	0-1	1-2	2-5	7-10	11-13	15-19	22-23	25-28	32-35	0-1	1-2	2-3	3-4	0-1	1-2	2-3	3-4	4-5	5-6	0-2	2-4	4-5
Pomatias elegans (>2mm)	-	1	1	-	1	-	-	-	-	2	1	-	1	-	1	1	1	1	1	3	2	1
Pomatias elegans (<2mm)	1	10	8	4	1	-	-	-	-	1	8	10	4	8	9	7	11	3	6	4	6	4
Carychium tridentatum	2	7	5	9	3	2	1	1	1	27	36	22	35	7	10	8	10	7	7	33	61	64
Cochlicopa lubrica	3	2	-	-	-	-	-	1	-	1	-	-	-	2	2	2	2	-	1	-	-	1
Cochlicopa lubricella	-	-	1	-	-	-	-	-	-	-	-	-	-	3	-	-	1	-	-	-	-	-
Cochlicopa spp.	29	26	13	19	7	6	7	1	5	20	26	19	19	38	22	21	16	9	14	18	34	35
Vertigo pusilla	-	-	-	-	-	-	-	-	-	-	-	-	-	-	-	-	-	-	-	-	-	-
Vertigo substriata	-	-	-	-	-	-	-	-	-	-	-	-	-	-	-	-	-	-	-	-	-	-
Vertigo pygmaea	-	2	-	1	1	1	1	-	-	2	2	6	8	4	1	1	2	-	1	2	3	3
Abida secale	-	-	-	-	-	1	1	1	2	-	-	-	-	-	-	-	-	-	-	-	-	-
Pupilla muscorum	-	-	-	-	-	1	1	-	1	4	3	1	1	-	-	-	-	-	-	6	4	6
Vallonia costata	59	70	27	23	12	12	3	3	-	21	49	62	59	82	67	47	27	14	14	39	52	73
Vallonia excentrica	2	8	5	10	4	-	2	-	-	7	18	17	14	1	6	4	2	3	4	15	12	26
Acanthinula aculeata	2	2	1	1	1	2	3	-	-	4	3	1	6	-	3	3	5	-	2	4	11	5
Ena montana	1	-	-	1	-	-	-	-	-	-	-	-	-	1	-	-	-	-	-	1	-	-
Ena obscura	1	1	-	-	-	-	-	-	-	2	2	1	1	1	-	2	-	1	1	1	5	2
Punctum pygmaeum	1	1	1	4	2	2	1	1	-	2	2	1	4	1	2	2	1	1	1	1	5	2
Discus rotundatus	53	47	9	5	1	5	3	3	2	8	6	13	6	57	25	22	7	4	2	10	19	24
Vitrina pellucida wp	9	3	1	2	-	3	-	-	1	2	4	2	1	12	7	6	4	1	1	1	-	3
Vitrina pellucida pp	-	-	-	-	-	-	-	-	-	-	-	-	-	-	-	-	-	-	-	-	-	-
Vitrea spp.	-	1	2	2	3	-	3	2	1	1	1	5	5	3	2	2	2	1	4	5	5	13
Nesovitrea hammonis	-	-	-	-	1	1	1	-	3	-	-	3	1	-	-	-	1	1	-	-	1	-
Aegopinella pura	-	5	3	2	-	7	-	-	3	2	3	3	2	2	-	1	1	-	2	3	5	7
Aegopinella nitidula	-	1	3	4	1	-	1	-	-	4	11	5	5	1	6	4	6	2	4	4	11	10
Oxychilus cellarius	13	14	5	3	4	1	-	-	2	1	-	4	2	31	21	12	5	2	-	-	-	-
Oxychilus alliarius	-	-	-	-	-	1	-	-	-	-	-	-	1	-	-	-	-	-	-	-	-	-
Euconulus fulvus	-	-	-	-	-	-	-	-	-	-	-	-	-	-	-	-	-	-	-	2	1	1
Cecilioides acicula	-	-	-	-	-	-	-	-	-	-	-	-	-	1	-	1	-	-	-	1	-	2
Cochlodina laminata	-	-	-	-	-	-	-	-	-	-	-	-	-	-	-	1	1	-	-	-	-	-
Clausilia bidentata wp	6	9	3	5	2	2	1	1	-	7	7	10	4	5	3	5	5	2	-	5	10	12
Clausilia bidentata pp	1	3	1	3	1	-	1	-	-	-	3	4	3	3	1	2	1	-	1	1	-	-
Balea perversa	-	-	-	-	-	-	1	-	-	-	-	-	1	-	-	-	-	-	-	-	-	-
Helicella itala	6	7	-	2	2	2	2	-	2	3	11	6	-	8	10	1	1	-	1	11	7	10
Helicellinae indet.	11	5	8	5	5	3	1	-	-	14	17	9	12	10	14	9	4	2	4	13	13	15
Trichia hispida	91	57	38	23	4	6	2	3	5	49	75	77	66	141	97	65	46	26	31	68	58	97
Helicigona lapicida	-	-	-	-	-	+	-	-	-	-	-	-	-	-	-	-	-	-	-	1	-	-
Arianta arbustorum	1	-	-	-	-	+	-	-	-	-	-	-	-	-	-	-	-	-	-	-	-	-
Cepaea hortensis	1	-	-	-	-	-	-	-	-	5	5	7	6	-	-	-	-	-	-	-	-	-
Cepaea/Arianta wp	1	3	-	2	2	2	2	1	-	5	5	4	4	4	4	3	4	5	5	5	3	7
Cepaea/Arianta pp	2	5	6	7	3	-	2	5	2	4	4	4	4	-	8	8	3	1	4	3	7	6
Slug plates	25	39	28	29	14	7	3	3	5	32	70	57	56	52	55	60	54	29	24	34	44	49
Eggs	1	-	-	-	-	-	-	-	-	-	-	-	-	-	-	-	-	-	-	1	-	-

Mark Fishpool

Table 55 continued: Pre-bank soil, molluscan analysis results.

	BB5 0-1	BB5 1-2	BB5 2-3	BB5 3-4	BB6 0-1	BB6 1-2	BB6 2-3	BB6 3-4	BB6 7-8	BB6 8-9	BB8 0-1	BB8 1-2	BB8 2-4	BB8 4-6	BB8 8-9	BB8 11-13	BB8 15-19	BB9 0-1	BB9 1-2	BB9 2-5	BB9 5-8
Pomatias elegans (>2mm)	3	8	7	2	3	9	9	-	3	1	2	1	3	9	2	2	-	3	1	3	1
Pomatias elegans (<2mm)	2	13	7	3	3	9	9	3	6	3	3	8	10	19	3	3	1	9	3	7	4
Carychium tridentatum	49	61	33	17	2	3	4	7	43	36	2	25	56	63	31	10	2	47	56	56	15
Cochlicopa lubrica	-	-	-	-	7	1	-	-	-	-	1	-	2	2	+	-	-	1	3	2	1
Cochlicopa lubricella	-	-	-	1	-	-	-	-	-	1	-	-	-	1	-	-	-	-	-	-	-
Cochlicopa spp.	29	25	19	9	68	15	14	14	27	33	24	21	40	43	12	10	2	21	51	21	13
Vertigo pusilla	-	-	1	-	-	-	-	-	-	-	-	-	-	-	-	-	-	-	-	-	-
Vertigo substriata	-	-	-	-	-	-	-	-	-	-	-	-	-	-	-	-	-	-	-	-	-
Vertigo pygmaea	2	6	7	3	-	2	2	1	5	4	1	2	7	9	2	2	-	4	4	6	6
Abida secale	-	-	-	-	-	-	-	-	-	-	-	-	-	-	-	-	-	-	-	-	-
Pupilla muscorum	2	4	2	2	1	1	2	-	2	2	-	-	-	2	-	-	-	1	-	-	-
Vallonia costata	28	34	27	25	102	48	22	20	53	53	86	69	99	119	45	19	1	40	102	80	19
Vallonia excentrica	9	13	14	10	-	2	7	6	20	24	19	29	46	60	34	5	4	29	30	24	12
Acanthinula aculeata	1	7	3	2	-	-	-	-	6	3	1	4	6	15	9	1	3	10	6	6	2
Ena montana	1	-	+	-	1	1	-	-	-	-	-	-	-	1	-	-	-	-	1	-	-
Ena obscura	-	1	1	-	-	-	-	-	-	-	1	-	2	2	2	1	-	-	-	1	-
Punctum pygmaeum	1	3	3	6	-	-	1	-	3	6	3	4	3	6	5	-	1	-	4	5	3
Discus rotundatus	13	8	2	3	117	25	15	19	15	12	32	16	36	22	11	1	1	9	10	9	6
Vitrina pellucida wp	1	-	-	-	12	3	1	1	1	2	1	1	6	3	1	1	1	2	3	3	1
Vitrina pellucida pp	1	1	1	2	2	-	-	-	-	-	1	-	-	-	-	-	-	-	-	-	-
Vitrea spp.	7	2	7	6	3	1	1	1	5	4	5	2	5	13	6	9	-	2	4	4	1
Nesovitrea hammonis	1	1	-	-	-	-	-	-	-	-	-	1	6	8	2	-	-	2	-	1	-
Aegopinella pura	2	2	3	2	3	-	-	-	4	3	1	3	4	5	-	-	1	2	4	3	3
Aegopinella nitidula	6	6	7	9	6	4	5	3	10	5	7	9	22	25	13	3	-	11	12	7	7
Oxychilus cellarius	-	1	-	4	15	7	6	2	1	1	3	-	1	6	-	1	1	-	2	1	1
Oxychilus alliarius	-	-	-	-	2	-	1	-	-	-	-	-	-	-	-	-	1	-	-	1	-
Euconulus fulvus	-	-	-	-	-	-	-	-	-	-	-	-	-	-	-	-	-	-	-	-	-
Cecilioides acicula	-	1	-	-	-	-	-	-	1	-	-	-	-	-	1	-	-	-	-	-	-
Cochlodina laminata	-	1	-	-	1	-	-	-	1	-	1	-	1	-	-	1	-	-	1	1	1
Clausilia bidentata wp	14	5	14	1	14	3	2	-	6	4	7	5	9	11	3	-	-	7	12	4	1
Clausilia bidentata pp	3	2	2	1	-	1	2	1	1	3	4	4	3	3	2	-	-	-	3	2	-
Balea perversa	-	-	-	-	-	-	-	-	-	-	-	-	-	-	-	-	-	1	-	-	-
Helicella itala	6	4	3	2	11	1	2	-	1	4	13	9	4	10	10	2	-	6	15	6	1
Helicellinae indet.	16	15	13	11	6	5	7	6	17	8	13	11	7	25	12	6	-	18	27	5	7
Trichia hispida	79	62	42	39	135	48	32	26	75	73	103	126	206	269	69	23	3	84	133	93	25
Helicigona lapicida	-	-	-	-	-	-	-	-	-	-	-	+	-	-	-	1	-	-	-	-	-
Arianta arbustorum	-	-	-	-	-	-	-	-	-	-	-	-	-	-	-	-	-	-	-	-	-
Cepaea hortensis	-	-	1	-	-	-	-	-	-	-	-	-	-	-	1	-	-	-	1	-	-
Cepaea/Arianta wp	9	8	10	1	9	5	6	5	7	4	6	6	16	15	5	3	1	2	11	8	1
Cepaea/Arianta pp	4	6	4	5	1	2	4	2	5	7	3	4	1	8	3	2	-	5	12	3	3
Slug plates	48	62	52	31	38	51	32	29	44	39	53	59	59	88	43	21	7	25	112	50	24
Eggs	-	-	-	-	-	-	-	-	-	-	-	-	-	-	-	-	-	1	-	-	-

than under grassland, but not to this extent. In effect, this can only mean severe disruption of the soil down to the chalk and bringing up the chalk to the soil surface. The surprise is that any stratification of snail species remains at all, although the top two centimetres of this are likely to be post-disturbance (as already discussed), and this is where the best stratification lies.

Discussion of the pre-bank environment

The natural vegetation was probably woodland, although there is no certain indication of this in the subsoil hollows. Even so, the high diversity of the fauna indicates nearby woodland, and this is also shown by the speed and completeness with which woodland regenerated in the outer ditch (see below). There is good evidence for woodland from Avebury and Easton Down in the pre-Neolithic period (Evans *et al.* 1985; Whittle *et al.* 1993) so there is no reason why it should not have existed on Windmill Hill as well.

For the actual environment of the pre-bank soil, one scenario would be some kind of grassland but with considerable diversity, which could be close bushes of scrub like juniper and hawthorn as one gets on some areas of regenerating chalk today (Stockbridge Down in Hampshire is a very good example of this). Later there was a trend to denser scrub. However, the fauna seems too diverse for this. An implication of this scenario is that, if we allow the natural vegetation to have been woodland, then the hilltop must have had a history of woodland clearance and subsequent landuse, the establishment of grassland and then severe turbation of the soil, prior to an episode of scrub regeneration.

Another scenario would be grassland among woodland: a kind of park landscape. This is currently in favour both among archaeologists who like to see Neolithic people using the woodlands in a controlled way as a routine part of their economy (e.g. Whittle 1997b), and palaeobotanists who are creating models of forest farming, especially for the pre-elm decline period, in which grassland plays a role (Edwards 1993). It might also accommodate the snail fauna better. Low intensity landuse of this kind, away from main areas of settlement and arable, would also fit in with the future role of Windmill Hill as the siting of a causewayed enclosure on land between settlements.

Whatever the case, there was subsequently a period of substantial disturbance, explicable in several possible ways: by pigs taking over the woodland grassland and rooting up the chalk subsoil; by ritual ploughing say with a rip ard of the kind suggested by the South Street evidence (Fowler and Evans 1967) to prepare the area for the future enclosure (a kind of consecration); or by clearance of woodland itself in advance of enclosure construction and the dragging of trees across the area. One still has to allow for the slight interval between disturbance and enclosure construction (the thin worm zone at the surface of the soil and the trend away from grassland, probably to scrub), but

perhaps the outer bank was built later than the other two circuits and the disturbance relates to them (see also chapter 17).

Even so, there are many peculiarities about the pre-bank snails and soils: the rubbly nature of the soil; the high diversity of the fauna; and the predominance of catholic species and the absence of any clear ecological picture. Other Neolithic soils in the area have given a much clearer picture.

The outer ditch fill *(figs 102–3; table 56)*

Trench B, column B1: a complete outer ditch sequence

The species were grouped in the histograms according to their behaviour through the sequence, and these were different from those in the buried soil under the bank. Species in very low abundance were ordered according to their ecology. Essentially this is a more conventional grouping, with woodland species on the left, intermediate species in the middle, and obligate xerophiles on the right; *Vallonia costata*, whose behaviour can be in common with any of these ecological groupings, is plotted separately.

The primary fill is from the bottom up to 185 cm on the basis of the fill itself. The fauna is a woodland one from the beginning with practically no open-country species and huge numbers of *C. tridentatum, D. rotundatus* and zonitids. This is quite different from the situation in the South Street long barrow where open-country species were common (Evans 1972; Evans in Ashbee *et al.* 1979), and is good evidence for a generally wooded environment around the enclosure.

Additionally, rock-rubble species, *Vitrea* and *Oxychilus* (Evans and Jones 1973), are common by comparison with their later decline and in contrast to the paucity of some other woodland species which later become common (e.g. *Aegopinella, Acanthinula* and a number of species of low abundance). This implies that the fauna of the primary fill had characteristics which were peculiar to the fill material itself (for example, loose rock rubble with interstices into which the snails could burrow, and a paucity of plant food; both *Oxychilus* and *Vitrea* are carnivores).

From 185 to 170 cm, numbers of shells are low and this may still be primary fill, as indicated by the lens of chalk at 170 cm. The fauna is also extremely rich in species. Hence it is not just the relative abundance of woodland snails and the virtual absence of open-country ones but also the species richness of the fauna that indicates woodland.

Up to 100 cm the fauna remains consistent although there are marked fluctuations in abundance, especially a drop between about 145 and 130 cm, which corresponds to an increase of rubble. Since there was no recalculation of numbers for rubble weight this drop might be due to low sample size, but it seems too large for that and there is probably a response to adverse environmental conditions as well. On recovery, there is no difference in relative species abundances, as the percentage diagram shows.

There is little doubt that woodland was growing in the ditch during its infilling.

At 100 cm there is a substantial change, with a drop in almost all the woodland species and an increase in open-country species. This is really quite sharp, and these trends continue up to 63 cm. This looks like a soil A-horizon since it is so humic, and it is noteworthy how many residual shells of *Pomatias elegans* there are in contrast to the layers lower down. Also, the clear gradations of the woodland species suggest a soil and the peak of *Vallonia costata* at 67–72 cm its surface. What sort of change is indicated? It was a gradual one because the changes in the snails are gradual; woodland species are substantially abundant at the bottom although declining to practically zero at the top, and there is no great and sudden influx of open-country species. Diversity increases too and this is a sign of gradual faunal change. Ploughing was not involved, and that is also clear from the ditch section (fig. 77) which shows an irregular base to the soil across the ditch and no continuation of this horizon on to a weathering ramp (note exactly the opposite situation in all these respects at South Street: Ashbee *et al.* 1979). So gradual opening up of the woodland can be suggested, but without the establishment of pure grassland. It is only at the surface, 67–72 cm, that open-country species appear in any significance, and grassland is implied.

At 67 cm there is a thin layer of chalk rubble which signals disturbance on the ditch sides although it does not actually continue to the ditch edges in the section. At this point, there is a dramatic drop in diversity, woodland species become practically absent, there is a decline in *V. costata*, open-country species begin to increase quite sharply and there is a huge increase of *Trichia hispida*. The environment has obviously become much more open, and quite – but not altogether – suddenly, but the causes of the change, especially why it is so sudden, are unknown.

The fauna as a whole from 67 to 47 cm is actually very distinctive and implies environmental stability of some sort or another (note the consistent low in the rubble histogram), certainly open grassland, and perhaps moderate or light grazing.

At 47–40 cm, there is an inwash of fine chalky and loamy material which is a Romano-British ploughsoil going right across the ditch. Initially it has absolutely no effect on the fauna at all but at its surface, *V. costata* more or less dies out.

At 28 cm two species of helicellines, *Cernuella virgata* and *Candidula intersecta* appear (the few occurrences lower down are probably contaminants down wormholes), and these are probably Roman or later introductions into the English fauna.

Trenches A and C, columns A3 and C2: sequences from the secondary fill

These samples came from the secondary fill and were made up entirely of woodland species, the faunas being virtually identical to the zone in B1 between 170 and 100 cm.

The middle and inner ditch fills *(figs 104–5; table 57)*

For the middle ditch, 0.4 kg samples were analysed from Trench D, column D1 (fig. 104). The samples came from the secondary fine chalky fill, up to the Romano-British ploughsoil. For the inner ditch, 0.4 kg samples were analysed from Trench F, column F2 (fig. 105). The samples came from the secondary fine chalky fill, up to the base of the modern turf.

The fills were very conflated by comparison with that of the outer ditch, although the same basic sequence was present in both. The fauna is a mixed one of woodland, intermediate and open-country species. Woodland species are declining but open-country ones are not especially abundant. It appears to be equivalent to the zone of the outer ditch between 100 and 67 cm.

Discussion of the ditch sequence

The beginning of the ditch sequence confirms the picture given by the pre-bank soil, that the dominant environment surrounding the enclosure was not an open-country one, whatever the precise nature of the vegetation may have been. As already discussed in considerable detail elsewhere (Whittle *et al.* 1993), this contrasts with other sampled situations in the area, principally under long barrows, which, as at Easton Down, South Street, Horslip and Beckhampton Road, have evidence for longer periods of grassland at the end of their pre-construction sequences. Taken at face value, therefore, the differences between the evidence from Windmill Hill and other sites sampled in this area could imply that a less open situation was deliberately chosen for the construction of the enclosure (cf. Whittle 1993). This appears to match the situation also being suggested for at least some other enclosures recently investigated, including Maiden Castle (Sharples 1991; Evans *et al.* 1988).

Does this simple model stand up? There is variation among the Avebury area long barrow sites too (Evans 1972, *passim*), and indeed within the situations under individual long barrows (e.g. at Easton Down: Whittle *et al.* 1993; cf. Dimbleby and Evans 1974), just as there is further variation demonstrable from what is known of the Kennet valley-bottom at this time (Evans *et al.* 1993). It is at least as likely that the Windmill Hill sequence is different merely in its timescale or its final sequence of events. It too may have seen earlier disturbance including clearance and perhaps cultivation (see also chapter 6), and the overall regional picture may be of an unstable and fluctuating mosaic of woodland, scrub and small, short-lived clearances.

It is disappointing that the fills of the middle and inner ditches were conflated by comparison with that of the outer ditch. It is possible to argue that a slower rate of woodland regeneration can be seen in those fills compared to the situation in the outer ditch (Fishpool 1992), and, if the

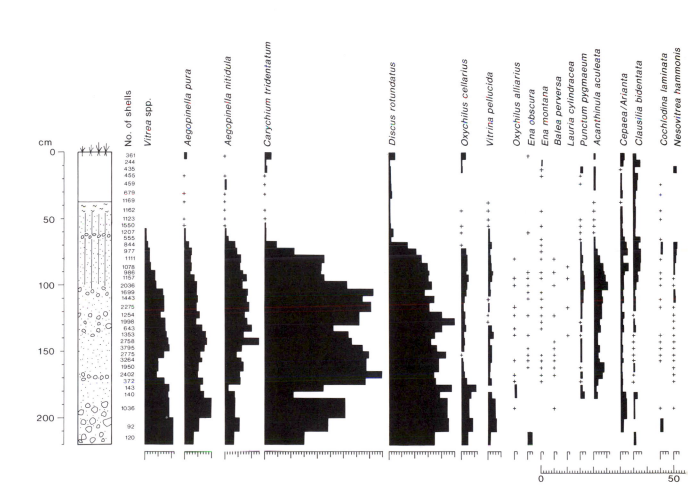

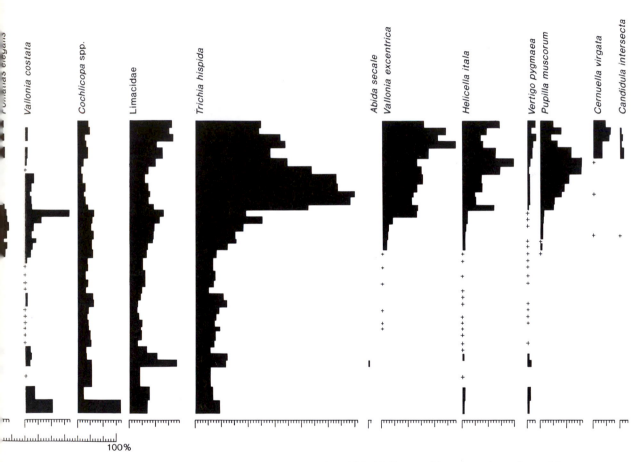

Fig. 103. Molluscan histogram for column B1, percentages.

Table 56: outer ditches, molluscan analysis results.

BB1

	0-5	5-10	10-15	15-20	20-28	28-34	34-40	40-47	47-53	53-57	57-63	63-67	67-72	72-77	77-83	83-89	89-92	92-97	97-103	103-108	108-113	113-120
Pomatias elegans (>2mm)	3	1	2	–	2	3	2	–	4	4	8	1	15	13	14	19	13	17	34	8	10	10
Pomatias elegans (<2mm)	4	3	7	6	9	3	9	7	14	7	9	11	10	15	29	13	4	20	17	10	4	9
Carychium tridentatum	9	1	3	1	1	–	–	1	3	6	8	3	37	109	250	230	208	260	636	702	532	921
Cochlicopa lubrica	1	–	–	–	2	2	2	–	4	1	–	1	5	4	2	–	2	2	3	5	4	9
Cochlicope lubricella	–	–	–	3	1	4	4	4	4	2	1	–	1	2	1	–	–	3	3	4	–	1
Cochlicopa spp.	15	12	12	15	16	15	10	21	28	34	36	21	49	50	55	67	53	60	120	60	57	59
Columella edentula	–	–	–	–	–	–	–	–	–	–	–	–	–	–	–	–	–	–	–	–	–	1
Vertigo pygmaea	11	3	14	9	9	7	6	8	8	12	11	3	–	3	1	–	3	2	1	1	1	1
Abida secale	–	–	–	–	–	–	–	–	–	–	–	–	–	–	–	–	–	–	–	–	–	–
Pupilla muscorum	17	19	16	29	53	105	180	123	101	121	62	27	11	10	9	9	2	5	2	–	1	2
Lauria cylindracea	–	–	–	–	–	–	–	–	–	–	–	–	–	–	–	1	–	1	–	–	1	1
Vallonia costata	2	3	3	3	3	4	4	36	24	15	25	13	139	57	32	24	39	29	33	8	2	1
Vallonia excentrica	56	58	91	125	79	86	172	175	145	182	131	75	109	36	25	37	16	50	104	47	47	69
Acanthinula aculeata	2	1	3	3	3	4	4	3	2	3	4	3	1	2	2	–	1	1	3	4	2	3
Ena montana	–	1	1	–	–	–	–	1	–	–	–	–	–	–	2	–	1	–	–	–	–	–
Ena obscura	1	–	–	–	–	–	–	–	–	–	3	1	1	–	–	–	1	–	3	1	2	3
Punctum pygmaeum	9	3	3	1	1	–	–	–	–	1	4	1	3	4	9	6	10	15	30	15	17	11
Discus rotundatus	–	3	3	4	9	5	5	5	11	22	5	62	102	139	161	153	175	333	230	250	351	7
Vitrina pellucida wp	–	–	–	–	–	2	2	1	4	1	4	7	6	7	11	14	14	3	2	15	5	165
Vitrina pellucida pp	–	–	–	–	–	–	1	2	2	2	1	2	3	3	3	2	2	2	2	2	2	7
Vitrea spp.	–	5	–	–	–	–	–	–	–	–	5	10	12	13	10	9	4	44	85	9	10	100
Nesovitrea hammonis	4	–	–	1	–	1	–	–	1	1	7	3	12	13	28	29	23	44	90	77	71	203
Aegopinella pura	1	–	–	3	8	1	4	4	5	4	6	7	14	26	66	60	66	94	131	144	117	16
Aegopinella nitidula	6	1	2	1	1	1	4	2	3	3	1	2	30	44	24	24	17	31	44	30	15	1
Oxychilus cellarius	4	–	–	–	–	–	2	2	1	1	1	–	2	19	2	1	1	1	1	–	–	–
Oxychilus alliarius	–	–	–	–	–	–	–	–	–	–	–	–	–	–	–	–	–	–	–	–	–	1
Euconulus fulvus	4	2	2	9	2	2	2	2	1	1	1	1	1	1	2	3	3	3	7	3	3	14
Cecilioides acicula	1	1	–	3	2	2	3	1	4	4	4	4	5	5	22	24	14	15	15	6	9	2
Cochlodina laminata	2	–	3	2	1	–	4	3	4	7	5	10	21	21	24	4	14	2	5	1	1	–
Clausilia bidentata wp	2	5	5	5	5	5	5	9	7	3	2	10	4	4	5	1	1	5	1	1	1	–
Clausilia bidentata pp	–	–	–	–	–	–	–	–	–	–	–	–	1	1	1	1	–	–	1	–	1	–
Balea perversa	–	–	–	–	1	1	–	1	–	–	–	–	–	–	–	–	–	–	–	–	–	–
Candidula intersecta	5	1	6	1	8	–	–	–	1	1	–	42	6	2	1	1	–	–	–	–	–	3
Cernuella virgata	16	7	8	3	8	2	1	2	2	67	43	25	11	8	9	9	6	10	4	1	–	3
Helicella itala	46	10	16	30	112	143	70	63	67	8	19	235	158	11	5	3	5	3	4	–	–	166
Helicellinae indet.	89	22	29	38	21	22	21	21	598	924	700	158	245	198	161	151	138	138	159	111	93	–
Trichia hispida	–	58	42	153	128	233	509	612	1	1	2	1	1	–	1	1	1	1	1	1	–	–
Arianta arbustorum	–	–	–	–	–	–	–	–	–	–	–	–	–	–	–	–	–	1	–	1	–	–
Cepaea nemoralis	–	–	–	–	–	–	1	2	2	4	3	2	9	16	8	21	8	9	17	5	12	9
Cepaea hortensis	2	–	1	–	2	3	1	6	5	3	4	6	7	7	6	6	2	2	3	4	3	1
Cepaea/Arianta wp	3	2	2	2	4	3	6	5	77	118	83	50	108	109	85	10	6	76	128	82	66	132
Cepaea/Arianta pp	57	36	71	45	56	63	50	64	77	118	83	50	108	109	103	97	85	76	128	82	66	132
Slug plates	3	1	1	1	2	1	1	–	1	2	2	–	1	1	1	1	1	1	1	–	–	–
Eggs	3	1	1	1	2	1	1	–	1	2	2	–	1	–	1	1	1	1	1	–	–	–

Table 56 continued: outer ditches, molluscan analysis results.

	BB1																A3			C2
	120-125	125-130	130-135	135-140	140-145	145-150	150-155	155-158	158-165	165-170	170-175	175-180	180-185	185-200	200-210	210-220	94-100	110-116	115-120	125-130
Pomatias elegans (>2mm)	5	12	1	2	10	16	11	23	16	5	1	-	-	-	-	-	6	11	-	-
Pomatias elegans (<2mm)	6	6	-	3	6	6	7	12	5	2	1	+	-	-	-	-	1	5	1	-
Carychium tridentatum	451	719	165	428	913	1408	1095	1261	752	1078	142	32	15	316	22	15	164	356	113	157
Cochlicopa lubrica	2	4	2	5	15	13	8	19	4	10	2	2	-	3	2	-	1	1	3	1
Cochlicope lubricella	2	1	-	4	5	4	8	2	10	4	-	-	-	6	1	1	-	-	3	2
Cochlicopa spp.	45	57	38	77	97	129	102	121	84	114	10	8	8	51	2	17	24	31	37	27
Columella edentula	-	-	-	-	-	-	-	-	-	-	-	-	-	-	-	-	-	1	-	-
Vertigo pygmaea	2	-	-	-	-	-	3	-	-	1	-	1	1	-	1	1	-	-	-	-
Abida secale	-	-	-	-	-	-	-	-	-	-	-	-	-	-	-	-	2	-	-	-
Pupilla muscorum	-	-	-	-	-	-	-	-	-	-	-	-	-	-	-	-	2	-	-	-
Lauria cylindracea	-	-	1	-	-	-	-	-	-	-	-	-	1	-	-	-	-	-	-	-
Vallonia costata	3	1	4	7	4	9	8	11	5	5	3	3	2	2	3	12	14	6	5	7
Vallonia excentrica	-	-	-	-	1	2	2	2	1	1	-	-	-	-	-	1	2	-	2	2
Acanthinula aculeata	37	39	16	15	39	50	44	66	77	50	6	1	2	-	3	-	31	46	20	15
Ena montana	1	2	1	1	-	2	1	-	2	1	1	-	-	-	-	-	1	1	-	1
Ena obscura	-	2	-	1	-	2	1	2	2	-	-	-	2	-	-	2	3	1	3	-
Punctum pygmaeum	6	6	3	3	11	15	10	15	5	17	1	1	2	-	-	-	6	3	1	1
Discus rotundatus	252	497	129	237	441	659	602	621	370	410	66	34	27	231	21	21	60	150	130	93
Vitrina pellucida wp	3	4	8	28	17	53	35	43	16	17	5	2	2	26	3	1	2	5	9	15
Vitrina pellucida pp	1	1	1	-	-	-	-	1	1	1	1	-	-	2	-	-	-	1	-	-
Vitrea spp.	73	152	50	110	239	350	195	158	98	112	28	13	12	95	10	13	48	47	36	63
Nesovitrea hammonis	4	3	2	5	2	2	4	2	1	2	-	-	-	1	-	-	1	-	-	1
Aegopinella pura	69	86	42	107	224	272	156	210	99	115	25	8	10	100	5	4	29	40	21	42
Aegopinella nitidula	92	166	64	92	352	235	115	195	134	133	21	2	5	35	5	4	41	91	43	49
Oxychilus cellarius	19	27	11	13	34	39	3	20	15	29	8	5	5	30	4	3	7	4	3	8
Oxychilus alliarius	1	-	1	1	-	2	-	2	-	1	1	1	2	-	-	-	2	1	-	-
Euconulus fulvus	-	-	-	-	-	-	-	-	-	1	-	-	-	-	-	-	1	-	-	-
Cecilioides acicula	-	-	-	-	-	-	-	-	-	-	-	-	-	-	-	-	-	-	-	-
Cochlodina laminata	-	-	-	-	-	-	1	-	-	1	-	-	-	1	-	-	1	1	1	1
Clausilia bidentata wp	2	7	3	3	3	3	6	-	5	1	1	2	2	3	1	1	3	6	2	-
Clausilia bidentata pp	2	3	2	-	2	-	5	10	-	-	-	-	-	2	-	-	-	-	-	-
Balea perversa	2	-	-	-	2	1	1	1	2	-	-	-	3	3	-	1	1	1	1	-
Candidula intersecta	-	-	-	-	2	2	4	-	-	-	-	-	-	-	-	-	-	-	-	-
Cernuella virgata	-	-	1	-	-	-	-	-	-	1	1	-	-	2	1	-	2	1	-	-
Helicella itala	-	1	-	-	3	7	1	1	-	-	-	1	-	-	-	-	1	-	-	-
Hellicellinae indet.	-	2	-	3	3	-	-	2	-	1	-	-	-	-	-	-	4	-	-	-
Trichia hispida	85	95	67	159	241	290	192	299	144	166	20	17	16	55	6	11	34	75	43	30
Arianta arbustorum	-	1	-	-	-	1	-	-	1	1	-	-	1	1	-	-	-	-	-	-
Cepaea nemoralis	-	-	-	-	-	-	1	-	-	-	-	-	-	-	-	-	-	-	-	-
Cepaea hortensis	-	-	-	-	1	-	-	-	-	-	-	-	-	-	-	-	-	-	-	-
Cepaea/Arianta wp	11	13	6	6	10	24	14	28	11	14	1	3	3	22	1	3	3	10	5	3
Cepaea/Arianta pp	5	3	1	1	7	7	1	4	-	2	2	1	1	1	-	4	-	-	-	-
Slug plates	71	90	26	39	75	134	130	135	85	71	24	15	25	40	7	8	38	44	33	27
Eggs	-	-	-	3	-	-	-	-	-	-	-	-	-	-	-	-	1	-	1	-

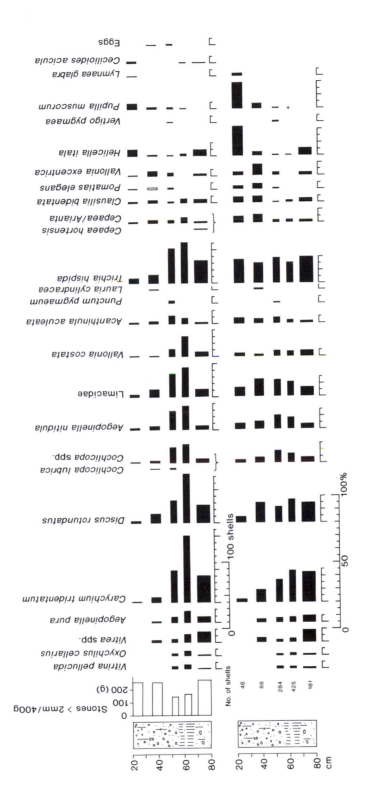

Fig. 104. Middle ditch, molluscan histogram for column D1, absolute numbers above, percentages below.

Mark Fishpool

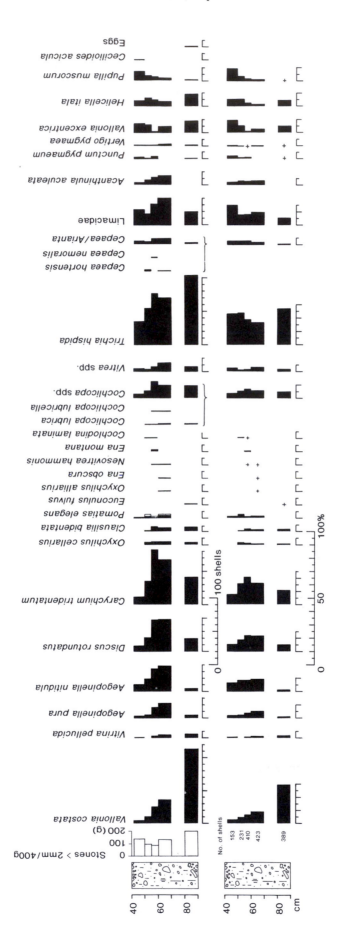

Fig. 105. Inner ditch, molluscan histogram for column F2, absolute numbers above, percentages below.

Table 57: Middle and inner ditches, molluscan, analysis results.

Sample size 400 g.

	D1					F2				
	20-27.5	25-42.5	50-55	60-65	70-80	42-50	50-55	55-60	60-70	80-90
Pomatias elegans (>2mm)	1	-	1	-	-	1	2	1	3	-
Pomatias elegans (<2mm)	-	3	1	-	-	-	5	1	2	-
Carychium tridentatum	1	8	48	100	40	11	35	82	67	41
Lymnaea glabra	1	-	-	-	-	-	-	-	-	-
Cochlicopa lubrica	-	1	2	-	-	-	1	1	2	2
Cochlicopa lubricella	-	-	-	-	-	-	-	1	1	-
Cochlicopa spp.	1	3	23	27	6	6	11	25	19	18
Vertigo pygmaea	-	-	1	-	-	1	1	1	2	1
Pupilla muscorum	9	3	2	1	-	14	8	6	4	1
Lauria cylindracea	-	1	-	-	-	-	-	-	-	-
Vallonia costata	1	1	11	15	7	4	10	25	36	113
Vallonia eccentrica	1	7	5	-	3	14	12	2	10	18
Acanthinula aculeata	2	3	12	9	2	3	7	11	13	-
Ena montana	-	-	-	-	-	-	-	3	-	-
Ena obscura	-	-	-	-	-	-	-	-	1	-
Punctum pygmaeum	-	-	2	-	-	3	1	4	-	1
Discus rotundatus	2	13	33	73	26	8	20	47	48	19
Vitrina pellucida	-	-	4	7	2	1	-	3	5	6
Vitrea spp.	-	3	5	12	16	4	3	7	13	7
Nesovitrea hammonis	-	-	-	-	-	-	-	1	1	-
Aegopinella pura	-	2	9	17	9	3	5	16	22	4
Aegopinella nitidula	2	5	25	35	6	10	19	34	38	4
Oxychilus cellarius	-	-	3	7	1	-	3	4	3	3
Oxychilus alliarius	-	-	-	-	-	-	-	-	1	-
Euconulus fulvus	-	-	-	-	-	-	-	-	-	1
Cecilioides acicula	3	-	-	1	1	1	-	-	-	-
Cochlodina laminata	-	-	-	-	-	-	1	1	-	-
Clausilia bidentata	2	4	2	6	5	-	1	7	5	6
Helicella itala	9	1	1	2	6	5	6	5	3	10
Helicellinae indet.	1	1	-	1	3	3	6	4	4	8
Trichia hispida	8	13	52	61	34	35	54	77	70	104
Cepaea nemoralis	-	-	-	-	-	-	-	1	-	-
Cepaea hortensis	-	-	-	-	1	-	2	-	1	-
Cepaea/Arianta	2	5	4	8	2	4	3	8	8	2
Slug plates	3	11	35	44	12	23	17	32	41	20
Eggs	-	1	2	-	-	-	-	-	-	1

inner and middle circuits preceded the outer circuit, the contrast between the inner and outer parts of the enclosure – between an inner, more open area of perhaps more intense activity and an outer area closer to woodland, park woodland or woodland/scrub – is all the more accentuated. Such possible environmental variation across a causewayed enclosure appears not to have been investigated elsewhere, and it remains somewhat uncertain at Windmill Hill.

Apart from the issues already discussed of the environment preceding and contemporary with enclosure construction, the ditch sequences as a whole raise an important question about the subsequent regional environment. Why did closed or dense woodland unrelieved by any open-country go on for so long in the ditches when the area as a whole (as seen at Avebury, the West Kennet enclosure and Silbury Hill: Smith 1965a; Whittle 1997a) is so

important and used in the Later Neolithic? Was there a later taboo on Windmill Hill, after the first main phase of its construction and primary use? Clearly some activity was taking place at the site because there are the strong rubble layers in the outer ditch during the woodland stage, but apart from fluctuations in shell numbers they have no effect on the fauna or, by inference, the vegetation. The kind of activity that this may represent remains to be established (cf. Evans 1990).

The greater openness of the environment at an approximately equivalent stage at South Street and Millbarrow (Ashbee *et al.* 1979; Whittle 1994) may be due to the fact that the areas around those sites, to the south and north of Windmill Hill respectively, were more used or that they had been more substantially cleared of woodland initially, but the contrast with Windmill Hill remains.

In the outer ditch sequence, a trend is set in motion at 100 cm to more open conditions and is maintained, though gradually, through the layer up to 67 cm. This is nothing to do with taphonomy *sensu stricto*; the changes are ecological. What was the nature and cause of the change at 100 cm ? This and the subsequent gradual changes to 67 cm remain unclear. The Later Neolithic use of the outer ditch is discussed also in chapters 6, 13 and 17.

The change at 67 cm (in the top part of the upper secondary fill) is clearer, and the subsequent environment was grassland to 47 cm. But was this just a culmination of the previous progression or was it a real break caused by a new kind of land use ? This is the first time there is any grassland on the hill since the bank was built. At the Late Neolithic or Early Bronze Age date of this phase (see especially chapter 13) Windmill Hill can at last be aligned securely with the general regional trend, towards open-country, which has been widely documented in the area.

8

Charred Plant Remains

Andrew Fairbairn

Introduction

Cultivation of wheat and other domestic crops has tradition-ally been considered as one of the central characteristics of the Neolithic way of life and part of the 'Neolithic package' which replaced the gatherer-hunter Mesolithic societies across south-west Asia and Europe (Piggott 1954; Darvill 1987; Thomas 1996a). Windmill Hill causewayed enclos-ure played an important role in firmly establishing this version of events. Hans Helbaek's account (1952) of the pottery impressions of cultivated and wild plants from Windmill Hill provided the first detailed, quantitative study of plant use in Neolithic Britain. He firmly implanted the idea of the dominance of cereal agriculture in the British Neolithic, arguing that the overwhelming abundance of cultivated remains in the assemblage indicated that the population which used the site had a well developed farming economy; the active cultivation of wheats (especially emmer) and barley provided the main plant economic component supplemented by crops such as flax and gathered wild foods, including apple.

With the exception of the identification of some pre-viously unrecognised regional patterns of crop cultivation in a re-interpretation of the impressions on pottery (Dennell 1976), Helbaek's interpretation of the importance of arable agriculture was accepted through the period of processual archaeology. Subsequently Pryor doubted the prevalence of fields of corn in the Neolithic landscape (Pryor 1988a). This view was supported by Moffett *et al.* (1989) who also suggested that wild gathered foods played a much larger role in the Neolithic plant economy than had previously been thought, retaining an importance well into the Bronze Age. These interpretations have been part of a wholesale reconsideration of British Neolithic life which in contrast to the traditional model sees the subsistence economy as based on a suite of food acquisition strategies including hunting, gathering, herding and growing crops in a system of transient hoe-based agriculture practised by a mobile population (Entwistle and Grant 1989).

A more radical re-interpretation of the evidence has suggested that domestic plants (and animals) had a purely symbolic significance in Neolithic Britain making only a minimal contribution to the caloric intake (Thomas 1993, 388; 1996a). Use and adoption of cereals was essentially a small-scale affair linked more to the negotiation of social relations than the quest for calories in a Neolithic world diverse in its social, economic and cultural characteristics (Thomas 1993). The theoretical perspective adopted by Thomas endows plants with non-functional attributes as symbols and situates them within a conceptual order drawing on, in this case, an opposition between wild and tame. Such an approach accounts for active Neolithic individuals, siting their actions within a specific historical context. This account is important as it marks a funda-mental shift in the archaeological treatment of plants, moving away from the positivist techno-environmental perspective (*sensu* Bender 1978) of the previously cited authors who largely interpret plants as functional economic entities in systems of value and exchange identical to those in operation today (Edmonds 1993), the use of which is ultimately directed by long-term processes of cultural and economic evolution in response to environmental factors.

These more recent interpretations are not without their critics on methodological as well as theoretical grounds (Legge 1989; see also Barclay 1997). Recent discoveries of Neolithic longhouses at Balbridie, Scotland (Fair-weather and Ralston 1993), and Lismore Fields, Derby-shire (Glynis Jones *pers. comm.*), with evidence of large stores of domestic produce and long-term settlement must also bring into question the universal applicability of a mobile, gatherer-hunter Neolithic. In this context of re-evaluation of the role of plants in the Neolithic world and indeed of what constitutes the Neolithic as a whole, there is a certain historical resonance in the re-investigation of the evidence for plant usage at Windmill Hill causewayed enclosure, where the current debate on Neolithic plant use and significance has its empirical roots. The 1988

Andrew Fairbairn

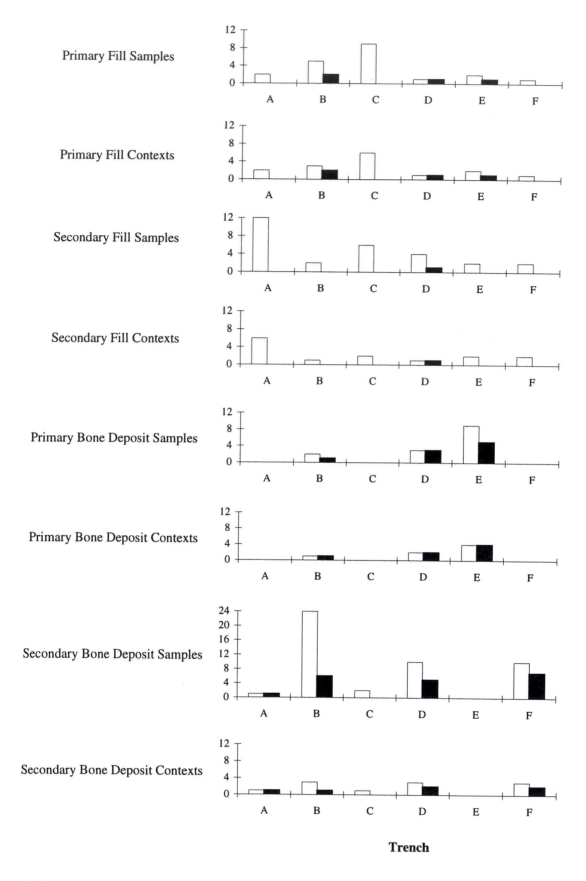

Fig. 106. Numbers of sampled contexts and charred plant remain samples collected, plotted by trench, context and fill types. White column represents total number of samples/contexts.

excavations at the causewayed enclosure provided an opportunity for a large-scale soil-sampling and flotation programme to recover charred plant remains and this report details the analysis and interpretation of the recovered material.

Site and laboratory methods

Bulk soil samples were collected throughout the excavation from each trench, and from every type of excavated context. A standard 10-litre sample size was used and a total of 139 samples were recovered from 54 contexts (fig. 106). Processing in the field consisted of Siraf-type flotation using a 0.3 mm mesh sieve to collect any floating charred material. The dry flots were sorted in the laboratory without sub-sampling using a binocular microscope, and all non-wood charred remains were removed for identification. A Wild M8 dissecting microscope was used during both sorting and identification operating at 10x-50x magnification. The reference collections of University College London Institute of Archaeology were used during the identifications; Gordon Hillman gave advice and verification of the cereal and seed identifications and Jon Hather identified the parenchymatous (i.e. root and tuber) remains using anatomical features observable on the scanning electron microscope (Hather 1993). The identifications are presented in tables 58–71 with nomenclature and taxonomic order for cereals largely following van Zeist (1984) and that for wild plant taxa following Stace (1991). The name *Hordeum vulgare* has been used to describe all domestic barley grains and does not refer specifically to any one variety. The assignation of barley type is discussed below.

Results

Although all the flots were carefully picked through, only 42 of the 139 contained non-wood charred plant remains, from 26 contexts. The individual sample assemblages contained few remains, all of which were badly preserved and represented relatively few species, a pattern of representation that is commonly recorded in investigations of

British Neolithic sites (Moffett *et al.* 1989). The grains and chaff of domestic cereals were present as were a number of wild species represented by the remains of seeds, fruits, nutshell, roots and tubers.

Identified taxa

The identified plant taxa from the site are summarised in table 58. Cereal remains consisted mostly of grains and grain fragments, many of which were badly preserved and beyond identification. Among these several whole and fragmented specimens were tentatively identified as einkorn wheat (*Triticum monococcum* L.). Einkorn is one of the first plant domesticates and an uncommon, although not unknown find in Britain (Moffett *et al.* 1989; Murphy 1988). Its grains were distinguished by their convex ventral and dorsal surfaces and attenuated distal and proximal apices. Grains of emmer wheat (*Triticum dicoccum* (Schrank) Schubl.) were also present as well as several grain specimens which could have been produced by either glume wheat species. The overlapping morphology of the grains of many of the wheat species may cast some doubt on the species level identifications of the wheat grains at the site due to the often single occurrence of the specimens in sampled contexts. Larger concentrations of grains would have provided some scope for the investigation of morphological variation using measurements and measurement ratios and could have made the identifications more certain. In this case only specimens with well developed, distinctive morphologies were given a species binomial.

Both symmetrical and asymmetrical grains of barley were identified. The presence of several distinctive asymmetrical, hulled lateral grains established the presence of six-row hulled barley (*Hordeum vulgare* L.), although the symmetrical hulled grains of barley may have derived from six-row or two-rowed forms. A single badly eroded wheat spikelet fork was the only piece of chaff identified at the site. The presence of primary and secondary keels, the sharp angles of the glumes and the overall size of the specimen suggested that the spikelet fork was from either einkorn or emmer wheat (Jacomet 1987; Gordon Hillman *pers. comm.*). Poor preservation prevented identification beyond this level.

Table 58: Plant taxa identified in the charred plant remain assemblages.

Latin name	Common name	Identified component
Triticum monococcum L.	einkorn wheat	grain
Triticum dicoccum (Schrank) Schubl.	emmer wheat	grain & glume base
Hordeum vulgare L.	six-row hulled barley	grain
Ranunculus flammula L.	lesser spearwort	fruit
Ranunculus ficaria L.	lesser celandine	tuber
Chenopodium album L.	fat hen	fruit
Polygonum cf. *arenastrum.* L.	knotweed	fruit
Conopodium majus (Gouan) Loret	pignut	tuber
Prunus spinosa L.	blackthorn	fruit stone
Corylus avellana L.	hazel	nut shell
Galium aparine L.	cleavers	fruit
Poa cf. *annua* L.	annual meadow-grass	fruit
Poa cf. *trivialis* L.	rough meadow-grass	fruit
Lolium L. sp.	rye grass	fruit

The remains of non-domestic plant taxa included several plants of disturbed habitats which may also be agricultural weeds such as cleavers (*Galium aparine* L.), fat hen (*Chenopodium album* L.), knotweed (*Polygonum arenastrum* L.), and poppy (*Papaver* L. sp.). A seed of the wetland plant lesser spearwort (*Ranunculus flammula* L.) was also identified along with a number of grass (Poaceae) taxa by Gordon Hillman. The lesser spearwort seed was small, poorly developed and may have been immature. Among the grass seeds were identified annual and rough meadow grass (*Poa annua* and *Poa trivialis* respectively) and an indeterminate rye grass species (*Lolium* L. sp.). Other remains included a single fragment of hazelnut shell (*Corylus avellana* L.) and an endocarp (fruitstone) of sloe (*Prunus spinosa* L.). Two types of charred vegetative parenchymatous tissue were identified, the first from the tubers of lesser celandine (*Ranunculus ficaria* L.) and a specimen which may have derived from the tuber of pignut (*Conopodium majus* (Gouan) Loret) or great pignut (*Bunium bulbocastanum* L.). Many small seeds and fruits were present which were unidentifiable due to the poor preservation of diagnostic features.

Plant remains distribution

Pre-bank features in Trench BB *(tables 59–60)*
Twenty samples were collected from 11 pre-bank contexts, four of which contained plant remains. The subsoil hollow 712 was the earliest sampled feature on the site and

produced no plant remains. Of the eight samples collected from the old land surface, only two produced charred plant remains. The sample from the turfline 741 contained one grain of einkorn wheat, with the charcoal concentration 743 yielding one emmer wheat grain, one indeterminate cereal grain and several seeds degraded beyond identification. The three postholes 760, 711 and 752 contained no identifiable remains. A six-row hulled barley grain and several unidentifiable cereals and seeds were present in one of three samples from the fill of the pre-bank grave and a barley grain was recovered from the single sample collected from pit 714.

Outer ditch, Trench B *(tables 61–62)*
Three natural fills in the primary deposits of this ditch segment were sampled, two of which (230 and 210) contained barley grains and unidentifiable seeds. Bone deposit 227 contained a single barley grain, with 224 (a natural fill from the secondary deposits) containing only an unidentifiable cereal grain. Five upper secondary strata were sampled; the only natural fill (215) contained no charred plant remains as did the two scoop fills of 216 and 219. 220 was a scoop or animal burrow and contained a small assemblage of whole and fragmented wheat and barley grains. The possible disturbance of this feature means that as with the tertiary fill 201, which included a mixture of Romano-British and Neolithic artefacts, there is considerable uncertainty about the date or security of the finds from that context. 202 was a deep deposit of charcoal-rich, chalky soil with a large variety of Later Neolithic artefacts and animal bone. Six of the 21 samples produced plant remains including cereal grains, all wheat, and many unidentifiable seeds, several goosefoot (*Chenopodium* spp.) seeds and the only specimen of hazelnut shell from the site.

Notes for Tables 59–71: For species names see Table 58. Abbreviations: W = whole specimens, F = fragments; OLS = old land surface; LN = Later Neolithic; RB = Romano-British contamination. Phases: 1 = primary; 2 = secondary; u2 = upper secondary; 3 = tertiary.

Table 59: Sample numbers and sampled contexts from Trench BB (pre-bank features).

Context	Context type	Total samples	Productive samples
704	primary bank	1	0
707	post-hole	3	1
711	posthole	2	0
712	treehollow	1	0
714	pit fill	1	1
734	grave fill	1	0
741	ols	5	1
743	ols with charcoal	3	1
745	posthole	1	0
752	posthole	1	0
760	posthole	1	0

Table 60: Plant remains from Trench BB (pre-bank features).

	Context	707		714		741		743	
	Sample	7308		7328		7767		7618	
	Context Type	grave		pit		OLS turfline		OLS (charcoal patch)	
Taxon	Component	W	F	W	F	W	F	W	F
Triticum cf. *monococcum*	grain	.	.	.	.	.	1	.	.
Triticum cf. *dicoccum*	grain	.	.	.	.	.	.	1	.
Hordeum vulgare	hulled twisted grain	1	.	.	.	.	.	.	.
Hordeum vulgare	grain	.	.	1	.	.	.	.	.
cereal indeterminate	grain	.	6	.	.	.	.	.	1
indeterminate	seed	.	3	.	8	.	.	.	3

Table 61: Sample numbers and sampled contexts from Trench B (outer circuit).

Phase	Context	Context type	Total samples	Productive samples
3RB	201	fill	4	4
u2	202	finds rich fill	21	6
u2	215	fill	1	0
u2	216	scoop fill (deposit)	2	0
u2	219	scoop fill (deposit)	1	0
u2	220	fill (with burrow?)	1	1
2	224	fill	1	1
1	210	fill	3	1
1	227	placed bone deposit	2	1
1	228	fill	1	0
1	230	fill	1	1

Table 62: Plant remains from Trench B (outer circuit).

Context		210		227		230		224		220		202		202		202		202		202		202		201		201		201		201	
Sample		23197		23159		23284		16576		16577		2502		2601		2651		2953		9001		9712		2203		2204		2381		2382	
Context Type		fill		deposit		fill		fill		scoop/ burrow		soil		soil		soil		soil		soil		soil		fill		fill		fill		fill	
Phase		1		1		1		2		u2		u2 LN		u2 LN		u2 LN		u2 LN		u2 LN		u2 LN		3 (RB)		3 (RB)		3 (RB)		3 (RB)	
Taxon / Component		W	F	W	F	W	F	W	F	W	F	W	F	W	F	W	F	W	F	W	F	W	F	W	F	W	F	W	F	W	F
Triticum cf *dicoccum*	grain	.	.	.	.	.	.	.	.	1	1	.	.	.	.	.	.	.	.	.	.	.	.	.	.	.	.	.	.	.	.
Triticum sp.	grain	.	.	.	.	.	.	.	.	.	.	1	.	.	.	2	.	.	.	1	.	.	.	.	.	.	.	.	.	1	.
Hordeum vulgare	hulled symmetrical grain	.	.	.	.	1	.	.	.	1	.	.	.	.	.	.	.	.	.	.	.	.	.	.	.	.	.	.	.	.	.
Hordeum vulgare	twisted grain	.	.	.	.	1	.	.	.	1	.	.	.	.	.	.	.	1	.	.	.	.	.	.	.	.	.	.	.	.	.
Hordeum vulgare	symmetrical grain	1	.	.	.	.	.	.	.	.	.	.	.	.	.	.	.	.	.	.	.	.	.	.	.	.	.	.	.	.	.
Hordeum vulgare	grain	.	.	1	.	.	.	.	.	.	.	.	.	.	.	.	.	.	.	.	.	.	.	.	.	.	.	.	.	.	.
cereal indeterminate	grain	.	.	.	.	11	.	.	.	2	.	3	.	2	.	1	.	2	.	1	.	.	.	3	.	.	.	1	.	2	.
Chenopodium album	seed	.	.	.	.	.	.	1	.	.	.	.	.	.	.	.	.	1	.	.	.	2	.	.	.	.	.	.	.	.	.
Chenopodium sp.	seed	.	.	.	.	.	.	.	.	.	.	.	.	.	.	.	.	.	.	1	.	.	.	.	.	.	.	.	.	.	.
Corylus avellana	nut shell	.	.	.	.	.	.	.	.	.	.	.	.	.	.	.	.	1	.	.	.	.	.	.	.	.	.	.	.	.	.
Polygonum sp.	seed	.	.	.	.	.	.	.	.	.	.	.	.	.	.	.	.	.	.	.	.	.	.	1	.	.	.	.	.	.	.
Galium sp.	seed	.	.	.	.	.	.	.	.	.	.	.	.	.	.	.	.	1	.	.	.	.	.	.	.	.	.	.	.	.	.
Lolium sp.	seed	.	.	.	.	.	.	.	.	.	.	.	.	.	.	.	.	.	.	.	.	.	.	.	.	.	.	.	.	3	.
Poaceae indeterminate	seed	.	.	.	.	.	.	.	.	1	.	.	.	.	.	.	.	.	.	.	.	.	.	.	.	.	.	.	.	.	.
indeterminate	seed	1	.	8	.	.	.	.	.	.	.	.	.	1	.	.	.	12	.	21	.	.	.	4	.	4	.	7	.	.	.
indeterminate	dicot. tuber	.	.	.	.	8	.	.	.	.	.	.	.	.	.	.	.	.	.	.	.	.	.	.	.	.	.	.	.	.	.

Table 63: Sample numbers and sampled contexts from Trench A (outer circuit).

Phase	Context	Context type	Total samples	Productive samples
3RB	102	fill/ploughsoil	2	1
2	104	fill	4	0
2	105	charcoal rich fill	1	1
2	106	fill	2	0
2	107	charcoal rich fill	1	0
2	108	fill	1	0
2	110	charcoal rich fill	2	0
1	116	fill	1	0
1	118	fill	1	0

Table 64: Plant remains from Trench A (outer circuit).

	Context	105		102	
	Sample	1399		-	
	Context Type	charcoal patch		fill	
	Phase	2		3 (RB)	
Taxon	Component	W	F	W	F
Triticum dicoccum	grain	.	.	1	.
Triticum sp.	grain	.	.	.	1
Ranunculus ficaria	tuber	[1]	6	.	.
indeterminate	seed	.	.	.	10

Outer ditch, Trench A *(tables 63–64)*
Samples from two primary natural fills (118 and 116) contained no remains, nor did those from the secondary natural fills 108, 106, 110, 107, 106 and 104. Fills 110 and 107 contained conspicuous charcoal but no seeds or fruits. The single sample from the charcoal-rich soil of secondary fill 105 produced a tuber of lesser celandine (*Ranunculus ficaria* L.) which was the only secure Neolithic plant remain from the ditch and associated with a sarsen rubber/grinder fragment. The date for the ditch fill at this point is uncertain, but is probably Later Neolithic. One of the two samples from the tertiary fill of the ditch segment (102) contained two wheat grains, one of which was identified as emmer wheat. This upper fill included Romano-British artefacts and the grains may be derived from contamination by later ploughing making the association with Neolithic activity insecure.

Outer ditch, Trench C *(table 65)*
A total of nine samples from six primary natural fill layers (324, 312, 311, 309, 307, 319) were processed as were

four samples from three secondary natural fill layers (303-305), two from an upper secondary natural fill (316) and two from an upper secondary bone deposit (317). None of the sampled contexts contained plant remains and 317 was one of the few bone deposits to produce no charred seeds and fruits at all.

Middle ditch, Trench D *(tables 66–67)*
Most of the sampled contexts from Trench D were bone deposits or contained large quantities of charcoal, pottery and other debris representing episodes of deposition. The single sample from the natural fill 416 in the primary deposits of the ditch contained only a single cereal grain, the fill also including an ox skull and a bone concentration. The single sample from 417 produced one of the largest concentrations of plant remains from the site. This layer comprised a charcoal concentration amongst chalk debris and included emmer and einkorn wheat grains, a single wheat spikelet fork and many unidentifiable cereal grains. Both samples from bone deposit 418 contained cereal grains including a wheat and barley grain associated with

Table 65: Sample numbers and sampled contexts from Trench C (outer circuit).

Phase	Context	Context type	Total samples	Productive samples
u2	316	fill	2	0
u2	317	bone deposit	2	0
2	303	fill	1	0
2	304	fill	1	0
2	305	fill	2	0
1	307	fill	1	0
1	309	fill	1	0
1	311	fill	1	0
1	312	fill	1	0
1	319	fill	3	0
1	324	fill	2	0

Table 66: *Sample numbers and sampled contexts from Trench D (middle circuit).*

Phase	Context	Context type	Total samples	Productive samples
2	404 spit 1	charcoal scattered fill	1	1
2	404 spit 3	charcoal scattered fill	1	0
2	404 spit 5	charcoal scattered fill	1	1
2	404 spit 6	charcoal scattered fill	1	1
2	404 other	charcoal scattered fill	2	0
2	406 spit 2	charcoal scattered fill	1	1
2	406 spit 4	charcoal scattered fill	2	1
2	411	fill	4	1
2	413	bone deposit	1	0
1	416	fill	1	1
1	417	bone deposit	1	1
1	418	bone deposit?	2	2

Table 67: *Plant remains from Trench D (middle circuit).*

	Context	416		417		404 spit1		404spit5		404spit6		406spit2		406spit4		418		418		411	
	Sample	4322		4350		-		4034		-		-		-		4122		4132		4153	
	Context Type	fill		spread		spread		spread		spread		spread		spread		deposit		deposit		fill	
	Phase	1		1		2		2		2		2		2		2		2		2	
Taxon	Component	W	F	W	F	W	F	W	F	W	F	W	F	W	F	W	F	W	F	W	F
Triticum monococcum	grain	·	·	1	1	·	·	·	·	·	·	·	·	·	·	·	·	·	·	·	·
Triticum cf. *monococcum*	grain	·	·	1	·	·	·	·	·	·	·	·	·	·	·	·	·	·	·	·	·
Triticum dicoccum	grain	·	·	4	2	·	·	·	·	·	·	·	·	·	·	·	·	·	·	1	·
Triticum cf. *dicoccum*	grain	·	·	·	·	·	·	·	·	·	·	·	·	1	·	·	·	·	·	·	·
Triticum monococcum or *T. dicoccum*	grain	·	·	·	·	·	·	·	·	·	·	·	·	1	·	·	·	·	·	·	·
Triticum monococcum or *T.dicoccum*	spikelet fork	·	·	1	·	·	·	·	·	·	·	·	·	·	·	·	·	·	·	·	·
Triticum sp.	grain	·	·	1	6	·	·	·	·	·	·	·	·	3	·	·	1	·	·	·	·
Hordeum vulgare	grain	·	·	·	·	·	·	·	·	·	·	·	·	·	·	·	·	·	1	·	·
cereal indeterminate	grain	·	1	·	21	·	·	·	4	·	1	·	·	·	7	·	3	·	2	·	·
Ranunculus cf. *flammula*	seed	·	·	·	·	·	·	·	·	·	·	1	·	·	1	·	·	·	·	·	·
Ranunculus ficaria	tuber	·	·	·	·	·	·	1	·	·	·	·	·	·	·	·	·	·	·	·	·
Papaver sp.	seed	·	·	·	·	·	1	·	·	·	·	·	·	·	·	·	·	·	·	·	·
Polygonum cf *arenastrum*	seed	·	·	·	·	·	·	·	·	·	·	1	·	·	·	·	·	·	·	·	·
Poa cf. *annua*	seed	·	·	·	·	·	·	·	·	·	1	·	·	·	·	·	·	·	·	·	·
Poa cf. *trivialis*	seed	·	·	·	·	·	·	·	1	·	·	·	·	·	·	·	·	·	·	·	·
Poa sp.	seed	·	·	·	·	·	·	·	·	·	·	1	·	·	·	·	·	·	·	·	·
Poaceae indeterminte	seed	·	·	·	·	·	·	·	·	·	·	·	·	1	·	·	·	·	·	·	·
indeterminate	seed	·	·	·	3	·	5	·	·	·	·	·	·	·	4	·	7	·	·	·	·

bone, antler and plain pottery. In the secondary fills the only sampled natural fill (411) contained a single wheat grain. The bone deposit 413 contained no plant remains. 404 and 406 contained a mixture of bone scatters, plain pottery and charcoal-rich soil. Of five samples from 404, three contained plant remains including a range of wild plants, comprising a lesser celandine tuber, a poppy seed and seeds of two meadowgrass species, as well as cereal grains. Both samples from 406 contained remains including possible emmer and einkorn wheats, one grass seed and one seed of lesser spearwort (*Ranunculus flammula*).

Middle ditch, Trench E *(tables 68–69)*

The primary deposits included several discrete episodes of deposition. The single primary natural fill sampled contained no plant remains. Two samples from the bone deposit 527 contained plant remains, one only containing an unidentifiable fragment of vegetative parenchymatous tissue and the other containing two cereal grains and a tuber of pignut/great pignut. The tuber was in several pieces, all of which fitted back together, suggesting that the specimen was broken during archaeological sample processing. Bone deposit 525 had only one sample collected from it, which contained a barley and another cereal grain with several indeterminate seeds. As with 527, the charred remains were associated with animal bone, plain pottery and in the case of 525, flint flakes. The fills of 504 and 518 contained charred plant remains. The small assemblage from 518 included several species including a sloe stone fragment, a probable cleavers seed fragment

and several cereal grains including barley. The three cereal grain fragments from 504 were associated with animal bones, flint flakes and plain pottery. The single sample from the natural fill 508 contained only unidentifiable cereal fragments.

Inner ditch, Trench F *(tables 70–71)*

The single sample from the primary fill context 613 produced no remains. The secondary fill contained several discrete bone deposits contained within natural fill layers. Neither of the sampled natural fills (604 and 605) produced any plant remains. Of the three sampled bone deposits, the uppermost, 627, produced no plant remains. Bone deposits 628 and 629 lay below this upper deposit and were preserved within a charcoal-rich soil that also included plain pottery and two broken antler combs in 628. Four of the five samples from 628 contained plant remains including a few wheat and barley grains and indeterminate seeds. Cleavers (*Galium aparine* L.) was preserved in three of the samples and was abundant in one of them. All three samples from 629 contained plant remains, the cereals being badly preserved but including barley and emmer wheat. Once again, all three samples contained the seeds of cleavers and one also two fragments of grass caryopsis. It is notable that cleavers was the most abundant species in the samples from this ditch fill and was more abundant than any of the other identified plants on the site (with the exception of indeterminate cereals). The tertiary fill 602 was also sampled, but this Romano-British ploughsoil contained no identifiable remains.

Table 68: Sample numbers and sampled contexts from Trench E (middle circuit).

Phase	Context	Context type	Total samples	Productive samples
2	502 (RB)	fill	2	0
2	503	charcoal rich fill	2	0
1	504	scoop with finds	1	1
1	508	fill	1	1
1	511	fill	1	0
1	518	scoop with finds	5	1
1	525	bone deposit	1	1
1	527	bone deposit	2	2

Table 69: Plant remains from Trench E (middle circuit).

	Context	504		508		518		525		527		527	
	Sample	-		12161		-		-		12376		12381	
	Context Type	scoop fill		fill		scoop fill		deposit		deposit		deposit	
	Phase	1		1		1		1		1		1	
Taxon	Component	W	F	W	F	W	F	W	F	W	F	W	F
Hordeum vulgare	grain	.	.	.	.	1	.	1	.	.	.	.	.
cereal indeterminate	grain	.	3	.	2	.	2	1	.	.	.	1	1
Prunus spinosa	stone	.	.	.	.	1	.	.	.	.	.	.	.
Conopodium majus	tuber	.	.	.	.	.	.	.	.	.	.	[1]	5
Galium cf *aparine*	seed	.	.	.	.	.	1	.	.	.	.	.	.
indeterminate	seed	.	.	.	.	.	9	.	7	.	.	.	.
indeterminate	parenchyma	.	.	.	.	.	.	.	.	.	1	.	.

Table 70: Sample numbers and sampled contexts from Trench F (inner circuit).

Phase	Context	Context type	Total samples	Productive samples
3RB	602	fill	1	0
2	604	fill	1	0
2	605	fill	1	0
2	627	bone deposit	2	0
2	628	bone deposit	5	4
2	629	bone deposit	3	3
1	613	fill	1	0

Table 71: Plant remains identified in Trench F (inner circuit).

	Context	628		628		628		628		610/629		610/629		629	
	Sample	6311		6332		6333		6360		6392		6393		6410	
	Context Type	deposit		deposit		deposit		deposit		deposit		deposit		deposit	
	Phase	1		1		1		1		1		1		1	
Taxon	Component	W	F	W	F	W	F	W	F	W	F	W	F	W	F
Triticum cf. *monococcum*	grain	.	.	1	.	.	.	.	.	.	.	.	.	.	.
Triticum cf. *dicoccum*	grain	.	.	.	.	.	.	.	.	1	.	.	.	.	.
Triticum sp.	grain	.	.	.	.	.	.	1	.	.	.	.	.	.	2
Hordeum vulgare	hulled symetrical grain	.	.	.	.	.	.	1	.	.	.	.	.	.	.
Hordeum vulgare	hulled grain	.	.	.	.	.	.	.	1	.	2	.	3	.	.
cf. *Hordeum vulgare*	grain	.	.	.	.	.	.	.	.	.	.	.	.	.	5
cereal indeterminate	grain	.	.	.	3	.	3	.	1	.	5	.	14	.	2
Galium aparine	seed	1	.	.	.	1	.	16	28	.	3	.	3	.	2
Poaceae indeterminate	seed	.	.	.	.	.	.	.	.	.	.	.	2	.	.
indeterminate	seed	1	.	.	7	1	11	.	8	.	.	.	.	.	13

Interpretations

Pre-bank features

Cereal remains were present in the old land surface turfline and in a charcoal spread within it, indicating the exposure of both wheat and barley grains to fire and their consequent deposition before the outer enclosure circuit was constructed. The charcoal spread and the charred cereals associated with animal bone in the soil of 741 might have been derived from middens or hearths, during periods of intermittent settlement and/or agricultural activity. The very disturbed nature of the buried soil is noted above (chapters 6 and 7). The cereals may have been charred during processing to remove chaff and free the grain (Hillman 1981) or during the cooking of food or preparation of ale.

Domestic and wild plant foods were preserved in abundance in the Earlier Neolithic pits outside the enclosure sampled during the 1993 excavations (Fairbairn in Whittle *et al.* forthcoming). Unlike these placed deposits and those of the deposits in the enclosure ditches (see below), the few remains from the pit 714 and grave fill were not derived from deliberate deposition of hearth ash and fire debris. In this case the plant remains are incidental inclusions through inward erosion of Neolithic topsoil which contained a 'charcoal bank', or the use of this soil as backfill for these features (see fig. 107). This low density of charred plant matter may have been accumulated in the soil through many years of low intensity activity and

has also been noted at Easton Down long barrow (Fairbairn 1993). The few finds from the old land surface and associated features add to the general picture of pre-enclosure cereal and wild plant use during occupation and/ or acts of deposition on the hill, prior to the formal laying out of the enclosure (or at least of the outer circuit: see further discussion of sequence in chapters 5 and 17).

The enclosure ditches: sources of plant remains

Charred cereals and wild plant fragments were preserved in small quantities throughout the fills of the enclosure ditch segments. It is important to consider how the plant remains came to be there.

Potential contamination. Sampled contexts 502 (Trench E), 102 (Trench A) and 201 (Trench B) contained Romano-British pottery indicating post-Neolithic re-working of the deposits. In the absence of AMS dating of individual specimens, all of the plant remains from these contexts may be of Romano-British date as plant remains from different archaeological periods are indistinguishable on morphological grounds, unlike many of the 'hard' artefacts such as pottery. Therefore, these contexts have not been considered in the analysis of the Neolithic features. The other plant remains were derived from secure Earlier and Later Neolithic contexts and it is assumed that they are not contaminants from later activity and are Neolithic in origin, although it is possible that some of the plant material was

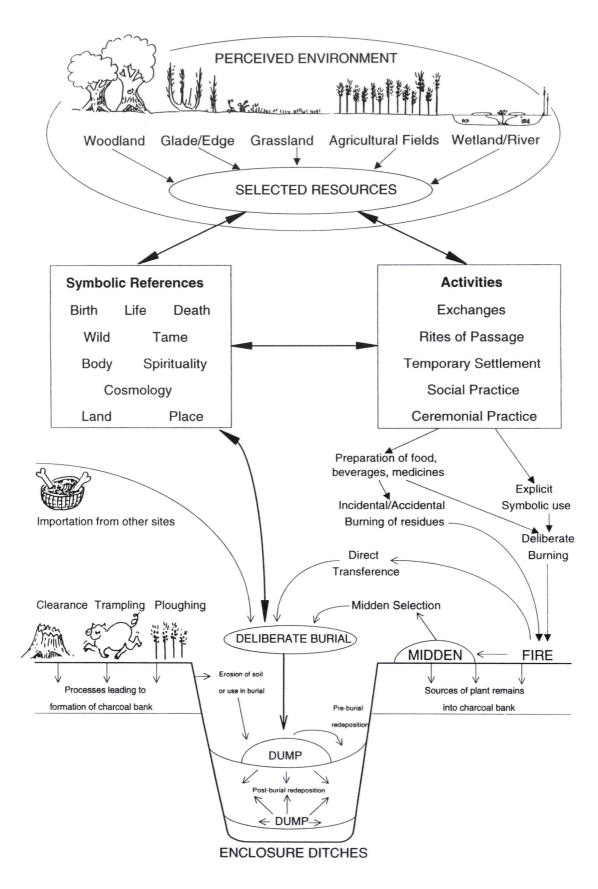

Fig. 107. Generalised model of the actions and processes leading to the incorporation of charred plant remains in the enclosure ditches.

derived from erosion of the 'charcoal bank' in the pre-enclosure soil (see above).

Natural ditch fills. These finds-poor deposits composed much of the ditch sediment, and would have accumulated mainly as the result of processes of natural weathering (as discussed in chapters 3, 4 and 17). Although extensively sampled, these deposits produced few plant remains per sample, if any, and the overall productivity of samples was low (see fig. 106). Only in the sample from context 230 (Trench B) were more than two plant fragments identified from a fill sample of certain Neolithic provenance. In view of the genesis of these deposits, much of this material would have derived from the eroded topsoil charcoal bank (see above). It is also possible that some remains may have been re-deposited by pre-burial weathering and/or post-burial earthworm movement from deposits within the ditch segments, although such remains are indistinguishable from those of the charcoal bank. This is a likely source in contexts 416 (Trench D, possible redeposition from 417/418), 508 (Trench E, re-deposition from 225) and 224 (Trench B, re-deposition from 228/229). Therefore, the remains from these contexts are of uncertain provenance and are grouped with the pre-bank contexts as providing a generalised background picture of Neolithic plant-based activity on the hill.

Deposits. One of the characteristic features of the site was the presence of artefact, bone and charcoal concentrations, which have been interpreted in general terms as the results of episodes of deliberate deposition of material in the ditches (see chapters 3, 4 and 17). Charcoal bank erosion is a less likely source of plant remains in these deposits as the remains were intimately associated with concentrations of ash and charcoal. Although some intrusive plant remains may have become incorporated with the deposits as they were buried or silted over, it has been assumed that the contribution of this source was insignificant.

Sampling of these deposits was more productive than that of the natural fills as shown in fig. 106 (which excludes the Romano-British samples) and individual samples contained more preserved remains. A total of 109 samples were collected from 49 enclosure ditch contexts, of which 48 samples contained plant remains from 18 contexts. Of the total sample set, 61 were collected from 18 deposits (morphologically groups and spreads) and 48 samples were from 31 natural fill contexts. Only 10 percent of the samples from natural fills produced plant remains, with 16 percent of this category of sampled contexts yielding remains. The total success rate of samples from the artefact/bone deposits was 46 percent, with 76 percent of the sampled contexts containing plant remains. Although the deposits were more intensively sampled, the pattern of greater sample success was maintained for total numbers of sampled contexts as well as total numbers of samples.

Since charred plant remains require exposure to heat to be transformed into a preservable state, in the absence of any direct evidence for *in situ* burning it is assumed that the charred plant remains were incorporated into the ditches after being charred in fires which burnt elsewhere. It is impossible to be sure that this burnt debris was generated exclusively at the site prior to its transference into the ditches, although burning at the site seems likely (see below). If such an assumption is accepted, the charred plant remains from the deposits were burnt as a result of the activities which occurred during the life of the enclosure. How they were transferred from the site of burning to the site of deposition is open to conjecture. The intimate association of the remains with wood charcoal and ash suggest that quantities of burning debris were collected from fireplaces and placed in the deposits or middens. Baskets or bags may have been used to carry the material, and possibly used to contain the material with the artefacts and bones in the ditches, as suggested by the discrete deposits of the primary fill (fig. 107).

Some of the remains may have also gone through a stage of transformation in middens at the site or elsewhere prior to burial. Many of the pot sherds were heavily eroded, and some bones also showed patterns associated with sub-aerial weathering. Some deposits might be derived from middens, although some, for example in the primary fills, could be derived from discrete episodes of burning and artefact deposition. Such a source would also explain the poor preservation of the charred plant remains, which are extremely sensitive to wind, water and frost damage, although this could also be explained by the location of the site. Chalk is highly water-permeable and clay soils are prone to shrinkage and cracking. Such mobile soils and free-drainage would cause weakening and ultimately the destruction of fragile charred plant matter.

Suggesting middens as the source of the plant remains has several important effects on subsequent interpretation. Midden accumulation would conflate temporally distinct episodes of burning and depositing, blurring the archaeological traces of separate activities. If those middens were located elsewhere and the ash and other debris were imported into the site as markers of activities carried out there, the spatial as well as temporal resolution of the deposits would be reduced. Instead of identifying discrete episodes of burning and deposition, a more generalised picture of plant use would emerge. As with the process of collecting burnt residues from fires, the act of collecting material from putative middens to include in ditch deposits would have been highly selective. Unlike the bones and other large artefacts, the almost invisible charred plant remains are unlikely to have been deliberately selected for inclusion, but rather incorporated with the ash and charcoal as representative elements of burning events relevant to the concepts which drove depositional practice. Therefore, the recovered plant remains may be quantitatively and qualitatively unrepresentative of the plants used in Neolithic activities and while the plant remains from the deposits are identifiable as being present in the enclosure ditches as the result of deliberate episodes of temporally discrete deposition, the separation of individual, temporally and spatially distinct episodes of plant use and burning is difficult. It is to these episodes of use and burning that we must now turn.

The enclosure ditches: functions and activities

The plant remain assemblages were charred through exposure to heat, which is usually assumed to have occurred accidentally during activities linked to the production, processing and consumption of plant products (Hillman 1981; Moffett *et al.* 1989). This assumption has recently been challenged by Thomas (1993, 388) who re-interpreted the grain concentrations in the Coneybury henge as representing a deliberate act of burning and spoilage. It has also been questioned and discussed in more detail in the consideration of two pit groups at Windmill Hill outside the enclosure (Fairbairn forthcoming). The assemblages in the enclosure ditches at Windmill Hill contained very few charred plant remains suggesting that there was no deliberate large-scale burning of plants prior to inclusion in the ditches, in contrast to the remains from the exterior pit groups. Deliberate burning is possible if only small quantities of plants were burnt or if those burnt contained few seeds. What would be the archaeological signature of a burnt straw effigy or a handful of grain when represented in the floating fraction of a soil sample after being cast on to the fire?

The plant remains from two discrete charcoal deposits may have been the result of deliberate burning. A tuber of lesser celandine (*Ranunculus ficaria*) was preserved in a discrete charcoal patch in association with a fragment of sarsen grinder in context 105 in the secondary fill of the outer circuit (Trench A). Context 417 contained charcoal and few bone fragments mixed with chalk rubble, suggesting a discrete act of ash disposal which preserved the largest, albeit still small assemblage of cereals in association with several unidentifiable seeds. In both cases the presence of plant remains can be explained as the result of deliberate burning and deposition of the resulting ash, paralleling the deposition of whole animal limbs in the ditches, and representing ceremonial consumption of plants as opposed to physical consumption.

With the exception of the remains from the natural fills and deposit contexts 417 and 105 the plant remains were generated as the result of the exposure to fire of the residues of food, beverage or medicine preparation, and the usual assumptions about plant remain generation are accepted. This interpretation is based on the repeated association of plant remains in the deposits with animal bones, which had been used as food and are interpreted as feasting debris. The remains of cereals were generated by the preparation of food and drinks from grain, including the picking through of prime grain or the processing of stored wheat spikelets prior to use, while wild plants may have been used as medicines or food (see below). Consumption itself may have taken several forms including cereal grain consumed as a coarsely ground meal, as in modern bulgur, as bread, gruel/porridge or as brewed beverages including beer. Burning of crop processing residues from large-scale processing of cereal grain from a standing crop was rejected as a source, due to the overall lack of remains and especially those of chaff/weed seed mixtures, which may indicate the lack of burning of crop processing residues from the threshing, winnowing and sieving stages of crop processing (Hillman 1981). This suggestion has been put forward elsewhere to account for the unsuitability of many plant remain assemblages to be used in agricultural reconstruction (Legge 1989), although differential preservation should again be noted.

Several wild taxa were present which may be agricultural weeds including cleavers (*Galium aparine*), knotweed (*Polygonum arenastrum*), poppy (*Papaver* sp.), goosefoots (*Chenopodium* sp. including *C. album*) and the grasses *Poa* and *Lolium*. These taxa are also very common weeds of disturbed places and so an agricultural origin cannot be certain, indeed they all may have grown in the disturbed conditions around the enclosure, and formed a soil seed bank which was burnt by fires on the surface and then included in the deposits when ash was collected. Cleavers (*Galium aparine*) was the single most common species identified in the assemblages and had a constant association with cereal crop products and may be a more certain agricultural weed. If an agricultural source is accepted, the seeds of this plant, as with the others mentioned above, may have been exposed to fire during the picking over and cleaning of wheat spikelets and cereal grain prior to use. The association of cleavers with cereal products and by-products has been used to interpret an autumn crop-sowing regime in later prehistory (Jones 1980) on the basis of its tendency to autumn germination. While this plant does often germinate in autumn it can also germinate throughout the year as long as the seeds have been exposed to cold (Hanf 1983; Grime *et al.* 1988), casting doubt on this interpretation.

The seeds of lesser spearwort (*Ranunculus flammula*) were present in two samples from the deposit context 406. The nearest possible source of this semi-aquatic plant would have been at least one kilometre away on the edges of one of the local rivers. This indicates (as with the lesser celandine tubers) inputs to the site from beyond the limits of its immediate setting, a pattern repeated in the Later Neolithic pits excavated outside the enclosure circuit (Fairbairn forthcoming). Why it was brought to the site is hard to tell, as accidental transportation seems unlikely, although the whole plant is recorded as being used in traditional medicine to induce mild vomiting, among other treatments (Grieve 1931). The specimen was very small and may be immature. In such a case it may have been burnt after collection of the parent plant for medicinal reasons, the immature fruits being present when the plant was still in leaf.

Several other wild taxa were identified which may have been present on the site functioning as food or for other purposes. Hazelnut was present in a single Later Neolithic context (202) in association with domestic plant produce and artefacts. A sloe (*Prunus spinosa*) fragment was present in an Earlier Neolithic deposit as were the other possible wild foods, the tubers of lesser celandine (*Ranunculus ficaria*) and pignut (*Conopodium majus/Bunium bulbocastanum*). Pignut has been found in Bronze Age barrows, evidently used in association with burial activities (Moffett 1991) and lesser celandine has been found in Neolithic contexts in Holland (Bakels 1988) as well as at a recently excavated Mesolithic site in the Hebrides (Sarah Mason *pers. comm.*). Pignut is a well known wild food which is gathered in late spring and early summer when its slender stalks and delicate umbels are visible in open woodland. It is a common chalk plant and may have been abundant in glades and pasture of the partially cleared Neolithic landscape of Wiltshire. Lesser celandine is a possible food although it is better known as an ancient herbal remedy for haemorrhoids dating from at least Roman times (Grieve 1931; Sell 1994). Its yellow flowers are some of the first to appear in spring and it is found in damp open grassland and pasture.

All the wild plants may have derived from deliberate burning of waste from the processing of resources for consumption, either from the picking out of weeds from processed grain or the trimmings and leftovers from wild food and medicine preparation. The occurrence of wild plants was sporadic and they were both outnumbered by cereal remains and less widely distributed. Hazelnut and sloe may indicate the use of woodland or scrub resources, possibly from the immediate environs of the site. As mentioned above, the seeds of lesser spearwort indicate inputs from beyond the limits of the site in wetland, and the tubers of lesser celandine and pignut indicate the use of lower-lying damp grasslands and/or woodland glades. The collection of pignut would have been confined to the late spring and summer suggesting, in the absence of storage of this delicious food, use of the site during that season. Many of the other possible foods may have been stored after collection in autumn in the case of the seeds and fruits, or from spring to autumn in the case of lesser celandine.

Context and Meaning

Social Context. Deliberate plant use led to the charring and incorporation of plant remains into the enclosure ditches, whether the plants were used and burnt at the site or elsewhere. This raises further questions including who used these plants and what the impact was of that use in the short and long term on the groups who visited the site and deposited material within its ditch circuits. Discussion of these questions requires a more detailed consideration of the social context of these acts of consumption and deposition in the Neolithic world.

The enclosure was situated in a woodland clearing, marginal to normal domestic activity, a setting not unusual for such sites (see especially chapters 7 and 17). It was a focal point in the landscape, the activities carried out there being important in the definition and consolidation of the local community from a population of mobile, disparate groups with flexible subsistence regimes who were perhaps only gradually becoming Neolithic (Whittle 1993; 1996, 274). Recent interpretations of these activities stress a multiplicity of possible uses for the site including some possible short-term settlement, but stress the role of the site as an arena for social exchange and a context for ceremonies involving rites of passage in life or from life to death (Edmonds 1993; Whittle 1993; 1996). They stress the symbolism of the form of the enclosures and the deposits incorporated in the concentric ditches in terms of attitudes to land and concepts of nature and culture (C. Evans 1988a). The account here (chapters 17 and 18) stresses the possible integrative role of the Windmill Hill enclosure by reading the deposits as a celebration of Neolithic domesticity and other new concepts. As well as an initial integrative role for causewayed enclosures, Edmonds (1993) has suggested that later activity was marked by an increasing division and control of access to such sites and the activities carried out within them by lineages or other putative social groupings. This interpretation stresses the role of the enclosures in the emergence of lineage, gender or clan group dominance and locates the sacred space of enclosures within this power struggle.

Theoretical considerations. This raises the subject of how and why plants were used in this arena of social power (*sensu* Chapman 1997). A review of plant remain interpretations for the Neolithic and for prehistory as a whole reveals a narrow interpretative focus, which assumes that archaeological botanical residues represent a limited range of human activities deployed only to fulfil a limited range of needs and relationships in simplistically modelled systems of value and exchange. Plant remains are usually conceptualised as indicators of the prevailing economy. The economy is routinely interpreted (implicitly or explicitly) as a subsistence economy, production and procurement supplying domestic consumption. Consumption itself is for the basic needs of life, in the case of plants, primarily used for food to fulfil calorific requirements.

Not only do the plants preserved in charred plant remain assemblages have a wide potential range of functional uses (food, brewing, medicines, drugs, cosmetics, dyes, perfumes and adornments), the use of these plants within specified social contexts may have symbolised ideas concerning the identity, position and power of individuals and groups. As well as being consumed by the producers of the plants and plant products, plants are routinely exchanged in non-industrial societies (Moore 1986; Campbell 1995) in systems of value which owe little to modern western economic concepts (Appadurai 1986). Ethnographic examples of social gatherings where culturally and linguistically separate mobile groups of gatherer-hunters come together are known, these gatherings often being synchronous with seasonal rounds of resource production and procurement (Allen 1973; Couture *et al.* 1988). Exchanges of food and other material goods take place in such contexts, as well as important social events including religious rites and competitive sports. Unfortunately few details are recorded of the role of plants within these gatherings, but it is beyond doubt that they are accorded more significance than as a convenient source of sustenance. In the context of the Neolithic the use and exchange of certain plants and plant products in the arena of social power of the causewayed enclosure by dispersed groups would position individuals within the social matrix and influence the interpretation of that position by other individuals and other groups (Edmonds 1993). Instead of conceptualising the plant remains as passive indicators of a plant economy it may be more appropriate in this context to consider the role of plants as active elements of the Neolithic society which utilised the enclosure.

Plant use in the context of the Windmill Hill causewayed enclosure

Charring during activities related to consumption has been accepted as the main reason for the preservation of the remains in the enclosure ditches. Several scenarios for consumption can be suggested including the preparation of foods, drink and medicines for feasts, meals shared between social groups during exchanges or marriage ceremonies, and for everyday life if the enclosure saw non-ceremonial occupation. None of these options need be mutually exclusive and all may have been situated in a seasonal round of activities by a mobile population (Thomas 1991) in which the enclosure was a focal point. The timing of occupancy of the enclosure may have served a number of functions, being intimately linked to the beliefs of the groups involved. Spring occupancy may have conceptually and practically linked to cosmology, the bountiful production of leafy foods and tubers after the dearth of fresh produce over winter, celebrations of the re-birth and the awakening of life and the re-establishment of social ties between kin groups. Summer or autumnal gatherings may have celebrated the productivity of domestic crops and the autumnal wild harvest, celebrating again the bounty of the seasons while maintaining practices which ensured that the seasonal cycles of productivity continued.

The preparation and consumption of food may have held explicit symbolic meaning itself (Tilley 1996) as well as more subtle expressions of social relations and position as reflected in the access to that food and the identity of those who served and ate it (Hastorf 1991). Cereals were the most widely found plant remains at the site. Overt consumption of cereal products in the feasts and exchanges which are represented at the enclosure could have acted as an explicit demonstration of control and ownership of these new resources and the land on which they grew. Cereal production demands a change in land relations from one of gathering or tending of untamed, although probably socialised, vegetation, to the removal of the natural vegetation and replacement of a group of plants entirely dependent on humans and in this case totally alien to the British Isles (C. Evans 1988a). In the absence of clear evidence of large-scale agricultural invasion, acculturation of the Mesolithic native population must have occurred (Whittle 1996). In

such a scenario, in at least the early stages of uptake, cereal consumption could have had powerful symbolic resonance as a metonym for access to and control of land that cereal cultivation demands. The novelty value of this suite of resources may also have endowed status and prestige within and between groups and lineages, favouring those who adopted the new ways and advancing their claims to influence and dominance. The presence of cereals in exchanges, ceremonies and feasts during important points in social life such as marriage, births, passage into adulthood or death, might have been valued above traditionally employed wild plants as explicit expressions of domesticity. While cereal consumption and exchange could have been laden with symbolic associations to land and social position, the burial of the residues of that consumption would have provided a metonym for completed social exchanges. Incorporation of these deposits would have been important in influencing future interpretations of the acts occurring in the enclosure by the population and thus important also in the creation and re-negotiation of tradition (Edmonds 1993).

Although cereals could have possessed symbolic power as new and initially unfamiliar goods, the consumption of wild resources may have symbolised tradition and in the early phases of cereal use 'the right thing to do'. Wild plant consumption may also have symbolised traditional lifeways in opposition to the new, as represented by the tamed, domestic cereals. This would mirror the presencing of ancestors in the enclosure in the form of placed human remains in the validation of activities and claims to social position through tradition (Edmonds 1993). Traditional associations with land may also have been expressed through the use of certain plants in the arena of the enclosure. Rights of access to land for gathering and hunting are an obvious functional association. Cosmological reference points in the landscape may also have been symbolised through the use of specific plants with an association or source to those areas of land and resident cosmological entities. These more subtle metaphors and metonyms may have invoked tradition, ancestors, or the presence of the spirits to validate specific activities and re-affirm traditional relationships of social groups to land.

If used as medicines the tubers of lesser celandine may have drawn on symbolic reference to the body, whether applied, eaten or deliberately burnt as a form of ceremonial consumption. Similar meanings may underlie the events leading to the charring of pignut tubers in Bronze Age cremations at Barrow Hills, Oxfordshire (Moffett 1991), which suggest a connection of this possible food with death, burial or religion. If the lesser celandine tubers and plants such as lesser spearwort (*Ranunculus flammula*) were charred simply as the residue of medicinal use, do we conceptualise this as purely functional, being used in the repair of the body, or linked to the practices within the liminal phase of rights of passage (Edmonds 1993)? The presence of the mild emetic lesser spearwort, which causes vomiting, may be such a case, being used to purge the body in a very visible manner and helping to attain the separation from normal conditions required in the rites of passage which may have occurred at the site.

While consumption of plants would have had a role in lineage or other group relations it is also possible that they were implicated in the definition of position within groups through the association of individuals with specific activities. The issue of who was involved in the activities that led to the charring of the plant remains could raise questions of individual identity. Among the ways in which individual identity may be defined and societies may be conceptually structured, gender is one of the most well discussed in archaeology (Conkey and Gero 1991; Moore and Scott 1997). Gender as a structure is a contingent and not necessarily relevant conceptual system and its application to individuals may vary with age (Lesick 1997). The representation of plants in the acts of consumption and destruction symbolised by the ditch deposits may have been totally without gender or age associations, although plants may have been important signifiers of gender groups (see also chapter 18). The cyclical annual re-growth of plants may have been the reference point for symbolic plant associations with birth, life and fertility, seen later in traditional European agricultural rites including various ploughing and harvesting festivals. Several associations can be suggested, including those with women and children, but especially with the newborn. The deliberate burning of cereals or wild plants (for example in contexts 417 and 105 respectively) may have symbolised new births and so the passage into life. Conversely, the emphasis on re-birth may have accompanied the passage into death.

Although plots for growing plants may be cleared by men, the cultivation and gathering of plants are often considered within the female sphere, as is the preparation of plants for consumption as food or beer (Hastorf 1991; Moore 1986; Campbell 1995). Ancient plant food gathering, growing and processing have been associated with female gender, conceptually (Hodder 1990) and functionally (Hastorf 1991; Molleson 1994). Molleson's study of Neolithic human bones from Tell Abu Hureyra in Syria provides a single example of an empirically supported association of gender with activity, in this case seed grinding. Food processing is often, although not exclusively, a female activity (Hastorf 1991) and, if this albeit essentialist assumption is accepted (cf. Gilchrist 1991), we may position female productivity and activities within the enclosure. Female power may have been represented through the deposition of ash from domestic fires, or those used to cook food in the rites at the enclosure. The meaning of such deposits might range from explicit expressions of female power within the political exchanges that characterised the activities at the site to symbolic representation of the tame, domestic and new ways of being, embodied by females and the hearth, deployed in opposition to the widely found remains of cattle which may have an association with maleness and male power (Hodder 1990). This might have been a deliberate and realistic reflection of power relations or might have been manipulated in the context of the enclosure to reflect idealised types and social relations somewhat distant from those actually in operation (cf. Shanks and Tilley 1982).

Spatial and temporal patterns of plant use on Windmill Hill

Distinguishing spatial and temporal patterns of plant use at the enclosure is difficult because of the poor representation of plant remains at the site and the probable unrepresentativeness of the assemblages. The range of plant taxa and potential range of activities in which they were employed are not evidenced in all of the sampled deposits. It is impossible to determine whether this indicates inconsistency in plant use in the activities associated with the enclosure, or is simply due to the vagaries of preservation. Plant remains are present within the deposits of both the primary and secondary deposits in all three ditch circuits, with the exception of the primary fill of the inner circuit, from which only natural fills were sampled. Samples from the natural layers and formalised deposits of the primary fills were more productive than those from the secondary deposits (fig. 106), although this may be an artefact of sampling and preservation rather than having any significance in terms of ancient plant use. Wheat and barley grains were present in formalised deposits in all three ditches in primary and secondary contexts and in the single sampled Later Neolithic context 202 as well as the Earlier Neolithic contexts. Wild plants without agricultural origin were present only in the outer and middle ditch segments, and were mainly found in secondary deposits, including those of Later Neolithic date.

Looking at the whole complex of Neolithic features on the hill, charred plants are present from the earliest to the latest deposits. The pre-bank land surface and associated features contained plant remains which had been incorporated into the soil through unidentifiable pre-enclosure activity, possibly including intermittent settlement and cultivation. Earlier Neolithic pits from the 1993 excavations (whose precise date is uncertain) contained rich assemblages of both wheat and barley remains mixed with those of wild plants, including hazelnut and sloe, and were deliberately placed in the pits with artefacts including grinders. Deliberate burial mimics that of the enclosure deposits, with the difference that the plants were not deliberately burnt and selected for burial in most cases in the enclosure, but incorporated incidentally with selected, buried ash and charcoal. Plant remains from these Earlier Neolithic extra-enclosure pits were charred through deliberate burning as a form of ceremonial consumption in comparison to the plant remains from the enclosure which were charred as the result of actual physical consumption as food, beverages or medicine. Therefore, cereal consumption continued to have a significance in the life of the enclosure, but mainly as consumed foods in periodic meetings, exchanges and ceremonies at the site. The change in emphasis may be significant and the enclosure deposits may signify that at this point cereals were considered a resource suitable for wide consumption as a food as well as a symbolic resource, and not mainly the latter.

Such consumption is seen throughout the main phase of enclosure use, mixed with cases of deliberate destruction for specified ceremonial purposes, including rites of passage through birth, life and death. The later phase of enclosure use going into the Later Neolithic sees sporadic depositions of plant matter and a lower intensity of deliberate deposition, alongside the formation of a large flint scatter on the southern slope of the hill (Whittle *et al.* forthcoming). Both wild and domestic species were identified, in contrast to Later Neolithic pits outside the enclosure where only wild plant remains were found in placed deposits. The plant remains in this later pit group were totally different to the Earlier Neolithic extra-enclosure pits and all but context 105 in the enclosure. This undoubtedly represents a different set of practices, including consumption of tubers from wetland plants. While possibly a result of the distortions of the archaeological record, a contrast can be drawn between plant usage in the pits outside the enclosure and that represented in the enclosure ditches. The pit assemblages emphasise wild, traditional plants and those from the enclosure domestic plants. This picture is enhanced in the distribution of wild and domestic plants within the enclosure ditches, with definite wild foods and medicines found in the outer and middle ditch, and domestic in all three ditches, but on their own in the inner.

If the spatial patterns in the distribution of plant remains at the enclosure are not due entirely to differential preservation, plants can be placed within the conceptual scheme drawing on wild and tame which may have been objectified in the form of the enclosure itself (see chapters 17 and 18). The presence of domestic resources only in the Later Neolithic deposits might support the idea of a control of access to the sacred space of the enclosures (Edmonds 1993), linked in this case to those controlling ceremonial use of domestic plant resources. Alternatively, the pattern may be better linked to a conceptual division objectified in the use of space between wild and tame and in this case reflected also in the pattern of plant use.

In his study of plant impressions in pottery recovered from Keiller's excavations of the enclosure, Helbaek (1952, 197–99) identified several species not present in the charred assemblages at the site, namely naked barley (*Hordeum vulgare* var. *nudum*), apple (*Malus sylvestris*) and flax (*Linum usitatissimum*). The simple quantitative approach which underlay both Helbaek's and Dennell's (1976) assessments of economic importance must now be considered redundant, as such an approach does not take into account the many factors altering the proportions of taxa represented in these assemblages. Dennell's study was important in taking account of the provenance of the different pottery types in which impressions were preserved. In his account, following Smith (1965a), pots were divided into those produced nearby

and those from the Bath/Frome region; subsequent analysis (Darvill 1983 and chapter 13 here) suggests that pottery with oolitic filler could have come from closer than Bath/Frome. This reinforces the likelihood that most plant impressions do derive from the surrounding area and that wheat, barley, flax and apple were present in both regions.

The deliberate inclusion of cereals in pot fabrics to provide a symbolic link between practical and conceptual realities and to express the distinction between the realm of people and the wild has recently been mooted (Tilley 1996, 188–89). The sherds from Windmill Hill often contain numerous grain impressions, and while isolated impressions may be explained away by accidental inclusion, the presence of several impressions on a single sherd cannot be dismissed so easily. It is consistent to suggest that some pots did have grains and other seeds deliberately included in their fabrics for symbolic and possibly decorative purposes. The association between pots and cereals was not necessarily practical but part of the conceptual order through which society structured itself. No grain or seed impressions were recorded in Grooved Ware sherds from the site, a phenomenon which is seen across Britain (Jones 1980). This difference may support the suggestion made above that the symbolic emphasis of plant use had shifted during the later phases of deposition on the hill. Earlier use made explicit and direct symbolic links between domesticity, plants and pots. Later use sees no such symbolic reference, although the control and use of cereals as a resource still held a significance in the negotiation of social relations as evidenced in the Later Neolithic enclosure deposits. The absence of domesticates and presence only of wild plants in the Later Neolithic extra-enclosure pits suggest that wild plants may have become more explicit symbolic resources in a domesticated Later Neolithic world.

Wider contexts

In a summary of finds of charred plant remains from Neolithic contexts by Moffett *et al.* (1989) almost all were from non-settlement sites, including many pit groups, enclosures and contexts associated with barrows. One of the few published examples of Neolithic plant remains from a causewayed enclosure is that from Briar Hill, Northamptonshire (Bamford 1985). The plant remains from the site were similar to those from Windmill Hill, being few in number and poorly preserved, although woodland plants were well represented alongside cereals. At Hambledon Hill, cereals including emmer wheat from burnt spikelets have been recovered from pits in association with the two enclosures. The Windmill Hill material seems to fit in to a pattern for much of southern Britain, with charred plant remains being an inconspicuous but constant presence when flotation recovery is extensively applied during archaeological excavations. That few remains are forthcoming is in part the result of the fragility of plants and the complex route to preservation which all charred remains in secondary contexts follow (Hubbard and Clapham 1992). Plants were evidently widely used in ceremonial and social events over southern Britain and may have had a significant role as a symbolic resource as the Neolithic world took shape and as social strategies were played out, a significance that extends beyond the visibility of plant remains in the archaeological record.

Subsistence practice as such is not best reconstructed from the remains recovered from sites such as Windmill Hill where everyday domestic refuse was unlikely to accumulate, except in a highly selected form as symbolic packages deposited for ceremonial purposes. Many of the contexts described by Moffett *et al.* (1989) could be seen as non-domestic in nature, and the use of these contexts to reconstruct the Neolithic plant economy has been criticised (Legge 1989). This critique, however, as with other commentaries on the subject, avoids discussion of what these non-domestic activities may have been and how they may have fitted into the Neolithic world. The analysis of the Windmill Hill botanical residue suggests that these plants were used in a variety of ways, both practically and symbolically, in the causewayed enclosure and associated contexts. Analysis of the archaeobotanical record from non-domestic sites across Britain suggests that plants may have been deployed for these purposes in many arenas of social interaction throughout the period. The homogeneous interpretation of the archaeobotanical record from varied archaeological and social contexts (e.g. Moffett *et al.* 1989) is theoretically naive and methodologically suspect. As with the much more widely imposed restriction of archaeobotanical discussions to subsistence, it also denies the possibility of a variety of experience which undoubtedly coloured the human past and the investigation of which should be the main subject of archaeological study.

The conclusions of Moffett *et al.* (1989) along with the observations of Entwistle and Grant (1989) have been influential in providing empirical support for more recent interpretations of the sustained importance of wild taxa in the domestic (i.e. food) plant economy and movement away from the rapid agricultural 'acculturation' of more traditional models. Although there are considerable reservations about the suitability of the evidence used to support this model (see above), the conclusions do fit in to the general picture of the Neolithic constructed from the results of large-scale survey and excavations both in the Avebury region (Whittle 1993) and elsewhere (e.g. Barrett *et al.* 1991). Where plant remains from unambiguous domestic contexts have been reported the picture of plant usage is variable. At the Stumble in Essex, mixtures of wild and domestic plant species have been found (Murphy 1988, and *pers. comm.*) including vegetable tubers and several cereal species. Large caches of grain were discovered at Balbridie, Scotland, in association with a longhouse, indicating that large-scale cultivation and storage of cultivated cereals was taking place (Fairweather and Ralston 1993). Another recent find at Lismore Fields

contained a similar hoard (Glynis Jones *pers. comm.*). It seems inconceivable in both of these latter cases to suggest that the abundant cereals were not important food resources, whatever the symbolic and social status of crops may have been. Such rich finds sit outside the general model of Entwistle and Grant and it is clear that the pattern of plant use was more varied.

Site destruction aside (cf. Legge 1989; Darvill 1996) and accepting the presence of mobile groups and long-houses, the conclusion must be that there was both inter- and intra-regional variation in the settlement pattern spatially and temporally in Neolithic Britain. The use of plant resources was similarly varied at any one point in time, domestic needs in some areas being fulfilled by traditional means through the gathering of plants, some perhaps even tended and encouraged. Some settlements may have been permanent, even in the Earlier Neolithic (perhaps Balbridie for example), their inhabitants growing cereals and living settled 'longhouse lives' (cf. Whittle 1996, 144). Over much of Britain there may have been a varied lifestyle, as suggested by Entwistle and Grant (1989), based on small-scale shifting cultivation, herding, gathering and hunting. The groups that we have evidence for at Windmill Hill had the knowledge to exploit both wild and domestic plant species. The ability to exploit wild species should not be taken for granted, especially knowledge of tubers and other less obvious plant resources. These traditional paths of knowledge still lay open throughout the period of deposition at Windmill Hill and maintained a relevance over much of Britain into the Bronze Age alongside the newer knowledge relating to domestic plant use.

Relations between groups that could have differed in subsistence practice, traditions and perhaps even language, may have been complex. New products, including domestic plants, may have been exchanged between cultivators and gatherer-hunters at sites like Windmill Hill causewayed enclosure, whether or not those exchanges occurred within or outside complex ceremonial practice. Such exchanges are not uncommon where agriculturalists and gatherer-hunters live side-by-side today and interaction does not necessarily lead to full-blown acculturation of one group by another (Kent 1992). Although the exchanges may not have led to the acculturation implicit in the traditional model of Neolithic origins, they would have exposed groups to new resources, including crops. Sites such as Windmill Hill might have played a vital role in the exchanges which allowed crops to spread in the Avebury region and, considering the repeated occurrence of crop plants in enclosures and pits, over much of southern Britain.

That crops were present over much of the British Isles early in the Neolithic and throughout the period seems undeniable. At Windmill Hill it is possible that the cereals were produced specifically for use in ceremonial and social activities by an indigenous local population (cf. Thomas 1993; 1996a), or that they were obtained by exchange. Direct cultivation would have imposed constraints on movement, fixing groups to specific areas of land during the period of soil preparation and crop harvest. Tending would have been required to obtain good yields and fencing would be necessary to prevent the total destruction of crops by untethered grazing animals. That they were used on a large scale is unlikely, except in some localities, and the archaeological evidence points to no such agricultural dominance in the economy or landscape in the Avebury region.

Change in the Neolithic and specifically the adoption of domestic crops has typically been characterised as driven by the need for calories to feed an increasing population (Legge 1989). In the interpretation here of the plant remains from Windmill Hill, plants, especially cereals, were deployed primarily as a symbolic and social resource in the activities which were carried out at the site, by a population that was mobile, small and dispersed in a little altered environment. In this context of untapped resources and a small population which retained its gatherer knowledge, the use of cereals was calorifically unnecessary, but was an encouraged and vital part of life due to the need to take part in and succeed in the increasingly complex and elaborate social exchanges which may have characterised the Neolithic. At Windmill Hill and elsewhere it is possible that for large spans of the Neolithic cereal use endowed status upon the user as well as calories, and this social dimension may have been as much a stimulus to the adoption of cereal agriculture as any calorific needs.

Acknowledgements

Thanks are due to: Gordon Hillman for help with the identifications of cereals, seeds and some useful discussion; Jon Hather for the identification of vegetative parenchyma; Phil Austen, Louise Martin, Helen Wickstead and John Chapman for inspiration, ideas and discussion; and Amanda Kennedy for encouragement and assistance with the final text.

9

The Charcoal Assemblages

Caroline Cartwright

Introduction

All ditch circuits and the old land surface under the outer bank were sampled for wood charcoal in the 1988 excavations. Over 315 charcoal samples were submitted for identification. In general, the charcoal samples from each context were fairly small. Table 80 summarises the taxa present for the main fills of ditch, bank and other structural contexts; tables 72–79 give the weight of charcoal in grams from each context.

In common with many other archaeological sites, interpretation of the charcoal is constrained by the fact that the fragments may have become incorporated into the deposits through a variety of taphonomic processes. They may at the same time be representative both of past environments concurrent with phases of the site's habitation and of timber specifically selected for particular domestic, structural or artefactual purposes. Consequently, in this report, it has been decided not to quantify the roundwood charcoal fragments according to the conventional percentage by weight basis, but on a presence/absence notation (table 80), with indications in the text as to relative frequencies which may have, according to individual contexts, greater or lesser significance.

Any vegetational reconstruction must be seen as part of wider environmental research comprising evidence from land molluscs, charred plant remains, pollen, soil micromorphology and microfauna.

Contexts sampled

The old land surface *(tables 72–73)*

The old land surface in Trench BB of the outer circuit, from base to surface, produced a predominance of *Quercus* sp. (oak) roundwood charcoal fragments. *Corylus* sp. (hazel) roundwood charcoal is also present, notably at the base of the old land surface. *Crataegus* sp. (hawthorn), *Betula* sp. (birch) and *Taxus baccata* (yew) roundwood charcoal was recovered from the old land surface. Whilst certain of these taxa, such as hawthorn, birch and hazel, may form part of chalk scrub (see below), they are also present in oak woodland on calcareous soils.

Prunus spp. (plum/cherry), including *P. spinosa* (sloe/blackthorn), *Fraxinus* sp. (ash) and *Corylus* sp. (hazel) are present in both scrubby and woodland environments. The grave (707) and its associated fill displays a dominant oak woodland character, as do the taxa from the primary bank contexts. There appears to be no significant change of source of the roundwood charcoal fragments from the main bank.

The outer ditch *(tables 74–76)*

The primary fill of Trench B only yielded a small amount of *Quercus* sp. The secondary and upper secondary fills displayed a predominance of *Quercus* sp. with *Corylus* sp., *Crataegus* sp. and *Prunus* sp./*Prunus spinosa* roundwood charcoal fragments. This may signify a more open type of woodland where the understorey elements are more in evidence. Alternatively, material from chalk scrubland or from field boundaries and hedgerows may be present. It is not inconceivable that material from both scrub and oak woodland may have been selected for particular purposes within the site-complex. The tertiary fill contained a small quantity of *Quercus* sp. and *Fraxinus* sp. bark.

The primary fill of Trench A only yielded a small amount of *Crataegus* sp. roundwood charcoal fragments. The secondary fill displayed a predominance of *Quercus* sp. with *Corylus* sp. and *Crataegus* sp. charcoal. No significant change can be seen amongst the taxa from the tertiary fill.

There is a noticeable representation of *Corylus* sp. roundwood charcoal fragments in the primary fill of Trench C, by comparison with the primary fill in Trenches A and B. *Quercus* sp. is also important. In the secondary fill, scrub or understorey elements are present: *Crataegus* sp., *Corylus* sp. and *Prunus spinosa* with *Fraxinus* sp. (which, in certain cases, can indicate secondary woodland) forming a significant proportion of the total roundwood

Table 72: Old land surface in Trench BB.

Context	Grams	Identification	Description
749	01.4	*Corylus* sp. (hazel)	OLS
743	21.6	*Quercus* sp. (oak)	"
741	19.7	*Quercus* sp.	"
	03.4	*Taxus baccata* (yew)	
	02.6	*Corylus* sp.	
	02.3	*Betula* sp. (birch)	
	02.0	*Crataegus* sp. (hawthorn)	
741/750	03.7	*Quercus* sp.	"
	01.6	*Corylus* sp.	
705	05.4	*Quercus* sp.	"
	04.5	*Crataegus* sp.	
	01.2	*Corylus* sp.	

Table 73: Other Trench BB contexts.

Context	Grams	Identification	Description
710	02.6	*Prunus* sp. (plum/cherry/sloe)	posthole
726	01.4	*Fraxinus* sp. (ash)	pit-fill
	00.5	*Corylus* sp.	
707	05.1	*Corylus* sp.	grave
	04.8	*Quercus* sp.	
	03.3	*Crataegus* sp.	
	03.3	*Prunus* sp.	
	01.2	*Fraxinus* sp. (including bark)	
707/732	03.0	*Quercus* sp.	grave-fill
	01.3	*Crataegus* sp.	
707/734	09.1	*Quercus* sp.	" "
	07.8	*Crataegus* sp.	
746	15.2	*Quercus* sp.	primary bank
	03.7	*Corylus* sp.	
704	01.0	*Corylus* sp.	" "
701	05.1	*Fraxinus* sp.	main bank
	01.1	bark	
702	06.0	*Quercus* sp.	" "
703	09.3	*Quercus* sp.	" "
	00.2	*Crataegus* sp.	

Table 74: The outer ditch, Trench B.

Context	Grams	Identification	Description
228	01.8	*Quercus* sp.	primary fill
225	01.9	*Quercus* sp.	secondary "
	01.8	*Corylus* sp.	
206	06.7	*Quercus* sp.	" "
203	11.8	*Quercus* sp.	" "
204	01.5	*Corylus* sp.	" "
	00.8	*Quercus* sp.	
212	01.6	*Corylus* sp.	upper " "
	01.5	*Crataegus* sp.	
	01.3	*Quercus* sp.	
214	08.7	*Quercus* sp.	" " "
215	80.1	*Quercus* sp.	" " "
	10.1	*Prunus spinosa/Prunus* sp.	
	08.4	*Corylus* sp.	
	04.8	*Crataegus* sp.	
216	26.7	*Quercus* sp.	" " "
	09.3	*Corylus* sp.	
	02.8	*Prunus* sp.	
	01.9	*Crataegus* sp.	
217	03.0	*Quercus* sp.	" " "
220	01.7	*Quercus* sp.	" " "
	01.4	*Crataegus* sp.	
202	57.9	*Quercus* sp.	soil
	31.1	*Crataegus* sp.	
	13.7	*Corylus* sp. (including hazel-shell fragment)	
	04.8	*Prunus* sp.	
	04.5	*Fraxinus* sp.	
201	04.5	*Quercus* sp.	tertiary fill
	01.2	*Fraxinus* sp. (bark)	

Table 75: The outer ditch, Trench A.

Context	Grams	Identification	Description
112	02.0	*Crataegus* sp.	primary fill
103	11.4	*Quercus* sp.	secondary "
	08.6	*Corylus* sp.	
104	35.0	*Quercus* sp.	" "
	05.2	*Crataegus* sp.	
	01.0	*Corylus* sp.	
105	15.0	*Quercus* sp.	" "
106	12.7	*Quercus* sp.	" "
109	02.8	*Quercus* sp.	" "
110	06.9	*Quercus* sp.	" "
	04.2	*Corylus* sp.	
	02.7	*Crataegus* sp.	
102	22.2	*Quercus* sp.	tertiary fill
	07.0	*Corylus* sp.	
	03.0	*Crataegus* sp.	
	02.2	*Prunus* sp.	

Table 76: The outer ditch, Trench C.

Context	Grams	Identification	Description
308	11.9	*Corylus* sp.	primary fill
	05.0	*Quercus* sp.	
312	02.8	*Quercus* sp.	" "
311/315	07.0	*Corylus* sp.	" "
315	02.0	*Quercus* sp.	" "
324	03.6	*Quercus* sp.	" "
303	03.4	*Prunus spinosa*	secondary fill
	02.0	*Quercus* sp.	
303/316	00.3	*Quercus* sp.	" "
304	19.0	*Quercus* sp.	" "
	13.9	*Fraxinus* sp.	
	07.5	*Corylus* sp.	
	02.0	*Crataegus* sp.	
305	06.8	*Quercus* sp.	" "
	02.7	*Crataegus* sp.	
302	06.2	*Quercus* sp.	tertiary fill
	01.0	*Corylus* sp.	

Table 77: The middle ditch, Trench D.

Context	Grams	Identification	Description
416	12.9	*Quercus* sp.	primary fill
417	05.0	*Quercus* sp.	" "
	02.1	*Corylus* sp. (half hazelnut shell)	
406	01.0	*Corylus* sp.	secondary fill
411	01.5	*Quercus* sp.	" "
	00.7	*Crataegus* sp.	
414	02.0	*Crataegus* sp.	" "
401	03.0	*Quercus* sp.	tertiary fill

Table 78: The middle ditch, Trench E.

Context	Grams	Identification	Description
508	09.0	*Quercus* sp.	primary fill
	01.5	*Corylus* sp.	
510	42.0	*Quercus* sp.	" "
512	02.0	*Quercus* sp.	" "
	01.5	*Corylus* sp.	
518	03.1	*Quercus* sp.	" "
524	02.5	*Quercus* sp.	" "
525	09.0	*Quercus* sp.	" "
503	03.0	*Prunus* sp.	secondary fill

Table 79: The inner ditch, Trench F.

Context	Grams	Identification	Description
610	03.0	*Corylus* sp.	primary fill
610/629	01.6	*Quercus* sp.	" "
604	06.3	*Quercus* sp.	secondary fill
605	02.0	*Corylus* sp.	" "
627	03.7	*Quercus* sp.	" "
628	04.2	*Quercus* sp.	" "
	01.0	*Corylus* sp.	
629	08.9	*Quercus* sp.	" "
630	05.7	*Quercus* sp.	" "

charcoal fragments. The tertiary fill is dominated by *Quercus* sp. charcoal (albeit in small quantities).

The middle ditch *(tables 77–78)*
The primary fill of Trench D of the middle circuit ditch produced *Quercus* sp. roundwood charcoal fragments and a charred *Corylus* sp. nut shell half. The secondary fill shows a small amount of charcoal which is mostly *Crataegus* sp. with a little *Quercus* sp. and *Corylus* sp.. The tertiary fill has a modest quantity of *Quercus* sp. charcoal.

The primary fill of Trench E produced *Quercus* sp. roundwood charcoal fragments and a small amount of *Corylus* sp. charcoal. The secondary fill contained only 3 g of *Prunus* sp. charcoal.

The inner ditch *(table 79)*
A small quantity of *Corylus* sp. and *Quercus* sp. roundwood charcoal fragments was retrieved from the primary fill of Trench F. The same taxa are present in the secondary fill, *Quercus* sp. dominating.

Discussion

When considering the roundwood charcoal fragments from the site contexts as a whole, it can be seen that the diversity of taxa is not great. Although it has to be noted that such categories as pits and ditches, for example, may draw upon a wide range of source material for their infills, some general comments can nevertheless be made about the distribution and quantity of particular taxa in the charcoal assemblage. In forming an environmental reconstruction, the interpretation must account, in part, for taxa absent as well as present. For example, according to comparable present-day models, in a *Quercus-Pteridium-Rubus* woodland with a sub-community of *Hedera helix* (ivy), *Fraxinus excelsior* (ash) is an important canopy element and *Acer campestre* (field maple) is frequent in the canopy or understorey (Rodwell 1991). The absence of *Acer campestre* may be significant when attempting a reconstruction of woodland exploited by the users of the enclosure. *Fraxinus* sp. is only sparsely present in the deposits: in the grave, on the main bank and in the pit fill under the Trench BB bank, and sporadically in the secondary fill, soil and tertiary fill of the ditch trenches in the outer circuit. An alternative present-day woodland analogue is provided by the association of *Quercus-Pteridium-Rubus* with constant *Fraxinus excelsior*, *Carpinus betulus* (hornbeam), *Tilia cordata* (lime) in the canopy and *Acer campestre*, *Euonymus europaeus* (spindle) and *Cornus sanguinea* (dogwood) in the understorey. However, only the scrub elements cf. *Corylus avellana* (hazel) and *Crataegus monogyna* (hawthorn) are represented from this vegetational association (*ibid.*) for the Windmill Hill charcoal assemblage. Ash, oak and hazel are highly suitable timbers for fences, hurdles, ditch enclosures and wattling (Rackham 1993; Edlin 1956). Ash and oak are excellent all-purpose timber for beams, stakes, posts and general building; hazel has also been well utilised for these purposes.

The *Crataegus monogyna-Hedera helix* (chalk) scrub community described by Rodwell (1991), is a diverse vegetation 'sometimes difficult to separate from more open herbaceous vegetation with scattered woody plants on the one hand and woodland on the other' (Rodwell 1991, 333). In this community *Crataegus monogyna* and *Prunus spinosa* dominate and saplings of *Fraxinus* sp., *Quercus* sp. and *Betula* sp. may be common locally. Even the occasional *Taxus baccata* (yew) sapling may be present. In the *Crataegus-Hedera* scrub, however, *Corylus* sp. is not found with any frequency. As a constant species,

coppice *Corylus* sp. is more common in the *Fraxinus excelsior-Acer campestre-Mercurialis perennis* woodland (Rodwell 1991). Table 80 displays the importance of *Corylus* sp. in the Windmill Hill charcoal assemblage. Whilst not invariably found in primary ditch fills, hazel nevertheless ranks second only to *Quercus* sp. in its frequency of occurrence. The taxa present in the assemblage seem to concentrate primarily on woods suitable for fencing and structures. All the woods could have been used as fuel, however, or may even be subject to the initial qualification noted above, that the deposits in question may draw upon a wide range of source material for their infills.

It is not clear from the taxa present whether or not there was a need for some form of woodland management to sustain timber resources for the requirements of the site. The study of species diversity is a complex issue as it deals in a wide range of ecological and historical factors which may determine richness. Studies of species diversity reveal a further complexity relating to spatial scales and patterns; many quite localised variants may occur. Niches of endemic species may be present; also regeneration niches where vegetation reflects particular responses to disturbance. There may be overwhelming edaphic factors

Table 80: Wood charcoal assemblage summary.

Context	*Quercus* sp. oak	*Corylus* sp. hazel	*Crataegus* sp. hawthorn	*Fraxinus* sp. ash	*Prunus* sp. (including *P. spinosa*) plum/cherry/sloe (blackthorn)	*Betula* sp. birch	*Taxus baccata* yew
OUTER CIRCUIT							
Trench BB bank							
old land surface	X	X	X			X	X
posthole					X		
pit fill		X		X			
grave	X	X	X	X	X		
grave fill	X		X				
primary bank	X	X					
main bank	X		X	X			
Trench B ditch							
primary fill	X						
secondary fill	X	X					
upper secondary fill	X	X	X		X		
soil	X	X	X	X	X		
tertiary fill	X			X			
Trench A ditch							
primary fill			X				
secondary fill	X	X	X				
tertiary fill	X	X			X		
Trench C ditch							
primary fill	X	X					
secondary fill	X	X	X	X	X		
tertiary fill	X	X					
MIDDLE CIRCUIT							
Trench D ditch							
primary fill	X	X					
secondary fill	X	X	X				
tertiary fill	X						
Trench E ditch							
primary fill	X	X					
secondary fill					X		
INNER CIRCUIT							
Trench F ditch							
primary fill	X	X					
secondary fill	X	X					

such as soil type, moisture and so on which operate a selective force which will determine high proportions of particular species. Invaders and pioneer species (such as birch) may compete in particular habitats especially where there is not a steady-state of vegetation growth and maintenance or where the pressure of agriculture and grazing takes hold. It is noteworthy that some of the taxa are either self-coppicing (hazel) or are suitable for coppicing, for example oak and ash (Rackham 1993). This observation is of consequence when evaluating the extent of utilisation of timber for wattling, fencing and hedging. Many of the taxa are natural components of hedgerows: hazel, hawthorn, blackthorn (sloe), oak and ash (Rackham 1993; Stace 1997). Some of the taxa are suitable for pollarding: hawthorn, oak and ash (Rackham 1993). Although the different species of *Prunus* cannot usually be distinguished on anatomical grounds, in the wood charcoal assemblage from Windmill Hill a close match with reference material for *Prunus spinosa* could be obtained. It is a fact that *Prunus* spp. are often associated with woodland margins and secondary woodland (Rackham 1993; Rodwell 1991) and it should be noted that it is possible that more than one species of *Prunus* could be present in this assemblage.

A few of the taxa represented are tolerant of a wide range of soils, such as oak and birch (Edlin 1953; 1956). Some are found widely in shrub and tree form, including hawthorn, hazel and *Prunus* spp., and are distributed in hedgerows, wood-borders, copses, scrub and woodland (Stace 1997). Certain of the taxa have more specific preferences in terms of habitat or soil type, such as ash which flourishes on damp or base-rich soils (Stace 1997; Rodwell 1991; Edlin 1956). It is also worth noting that many of the taxa may be destroyed easily by animal-browsing, for example hazel and ash (especially by young deer); some are less readily affected, such as oak (Edlin 1956; Rackham 1993). These observations gain significance when considering the impact of domesticated and non-domesticated animal grazing and browsing coupled with the effects of the spread of agriculture at the expense of woodland.

Whilst many features such as the elm decline and the increased diversity and quantity of herbs following land clearance for agriculture remain important markers within Neolithic pollen sequences, the evidence from the Windmill Hill wood charcoal seems to indicate that a mosaic of woodland, scrub and cleared land was available for exploitation (and management). The proximity of such resources to settlement or ritual activity areas cannot be established with any accuracy, but modern vegetational community analogues, such as exemplified by Rodwell's *Fraxinus excelsior-Acer campestre-Mercurialis perennis* (W8) category (1991) can be seen to contain woodland, coppice-with-standards and scrub elements including (amongst others) the seven taxa present as wood charcoal at Windmill Hill. Whether *Quercus* sp. indicates a dominant vegetational element or a specifically-selected (all-purpose) timber, or even a combination of the two factors, its importance in the Windmill Hill wood charcoal assemblage is not under dispute.

10

Pollen Analysis

Michael Walker

Introduction

In some circumstances, pollen grains can be recovered in reasonable condition and in more or less countable numbers from chalk soils. Sites where this has been achieved in the region around Windmill Hill include Beckhampton Road, South Street and Horslip or Windmill Hill long barrows, Knap Hill and Avebury (Dimbleby and Evans 1974). Pollen was extracted from thin sections of the buried soil under the Easton Down long barrow (Cruise 1993). Pollen was also found in greater quantities in the non-calcareous soil – brownearth on clay-with-flints – buried under Silbury Hill (Dimbleby 1997). Preservation, however, may be extremely variable in chalk soils. A mere 32 years after the construction of the Overton Down experimental earthwork, pollen counts from the old land surface beneath it were reported as sparse and poorly preserved (Crabtree 1996).

In 1957 and 1966, Dimbleby succeeded in extracting pollen from the old land surface under the outer bank in cutting V (Dimbleby 1965; Dimbleby and Evans 1974). Counts were not reported in detail, but were described as 'adequate' (Dimbleby and Evans 1974, 128); no direct comment on preservation was reported, though there was discussion of the issue of differential preservation (Dimbleby and Evans 1974). There were very low tree counts, including traces of *Alnus*, *Betula*, *Pinus*, *Quercus*, *Tilia* and *Ulmus*, and higher counts of *Corylus*. The assemblage was dominated by *Pteridium*, Gramineae (Poaceae) and Liguliflorae (Lactuceae type), and taken to suggest an open environment; cereal pollen was found in extremely small quantities. The reliability of these results was accepted. Differential preservation was discussed but rejected, on the grounds that the values of the most decay-resistant species varied considerably from site to site within the region (Dimbleby and Evans 1974, 130). To explain the discrepancy between the pollen results and the molluscan results, it was suggested that the pollen rain reflected the most recent history of the soil before burial (Dimbleby and Evans 1974). Bracken infestation of cultivated plots was also suggested (Dimbleby and Evans 1974), and later elaborated by R. Smith (1984).

1988 results

In 1988, the old land surface under the outer bank in Trench BB was sampled for pollen in several places: the subsoil hollow, and the buried soil in the molluscan sampling points BB3, BB4 and BB5, along the exposed north section of Smith cutting V. The primary fill of the outer ditch in Trench B was also sampled.

There was no countable pollen in the samples. There were occasional grains of Poaceae, *Corylus* and *Pteridium*, but these were all very badly degraded. The discrepancy with Dimbleby's results may reflect, in part, small-scale variations in the conditions of preservation.

The modern soil was also sampled in BB3, at the crest of the outer bank on the north section of Smith cutting V (table 81). This yielded broad similarities with the counts from the modern soils obtained by Dimbleby. The contrast is striking between the surface layer (sample 1) and the three layers beneath (samples 2–4). The dominant component of the surface horizon is grass (Poaceae), which is expected given the nature of the contemporary vegetation. The Poaceae count exceeds 50 percent of the total land pollen. The other major component is Lactuceae (20 percent), which is a far higher value than might be expected on purely ecological grounds. Lactuceae pollen possesses an extremely robust outer coating which makes it very resistant to decay, and hence differential preservation often leads to a bias in favour of this type of grain. The effect is more clearly seen in samples 2–4 where over 40 percent of the spectra consist of Lactuceae pollen. In these samples, grass pollen values are reduced to less than 30 percent, again most probably reflecting differential pollen preservation. Dimbleby also obtained high counts for Compositae pollen (including Lactuceae), which tend to dominate the

Table 81: Percentage pollen analysis of the modern soil profile on the outer bank (sample point BB3, Trench BB/cutting V).

Sample (cm below surface)	1	2	3	4
Betula	0.6	0.5	2.5	2.5
Pinus	2.3	4.0	0.5	0.5
Abies	-	-	0.5	0.5
Alnus	0.6	1.0	-	1.0
Picea	2.0	2.0	2.0	3.0
Corylus	1.6	1.0	1.0	1.5
Ericaceae	0.3	1.0	0.5	-
Ilex	-	1.0	-	-
Poaceae	52.6	22.5	28.5	25.5
Cerealia type	1.6	1.0	2.0	3.0
Cyperaceae	2.3	3.0	4.0	3.5
Caryophyllaceae	0.3	0.5	-	-
Chenopodiaceae	0.6	0.5	-	-
Lactuceae type	21.6	40.5	39.5	46.0
Asteraceae type	2.3	2.5	4.0	3.0
Hypericum	-	0.5	-	-
Leguminosae	0.3	-	-	-
Plantago lanceolata	0.6	0.5	1.0	1.5
Plantago media/major	1.0	-	0.5	1.0
Ranunculus	-	1.0	-	0.5
Rumex	0.3	0.5	0.5	-
Saxifraga	0.5	0.5	-	-
Succisa	-	-	1.0	-
Urtica	0.6	-	-	-
Valeriana	1.0	-	-	-
Pteropsida monolete (undiff.)	3.6	4.0	4.5	-
Polypodium	0.3	0.5	-	0.5
Lycopodium	-	-	-	0.5
Pteridium	-	0.5	-	-
Unknown/indeterminate	2.0	6.5	8.5	6.5
Pollen sum (Total land pollen)	300	200	200	200

spectra largely, perhaps, because of their greater resistance to decay.

In all the modern 1988 samples a relatively high number of pollen grains were degraded, the majority exhibiting the type of exine damage usually associated with chemical destruction in aerobic environments. In samples 2-4, the numbers of indeterminate grains exceed 6 percent. Most of these were so badly deteriorated that identification was impossible. Clearly, a considerable amount of post-depositional damage has taken place, yet in only a modern soil. It is scarcely surprising, therefore, that in the buried soil, of Neolithic date, virtually no pollen has managed to survive.

Conclusion

It is almost impossible to obtain pollen counts from this type of deposit that are a true reflection of the former pollen rain and hence of former vegetation cover. As there is no way of knowing the extent to which post-depositional processes within these calcareous soils have combined to change the nature of the original pollen assemblage, any palaeoecological inference that is drawn from such a data set must rest on very insecure foundations. The counts obtained by Dimbleby might be taken to reflect an essentially open, grassland environment, but apart from seeming to contradict other evidence from the site for the Neolithic pre-bank environment, there is no way of telling whether the low counts for tree pollen indicate relatively sparse woodland cover in the original landscape or are merely due to the differential destruction of arboreal pollen grains.

11

The Mammalian Remains

Caroline Grigson

PART 1: INTRODUCTION

The aim of the faunal analysis is to illuminate the activities of the people of Windmill Hill in relation to their domestic animals and to the wild animals living in the surrounding landscape. As the main thrust of the present volume is the analysis of the finds of all types from the 1988 excavations in terms of their spatial distribution within the different contexts of the site, rather than the more usual attempt to establish a hard and fast chronological framework within which the features and their contents can be grouped, Part 2 of this chapter is an attempt to quantify the 1988 bone data in contextual terms, context by context, level by level and trench by trench. Part 3 is taken up with a faunal analysis of the more usual kind and includes material from the earlier excavations by Alexander Keiller and Isobel Smith.

Excavation, retrieval and curation

Every piece of bone and tooth that was seen in the excavation was retrieved; there was no on-site sorting. All bones and teeth, except for a few which were too fragile or too small, were washed, dried, marked with site and year code, and with find, context and trench number, and then packed in separate bags for each find. The standard of retrieval and curation was exceptionally high. The deposits of suitable contexts were subject to flotation for charred plant remains (see chapter 8), the bone fragments being extracted in a 3 mm sieve. They were of course too small to be marked individually, but were packed into separate bags for each find. A few of the bones were broken in or after excavation and where feasible most of these were repaired in the course of the faunal analysis.

Storage

The bones from all three Windmill Hill excavations are stored in the Alexander Keiller Museum, Avebury.

Preservation

One might expect bone preservation in the alkaline conditions of the chalky deposits of Windmill Hill to be good, and indeed the clean whitish appearance of the majority of the bones suggests that this is the case, but preservation in such conditions can in fact be poor (Locock *et al.* 1992). In particular the surface of the bones has to a large extent been eroded away, thus removing almost all surface modifications such as cutmarks and traces of gnawing. In such conditions one would expect teeth and the denser bone elements to survive better than softer elements.

The colour of bones is a variable which can be of taphonomic interest, so in the early stages of the present faunal analysis an attempt was made to record the colour of each bone fragment. This was abandoned, partly because the bone fragments had not all been washed to the same degree, and some were too fragile or too fragmentary to clean, but largely because many were not uniform in colour.

Methods

Identification

Wherever possible each bone was identified to taxon, bone, and part of bone, using the reference collection in the Mammalian Osteology Room of the Natural History Museum. All bone fragments, whether identified or not, were counted and recorded and a note was made of the size (to the nearest 1 cm) of each fragment, except for those taken for radio-carbon dating and the very few which had clearly been broken during or since excavation, or were too crumbly to be measured.

Quantification

Simple counts of the *numbers of bones* (NISP in the American literature) have been made for the present analysis. However, a second category of numbers, *bone finds*, has also been included when it was clear that any particular bone came from the same individual animal as another. For example, a set of articulating wrist or ankle bones or articulating vertebrae would be counted as one find.

Although methods such as those suggested by Davis (1992) and by Watson (1979), in which only a limited range of bone elements is identified or counted, are gaining in popularity because they help to speed the recording and to facilitate the quantification of the relative numbers of the different species present, they have not been used in the present analysis. This is because body part analysis means very little unless all parts of the skeleton are included and because it is the entire content of individual contexts which is of interest at Windmill Hill. For example many of the assemblages within particular contexts are dominated by cattle vertebrae and ribs, elements which would have been excluded in any analysis based on a few standard bone elements. A second objection is that the underlying assumption of these methods is that non-adjacent parts of the same bone element are counted as one – on the assumption that they come from the same bone. This is a minimal number approach, similar to the minimum number of individuals, which is discussed below, and has not been utilised for the same reasons.

The use of *minimum numbers of individuals* (MNI) is frequent in faunal analysis, particularly in North America. Although calculations of MNI may be useful in small closed features, such as pits, both Gautier (1984) and Ducos (1983) have shown that the statistical chance of any one bone found in an archaeological site belonging to the same individual as another is minute, particularly on sites which were occupied for several hundred years. Therefore MNI counts have been used only in the bone element analyses (as a basis for estimating which elements are under-represented in the assemblage), not as a means of quantifying the relative numbers of the various taxa.

It is a common practice in faunal analysis not only to count bones, but to record *the weight of each bone*. This allows for the relative contribution of each taxon to the diet to be very crudely recorded in terms of body weight. Although apparently logical this is in fact highly misleading because it is not possible to clean each bone in such a manner that all particles of deposit are removed from its interstices, some bone elements are much heavier than others from the same skeleton, and in many sites, including Windmill Hill, bones have undergone varying degrees of destruction and of mineralisation.

PART 2: CONTEXTUAL ANALYSIS

Introduction

The following is an attempt to quantify some of the taphonomic bone data in various ways, context by context, in order to establish criteria by which the modes of deposition can be distinguished and to see whether the resulting patterns correspond with those observed in the field or established in subsequent analysis; these have already been designated bone groups, spreads and scatters on morphological criteria (see chapters 3 and 4). Summaries of this contextual information about the animal remains have been set out with the results of other classes of contextual analysis in chapters 3 and 4, and further discussion will follow in chapter 17.

The contextual information is presented in twelve main categories: fragment size – statistical parameters and distribution of frequencies; the numbers of burnt bones; the numbers of gnawed bones; the percentage of bones identified to taxon; the relative numbers of domestic ungulates represented; the relative numbers of wild and domestic animals; species richness; the numbers of matching bones – that is bones clearly from the same individual animal; bone element analysis; body part analysis; the side of the body; and, lastly, special finds. In some contexts the numbers of bones are too small for particular analyses, but they are all included in summaries of the larger groupings

by level, such as primary, secondary and tertiary in the ditches. The main faunal data for each trench are set out in summary form in tables 82–88.

Fragment size: statistical parameters and distribution of frequencies

The maximum diameter of each bone fragment, whether identified or not, was recorded wherever possible and the main statistical parameters of fragment size calculated for each context. The pattern of distribution of fragment size within the contexts was plotted for the larger samples. A similar method, using fragment weight instead of length has been used by Morel (1987). The small fragments of bone retrieved from flotation were counted and measured, but they have not been included in the contextual analysis as not all contexts were suitable for flotation. It can be seen in all the charts that there is a dearth of fragments in the 0–1 cm class, 1–2 cm being the size at which fragments were rarely retrieved by hand.

Trench BB: old land surface and bank
Summaries of the main statistical parameters of fragment size for the larger contexts are set out in table 89. Fig. 108 is a plot of mean fragment size and variability. Mean

Table 82: Trench BB, main faunal data.

Context	Feature	Cattle finds	nos	large rib	Pig finds	nos	Shp/gt finds	nos	medium rib	Red deer antler	Roe deer antler	Fragments nos	FLOT frags
712	tree hollow	*4*	4	2	-	-	-	-	-	1	-	6	-
705	OLS	*21*	21	8	*5*	5	*4*	4	2	-	-	116	-
741	OLS	-	-	-	*1*	1	*1*	1	1	-	1	22	8
743	OLS	-	-	-	-	-	-	-	-	-	-	1	-
742	OLS	*1*	1	-	*1*	1	*1*	1	-	-	-	4	-
761	posthole 760	*1*	1	-	-	-	-	-	1	-	-	-	-
711	posthole 711	-	-	-	-	-	-	-	-	-	-	-	6
722	posthole 711	-	-	-	-	-	-	-	-	-	-	1	-
756	posthole 755	-	-	-	-	-	-	-	-	-	-	3	-
710	posthole 710	-	-	1	-	-	-	-	-	-	-	3	-
709	posthole 709	-	-	-	-	-	-	-	-	-	-	3	-
752	posthole 751	-	-	-	-	-	-	-	-	-	-	2	-
714	pit 715	*1*	1	-	-	-	-	-	-	-	-	4	-
726	pit 715	2	2	-	-	-	-	-	-	-	-	9	-
707	grave	6	6	-	2	2	*1*	1	-	-	-	45	2
733	grave fill	2	2	-	*1*	1	-	-	-	-	-	4	-
734	grave fill	2	2	-	-	-	*3*	3	-	-	-	32	-
717	base of bank	*1*	1	-	-	-	-	-	-	-	-	2	-
746	primary bank	5	5	6	*1*	1	*1*	1	-	-	-	27	-
765	primary bank	5	5	2	*1*	1	*2*	2	-	2	-	63	-
703	main bank	5	5	1	*1*	1	-	-	-	1	-	22	-
702	main bank	-	-	-	-	-	-	-	-	-	-	6	-
701	main bank	4	4	1	*5*	5	*1*	1	-	-	-	35	-
700	turf	5	5	-	*1*	1	*1*	3	-	-	-	2	-

Table 83: Trench B, main faunal data (continued on opposite page).

Context	Cattle finds	nos	large rib	Pig finds	nos	Shp/gt	Sheep	Goat	medium rib	Dog finds	nos	Wild cattle	Red deer antler	bone
PRIMARY														
228	*31*	34	-	*5*	5	8	-	-	-	-	-	-	2	3
229	*17*	18	-	*2*	2	1	-	1	-	-	-	-	-	-
230	*1*	1	-	-	-	-	-	-	-	-	-	-	-	-
210	*9*	13	3	*1*	8	4	1	-	1	-	-	-	1	-
227	*27*	28	10	*6*	7	2	-	-	15	*1*	6	-	3	-
SECONDARY														
207	*4*	4	2	-	-	-	-	-	5	-	-	-	4	-
207/208	*5*	5	2	*1*	1	-	-	-	-	-	-	-	-	-
208	-	-	-	*2*	2	1	-	-	-	-	-	-	-	1
225	*10*	11	2	*17*	17	3	-	1	2	*1*	1	-	-	-
224	-	-	-	-	-	-	-	-	-	-	-	-	-	-
206	*2*	2	1	-	-	-	-	-	-	-	-	-	-	-
206/213	-	-	-	-	-	-	-	-	-	*1*	1	-	-	-
213	-	-	-	-	-	-	-	-	-	-	-	-	-	-
205	*4*	4	8	*2*	2	1	-	-	-	-	-	-	-	2
204	*3*	3	-	*1*	1	-	-	-	-	-	-	-	1	-
203	*37*	40	-	*16*	16	3	-	-	2	*2*	2	-	1	3
total	**65**	**69**	**15**	**39**	**39**	**8**	-	**1**	**9**	**4**	**4**	-	**6**	**6**
UPPER SECONDARY														
222	*2*	2	-	-	-	-	-	-	2	-	-	-	-	-
221	-	-	-	-	-	-	-	-	-	-	-	-	-	-
220	*3*	4	-	-	-	-	-	-	-	-	-	-	-	-
219	*2*	2	-	*1*	1	-	-	-	1	-	-	-	-	-
217	*5*	5	-	*2*	2	-	-	-	1	*1*	1	-	-	-
216	*15*	15	3	*12*	14	5	2	-	5	*1*	1	-	2	-
214	*23*	23	-	*19*	20	4	-	-	6	-	-	-	1	-
215	*11*	15	2	*9*	9	3	-	-	1	-	-	1	1	-
212	*1*	1	-	*1*	1	-	-	-	1	-	-	-	-	-
211	*1*	1	-	*1*	1	-	-	-	-	-	-	-	-	-
SOIL														
202	*82*	83	9	*79*	81	24	-	-	25	-	-	-	-	4
TERTIARY														
201	*25*	25	-	*14*	14	12	-	-	4	*1*	1	-	-	1

Table 84: Trench A, main faunal data.

Context	Bos finds	Bos nos	large rib	Pig finds	Pig nos	Shp /Gt	medium rib	Dog finds	Dog nos	Wild cattle	Wild? pig	Red deer antler	Red deer bone	Frag. nos	TOTAL ID finds	TOTAL ID nos	TOTALS finds	TOTALS nos	Flot frags	Flot bos	Flot pig
PRIMARY																					
112	1	1	-	-	-	1	-	-	-	-	-	-	-	6	2	2	8	8	-	-	-
117	7	10	-	-	-	1	-	-	-	-	-	-	-	3	8	11	11	14	-	-	-
SECONDARY																					
109	-	-	-	-	-	1	-	-	-	-	-	-	-	-	1	1	1	1	-	-	-
111	1	1	-	1	1	-	-	-	-	-	-	-	-	1	2	2	3	3	-	-	-
115	2	3	3	-	-	-	-	-	-	-	-	-	-	6	5	6	11	12	-	-	-
106	12	13	-	8	8	-	2	-	-	-	-	-	-	88	22	23	110	111	-	-	-
110	4	4	-	-	-	-	-	-	-	-	-	-	-	66	4	4	70	70	1	-	-
110/103	1	1	-	-	-	-	-	-	-	-	-	-	-	-	1	1	1	1	-	-	-
107	1	1	-	-	-	1	-	-	-	-	-	-	-	3	2	2	5	5	-	-	-
103	6	7	-	5	5	-	-	1	1	1	1	-	-	42	14	15	56	57	-	-	-
104	12	13	5	3	3	2	-	2	2	-	-	3	1	84	28	29	112	113	1	-	-
? 108	3	3	-	-	-	1	-	-	-	-	-	-	-	5	4	4	9	9	-	-	-
? 108/9	1	1	-	-	-	-	-	-	-	-	-	-	-	-	1	1	1	1	-	-	-
TERTIARY																					
102	14	14	1	3	3	-	-	-	-	-	-	-	1	60	19	19	79	79	7	1	1
101	1	1	-	-	-	-	-	-	-	-	-	-	-	-	1	1	1	1	-	-	-

Roe deer antler	Roe deer bone	Fox	Cat	Mustelid	Otter	Bird	Fragments finds	Fragments nos	TOTALS finds	TOTALS nos	FLOT cattle	FLOT pig	FLOT shpgt	FLOT roe	FLOT frags	FLOT total
-	1	-	-	-	-	-	63	63	113	116	-	-	-	-	29	29
-	-	-	-	-	-	-	9	9	30	31	-	-	-	-	-	-
-	-	-	-	-	-	-	-	-	1	1	-	-	-	-	-	-
-	-	-	-	-	-	3	12	13	36	47	-	-	-	-	1	1
-	-	-	-	-	-	-	96	96	160	167	-	-	-	-	-	-
-	-	-	-	-	-	-	22	22	37	37	-	-	-	-	-	-
-	-	-	-	-	-	-	9	9	17	17	-	-	-	-	-	-
-	-	-	-	-	-	-	3	3	7	7	-	-	-	-	-	-
-	-	-	-	1	-	2	274	274	313	314	-	-	-	-	13	13
-	-	-	-	-	-	-	10	10	10	10	-	-	-	-	-	-
-	1	-	-	-	-	-	9	9	13	13	-	-	-	-	2	2
1	-	-	-	-	-	-	-	-	2	2	-	-	-	-	-	-
-	-	-	-	-	-	-	5	5	5	5	-	-	-	-	-	-
-	-	-	-	2	-	-	38	38	57	57	-	-	-	-	-	-
-	1	-	-	-	-	-	14	14	20	20	-	-	-	-	-	-
2	1	-	-	-	-	-	82	82	149	152	-	-	-	-	-	-
3	**3**	-	-	**3**	-	**2**	**466**	**466**	**630**	**634**	-	-	-	-	-	-
-	-	-	-	-	-	-	5	5	9	9	-	-	-	-	-	-
-	1	-	-	-	-	-	4	4	5	5	-	-	-	-	-	-
-	-	-	-	-	-	-	14	14	17	18	-	-	-	-	3	3
1	-	-	-	-	-	-	1	1	6	6	-	-	-	-	1	1
-	1	-	-	-	-	-	51	51	61	61	-	-	-	-	-	-
-	1	-	-	1	-	1	143	143	191	193	-	1	-	-	19	20
-	-	-	-	-	-	-	227	227	280	281	-	-	-	-	-	-
-	-	-	-	-	-	-	110	110	138	142	-	-	-	-	4	4
-	-	-	-	-	-	-	58	58	61	61	-	-	-	-	-	-
-	-	-	-	-	-	-	11	11	13	13	-	-	-	-	-	-
-	1	3	-	-	1	-	**788**	**788**	**1016**	**1019**	1	2	2	1	168	174
-	1	1	1	-	-	-	216	216	276	276	-	-	-	-	-	-

Table 85: Trench C, main faunal data.

Context	Cattle finds	Cattle nos	large rib	Pig	Shp/Gt	Sheep	Goat	medium rib	Dog finds	Dog nos	Wild? cattle	Red deer	Roe deer	Fox	Cat finds	Cat nos	Bird	Fragments	TOTAL ID finds	TOTAL ID nos	GRAND TOTAL finds	GRAND TOTAL nos	Flot
PRIMARY																							
324	3	3	-	-	-	-	-	-	-	-	-	-	-	-	-	-	-	1	3	3	*4*	4	-
323	-	-	1	-	-	-	-	-	-	-	-	-	-	-	-	-	-	-	1	1	*1*	1	-
315	-	-	1	-	-	-	-	-	-	-	-	-	-	-	-	-	-	7	1	1	*8*	8	-
312	3	3	1	1	1	-	-	-	-	-	-	-	-	-	-	-	-	7	6	6	*13*	13	-
322	-	-	-	1	-	-	-	-	-	-	-	-	-	-	-	-	-	3	2	2	*5*	5	-
314	3	3	1	-	-	-	-	-	-	-	-	-	-	-	-	-	1	18	5	5	*23*	23	-
311	-	-	-	-	-	-	-	-	-	-	-	-	-	-	-	-	-	-	-	-	*-*	-	2
308	13	14	1	3	1	-	-	-	-	-	-	-	-	-	1	1	-	39	19	20	*58*	59	-
309	8	8	-	1	2	-	-	-	-	-	-	-	-	1	-	-	-	10	12	12	*22*	22	2
306	2	2	-	1	-	1	-	-	-	-	-	-	-	-	-	-	-	12	4	4	*16*	16	-
313	1	1	-	-	-	-	-	-	-	-	-	-	-	-	-	-	-	2	1	1	*3*	3	-
319	6	7	3	-	4	2	1	2	-	-	-	-	-	-	-	-	-	15	18	19	*33*	34	-
? 382	1	1	-	-	-	-	-	-	-	-	-	-	-	-	-	-	-	-	1	1	*1*	1	-
308/312	-	-	-	-	-	-	-	-	-	-	-	-	-	-	-	-	-	3	-	-	*3*	3	-
308/315	-	-	1	-	-	-	-	-	-	-	-	-	-	-	-	-	-	-	1	1	*1*	1	-
311/315	9	9	1	3	2	-	-	1	-	-	-	-	1	-	-	-	-	19	17	17	*36*	36	-
312/315	-	-	1	-	-	-	-	-	-	-	-	-	-	-	-	-	-	5	1	1	*6*	6	-
307	2	2	-	-	-	-	-	-	-	-	-	-	-	1	1	2	-	5	4	5	*9*	10	-
SECONDARY																							
321	13	68	1	-	2	-	-	2	-	-	-	-	-	-	-	-	-	32	18	73	*50*	105	-
UPPER SECONDARY																							
317	23	33	3	1	-	-	-	-	1	3	1	-	-	-	-	-	-	18	29	41	*47*	59	-
TERTIARY																							
302	47	47	7	16	6	1	-	1	1	3	-	1	1	-	-	-	-	205	81	83	*286*	288	-
301	5	5	2	1	-	-	-	-	-	-	-	-	-	-	-	-	-	33	8	8	*41*	41	-
300	1	1	-	1	-	-	-	-	-	-	-	-	-	-	-	-	-	15	2	2	*17*	17	-

Table 86: Trench D, main faunal data.

Context	Cattle finds	Cattle nos	large rib	Pig	Shp/Gt	Sheep	medium rib	Dog? nos	Wild? cattle	Red deer	Frags	TOTAL ID finds	TOTAL ID nos	GRAND TOTAL finds	GRAND TOTAL nos	Flot frags
PRIMARY																
416	12	14	5	3	2	2	2	-	-	-	20	20	24	*44*	46	-
417	-	-	1	-	-	-	-	-	-	-	-	1	1	*1*	1	-
415	3	3	-	1	-	-	-	-	-	-	5	4	4	*9*	9	-
409	-	-	2	-	1	-	-	-	-	-	2	1	1	*3*	3	-
408	-	-	2	-	-	-	-	1	-	1	5	3	3	*8*	8	-
418	10	10	-	2	-	-	-	-	-	1	-	13	13	*13*	13	-
SECONDARY																
411	5	5	2	2	-	-	-	-	3	-	18	12	12	*30*	30	32
414	13	13	6	-	-	-	-	-	2	-	30	21	21	*51*	51	-
413	16	18	9	9	3	3	12	-	12	1	154	41	41	*195*	197	9
406	14	14	11	1	2	2	5	-	5	-	46	33	33	*79*	79	20
405	-	-	-	-	-	-	-	-	-	1	1	1	1	*2*	2	-
404	2	2	-	1	-	1	-	1	-	2	17	5	5	*22*	22	3
TERTIARY																
401	1	1	1	-	-	1	-	-	-	-	3	2	2	*5*	5	-

Table 87: Trench E, main faunal data.

Context	Cattle finds	Cattle nos	large rib finds	large rib nos	Pig finds	Pig nos	Goat	Sheep	Shp/Gt	medium rib	Dog? finds	Dog? nos	Wild? cattle finds	Wild? cattle nos	Red deer antler	Red deer bones	Roe deer	Frags	TOTAL ID finds	TOTAL ID nos	GRAND TOTAL finds	GRAND TOTAL nos	Flot frags	Flot bos	Flot pig	Flot mm rib	Flot dog?
PRIMARY																											
514	3	3	1	1	-	-	-	-	2	-	-	-	-	-	-	-	-	2	6	6	8	8	-	-	-	-	-
515	-	-	3	3	-	-	-	-	-	-	-	-	-	-	-	-	-	7	3	3	10	10	-	-	-	-	-
527	2	2	-	-	5	5	-	1	4	6	-	-	-	-	-	-	-	27	18	18	45	45	-	-	1	-	-
512	2	2	7	7	-	-	-	-	-	-	-	-	-	-	-	-	-	4	9	9	13	13	-	-	-	-	-
522	30	31	13	13	10	11	-	12	-	4	1	-	-	-	-	-	-	76	70	72	146	148	-	-	-	-	-
524	11	11	2	2	1	1	-	1	-	1	-	-	-	-	-	-	-	4	16	16	20	20	-	-	-	-	-
523	13	13	4	4	3	3	-	-	1	1	-	-	-	-	-	-	-	6	22	22	28	28	-	-	-	-	-
506	1	1	1	1	2	2	-	1	1	-	-	-	-	-	-	-	-	14	5	5	19	19	-	-	-	-	-
513	1	1	1	1	-	-	-	-	-	-	-	-	-	-	-	-	-	1	1	1	2	2	-	-	-	-	-
511	-	-	-	-	3	3	-	1	1	1	-	-	-	-	-	-	-	3	4	4	7	7	-	-	-	-	-
509	2	2	-	-	1	1	-	1	1	1	-	-	-	-	-	-	-	6	3	3	9	9	-	-	-	-	-
508	17	17	-	-	-	-	-	-	-	-	-	-	-	-	-	1	-	13	20	20	33	33	5	-	-	-	-
525	28	36	4	4	12	12	1	6	4	-	-	-	-	-	-	-	-	21	55	63	76	84	13	-	-	-	-
518	2	2	1	1	1	1	-	-	-	2	-	-	-	-	-	-	-	16	6	6	22	22	7	-	-	-	-
516	2	2	-	-	2	2	-	1	1	-	3	3	-	-	-	-	-	-	8	8	8	8	-	-	-	-	-
SECONDARY																											
503	15	15	3	3	2	2	-	3	3	-	1	-	1	1	-	1	-	22	28	28	50	50	-	-	-	-	-
502	5	5	1	1	2	2	-	-	-	-	1	-	1	-	-	-	-	21	9	9	30	30	8	-	-	-	-
TERTIARY																											
501	23	23	2	2	5	5	-	3	3	2	-	-	-	-	-	1	1	159	38	38	197	197	-	-	-	-	-
500	1	1	-	-	-	-	-	-	-	-	-	-	-	-	-	1	-	5	1	1	6	6	-	-	-	-	-

Table 88: Trench F, main faunal data.

Context	Cattle finds	Cattle nos	large rib finds	large rib nos	Pig finds	Pig nos	Goat	Sheep	Shp/Gt	medium rib	Dog? finds	Dog? nos	Wild? cattle finds	Wild? cattle nos	Red deer bones	Frags	TOTAL ID finds	TOTAL ID nos	GRAND TOTAL finds	GRAND TOTAL nos	Flot frags	Flot bos	Flot pig	Flot mm rib	Flot dog?
PRIMARY																									
613	1	1	-	-	-	-	-	-	-	-	-	-	-	-	-	-	1	1	1	1	-	-	-	-	-
610	5	5	-	-	2	2	-	-	-	-	-	-	-	-	-	17	8	8	25	25	-	-	-	-	-
611	1	1	-	-	-	-	-	-	-	-	-	-	-	-	-	-	1	1	1	1	-	-	-	-	-
SECONDARY																									
630	15	15	3	-	4	4	1	-	6	-	2	2	-	-	-	55	32	33	87	88	1	-	1	-	-
629	16	16	-	-	3	3	-	2	3	-	-	2	-	-	-	8	26	26	34	34	-	-	-	-	-
627	3	3	4	-	6	7	-	-	4	-	1	1	-	-	-	11	18	19	29	30	45	1	1	-	1
604	15	15	3	-	4	4	-	-	3	-	1	-	-	-	-	13	26	26	39	39	288	-	1	1	-
605-626	6	6	-	-	2	2	-	-	-	-	-	-	-	-	-	9	8	8	17	17	3	-	-	-	-
TERTIARY																									
602	20	20	-	-	2	2	-	-	4	-	1	1	1	1	1	110	30	30	140	140	2	-	-	-	-
601	5	5	-	-	1	1	-	-	3	-	1	1	-	-	-	59	10	10	69	69	-	-	-	-	-
600	-	-	-	-	-	-	-	-	3	-	-	-	-	-	-	19	3	3	22	22	-	-	-	-	-

Table 89: Trench BB, statistical parameters of fragment size for the larger contexts.

	Context							
	705	**741**	**707**	**734**	**746**	**765**	**703**	**701**
N	143	25	53	33	35	53	29	46
mean	4.22	2.60	2.77	2.61	5.54	4.64	4.14	3.46
s	3.26	1.29	2.14	1.03	4.14	3.18	3.11	2.23
V	77.34	49.65	77.02	39.48	74.69	68.53	75.25	64.46
median	3	2	2	2	3	4	3	3
skew	1.12	1.39	1.09	1.77	1.84	0.60	1.10	0.61

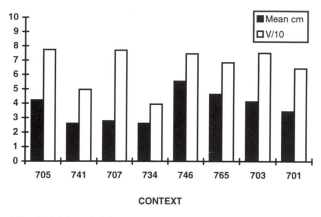

Fig. 108. Trench BB: mean size and variability in size of the bone fragments within the larger contexts. Variability is expressed as the coefficient of variation V divided by 10. Mean size is generally low, reaching 5 cm only in 746 (the base of the primary bank), with no apparent patterning in variability.

fragment size is quite low reaching 5 cm only in context 746 (the base of the primary bank). No patterning in variability can be discerned.

Fig. 109 shows the distribution of fragment size within the larger contexts of Trench BB. The distribution of fragment size within the bank contexts (746, 765, 703 and 701) is uneven as in the first type identified in Trench B, suggesting that they were incorporated into the bank soon after being discarded. One of the contexts in the old land surface (741) and the grave fill (734) show the second, smoother type of distribution, with a marked concentration at the smaller end of the scale, suggesting that these assemblages were subjected to marked degradation subsequent to deposition.

Trench B: outer ditch

Summaries of the main statistical parameters of fragment size for the larger contexts are set out in table 90. Fig. 110 is a plot of two of these parameters, mean fragment size and variability, expressed in terms of the coefficient of variation divided for convenience by 10, and set out in context order. Four contexts (210, 229, 228 in the primary level and 203 in the secondary level) are distinguished from the remainder by the larger mean size of the bone fragments; and in general there is a gradual reduction in mean fragment size over time. Variability also seems to decline slightly over time. It seems that the higher contexts have been more degraded than the lower ones, that is the bones have been more broken up, so that a much higher proportion is concentrated in the small size groups. This is confirmed by the graphical analysis of the distribution of fragment size.

Figs 111.1–111.4 show the distribution of fragment size within the larger contexts of Trench B. Comparison of the different graphs suggests two main types of deposit. In one there is a smaller proportion of small fragments and an uneven distribution of fragments of larger size (e.g. 210, 228, 229 primary, and 204 and 203 secondary). In the others fragment sizes are heavily concentrated at the smaller end; the curve then drops fast towards the larger end with a smooth distribution of fragment size, and with few, if any, large fragments (e.g. 225 secondary and all the upper secondary and tertiary contexts). It is, however, difficult to make a hard and fast distinction between these two main categories as the remaining contexts are intermediate between the two.

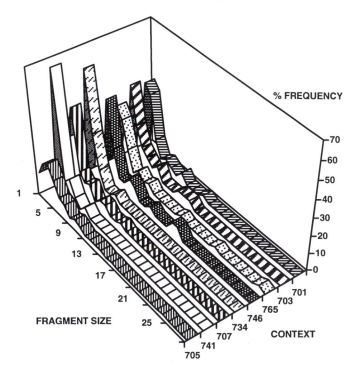

Fig. 109. Trench BB: distribution of bone fragment size. The old land surface (741) and the grave fill (734) have a smooth pattern of distribution, concentrated at the smaller end of the scale, suggesting marked degradation after deposition. Whereas the pattern within the bank (746, 765, 703 and 701) is uneven, indicating incorporation into the bank soon after discard.

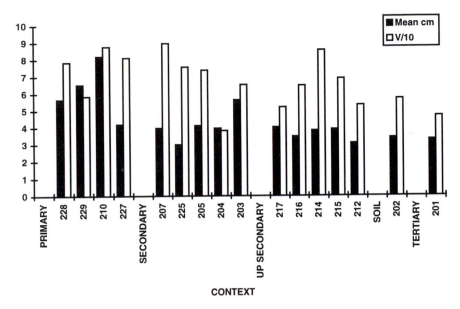

Fig. 110. Trench B: mean size and variability in size of the bone fragments within the larger contexts. Variability is expressed as the coefficient of variation V divided by 10. 210, 229, 228 (primary) and 203 (secondary) are distinguished the large mean fragment size. There seems to be reduction in mean fragment size and in variability over time, indicating a greater degree of degradation within the later contexts.

Trench A: outer ditch

Summaries of the main statistical parameters of fragment size for the larger contexts are set out in table 91. The numbers of bones retrieved in each context were small and only four secondary and one tertiary context contained enough bones for fragment size analysis. Fig. 112 shows that mean fragment size is quite low in Trench A, never reaching 5 cm. Variability is high, particularly in context 110, where it is due to the unusually high number of fragments of less than 1 cm (fig. 113); this is probably an artifact of particularly conscientious retrieval.

Fig. 113 shows that all the contexts in Trench A have a slightly uneven size distribution, intermediate between the two main types. Unevenness is most marked in context 103, which also has a larger mean size than the remainder of the contexts.

Trench C: outer ditch

Summaries of the main statistical parameters of fragment size for the larger contexts are set out in table 92. Fig. 114 is a plot of mean fragment size and variability. Fragment size is high in primary context 319 and the upper secondary context 317, and low in the tertiary contexts, suggesting greater degradation in the more superficial deposits.

Fig. 115, however, shows that the distribution of fragment size is markedly uneven in all the primary, secondary and upper secondary contexts, with the two tertiary contexts (302 and 301) of intermediate type.

Trench D: middle ditch

Summaries of the main statistical parameters of fragment size for the larger contexts are set out in table 93. Fig. 116

Table 90: Trench B, statistical parameters of fragment size for the larger contexts.

PRIMARY			Context	
	228	**229**	**210**	**227**
N	113	29	38	145
mean	5.65	6.52	8.18	4.18
s	4.42	3.80	7.17	3.38
V	78.35	58.37	87.55	80.98
median	4	6	5	3
skew	1.12	0.41	1.33	1.05

SECONDARY					
	207	**225**	**205**	**204**	**203**
N	34	312	54	20	148
mean	3.97	3.00	4.11	3.95	5.61
s	3.55	2.27	3.03	1.50	3.65
V	89.52	75.62	73.76	38.06	65.07
median	3	3	3	4	4
skew	0.82	0.00	1.10	-0.10	1.32

UPPER SECONDARY					
	217	**216**	**214**	**215**	**212**
N	59	185	281	132	59
mean	4.02	3.46	3.81	3.89	3.07
s	2.08	2.24	3.26	2.67	1.63
V	51.79	64.68	85.38	68.75	53.07
median	4	2	3	3	3
skew	0.02	1.96	0.75	1.00	0.12

	SOIL	TERTIARY
	202	**201**
N	1009	276
mean	3.40	3.28
s	1.93	1.53
V	56.89	46.58
median	3	3
skew	0.61	0.55

Caroline Grigson

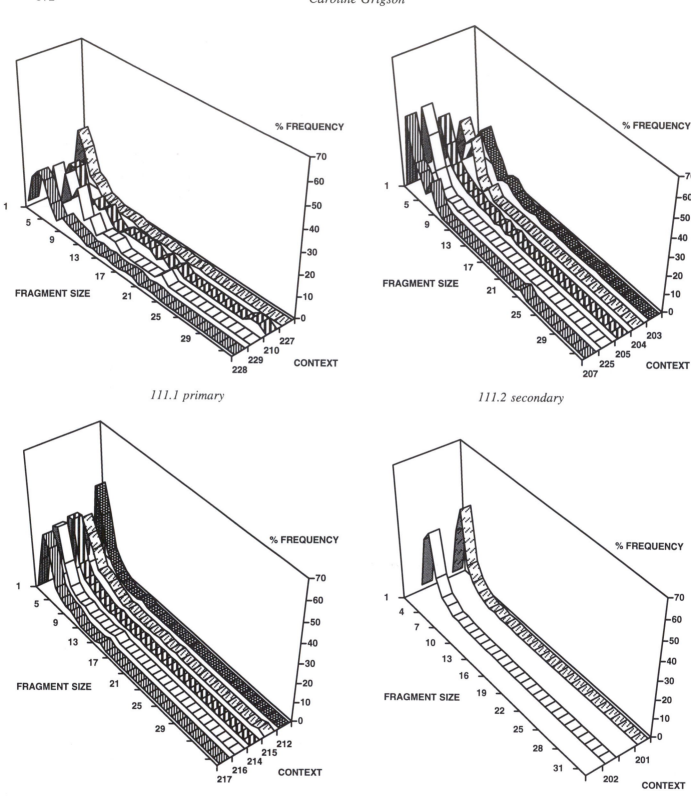

111.1 primary

111.2 secondary

111.3 upper secondary

111.4 soil and tertiary

Fig. 111. *Trench B: distribution of bone fragment size. Contexts 210, 228 and 229 (primary) and 204 and 203 (secondary) have a low percentage of small fragments and an uneven distribution of fragments of larger size indicating incorporation into the bank soon after discard. In most of the later contexts (including 225 secondary) fragment size is heavily concentrated at the smaller end, with a smooth distribution and few, if any, large fragments, confirming the greater degree of degradation within the later contexts suggested above. The distribution of fragment size within the remaining contexts seems to be intermediate between these two main types.*

Table 91: Trench A, statistical parameters of fragment size for the larger contexts.

	Context				
	106	**110**	**103**	**104**	**102**
N	108	70	54	111	76
mean	3.46	1.73	4.35	4.05	4.46
s	2.92	1.65	3.37	2.20	3.71
V	84.44	95.45	77.46	54.51	83.20
median	3	1	3	3	3
skew	0.47	1.32	1.20	1.42	1.18

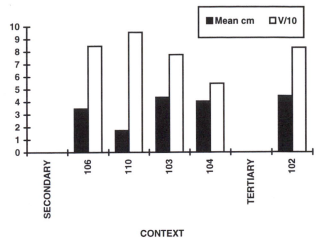

Fig. 112. Trench A: mean size and variability in size of the bone fragments within the larger contexts. Variability is expressed as the coefficient of variation V divided by 10. Mean fragment size is quite low in Trench A never reaching 5 cm. Variability is high, particularly in context 110, where it is due to the unusually high number of fragments of less than 1 cm, probably an artifact of particularly conscientious retrieval.

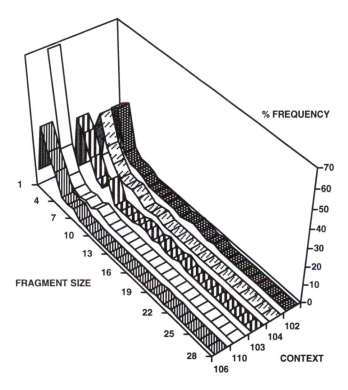

Fig. 113. Trench A: distribution of bone fragment size. All the larger contexts in Trench A have a slightly uneven distribution of size, intermediate between the two main types. Unevenness is most marked in context 103, which also has a larger mean size than the remainder of the contexts.

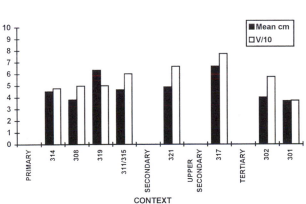

Fig. 114. Trench C: mean size and variability in size of the bone fragments within the larger contexts. Variability is expressed as the coefficient of variation V divided by 10. Fragment size is high in primary context 319 and the upper secondary context 317, and low in the tertiary contexts, suggesting greater degradation in the more superficial deposits.

Table 92: Trench C, statistical parameters of fragment size for the larger contexts.

	Context							
	314	**308**	**319**	**311/315**	**321**	**317**	**302**	**301**
N	21	58	27	31	98	46	277	40
mean	4.52	3.79	6.33	4.65	4.88	6.65	3.99	3.68
s	2.16	1.89	3.17	2.80	3.24	5.13	2.30	1.37
V	47.73	49.82	50.12	60.26	66.50	77.19	57.48	37.17
median	4	3	6	4	4	5	3	3
skew	0.73	1.26	0.32	0.69	0.81	0.97	1.30	1.48

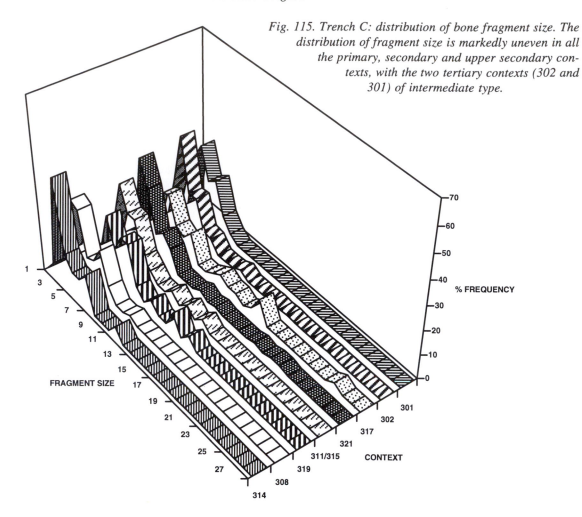

Fig. 115. Trench C: distribution of bone fragment size. The distribution of fragment size is markedly uneven in all the primary, secondary and upper secondary contexts, with the two tertiary contexts (302 and 301) of intermediate type.

Table 93: Trench D, statistical parameters of fragment size for the larger contexts.

| | Context | | | | | |
	416	**411**	**414**	**413**	**406**	**404**
N	46	46	60	216	109	23
mean	6.70	3.85	4.63	2.37	4.43	4.52
s	4.73	3.11	2.85	1.47	3.78	2.56
V	70.68	80.70	61.56	61.97	85.24	56.53
median	4	2	3	2	2	4
skew	1.71	1.79	1.72	0.75	1.93	0.61

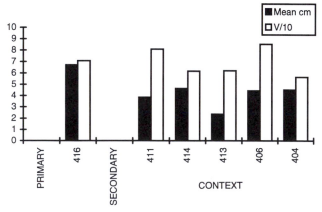

Fig. 116. Trench D: mean size and variability in size of the bone fragments within the larger contexts. Variability is expressed as the coefficient of variation V divided by 10. Mean size was particularly high in primary context 416 at the base of the ditch, but low in all contexts above it, particularly 413, which is the context showing the smoothest distribution of size (fig. 117).

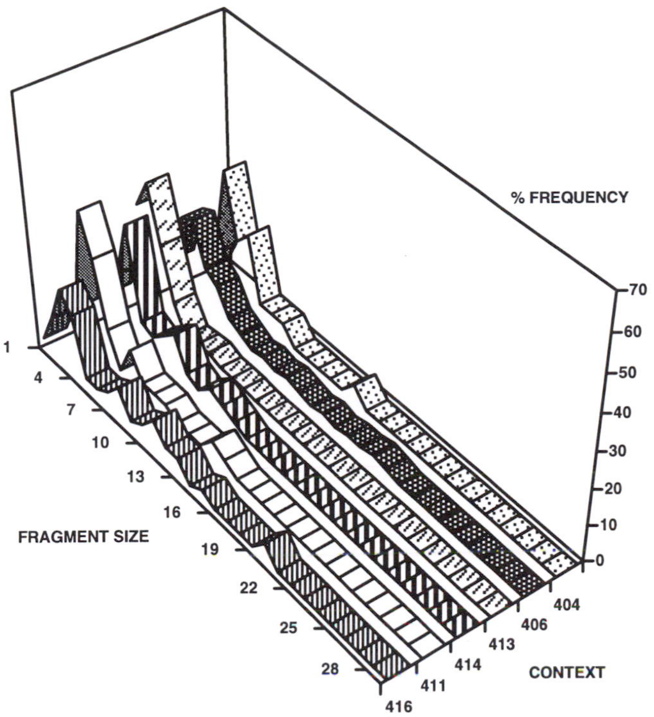

Fig. 117. Trench D: distribution of bone fragment size. 416, 411, 414 and 404 have an uneven distribution of size suggesting incorporation into the bank soon after discard, whereas in context 413 the pattern is particularly smooth, indicating marked degradation.

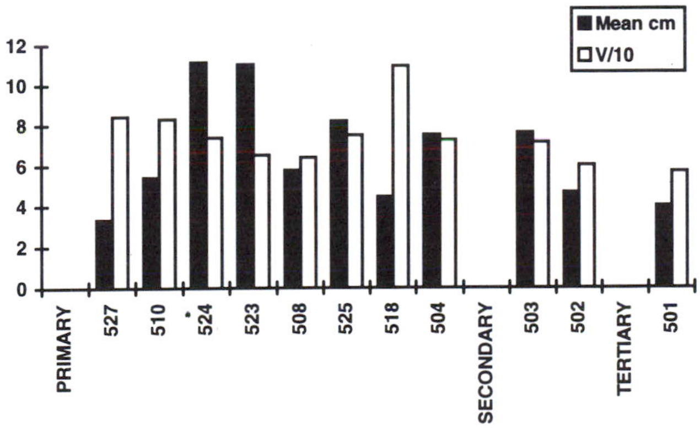

Fig. 118. Trench E: mean size and variability in size of the bone fragments within the larger contexts. Variability is expressed as the coefficient of variation V divided by 10. Mean size is particularly high in almost all the primary contexts and in secondary context 503, tailing off as usual in the later contexts. Variability is low in most contexts.

is a plot of mean fragment size and variability. Only two primary and four secondary contexts in the middle ditch excavation contained enough bones for fragment size analysis. Mean size was particularly high in primary context 416 at the base of the ditch, but low in all contexts above, particularly 413, which is the context showing the smoothest distribution of size (fig. 117). All the other contexts have uneven distribution curves.

Trench E: middle ditch

Summaries of the main statistical parameters of fragment size for the larger contexts are set out in table 94. Fig. 118 is a plot of mean fragment size and variability. Mean fragment size is particularly high in almost all the primary contexts and in secondary context 503, tailing off as usual in the tertiary fill (context 501), and this is matched by generally low variability and an uneven distribution of size in all primary contexts (fig. 119.1); the same is true of the secondary contexts, but the curve is smooth in the tertiary (fig. 119.2). Primary contexts 524, 523 and 525 and secondary context 503 are marked by their low proportion of small fragments, suggesting minimal degradation since deposition.

The patterns of bone fragmentation in Trench E are similar to those of the other middle ditch cutting, Trench D.

Trench F: inner ditch

Summaries of the main statistical parameters of fragment size for the larger contexts are set out in table 95. Fig. 120 is a plot of mean fragment size and variability. Mean fragment size is quite high in the single primary context and in the three secondary contexts, particularly 629. Both mean size and variability are low in the three tertiary contexts.

The distribution of fragment size (fig. 121) is uneven in all the primary and secondary contexts and smoother in the tertiary. Contexts 629 and 604 (both secondary) resemble some of those in Trench E in having few small fragments, again suggesting minimal degradation since deposition in the inner and middle ditches.

Table 94: Trench E, statistical parameters of fragment size for the larger contexts.

	Context										
	527	510	524	523	508	525	518	504	503	502	501
N	42	78	20	27	30	64	22	35	44	29	188
mean	3.33	5.41	11.15	11.04	5.77	8.20	4.45	7.51	7.61	4.66	4.00
s	2.81	4.49	8.23	7.20	3.69	6.16	4.88	5.45	5.42	2.79	2.28
V	84.25	83.06	73.80	65.21	64.03	75.06	109.48	72.56	71.22	60.02	56.94
median	3	4	8	9	4	6	3	5	6	4	3
skew	0.36	0.94	1.15	0.85	1.44	1.07	0.89	1.38	0.89	0.70	1.32

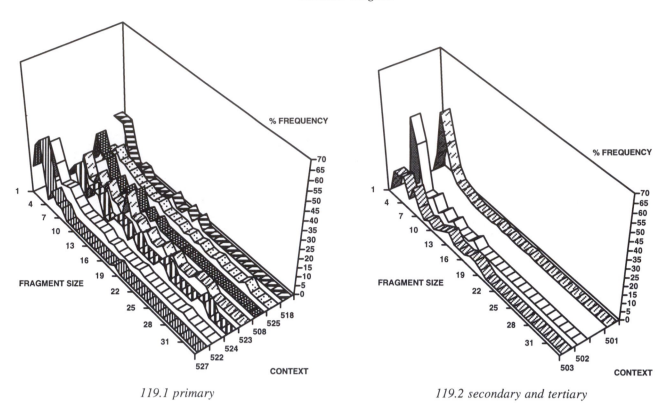

119.1 primary   *119.2 secondary and tertiary*

Fig. 119. Trench E: distribution of bone fragment size. All primary contexts and 503 (secondary) show an uneven distribution of size with a low percentage of small fragments, suggesting minimal degradation since deposition. The curve is smooth in the tertiary and that in 502 (secondary) seems intermediate.

Table 95: Trench F, statistical parameters of fragment size for the larger contexts.

		Context						
	610	**630**	**629**	**627**	**604**	**602**	**601**	**600**
N	24	95	37	28	38	140	68	22
mean	4.92	5.19	9.19	7.43	5.97	4.16	3.22	3.23
s	2.83	4.36	5.67	5.64	2.89	2.07	1.55	1.15
V	57.50	84.10	61.66	75.92	48.37	49.69	48.24	35.69
median	5	3	7	7	4	4	3	3
skew	-0.09	1.50	1.16	0.23	2.05	0.24	0.43	0.59

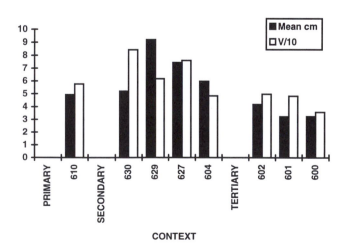

Fig. 120. Trench F: mean size and variability in size of the bone fragments within the larger contexts. Variability is expressed as the coefficient of variation V divided by 10. Mean fragment size is quite high in 610 (primary) and in the three secondary contexts, particularly 629. Both mean size and variability are low in the tertiary.

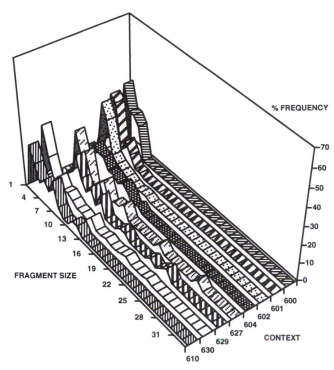

Fig. 121. Trench F: distribution of bone fragment size. The distribution of fragment size is uneven in all the primary and secondary contexts, but smoother in the tertiary. 629 and 604 (secondary) have few small fragments, suggesting minimal degradation since deposition.

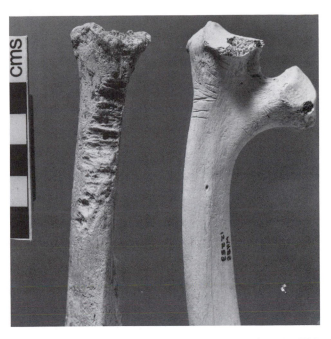

Fig. 122. A (left): Gnaw marks on a pig's tibia, in 516, middle ditch (Trench E). Early Neolithic. Probably made by a mouse. B (right): Cut marks on the proximal end of the first rib of an ox, in 512, middle ditch (Trench E). Early Neolithic. Such marks are produced in the removal of the longissimus dorsi muscle.

The numbers of burnt and gnawed bones

One or two contexts excavated at Windmill Hill have a significant proportion of burnt fragments. As burning seems to be confined to small fragments it is likely that they were accidentally incorporated into fires well after the time of their initial deposition. There are no bones that have been partially burnt as found by Vigne and Marinval-Vigne (1983) for the bones of *Prolagus* (a rabbit-like creature formerly inhabiting Sardinia) in which the distal ends of the longbones were burnt whilst the proximal ends were not, suggesting that they had been protected by flesh during roasting. This does not mean that the meat at Windmill Hill had not been cooked, merely that it was not roasted.

It is clear that dogs have played a role in the destruction of bone at Windmill Hill. The obvious signs of this are gnaw marks, the reduction of long bones to shaft cylinders (the ends of the bones have been gnawed off) and occasionally the presence of bones so eroded as to suggest that they have been voided in dog faeces (coprolites were also found in the excavations). Dog bones are present in some of the contexts and complete and partial dog skeletons were found in the Keiller excavations.

Very few bones showed any traces of gnawing by animals other than dogs; one exception was a pig's tibia, in 516, (middle ditch, Trench E), with massive traces of gnawing, made by a lagomorph or rodent, most probably a mouse. It is illustrated in fig. 122A.

Table 96: Trench BB, burnt bones.

Context	Feature	total nos	nos burnt	% burnt
712	tree hollow	13	-	-
705	OLS	156	3	1.9
741	OLS	26	-	-
743	OLS	1	-	-
742	OLS	7	-	-
761	posthole 760	2	-	-
722	posthole 711	1	-	-
756	posthole 755	3	1	33.3
710	posthole 710	4	3	75.0
709	posthole 709	3	-	-
752	posthole 751	2	-	-
714	pit 715	5	-	-
726	pit 715	11	2	18.2
707	grave	54	3	5.6
733	grave fill	7	-	-
734	grave fill	37	2	5.4
717	base of bank	3	-	-
746	primary bank	40	-	-
765	primary bank	75	3	4.0
703	main bank	30	2	6.7
702	main bank	6	-	-
701	main bank	46	2	4.3
700	turf	11	-	-
	TOTAL	543	21	3.9

Trench BB: old land surface and bank

Table 96 shows that burnt fragments of bone were present in many contexts in Trench BB, albeit in very small numbers. Their apparently haphazard presence suggests accidental incorporation rather than deliberate burning.

Table 97: Trench B, burnt and gnawed bones.

Context	TOTAL nos	burnt no	gnawed no	burnt %	gnawed %
PRIMARY					
228	116	-	6	-	5.2
229	31	-	4	-	12.9
230	1	-	-	-	-
210	47	-	-	-	-
227	167	4	2	2.4	1.2
total	**362**	**4**	**12**	**1.1**	**3.3**
SECONDARY					
207	37	2	1	5.4	2.7
207/208	17	-	2	-	11.8
208	7	-	-	-	-
225	314	53	1	16.9	0.3
224	10	1	-	10.0	-
206	13	-	1	-	7.7
206/213	2	-	-	-	-
213	5	-	-	-	-
205	57	-	2	-	3.5
204	20	2	-	10.0	-
203	152	4	17	2.6	11.2
total	**634**	**62**	**24**	**9.8**	**3.8**
UPPER SECONDARY					
222	9	-	-	-	-
221	5	-	-	-	-
220	18	-	1	-	5.6
219	6	-	-	-	-
217	61	-	-	-	-
216	193	1	4	0.5	2.1
214	281	2	2	0.7	0.7
215	142	1	3	0.7	2.1
212	61	-	-	-	-
211	13	1	-	7.7	-
total	**789**	**5**	**10**	**0.6**	**1.3**
SOIL					
202	1019	7	16	0.7	1.6
TERTIARY					
201	276	2	2	0.7	0.7
TOTAL	**3080**	**80**	**64**	**2.6**	**2.1**

Table 98: Trench A, burnt and gnawed bones.

Context	TOTAL nos	burnt no	gnawed no	burnt %	gnawed %
PRIMARY					
112	8	-	-	-	-
117	14	-	-	-	-
total	**8**	**-**	**-**	**-**	**-**
SECONDARY					
109	1	-	-	-	-
111	3	-	-	-	-
115	12	-	-	-	-
106	111	16	4	14.4	3.6
110	70	64	-	91.4	-
110/103	1	-	-	-	-
107	5	-	-	-	-
103	57	-	2	-	3.5
104	114	1	2	0.9	1.8
? 108	3	-	-	-	-
? 108/9	1	-	-	-	-
total	**378**	**81**	**8**	**21.4**	**2.1**
TERTIARY					
102	79	1	-	1.3	-
101	6	-	-	-	-
108	1	-	-	-	-
total	**86**	**1**	**-**	**1.2**	**-**
TOTAL	**472**	**82**	**8**	**17.4**	**1.7**

There were no bones in Trench BB with obvious signs of gnawing, but as already pointed out, this does not mean that the bones were not subject to depredation by dogs, merely that the condition of preservation was not good enough for superficial marking to survive.

Trench B: outer ditch

It can be seen from table 97 that only one context on Trench B had a substantial proportion of burnt bone; 53 small unidentified fragments were retrieved from secondary context 225, which are probably the result of accidental incorporation into a fire.

Table 97 also shows that the number of bones with obvious gnawmarks was very low, but their presence, albeit in small numbers, in most contexts confirms the suspicion that dogs played a role in the depredation of the bone in Trench B.

Trench A: outer ditch

In contrast to Trenches B and BB, Trench A has two adjacent contexts with high proportions of burnt bone, secondary context 110 with 91 percent of burnt fragments

(although many of these may be fragments of the same bone) and 106 with 14 percent (table 98). A few bones showed signs of gnawing.

Trench C: outer ditch

There were very few burnt or obviously gnawed bones in Trench C, except in the uppermost tertiary context (300) with 29 percent of burnt bones and 76 percent gnawed (table 99).

Trench D: middle ditch

There were very few burnt or obviously gnawed bones in Trench D (table 100).

Trench E: middle ditch

There were particularly few burnt bones in Trench E, but a few gnawed bones were present in many of the contexts, including one (523) of the four which, on the basis of fragment size analysis, appear to have suffered the least degradation (table 101).

Trench F: inner ditch

As in Trench E there were particularly few burnt bones in Trench F, but a few gnawed bones were present in many of the contexts (table 102).

Percentage of bones identified to taxon

The percentage of bones identified to taxon is of course a rather subjective variable since different faunal analysts have different skills and knowledge of identification. Nevertheless it can be useful when all the analysis is done by the same person.

Table 99: Trench C, burnt and gnawed bone.

Context	TOTAL nos	burnt no	gnawed no	burnt %	gnawed %
PRIMARY					
324	4	-	-	-	-
323	1	-	-	-	-
315	8	-	-	-	-
312	13	-	1	-	7.7
322	5	-	-	-	-
314	23	1	-	4.3	-
308	59	-	-	-	-
309	22	-	1	-	4.5
306	16	1	-	6.3	-
313	3	-	-	-	-
319	34	-	-	-	-
? 382	1	-	-	-	-
308/312	3	1	1	33.3	33.3
308/315	1	-	-	-	-
311/315	35	-	-	-	-
312/315	6	-	-	-	-
307	10	-	-	-	-
total	244	3	3	1.2	1.2
SECONDARY					
321	105	-	-	-	-
UPPER SECONDARY					
317	59	-	6	-	10.2
TERTIARY					
302	287	2	4	0.7	1.4
301	41	-	-	-	-
300	17	5	13	29.4	76.5
total	345	7	17	30.1	77.9
TOTAL	753	10	26	1.3	3.5

Table 100: Trench D, burnt and gnawed bones.

Context	total nos	burnt no	gnawed no	burnt %	gnawed %
PRIMARY					
416	44	-	5	-	11.4
417	1	-	-	-	-
415	9	-	1	-	11.1
409	3	-	-	-	-
408	8	-	-	-	-
418	13	-	2	-	15.4
total	78	-	8	-	10.3
SECONDARY					
411	30	-	-	-	-
414	51	-	1	-	2.0
413	197	-	1	-	0.5
406	79	1	2	1.3	2.5
405	2	-	-	-	-
404	21	2	-	9.5	-
total	380	3	4	0.8	1.1
TERTIARY					
401	5	-	-	-	-
TOTAL	463	3	12	0.6	2.6

Table 101: Trench E, burnt and gnawed bones.

Context	TOTAL nos	burnt no	gnawed no	burnt %	gnawed %
PRIMARY					
514	8	-	1	-	12.5
515	10	-	-	-	-
527	45	-	1	-	2.2
512	13	-	1	-	7.7
522	148	-	13	-	8.8
524	20	-	-	-	-
523	28	1	4	3.6	14.3
506	19	-	-	-	-
513	2	-	-	-	-
511	7	-	-	-	-
509	9	-	1	-	11.1
508	33	2	4	6.1	12.1
525	84	-	3	-	3.6
518	22	-	-	-	-
516	8	-	1	-	12.5
total	456	3	29	0.7	6.4
SECONDARY					
503	50	-	-	-	-
502	30	-	-	-	-
total	80	-	-	-	-
TERTIARY					
501	197	-	1	-	0.5
500	6	-	-	-	-
total	203	-	1	-	0.5
TOTAL	739	3	30	0.4	4.1

Table 102: Trench F, burnt and gnawed bones.

Context	TOTAL nos	burnt no	gnawed no	burnt %	gnawed %
PRIMARY					
610	25	-	2	-	8.0
611	1	-	1	-	100.0
total	26	-	3	-	11.5
SECONDARY					
630	88	-	3	-	3.4
629	34	-	5	-	14.7
627	30	-	-	-	-
604	39	1	2	2.6	5.1
605-626	17	-	1	-	5.9
total	208	1	11	0.5	5.3
TERTIARY					
602	140	-	4	-	2.9
601	69	1	1	1.4	1.4
600	22	-	-	-	-
total	231	1	5	0.4	2.2
TOTAL	465	2	19	0.4	4.1

Table 103: Trench BB, percentage bones identified.

Context	Feature	total ident	total frags	% ident
712	tree hollow	7	6	54
705	OLS	40	116	26
741	OLS	4	22	15
743	OLS	-	1	-
742	OLS	3	4	43
761	posthole 760	2	-	100
722	posthole 711	-	1	-
756	posthole 755	-	3	-
710	posthole 710	1	-	100
709	posthole 709	-	3	-
752	posthole 751	-	2	-
714	pit 715	1	4	20
726	pit 715	2	9	18
707	grave	9	45	17
733	grave fill	3	4	43
734	grave fill	5	32	14
717	base of bank	1	2	33
746	primary bank	13	27	33
765	primary bank	12	63	16
703	main bank	8	22	27
702	main bank	-	6	-
701	main bank	11	35	24
700	turf	9	2	82
	TOTAL	**131**	**409**	**24**

Table 104: Trench B, percentage bones identified.

Context	total ident	total frags	% ident
PRIMARY			
228	50	63	44
229	21	9	70
230	1	-	100
210	29	13	71
227	64	96	40
total	**165**	**181**	**48**
SECONDARY			
207	15	22	41
207/208	8	9	47
208	4	3	57
225	39	274	12
224	-	10	-
206	4	9	31
206/213	2	-	100
213	-	5	-
205	19	38	33
204	6	14	30
203	67	82	45
total	**164**	**466**	**26**
UPPER SECONDARY			
222	4	5	44
221	1	4	20
220	3	14	18
219	5	1	83
217	10	51	16
216	48	143	25
214	53	227	19
215	28	110	20
212	3	58	5
211	2	11	15
total	**157**	**624**	**20**
SOIL			
202	228	788	22
TERTIARY			
201	60	216	22
TOTAL	**774**	**2275**	**25**

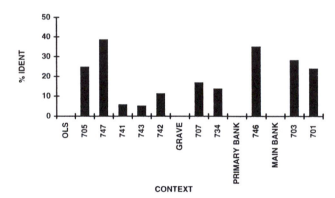

Fig. 123. Trench BB: percentages of bones identified within the larger contexts (n=>20). The percentages were all low in all contexts, the highest being in 746 (primary bank).

Trench BB: old land surface and bank

The percentages of bones identified in the various contexts of Trench BB were all low, but the highest was context 746 (primary bank), which was also marked by having the highest mean fragment size in this trench and its uneven fragment size distribution (table 103 and fig. 123).

Trench B: outer ditch

Table 104 and fig. 124 show that in the contexts containing more than 20 bones, the highest percentages, with over 70 percent identified, occur in the primary contexts (229 and 210), followed by the two other primary contexts (228 and 227) and two secondary contexts (207 and 203), in which about 40–50 percent were identified. The lumped per-

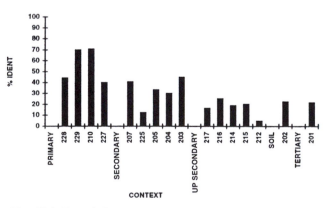

Fig. 124. Trench B: percentages of bones identified within the larger contexts (n=>20). The highest percentages, over 70 percent identified, occur in 229 and 210 (primary), followed by 228 and 227 (also primary) and 207 and 203 (secondary) in which about 40–50 percent were identified, contrasting with less than 20 percent in the upper secondary and tertiary levels.

centages were highest in primary levels, tailing off through the secondary levels to less than 20 percent in the upper secondary and tertiary levels. These marked contrasts suggest varied modes of deposition.

Table 105: Trench A, percentage bones identified.

Context	total ident	total frags	% ident
PRIMARY			
112	2	6	25.0
117	11	3	78.6
SECONDARY			
109	1	-	100.0
111	2	1	66.7
115	6	6	50.0
106	23	88	20.7
110	4	66	5.7
110/103	1	-	100.0
107	2	3	40.0
103	15	42	26.3
104	30	84	26.3
? 108	3	-	100.0
? 108/9	1	-	100.0
TERTIARY			
102	19	60	24.1
101	1	5	16.7
108	1	-	100.0
TOTAL	**122**	**364**	**25.1**

Table 106: Trench C, percentage bones identified.

Context	total ident	total frags	% ident
PRIMARY			
324	3	1	75.0
323	1	-	100.0
315	1	7	12.5
312	6	7	46.2
322	2	3	40.0
314	5	18	21.7
308	20	39	33.9
309	12	10	54.5
306	4	12	25.0
313	1	2	33.3
319	19	15	55.9
? 382	1	-	100.0
308/312	-	3	-
308/315	1	-	100.0
311/315	16	19	45.7
312/315	1	5	16.7
307	5	5	50.0
total	98	146	40.2
SECONDARY			
321	73	32	69.5
UPPER SECONDARY			
317	41	18	69.5
TERTIARY			
302	82	205	28.6
301	8	33	19.5
300	2	15	11.8
total	92	253	26.7
TOTAL	**304**	**449**	**40.4**

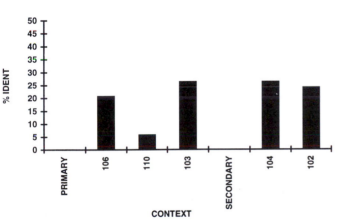

Fig. 125. Trench A: percentages of bones identified within the larger contexts (n=>20). The percentages in Trench A contexts were all low, the two highest being in 103 and 104.

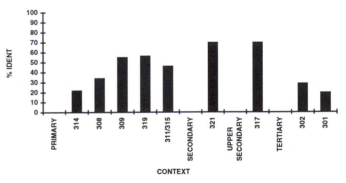

Fig. 126. Trench C: percentages of bones identified within the larger contexts (n=>20). The highest percentages, with over 60 percent identified, occur in the secondary and upper secondary (321 and 317), with about 50 percent in two primary contexts (309 and 319). The percentages were lowest in one primary context (314) and the tertiary levels.

Trench A: outer ditch

The percentages of bones identified in the various contexts of Trench A were all low; the two highest percentages were in contexts 103 and 104. One of these (103) was also marked by having the highest mean fragment size in this trench and an uneven fragment size distribution (table 105 and fig. 125).

Trench C: outer ditch

In the contexts containing more than 20 bones, the highest percentages, with over 60 percent identified, occur in the secondary (321) and upper secondary (317) levels, followed by the two primary contexts (309 and 319) in which about 50 percent were identified. The percentages were lowest in one primary context (314) and the tertiary levels (table 106 and fig. 126).

Trench D: middle ditch

The highest percentage of identified bones in the larger contexts of Trench D occurs in the primary levels, with that of 416 being over 50 percent; 416 also had a particu-

Table 107: Trench D, percentage bones identified.

Context	total ident	total frags	% ident
PRIMARY			
416	24	20	54.5
417	1	-	100.0
415	4	5	44.4
409	1	2	33.3
408	3	5	37.5
418	13	-	100.0
total	46	32	59.0
SECONDARY			
411	12	18	40.0
414	21	30	41.2
413	43	154	21.8
406	33	46	41.8
405	1	1	50.0
404	4	17	19.0
total	114	266	30.0
TERTIARY			
401	2	3	40.0
TOTAL	162	301	35.0

Table 108: Trench E, percentage bones identified.

Context	total ident	total frags	% ident
PRIMARY			
514	6	2	75.0
515	3	7	30.0
527	18	27	40.0
512	9	4	69.2
522	72	76	48.6
524	16	4	80.0
523	22	6	78.6
506	5	14	26.3
513	1	1	50.0
511	4	3	57.1
509	3	6	33.3
508	20	13	60.6
525	63	21	75.0
518	6	16	27.3
516	8	-	100.0
total	256	200	56.1
SECONDARY			
503	28	22	56.0
502	9	21	30.0
total	37	43	46.3
TERTIARY			
501	38	159	19.3
500	1	5	16.7
total	39	164	19.2
TOTAL	332	407	44.9

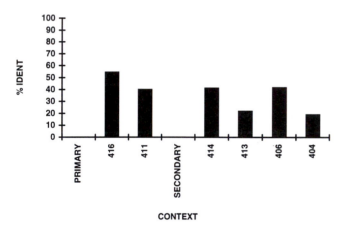

Fig. 127. Trench D: percentages of bones identified within the larger contexts (n=>20). The highest percentages occur in the primary levels, with that of 416 being over 50 percent. 411 (primary) and 414 and 406 (secondary) have just over 40%, with lower levels in 413 and 404. There are too few bones in the tertiary level for the percentage to be significant.

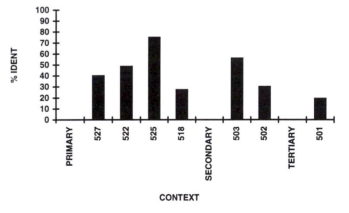

Fig. 128. Trench E: percentages of bones identified within the larger contexts (n=>20). 525 (primary) has a very high proportion of identified fragments, over 70 percent, followed by 503 (secondary) with 56 percent and 522 (primary) with nearly 50 percent, with lower percentages in the remaining contexts, particularly in the tertiary ones.

larly high mean fragment size. The other primary context (411) and two of the secondary contexts (414 and 406) have just over 40 percent, with lower levels in 413 and 404. There are too few bones in the tertiary level for the percentage to be significant (table 107 and fig. 127).

Trench E: middle ditch
A particularly high percentage of identified bones in the larger contexts of Trench E occurs in the primary context 525 with over 70 percent and secondary context 503 with 56 percent. Both contexts were also marked by high mean fragment size and a low proportion of small fragments.

Another primary context (522) had nearly 50 percent, with lower levels in the remaining contexts, particularly in tertiary context 501 (table 108 and fig. 128).

Trench F: inner ditch
Two secondary contexts (629 and 604) had over 60 percent of identified bones; the other secondary context (630) and the primary (610) had over 30 percent, with, as usual, lower percentages in the tertiary levels (table 109 and fig. 129).

Table 109: Trench F, percentage bones identified.

Context	total ident	total frags	% ident
PRIMARY			
613	1	-	100.0
610	8	17	32.0
611	1	-	100.0
total	**10**	**17**	**37.0**
SECONDARY			
630	33	55	37.5
629	26	8	76.5
627	19	11	63.3
604	26	13	66.7
605-626	8	9	47.1
total	**112**	**96**	**53.8**
TERTIARY			
602	30	110	21.4
601	10	59	14.5
600	3	19	13.6
total	**43**	**188**	**18.6**
TOTAL	**165**	**301**	**35.4**

The relative numbers of the domestic ungulates represented

Domestic ungulates are the only species represented in significant numbers in the Windmill Hill faunal assemblages. It is particularly important to ascertain whether the high proportion of cattle said by many authors (e.g. Grigson 1981b; Grigson *et al.* 1987) to typify Early Neolithic assemblages in Britain (and elsewhere) is a characteristic that reflects economic activity or whether the high proportions of particular species are confined to contexts which may be said to represent special activities (e.g. Richards and Thomas 1984 for the Later Neolithic).

Trench BB: old land surface and bank

Details of the ungulates identified in Trench BB are set out in table 110; the individual contexts were too small for individual analysis, so only the totals of the combined assemblage can be figured (fig. 130), which shows that the proportions of cattle, pigs and sheep/goats are similar to those of the primary level of Trench B.

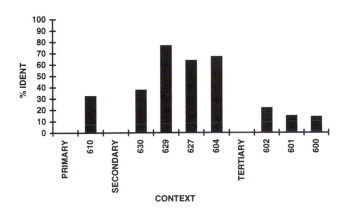

Fig. 129. Trench F: percentages of bones identified within the larger contexts (n=>20). 629 and 604 (secondary) had over 60 percent of identified bones; 630 (also secondary) and the primary (610) had over 30 percent, with, as usual, lower percentages in the tertiary levels.

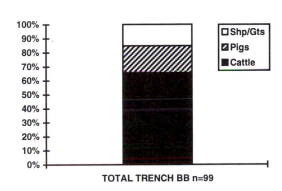

Fig. 130. Trench BB: percentages of domestic ungulates identified in all contexts; the individual contexts being too small for individual analysis. The proportions of cattle, pigs and sheep/goats are similar to those of the primary level of Trench B (see below).

Table 110: Trench BB, domestic ungulates.

Context	Features	Cattle finds	Cattle %	Pigs finds	Pigs %	Shp/Gt finds	Shp/Gt %	Total
712	tree hollow	4	100.0	-	-	-	-	4
705	OLS	21	70.0	5	16.7	4	13.3	30
741	OLS	-	-	1	50.0	1	50.0	2
742	OLS	1	33.3	1	33.3	1	33.3	3
761	posthole 760	1	100.0	-	-	-	-	1
714	pit 715	1	100.0	-	-	-	-	1
726	pit 715	2	100.0	-	-	-	-	2
707	grave	6	66.7	2	22.2	1	11.1	9
733	grave fill	2	66.7	1	33.3	-	-	3
734	grave fill	2	40.0	-	-	3	60.0	5
717	base of bank	1	100.0	-	-	-	-	1
746	primary bank	5	71.4	1	14.3	1	14.3	7
765	primary bank	5	62.5	1	12.5	2	25.0	8
703	main bank	5	83.3	1	16.7	-	-	6
701	main bank	4	40.0	5	50.0	1	10.0	10
700	turf	5	71.4	1	14.3	1	14.3	7
TOTAL		**65**	**65.7**	**19**	**19.2**	**15**	**15.2**	**99**

Caroline Grigson

Table 111: Trench B, domestic ungulates.

Context	Cattle		Pigs		Shp/Gt		Total
	finds	*%*	*finds*	*%*	*nos*	*%*	
PRIMARY							
228	*31*	70.5	*5*	11.4	8	18.2	**44**
229	*17*	81.0	*2*	9.5	2	9.5	**21**
230	*1*	100.0	-	-	-	-	**1**
210	*9*	60.0	*1*	6.7	5	33.3	**15**
227	*27*	77.1	*6*	17.1	2	5.7	**35**
total	*85*	73.3	*14*	12.1	17	14.7	**116**
SECONDARY							
207	*4*	100.0	-	-	-	-	**4**
207/208	*5*	83.3	*1*	16.7	-	-	**6**
208	-	-	*2*	66.7	1	33.3	**3**
225	*10*	32.3	*17*	54.8	4	12.9	**31**
224	-	-	-	-	-	-	**-**
206	*2*	100.0	-	-	-	-	**2**
206/213	-	-	-	-	-	-	**-**
213	-	-	-	-	-	-	**-**
205	*4*	57.1	*2*	28.6	1	14.3	**7**
204	*3*	75.0	*1*	25.0	-	-	**4**
203	*37*	66.1	*16*	28.6	3	5.4	**56**
total	*65*	57.5	*39*	34.5	9	8.0	**113**
UPPER SECONDARY							
222	*2*	100.0	-	-	-	-	**2**
221	-	-	-	-	-	-	**-**
220	*3*	100.0	-	-	-	-	**3**
219	*2*	66.7	*1*	33.3	-	-	**3**
217	*5*	71.4	*2*	28.6	-	-	**7**
216	*15*	44.1	*12*	35.3	7	20.6	**34**
214	*23*	50.0	*19*	41.3	4	8.7	**46**
215	*11*	47.8	*9*	39.1	3	13.0	**23**
212	*1*	50.0	*1*	50.0	-	-	**2**
211	*1*	50.0	*1*	50.0	-	-	**2**
total	*63*	51.6	*45*	36.9	14	11.5	**122**
SOIL							
202	*82*	44.3	*79*	42.7	24	13.0	**185**
TERTIARY							
201	*25*	49.0	*14*	27.5	12	23.5	**51**
TOTAL	***320***	**54.5**	***191***	**32.5**	**76**	**12.9**	**587**

Trench B: outer ditch

The identifications of the animals represented by the bones in Trench B are set out in the main table (table 82). The numbers of bone finds of domestic ungulates, cattle, pigs, sheep and goats, are detailed in table 111. The numbers in which these are represented in contexts with 20 bone finds are set out in fig. 131, which suggests a marked predominance of cattle in the primary levels (228, 229 and 227), after which cattle decrease in an irregular manner. The secondary context 225 has a particularly large proportion of pig. The simpler fig. 132, which shows the totals for each main level, suggests a steady increase in the proportion of pigs and sheep/goats at the expense of cattle from the secondary level onwards. In the tertiary level sheep/goats increase slightly at the expense of pig.

Trench A: outer ditch

Details of the ungulates identified in Trench A are set out in table 112. As in Trench BB the individual contexts in Trench A were too small for individual analysis, and this is also true of the primary and tertiary levels as a whole, so only the totals of the whole assemblage in the secondary level can be figured. Fig. 133 shows that the high proportion of cattle to pigs and sheep/goats is similar to those in the primary level of Trench B and the total assemblage for Trench BB, though with a slightly higher proportion of pig.

Trench C: outer ditch

Details of the ungulates identified in Trench C are set out in table 113. With the exception of the single context within the upper secondary level, the individual contexts in Trench C were too small for individual analysis, and this is also true of the secondary level as a whole, so only the totals of the assemblages in the primary, upper secondary and tertiary levels can be figured. Fig. 134 shows that

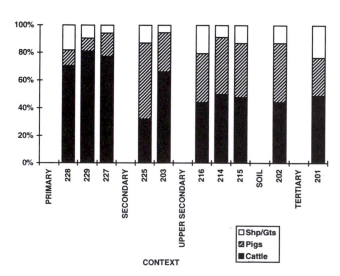

Fig. 131. Trench B: percentages of domestic ungulates identified in all larger contexts (n=>20). There is a marked predominance of cattle in the primary levels (228, 229 and 227), after which cattle decrease in an irregular manner. 225 (secondary) has a high proportion of pig bones.

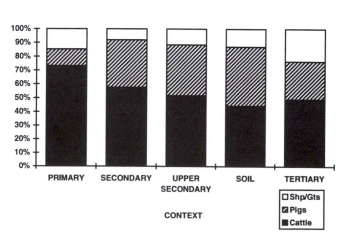

Fig. 132. Trench B: percentages of domestic ungulates identified in the main levels, showing a steady increase in the proportion of pigs and sheep/goats at the expense of cattle from the secondary level onwards. In the tertiary sheep/goats increase slightly at the expense of pigs.

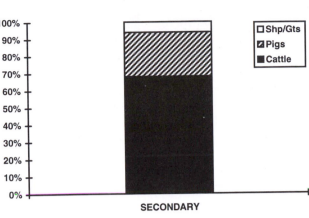

Fig. 133. Trench A: percentages of domestic ungulates identified in all contexts; the individual contexts being too small for individual analysis. Showing a high proportion of cattle to pigs and sheep/goats similar to that in the primary level of Trench B, though with a slightly higher proportion of pig.

Table 112: Trench A, domestic ungulates.

Context	Cattle		Pigs		Shp/Gt		Total
	finds	%	finds	%	nos	%	
PRIMARY							
112	1	50.0	-	-	1	50.0	2
117	7	-	-	-	1	12.5	8
total	8	80.0	-	-	2	20.0	10
SECONDARY							
109	-	-	-	-	1	100.0	1
111	1	50.0	1	50.0	-	-	2
115	4	100.0	-	-	-	-	4
106	12	60.0	8	40.0	-	-	20
110	4	100.0	-	-	-	-	4
110/103	1	100.0	-	-	-	-	1
107	1	50.0	-	-	1	50.0	2
103	6	54.5	5	45.5	-	-	11
104	12	70.6	3	17.6	2	11.8	17
? 108	3	100.0	-	-	-	-	3
? 108/9	1	100.0	-	-	-	-	1
total	45	68.2	17	25.8	4	6.1	66
TERTIARY							
102	14	82.4	3	17.6	-	-	17
101	1	100.0	-	-	-	-	1
108	-	-	-	-	1	100.0	1
total	15	78.9	3	15.8	1	5.3	19
TOTAL	**23**	**79.3**	**3**	**10.3**	**3**	**10.3**	**29**

Fig. 134. Trench C: percentages of domestic ungulates identified in the primary, upper secondary and tertiary levels; the individual contexts, and the secondary level as a whole, were too small for individual analysis. The high proportion of cattle in both the primary and tertiary levels resembles that in the primary level of Trench B.

Table 113: Trench C, domestic ungulates.

Context	Cattle		Pig		Shp/Gt		Total
	finds	%	nos	%	nos	%	
PRIMARY							
324	3	100.0	-		-	-	3
315	-	-	1	100.0	-	-	1
312	3	60.0	1	20.0	1	20.0	5
322	-	-	1	100.0	-	-	1
314	3	100.0	-	-	-	-	3
308	13	76.5	3	17.6	1	5.9	17
309	8	72.7	1	9.1	2	18.2	11
306	2	50.0	1	25.0	1	25.0	4
313	1	100.0	-	-	-	-	1
319	6	46.2	-	-	7	53.8	13
? 382	1	100.0	-	-	-	-	1
311/315	9	64.3	3	21.4	2	14.3	14
307	2	100.0	-	-	-	-	2
total	51	67.1	11	14.5	14	18.4	76
SECONDARY							
321	13	86.7	-	-	2	13.3	15
UPPER SECONDARY							
317	23	95.8	1	4.2	-	-	24
TERTIARY							
302	47	67.1	16	22.9	7	10.0	70
301	5	83.3	1	16.7	-	-	6
300	1	50.0	1	50.0	-	-	2
total	53	67.9	18	23.1	7	9.0	78
TOTAL	**140**	**72.5**	**30**	**15.5**	**23**	**11.9**	**193**

Table 114: Trench D, domestic ungulates.

Context	Cattle finds	%	Pig nos	%	Shp/Gt nos	%	Total
PRIMARY							
416	12	70.6	3	17.6	2	11.8	17
415	3	75.0	1	25.0	-	-	4
409	-	-	-	-	1	100.0	1
418	10	83.3	2	16.7	-	-	12
total	25	**73.5**	6	**17.6**	3	**8.8**	34
SECONDARY							
411	5	71.4	2	28.6	-	-	7
414	13	68.4	6	31.6	-	-	19
413	16	84.2	-	-	3	15.8	19
406	14	82.4	1	5.9	2	11.8	17
404	2	25.0	1	12.5	5	62.5	8
total	50	**71.4**	10	**14.3**	10	**14.3**	70
TERTIARY							
401	1	50.0	1	50.0	-	-	2
TOTAL	76	**71.7**	17	**16.0**	13	**12.3**	106

Table 115: Trench E, domestic ungulates.

Context	Cattle finds	%	Pig finds	%	Shp/Gt nos	%	Total
PRIMARY							
514	3	60.0	-	-	2	40.0	5
527	2	16.7	5	41.7	5	41.7	12
512	2	100.0	-	-	-	-	2
522	30	57.7	10	19.2	12	23.1	52
524	11	84.6	1	7.7	1	7.7	13
523	13	76.5	3	17.6	1	5.9	17
506	1	25.0	2	50.0	1	25.0	4
513	1	100.0	-	-	-	-	1
511	-	-	3	75.0	1	25.0	4
509	2	66.7	1	33.3	-	-	3
508	17	94.4	-	-	1	5.6	18
525	28	54.9	12	23.5	11	21.6	51
518	2	66.7	1	33.3	-	-	3
516	2	40.0	2	40.0	1	20.0	5
total	114	**60.0**	40	**21.1**	36	**18.9**	190
SECONDARY							
503	15	75.0	2	10.0	3	15.0	20
502	5	71.4	2	28.6	-	-	7
total	20	**74.1**	4	**14.8**	3	**11.1**	27
TERTIARY							
501	23	74.2	5	16.1	3	9.7	31
500	1	100.0	-	-	-	-	1
total	24	**75.0**	5	**15.6**	3	**9.4**	32
TOTAL	158	**63.5**	49	**19.7**	42	**16.9**	249

Table 116: Trench F, domestic ungulates.

Context	Cattle finds	%	Pig finds	%	Shp/Gt nos	%	Total
PRIMARY							
610	5	71.4	2	28.6	-	-	7
611	1	100.0	-	-	-	-	1
total	6	**75.0**	2	**25.0**	-	-	8
SECONDARY							
630	15	57.7	4	15.4	7	26.9	26
629	16	66.7	3	12.5	5	20.8	24
627	3	30.0	6	60.0	1	10.0	10
604	15	68.2	4	18.2	3	13.6	22
605-626	6	75.0	2	25.0	-	-	8
total	55	**61.1**	19	**21.1**	16	**17.8**	90
TERTIARY							
602	20	76.9	2	7.7	4	15.4	26
601	5	55.6	1	11.1	3	33.3	9
600	-	-	-	-	3	100.0	3
total	25	**65.8**	3	**7.9**	10	**26.3**	38
TOTAL	86	**63.2**	24	**17.6**	26	**19.1**	136

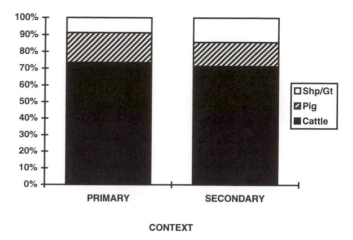

Fig. 135. Trench D: percentages of domestic ungulates identified in the primary and secondary levels; the individual contexts, and the tertiary level as a whole, were too small for individual analysis. The high proportion of cattle to pigs and sheep/goats in the primary and secondary levels is similar to that in the primary level of Trench B.

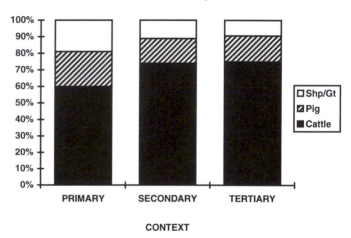

Fig. 136. Trench E: percentages of domestic ungulates identified in the main levels; the individual contexts were too small for individual analysis. The proportion of cattle in the secondary and tertiary levels is similar to that in the primary of Trench B, whereas that in the primary is slightly lower.

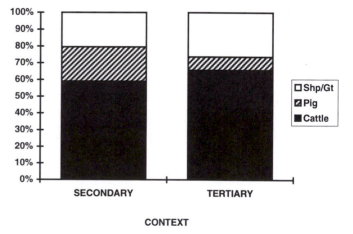

Fig. 137. Trench F: percentages of domestic ungulates identified in the secondary and tertiary levels; the individual contexts, and the primary level as a whole, were too small for individual analysis. Showing a similar proportion of cattle in the secondary level to that in the primary level of Trench E, with an increase in sheep/goats in the tertiary as in Trench B.

the high proportion of cattle to pigs and sheep/goats in the primary level and, surprisingly, the tertiary level is similar to those in the primary level of Trench B and the total assemblage for Trench BB.

Trench D: middle ditch

Details of the ungulates identified in Trench D are set out in table 114. Once again the individual contexts were too small for individual analysis, and this is also true of the secondary level as a whole, so only the totals of the assemblages in the primary and secondary levels can be figured. Fig. 135 shows that the high proportion of cattle to pigs and sheep/goats in the primary and secondary levels is similar to those in the primary level of Trench B and the total assemblage for Trench BB.

Trench E: middle ditch

Details of the ungulates identified in Trench E are set out in table 115. Once again the individual contexts were too small for individual analysis, so only the totals of the assemblages in the three main levels can be figured. Fig. 136 shows a slightly lower proportion of cattle in the primary levels, whereas that in secondary and tertiary levels is similar to those in the primary level of Trench B and the total assemblage for Trench BB.

Trench F: inner ditch

Details of the ungulates identified in Trench F are set out in table 116. Once again the individual contexts were too small for individual analysis, so only the totals of the assemblages in the secondary and tertiary levels can be figured. Fig. 137 shows a similar proportion of cattle in the secondary level to that in the primary level of Trench E, with an increase in sheep/goats in the tertiary as in Trench B.

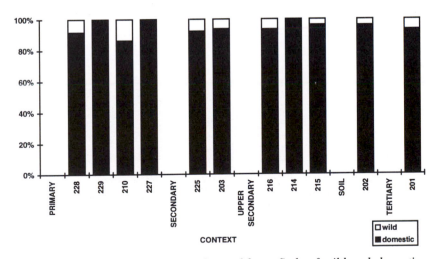

Fig. 138. Trench B: relative numbers of bone finds of wild and domestic animals in the larger contexts. There is no obvious patterning in the proportion of wild animal bones found; the only possible exception being the slightly high percentage in context 210, in which three bones of wild animals all derive from birds, but these may well be from the same individual.

The proportions of bone finds of wild to domestic ungulates

Trench B: outer ditch

Neither table 117 nor figs 138–39 indicate any obvious patterning in the proportion of wild animal bones found,

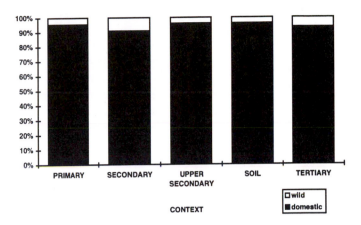

Fig. 139. Trench B: relative numbers of bone finds of wild and domestic animals in the main levels. The proportion of wild animal bones found is consistently low.

Table 117: Trench B, domestic and wild.

Context	TOTAL domestic	wild	% wild
PRIMARY			
228	44	4	8.3
229	21	-	-
230	1	-	-
210	19	3	13.6
227	61	-	-
total	146	7	4.6
SECONDARY			
207	11	-	-
207/208	8	-	-
208	3	1	25.0
225	36	3	7.7
224	-	-	-
206	3	1	25.0
206/213	1	-	-
213	-	-	-
205	15	4	21.1
204	4	1	20.0
203	60	4	6.3
total	141	14	9.0
UPPER SECONDARY			
222	4	-	-
221	-	1	100.0
220	3	-	-
219	4	-	-
217	9	1	10.0
216	43	3	6.5
214	52	-	-
215	26	1	3.7
212	3	-	-
211	2	-	-
total	146	6	3.9
SOIL			
202	219	9	3.9
TERTIARY			
201	56	4	6.7
TOTAL	708	40	5.3

the only possible exception being the slightly high percentage in context 210, in which three bones of wild animals all derive from birds. However, they may well be from the same individual.

Other trenches

The number of bones of wild animals in these trenches is so small as to make any analysis of the differences between them meaningless.

Species richness

Another way of assessing the significance of differences in the numbers of taxa represented in a particular context is to look at their diversity. Although frequently used, a simple count of the taxa present is not a good way of assessing this, because the number of species represented increases with increasing sample size. A better method is to use Simpson's diversity index as defined by Odum (1983) and Clark and Yi (1983):

$$d = \frac{100}{\sqrt{(\Sigma\ b^2)}}$$

where d is the diversity index and b is the percentage of each taxon in the total assemblage. In using this method I have omitted ribs not definitely identified to species, as well as antler fragments, and I have lumped all the sheep, goat and sheep/goat bones as a single taxon.

Trench BB: old land surface and bank

The contexts have too few bones for the calculation of individual diversity indices. The index for Trench BB assemblage as a whole is again very low; d = 1.44.

Trench B: outer ditch

The diversity indices, calculated for each context and level, are given in table 118. The indices vary from 1.00 to 2.04 and there is a slight suggestion that, taken as a whole, the primary level, where d = 1.41, is less rich in species than the higher levels, but as d rises to a maximum of only 1.8 in the tertiary, the results suggest marked dependence on a single species: domestic cattle. For the Trench B assemblage as a whole, d = 1.67.

Trench A: outer ditch

The diversity indices, calculated for each context and level, are given in table 119. The indices vary from 1.00 to 1.75. As in Trench B, there is a slight suggestion that, taken as a whole, the primary level (d = 1.21) is less rich in species than the higher levels, but as d rises to a maximum of only to 1.51 in the secondary, the results again suggest marked dependence on a single species: domestic cattle. For the Trench A assemblage as a whole, d = 1.44.

Trench C: outer ditch

The diversity indices, calculated for each context and level,

Table 118: Trench B, diversity indices.

Context	Diversity
PRIMARY	
228	1.47
229	1.22
230	1.00
210	1.67
227	1.30
total	**1.41**
SECONDARY	
207	1.00
207/208	1.18
208	1.63
225	1.73
206	1.34
206/213	1.00
205	2.04
204	1.51
203	1.53
total	**1.71**
UPPER SECONDARY	
222	1.00
221	1.00
220	1.00
219	1.34
217	1.62
216	1.85
214	1.53
215	1.65
212	1.41
211	1.41
total	**1.65**
SOIL	
202	1.67
TERTIARY	
201	1.80
TOTAL	**1.67**

Table 120: Trench C, diversity indices.

Context	Diversity
PRIMARY	
112	1.41
117	1.13
total	**1.21**
SECONDARY	
109	1.00
111	1.41
115	1.00
106	1.39
110	1.00
110/103	1.00
107	1.41
103	1.75
104	1.63
? 108	1.00
? 108/9	1.00
total	**1.51**
TERTIARY	.
102	1.25
101	1.00
108	1.00
total	**1.30**
TOTAL	**1.44**

Table 119: Trench A, diversity indices.

Context	Diversity
PRIMARY	
324	1.00
315	1.00
312	1.51
322	1.00
314	1.26
308	1.34
309	1.43
306	1.63
313	1.00
319	1.41
? 382	1.00
311/315	1.54
307	1.63
total	**1.52**
SECONDARY	
321	1.14
UPPER SECONDARY	
317	1.13
TERTIARY	
302	1.46
301	1.18
300	1.41
total	**1.44**
TOTAL	**1.41**

Table 121: Trench D, diversity indices.

Context	Diversity
PRIMARY	
416	1.36
415	1.26
408	1.00
418	1.27
total	**1.39**
SECONDARY	
411	1.30
414	1.33
413	1.23
406	1.20
405	1.00
404	1.63
total	**1.32**
TOTAL	**1.35**

Table 122: Trench E, diversity indices.

Context	Diversity
PRIMARY	
514	1.39
527	1.63
512	1.00
522	2.07
524	1.17
523	1.27
506	1.63
513	1.00
511	1.26
509	1.34
508	1.06
525	1.57
518	1.34
504	1.91
516	1.89
total	**1.54**
SECONDARY	
503	1.42
502	1.46
total	**1.45**
TERTIARY	
501	1.39
500	1.00
total	**1.37**
TOTAL	**1.43**

Table 123: Trench F, diversity indices.

Context	Diversity
PRIMARY	
610	1.30
611	1.00
total	**1.26**
SECONDARY	
630	1.58
629	1.52
627	1.60
604	1.39
605-626	1.26
total	**1.58**
TERTIARY	
602	1.41
601	1.67
600	1.00
total	**1.54**
TOTAL	**1.49**

are given in table 120. The indices vary from 1.00 to 1.63; the lowest indices are in the secondary level (d = 1.14) and upper secondary level (d = 1.13), each represented by a single context, 321 and 317 respectively. For the Trench C assemblage as a whole, d = 1.41.

Trench D: middle ditch

The diversity indices, calculated for each context and level, are given in table 121. As in Trench C the indices vary from 1.00 to 1.63. There were too few tertiary identifications for d to be calculated, but for the Trench D primary and secondary assemblage as a whole the index (d = 1.35) is very low.

Trench E: middle ditch

The diversity indices, calculated for each context and level, are given in table 122. The indices vary from 1.00 to 1.89. For the Trench E assemblage as a whole, d = 1.43. The highest indices are in primary contexts, though this is probably not significant.

Trench F: inner ditch

The diversity indices, calculated for each context and level, are given in table 123. The indices vary from 1.00 to 1. 73. For the Trench F assemblage as a whole, d = 1.49. The lowest indices are in primary contexts, though this may not be significant.

The numbers of matching bones

A few contexts had several bones which were clearly from the same individual and in some cases some were in still in articulation, or partial articulation, suggesting that they were deposited with the flesh intact, and soon covered over, thus preventing degradation by dogs. Complete, or near complete, skeletons of cattle, a goat, a pig and dogs were found in the Keiller excavations. The numbers of matching bones from the 1988 excavations have been quantified by expressing the difference between the number of bone finds of each taxon and the number of bones identified as a percentage of the numbers identified.

Trench BB: old land surface and bank

There were no matching bones in Trench BB.

Trench B: outer ditch

Table 124 and fig. 140 show that within the contexts containing large enough numbers of bones for quantification the numbers of bones from the same individual skeleton are highest in the primary levels, in contexts 227 and 210. 227 contains dog footbones which seem to come from the same animal and two matching pig bones which are fragments of the same ulna divided by an ancient break. 227 also contained a large number of very broken fragments of cattle vertebrae and large mammal ribs, almost certainly of cattle, which probably all derive from the same animal. The remains of many new-born pig bones, very probably from the same piglet, were found in 210; 210 also contained some cattle bones which seem to be from the same ankle. The remaining larger contexts have a few very unspectacular matches, parts of the same pig skull and mandible in 216 and some teeth from the same ox mandible in 215.

Trench A: outer ditch

The matching bones in Trench A were all of cattle and are unremarkable: two sets of ankle bones (contexts 117 and 115), one set of wrist bones (103) and a loose tooth associated with a mandibular fragment in 104 (table 125 and fig. 141).

Trench C: outer ditch

The data on matching bones in Trench C are set out in table 126 and fig. 142. The matches are concentrated in the uppermost part of the secondary context, the upper secondary and the lowest tertiary context.

The secondary context 321 has so many matching cervical, dorsal, lumbar and sacral cattle vertebrae, as well as paired loose teeth and bones from the left and right hindlimbs, that it is tempting to assume that they are all from the same very broken ox skeleton. However, there is no way in which the vertebrae and limb bones can be articulated, so this cannot be ascertained. There are also many cattle vertebrae in the single upper secondary deposit (317) immediately above, which makes one wonder whether they might all be from the same individual ox.

Caroline Grigson

Table 124: Trench B, matching bones.

Context	Cattle			Pigs			Dogs		
	finds	nos	% matches	*finds*	nos	% matches	*finds*	nos	% matches
PRIMARY									
228	*31*	34	8.8	*5*	5	-	-	-	-
229	*17*	18	5.6	*2*	2	-	-	-	-
230	*1*	1	-	-	-	-	-	-	-
210	*9*	13	30.8	*1*	8	87.5	-	-	-
227	*27*	28	3.6	*6*	7	14.3	*1*	6	83.3
total	*85*	94	**9.6**	*14*	22	**36.4**	*1*	6	**83.3**
SECONDARY									
207	*4*	4	-	-	-	-	-	-	-
207/208	*5*	5	-	*1*	1	-	-	-	-
208	-	-	-	*2*	2	-	-	-	-
225	*10*	11	9.1	*17*	17	-	*1*	1	-
224	-	-	-	-	-	-	-	-	-
206	*2*	2	-	-	-	-	-	-	-
206/213	-	-	-	-	-	-	*1*	1	-
213	-	-	-	-	-	-	-	-	-
205	*4*	4	-	*2*	2	-	-	-	-
204	*3*	3	-	*1*	1	-	-	-	-
203	*37*	40	7.5	*16*	16	-	*2*	2	-
total	*65*	69	**5.8**	*39*	39	**-**	*4*	4	**-**
UPPER SECONDARY									
222	*2*	2	-	-	-	-	-	-	-
221	-	-	-	-	-	-	-	-	-
220	*3*	4	25.0	-	-	-	-	-	-
219	*2*	2	-	*1*	1	-	-	-	-
217	*5*	5	-	*2*	2	-	*1*	1	-
216	*15*	15	-	*12*	14	14.3	*1*	1	-
214	*23*	23	-	*19*	20	5.0	-	-	-
215	*11*	15	26.7	*9*	9	-	-	-	-
212	*1*	1	-	*1*	1	-	-	-	-
211	*1*	1	-	*1*	1	-	-	-	-
total	*63*	68	**7.4**	*45*	48	**6.3**	*2*	2	**-**
SOIL									
202	*82*	83	1.2	*79*	81	2.5	-	-	-
TERTIARY									
201	*25*	25	-	*14*	14	-	*1*	1	-
TOTAL	*320*	339	**5.6**	*191*	204	**6.4**	*8*	13	**38.5**

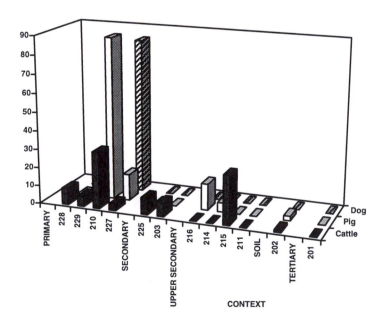

Fig. 140. Trench B: percentages of matching bones (i.e. bones from the same individual animal) compared with the numbers identified in each context. The proportions of bones from the same individual skeleton are highest in the primary contexts 227 (many cattle vertebrae and ribs, dog foot bones and two fragments of the same pig ulna divided by an ancient break) and 210 (piglet skeleton). There were parts of the same pig skull in 216 and some teeth from the same ox mandible in 215.

Table 125: Trench A, matching bones.

Context	Cattle finds	nos	% matches
PRIMARY			
112	*1*	1	-
117	*7*	10	30.0
total	*8*	11	**27.3**
SECONDARY			
111	*1*	1	-
115	*4*	6	33.3
106	*12*	13	7.7
110	*4*	4	-
110/103	*1*	1	-
107	*1*	1	-
103	*6*	7	14.3
104	*12*	13	7.7
? 108	*3*	3	-
? 108/9	*1*	1	-
total	*45*	50	**10.0**
TERTIARY			
102	*14*	14	-
101	*1*	1	-
total	*15*	15	**-**
TOTAL	*68*	76	**10.53**

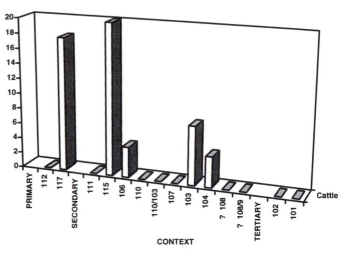

Fig. 141. Trench A: percentages of matching bones (i.e. bones from the same individual animal) compared with the numbers identified in each context. The only matching bones in Trench A were of cattle: two sets of ankle bones (117 and 115), one of wrist bones (103) and a loose tooth associated with a mandibular fragment in 104.

Table 126: Trench C, matching bones.

Context	Cattle finds	nos	% matches	Dogs finds	nos	% matches	Cats finds	nos	% matches
PRIMARY									
324	*3*	3	-	-	-	-	-	-	-
323	-	-	-	-	-	-	-	-	-
315	-	-	-	-	-	-	-	-	-
312	*3*	3	-	-	-	-	-	-	-
322	-	-	-	-	-	-	-	-	-
314	*3*	3	-	-	-	-	-	-	-
308	*13*	14	7.1	-	-	-	*1*	1	-
309	*8*	8	-	-	-	-	-	-	-
306	*2*	2	-	-	-	-	-	-	-
313	*1*	1	-	-	-	-	-	-	-
319	*6*	7	14.3	-	-	-	-	-	-
? 382	*1*	1	-	-	-	-	-	-	-
308/315	-	-	-	-	-	-	-	-	-
311/315	*9*	9	-	-	-	-	-	-	-
312/315	-	-	-	-	-	-	-	-	-
307	*2*	2	-	-	-	-	*1*	2	50.0
total	*51*	53	**3.8**	-	-	**-**	*2*	3	**33.3**
SECONDARY									
321	*13*	68	80.9	-	-	-	-	-	-
UPPER SECONDARY									
317	*23*	33	30.3	*1*	3	66.7	-	-	-
TERTIARY									
302	*47*	47	-	*1*	2	50.0	-	-	-
301	*5*	5	-	-	-	-	-	-	-
300	*1*	1	-	-	-	-	-	-	-
total	*53*	53	**-**	*1*	2	**50.0**	-	-	**-**
TOTAL	*140*	207	**32.4**	*2*	5	**60.0**	*2*	3	**33.3**

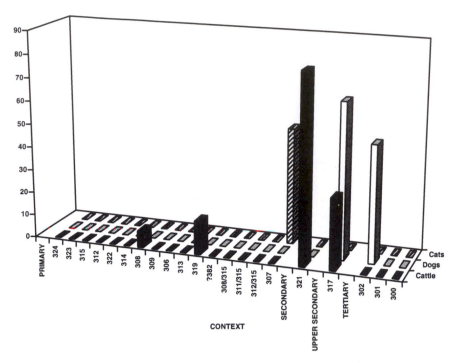

Fig. 142. Trench C: percentages of matching bones (i.e. bones from the same individual animal) compared with the numbers identified in each context. The matches are concentrated in secondary, upper secondary and the lowest tertiary contexts. 321 (secondary) has many matching vertebrae, paired loose teeth and bones from the left and right hindlimbs, possibly all from the same ox skeleton. 317 (upper secondary) immediately above, also had many cattle vertebrae perhaps from the same skeleton as those in 321. Similarly three neck vertebrae in 317 (upper secondary) and three lumbar vertebrae immediately above in 302 (tertiary) may derive from the same dog. Two cat metapodials in 307 are probably from the same foot.

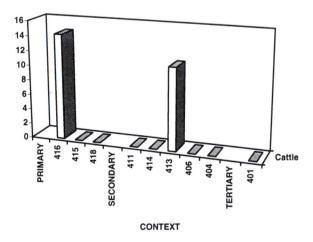

Fig. 143. Trench D: percentages of matching bones (i.e. bones from the same individual animal) compared with the numbers identified in each context. The few matching bones were all of cattle: articulating radius and ulna fragments and two teeth from the same jaw in 416 and a few vertebrae which appear to be from the same animal in 413.

There is a rather similar situation with the dog bones: three neck vertebrae from the same animal in 317 and three lumbar vertebrae immediately above, in tertiary context 302.

There are two cat metapodials in 307, which may come from the same foot.

Table 127: Trench D, matching bones.

Context	finds	Cattle nos	% matches
PRIMARY			
416	*12*	14	14.3
415	*3*	3	0.0
418	*10*	10	0.0
total	*25*	27	**7.4**
SECONDARY			
411	*5*	5	0.0
414	*13*	13	0.0
413	*16*	18	11.1
406	*14*	14	0.0
404	*2*	2	0.0
total	*50*	52	**3.8**
TERTIARY			
401	*1*	1	0.0
TOTAL	-	-	**5.0**

Trench D: middle ditch

The matching bones in Trench D were all of cattle and are unspectacular: articulating radius and ulna fragments and two teeth from the same jaw in 416 and a few vertebrae which appear to be from the same animal in 413 (table 127 and fig. 143).

Trench E: middle ditch

The only notable matches are of cattle bones in the primary context 525, some lumbar and sacral vertebrae which articulate and a set of wrist bones (table 128 and fig. 144).

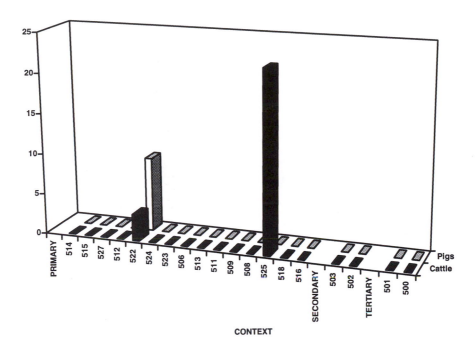

Fig. 144. Trench E: percentages of matching bones (i.e. bones from the same individual animal) compared with the numbers identified in each context. The only notable matches are of cattle bones in 525 (primary): some lumbar and sacral vertebrae which articulate and a set of wrist bones.

Table 128: Trench E, matching bones.

Context	Cattle			Pigs		
	finds	nos	% matches	*finds*	nos	% matches
PRIMARY						
514	*3*	3	-	-	-	-
527	*2*	2	-	*5*	5	-
512	*2*	2	-	-	-	-
522	*30*	31	3.2	*10*	11	9.1
524	*11*	11	-	*1*	1	-
523	*13*	13	-	*3*	3	-
506	*1*	1	-	*2*	2	-
513	*1*	1	-	-	-	-
511	-	-	-	*3*	3	-
509	*2*	2	-	*1*	1	-
508	*17*	17	-	-	-	-
525	*28*	36	22.2	*12*	12	-
518	*2*	2	-	*1*	1	-
516	*2*	2	-	*2*	2	-
total	*114*	123	7.3	*40*	41	2.4
SECONDARY						
503	*15*	15	-	*2*	2	-
502	*5*	5	-	*2*	2	-
total	*20*	20	-	*4*	4	-
TERTIARY						
501	*23*	23	-	*5*	5	-
500	*1*	1	-	-	-	-
total	*24*	24	-	*5*	5	-
TOTAL	*158*	167	-	*49*	50	-

Table 129: Trench F, matching bones.

Context	Pigs			Dogs		
	finds	nos	% matches	*finds*	nos	% matches
PRIMARY						
610	*2*	2	-	-	-	-
SECONDARY						
630	*4*	4	-	*1*	2	50.0
629	*3*	3	-	*2*	2	-
627	*5*	5	-	*1*	1	-
604	*4*	4	-	-	-	-
605-626	*2*	2	-	-	-	-
total	*18*	18	-	*4*	5	20.0
TERTIARY						
602	*2*	2	-	*1*	1	-
601	*1*	1	-	*1*	1	-
total	*2*	2	-	*1*	1	-
TOTAL	**22**	**22**	-	**5**	**6**	**16.7**

Trench F: inner ditch

The only matches are a skull fragment in secondary context 627, which could be from the same skull as one in 630 and a dog's radius and ulna in 630. The data are set out in table 129 but have not been figured.

Bone element analysis

What we are looking for here is any suggestion that the pattern of representation is not related to normal taphonomic processes, but that particular parts of the body have been selected for deposition.

The analysis of the patterns of representation of individual bones (and parts of bones) at Windmill Hill was attempted only on cattle bones, which are the most numerous. The results yielded little information, probably because when broken down into 40 or more categories the size of the samples was too small. The results obtained on the largest sample, the soil in the upper secondary level of Trench B, with, for the sake of comparison, all the contexts in the primary level of Trench B, are presented below.

It is clear that the survival of bone elements is related to the density of that bone, or part of bone (Brain 1967; Binford and Bertram 1977; Lyman 1994). This may be due to depredation by dogs, who will chew off the softer parts of bones, but is probably also related to destruction by trampling and to *in situ* destruction by chemical and physical weathering. Thus there should be a correlation

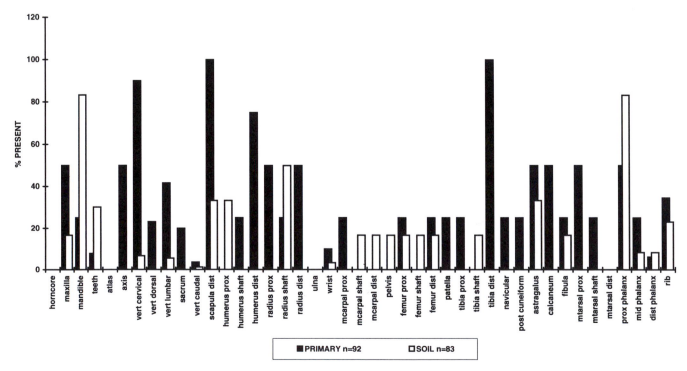

Fig. 145. Trench B: cattle bone element representation, in the largest samples: all contexts within the primary level (n=92) and context 202 (the soil, upper secondary). There is no obvious patterning, probably because the samples are too small when broken down into so many categories.

between the numbers of bone elements found and their density. I have not been able to find good estimates of bone density for domestic cattle, so mineral bone densities of a similar species, North American bison, established by Kreutzer (1992) were used instead. However, no correlation was apparent; whether this is due to inappropriate comparisons, or to the special conditions of deposition and preservation at Windmill Hill, is not possible to determine. Positive correlation of numbers of surviving bones with their density is apparent in some other Neolithic sites, for example the sheep and goat bones at Arjoune in Syria (Grigson forthcoming).

Trench B: outer ditch

The data on cattle bone element representation in the primary level of Trench B (n=92) and from the soil (context 202, n=77) in the upper secondary fill are set out in table 131 and fig. 145; there seems to be no discernible patterning in the histograms that could have been caused either by differential preservation or by deliberate selection. With such small minimum number of individuals in each case, it is clear that the samples are far too small for analysis on this basis.

The frequencies of bone elements from both these levels were tested against their mineral density, but, as with all other levels in other trenches as well, there was no correlation.

Body part analysis

Information of a simpler kind than that potentially yielded by bone element representation may be yielded when bones are grouped into larger parts of the body:

Cranial: horncore, maxilla, other cranial parts, mandible
Teeth: loose teeth
Trunk: all vertebrae, sacrum, ribs
Forelimb: scapula, humerus, radius, ulna
Hindlimb: pelvis, femur, patella, tibia
Feet: wrist, astragalus, calcaneum, navicular and other ankle bones, including fibula, metapodials, phalanges.

Of these categories only the teeth and feet can be thought of as non-meat bearing.

Trench BB: old land surface and bank

The data on body part analysis for Trench BB are summarised in table 130 and illustrated in fig. 146. The

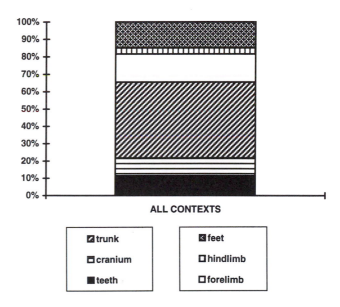

Fig. 146. Trench BB: cattle body part representation. The individual contexts were too small for individual analysis, so they have been grouped together. The resulting pattern is similar to that found in the secondary level of Trench B (fig. 148 below).

Table 130: Trench BB, cattle body parts.

context	feature	teeth	cranium	trunk	forelimb	hindlimb	feet	total
712	tree hollow	-	-	5	-	-	1	6
705	OLS	1	4	1	7	1	5	19
742	OLS	-	-	12	-	-	-	12
761	posthole 760	-	-	1	-	-	-	1
710	posthole 710	-	-	1	-	-	-	1
714	pit 715	-	-	1	-	-	-	1
726	pit 715	-	1	-	1	-	-	2
707	grave	1	1	1	1	-	2	6
733	grave fill	-	-	1	-	-	-	1
734	grave fill	1	-	-	-	-	1	2
746	primary bank	-	1	9	-	1	-	11
765	primary bank	-	1	2	2	-	2	7
703	main bank	1	1	1	1	1	1	6
701	main bank	2	-	2	-	-	1	5
700	turf	4	-	-	2	-	-	6
717	base of bank	-	-	1	-	-	-	1
	TOTAL	**10**	**9**	**38**	**14**	**3**	**13**	**87**

Table 131: Trench B, cattle bone element representation.

bone element	no found	PRIMARY (MNI=2)			no found	SOIL (MNI=3)		
		no exp	no exp x2	% present		no exp	no exp x3	% present
horncore	-	2	4	-	-	2	6	-
maxilla	2	2	4	50.0	1	2	6	16.7
mandible	1	2	4	25.0	5	2	6	83.3
teeth	5	32	64	7.8	29	32	96	30.2
atlas	-	1	2	-	-	1	3	-
axis	1	1	2	50.0	-	1	3	-
vert cervical	9	5	10	90.0	1	5	15	6.7
vert dorsal	6	13	26	23.1	-	13	39	-
vert lumbar	5	6	12	41.7	1	6	18	5.6
sacrum	2	5	10	20.0	-	5	15	-
vert caudal	2	28	56	3.6	1	28	84	1.2
scapula dist	4	2	4	100.0	2	2	6	33.3
humerus prox	-	2	4	-	2	2	6	33.3
humerus shaft	1	2	4	25.0	-	2	6	-
humerus dist	3	2	4	75.0	-	2	6	-
radius prox	2	2	4	50.0	-	2	6	-
radius shaft	1	2	4	25.0	3	2	6	50.0
radius dist	2	2	4	50.0	-	2	6	-
ulna	-	2	4	-	-	2	6	-
wrist	2	10	20	10.0	1	10	30	3.3
mcarpal prox	1	2	4	25.0	-	2	6	-
mcarpal shaft	-	2	4	-	1	2	6	16.7
mcarpal dist	-	2	4	-	1	2	6	16.7
pelvis	-	2	4	-	1	2	6	16.7
femur prox	1	2	4	25.0	1	2	6	16.7
femur shaft	-	2	4	-	1	2	6	16.7
femur dist	1	2	4	25.0	1	2	6	16.7
patella	1	2	4	25.0	-	2	6	-
tibia prox	1	2	4	25.0	-	2	6	-
tibia shaft	-	2	4	-	1	2	6	16.7
tibia dist	4	2	4	100.0	-	2	6	-
navicular	1	2	4	25.0	-	2	6	-
post cuneiform	1	2	4	25.0	-	2	6	-
astragalus	2	2	4	50.0	2	2	6	33.3
calcaneum	2	2	4	50.0	-	2	6	-
fibula	1	2	4	25.0	1	2	6	16.7
mtarsal prox	2	2	4	50.0	-	2	6	-
mtarsal shaft	1	2	4	25.0	-	2	6	-
mtarsal dist	-	2	4	-	-	2	6	-
prox phalanx	2	2	4	50.0	5	2	6	83.3
mid phalanx	4	8	16	25.0	2	8	24	8.3
dist phalanx	1	8	16	6.3	2	8	24	8.3
rib	18	26	52	34.6	18	26	78	23.1
total	**92**	**205**	**410**		**83**	**205**	**615**	

samples in the individual contexts were too small for individual analysis, so they have been grouped together. The resulting pattern is similar to that found in the secondary level of Trench B (fig. 148).

Trench B: outer ditch

The data on body part analysis are summarised in table 132. A detailed analysis of the body parts represented in the primary levels as a whole and in the soil is set out above in fig. 145. No consistent patterning emerges, probably because despite their relatively large size the samples are too small when broken down into so many categories. In fig. 147 one can see a predominance of bones of the trunk, that is vertebrae, or ribs, or both, in contexts 227 (primary) and 225 and 205 (secondary), and a predominance of

footbones in 228, 229 and 210 (primary).

When the contexts are grouped into levels (fig. 148), a much clearer pattern emerges. The soil in context 202 and the other upper secondary contexts have an almost identical pattern, and there is a marked increase in the number of loose teeth from the primary to the tertiary levels, presumably related to a much greater degree of destruction, or at least fragmentation, of bone in the upper levels.

Trench A: outer ditch

The data on body part analysis for Trench A are summarised in table 133. There were too few data in the individual primary level contexts for analysis, but the results from two secondary and tertiary contexts are illustrated in fig. 149. The uppermost secondary level

Pl. 1. Windmill Hill at dawn, from the west, with the Marlborough Downs behind.

Pl. 3. Windmill Hill from the air from the north-east. RCHME © Crown copyright.

Pl. 4. The 1957–58 excavations on the outer circuit, painted by Dennis Grant King. The figures include Isobel Smith (far right), Lady Wheeler, Margaret Nurse and Dennis Grant King. Reproduced by kind permission of Margaret Nurse and Devizes Museum.

Pl. 2. Windmill Hill from the north, seen over one of the cuttings across the outer ditch at Millbarrow.

Pl. 30. Bone deposit 630 in the lower secondary fill of the inner ditch in Trench F. The human child femur inserted into a cattle humerus is visible at top left of the deposit.

Pl. 32. The south section of the inner ditch in Trench F.

Pl. 29. Bone deposit 629 in the lower secondary fill of the inner ditch in Trench F.

Pl. 31. The upper part of bone deposit 627/628 in the lower secondary fill of the inner ditch in Trench F. In the foreground is the emptied cutting of Inner Ditch XVII of the 1957–58 excavations.

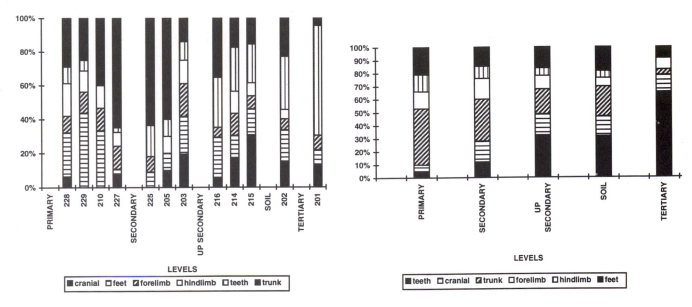

Fig. 147. Trench B: cattle body part representation in the larger contexts (n=>10). 227 (primary) and 225 and 205 (secondary) contain mainly bones of the trunk, and in 228, 229 and 210 (primary) footbones predominate.

Fig. 148. Trench B: cattle body part representation in the main levels. The soil (202) and the other upper secondary contexts have an almost identical pattern. There is a marked increase in the proportion of loose teeth from the primary to the tertiary levels.

Table 132: Trench B, cattle body parts.

Context	teeth	cranial	trunk	forelimb	hindlimb	feet	total
PRIMARY							
228	3	2	9	3	6	8	31
229	1	-	4	2	2	7	16
230	-	-	-	1	-	-	1
210	-	-	6	2	2	5	15
227	1	3	24	5	3	1	37
total	5	5	43	13	13	21	100
SECONDARY							
207	-	2	3	-	-	1	6
207/208	-	1	2	2	1	-	6
225	2	-	7	1	-	1	11
206	-	1	1	1	-	-	3
205	1	1	6	-	1	1	10
204	2	-	-	1	-	-	3
203	4	7	5	7	5	8	36
total	9	12	24	12	7	11	75
UPPER SECONDARY							
220	4	-	1	1	-	-	6
219	1	-	-	1	-	-	2
217	2	2	-	-	-	1	5
216	5	1	6	1	-	4	17
214	6	4	4	3	3	3	23
215	3	4	2	1	1	2	13
212	-	-	-	-	-	1	1
211	1	-	-	-	-	-	1
total	22	11	13	7	4	11	68
SOIL							
202	29	14	21	6	5	17	92
TERTIARY							
201	15	3	1	2	-	2	23

Table 133: Trench A, cattle body parts.

Context	teeth	cranial	trunk	forelimb	hindlimb	feet	total
PRIMARY							
112	-	-	-	-	-	1	1
117	-	3	-	1	2	3	9
total	-	3	-	1	2	4	10
SECONDARY							
115	-	-	4	-	-	3	7
106	2	-	4	1	2	4	13
110	1	-	1	1	-	1	4
110/103	-	-	1	-	-	-	1
103	-	-	-	-	-	5	5
104	5	1	-	2	2	1	11
total	8	1	10	4	4	14	41
TERTIARY							
102	5	1	-	4	-	2	12
101	1	-	-	-	-	-	1
108	1	-	-	-	-	2	3
108/9	-	-	-	-	-	1	1
total	7	1	-	4	-	5	17
TOTAL	15	5	10	9	6	23	68

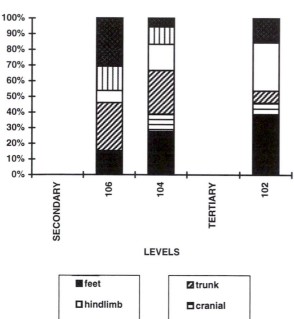

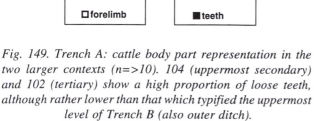

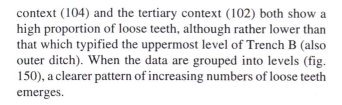

Fig. 149. Trench A: cattle body part representation in the two larger contexts (n=>10). 104 (uppermost secondary) and 102 (tertiary) show a high proportion of loose teeth, although rather lower than that which typified the uppermost level of Trench B (also outer ditch).

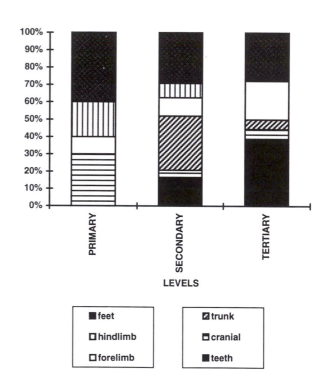

Fig. 150. Trench A: cattle body part representation in the primary, secondary and tertiary levels. There is a clear pattern of increasing numbers of loose teeth from primary to tertiary.

context (104) and the tertiary context (102) both show a high proportion of loose teeth, although rather lower than that which typified the uppermost level of Trench B (also outer ditch). When the data are grouped into levels (fig. 150), a clearer pattern of increasing numbers of loose teeth emerges.

Trench C: outer ditch

The data on body part analysis for Trench C are summarised in table 134 and illustrated in figs 151–52. The high proportion of bones of the trunk in contexts 308 (primary) and 321 (secondary) is notable. As in Trenches B and A, there is an increasing proportion of loose teeth in the higher levels.

Table 134: Trench C, cattle body parts.

Context	teeth	cranial	trunk	forelimb	hindlimb	feet	total
PRIMARY							
308	1	1	10	-	1	2	**15**
SECONDARY							
321	3	2	44	4	10	13	**76**
UPPER SECONDARY							
317	5	3	14	7	1	6	**36**
TERTIARY							
302	26	4	11	2	5	6	**54**
TOTAL	35	10	79	13	17	27	**181**

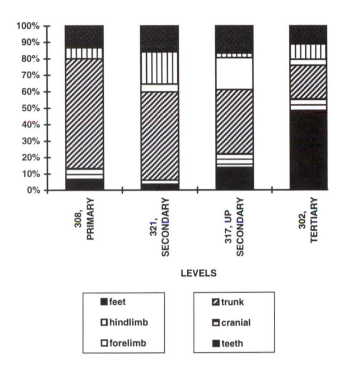

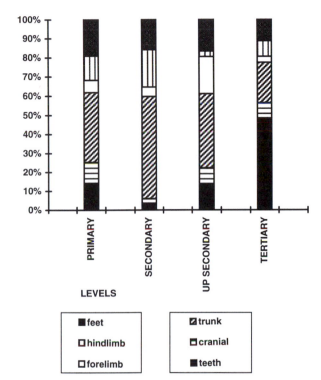

Fig. 151. Trench C: cattle body part representation in the larger contexts (n=>10). 308 (primary) and 321 (secondary) have a high proportion of bones of the trunk; there is an increasing proportion of loose teeth in the higher levels.

Fig. 152. Trench C: cattle body part representation in the main levels. The secondary level has a high proportion of bones of the trunk and there is an increasing proportion of loose teeth from the secondary to the tertiary.

Trench D: middle ditch

The data on body part analysis for Trench D are summarised in table 135 and illustrated in figs 153–54. There were no data for the tertiary. Context 413 (secondary) has a particularly high proportion of bones of the trunk.

Trench E: middle ditch

The data on body part analysis for Trench E are summarised in table 136 and illustrated in figs 155–56. The primary contexts 522 and 525 contain a high proportion of bones of the trunk; primary context 508 has many cranial fragments, matched by a fairly high proportion of loose teeth, and, as now familiar, the proportion of loose teeth increases in the higher levels.

Trench F: inner ditch

The data on body part analysis for Trench F are summarised in table 137 and illustrated in figs 157–58. There are too few data in the primary contexts for individual analysis. There are high proportions of cranial fragments in the secondary context 630 and of footbones in the tertiary context 602. The tertiary had a higher proportion of loose teeth than the primary and secondary levels taken together, but it is less high than in the uppermost levels of the other ditches.

The side of the body

Faunal assemblages in which bones from one side of the body are more frequent than those of the other are not unknown in archaeological assemblages and suggest some

Table 135: Trench D, cattle body parts.

Context	teeth	cranial	trunk	forelimb	hindlimb	feet	total
PRIMARY							
416	2	1	5	5	-	4	17
417	-	-	1	-	-	-	1
415	-	-	1	-	-	2	3
408	-	-	2	-	-	-	2
418	-	1	-	-	5	4	10
total	2	2	9	5	5	10	33
SECONDARY							
411	1	-	4	-	-	1	6
414	1	2	5	2	1	-	11
413	-	-	21	1	1	1	24
406	4	-	12	2	4	3	25
404	1	-	-	-	1	-	2
total	7	2	42	5	7	5	68
TERTIARY							
401	-	-	-	-	-	1	1
TOTAL	9	4	51	10	12	16	102

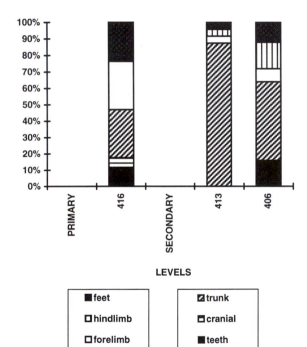

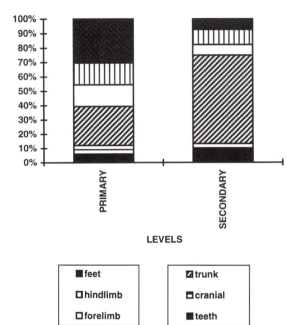

■ feet	▨ trunk
☐ hindlimb	☐ cranial
☐ forelimb	■ teeth

Fig. 153. Trench D: cattle body part representation in the larger contexts (n=>10). 413 (secondary) has a particularly high proportion of bones of the trunk.

■ feet	▨ trunk
☐ hindlimb	☐ cranial
☐ forelimb	■ teeth

Fig. 154. Trench D: cattle body part representation in the main levels. The secondary level has a high proportion of bones of the trunk.

kind of deliberate selection. Indeed there is a possible indication of this in part of the Late Neolithic site at West Kennet (Edwards and Horne 1997).

All Trenches

The numbers of bones which could be confidently assigned to one side of the body or the other is rather small (tables 138–44) and in the larger groupings the apparent differences between numbers of right and left are statistically insignificant.

Possible exceptions are the pig bones in the secondary context 203 in Trench B and the cattle bones in primary context 525 in Trench E. In 203 there were five bones

from the right side and none that could be allocated to the left. Those from the right were two femur shafts (one a classic shaft cylinder produced by gnawing), a tibia shaft (also gnawed), a cuboid and a maxilla fragment. It is probable that the disparity is due to chance, as deliberate selection for body side seems unlikely with such unprepossessing material.

Of the cattle bones that could be assigned to side in context 525, 11 were from the left and three from the right. However, once these are broken down into elements, that is three left pelves, two left scapulae and bones from the same left wrist, it seems unlikely that any special significance can be attached to this asymmetry.

Table 136: Trench E, cattle body parts.

Context	teeth	cranial	trunk	forelimb	hindlimb	feet	totals
PRIMARY							
514	-	1	1	-	-	2	4
515	-	-	3	-	-	-	3
527	-	-	1	-	1	-	2
512	-	-	8	-	-	1	9
522	1	5	23	7	6	3	45
524/510	1	1	-	-	-	-	2
524	-	2	4	3	-	3	12
523	1	-	6	6	3	1	17
506	1	-	1	-	-	-	2
513	-	2	-	-	-	-	2
509	-	-	2	-	-	-	2
508	3	4	3	6	1	-	17
525	1	3	16	4	6	4	34
518	-	-	2	-	1	-	3
516	1	-	1	-	-	-	2
total	9	18	71	26	18	14	156
SECONDARY							
503	-	-	5	8	3	2	18
502	2	-	1	-	2	1	6
total	2	-	6	8	5	3	24
TERTIARY							
501	11	-	2	4	3	3	23
500	1	-	-	-	-	-	1
total	12	-	2	4	3	3	24
TOTAL	23	18	79	38	26	20	204

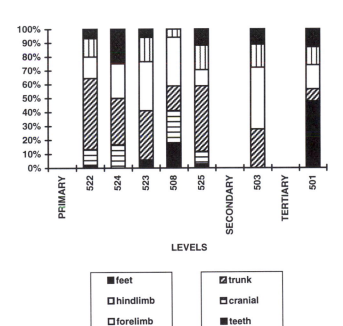

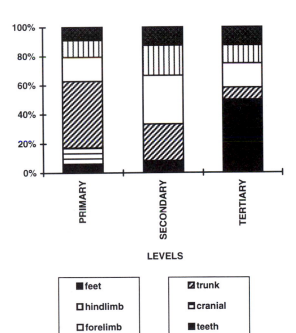

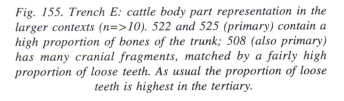

Fig. 155. Trench E: cattle body part representation in the larger contexts (n=>10). 522 and 525 (primary) contain a high proportion of bones of the trunk; 508 (also primary) has many cranial fragments, matched by a fairly high proportion of loose teeth. As usual the proportion of loose teeth is highest in the tertiary.

Fig. 156. Trench E: cattle body part representation in the main levels. The primary level has a high proportion of bones of the trunk; as usual the proportion of loose teeth is highest in the tertiary.

Table 137: Trench F, cattle body parts.

Context	teeth	cranial	trunk	forelimb	hindlimb	feet	totals
PRIMARY							
613	-	-	1	-	-	-	1
610	-	2	2	-	1	1	5
611	-	-	-	1	-	-	1
total	-	2	3	1	1	1	7
SECONDARY							
630	-	10	7	1	3	4	16
629	-	2	3	10	4	-	18
627	-	-	4	1	2	-	7
604	-	2	7	-	6	2	17
626	1	-	1	2	-	2	6
total	1	14	22	14	15	8	64
TERTIARY							
602	4	-	-	7	1	9	21
601	1	-	1	1	-	2	5
total	5	-	1	8	1	11	26
TOTAL	6	16	26	23	17	20	97

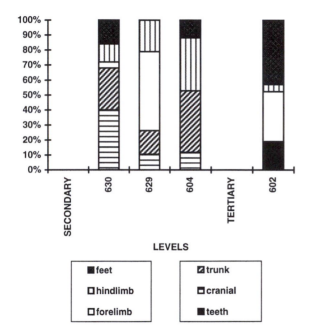

Fig. 157. Trench F: cattle body part representation in the larger contexts (n=>10). 630 (secondary) has a high proportion of cranial fragments and 602 (tertiary) has an unusually high number of footbones.

Fig. 158. Trench F: cattle body part representation in the main levels. The tertiary had a higher proportion of loose teeth than the primary and secondary levels taken together, but it is less high than in the uppermost levels of the other ditches.

Table 138: Trench BB, side of body.

Context	Feature	Cattle L	Cattle R	Pigs L	Pigs R	Shp/Gt L	Shp/Gt R	Totals L	Totals R
712	tree hollow	-	1	-	-	-	-	-	1
705	OLS	3	4	-	1	-	1	3	6
741	OLS	-	-	1	-	-	1	1	1
742	OLS	-	-	1	-	-	-	1	-
707	grave	4	-	-	-	-	-	4	-
733	grave fill	-	-	1	-	-	-	1	-
734	grave fill	-	-	-	-	1	-	1	-
746	primary bank	-	1	-	-	-	-	-	1
767	primary bank	3	-	-	-	-	-	3	-
703	main bank	1	2	-	-	-	-	1	2
701	main bank	-	1	-	-	-	-	-	1
700	turf	2	2	-	-	-	-	2	2
	Totals	13	11	3	1	1	2	17	14

Table 139: Trench B, side of body.

Context	Cattle L	R	Pigs L	R	Shp/Gt L	R	Totals L	R
PRIMARY								
228	6	6	-	1	2	1	8	8
229	4	2	1	-	1	1	6	3
230	1	-	-	-	-	-	1	-
210	2	3	1	1	-	1	3	5
227	4	2	-	4	-	2	4	8
total	17	13	2	6	3	5	22	24
SECONDARY								
207	1	-	-	-	-	-	1	-
207/208	-	2	-	-	-	-	-	2
225	2	2	2	4	1	1	5	7
205	1	-	-	1	-	-	1	1
204	-	-	-	-	-	-	-	-
203	6	4	-	5	-	-	6	9
total	10	8	2	10	1	1	13	19
UPPER SECONDARY								
222	-	2	-	-	-	-	-	2
219	-	2	-	-	-	-	-	2
217	-	-	1	-	-	-	1	-
216	2	3	3	3	2	2	7	8
214	3	3	5	1	-	1	8	5
215	5	3	2	1	-	1	7	5
212	1	-	-	1	-	-	1	1
total	11	13	11	6	2	4	24	23
SOIL								
202	5	6	9	9	3	2	17	17
TERTIARY								
201	1	2	2	3	1	1	4	6
TOTAL	44	42	26	34	10	13	80	89

Table 140: Trench A, side of body.

Context	Cattle L	R	Pigs L	R	Shp/Gt L	R	Totals L	R
PRIMARY								
112	-	1	-	-	1	-	1	1
117	2	6	-	-	-	-	2	6
SECONDARY								
109	-	-	-	-	-	1	-	1
111	-	1	-	-	-	-	-	1
115	2	-	-	-	-	-	2	-
106	2	4	2	1	-	-	4	5
110	1	2	-	-	-	-	1	2
103	-	4	2	2	-	-	2	6
104	5	3	-	1	1	1	6	5
? 108	1	2	-	-	-	-	1	2
? 108/9	1	-	-	-	-	-	1	-
TERTIARY								
102	2	5	1	1	-	-	3	6
TOTAL	16	28	5	5	2	2	23	35

Table 141: Trench C, side of body.

Context	Cattle L	R	Pigs L	R	Shp/Gt L	R	Totals L	R
PRIMARY								
324	1	-	-	-	-	-	1	-
315	1	1	-	1	-	-	1	2
312	1	-	-	-	-	-	1	-
308	2	2	-	1	-	1	2	4
309	3	3	1	-	-	-	4	3
306	2	-	1	-	-	1	3	1
319	2	-	-	-	1	3	3	3
311/315	2	3	1	-	-	1	3	4
307	-	1	-	-	-	-	-	1
total	14	10	3	2	1	6	18	18
SECONDARY								
321	10	9	-	-	-	1	10	10
317	8	5	-	-	-	-	8	5
total	18	14	-	-	-	1	18	15
TERTIARY								
302	7	6	1	3	-	2	8	11
301	1	1	-	-	-	-	1	1
total	8	7	-	-	-	2	8	9
TOTAL	40	31	3	2	1	9	44	42

Table 142: Trench D, side of body.

Context	Cattle L	R	Pigs L	R	Shp/Gt L	R	Totals L	R
PRIMARY								
416	3	6	-	1	2	1	5	8
415	-	1	-	-	-	-	-	1
418	3	5	-	1	-	-	3	6
total	6	12	-	2	2	1	8	15
SECONDARY								
411	-	1	1	-	-	-	1	1
414	-	1	-	-	-	1	-	2
413	-	2	-	-	1	-	1	2
406	4	1	-	-	1	-	5	1
total	4	5	1	-	2	1	7	6
TOTAL	10	17	1	2	4	2	15	21

Table 143: Trench E, side of body.

Context	Cattle L	R	Pigs L	R	Shp/Gt L	R	Totals L	R
PRIMARY								
514	2	-	-	-	1	-	3	-
527	-	1	1	2	1	1	2	4
512	-	1	-	-	-	-	-	1
522	8	8	1	4	-	3	9	15
524	4	2	-	1	-	-	4	3
523	2	3	1	-	-	1	3	4
508	4	2	-	-	-	1	4	3
525	11	3	3	1	3	1	17	5
total	31	20	6	8	5	7	42	35
SECONDARY								
503	6	3	-	-	2	-	8	3
502	1	-	-	-	-	-	1	-
total	7	3	-	-	2	-	9	3
TERTIARY								
501	2	3	1	-	1	-	4	3
TOTAL	40	26	7	8	8	7	55	41

Table 144: Trench F, side of body.

Context	Cattle L	R	Pigs L	R	Shp/Gt L	R	Totals L	R
PRIMARY								
610	-	-	-	2	-	-	-	2
611	-	1	-	-	-	-	-	1
total	-	1	-	2	-	-	-	3
SECONDARY								
630	2	4	-	-	-	3	2	7
629	4	6	1	1	-	1	5	8
627	1	2	-	-	-	-	1	2
604	-	4	-	-	2	-	2	4
605-626	1	-	1	-	-	-	2	-
total	8	16	2	1	2	4	12	21
TERTIARY								
602	4	4	-	-	-	-	4	4
601	1	-	-	-	-	-	1	-
total	5	4	-	-	-	-	5	4
TOTAL	13	21	2	3	2	4	17	28

Special finds

The only individual finds from the 1988 excavations at Windmill Hill that can be considered 'special' are cattle skulls, sheep horncores and, in one instance, a human bone inserted into the marrow cavity of an ox humerus. Shed roe deer antlers can also be categorised as special. The Keiller excavations also produced several complete skeletons of cattle and other species which are described in Part 3 of this chapter.

A marked feature of the faunal assemblage from the Keiller excavations was the large number of complete, or nearly complete, skulls and horncores of cattle (Grigson 1982a). The same is true of the 1988 material, although less spectacularly. Fragments of cattle skulls and teeth derived from them are scattered throughout all the trenches, but certain contexts had particular concentrations of large pieces of skull or horncore, or of fragments appearing to derive from the same skull.

There were no such concentrations in Trenches BB or B, but in the outer ditch in Trench A in the primary context 117 a right and a left horncore were preserved almost entire (fig. 159). They both derive from old cows, but do not exactly match each other, so probably derive from two different individuals. In addition this context contained the frontlet of a ox, probably male (fig. 160A). That the skull was that of a young animal is shown by open porous surfaces of the horncores and by the open sutures between the cranial

elements. The suture between the left and right frontal was open, the frontal/parietal suture on the poll seems to have been partially open, though the erosion of the surface makes this uncertain, the frontal/parietal sutures in the temporal grooves were open and those between the occipital and parietal on the occipital surface were partially open. The shape and size of the horncores suggest that the skull came from a bull; the measurements are given in Appendix 1.3. The presence of multiple cutmarks on the frontal (fig. 160B), may imply that the skin had been removed prior to deposition; they might also relate to dehorning.

A complex situation arises from the ox skull fragments found in the middle ditch in Trench D, in contexts 416 and 418 (primary) and 411 and 414 (secondary). The remains of at least two and more probably three skulls were found scattered through these contexts; the problem is that fragments thought to come from the same skull were found in different contexts. Parts of the skull of the oldest animal, probably a cow, were found in 418, 411 and 414; skull parts of a younger animal were in 416 and 414; and a large piece of the posterior part of a skull of a possible third animal was in 416.

That some particular activity characterised these contexts in Trench D is further emphasised by the presence of two almost intact horncores of young male sheep in 416. Although very similar to one another, they certainly come from two individual rams, as both are from the left side. Sheep horncores are notoriously rare in archaeological

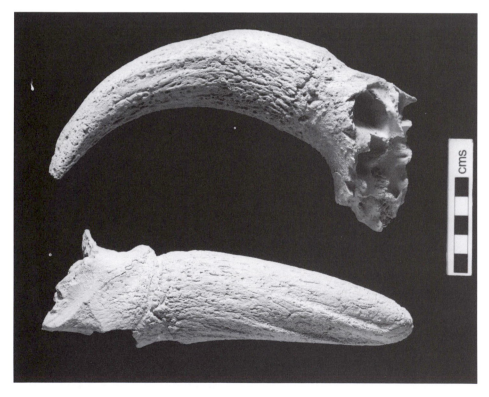

Fig. 159. Context 117, Trench A. Early Neolithic. This context was unique in containing two intact cattle horncores, seen here, and an ox frontlet (fig. 160). Both the right horncore (above) and the left (below) derive from old females, but as they do not match one another, they are probably from two different cows.

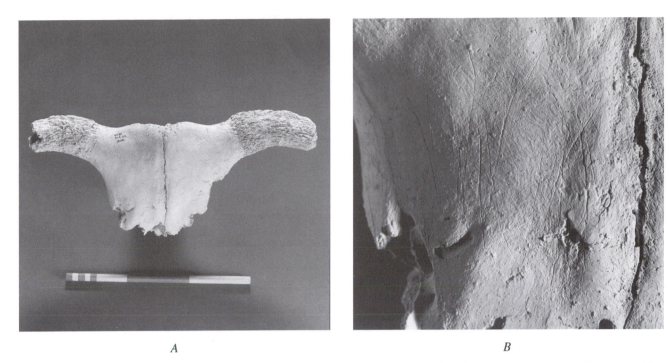

A   B

Fig. 160. Context 117, Trench A. Early Neolithic. This context contained an ox frontlet, seen here, and two horncores (fig. 159). A: The frontlet of a young ox, probably male. B: The same frontlet, enlarged to show multiple cutmarks, suggestive of both skinning and perhaps dehorning.

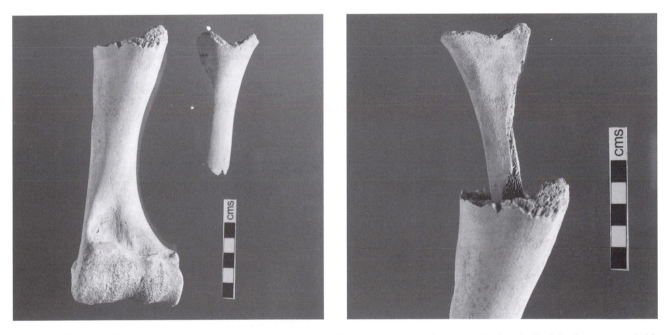

Fig. 161. Context 630, Trench F. Early Neolithic. The distal half of the humerus of an ox, with the shaft of the femur of a child, inserted into the marrow cavity. The ox bone seems to have been chopped in half and cutmarks suggest it was from a dismembered carcass. The same context contained the very broken remains of an ox skull.

deposits, probably due to differential preservation, as they have a particularly soft, open texture, especially in young animals.

The survival of these cattle skulls, albeit in a very broken state, and of the sheep horncores, suggests that they were protected from destruction by dogs by being covered with earth, probably deliberately soon after being placed in the ditch, and then suffered a degree of destruction by trampling and weathering, or that material was repeatedly drawn from the same source, perhaps a midden.

The presence of fragments of the same skulls in different contexts, in different levels, suggests that the contexts and indeed the levels may not actually be as discrete as they appeared to be in the course of excavation.

Another context in which an ox skull appears to have been deliberately placed is 630 in the secondary levels of the inner ditch. Here 10 fragments of a very young animal appear to derive from the same skull. None can be fitted together, but the presence of matching left and right petrous bones and other temporal fragments is highly suggestive.

The same context contained an extraordinary combination of human and animal bone: the distal half of the humerus of an ox, with the shaft of a femur of an immature human, inserted into the marrow cavity (fig. 161). The humerus appeared to have been chopped in half and distal cutmarks suggest it was from a dismembered carcass.

A few fragments of antler of both red and roe deer were found in various contexts in the 1988 excavations at Windmill Hill. Although noted in the summary tables (tables 82–88) they have not been included in the counts as one cannot be sure whether they derive from unshed antler (animals killed and therefore probably eaten) or from shed antler (collected in the wild).

Basal fragments of shed roe deer antler were retrieved only from the outer ditch, in Trench B in secondary contexts 203 and 213/206. Being shed these were not from hunted animals, but were collected for some perceived intrinsic value, probably in October, since that is the time of year when roe deer bucks shed their antlers. This is *not* an indication of seasonal use of the site, since the antler may well have been curated.

Roe deer antler appears to have had a special connotation for some groups of people. For example, a complete antler was found with the burial of a man in the Beaker site of Hemp Knoll (see Grigson 1980). One can only guess at the significance of the inclusion of such an item, with little or no economic relevance, but it should be remembered that in red and roe deer antlers are present only in the male.

Patterns of deposition

So far, bone deposits have been put under the working headings, defined on morphological criteria, of groups, spreads and scatters. As set out briefly in chapter 4 and in much more detail here, other criteria can be brought to bear on the analysis of these deposits. On the basis of these criteria, it is possible to outline three main sets of deposit, in terms of the intentionality behind them and the histories which they contain. The term 'set' is preferred to 'type', in that its use may keep issues of diversity and overlap more open. One set, 1, may be bound up with deliberate placement, another, 3, with less formalised deposition. Constituting yet another set, 2, there are also assemblages which appear to be intermediate between these two extremes. Many contexts in each trench had assemblages which were too small to be assigned to any particular type of activity. These suggested sets do not coincide exactly or neatly with the morphology of the deposits. For example, both 522 and 523 in Trench E are morphologically spreads,

but 523 may be a deliberate placement while 522 seems to be of intermediate character. These sets are also the subject of further discussion in chapter 17.

Set 1: deliberate placements

Deliberate placements are characterised by the large mean size of the bone fragments within them and an uneven frequency distribution of fragments of larger size, suggesting that they were incorporated into the ditch deposits soon after being discarded, and that they may have been deliberately covered. They have a high proportion of identified bones and usually a marked predominance of cattle bones, many of which appear to be from the same individual. In some contexts, morphologically mainly groups, these bones were so neatly arranged that it has been suggested that they had been bound together prior to deposition; a more likely explanation is that whole rib cages, or sections of legs and feet, held together by tendons and probably even muscle, that is meat, were deposited. This means that such deposits are not the remains of meals, since the consumption of food almost invariably involves dismemberment. However, it is likely that the skin was removed prior to deposition as there were conspicuous cutmarks on the frontal of one of the ox skulls. Such deposits were also found in the earlier excavations at Windmill Hill and at Hambledon Hill, where Legge (1981) noted articulating sets of ankle bones. Sets of articulating bone have been found in some other Early Neolithic sites and are discussed in Part 3 of this chapter.

The range of species represented in the deliberate placements is also described in more detail in Part 3; the numbers of bones of each species are set out in table 146 and the relative numbers of the domestic ungulates in fig. 181. Domestic cattle predominate, but pigs and sheep/goats form a significant proportion of the assemblages. Dogs, wild cattle, red deer, roe deer and wild cat are also present, but in very small numbers.

Four contexts in the primary level of the outer ditch in Trench B (210, 229, 228 and 227) and two in the secondary level (204 and 203) seem to be placed deposits. Of those in the primary fills, two (210 and 228) are morphologically spreads and two (227 and 229) scatters. 229, 210, 228, 227 and 203 have a high proportion of identified bones. 228 and 229 have a marked predominance of cattle bones, particularly foot bones, with many trunk bones in 227, and with foot and other bones from the same individual skeleton in 210. 227 also contains dog footbones and fragments of the same pig ulna divided by an ancient break. The remains of a skeleton of a new-born piglet were found in 210 and of shed roe deer antler in 203.

In the outer ditch in Trench A the primary context 117 (a bone group) is notable for containing two ox horncores and an ox frontlet; all the other bones in this context, except for one, were unidentified fragments, too fragile for measurement.

In Trench C in the outer ditch the distribution of fragment size was markedly uneven in all the primary, secondary and upper secondary contexts. The percentages of identified bones were highest in the secondary (321) and upper secondary (317) and these two contexts also had many matching cattle bones, possibly all from the same animal. Morphologically, 321 is a bone group and 317 a spread. 317 also had three neck vertebrae from the same dog skeleton and there were three articulating dog lumbar vertebrae immediately above, in tertiary context 302. The high proportion of cattle bones of the trunk in contexts 308 (primary) and 321 (secondary) is notable.

Deliberate placements occur in the middle ditch in Trench D in the primary levels (contexts 416 and 418), and in the secondary levels (414); two being spreads and one (416) a scatter. The remains of at least two and more probably three ox skulls were found in these contexts, with fragments thought to come from the same skull in different contexts, suggesting that these contexts may not be as discrete as they appeared in excavation. 416 was also notable for the presence of two almost intact horncores of young male sheep.

Like Trench D, Trench E, also in the middle ditch, had deliberate placements of cattle bones in the primary and secondary levels (contexts 524, 523, 525 in the primary and 503 in the secondary). Of these, 524 might be defined as a group and the rest as spreads. 525 contained a high proportion of cattle trunk bones, including lumbar and sacral vertebrae which articulate and a set of wrist bones. Primary context 508 should probably be included here as it had many cranial fragments possibly from the same skull.

Deliberate placements in Trench F in the inner ditch were identified in the single primary context (610) and in the three secondary contexts (630, 629 and 627/628). 630 and 629 are morphologically groups and 627/628 a spread. Fragments of what may be the same ox skull were found in two different secondary contexts 627 and 630, with a dog's radius and ulna in 630.

Set 3: less formalised deposits
In these assemblages there is a smooth distribution of fragment sizes, heavily skewed towards the smaller end. It is suggested that this type of fragment size distribution, indicates that the bone assemblages were subjected to marked degradation subsequent to deposition. These contexts show no particular features in the other classes of variation, except that they often have a high proportion of loose cattle teeth, which is also suggestive of degradation. Almost all of them have high proportions of cattle bones, though not as high as those in the deliberate placements, with correspondingly slight higher proportions of the other species. Fox and mustelid bones are present in one or two of the less formalised deposits, but absent from the deliberate placements, but in such small numbers that this is almost certainly due to chance (table 146 and fig. 181).

In Trench B (outer ditch) less formalised deposits characterise all the larger upper secondary contexts (including, as one would expect, the soil) and the tertiary contexts, and in BB one of the contexts in the old land surface (741)

and the grave fill (734). In context 501 in the tertiary level of Trench E (middle ditch) the smoothness of the curve was matched by a high proportion of loose teeth. The bone deposits in the tertiary levels of Trench F can be classed as less formalised, although the distribution of fragment size is a little uneven. The tertiary had a higher proportion of loose teeth than the primary and secondary levels taken together, but it is rather less than in the uppermost levels of the other trenches. Tertiary context 602 had an unusually high proportion of cattle footbones.

Set 2: intermediate type deposits
Many of the larger bone assemblages are intermediate in most respects between deliberate placements and less formalised deposits. Mean fragment size is quite low in all the contexts in Trench BB, reaching 5 cm only in 746 (the base of the primary bank), but the distribution of fragment size within the bank contexts (746, 765, 703 and 701) is uneven as in deliberate placements, so these appear to be of intermediate type. Context 746 was also marked by having the highest percentages of identified bones in Trench BB.

In Trench B the secondary context 225 has a smooth distribution of fragment size, but a minor concentration of cattle trunk bones and a particularly large proportion of pig, so it should perhaps be classed as intermediate.

Mean fragment size is quite low in Trench A in the outer ditch, never reaching 5 cm, although variability is high. All the larger contexts have a slightly uneven distribution of size, intermediate between the two main types. The percentages of bones identified in the various contexts of Trench A were all low; the two highest percentages were in the secondary contexts 103 and 104 (both scatters). 103 was also marked by having the highest mean fragment size in this trench, the most uneven fragment size distribution and a set of cattle wrist bones. 104 and the tertiary context 102 had a high proportion of loose teeth.

In Trench C in the outer ditch the two tertiary contexts (302 and 301) are of intermediate type in terms of fragmentation. The lowest percentages of identified bones in Trench C were in the tertiary and also in primary context 314, so this should probably be classed as intermediate. There was an increasing proportion of loose teeth in the higher levels.

There was one deposit of intermediate type in the secondary level of Trench D in the middle ditch, context 413 (a group). It had a few ox vertebrae which appear to be from the same animal, but mean size was particularly low and it had a smooth distribution of fragment size. This was also true of context 522 (a spread) in the primary level of Trench E, which is also middle ditch.

Fragmentation: conclusion
The contextual analysis confirms that the faunal material at Windmill Hill was deposited in various ways. Deliberate placements of domestic cattle bones are frequent in the

primary and secondary levels of the ditches, with very degraded, less formalised deposits in the tertiary and sometimes in the uppermost contexts in the secondary level. Deposits which seem to be intermediate between these two extremes occur sporadically in the ditches and particularly in the bank deposits in Trench BB.

Clearly the morphological and compositional variation in the deposits indicates a range of depositional practices. Likewise, the condition of the bones (whether fragmentary or not) indicates varied sources and histories prior to deposition. Whilst many were discarded as bone, some others, particularly those of cattle, seem to have been deposited with the flesh intact. The burial of cattle parts complete with meat constitutes a form of behaviour involving what might be called conspicuous non-consumption of potential food. The less formalised deposits and most, if not all, of the intermediate deposits, which are also dominated by cattle bones, have rather more pig, sheep and goat bones than the deliberate placements, and are probably the relics of activities largely related to the consumption of meat. Further interpretation of these deposits is offered in chapter 17.

PART 3: FAUNAL ANALYSIS

The excavations of Keiller and Smith

As this part of the present chapter, while being primarily concerned with the animal remains from the 1988 excavations, also draws on the more copious material from the previous excavations, it is necessary to give a brief outline of the work done on the earlier material. The animal remains from the excavations of 1925–29 by Keiller and from some minor re-excavations in the 1930s were studied by D.M.S. Watson; it is not clear whether his work was ever completed, but it was certainly not published.

The first detailed report on the animal remains appeared in 1965 and consisted of two main sections, the first on the identification and quantification of the finds from Isobel Smith's excavations in 1957–58 by Margaret Jope and the second on the measurements of the bones from all the excavations by the author. In 1978–79 and 1987 I re-studied the material from all these excavations, which is preserved in the Alexander Keiller Museum in Avebury. Some of the results have already appeared (Grigson 1982a; Grigson 1984). Additional data, which were presented at a meeting of the Neolithic Studies Group at the British Museum in November 1987, have not been published.

Joshua Pollard's recent meticulous analysis of the records and surviving artifacts has allowed much of the material from the earlier excavations to be assigned to period. Almost all the Keiller animal remains are from the primary contexts (Early Neolithic), with a smaller quantity of Late Neolithic/Early Bronze Age material.

Jope's study of the material from the 1957–58 excavations, was confined to three main periods: Pre-Enclosure (Early Neolithic) from under the outer bank, primary (also Early Neolithic but thought to post-date the pre-enclosure phase) and Late Neolithic/Early Bronze. However, her primary sample also included some material from Keiller's 1929 excavations chosen from boxes of unsorted material from the middle ditch: MD VII and MD XI (Smith 1965a, 141 and *pers. comm.*). Jope's Late Neolithic/Early Bronze sample was confined to material from OD V in the outer ditch; material from other Late Neolithic contexts excavated in 1957–58 was not included. It is not now possible to discover exactly which bones were studied by Jope, largely because no detailed records were kept. As we shall see below, Jope's samples were larger than those that can be now be assigned to period, perhaps because Pollard's conservative phasing differs occasionally from that worked out by Smith.

The work on the measurements (Grigson 1965) and my subsequent re-study were based on the entire Windmill Hill material from both the pre-war and the 1957–58 excavations. In the course of the re-study all the surviving material was curated and catalogued.

In order to make comparisons between the 1988 and earlier material it is necessary to realise that although broadly similar the terminology of the main phases at Windmill Hill in the present volume differs slightly from that used by myself, Margaret Jope and the other contributors to Smith (1965a):

Phase 1, Early Neolithic. The 1988 old land surface or pre-bank phase beneath the outer bank (Trench BB) is equivalent to Smith's pre-enclosure phase from an adjacent section.

Phases 2 and 3, Early Neolithic and Late Neolithic/Early Bronze Age. The 1988 primary and secondary fills are broadly equivalent to Smith's 'Primary' Early Neolithic. The upper secondary fill, confined to the outer ditch (Trenches B and C), contains Late Neolithic, Beaker and Early Bronze Age material and is therefore equivalent to Smith's 'Late Neolithic/EBA'. However, in Trench A, which is also outer ditch, some of the secondary contexts contain Late Neolithic material.

Phase 4, later, often mixed, tertiary and other ditch contexts, usually including Romano-British pottery equate with Smith's 'Ploughsoil' (not studied by Jope).

Pollard has been able to assign much of the material from the pre-war excavations to Phases 2 and 3.

Fig. 162. Animal bones being examined by Keiller, possibly by one of the middle
ditch cuttings in 1929 (photo: Alexander Keiller Museum, Avebury).

Fig. 163. Animal bones laid out beside one of the cuttings, probably of the outer ditch, OD I, in 1928
(photo: Alexander Keiller Museum, Avebury).

Fig. 164. Animal bones laid out beside one of the cuttings, probably of the outer ditch, in 1929
(photo: Alexander Keiller Museum, Avebury).

Jope's report does not mention the unidentified fragments, but it is clear from the re-study of the material, and Smith's statement (Smith 1965a, 141) that almost all those from Gray's and Keiller's excavations were discarded, if indeed they were ever retrieved. It seems that after examination by Watson only the most complete identified bones were kept, so the sample surviving may be subject to unintentional bias. Some of the unidentified fragments from the 1957–58 excavations survive, but have not been measured or quantified, since it is clear from comparison with the 1988 material that many were discarded at some stage.

Although with hindsight one may be critical of this apparent lack of care in the retrieval and curation of the faunal material from the pre-war excavations and of the rather sketchy subsequent faunal analyses, these need to be seen in the contexts of their times.

Figs 162–64 are photographs, probably taken in 1928 and 1929, showing piles of animal bones laid out beside the cuttings. One would expect most of the smaller bones to have been lost in these circumstances. Fig. 165 is particularly interesting since it shows the bones of a complete forelimb and a semi-complete hindlimb of an ox still in articulation.

It is only quite recently that animal remains have begun to be excavated with as much care as artifacts. It is to Keiller's credit that he not only collected the animal remains, but kept many of them in Avebury, having had several of the complete skeletons articulated and the more complete ox skulls mounted like hunting trophies on wooden shields. This was at a time when the excavator of Belas Knap (Berry 1929) was able to dismiss the faunal remains as mere 'animal bones and teeth, of no importance'. Thanks to Keiller, Isobel Smith and the curators of the Alexander Keiller Museum, the Windmill Hill material

and records are far more accessible than those from many other excavations, which are buried within the large, off-site storage facilities of our national museums. Taken together, Jope's and my 1965 reports were far more detailed than any previous reports on English Neolithic animal remains.

Representation of animal taxa

The numbers of remains of the various taxa of animals identified in each of the contexts excavated in 1988 are presented in tables 82–88 in Part 2 above; those dating from the Neolithic are summarised in table 145.1 below. It is clear that domestic animals are of far more importance than wild (the criteria used for the distinction of wild and domestic cattle, pigs, sheep and goats are outlined below) in all trenches and in almost all contexts. The presence of dogs is indicated not only by their bones but also by the presence of their coprolites and signs of gnawing of bones. Red and roe deer are represented by both antlers and bones. Since many of the antler fragments derive from collected shed antler rather than from animals which had been killed, and since antler played a very different role in the activities at Windmill Hill from that of carcasses, it is categorised separately; antler working is noted in chapter 15. Other wild animals represented by very small numbers of bones are wild cattle, wild pig, fox, wild cat, polecat, and a few birds which have not been further identified.

In order to compare the representation of taxa in the 1988 sample (table 145.1) with those from the earlier excavations, three other tables summarising all the data which can be assigned to the Neolithic have been added. Table 145.2 is based on Jope's (1965) tables of identifications of the 1957–58 material (to which she added a small proportion of pre-war material) and table 145.3 shows the

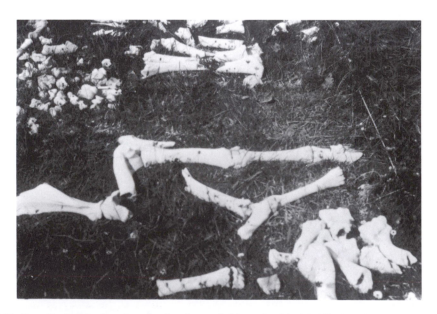

Fig. 165. Detail of articulated and other bones laid out beside Middle Ditch VII (from layer 5)
(photo: Alexander Keiller Museum, Avebury).

results of the re-examination of the faunal collection from the pre-war excavations.

When the results from 1988 are compared with those from 1957–58 and with those from the pre-war excavations, the broad pattern is similar. The higher proportions of cattle bones and red deer antler in the pre-war material are probably due to differential collection – both being more conspicuous and obviously interesting than the bones of smaller animals.

However, some anomalies were apparent between the species identified by Jope and those in my re-examination of the entire collection. Jope identified the remains of two taxa which I have been unable to find: five teeth and some skull fragments of badger and two sternebrae of horse, all from the primary levels. The presence of badger remains, which could derive from a single skull and which might even be intrusive, is less important than that of horse.

Wild horses were part of the British Late Glacial fauna; the most recent direct dates are 9770 ± 80 BP (BM-1619) for a horse bone from the Darenth gravels (Burleigh 1986; Clutton-Brock 1986) and 9790 ± 180 BP (BM-2350) for a mandible from Seamer Carr (Ambers *et al.* 1987; Clutton-Brock and Burleigh 1991a). The earliest direct date for a domestic horse is that from Grime's Graves at 3740 ± 210 BP (BM-1546) (Clutton-Brock and Burleigh 1991b; Clutton-Brock 1992); the horses at Newgrange in Ireland date from about the same time (Wijngaarden-Bakker 1974; 1986) and, since horse were not native to Ireland they must have been introduced as domestic animals, so it is reasonable to assume that this was also true of the horse whose remains were found in the Late Neolithic at Durrington Walls, in Wiltshire (Harcourt 1971; Albarella and Serjeantson forthcoming). However, the presence or absence of either wild or domesticated horses in the British Early Neolithic has yet to be definitely established (Clutton-Brock 1986; 1992; Grigson 1966; 1978b; 1981a; 1981b). All the larger sternebrae from the early excavations have been re-studied in great detail and none are of horse; it is not possible to say whether the bones are missing from the collection or whether they were misidentified. There were no horse remains in the 1988 assemblage from Windmill Hill.

No roe deer were noted by Jope, although both antlers and bones are present in the collection; perhaps there were none in the limited material which she studied. Similarly she found wild ox only in the Late Neolithic/Early Bronze level and did not identify any wild pig (however, only one tooth from the earlier excavations was noted in the re-study).

Problems also arise from the use of different methods of quantification. Although she gives their numbers, Jope did not include teeth, vertebrae or ribs in her percentages of the taxa present, so these have been recalculated in various ways in table 145.2. Jope made no allowance for the fact that many of the bones clearly derive from the same individual animals. Thus her figure of 50 bones of cat in the primary levels has to be discounted since the re-study makes clear that they were all from the same skeleton. Similarly the number of dog bones in the primary level is probably inflated as it seems to includes bones derived from several complete or incomplete skeletons. Even with the re-study this is a recurrent problem; one suspects that many more bones than those which can actually be matched or articulated, derive from the same complete or partial skeletons, but are too damaged for this to be done. The problem is compounded by incomplete retrieval, discard and, most importantly, destruction both before and after deposition in the ground.

Diachronic changes in taxonomic representation

Tables 145.1–145.3 show that there were no dramatic changes over time in the fauna between the pre-bank (pre-enclosure) phase, the Early Neolithic fill of the ditches (primary) and the Late Neolithic/Early Bronze Age fill of the ditches. All three phases are dominated by domestic animals, especially cattle. The apparent dearth of wild animal remains in the pre-bank/pre-enclosure phase, apart from one red deer bone in Jope's material, might be due to the small sample sizes from this level. The most obvious diachronic change is the increase of pigs, which is particularly marked in the 1988 material; its significance in relation to the numbers of the other domestic ungulates is discussed below in the section on the domestic economy, where they are set out in graphic form in figure 181.

Diversity indices for the 1988 faunal sample (table 145.1) show an increase in diversity with time, rising from 1.36 in the pre-bank material (n=99) to 1.50 in the Early Neolithic (n=1039) and 1.64 in the Late Neolithic (n=533). This is not an effect of sample size as the Early Neolithic sample is the largest. The increase in diversity is small and probably results largely from the increased proportion of pigs, rather than the presence of two additional species, wild pig and otter, which is counter-balanced by the absence of cat. Indices were also calculated for all the material summarised in tables 145.2 and 145.3, but will not be discussed further because of the problems outlined above.

Taxonomic representation within different types of deposit

It has been claimed that faunal assemblages excavated from various Neolithic sites reflect selection of particular animals for ceremonial activities and cannot therefore be used to ascertain their economic importance (e.g. Richards and Thomas 1984 for the Later Neolithic). The differences of the faunal assemblages within various individual contexts of each trench excavated in 1988 were discussed at length in the first part of this chapter, and it was concluded on the basis of several criteria, particularly relating to fragmentation, that some of the contexts represented deliberately placed deposits, which probably reflect symbolic or ritualistic behaviour, rather than more day to day activity. Whether or not such a dichotomy can legitimately be drawn between these behaviours, it is clear that the

Caroline Grigson

Table 145.1: 1998 representation of taxa.

period	Cattle finds	large rib	Pig finds	Shp/Gt	medium rib	Dog finds	Wild cattle	Wild? pig	Red deer bone	Roe deer bone	Mustelid	Cat	Fox	Otter	Bird	TOTAL ID
PRE-BANK																
numbers	51	19	12	13	4	-	-	-	-	-	-	-	-	-	-	99
%	70.7		12.1	13.1	4.0											100.0
EARLY NEOLITHIC																
numbers	523	127	151	114	74	15	5	-	11	5	3	2	2	-	6	1038
%	62.6		14.5	11.0	7.1	1.4	0.5	-	1.1	0.5	0.3	0.2	0.2	-	0.6	100.0
LATE NEOLITHIC/EARLY BRONZE AGE																
numbers	230	25	158	44	46	8	3	1	6	4	1	-	3	1	1	531
%	48.0		29.8	8.3	8.7	1.5	0.6	0.2	1.1	0.8	0.2	-	0.6	0.2	0.2	100.0

Table 145.2 1957–58* representation of taxa.

	Cattle bones	Cattle teeth	large ribs+vert	Pig bones	Pig teeth	Sheep/Goat bones	Sheep/Goat teeth	medium ribs+vert	Dog bones	Dog teeth	Wild cattle	Red deer antler	Red deer bone	Red deer teeth	Totals	Wild Cattle	Cat bones	Cat teeth	Fox	Badger bones	Badger teeth	Hare	Horse	Totals
PRE-BANK 1957/58																								
nos Jope 1965	90	25	41	22	9	16	9	5	5		3	5		1	226									226
% Jope 1965	66.2			16.0		11.7			2.2			3.7			100									100
re-calculated nos	115		41	31		25		5	5		3		1		221									221
re-calculated %	52.0		18.6	14.0		11.3		2.3	1.4				0.5		100									100
re-calculated %	70.6			15.3		12.3			1.4				0.5		100									100
PRIMARY 1957/8 + some KEILLER 1929?																								
nos Jope 1965	292	50	74	74	16	121	17	170	159	40		9		1	1223		50	5	8	2	5	10	2	1305
% Jope 1965	40.2		10.2	10.2		16.6		13.1	21.9						100		6.9		1		0.2	1.4	0.2	100
re-calculated nos	342		274	90		138		170	199				1		1214		55		8	7		10	2	1296
re-calculated %	26.4		21.1	6.9		10.6		13.1	15.4				0.04		0.0		4.2		0.6	0.54		0.77	0.15	100
re-calculated %	47.5			12.1		18.5			15.4				0.04				4.2		0.6	0.54		0.77	0.15	100
LATE NEOLITHIC/EARLY BRONZE 1957/58 Outer Ditch V only																								
nos Jope 1965	30	20	10	12	3	7	1	9	9		10			4	107	3	2							112
% Jope 1965	46.1		18.5	18.5		10.7		8.0	15.3					1.5	100	4.6	3.0							100
re-calculated nos	50		10	15		8		9	9				5		96	3	2							107
re-calculated %	44.6		8.9	13.4		7.1		8.0	8.9				4.5		95	2.7	1.8							100
re-calculated %	53.6			19.4		9.1			8.9				4.5			2.7	1.8							100

* includes some material from Keiller excavations

Table 145.3: 1925–29 representation of taxa.

	Cattle	l mamm ribs	Pig	Sheep/ goat	m mam ribs	Dog	Red deer antler	Roe deer antler	Red deer bone	Wild Cattle	Cat	Fox	Hedge-hog	Bird	Small mammal	TOTALS
PRIMARY																
numbers	404	13	40	85	8	27	58	6	4	6	1	1	1		6	662
%	63.0		6.0	12.8	1.2	4.1	8.8	0.9	0.6	0.9	0.2	0.2	0.2		0.9	100
LATE NEOLITHIC/EARLY BRONZE																
numbers	44	3	11	5	1	8	10	5	1	3	4	4		3		107
%	43.9		10.3	4.7	0.9	7.5	9.3	4.7	0.9	2.8	3.7	3.7		2.8		100
TOTAL																769

Table 146: 1988 representation of taxa in placed and other deposits.

	Cattle finds	large rib	Pig finds	Shp/Gt	medium rib	Dog finds	Wild cattle	Red deer bone	Roe deer bone	Fox	Cat	Mustelid	Bird	TOTAL ID
PLACED DEPOSITS														
numbers	365	52	85	72	36	8	2	8	3	0	1	-	3	635
%	65.7		13.4	11.3	5.7	1.3	0.3	1.3	0.5	0.0	0.2	-	0.5	100.0
SCATTERS etc														
numbers	158	75	66	42	38	7	4	3	2	2	1	3	3	404
%	57.7		16.3	10.4	9.4	1.7	1.0	0.7	0.5	0.5	0.2	0.7	0.7	100.0

deliberately placed deposits at Windmill are quite distinct from the others. It is necessary to discover whether deliberately placed deposits as a whole, which all probably relate to Early Neolithic activity, differ from the remainder of the fauna from the same period. As no such distinctions were made in the earlier excavations the present discussion is confined to the 1988 material, which is outlined in table 146.

It is clear from this table that the taxonomic representation and diversity within the two main types of context do not differ dramatically. Both are dominated by domestic animals, particularly cattle. The bones of two wild taxa (fox and mustelids) are present in the less formalised deposits, but absent from the deliberately placed deposits, but in such small numbers that this is may be due to chance. What may be of more significance is the slightly higher proportion of cattle finds within the deliberately placed deposits and this is discussed further below in the section on ungulate proportions.

Criteria for the distinction of wild and domestic ungulates

The main criterion used to distinguish wild from domestic ungulates in archaeological assemblages is the smaller size of the domestic animals (Boessneck 1958; Jewell 1963; Degerbøl 1963; von den Driesch and Boessneck 1978; Uerpmann, 1979; Grigson 1969; 1978a; 1982c; 1989; Flannery 1983; Davis 1987; and many others). The second important criterion is the presence of a species outside the geographical range of its wild forebear. Other criteria include a sudden diachronic increase of a species within a faunal spectrum (Clutton-Brock 1981; Davis 1982; 1987) and, much less certainly, indications of a demographic structure differing from that found in the wild (Ducos 1968, 1978; Hesse 1978; 1982; Bökönyi 1977).

Sheep and goat remains from British and European sites are bound to be of domestic animals, since the wild forms have never been native. However, both wild cattle and wild pigs were present in Britain; cattle probably died out during the Bronze Age, but pigs survived into medieval times, if not later. For cattle and pigs the main criterion for the distinction of the remains of wild and domestic animals in the Neolithic is diminution in size.

Since both wild and domestic cattle and pigs were present in England during the Neolithic the question arises as to whether cattle were actually undergoing domestication at this time in Britain. This is not the place for a detailed discussion of autochthonous domestication; suffice it to say that the notion is illogical since it implies that when domestic sheep and goats were imported into Britain, domestic cattle and pigs were left behind. As the main criterion for domestication is reduction in body size, if domestication was actually happening one would expect to see a gradual diminution in assemblages from sites with levels spanning the periods in question. Such intermediate stages have not been found in Britain (Grigson 1969; 1982a; 1982d; 1984; Serjeantson forthcoming; Albarella and Payne, n.d.; Albarella and Serjeantson forthcoming) or in northern Europe (Degerbøl 1963). Such evidence as there is for local domestication of taurine cattle and pigs of the appropriate sub-species is confined to south-west Asia (Grigson 1989; Flannery 1983).

Cattle (*Bos taurus*)

The distinction between wild and domestic cattle
When size is used as a criterion for the distinction between wild and domestic cattle there are three main approaches that can be pursued: comparisons of absolute size, comparisons of size compared with that of a standard animal and comparisons of shape.

The size of wild cattle and early domestic cattle in the Holocene of northern Europe has been established using the data set out by Degerbøl (Degerbøl and Fredskild 1970) in his classic work on finds of complete skeletons of bulls and cows from Danish bogs and of fragmentary material from Mesolithic and Neolithic sites, with the addition of further data from Danish and British sites (Grigson 1982a; 1989). The main problem is that the ranges of many of the dimensions of domestic bulls and wild cows overlap, so it is important to establish sexual differences. Some complete bones can be sexed on the basis of shape, those of cows tending to be more slender than those of bulls. Sexual differences are particularly marked in the horncores.

Measurements of the cattle bones from the 1988 excavations are set out in Appendix 1.1–1.4; those from the Keiller and Smith excavations are in Grigson (1965). Appendices 1.2 and 1.3 contain revised versions of the tables of the measurements of skulls and horncores from the earlier excavations, as well as the scanty material from 1988.

Measurements of the bones from the most recent levels in the Windmill Hill excavations which contain Romano-British material are included in the Appendix, but have not been used in the present analysis.

Absolute size

The distribution of the proximal breadth of the middle phalanx of wild cattle is set out in fig. 166.1. The four peaks of the curve represent (from left to right), female posterior phalanges, female anterior phalanges, male posterior and male anterior phalanges. It can be seen immediately that the majority of the Windmill Hill phalanges, represented by columns, are from much smaller animals than the wild cattle and are therefore likely to be of domestic animals. A much smaller group falls within the area of apparent overlap of domestic bulls and wild females, whilst two phalanges are clearly derived from wild males.

A similar result is obtained when the distal breadth of the astragalus is compared (fig. 166.2), but as this bone is only in the hind limb there is no complication due to an anterior/posterior difference.

Windmill Hill is almost unique in the large number of cattle skulls and horncores included in the faunal assemblage. As measurements of 97 wild bulls' horncores and 37 of wild cows are available for comparison, as well as 24 complete Neolithic domestic skulls of known sex from Denmark (Degerbøl and Fredskild 1970), this allows a detailed analysis to be made of their absolute size; their shape is dealt with below. Fig. 167 consists of plots of the basal circumference of the horncores from these three groups, and a fourth from Neolithic habitation sites in northern Europe (Nobis 1954). It shows that the majority

of the Windmill Hill skulls and horncores are from domestic cows, while the remainder all fall within the area of overlap of wild cows and domestic bulls.

The height at the withers of cattle can be estimated from the lengths of longbones by using the indices established by Fock and Matolsci (von den Driesch and Boessneck 1974). The main difficulty is that the indices are different for the different sexes and in some cases it is not possible to say whether a particular bone from an archaeological assemblage is from a cow or a bull. Two complete cattle longbones from the 1988 excavations and 17 from the earlier ones can be used to estimate withers heights utilising both sets of indices, as well as the mean between them. They indicate animals ranging upwards in size from just over a metre, 1.1 m, to about 1.4 m. When the calculations are confined to bones which can be sexed, for example the metacarpals, use of Fock's indices of 6.25 for males and 6.00 from females, indicates that the withers height for the Windmill Hill cows is 1.1–1.3 m (n=8) and for the single male metacarpal 1.4 m (n=1). Equivalent ranges calculated from measurements of Danish wild cattle taken by Degerbøl and Fredskild (1970) are 1.4–1.5 m for cows (n=11) and for wild bulls 1.5–1.7 m (n=22).

Comparison with a standard animal

The chief advantage of this method is that the measurements of different bones can be lumped together, whereas plots of the absolute size of individual bone measurements are often too small for any patterning to be discerned.

A skeleton of *Bos primigenius* from Ullerslev was used as a standard animal first by Buitenhuis (1985) and then by Grigson (1989). It is the complete skeleton of an adult

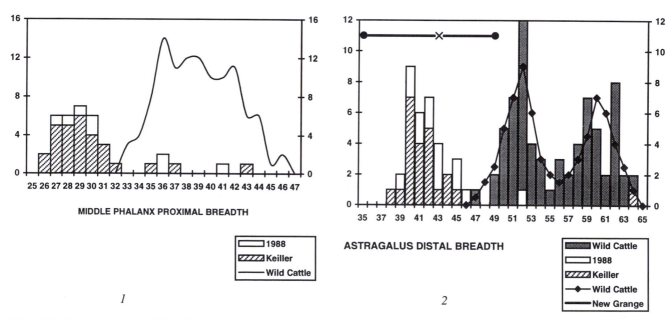

Fig. 166. Absolute size in wild and domestic cattle: phalanges and astragali. 1, The proximal breadth of the middle phalanx. 2, The distal breadth of the astragalus. Most of the Windmill Hill measurements are smaller than those of wild cattle and are considered to be of domestic animals. A smaller group falls within the area of apparent overlap of domestic bulls and wild cows, whilst two phalanges and one astragalus are clearly derived from wild males.

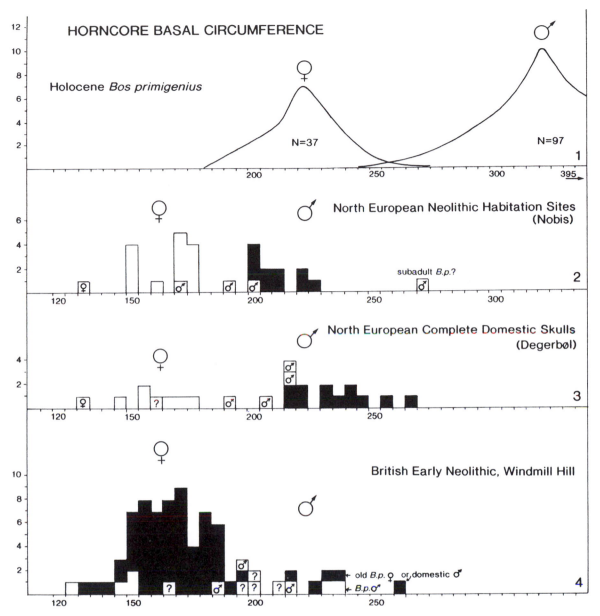

Fig. 167. Absolute size in wild and domestic cattle: horncore basal circumference. 1, Wild cattle (Bos primigenius). 2, Cattle, mainly domestic, from N. European habitation sites (after Nobis 1954). 3, Complete domestic cattle skulls from N. Europe (after Degerbøl 1963). 4, Cattle from Windmill Hill (1988 data). The majority of the Windmill Hill skulls and horncores are from domestic cows, while the remainder fall within the area of overlap of wild cows and domestic bulls.

wild cow, aged about 5–7 years, retrieved from a bog at Ullerslev, on what is now the Danish island of Fyn, and dates from the Early Boreal (pollen zone V). It was described in detail by Degerbøl and Fredskild (1970) and is kept in the Universiteits Zoologiske Museum in Copenhagen. The Ullerslev measurements used in the present study are (in mm):

lower third molar length LM3	48.8
humerus breadth of trochlea Bt	89
radius proximal breadth Bp	100
metacarpal proximal breadth Bp	74
metacarpal distal breadth Bd	73
tibia distal breadth Bd	78
calcaneum maximum length GL	165

astragalus maximum length GL	83
metatarsal proximal breadth Bp	62
metatarsal distal breadth Bd	68
navicular maximum breadth GB	67.

Fig. 168 is a histogram consisting of a plot of the measurements of the cattle bones from the 1988 and earlier excavations at Windmill Hill and another of wild cattle from Denmark. All measurements are expressed in terms of the difference of their logarithm from that of the equivalent measurement in the Ullerslev cow. It is clear that the majority of the bones from Windmill Hill are considerably smaller than those of wild cattle and can therefore be safely assigned to domestic animals. The sexual dimorphism of the wild cattle bones is obvious and

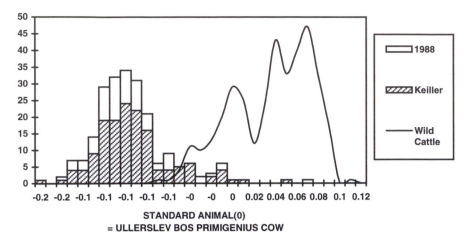

Fig. 168. Relative size in wild and domestic cattle: logarithmic differences from the dimensions of the standard wild animal (the Ullerslev wild cow). Most of the bones from Windmill Hill are considerably smaller than those of wild cattle and can therefore be safely assigned to domestic animals. The sexual dimorphism in both wild and domestic cattle is obvious. The two Windmill Hill dimensions on the extreme right appear to be from wild bulls and those in the intermediate group are probably either domestic bulls or wild cows.

as a similar dimorphism occurs in the domestic cattle, those on the left of the graph represent domestic cows. The two dimensions on the extreme right appear to be from wild bulls and those in the intermediate group are probably a mixture of domestic bulls and wild cows.

Shape

Metacarpals. The scattergram (fig. 169) of metacarpal length against distal breadth shows the very clear distinction between those of wild cattle of known sex and the much smaller, domestic, animals from Windmill Hill. If, as is reasonable, one presumes that sexual differences were similar in wild and domestic cattle, it is also clear that eight of the nine complete metacarpals from Windmill Hill

are from females and one is from a male. This last bone is the only complete metacarpal from the 1988 excavations.

Horncores. In the analysis of the absolute size of cattle horncores it was apparent that the basal circumference of those of domestic bulls overlapped with that of wild cows. Fig. 170 is a scattergram in which a logarithmic index of horncore size is plotted against a logarithmic index of shape for wild cattle of known sex and presumed domestic cattle from Neolithic sites (mostly Windmill Hill). It shows a distinct difference in both size and shape of the two sexes and the wild and domestic forms, with wild cows overlapping with domestic bulls in total size, but scarcely at all in shape. The difference in shape is also indicated in fig. 171, in which the basal circumference is plotted against the

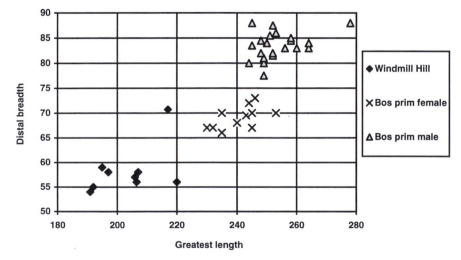

Fig. 169. Size and shape in wild cattle metapodials and those at Windmill Hill: metacarpal length plotted against distal breadth. There is a clear distinction between metacarpals of wild cattle of known sex and the much smaller, domestic, animals from Windmill Hill. If sexual differences were similar in wild and domestic cattle, eight of the nine complete metacarpals from Windmill Hill are from females and one is from a male.

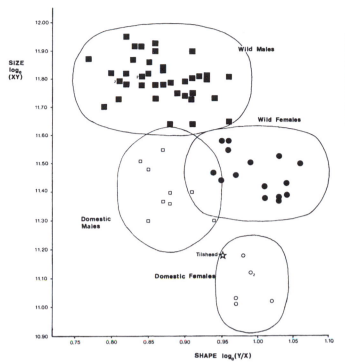

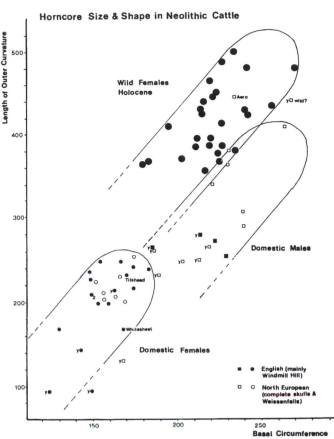

Fig. 170. Size and shape in cattle horncores: logarithmic indices of horncore size plotted against a logarithmic index of shape for wild cattle of known sex and presumed domestic cattle from English Neolithic sites (mostly Windmill Hill and Tilshead). There is a distinct difference in both size and shape of the two sexes in the wild and domestic forms, with wild cows overlapping with domestic bulls in total size, but scarcely at all in shape.

Fig. 171. Size and shape in cattle horncores: basal circumference plotted against the length of the outer curvature. Although there is a slight overlap, wild cows are quite distinct from domestic males at Windmill Hill and elsewhere in the Neolithic, in having much longer horncores. This suggests that most if not all those in the area of overlap of basal circumference are of domestic bulls, not of wild cows.

length of the outer curvature. It shows that although there is a slight overlap, wild cows are quite distinct from domestic males at Windmill Hill and elsewhere in the Neolithic, in having much longer horncores. From this it seems that most if not all those in the area of overlap of basal circumference are of domestic bulls, not of wild cows. Both Neolithic domestic cattle and wild cattle bulls had longer horncores than the cows; both differ from most cattle of later periods in Britain in which horncores (and therefore horns) are often shorter in bulls than in cows and castrates (Armitage and Clutton-Brock 1976). It seems that this change probably occurred in the Middle or Late Bronze Age.

Outline tracings of the shape of the more complete horncores of the Windmill Hill cattle of each sex at different ages are shown in figs 172.1 and 172.2. Information on complete horncores can be deduced by laying them on these outlines (when reproduced at their full size).

Cattle demography

The demographic data obtained on the Windmill Hill cattle are outlined below and the implications of the results are discussed in the section on the role of domestic ungulates.

Age

The age at death of the cattle represented in the faunal assemblage from Windmill Hill has been examined in three main ways: the state of fusion of the longbones, the state of wear of the teeth and the ageing of the horncores. It must be stressed that the criteria for ageing are not very precise; there is a wide degree of variation in the time of epiphysial fusion and age changes may have occurred at different rates in the past. However, most sexual differences are more discrete, and in fact reasonably consistent patterns emerge from the various methods utilised.

The survival curve based on epiphysial fusion of the domestic cattle at Windmill Hill is shown in fig. 173; it is based on the data set out in table 147. The pattern produced from the analysis of the bones from 1988 (n=172) is similar to that from the earlier excavations (n=265), but the fact that it is slightly lower throughout suggests that some of the unfused elements from the earlier excavations have been discarded. However, the 1988 curve is jagged, and actually rises in two places. In theory in any one population

Caroline Grigson

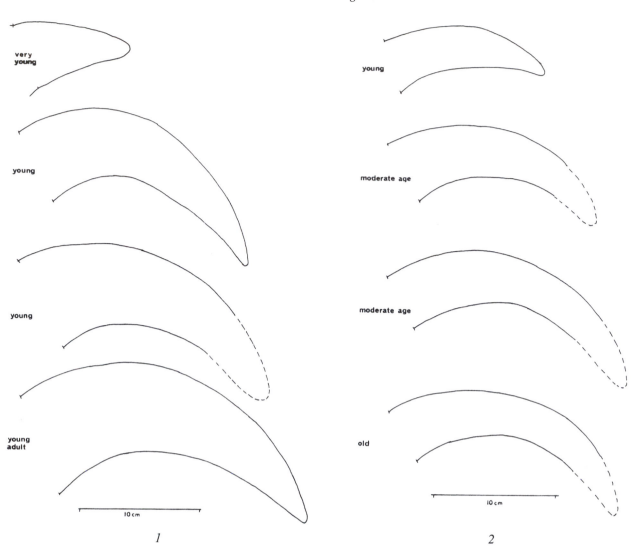

Fig. 172. Outline tracings of the shape of the more complete horncores of the Windmill Hill cattle at different ages. 1, Bulls. 2, Cows. Information on complete horncores can be deduced by laying them on these outlines (when reproduced at their full size).

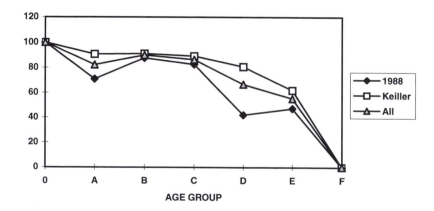

Fig. 173. Cattle survivorship at Windmill Hill, based on epiphysial fusion. The pattern produced from the analysis of the bones from 1988 (n=172) is similar to, but slightly lower than, that from the earlier excavations (n=265), suggesting that some of the unfused elements from the earlier excavations have been discarded. It is clear that after about 15 percent mortality in the first year, approximately 50 percent of the domestic cattle survived until aged at least 3½–4 years.

Table 147: Cattle age based on epiphysial and suture fusion.

age group	bone	part	age of fusion (Silver 1963)	fused?	1988 no	1988 % fused	Keiller/Smith no	Keiller/Smith % fused
A	pelvis	acetabulum	7-10 months	no	4	-	1	-
A	scapula	distal	7-10 months	no	1	-	2	-
A	pelvis	acetabulum	7-10 months	yes	7	-	16	-
A	scapula	distal	7-10 months	yes	10	77.3	13	90.6
B	radius	proximal	12-18 months	no	-	-	1	-
B	humerus	distal	12-18 months	no	4	-	6	-
B	radius	proximal	12-18 months	yes	21	-	22	-
B	humerus	distal	12-18 months	yes	14	89.7	49	91.0
C	prox phalanx	proximal	c. 18 months	no	3	-	4	-
C	mid phalanx	proximal	c. 18 months	no	3	-	1	-
C	prox phalanx	proximal	c. 18 months	yes	16	-	18	-
C	mid phalanx	proximal	c. 18 months	yes	12	82.4	23	89.1
D	tibia	distal	24-30 months	no	9	-	2	-
D	metacarpal	distal	c. 30 months	no	2	-	2	-
D	metatarsal	distal	c. 30 months	no	9	-	6	-
D	metapodial	distal	c. 30 months	no	1	-	3	-
D	tibia	distal	24-30 months	yes	7	-	21	-
D	metacarpal	distal	c. 30 months	yes	3	-	20	-
D	metatarsal	distal	c. 30 months	yes	5	-	13	-
D	metapodial	distal	c. 30 months	yes	1	43.2	0	80.6
E	radius	distal	42-48 months	no	6	-	7	-
E	femur	distal	42-48 months	no	8	-	1	-
E	femur	proximal	42 months	no	-	-	1	-
E	tibia	proximal	42-48 months	no	3	-	6	-
E	humerus	proximal	42-48 months	no	1	-	1	-
E	radius	distal	42-48 months	yes	10	-	8	-
E	femur	distal	42-48 months	yes	3	-	6	-
E	femur	proximal	42 months	yes	1	-	4	-
E	tibia	proximal	42-48 months	yes	3	-	3	-
E	humerus	proximal	42-48 months	yes	-	48.6	5	61.9
TOTAL AGEABLE LONG BONES					167	-	265	-
	calcaneum	tuber	c. 36 months	no	1	f	-	-
	calcaneum	tuber	c. 36 months	yes	2	-	-	-

the pattern should fall from left to right, any rise being caused either by sampling problems or by the introduction of new stock. The low percentage of fused elements in age group A is caused by the presence of five very young pelves, probably due to chance as the total number of pelves from the 1988 excavations that could be aged was only 12; similarly the trough in age group D is caused by the unexpected presence of 10 unfused metatarsals in a total of 15, perhaps exaggerated in appearance by the steep rise to age group E, which is due to the presence of 10 fused distal radii out of a total of 16. Although the curve from the earlier excavations appears the more reliable, it is possible that the trough in age group D (animals aged about 2½ years), followed by a rise in age group E (animals aged more than 3½-4 years), does represent the real state of affairs, in which case one would have to argue that the scarcity of unfused elements in age group D is due to biased discard in the older excavations.

Notwithstanding these problems it is clear from the longbone fusion data that after about 15 percent mortality in the first year, approximately 50 percent of the domestic cattle survived until aged at least 3½-4 years.

The mandibular teeth of cattle from the 1988 excavations (but not from the earlier excavations) were aged according to the wear stages established by Grant (1982); the data are set out in table 148. The sample is too small for any real conclusions to be drawn, but it is worth noting the presence of quite a few lower third molars. As those teeth are the last lower molars to erupt (probably at about 2½ years) and many were in an advanced state of wear, this suggests the presence of quite elderly animals. The lower fourth deciduous molars are replaced by the fourth pre-

Table 148: Cattle tooth wear stages (after Grant 1982).

lower cheek teeth	A	B	C	C/D	D	E	E/F	F	G	H	I	J	K	L	M
m4															1
P4			1		1										
M1										1					
M1/2		1												2	
M2						1								1	
M3			2					1	1				2	1	

arrows connect teeth from same jaw

molars at about three years; in the 1988 material there were 7 lower fourth deciduous molars and 11 fourth premolars, so animals of less than 3 years of age were also present at Windmill Hill.

Sex

The pelves of cattle can be sexed on the basis of the non-metrical character of the configuration of the inner surface of the acetabulum (Grigson 1982b). They can also be very roughly aged by the state of fusion of the three main pelvic elements: ilium, ischium and pubis within the acetabulum (the socket for the head of the femur) at 7–10 months, provided of course that the pelvic fragment includes the acetabulum. Table 149 shows that only one pelvis, of a male, could be assigned to the infant class, and that there were 19 of older cows and three of bulls. Clearly cows feature more strongly than bulls at Windmill Hill.

Table 149: Sexed cattle pelves.

Age	females	males
infant	-	1
? age	10	2
adult	9	1
total	**19**	**4**

NB: includes 4 adult females and 1 adult male from 1988 excavation

Age and sex

It was shown above in the discussion of the wild/domestic status of the cattle at Windmill Hill that horncores of cattle are sexually dimorphic; in wild cattle and Neolithic domestic cattle those of bulls are both longer and stouter than those of cows. In addition it is possible to age horncores by texture and by the state of closure of the frontal-parietal suture which fuses at 5–7 years within the temporal fossa, and at 7–10 years where it runs along the edge of the temporal fossa close to the base of the horncore. It is therefore sensible to consider age and sex together when dealing with horncores. Table 150 shows the numbers of horncores from the earlier excavations that can be aged and sexed. There are only a few of either sex that can definitely be assigned to ages of 3–4 years or younger, although the

Table 150: Sexed and aged cattle horncores.

Age		females	males
infant	less than 1 year	-	1
young	1-2 years	1 (?4)	2 (?7)
young adult	3-4 years	2	3
moderate age	5-6 years	27	-
old age	>5-6 years	27	-
total		**57 (?61)**	**6 (?13)**

number rises if the numbers of females, and particularly of males, which are more doubtfully assigned to the young age group, are included. The important fact is that there are no horncores of bulls in the 5–6 year or older class, whereas there are 27 of cows in each of these age classes. Clearly old and moderately old cows predominated in the life of the inhabitants of Windmill Hill. A similar preponderance of old animals was noted by Armour-Chelu (1992) for the causewayed enclosures at Etton and Maiden Castle, and by Legge (1981) at Hambledon Hill. It is worth noting the presence of a shed lower fourth deciduous molar of an ox in the Late Neolithic/Early Bronze Age soil horizon in the outer ditch (Trench B), since this indicates its loss by a live animal, aged about three years of age, within the confines of the site.

Castration

The effects of castration on the size and shape of the bones of domestic cattle have not been clearly established, though it is clear from the simple observation of live animals that longbones of male castrates (bullocks) tend to be longer than those of bulls. Thus one would expect univariate plots of measurements to be trimodal, whereas all those illustrated above are bimodal and similar in shape and extent to those of wild cattle in which castrates do not of course occur. Similarly with bivariate plots one would expect to find three concentrations of measurements, rather than the two recognised so far. On this rather negative evidence it seems unlikely that the bones of castrates were present in the assemblage at Windmill Hill. The main reason for castrating cattle is to produce strong, unaggressive animals that can be kept into old age and used for draught. Such usage, whether of bullocks or cows, produces arthritis in the joints, which scarcely occurs at Windmill Hill (see section on pathology below), so it seems likely that cattle were neither castrated, nor used for draught. It is true that there is evidence, in the form of ardmarks under a barrow, for the use of ploughs at the nearby Early Neolithic site of South Street long barrow (Fowler and Evans 1967; Evans 1971; Ashbee *et al.* 1979), but it does not follow that cattle were used to pull them.

Pigs (*Sus scrofa*)

Domestic status and size

In pigs, as with cattle, the main criterion for distinguishing domestic from wild animals is a diminution in size.

Measurements of the pig bones from the 1988 excavations are set out in Appendix 1.5; those from the Keiller and Smith excavations are in Grigson (1965). Measurements of the bones from the most recent levels in the Windmill Hill excavations which contain Romano-British material are included in the Appendix, but have not been used in the present analysis.

Unfortunately there is no body of data on the size of wild pigs equivalent to that used for cattle above. However, there are two sets of information which are of use. The first is the establishment of a standard animal as the mean of measurements of present-day wild boar in Turkey by Payne and Bull (1988), although it might be questioned whether such animals are suitable for comparisons with Neolithic British material. Bergmann's rule suggests that they would be smaller than English pigs; this probably is the case as the only two comparable measurements of wild pig bones from the Mesolithic site of Star Carr in Yorkshire (Legge and Rowley-Conwy 1988) are larger than the standard. Payne and Bull's means of measurements of wild pigs used here are (in mm):

scapula least length of neck SLC	29.8
radius distal breadth Bd	41.3

tibia distal breadth Bd	34.6
astragalus maximum length GL	48.7.

These elements have been selected because their measurements are represented in the Windmill Hill material.

The second source of comparative information is a huge unpublished database of measurements of pig bones from the Late Neolithic site of Durrington Walls in southern Wiltshire, kindly made available to me by Umberto Albarella and Sebastian Payne (Albarella and Payne n.d.).

When the data from Durrington Walls are compared on a logarithmic scale with the standard animal (fig. 174) it is clear that they are considerably smaller than the standard pig and there is little doubt that almost all stem from domestic animals. This must also be true of the Windmill Hill pigs as their size distribution appears to be identical; a student's t test shows no significant difference in size. One mandible fragment with a lower third molar length of 39.9 was large enough to have come from a wild pig, but it falls within the range of overlap of wild and domestic animals. It comes from a Late Neolithic context, 103, in the outer ditch (Trench B). The few comparable measurements (all of limb bones) from Star Carr (Legge and Rowley-Conwy 1988) are all considerably larger than those at Durrington and Windmill Hill.

Demography: age and sex

It is possible to age pig bones by the state of epiphysial fusion of the longbones. Details of those at Windmill Hill are given in table 151 and presented graphically in fig. 175. It is clear from the analysis of the 1988 sample that almost all of the pigs had been killed by the age of two years. The analysis of all the material from the earlier excavations gives a very different picture, with a much higher proportion of bones of older animals. The reason for this disparity is almost certainly differential collection

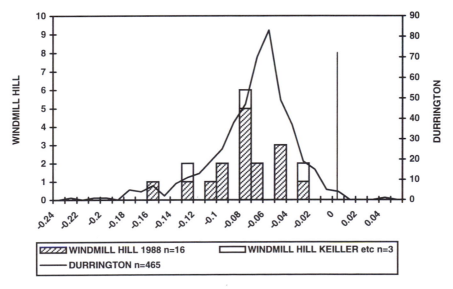

Fig. 174. Relative size of pigs at Windmill Hill and Durrington Walls, compared to that of a standard animal (based on a population of wild pigs in Turkey, after Payne and Bull 1988). Almost all the Durrington and Windmill Hill pigs are considerably smaller than the standard pig and there is little doubt that almost all stem from domestic animals.

Table 151: Pig age based on epiphysial fusion.

age group	bone	part	age of fusion (Silver 1963)	fused?	1988 no	% fused	Keiller/Smith no	% fused
B	humerus	distal	1 year	no	4	-	7	-
B	middle central phalanx	proximal	1 year	no	2	-	-	-
B	pelvis	acetabulum	1 year	no	-	-	-	-
B	radius	proximal	1 year	no	4	-	1	-
B	scapula	distal	1 year	no	-	-	-	-
B	humerus	distal	1 year	yes	1	-	7	-
B	middle central phalanx	proximal	1 year	yes	3	-	2	-
B	pelvis	acetabulum	1 year	yes	2	-	2	-
B	radius	proximal	1 year	yes	3	-	2	-
B	scapula	distal	1 year	yes	2	52.4	1	63.6
C	metapodial distal	distal	2 years	no	7	-	2	-
C	proximal central phalanx	proximal	2 years	no	2	-	5	-
C	tibia	distal	2 years	no	3	-	4	-
C	calcaneum	proximal	2 years	no	2	-	3	-
C	metapodial distal	distal	2 years	yes	-	-	2	-
C	proximal central phalanx	proximal	2 years	yes	-	-	1	-
C	tibia	distal	2 years	yes	1	-	3	-
C	calcaneum	proximal	2 years	yes	-	6.7	-	30.0
D	ulna	proximal	3½ years	no	2	-	4	-
D	femur	distal	3½ years	no	3	-	2	-
D	femur	proximal	3½ years	no	5	-	-	-
D	humerus	proximal	3½ years	no	2	-	1	-
D	radius distal	distal	3½ years	no	4	-	-	-
D	tibia	proximal	3½ years	no	2	-	-	-
D	ulna	proximal	3½ years	yes	-	-	-	-
D	femur	distal	3½ years	yes	-	-	1	-
D	femur	proximal	3½ years	yes	-	-	-	-
D	humerus	proximal	3½ years	yes	1	-	-	-
D	radius distal	distal	3½ years	yes	-	-	-	-
D	tibia	proximal	3½ years	yes	-	5.3	2	30.0
TOTAL AGEABLE LONG BONES					**55**	-	**52**	-

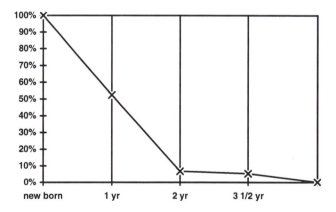

Fig. 175. Pig survivorship at Windmill Hill, based on epiphysial fusion. The 1988 sample shows that almost all of the pigs had been killed by the age of two years, but the material from the earlier excavations suggests a much higher proportion of bones of older animals. This disparity is almost certainly due to differential collection of the earlier material, bones lacking epiphyses being incomplete and therefore many fewer were retained. It is usual for the majority of pig bones in archaeological assemblages to be of young animals, but the extreme pattern at Windmill Hill might indicate the importation of piglets into the site rather than a breeding population.

of the earlier material, bones lacking epiphyses being incomplete, and therefore few were retained.

Although it is usual for the majority of pig bones in archaeological assemblages to be of young animals, the pattern at Windmill Hill seems to be more extreme and indicates perhaps the importation of piglets into the site rather than a breeding population. A few of the pig bones could be sexed. The 1988 sample contained three female and one male canine and one female pelvis, and the sample from the earlier excavations six female and two male canines. Although only a few pigs at Windmill Hill reached adulthood it seems that the majority of those that did were female.

Two rather unspectacular groups of pig bones were found in 1988 in the outer ditch in Trench B: the remains of what appears to be a newborn piglet in context 210 (Early Neolithic) and a fragmentary skull and mandible in 216 (Late Neolithic). A complete skeleton of a pig (fig. 176), was excavated in 1929, also from the outer ditch (OD IIIC layer 5, Early Neolithic).

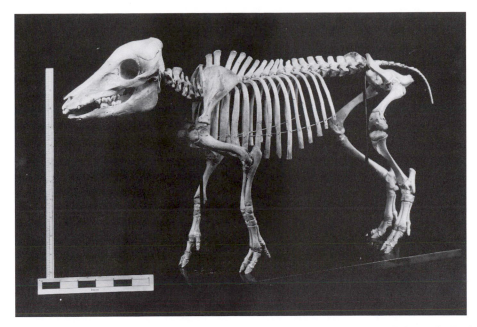

Fig. 176. Complete skeleton of a pig excavated in 1929, from the outer ditch (OD IIIC, layer 5: Early Neolithic). Plate IXb in Smith (1965a).

Sheep (*Ovis aries*) and goats (*Capra hircus*)

Although the bones of both sheep and goat at Windmill Hill were identified in the original studies (Jope 1965; Grigson 1965) on the basis of cranial material, the criteria for the distinction of postcranial bones had not at that time been established and were not published until 1969 (Boessneck 1969). Even in the material from the 1988 excavations, the numbers which could be assigned to species were so small that in most of what follows they have to be treated as a single category.

Domestic status and size

As neither wild sheep nor wild goats have ever been members of the British fauna their remains at Windmill Hill must be of domestic animals. Although comparison with the standard wild sheep and goat which are given by Uerpmann (1979) might be informative, there are too few measurable bones that can be assigned to species to make this significant. However, all the suitable dimensions of the sheep, goat and sheep/goat bones from Windmill are less than those of the standard animals, with the single exception of a large scapula of a sheep from the 1988 excavations. A complete radius of an Early Neolithic sheep excavated in 1988 (fig. 177) indicates a withers height of 57 cm, using the index established by Teicherdt (1975). Measurements of the sheep and goat bones from the 1988 excavations are set out in Appendix 1.6; those from the Keiller and Smith excavations are in Grigson (1965).

Relative numbers of sheep and goats

The relative numbers of bones identified as either sheep or goat are quite similar in the two sets of material (table 152) and show that about 75 percent were of sheep.

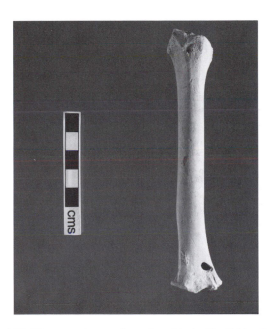

Fig. 177. The complete radius of an Early Neolithic sheep. From context 319, Trench C, outer ditch. One of the very few complete bones from the 1988 excavations at Windmill Hill, it shows the small gracile nature of the sheep from the Neolithic levels.

Table 152: Sheep and goat relative numbers.

excavation years	Goat no	%	Sheep no	%
1925-1957-58	15	26.8	41	73.2
1988	5	20.8	19	79.2

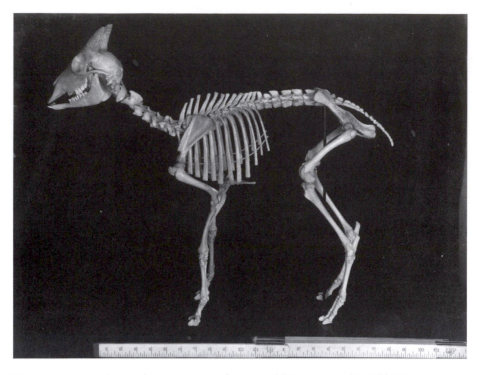

Fig. 178. A complete skeleton of a young goat (bone no. 206) excavated in 1929 from the outer ditch
(OD IIIB, layer 3: Early Neolithic). Plate Xa in Smith (1965a).

There were a few finds of bones of sheep and goat which perhaps qualify as deliberately placed deposits. In the 1988 excavations two almost intact left horncores of young male sheep were found in an Early Neolithic context, 416, in the middle ditch (Trench D). Sheep horncores are notoriously rare in archaeological deposits, probably due to differential preservation, as they have a particularly soft, open texture, especially in young animals. A complete skeleton of a young goat (fig. 178) was found in the Keiller excavations of 1929 in the outer ditch OD IIIB layer 3 (an Early Neolithic context). It was re-articulated and its photograph was published in Smith (1965a), where a shoulder height of 39.4 cm is given. There were also two collections of bones of a very young lamb or kid, one in the Early Neolithic in the middle ditch MD XIIB excavated in 1927 and another whose context was not recorded. A damaged goat skull, with intact horncores, was found in the middle ditch MD VI in an Early Neolithic level.

Pathology of the domestic animals

The cattle bones from the 1988 excavations have a variety of minor abnormal features such as are frequently encountered in archaeological material; details are given in Appendices 2.1 and 2.2. It is not possible in fragmentary material to give accurate scores of the rates of abnormality since the relevant parts, whether normal or abnormal, are often missing. However, there are very few signs of actual pathological conditions such as fracture or infection, suggesting that the animals were well cared for. A lower

molar of an ox from the tertiary level which had swollen roots may indicate the occurrence of actinomycotic infection. There are a few bones which show signs which could be interpreted as indicative of the use of the animals for draught or load-bearing, but these are conditions that also may develop with age, and, as they are not at all extreme, age is the more likely explanation. The most marked cases are a navicular fused to a posterior cuneiform and two pelves, both of old females. In one there is an exostosis on the pubis and in the other the inner surface of the acetabulum shows signs of porosis and has a slight polish (eburnation); both conditions are characteristic of arthritis of the hip joint. Of the 16 acetabula of cattle examined from the causewayed enclosure at Etton in Cambridgeshire by Armour-Chelu and Clutton-Brock (1985), four of adult cows and three cattle of uncertain sex were reported to have symptoms of arthritis. The authors took this as evidence for the use of cows for traction. However, in the re-examination of the cattle bones from the earlier excavations at Windmill Hill none of the 26 acetabula examined were in any way pathological. It is possible that eburnation might have been obscured by the destruction of the surface of the bone, but there was no sign of the other symptoms of arthritis.

Also in the older material were three cattle vertebrae each with a foramen piercing the centrum on the right side, a not unusual, though unexplained, anomaly. One proximal and one middle phalanx showed slight widening of the proximal articulation, though this is probably due to normal ageing. The most distinctively pathological ox bone was a metatarsal (bone 419 from the Keiller excava-

Fig. 179. The effects of traction on an ox bone in the tertiary (modern) context 601, inner ditch (Trench F). The proximal articular surface of a middle phalanx has been widened by heavy exostosis on its lateral edge.

tions of the Late Neolithic/Early Bronze Age level of the middle ditch, measured for the first time in 1987), which though mature had a maximum length of only 200 mm, with a proximal breadth of 45.6 and a distal breadth of 59.1; the other ox metatarsals with fused epiphyses at the site range in length from 232–57 mm. It is so short that it might derive from an achondroplastic dwarf. Achrondroplasia is a condition that characterises some modern breeds (Dexter cattle for example have similarly shortened leg and footbones) and may indicate a naturally occurring genetic mutation. Another markedly pathological bone was a tibia with a massive, bony lesion on the outer side of the distal third of the shaft; most of the surface is smooth, though it is rough and porous at the edges. It came from the mixed-Romano-British levels. A middle phalanx of an ox with marked exostosis of the proximal articular surface was found in a modern context (fig. 179).

Abnormalities were observed in only two pig bones: one in the 1988 assemblage and another from the earlier excavations. That from 1988 is an ulna with a groove in the articular surface. The other is a mandible from the earlier excavations with an alveolus for a supernumerary lower 4th premolar; it derives from the mixed, Romano-British level.

It is probably coincidental but the only sheep/goat tooth with swollen roots indicative of infection was, like the ox molar already mentioned, found in the tertiary level of the outer ditch. No such teeth were noted in the earlier phases. Two sheep/goat phalanges with exostoses were found in the 1988 material; whether this is due to excessive activity, load bearing or old age cannot be determined.

Treatment of domestic animal carcasses

Before discussing the evidence for the processing of carcasses at Windmill Hill it is necessary to understand that there are several processes which an animal undergoes from the moment of death to the utilisation of the required products and the formation of waste, not all of which are recognisable in the excavated faunal assemblage, though partial information can sometimes be gleaned or at least inferred.

Slaughter

The most visible osteological evidences of the mode of slaughter of domestic animals are those of pole-axing and decapitation. Pole-axing results in a jagged hole in the frontal bones of the skull, in the midline between the level of the horncore bases and the orbits. Several skulls are damaged in this region, and it used to be claimed, by for example Watson (1931) at the Neolithic site of Skara Brae in the Orkneys, that such damage was indicative of pole-axing. However, this is a fragile region of the frontal and it is more likely that the damage occurred after death, probably after deposition. Decapitation may be suspected when chopmarks occur vertically across the dorsal surfaces of one or more of the first cervical vertebrae, especially the atlas or the axis. It is also possible that animals may have been killed with spears or arrows, and indeed several skeletons of wild cattle preserved in bogs have been shown to have suffered in this way, by the presence of lesions within scapulae.

Skinning

Skinning usually involves cutting the skin away from the underlying soft tissue, which of course leaves no trace in the archaeological record, but there are several places on the body where the skin is very closely attached to underlying bone: wrists, ankles, feet, skull, the iliac crest of the pelvis, and the tips of the dorsal spines of the vertebral column. So cutmarks on the outer surfaces of the wrist bones, the distal radius and the proximal metacarpal, the ankle bones (especially the astragalus), the distal tibia and the proximal metatarsal, and the outer surface of the iliac crest probably indicate skinning. Cutmarks on the frontal may be related to skinning or the removal of hornsheaths or both.

Dehorning

It is sometimes possible to remove hornsheaths from their underlying horncores by gripping them firmly and twisting them off, especially if some time has elapsed since slaughter. If the horncore has been broken or chopped off the skull, this process can be facilitated by boiling or heating the horn. In either case the horn has to be cut from the surrounding skin and if the cut is deep enough cutmarks may be left on the frontal. It does not follow that the skull and footbones were necessarily removed from the skin. The well-known 'head and hoof' burials of the Neolithic (Piggott 1962b; Grigson 1966; 1980) seem to be the remains of hides buried complete with skull, horns and feet. It is also possible that the complete animal heads, or frontlets were prepared and used in various symbolic behaviours.

Removal of sinews

Sinews are an important animal product amongst pastoralists and hunters today and must have been even more utilised in the past. The most likely form of evidence for their removal would be the presence of cutmarks around their insertion points on bones, particularly the olecranon of the ulna and calcaneum and on the tops of the dorsal spines of the dorsal and lumbar vertebrae.

Dismemberment

The division of the animal's carcass is a pre-requisite of most forms of cooking, eating and the utilisation of bones. Although this may be facilitated by cutting, the most usual method is the simple chopping apart of bones, either at the joints or through the body of the bones, especially the shafts of long bones. Separation of the bones at the joints can be facilitated by cutting through the ligaments around them, and this might result in cutmarks on the underlying bone. Smaller joints may be separated at the time of consumption of the meat.

Evisceration

The removal of soft parts does not necessarily involve the bones at all, although extraction of the brain or of the mandibular nerve would necessitate bone damage. Cutmarks on the inner surfaces of the ribs might relate to the removal of the lungs and on the inner surfaces of the pelvis to the removal of the intestines.

Filletting

Filletting is the removal of meat from the bone prior to cooking. The most usual and valuable fillet is the *longissimus dorsi* muscle lying along the body on each side of the vertebral column; its removal results in cutmarks on the sides of the dorsal spines of the dorsal vertebrae and on the outer proximal surfaces of the ribs. Of course other muscles can also be removed from the underlying bone.

Marrow removal

Marrow is an important source of food most easily obtained by splitting or breaking longbones, though in Mesolithic sites in northern Europe so little was wasted that even the phalanges of large ungulates were treated in this way. Marrow-split long bones usually have spiral fractures which expose the marrow cavity for much of its length. Serjeantson (forthcoming) has suggested that small localised traces of burning may indicate use of fire to assist bone cracking for marrow.

Bone grease

Much has been made about the extraction of fat from bones by Binford (1978), Speth (1983) and Lyman (1994) leading to the creation of bone utility indices and so on. Although it cannot be ruled out, the relative completeness of the bones at Windmill Hill makes it doubtful that animal carcasses were subjected to such an intense level of processing.

Bone tool manufacture

Many bone tools were found in the earlier excavations at Windmill Hill and are described in some detail by Smith (1965a). They are usually made from the longbones of ruminants, cattle, sheep and goats, so it is very probable that some of the fragmentary bones found in the Windmill Hill excavations are the waste products of tool preparation, but a very careful study of the fracturing patterns would be needed before they could be distinguished with any degree of certainty. Tools made from bone and red deer antler are noted in chapters 15 and 17.

What do the chopmarks and cutmarks on the bones at Windmill Hill tell us about the processes of slaughter and bone processing? Chopmarks on some of the bones have been recorded, but there are so many ways in which bones can be broken that it is very difficult to distinguish whether it has been done accidentally or deliberately, and if deliberately whether by chopping, pounding or even stamping over an anvil. A more detailed study of such modifications might be rewarding. Serjeantson (1991) pointed out that at Runnymede, post-depositional damage was responsible for much of the fragmentation of bone, masking the effects of human usage and animal predation. Although such damage is obviously reduced when bones, with or without attached soft tissue, are protected by burial, it is clear that even in the deliberately placed deposits at Windmill Hill bones have been degraded and damaged.

Cutmarks are considered in a little more detail, but even here there are problems because, as mentioned in the first section of this chapter, the state of preservation of the Windmill Hill bones varies from poor to good, but in the majority the surface has been slightly eroded. This means that while the presence of cutmarks is obviously significant, their absence is not, and for this reason no attempt has been made at quantification or exact description; although as with breakage and chopmarks a more detailed study might be rewarding, particularly if cutmarks were examined by SEM. Notes of all the bones on which cutmarks were recorded are given in Appendices 3.1 and 3.2.

Slaughter

There are no definite chopmarks on the cervical vertebrae which might indicate decapitation, nor any other evidence for the mode of slaughter of the domestic ungulates in the Neolithic levels at Windmill Hill. However, as all parts of the body are represented it is likely that the animals were killed at or very close to the site.

Skinning

The bones which suggest that the cattle at Windmill Hill were skinned are the frontlet of a young bull with multiple cutmarks found in the outer ditch in Trench A in the primary context 117 which is illustrated in fig. 160. Other ox bones in the 1988 excavations which suggest skinning include several distal tibiae, six astragali, a navicular, two metatarsals with cutmarks right round the proximal end and a pelvis with distinct marks on the outer surface of the iliac crest. Among the cattle bones from the older excavations there was a proximal metacarpal with cutmarks and three astragali.

Dehorning
Cattle horncores are unusually common at Windmill Hill and it is likely that horn was removed from carcasses. Many of the horncores from the earlier excavations were entire, but detached from the skull. One from the 1988 excavations in a Late Neolithic/Early Bronze Age context in the outer ditch (Trench B) had clearly been chopped off the skull. Horn removal or skinning or both is indicated by two ox horncores from the earlier excavations with cutmarks around the base.

Dismemberment
Chopmarks and cutmarks around the distal end of the humerus (fig. 161) and the proximal end of the radius of cattle are quite common at Windmill Hill and suggest dismemberment through the elbow joint. Similar marks on the distal end of cattle scapulae, a goat's scapula and the proximal femora of cattle and a pig, also suggest dismemberment. Chopmarks on a distal metatarsal and a proximal phalanx indicate removal of the feet, probably as a prelude to skinning. Sinew removal, or dismemberment, is suggested by cutmarks on two lumbar vertebrae.

Evisceration
Fine, wavy cutmarks on the inner surface of the ilia of several ox pelves, and one of a pig, probably indicate evisceration, although they could also be caused by scraping off the *iliacus internus* muscle. Although the siting of the cutmarks noted on large mammal rib fragments, which almost certainly all derive from cattle, was not always recorded, most were on the inner side, indicating evisceration.

Filleting
Removal of the *longissimus dorsi* muscle is suggested by cutmarks on the upper surface of the proximal end of the first rib of an ox (fig. 122B), and pork tenderloins by two pigs' ribs with cutmarks on the outer side of the proximal ends. Cutmarks along the spine of an ox scapula might also be related to the removal of meat from the bone.

Marrow removal
Although some bones had been split vertically, almost certainly by people, it is difficult to be sure whether this is to do with tool manufacture, marrow extraction, or bone grease. No small localised traces of burning which might have assisted bone cracking for marrow were noted.

Bone tool manufacture
Certainly both bone and antler tools were made at Windmill Hill (chapter 15; and see also chapter 17 and Smith 1965a). One bone tool was made from a large long bone, almost certainly the tibia of an ox, and had deep grooves worked into it (fig. 217). It was in the inner ditch (Trench F), in a deliberately placed Early Neolithic deposit.

Although it is clear from the study of chopmarks and cutmarks that many of the domestic ungulates in the Neolithic levels at Windmill Hill were eaten, the section on fragmentation in the first part of this chapter indicates that a few whole carcasses and parts of carcasses of cattle were deposited entire, that is without the dismemberment or the removal of meat that precedes consumption. Nevertheless it seems that the skins were removed prior to deposition. The rather tentative conclusion therefore is that the processing of two products, leather and horn, which are in themselves invisible in the archaeological record, was one of the activities at Windmill Hill. Both materials have dozens of uses, but one would suspect that the leather was used mainly for clothing and for covering huts, and for straps and thongs with a multiplicity of uses. Horns can be used as drinking vessels, but horn can also be processed to form both useful and decorative objects.

Cooking
As stated in the first section of this paper there are no bones at Windmill Hill that have been partially burnt, which would indicate roasting. There are many traces of fire in the ditches and food must have been cooked, but there is no evidence as to how this was done. The rather slight indications of filleting outlined above suggest that small pieces of meat may have been cooked, but large joints were probably cooked and eaten as well, presumably by boiling in pots or skins.

Ungulate proportions

Differences in ungulate proportions over time
Figs 180.1–180.3 are based on the numbers of each taxon of domestic ungulates found in the different types of Early Neolithic deposit excavated in 1988 as set out in tables 145.1–145.3, but with ribs excluded, as those of medium sized mammals could derive from either pigs or sheep/goats. Figs 180.1–180.3 show that while that there is an increase in pigs in each of the three sets of Neolithic data (from the 1988, 1957–58 and pre-war excavations), it is particularly marked in the 1988 material. Although it might be tempting to explain this by the more careful retrieval of small bones in 1988, it should be noted that the numbers of sheep/goats diminish. Although pigs increase in number, cattle still predominate. Pigs do not reach the high proportions which seem to characterise Late Neolithic sites in which Grooved Ware is the dominant pottery, such as Durrington Walls (Harcourt 1971; Albarella and Payne n.d.; Albarella and Serjeantson forthcoming) and many others (Grigson 1981b; 1982d).

Differences in ungulate proportions in different types of deposit
It is particularly important to ascertain whether the high proportion of cattle said by many authors (for example,

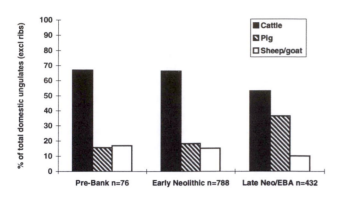

1

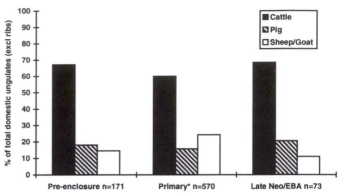

2

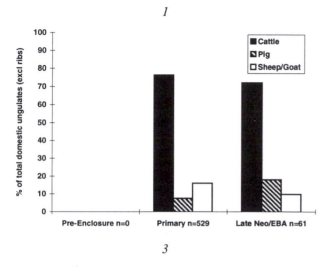

3

Fig. 180. Ungulate proportions at Windmill Hill: differences over time in the material from the three main excavations. Based on the numbers of bone finds of each taxon, with ribs excluded. 1, the 1988 excavations. 2, the 1957–58 excavations (after Jope 1965). 3, the 1925–29 excavations. While there is an increase in pigs in each of the three sets of Neolithic data, it is particularly marked in the 1988 material. This could be explained by the more careful retrieval of small bones in 1988, but the numbers of sheep/goats diminish.

Grigson 1981b; Grigson *et al.* 1987) to typify Early Neolithic assemblages in Britain (and elsewhere) is a characteristic that reflects economic activity or whether the high proportions of particular species are confined to contexts which may be said to represent special activities, that is to the deliberately placed deposits.

Fig. 181 is based on the numbers of each taxon of domestic ungulate found in the different types of Early Neolithic deposit excavated in 1988 as set out in table

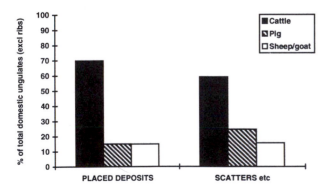

Fig. 181. Ungulate proportions at Windmill Hill: differences in different types of deposit excavated in 1988, with ribs excluded. Cattle bones predominate in all types of deposit, though at a slightly higher rate in the deliberate placements.

146, but with ribs excluded, as those of medium sized mammals could derive from either pigs or sheep/goats. Cattle bones predominate in both types of deposit, though at a slightly higher rate in the deliberately placed deposits.

The role of domestic ungulates

It is clear that cattle were by far the most important component of the animal economy at Windmill Hill, as well as having an importance which can be described as symbolic, or perhaps ritualistic, if indeed such activities were demarcated in the lives of the people of Windmill Hill.

The predominance of elderly cows may reflect the true demographic situation in the cattle killed at Windmill Hill, but it is also possible that most bulls were slaughtered when young, that is when their bones were too soft to survive the rigours of disturbance, time and weathering. It is usual for cows to be kept to a greater age than bulls as breeding animals, as one bull may service a larger number of cows, and cows are also more docile and easier to manage. The predominance of old animals suggests that the products which they produced in life were of greater importance than those which could be obtained only from slaughtered animals. Obviously herd maintenance by reproduction is the most basic necessity, but it is likely that secondary products such as milk, and perhaps blood, repaid this investment in older stock. There is no artifactual evidence for or against milking of cattle at Windmill Hill or elsewhere in the British Neolithic; however, pottery vessels or leather bags could have been used as milk containers.

Although much of the bone at Windmill Hill seems to be of the usual type of waste produced when animals are consumed, the contents of some contexts indicate an alternative treatment of some of the carcasses. Some of the deliberately placed deposits from the Early Neolithic are characterised by complete ox skulls, or by groups of cattle bones which can be articulated, or which appear to be from the same animal, indicating that the carcasses were placed in the ditches either entire or, more usually, as large sections of the body, complete with flesh and tendons. For example, the foreleg of an ox in MD VII layer 5 was complete from scapula to distal phalanges; it was accompanied by a large articulated part of a hindleg, comprising most of the tibia, the ankle bones and the complete metatarsal (fig. 165). The remains of at least eight individual cattle were retrieved from the same context, many of which survive and can be re-articulated. The lack of dismemberment which this suggests must indicate that much potential beef was not consumed; recognition of such 'conspicuous non-consumption', as Barker (1983) has termed it, is one of the most important results of the present analysis and is discussed further in chapter 17. It seems that the carcasses were not entirely wasted in economic terms, as the study of the limited range of visible cutmarks suggests that the production of leather was an important activity; when this is considered in conjunction with the large quantity of leather-working tools made from antler and bone found in the earlier excavations (Smith 1965a), it seems that processing this 'invisible' product may have been a major activity at Windmill Hill, at least during the primary phase of occupation.

However, it is clear from the numbers of unassociated and very fragmentary bones that much beef was eaten at Windmill Hill and the bone discarded as waste. Whether this consumption should be described as feasting is uncertain, as criteria for the distinction in archaeological assemblages between day-to-day eating on one hand and feasting on the other have not been established and indeed may not exist. The main components of the faunal remains retrieved from the Early Neolithic pit on Salisbury Plain, known as the Coneybury Anomaly, were 450 cattle bones and 304 roe deer bones, which may have been dumped in a single episode of butchery. The under-representation of the upper limb bones and of dorsal and lumbar vertebrae of cattle was thought to indicate that the main meat-bearing bones had been removed elsewhere, and this, together with the presence of a uniquely high proportion of roe deer bones, may perhaps indicate that they were the remains of food prepared for feasting (Maltby 1990). The presence of huge numbers of pig bones at Durrington Walls in the Late Neolithic does suggest massive consumption which might indicate feasting, but this is not matched at Windmill Hill. It is true that unless meat were preserved, in warm weather a large animal such as a cow would have had to be consumed rapidly and this implies consumption by many people. However, that would mean that any meat-bearing bone of an ox indicates a feast, which is unlikely.

The role of pigs, sheep and goats in the lives of the people of Windmill Hill was even more limited than their numbers suggest, as the meat weight (and the quantity of other potential products) of each animal is so much less than that of cattle. These smaller ungulates may have had a role as providers of small units of meat, and in risk management, should cattle herds fail. That conspicuous non-consumption was not confined to cattle is attested by the discovery of the complete skeletons of a goat and a piglet in the outer ditch during the pre-war excavations. Similarly the two almost intact horncores of young rams, perhaps deposited as horns, found in 1988 in the middle ditch in context 416, probably survive only because they were deliberately buried.

As in most archaeological assemblages, most of the pigs were slaughtered and presumably eaten when still young, though a few survived into breeding age. The very limited age data for sheep and goats give a rather older profile and it is possible that they were kept for fibre and milk production, as well as meat. It is unlikely that Neolithic sheep in Britain were wool sheep (Ryder 1983), but even hairy sheep have an undercoat of wool, so sheep's wool and the hair of both sheep and goats were probably utilised. It is not impossible that some of the smaller bone tools described by Smith (1965a), particularly the awls, may relate to weaving, but even if this were the case, such an activity was extremely limited compared with the production of ox leather. As with cattle there is no artifactual evidence for or against milking of sheep or goats in the British Neolithic.

No information on seasonality can be gathered from the analysis of ageing patterns of teeth or epiphyseal fusion in the bones of domestic animals at Windmill Hill as the methods employed are not fine-grained enough. However, on the assumption that they would have been born in about April the presence of some very young, probably new born pigs and lambs or kids suggests that the site was in use in the spring, but of course this does not preclude occupation at all other times of the year.

All four species of domestic ungulate are herd animals and in many parts of the world cattle and particularly sheep and goats move with their owners around the landscape. In Britain partial transhumance was a characteristic of the agricultural system of the highlands and islands of Scotland, as a response to harsh winter conditions. It usually involved a movement of flocks and herds accompanied by some members of each community to high ground during the summer, that is to summer shielings, with a return to lower-lying ground in the winter. Such partial transhumance lies on a spectrum from settled farming, in which the cultivation of plants and the raising of animals are completely integrated, to complete nomadism, usually involving only sheep, goats and camels in desert regions, in which domestic plant foods are obtained only by exchange

(Grigson 1995). It is not possible to say on the basis of faunal data that there was no seasonal movement in southern England during the Neolithic, but, as I pointed out in a paper on pig remains which are so common in Late Neolithic sites (Grigson 1982d), although pigs can travel short distances they are not a component of pastoral nomadism; an old verse contains the lines:

> You can poke, and you can shove,
> But a Sussex pig he won't be drove.

The fact that Windmill Hill appears to have been surrounded by woodland, with some natural clearings, and with clearances made for cultivation (chapter 17) implies a degree of movement within the landscape, but not necessarily on a seasonal basis. The presence of pigs implies that such movement would have been on a very small scale.

Given that agriculture was confined to a mosaic of small clearances within woodland one can speculate about the ways in which the various ungulates were managed. Cattle are browsers as well as grazers and would have been able to feed in the surrounding woodland, probably at all times of the year. They would have had to have been closely controlled to prevent damage to crops or escape into the wild and to thwart any tendency to interbreed with their wild cousins, the aurochs, which were particularly common. Pigs are particularly well adapted to woodland, where they would have utilised pannage. Like cattle, and for the same reasons, they would have had to have been closely watched; wild pigs would certainly have been present in the surrounding woods. Sheep and goats may have had the use of woodland, or they may have been kept within the clearances, perhaps grazing on stubble after harvest; they too would have required much care to prevent escape or damage to crops, but had no wild relatives in Britain with which to interbreed. Trampling by all or any of these animals may have been utilised in the maintenance of forest clearances. The likely small scale of the clearances suggests that only small herds of animals were kept, ownership being perhaps confined to small groups of people. Gatherings at such places as Windmill Hill may have helped in the exchange of live animals for breeding and thus helped to ensure the out-breeding essential for the genetic health of the herds.

Dogs (*Canis familiaris*)

Little can be said about the type of dog at Windmill Hill on the strength of the scanty 1988 material; the single measurement taken is included in Appendix 1.7. However, a fair number of dog bones survive from the earlier excavations and some of their measurements are given in Grigson (1965) and Harcourt (1974).

The most informative collection of dog remains is the complete skeleton (bone no. 134) excavated from the bottom of MD IX in 1928. It was re-articulated and displayed in the Alexander Keiller Museum (fig. 182). It was studied by Burleigh *et al.* (1977) and by Harcourt (1974); both papers include measurements of some of its limb bones and skull. Harcourt also gives indices for calculating the height at the shoulder from the greatest lengths of the longbones:

humerus greatest length	(GLx3.43) -26.54
radius greatest length	(GLx3.18) +19.51
humerus + radius greatest length	(GLx1.65) -4.32
ulna greatest length	(GLx2.78) +6.21
femur greatest length	(GLx3.14) -12.96
tibia greatest length	(GLx2.92) +9.41
femur + tibia greatest length	(GLx1.52) -2.47.

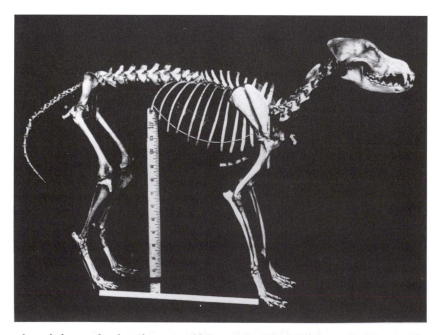

Fig. 182. A complete skeleton of a dog (bone no. 134) excavated in 1928 from the bottom of Middle Ditch IX;
Early Neolithic. Plate IXa in Smith (1965a).

Application of these indices to the complete skeleton (bone 134) gives a range of height of 43–47 cm; this agrees reasonably well with the shoulder height of the articulated skeleton, which is 42 cm. Burleigh *et al.* (1977) described the dog as nearly full grown, but less than a year old, and tentatively identified it as female, as although the skeleton appears to be complete, there was no penis bone.

Although no relationship should be implied, the shape of the skull of the complete skeleton and of the other more fragmentary skulls at Windmill Hill, as well as those from other British Neolithic sites, resembles that of a modern fox terrier. This is an unspecialised dog, with a face of medium length, similar to that of its wild progenitor, the wolf, but smaller (Miles and Grigson 1990; K. Clark 1996).

Harcourt (1974) and Burleigh *et al.* (1977) compared the dimensions of the Windmill Hill dogs with those of other Neolithic (and Beaker) dogs in Britain and Ireland and concluded that they showed little variation, probably because they formed part of a single freely interbreeding uncontrolled population.

Although there were occasional isolated finds of dog bones from the 1988 excavations in the Neolithic fills of the outer and inner ditches, some bones were found in groups appearing to derive from the same dog. In the outer ditch, the primary context 227 in Trench B contained matching footbones and the secondary context 317 in Trench C contained three articulating neck vertebrae, with three lumbar vertebrae, perhaps from the same animal, immediately above, in tertiary context 302. Although there were a few scattered dog bones in the material from the earlier excavations, the numbers of matching bones are higher. When the database resulting from the re-study of the material from the earlier excavations is sorted by find spot and level, it is clear that the majority of the dog bones come from only a few Early Neolithic contexts, each containing the remains of a single skeleton (fig. 185). This confirms the view stated above that the numbers of dogs may have been over-estimated by Jope. Four of the five more or less complete skeletons were in the middle ditch and one was in the inner ditch, with a skull in the inner ditch and an extra set of footbones in the middle ditch.

Only one dog bone had any signs of butchery or skinning, a distal humerus with possible cutmarks on the trochlea in the inner ditch (Trench B) in 629, a deliberately placed deposit and probably Early Neolithic; they could be related to dismemberment or skinning. The dearth of other indications of dog butchery could simply be due to chance or to poor preservation, although having been in deliberately placed deposits most of the bones are rather well preserved, so it suggests that dogs were not eaten at Windmill Hill, though some may have been skinned.

The evidence for the presence of numerous dogs at Windmill Hill consists not just of their bones, but of the traces of gnawing by dogs visible on many of the bones of other animals in the 1988 faunal assemblage. The effects of gnawing and estimates of the numbers of bones gnawed

in each context have been discussed in the first part of this chapter. Suffice it to say that the presence of gnawed bones in each of the ditches and of dog coprolites in the inner ditch, but probably also in the other ditches, suggests that dogs were allowed to mingle freely with the people of Windmill Hill.

Dogs could have been kept for a variety of reasons. They may have been pets, guard dogs, shepherd dogs, hunting dogs or simply casual camp followers like the pariah dogs of villages in many parts of the world today or dingos living in the camps of Australian aborigines. A few dead dogs seem to have been deliberately buried, which may have been a matter of simple disposal, or more probably may indicate special symbolic behaviour by their owners.

Wild animals
Wild cattle (aurochs) (*Bos primigenius*)

Wild cattle were an important part of the fauna of Britain for most of the Early Holocene, and seem to have been common during the Mesolithic and Neolithic. It is likely that they died out during, or soon after, the Early Bronze Age. Several direct dates for wild cattle in Britain cluster around 4000 BP, but the most recent is the skeleton of a bull from Charterhouse Warren Farm, Somerset, at 3245 ± 37 BP (BM-731) (Clutton-Brock 1986; Levitan and Smart 1989). Use of the indices for withers height mentioned above for domestic cattle, indicates that in the Danish Postglacial wild bulls ranged in height from about 1.53 to 1.75 m and cows from 1.38 to 1.52 m. British aurochs seem to have been of the same size (Grigson 1969; 1978a).

The problems of the distinction between wild and domestic cattle have been discussed above, where it was shown that it is often difficult to distinguish bones of wild cows from those of domestic bulls, but quite a number of cattle bones from Windmill Hill are so large that they must be from wild cattle, and the largest, which are very large indeed (see figs 166.2 and 168), undoubtedly derive from wild bulls. Proximal phalanges of wild and domestic cattle are illustrated in fig. 183. The bones from the Early Neolithic levels of the 1988 excavations which have been identified as wild cattle are all from the middle ditch (Trench D): a huge proximal phalanx (fig. 183A, left) and some teeth which all seem to come from the same mandible of an immature individual in context 404, and a calcaneum in 413. In the Late Neolithic/Early Bronze Age levels there was part of a very large femur in the outer ditch (Trench A), which had been split horizontally and gnawed, in context 103. Also in the outer ditch, but from Trench B context 215, was a very large, damaged proximal phalanx, with the proximal end of a radius in the middle ditch (Trench E) 503. Another proximal phalanx, of a smaller wild ox, probably a cow, came from context 602 in the inner ditch (Trench F), a context containing mixed Neolithic and Romano-British pottery (fig. 183A, right).

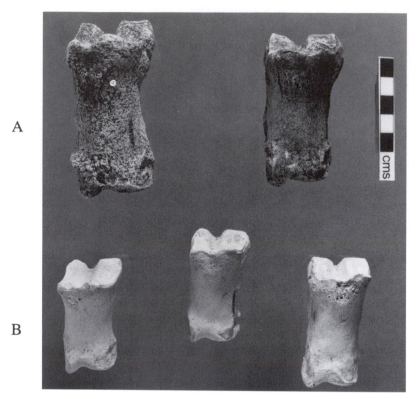

Fig. 183. Phalanges of wild and domestic cattle, showing the contrast in size. A: Wild ox (Bos primigenius) proximal phalanges. A Left: of a bull from a secondary context 404 in the middle ditch (Trench D), Early Neolithic. A Right: probably of a cow, from context 602 of the inner ditch (Trench F). This context contained Beaker, Early Bronze Age and Romano-British pottery. B: Domestic cattle (Bos taurus) proximal phalanges from Early Neolithic contexts in the middle ditch. Left and centre: both from context 522 (Trench E); right: context 416 (Trench D).

The finds of wild cattle from the Early Neolithic of the earlier excavations are a pair of upper third molars in the inner ditch ID I-II, a proximal phalanx from the outer ditch OD IIIA and a proximal radius from OD IB; two horncore bases, one from the inner ditch (ID I-II) and one from the middle ditch MD IIB, may derive from wild cows. Wild cattle bones were also scattered through the ditches in the Late Neolithic/Early Bronze Age levels, with an astragalus and an upper molar in the inner ditch ID XVB and ID XVII, a middle phalanx and a proximal phalanx in the middle ditch MD IX and a distal tibia in MD XII. A lower third molar, tentatively identified as wild, was in the outer ditch OD V.

One would expect that hunting wild cattle, which were extremely dangerous animals, and which could be nearly two metres high at the shoulder, was a matter of prestige. Nevertheless their remains are scattered through the various ditches and contexts, with no identifiable patterning and seem to have been accorded no special treatment.

Wild boar (*Sus scrofa*)

Wild pigs were part of the British fauna from the Late Glacial until only a few hundred years ago, but very few remains were found in Windmill Hill. It is likely that one bone from the 1988 excavations comes from a wild pig

and even that could be from a very large domestic animal. It is part of a mandible with a very large lower third molar, with a length of 39.9 mm, which falls within the area of overlap of wild and domestic pigs. It was in a Late Neolithic context, 103, in the outer ditch (Trench B). Another molar and the proximal end of a radius could possibly also be from wild boar, but as fig. 174 shows, even the largest measurements are a little smaller than the standard wild boar. There is a similar dearth of wild pig bones in the material from the earlier excavations, apart from an enormous lower canine (tusk) from the middle ditch MD I; unfortunately the level at which it was found was not recorded. Clearly little use was made of wild boar by the people of Windmill Hill.

Red deer (*Cervus elaphus*)

The red deer remains from Windmill Hill fall into two main categories, bones and antlers, whose inclusion in the assemblage results from two quite different, but overlapping human behaviours. Bones indicate the use of slain animals, of either sex, presumably hunted and killed in the locality, and used mainly for food, whereas antler was used as a raw material for the manufacture of various implements and could have been from antlers which had been shed by the stags. Red deer shed their antler annually between March and May (Clutton-Brock 1984), when it could have been collected by the people of Windmill Hill and curated for future use. Mature antler from killed animals could have been used in the same way.

The largest piece of antler found in the 1988 excavations was a pick from the old land surface (context 765) under the outer bank, which consisted of part of the beam with clear chevron-shaped cuts around its lower end, with one tine, probably the bez. A large flat section of antler beam, which also appeared to have been worked, was also found in the OLS and there was a small piece of worked antler in the tree hollow, perhaps derived from the old land surface. The middle ditch had a piece of antler consisting of the brow tine and part of the beam; it had been cut above the rosette and below the bez tine. Almost all the other antler finds were in the Early Neolithic contexts of the outer ditch; they were very fragmentary and in many cases showed signs of weathering, as though they had been left lying on the surface. 13 small fragments in context 227 appear to have come from the same very damaged antler.

114 pieces of antler, most of which were worked and quite substantial, survive from the earlier excavations, but the find spots and levels of much of the Keiller material were not recorded, and it seems likely that most smaller fragments of antler were discarded. As with the 1988 material much of the antler was decayed (Smith 1965a). The worked pieces of antler are described in detail, with some illustrations, by Smith (1965a), who considers that while many were digging tools, some were used as skin-dressing tools. Antler working is noted in chapter 15. The much higher proportion of red deer antler to bone in the Keiller material suggests the preferential retrieval of antler, with much of the bone having been discarded.

It is only possible to be sure whether antler fragments found in the excavations were from killed animals if the base of the antler is still attached to the pedicel, which is part of the frontal bone of the skull. In 11 of the 19 antlers from Early Neolithic levels in the earlier excavations in which the base was preserved, it is not attached to the pedicel, indicating that they had been collected. There was only one with the base intact in the Late Neolithic/Early Bronze Age levels and this had been shed. The seasonal implications of the antlers are discussed below.

Only seven definite and three less definite red deer bones were found in the Early Neolithic levels and five bone fragments and a tooth in the Late Neolithic/Early Bronze Age levels, including four from the soil (context 202) in the outer ditch. None of the bones were articulated or given any special treatment, with the possible exception of the remains of a cranium of a very young animal, with an unerupted upper third molar, and a mandibular fragment probably from the same animal, in context 205 in the outer ditch (Trench B). No cutmarks were noted on any of the red deer bones, but on such a small sample this is not significant. However, the proximal end of a metatarsal appeared to have been chopped off, possibly as a preliminary to tool manufacture; it was in the soil of the outer ditch, which is Late Neolithic/Early Bronze Age.

The most detailed description of a Holocene red deer is the complete skeleton of an adult stag, five or six years old, from Seamer Carr in Yorkshire (Tooley *et al.* 1982), which has an uncalibrated direct date of 4330 ± 100 BP (Birm-977); it is stored in the Archaeology Department of the University of Durham. Its measurements are used here as a standard for comparison with those of red deer from Windmill Hill; the results are plotted in fig. 184, which also includes measurements from the Mesolithic site of Star Carr in Yorkshire (Fraser and King 1954; Legge and Rowley-Conwy 1988). This is not the place to discuss the significance of the size distribution of the Star Carr deer, except to say that the presence of four peaks, rather than the expected two (one each for females and males), is due to the fact that the bones of the front limb seem to have a wider sexual dimorphism than those of the hind limb in that assemblage. The very scanty Windmill Hill size data suggest that at least seven deer were as large, or larger than the Seamer Carr stag, and four smaller deer were represented, presumably from male and female animals respectively, suggesting that both sexes were hunted, but with a probable preference for stags. This is hardly surprising, both for the value of their antlers and for the normal partiality of hunters for the more spectacular animals. Unfortunately it was not possible to compare the size of the Windmill Hill antlers with the very copious Neolithic material from Grime's Graves and Durrington Walls, described in detail by Clutton-Brock (1984), as different measurements were taken. No measurements were recorded for the antlers of the stag from Seamer Carr.

Measurements of the red deer bones from the 1988 excavations at Windmill Hill are given in Appendix 1.7 and of antler and bones from the earlier excavations in Grigson (1965).

Roe deer (*Capreolus capreolus*)

Like red deer stags roe deer bucks have antlers, but like the animals themselves the antlers are small and may not have been used for the manufacture of tools. However, one fragment in the old land surface (context 741) appears to have been deliberately snapped through the beam. The bases of at least two shed roe deer antlers were found in the 1988 material. One was found in the Early Neolithic level of the outer ditch (Trench B) in context 203 together with the base of an unshed antler, and the other in 206/213. Only one other antler fragment was identified as roe; it was in a Late Neolithic/Early Bronze Age context (219) of the outer ditch (Trench B). 25 pieces of roe deer antler were noted in the re-study of the material from the earlier excavations. All four antlers with intact bases from the Early Neolithic and all five from the Late Neolithic/Early Bronze Age levels were shed, that is they had been collected in or soon after October when roe deer shed their antlers.

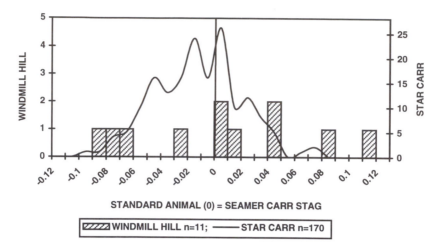

Fig. 184. The size of red deer at Windmill Hill compared with that of a standard animal (the stag from Seamer Carr: Tooley et al. 1982). Suggesting that at least seven deer as large, or larger than the Seamer Carr stag, and four smaller deer were represented at Windmill Hill, presumably from male and female animals respectively.

The collection of shed roe deer antlers by the people of Windmill Hill must have been for some purpose, not necessarily utilitarian. They are reminiscent of the complete roe deer antler buried with a man in the Beaker barrow at Hemp Knoll, in Wiltshire (Grigson 1980).

There were four fragments of roe deer bone, or five if the unshed antler is included, in the Early Neolithic levels excavated in 1988, including a nearly complete radius in context 206 (outer ditch, Trench B) with cutmarks, and four from the Late Neolithic/Early Bronze Age levels, including a tooth retrieved from the flot from the soil (context 202) in the outer ditch (Trench B). Only five roe deer bones were identified in the re-study of the earlier material, a tibia and a metatarsal in the middle ditch MD VIII, a middle phalanx in MD VII and a metacarpal in the Late Neolithic/Early Bronze Age level of the outer ditch OD IIIC; a frontlet with the antler still attached had no provenance data.

A nearly complete roe deer radius had cutmarks around its proximal end, probably related to dismemberment or stripping off of meat. It was in the outer ditch (Trench B) in an Early Neolithic context.

The much higher proportion of roe deer antler to roe deer bone in the Keiller material suggests the preferential retrieval of antler, with much of the bone having been discarded.

Comparison of the size of roe deer bones from the Mesolithic levels at Cherhill with that of roughly contemporary remains from Switzerland and with modern English material, showed that the English Mesolithic animals were considerably larger than the Swiss or the modern animals (Grigson 1983). An examination of the roe deer measurements from the Mesolithic site of Star Carr in Yorkshire (Legge and Rowley-Conwy 1988) confirms this superiority in size. Unfortunately there is no standard animal for roe deer, but the few measurements from Windmill Hill show that they were just as large as those from Star Carr.

Measurements of the roe deer bones from the 1988 excavations are given in Appendix 1.7 and some from the earlier excavations in Grigson (1965) where those of tibiae attributed to roe deer should be disregarded as some identified as roe, probably by D.M.S. Watson, may have been of sheep or goats.

Fox (*Vulpes vulpes*)

The fox remains found at Windmill Hill were very scanty. A complete metatarsal III of a fox was found in the 1988 excavations in the Early Neolithic level of the outer ditch (Trench C) context 309. Other canid remains, which are probably fox rather than dog, were a lower incisor in context 307 and a skull fragment in the inner ditch (Trench F) 627. Two teeth and a humerus fragment were found in the soil of the outer ditch (Trench B) context 202.

Two groups of fox bones were found in the early excavations which seem to be the remains of complete skeletons. Both were in the outer ditch OD IIIB layer 3 (Early Neolithic) and OD 1C level 3 (Late Neolithic/Early Bronze Age). It is possible that both are intrusive.

Cat (*Felis silvestris*)

The only cat bones from the 1988 excavations are four metapodials from the Early Neolithic of the outer ditch (Trench C). Although in three different contexts (305, 307 and 308), they all appear to come from the same hind foot. One was a complete metatarsal II, as large as that of a modern wild cat. All 55 cat foot and tail bones and teeth from the Keiller excavations noted by Jope (1965) seem to come from the same skeleton, which was found in 1929 in the middle ditch MD XIB in layers 4 and 5 (Early Neolithic). They may indicate the burial of a cat skin.

Wild cats are now confined to Scotland, but formerly had a much wider distribution.

Mustelids

Four fragmentary bones of mustelids were present in the 1988 material. All were from the outer ditch (Trench B) and comprised a very broken cranium and a left mandible of a polecat (*Mustela putorius*), possibly from the same individual, from 202 (Early Neolithic), a complete metapodial identified only as mustelid from 225 (Early Neolithic) and a right mandible of a polecat from 216 (Late Neolithic/Early Bronze Age). Since only head and foot bones were identified it is possible that these represent skins. There was also one uncertainly identified otter (*Lutra vulgaris*) bone, a proximal radius fragment, in the Late Neolithic/Early Bronze Age context 202.

Polecats are woodland animals now apparently confined to Wales; otters are rare in England, but were more common and more widely distributed in the past, living along river banks.

Hedgehog (*Erinaceus europaeus*)

A single bone of a hedgehog was found in the re-study of the material from the earlier excavations, a humerus from the Early Neolithic of the middle ditch MD VII, layer 3.

Other mammals

As already mentioned the badger (*Meles meles*) bones identified by Jope (1965) were not found when the material from the earlier excavations was re-studied. The same is true of the 10 hare (*Lepus capensis*) metapodials which she found, although it is possible that some of these are among the remains of the fragmentary small mammal bones which were not identified further. Both animals are common in Wiltshire to this day.

Birds

Six bones identified as bird, but not to species of bird, were found in the Early Neolithic levels excavated in 1988. In the Late Neolithic/Early Bronze Age there was one bird bone from 1988 and four from the earlier excavations. Although such a small number of bird remains is usual in Neolithic assemblages, it is surprising, since their meat, skins and particularly their feathers have many potential uses. One of the most important is the fletching of arrows. However, arrowheads were rare in the Early Neolithic levels at Windmill Hill; three leaf arrowhead fragments were retrieved from the pre-enclosure level of the 1957–58 excavations and eight from the primary fills of the inner ditch in 1928–29; there were none in the middle and inner ditches.

Environmental indicators

Whilst the remains of animals at Windmill Hill represent human activity, the remains of slain wild animals were presumably acquired within a reasonable distance of the site. The most telling parameter is the presence of very large red and roe deer; both animals are very susceptible to environmental degradation and their large size suggests that they lived within large tracts of woodland, a conclusion which is compatible with the evidence presented in chapters 6–9.

Seasonality: indications from wild animals

What little information on the season of occupation can be gathered from the remains of wild animals at Windmill Hill is provided by the state of the antlers of red and roe deer.

In southern England red deer stags grow their antlers from about April to September, when they are soft and covered with velvet. It is only useful for tool manufacture when it is hard, that is from late August or September until about April, when it is shed. Although the presence of shed antler is sometimes used to infer seasonal occupation of a site, it must be remembered that although it would have to be collected soon after being shed, since deer eat shed antler, it can be kept over a long period of time. Only antler that is in the *process* of being shed is a reliable indicator of season of use (i.e. March to May) and there was none in this state at Windmill Hill. One can be sure that the unshed antler at Windmill Hill came from animals killed between from August to March, April or May, and the shed antler must have been collected between March and May, or soon after.

Nine of the ten roe deer antlers from all the excavations were shed, that is almost all were collected in, or soon after October, the month in which roe deer in England shed their antlers. However, they could have been curated, and brought to the site at any time of the year. In order to demonstrate seasonality one has to prove that a site was *not* occupied at a particular time of year, and this cannot be done for Windmill Hill.

The role of hunting

The small numbers of bones of wild animals indicate that hunting was a minor activity in the lives of the inhabitants of Windmill Hill, although red deer antlers, both collected and from slain animals, were clearly an important resource for the manufacture of implements. The integration of material obtained from the wild with what can be described as domestic activity, is indicated by the use of many of the antler implements in the processing of domestic ox hides for leather. The skins of deer and wild cattle were probably utilised in the same way, but the number of fur-bearing animals, that is cats, mustelids and hares, is so low, that fur was probably little used, and the same seems to have been true of birds and their feathers.

Little can be said about the hunting methods employed. Small animals were probably trapped, and the larger animals, roe and red deer, were probably hunted individually, rather than being driven in groups. If the latter had been the case, one would expect a predominance of young and female animals from a nursery herd since these are the most easily targeted, whereas there seems to have been a preference for male animals at Windmill Hill, including for the acquisition of antler. It is not possible to establish a preference for wild bulls rather than cows, but bulls were certainly hunted, and their acquisition, as well as that of red deer stags, may well have conferred prestige on the hunters. As Harcourt (1971) has pointed out, wild cattle cannot have been killed solely for their meat; beef could be obtained far more easily from domestic animals.

Discussion

A mode of life in which domestic cattle played a major role, with significant contributions from pigs and sheep/ goats, seems to be a feature of virtually all Neolithic sites in England, particularly in the Early Neolithic. This seems to be true of the apparently domestic site at Runnymede (Serjeantson 1996), the pre-bank levels at Windmill Hill, and the soils beneath the barrows at Fussell's Lodge (Grigson 1966) and Hazleton North (Levitan 1990), which are arguably the product of domestic activity. However, the predominance of domestic cattle is more spectacular in most English causewayed enclosures and funerary monuments, as well as in the primary level of the pit known as the 'Coneybury Anomaly' where there were also many bones of roe deer, none of sheep or goats and only a few pigs (Maltby 1990). For a list of Early Neolithic sites with animal remains, which was then more or less complete, see Grigson (1984) and the more comprehensive and up-to-date review which is being prepared by Dale Serjeantson (forthcoming). In Late Neolithic Grooved Ware sites, whether domestic or 'ceremonial', pigs take on the major role (Albarella and Serjeantson forthcoming; Grigson 1982d), but in the causewayed enclosure at Etton in Cambridgeshire, which has Grooved Ware, cattle still predominate (Armour-Chelu 1992).

In all Early Neolithic sites in which demographic structures have been studied, for example Etton and Maiden Castle (Armour-Chelu 1992) and Hambledon Hill (Legge 1981), it seems that, as at Windmill Hill, adult cattle predominate, and where sex has been established the adult animals are mostly cows. The low proportion of bones of young cattle must to some extent be due to taphonomic factors, but the sexual imbalance is surely significant. The problem is that the only assemblages large enough for such parameters to be established come from causewayed enclosures; the situation may have been different at other types of site.

Collections of articulated, or semi-articulated cattle vertebrae, reminiscent of the many found at Windmill Hill, have been excavated from the ditches of several earthen long barrows in Wiltshire, such as Fussell's Lodge (Grigson 1966), and South Street (Ashbee *et al.* 1979). Ox skulls too are quite common in barrows, sometimes in ditches,

sometimes associated with the human burials and at Beckhampton Road placed under the mound (Ashbee 1979, 247; Carter and Higgs 1979, 248–50).

Windmill Hill is remarkable not only for numerous complete or semi-complete ox skeletons found within the ditches, but also skeletons of other animals, particularly in the earlier excavations; their locations within the site are mapped in fig. 185. Some have been described individually above. There was a particular concentration of cattle bones in the middle ditch (MD VII); it is not possible to be certain how many skeletons are present, but the remains of at least eight individuals are represented. A nearly complete skeleton of an ox, lacking provenience data, has been mounted and is stored in the Alexander Keiller Museum in Avebury. Substantial proportions of two complete ox skeletons were found, in the inner ditch (ID XVII) and the outer ditch (OD IV). The outer ditch also contained the skeleton of a goat, a pig and two foxes. The middle ditch contained the skeleton of a cat, a young lamb or kid and a large part of a sheep skeleton. Complete or partial dog skeletons were present in all three ditches.

The evidence for complete and partial skeletons in the 1988 material has been discussed in detail in the section on fragmentation. Four of the more complete were all in the outer ditch, three in the primary fill of Trench B: substantial portions of individual ox skeletons, vertebrae and ribs in 227, ox foot and other bones in 210, the skeleton of a new-born piglet in 210; with a probable ox skeleton in Trench C divided between the secondary and upper secondary contexts 321 and 317.

With the exception of the complete skeletons of foxes and a cat and the shed roe deer antler mentioned above there seems to have been little special treatment of the remains of wild animals at Windmill Hill. Even the selection of large red deer stags at Windmill Hill has a utilitarian explanation. The same seems to be true of most other Neolithic sites. However, skulls of wild, rather than domestic cattle were buried in the ditches at Horslip (Higham and Higgs 1979) and Thickthorn Down (Jackson 1936). The aurochs skull at Dorchester-on-Thames was that of a bull (Atkinson *et al.* 1951).

Although much has been written on the reasons why modern people keep cattle, and how they are managed, there is very little in the ethnographic literature that describes how these behaviours are reflected in the disposal of cattle remains. Skulls are an obvious exception, since there are many instances of skulls or heads of animals being conspicuously displayed. However, there seem to be no parallels for the deliberate deposition of carcasses, or parts of carcasses, as manifest at Windmill Hill and other Neolithic sites in southern Britain. As to feasting, these sites appear to be characterised less by lavish consumption than by conspicuous non-consumption.

Acknowledgements
Acknowledgements are due to: Alasdair Whittle for inviting me to work on the material from his 1988 excava-

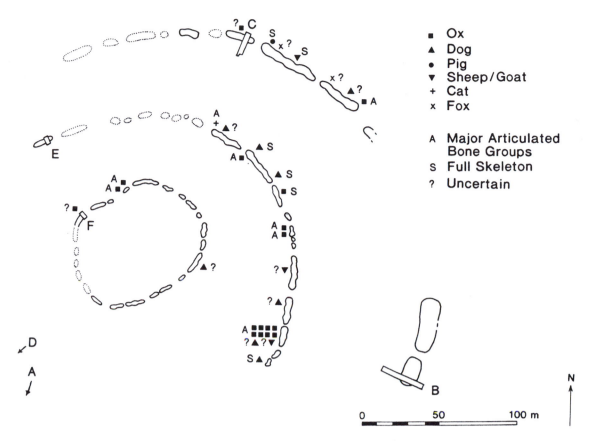

Fig. 185. The locations of some of the complete and partial skeletons of animals found in the earlier excavations at Windmill Hill. The information is derived from re-analysis of surviving faunal material and from excavation photographs and notebook references. All are from Earlier Neolithic contexts.

tions, and for endless patience and encouragement during the long gestation of the result; Joshua Pollard for entering the information from the handwritten data sheets from re-study of the material from the earlier excavations into a computer database, as well as answering queries and providing detail; the numerous diggers, who despite the wind, rain and cold of the so-called summer of 1988, managed to retrieve, record and curate the faunal material to a high standard rarely achieved elsewhere; Juliet Clutton-Brock, and the other staff of the Mammal Section of the Natural History Museum, for providing working space and allowing access to comparative material; Mike Pitts, then Curator of the Alexander Keiller Museum, for allowing and encouraging access to the material from the earlier excavations at Windmill Hill; Dr Isobel Smith for inviting me, as a very inexperienced research student, to work on the measurements of the animal remains from her own and the earlier Windmill Hill excavations, and for her help with details of stratigraphy as well as much informative discussion; and finally Peter Tate, the former custodian of the Alexander Keiller Museum, without whose warm welcome, not to mention tea, biscuits and chat, the re-study of the material from the earlier excavations would never have been completed.

Appendices

Notes for Appendices

All measurement abbreviations from von den Driesch 1976. All measurements in mm.

General:

e	=	estimated
c	=	circa
ant	=	anterior
post	=	posterior
out	=	outer
phal	=	phalanx
prox	=	proximal
mid	=	middle
ai	=	anterior inner (phlanx)
ao	=	anterior outer (phalanx)
pi	=	posterior inner (phalanx)
po	=	posterior outer (phalanx)
hcore	=	horncore
ep	=	epiphysis
circ	=	circumference
diam	=	diameter
max	=	maximum
min	=	minimum

b followed by a number is the bone number

arts	=	articulates
L	=	length

Under teeth:

C	=	canine
P	=	premolar
M	=	permanent molar
m	=	deciduous molar
low	=	lower
up	=	upper

an upper-case letter after a tooth abbreviation is the wear stage following Grant 1982

Under ageing:

vy	=	very young
y	=	young
m or mod	=	moderate age
o	=	old

Appendix 1.1: Measurements of cattle bones from Windmill Hill 1988.

* = bone destroyed in dating

bone no.	trench	context no.	find no.	ditch	level	bone	measurements	notes
5859	E	524/510	12120	middle	primary	horncore	basal circ c205; max diam e68; min diam 57.2; L out curve >210 c235	
2595	B	216	161221	outer	up secondary	M3 low	LM3 37.2	
3915	B	214	9930	outer	up secondary	mandible	LM3 38.5	
3757	BB	765	7334		primary bank	mandible	Lm4 28.9	
3656	BB	700	7012		turf	M3 low	LM3 39.5	
5352	A	110	1640	outer	secondary	M3 low	LM3 35.7	
4671	C	311/315	10584	outer	primary	mandible	LM3 36.8	
1540	D	406	4058	middle	secondary	mandible	LM3 37.6	?same jaw as b1648; Bos primigenius
1656	D	405	4046	middle	secondary	m4 low	Lm4 31.1	shed
2703	B	202	2631	outer	soil	m4 low	L m4 low 17.9	
1648	D	404	4037	middle	secondary	M3 low	LM3 44.8	?same jaw as b1656; Bos primigenius
66	E	525	12222	middle	primary	mandible	LM3 38.2	
791	E	501	5549	middle	RB	M3 low	LM3 36.6	
80	BB	746	7701		primary bank	axis	b ant art surface 90.4	
5174	C	302	3232	outer	tertiary	axis	b ant art surface 104.0	
290	BB	705	7807		OLS	scapula	SLC 47.3; Bd 65.9	
198	C	317	3950	outer	up secondary	scapula	GLP e76	*Bos primigenius ? ?pair b7*
7	C	317	3915	outer	up secondary	scapula	SLC 60.0	*Bos primigenius ? ?pair b198*
5885	E	524	12166	middle	primary	scapula	SLC 50.2; GLP 70.5; LG 58.0; BG 48.9	
88	E	525	12283	middle	primary	scapula	SLC 47.5; GLP 66.1; LG 54.0; BG 45.5	
67	E	525	12216	middle	primary	scapula	SLC 46.8	
713	E	503	5808	middle	secondary	scapula	SLC 52.0	
663	E	503	5736	middle	secondary	scapula	SLC 51.4	
1378	F	629	6360	inner	secondary	scapula	SLC 56.2	
4586	B	230	23292	outer	primary	humerus	Bd 83.6	
15*	B	227	23368	outer	primary	humerus	Bd 79.9	
33	BB	765	7284		OLS	humerus	Bd 80.7; Bt 71.7	
1800	E	508	12139	middle	primary	humerus	Bd 82.6; Bt 75.6	
5	E	525	12278	middle	primary	humerus	Bd 84.5; Bt 76.8	
11	F	629	6389	inner	secondary	humerus	Bd 94.2; Bt e86.3	
10	F	629	6389	inner	secondary	humerus	Bd 76.1; Bt 68.9	
4327	B	228	23359	outer	primary	radius	Bp 74.1	
16*	B	227	23368	outer	primary	radius	Bd 68.2	
5693	A	106	1555	outer	secondary	radio-ulna	Bd 74.7	
2276	B	222	16600	outer	up secondary	radius	Bp 77.0	
3714	BB	705	7523		OLS	radius	Bp 79.8	
4935	C	315	10634	outer	primary	radius	Bp 74.7	
1731	D	416	4385	middle	primary	radius	Bd (loose ep) 69.3	
1743	D	416	4330	middle	primary	radius	Bp 73.7	
1599	D	413	4172	middle	secondary	radius	Bd 66.9	
1691	D	406	4082	middle	secondary	radius	Bp 79.9	

Appendix 1.1 (continued): Measurements of cattle bones from Windmill Hill 1988.

* = bone destroyed in dating

bone no.	trench	context no.	find no.	ditch	level	bone	measurements	notes
5865	E	522	5904	middle	primary	radius	Bd 67.6	
1854	E	522	5997	middle	primary	radius	Bd 68.6	
5903	E	524	12341	middle	primary	radius	Bd (loose ep) 78.2	
5886	E	524	12225	middle	primary	radius	Bp 77.4	
1485	E	523	12090	middle	primary	radius	Bp 76.0	
701	E	503	5807	middle	secondary	radius	Bp 93.0	*Bos primigenius ?*
2042	F	611	6321	inner	primary?	radius	Bd 87.1	
1292	F	629	6374	inner	secondary	radius	Bp 76.6	
11150	F	627	6317	inner	secondary	radius	Bd 74.0	loose epiphysis
2247	F	602	6217	inner	RB	radius	Bd 74.2	
2631	B	207	23028	outer	secondary	metacarpal	GL 217; Bp 70.6; SD 37.5; Bd 70.7	
5542	A	103	1563	outer	secondary	metacarpal	Bp 58.8; SD 33.2	
5516	A	102	1137	outer	tertiary	metacarpal	Bp e50.8	
5173	C	302	3450	outer	tertiary	metacarpal	Bp 52.0; SD 28.6	young?
1734	D	416	4300	middle	primary	metacarpal	Bp 63.4	
1930	E	512	12191	middle	primary	metacarpal	Bp 63.7	
8	E	525	12224	middle	primary	pelvis	LA 76.4; SB 22.1; SH 40.1	female?
9	F	630	6416	inner	secondary	pelvis	LA 72.8; SB 24.0; SH 44.3	old female
5562	A	103	1483	outer	secondary	femur	SD 49.5	*Bos primigenius*
4323	B	228	23317	outer	primary	tibia	Bd 59.7	
4328	B	228	23261	outer	primary	tibia	Bd 60.5	
14*	B	229	23200	outer	primary	tibia	GL – both eps c305	
279	BB	746	7759		primary bank	tibia	GL 311; Bd 58.9	
5329	A	117	1717	outer	primary	tibia	SD 33.9; Bd 58.0	arts with b5331 (astragalus) & 5339 (calcaneum)
12	D	418	4374	middle	primary	tibia	Bd 59.7	
1412	D	418	4384	middle	primary	tibia	Bd 61.4	loose epiphysis
1411	D	418	4364	middle	primary	tibia	Bd 58.8	loose epiphysis
13	D	414	4362	middle	secondary	tibia	Bd 61.0	
1962	E	522	12063	middle	primary	tibia	Bd 61.0	
662	E	503	5736	middle	secondary	tibia	Bd 57.2	
1384	F	629	6369	inner	secondary	tibia	Bp 91.3	
3822	B	210	23188	outer	primary	astragalus	GL 70.8; Bd 46.0	
4265	B	205	16872	outer	secondary	astragalus	GL 80.8; Bd e52	
4176	B	203	16707	outer	secondary	astragalus	GL 60.0; Bd 39.2	
4146	B	203	16830	outer	secondary	astragalus	GL 65.7; Bd 40.9	
4312	B	203	16818	outer	secondary	astragalus	GL 68.9; Bd 41.1	
3734	BB	705	7340		OLS	astragalus	GL 65.4; Bd 39.9	
5343	A	112	1691	outer	primary	astragalus	GL 67.5; Bd 41.0	?pair b5331
5331	A	115	1697	outer	secondary	astragalus	GL 66.6; Bd 39.0	arts with b5329 (tibia) & 5339 (calcaneum); ? pair 5343

Appendix 1.1 (continued): Measurements of cattle bones from Windmill Hill 1988.

* = bone destroyed in dating

bone no.	trench	context no.	find no.	ditch	level	bone	measurements	notes
5591	A	104	1284	outer	secondary	astragalus	GL e67.9; Bd 44.4	
5460	A	102	1071	outer	tertiary	astragalus	GL e65.4	
4717	C	306	10488	outer	primary	astragalus	GL 67.1; Bd 42.1	
171	C	319	10649	outer	primary	astragalus	GL 68.0; Bd e42.8	arts with b130 (navicular)
27	C	321	10457	outer	secondary	astragalus	GL 63.6; Bd 41.4	
113	C	317	3922	outer	up secondary	astragalus	GL 64.4; Bd 42.8	
1424	D	418	4363	middle	primary	astragalus	GL 64.6; Bd 44.4	same foot? as b1413 (metatarsal)
5339	A	115	1672	outer	secondary	calcaneum	GL 120.9	arts with b5331 (astragalus) & 5329 (tibia)
4714	C	306	10496	outer	primary	calcaneum	GL 125.1	
25	D	413	4179	middle	secondary	calcaneum	GL 135.8	Bos primigenius?
4593	B	229	23206	outer	primary	navicular	GB 57.4	
19*	A	117	1712	outer	primary	navicular	GB 50.4	
199	C	321	10464	outer	secondary	navicular	GB e45.4	v small but definitely ox; young; arts with 74 (metatarsal)
130	C	317	3927	outer	up secondary	navicular	GB 54.0	arts with b171 (astragalus)
1625	D	415	4265	middle	primary	navicular	GB 52.5	
1342	F	630	6420	inner	secondary	navicular	GB 55.8	
4362	B	228	23272	outer	primary	metatarsal	Bp 46.5	
3823	B	210	23171	outer	primary	metatarsal	Bd 48.2	
4463	B	225	16890	outer	secondary	metatarsal	GL 211; Bp 46.8; SD 25.8	
302	BB	712	7869		tree hollow	metatarsal	Bd 54.6	
18*	A	117	1712	outer	primary	metatarsal	Bp 43.6	
5353	A	110	1638	outer	secondary	metatarsal	Bp 44.6; SL 25.8	
74	C	321	10455	outer	secondary	metatarsal	GL-ep 172; Gl+ep 196.1; Bp 40.0; SD 19.4; Bd 47.5	loose epiphysis; arts w+ b199 (navicular)
155	C	317	3928	outer	up secondary	metatarsal	Bp 46.4, SD 26.1	
1768	D	416	4296	middle	primary	metatarsal	Bp 47.0;	
1413	D	418	4361	middle	primary	metatarsal	Bp 47.6	same foot as b1424 (astragalus)
1718	D	406	4065	middle	secondary	metatarsal	B condyle 26.9	
5902	E	524	12198	middle	primary	metatarsal	Bp 43.6	
526	B	227	23100	outer	primary	phal prox p	Bp 30.3; GLpe 66.3	
2391	B	216	16218	outer	up secondary	phal prox ao	GLpe 62.4; Bp 35.6	
2530	B	215	9758	outer	up secondary	phal prox a	Bp 43.9	Bos primigenius
3172	B	201	2164	outer	tertiary	phal prox ao	GLpe 62.5; Bp 30.3	
3601	BB	705	7498		OLS	phal prox ai	GLpe 55.8; Bp 30.3	
4754	C	308	10400	outer	primary	phal prox po	GLpe e58.5; Bp 28.9	
1745	D	416	4298	middle	primary	phal prox ao	GLpe 66.6; Bp 32.7	
1569	D	406	4074	middle	secondary	phal prox ao	GLpe 59.3; Bp 27.6	
1663	D	404	4036	middle	secondary	phal prox pi	GLpe 88.2; Bp 42.6	Bos primigenius
1916	E	514	12338	middle	primary	phal prox po	GLpe 58.2; Bp e27.2	

Appendix 1.1 (continued): Measurements of cattle bones from Windmill Hill 1988.

* = bone destroyed in dating

bone no.	trench	context no.	find no.	ditch	level	bone	measurements	notes
1852	E	522	5980	middle	primary	phal prox ao	GLpe 57.6; Bp 30.9	
1851	E	522	12010	middle	primary	phal prox pi	GLpe 59.4; Bp 30.9	
5887	E	524	12194	middle	primary	phal prox ao	GLpe 66.6; Bp 37.4	
2045	F	604	6269	inner	secondary	phal prox pi	GLpe 57.7; Bp e37.6	*Bos primigenius?*
2245	F	602	6216	inner	RB	phal prox ao	GLpe 75.3; Bp 41.0	
4404	B	228	23304	outer	primary	phal mid pe	Bp 28.7; GLpe 41.1	
3989	B	214	9811	outer	up secondary	phal mid ao	Bp 28.4; GLpe 36.1	
2454	B	215	9759	outer	up secondary	phal mid ao	GLpe 42.0; Bp 36.3	
3876	B	212	9623	outer	up secondary	phal mid ao	Bp 30.7	
3592	BB	705	7489		OLS	phal mid ai	GLpe 38.9; Bp 27.9	
3654	BB	703	7051		main bank	phal mid	GLpe 36.0; Bp 26.7	
4625	C	309	19522	outer	primary	phal mid po	Bp 29.0	
2781	B	202	9394	outer	soil	phal mid p	GLpe 39.3; Bp 27.6	
1414	D	418	4365	middle	primary	phal mid ai	GLpe 38.5; Bp 30.8	
1878	E	522	5947	middle	primary	phal mid ao	GLpe 37.6; Bp 28.8	
2148	F	601	6021	inner	tertiary	phal mid	GLpe 39.3; Bp 37.2	incl exostosis

Appendix 1.2: Measurements of cattle skull's from from Keiller and Smith excavations.
(Modified from Grigson 1965)

skull no	1	2	3	4	5	6	7	8
minimum breadth between horncores	182	145	137	176	e174	193	e178	169
minimum frontal breadth	c187	e162	-	-	e168	-	-	-
maximum frontal breadth	-	e202	-	-	-	-	-	-
breadth between occ notches of temporal fossae	e167	122	132	e144	e140	153	e174	134
occipital region maximum breadth	>200	c200	-	-	c195	-	c208	c198
occipital condyles maximum breadth	e96	78	103	e102	100	110	111	101
occipital height from basion	e161	-	e151	e160	-	170	-	e164
occipital height from opisthion	121	109	e111	120	-	126	c126	125
horncore base max diameter L/R	70/73	57/56	65/-	58	-/61	-/77	-	68/67
horncore base min diameter L/R	60/58	-/44	48/46	45	-/44	-/57	57	55/55
horncore basal circumference L/R	215/215	-/160	180/-	170	-/175	-/175	c200	195/195
horncore length outer curvature L/R	-	-	-	-	e241 (>180)	e280 (>220)	-	-
sex/taxon	F wild/M dom	F dom	F dom	F dom	F dom	M dom?	M dom?	M dom
age	young/mod	moderate	moderate	moderate	moderate	young?	young?	young

skull no	9	10	11	12	13	14	15
minimum breadth between horncores	172	e142	e134	160	e152	176	e180
minimum frontal breadth	e162	-	-	-	e172	-	-
maximum frontal breadth	-	-	-	-	-	-	-
breadth between occ notches of temporal fossae	148	e136	e120	-	-	c132	e148
occipital region maximum breadth	-	-	-	-	-	-	e186
occipital condyles maximum breadth	c100	-	-	-	-	-	108
occipital height from basion	-	-	-	-	-	-	157
occipital height from opisthion	114	-	-	-	-	-	119
horncore base max diameter L/R	48/48	55	e59	60/58	60/-	-	-/59
horncore base min diameter L/R	39/38	46	46	47/46	47/-	-	-/46
horncore basal circumference L/R	140/140	160	160	170/170	170/-	c155	-/163
horncore length outer curvature L/R	-/190	>198	-	e210 (>186)	-	-	-
sex/taxon	F dom	F dom	F dom	F dom	F dom	F dom	F dom
age	moderate	old	old	young/mod	moderate	moderate	moderate

Appendix 1.3: Measurements of cattle horncores from Keiller and Smith excavations.
(Modified from Grigson 1965; with addition of 1988 material)

horncore no	horncore base max diameter	horncore base min diameter	horncore basal circumference	horncore length outer curvature	sex/taxon	age
1	33	25	-	e60	F dom	vy
2	65	46	e185	265	M dom	y
3	50	45	155	c250(>180)	F dom	o
4	59	46	168	e250(>215)	F dom	m
5	42	34	125	97	F dom	vy
6	80	63	230	255	M dom	m
7	63	49	178	>>230	F dom	m?
8	54	e42	e154	e200(>160)	F dom	m
9	64	49	184	e240(>215)	F dom	m
10	52	42	150	e230(>220)	F dom	m
11	53	43	e150	e210(>200)	F dom	m?
12	57	47	168	>>140	F dom	o
13	55	46	165	215	F dom	y
14	e59	e50	e175	e220(>210)	F dom	m?
15	52	43	149	e237(>193)	F dom	o
16	58	45	160	200	F dom	m
17	81	63	235	-	F wild	vy
18	56	46	164	-	F dom	m
19	54	42	150	-	F dom	y
20	69	50	195	-	M dom	y
21	70	49	190	-	F dom	m
22	62	49	180	-	F dom	o
23	53	42	155	-	F dom	m
24	50	40	145	-	F dom	m
25	66	50	186	-	F dom	m
26	62	51	185	-	F dom	m
27	58	51	173	-	F dom	o
28	64	48	181	-	F dom	o
29	59	44	165	-	F dom	m?
30	54	45	160	-	F dom	o
31	53	45	155	-	F dom	o
32	45	35	130	-	F dom	
33	51	42	154	-	F dom	o
34	e57	45	e165	-	F dom	m?
35	56	43	160	-	F dom	o
36	58	43	165	-	F dom	vy
37	50	42	145	-	F dom	m?
38	55	40	150	-	F dom	o
39	65	48	185	-	F dom	m
40	62	50	180	-	F dom	m?
41	53	43	155	-	F dom	o
42	65	e47	180	-	F dom	o
43	58	45	170	-	F dom	o
44	60	42	165	-	F dom	m?
45	60	47	170	-	F dom	o
46	63	46	180	-	F dom	o
47	80	64	228	-	M dom	y
48	62	47	170	-	F dom	o
49	71	54	200	-	M dom	y
50	50	42	148	-	F dom	o
51	69	59	210	-	M? dom?	y?
52	61	47	170	-	F dom	o
53	60	47	174	-	F dom	m
54	70	50	195	-	F dom	o
55	54	42	158	-	F dom	o
56	70	c46	e186	-	F dom	m?
57	57	47	165	-	F dom	o
58	94	70	260	-	M? dom?	o
59	80	66	235	-	F wild	y
60	47	39	136	-	F dom	o
61	53	40	155	-	F dom	m
62	57	45	165	-	F dom	o
63	52	45	-	-	F dom	y
64	e55	42	-	-	F dom	m?
65	49	45	145	145	F dom	vy
66	55	-	c155	-	F dom	vy
67	53	45	150	e95	F dom	vy
68	78	61	223	278	M dom	m
69	67	-	-	-	M dom	y
70	-	43	-	-	F dom	m?
71	-	44	-	-	F dom	o
72	e54	-	-	-	F dom	vy
73	-	-	-	e210	F dom	o
1988						
5859	e68	57.2	c205	c235(>210)	M dom	y?

Appendix 1.4: Additional measurements of cattle metatarsals from Keiller and Smith excavations.

bone no	419	422
metatarsal no (1965)	-	4
year excavation	1928	1957/8
period	Early Neo	Late Neo
trench	MD IB	OD V
level	2	6
maximum length GL	200	e257*
proximal breadth Bp	45.6	55
distal breadth Bd	59.1	30
notes	dwarf	*published as e157

Appendix 1.5: Measurements of pig bones from Windmill Hill 1988.

bone no.	trench	context no.	find ditch no.	level	bone	measurements	notes
3827	B	210	23064 outer	primary	cranium	Lm4 up 15.4; LM1 up 18.3	M1 crypt open
3817	B	210	23067 outer	primary	skull	Lm4 low 20.6; Lm4 up 15.4	m4A; M1 unworn
3065	B	203	16672 outer	secondary	maxilla	LM2 up 18.6	unworn
3960	B	214	16098 outer	up secondary	cranium	LM1 up 17.0	M1 v sl wear
4044	B	214	9763 outer	up secondary	M3 up	LM3 up 30.9	M3 unerupted
3210	B	201	2237 outer	tertiary	cranium	LM2 up 21.1; M1 up 17.3	v sl wear all teeth
3175	B	201	2110 outer	tertiary	M2 up	LM2 up 22.3	M2 unerupted
5055	C	302	3567 outer	tertiary	maxilla	LM2 up 19.9	M1 v sl wear; M2 unworn
36	E	525	12290 middle	primary	cranium	LM1 up 16.9; LM2 up 21.6	M3 erupting; palatal suture open
1297	F	630	6458 inner	secondary	cranium	LM2 up 20.4	M2 unworn
2348	B	216	16261 outer	up secondary	M1 low	LM1 low 18.7	M1 unerupted
2625	B	216	16427 outer	up secondary	mandible	L M1 low 17.0; LM2 low 22.8	m4D; M1B; M2A (erupting)
2345	B	216	16413 outer	up secondary	mandible	LM1 low 15.9; LM2 low 19.9	M1D; M2B; M3A
2662	B	202	9311 outer	soil	mandible	LM1 low 16.1; LM2 low 20.8	
2635	B	202	9324 outer	soil	mandible	LM1 low 16.1; LM2 low 21.2	
2828	B	202	9067 outer	soil	mandible	LM1 low 16.2; LM2 low 21.0	
2491	B	215	9880 outer	up secondary	mandible	Lm4 low 18.8; LM1 low 17.1; LM2 low 18.8	m4D; M1A; M2 unerupted
2449	B	215	9733 outer	up secondary	mandible	Lm4 low 19.8; LM1 low 18.0; LM2 low 21.8	m4D; M1B; M2 beginning to erupt
5545	A	103	1464 outer	secondary	mandible	Lm4 low 19.5	
5561	A	103	1620 outer	secondary	mandible	LM3 low 39.9	M3C; wild? pig
5138	C	302	3449 outer	tertiary	M3 low	LM3 low 35.7	M3F v worn
5080	C	302	3249 outer	tertiary	P4 low	LP4 low 13.9	P4 unworn
38	E	525	12303 middle	primary	mandible	L lower canine alveolus c12	P2-1 (C) i3 (I2) I1: I1 (I2) i2 i3 (C) P1-3
32	BB	733	7393	grave fill	scapula	S_C 24.4	
477	B	227	23073 outer	primary	scapula	S_C 23.4	
22	E	527	12369 middle	primary	scapula	SLC 20.4	
2942	B	202	2889 outer	soil	scapula	SLC 23.5	
2857	B	202	9351 outer	soil	scapula	SLC 24.4	
2002	E	522	12042 middle	primary	radius	Bp 29.0	
2612	B	216	16416 outer	up secondary	radius	Bp 26.5	
2325	B	217	16626 outer	up secondary	tibia	Bd 29.2	
301	BB	741	7720	OLS	astragalus	GL 43.0; Bd 24.1	
4934	C	315	10635 outer	primary	astragalus	GL 39.8	
5404	A	106	1609 outer	secondary	astragalus	GL 40.3	
4005	B	214	16006 outer	up secondary	astragalus	GL 42.9	
2725	B	202	2625 outer	soil	astragalus	GL 42.6	
3103	B	201	2361 outer	tertiary	phal mid cent	GLpe 24.5; Bp 16.8	
3260	B	201	2106 outer	tertiary	phal mid cent	GLpe 23.0; Bp 16.2	
3913	B	214	16166 outer	up secondary	phal mid cent	Bp 17.2	
2752	B	202	2693 outer	soil	phal mid cent	GLpe 21.8; Bp 15.6	
3419	B	202	2449 outer	soil	phal mid cent	GLpe 23.0; Bp 16.1	

Appendix 1.6: Measurements of sheep and goat bones from Windmill Hill 1988.

bone no.	trench	context no.	find no.	ditch	level	taxon	bone	measurements	notes
4716	C	306	10496	outer	primary	sheep	frontal+hcore	basal diam max 28.8	
1732	D	416	4299	middle	primary	sheep	horncore	basal diam max 29.9, min 17.6; L in front 9	male
1740	D	416	4327	middle	primary	sheep	horncore	basal diam max 29.9, min 20.5	male
41	E	525	12298	middle	primary	goat	horncore	basal diam max 32.2, min 19.7	male?
3807	B	210	23170	outer	primary	sheep	scapula	SLC 19.8	
3751	BB	705	7571		OLS	sheep	scapula	SLC 17.2	
176	C	319	10650	outer	primary	goat	scapula	SLC 17.3; GLP 27.2	
1321	F	630	6439	inner	secondary	goat	scapula	SLC 17.9	
1488	E	523	12104	middle	primary	sheep	humerus	Bd 25.4; Bt 25.4	
108	E	525	12327	middle	primary	sheep	humerus	Bt 28.0	lateral exostosis
793	E	501	5475	middle	RB	shpgt	humerus	Bt e30.1	
2038	F	604	6276	inner	secondary	shpgt	humerus	Bt 27.0	
2561	B	216	16206	outer	up secondary	sheep	radius	GL-ep 109; Bp 24.6; SD 13.1	
164	C	319	10601	outer	primary	sheep	radius	GL 142.3; Bp 28.3; SD 14.2; Bd 25.2	
1919	E	514	12390	middle	primary	shpgt	radio-ulna	SD 17.3; Bd 28.2	
5920	E	527	12373	middle	primary	sheep	radius	Bp 29.5	
157	C	319	10524	outer	primary	sheep	metacarpal	GL-ep 91.7; Bp 17.3; SD 8.8	
4337	B	228	23355	outer	primary	shpgt	tibia	Bd c24	
1329	F	630	6428	inner	secondary	shpgt	tibia	Bd 25.6	similar to Soay
1748	D	416	4371	middle	primary	shpgt	astragalus	GL 24.9; Bd 16.4	
4516	B	225	16936	outer	secondary	goat	phal prox	GLpe 36.3; Bp 12.3	female?
110	E	525	12289	middle	primary	shpgt	phal mid	Bp 10.9	

Appendix 1.7: Measurements of red and roe deer, dog, fox and mustelid bones from Windmill Hill 1988.

bone no	trench	context no	find no	ditch	level	taxon	bone	measurements
572	E	503	5709	middle	secondary	red deer	astragalus	GL 50.4; Bd 33.4
853	B	202	9213	outer	soil	red deer	metatarsal	Bp 43.8
3414	B	202	2917	outer	soil	red deer	metatarsal	Bd 40.1
853	B	202	9213	outer	soil	red deer	metatarsal	Bp 43.8; v deep sag grooves
3414	B	202	2917	outer	soil	red deer	metatarsal	Bd 40.1
4667	C	311/315	10587	outer	primary	roe deer	humerus	Bd 28.0; Bt 27.4
4261	B	206	16858	outer	secondary	roe deer	radius	GL e182; Bp 26.8; SD 16.6; Bd 25.2
2587	B	216	16539	outer	up secondary	roe deer	phal prox	GLpe 34.5; Bp 10.1
845	E	501	5537	middle	RB	roe deer	phal mid	GLpe 24.1; Bp 10.5
1400	F	629	6361	Inner	secondary	dog	humerus	Bd 29.7
1039	B	202	2944	outer	soil	fox	P3 low	L P3 low 8.8
3069	B	205	16850	outer	secondary	mustelid	mandible	L cheektooth row 21.3; pine marten?

Appendix 2.1: Bones with abnormalities from the 1988 excavations at Windmill Hill.

year excavation	bone no	trench	context	find no	ditch	level	taxon	bone	part	ant/prox fused	post/dist fused	age	abnormality
1988	1951	E	522	12026	middle	primary	bos	skull	intercornual ridge				hole in parietal
1988	4937	C	315	10632	outer	primary	bos	M1 upper	nearly complete				1 root swollen with drainage channel
1988	5045	C	302	3595	outer	tertiary	bos	M1/2 lower	complete				swollen roots
1988	112	C	317	3963	outer	up secondary	bos	cervical vertebra V	centrum+arch	y	y		slight groove in anterior epiphysis
1988	21	F	613	6464	inner	primary	bos	cervical vertebra VI	damaged	y	n		ant epiphysis w+ raised conical centre
1988	425	B	227	23079	outer	primary	bos	dorsal vertebra	centrum+arch	n	n		odd groove on posterior articulation
1988	293	BB	761	7967	OLS	posthole 760	bos	dorsal vertebra	base of dorsal spine				post articulation asymmetrical
1988	4577	B	225	16981	outer	secondary	bos	lumbar vertebra	centrum+arch	n	n		foramen low centrum, right *
1988	4590	B	229	23242	outer	primary	bos	lumbar vertebra VI	centrum+arch	yn	yn		foramen low centrum, right *
1988	479	B	227	2310	outer	primary	bos	scapula	distal				anterior foramen very large
1988	2529	B	215	9734	outer	up secondary	bos	humerus	distal half		y		hole above condyle, ?pmortem
1988	1691	D	406	4082	middle	secondary	bos	radius	proximal	y			slight osteitis inner side articular surface
1988	2631	B	207	23028	outer	secondary	bos	metacarpal	complete		y		slight anterior bulge proximal end
1988	5542	A	103	1563	outer	secondary	bos	metacarpal	proximal half				slight exostosis anteriorly below art
1988	60	E	525	12229	middle	primary	bos	pelvis	acetabulum etc	y		old	exostosis on pubis
1988	9	F	630	6416	inner	secondary	bos	pelvis	ilium+acetabulum	y		old	slight eburnation and porosis
1988	130	C	317	3927	outer	up secondary	bos	navicular	complete			old?	fused to cuneiform
1988	1342	F	630	6420	inner	secondary	bos	navicular	complete				hole in proximal articular surface
1988	2148	F	601	6021	inner	tertiary	bos	middle phalanx	complete	y			proximal exostosis
1988	2454	B	215	9759	outer	up secondary	bos	middle phalanx ao	complete				v slight proximal expansion, ?normal
1988	3876	B	212	9623	outer	up secondary	bos	middle phalanx ao	nearly complete	y			slight proximal lipping
1988	11109	F	627	6308	inner	secondary	pig	ulna	proximal+shaft	n			groove in articular surface
1988	3111	B	201	2006	outer	tertiary	shpgt	M1/2 lower	complete				swollen roots
1988	108	E	525	12327	middle	primary	sheep	humerus	distal		y		lateral exostosis on condyle
1988	11104	F	627	6312	inner	secondary	shpgt	proximal phalanx	distal				possible distal osteitis
1988	110	E	525	12289	middle	primary	shpgt	middle phalanx	complete	y			posterior distal exostosis

* 4577/4590 could be same animal

Appendix 2.2: Bones with abnormalities from the earlier excavations at Windmill Hill.

year excavation	bone no	level	ditch + segment	layer	taxon	bone	part	prox/ant	dist/post	abnormality
1957/8	1402	late neo/EBA	OD V	3	bos	middle phalanx	complete			expanded proximal articular surface
1957/8	1393	late neo/EBA	OD V	3	bos	proximal phalanx	complete			expanded proximal articular surface
1929	181	Romano-British/mixed	MD XB	1	bos	tibia	distal half		y	severe lesion
1928	419	late neo/EBA	MD IB	2	bos	metatarsal	complete		y	dwarf?
1928	549	primary	MD VII	4&5	bos	lumbar vertebra	centrum	y	y	hole right side centrum
1957/8	589	primary	ID XVII	4	bos	lumbar vertebra	centrum	y	y	hole right side centrum
1928	560	primary	MD VII	4&5	bos	lumbar vertebra VI		n	n	hole right side centrum
1926	1490	primary	ID VII	4	bos primigenius	metacarpal	distal		y	distal foramina connect
1929	171	late neo/EBA	MD XA	2	pig	mandible	tooth row			alveolus for extra P4

Caroline Grigson

Appendix 3.1: Bones (excluding antler) with cutmarks from the 1988 excavations at Windmill Hill.

bone no	trench	context	find no	ditch	level	taxon	bone	part	cut marks, etc.
86	A	117	1709	outer	primary	bos	skull	frontlet	multiple cut marks on frontal
5899	E	524	12168	middle	primary	bos	skull	nasal	cut marks upper surface
2619	B	216	16415	outer	up secondary	bos	horncore	basal fragment	chop marks indicating horn removal?
348	BB	726	7401		pit 715	bos	mandible	diastema fragment	vertical cut mark?
125	C	317	3952	outer	up secondary	bos	mandible	molar row	chopped anteriorly
290	BB	705	7807		OLS	bos	scapula	distal	chopped off?
17*	A	117	1711	outer	primary	bos	scapula	spine	slight ?scrape marks
713	E	503	5808	middle	secondary	bos	scapula	distal	cut marks on anterior edge
67	E	525	12216	middle	primary	bos	scapula	distal half	cut marks diag on inner edge distal epiphysis
15*	B	227	23368	outer	primary	bos	humerus	distal	chopped horizontally
4586	B	230	23292	outer	primary	bos	humerus	distal	slight cut mark
33	BB	765	7284		OLS	bos	humerus	distal	3 slight horizontal cut marks posteriorly
1800	E	508	12139	middle	primary	bos	humerus	distal	cut marks posterior articulation
1370	F	630	6422	inner	secondary	bos	humerus	distal half	chopped horizontally, cut marks, human bone in shaft
10	F	629	6389	inner	secondary	bos	humerus	distal half	chopped horizontally
11	F	629	6389	inner	secondary	bos	humerus	distal	cut marks; chopped horizontally
5	E	525	12278	middle	primary	bos	humerus	distal half	cut marks on trochanter
16*	B	227	23368	outer	primary	bos primigenius?	radius	distal	chopped horizontally
701	E	503	5807	middle	secondary	bos	radius	proximal	cut mark?
1485	E	523	12090	middle	primary	bos	radius	proximal	cut marks proximally
8	E	525	12224	middle	primary	bos	pelvis	ilium+acetabulum	cut marks inner side ilium wing
9	F	630	6416	inner	secondary	bos	pelvis	ilium+acetabulum	cut marks outer side ilium wing
42	E	525	12291	middle	primary	bos	pelvis	ilium	cut mark across outer face of wing
1401	F	629	6370	Inner	secondary	bos	pelvis	acetabulum frag	cut mark
1487	E	523	12081	middle	primary	bos	pelvis	pubic symphisis frag	cut marks
1861	E	522	5011	middle	primary	bos	pelvis	ilium	cut marks
4617	C	309	10515	outer	primary	bos	pelvis	ilium blade	cut marks inner surface & lower edge
4668	C	311/315	10536	outer	secondary	bos	pelvis	ischium fragment	cut mark near inner edge
11182	F	627	6344	Inner	primary	bos	pelvis	acetabulum	chop marks
1881	E	518	5880	middle	primary	bos	pelvis	ilium blade	cut marks
457	B	227	23146	outer	primary	bos?	femur	proximal shaft frag	2 horizontal cut marks below articulation
12	D	418	4374	middle	primary	bos	tibia	distal	chopped horizontally
13	D	414	4362	middle	secondary	bos	tibia	distal half	chopped diagonally
75	C	321	10452	outer	secondary	bos	tibia	nearly complete	multiple horizontal cut marks posteriorly
2043	F	610	6327	Inner	primary?	bos	tibia?	shaft fragment	very deep grooves - COMB?
5343	A	112	1691	outer	primary	bos	astragalus	complete	?cut mark on trochlea
4146	B	203	16830	outer	secondary	bos	astragalus	nearly complete	horizontal cut marks
4717	C	306	10488	outer	primary	bos	astragalus	complete	cut marks anterior & posterior surface
171	C	319	10649	outer	primary	bos	astragalus	nearly complete	cut mark outer surface
1424	D	418	4363	middle	primary	bos	astragalus	complete	cut mark anterior face
27	C	321	10457	middle	secondary	bos	astragalus	complete	horizontal cut marks anteriorly on trochlea
4714	C	306	10496	outer	primary	bos	calcaneum	complete	?cut mark anteriorly
1413	D	418	4361	middle	primary	bos	metatarsal	proximal half	proximal cut mark around diameter
5364	A	107	1432	outer	secondary	bos	metatarsal	distal shaft	??scoop
155	C	317	3928	outer	up secondary	bos	metatarsal	proximal half	chopped horizontally

Appendix 3.1 (continued): Bones (excluding antler) with cutmarks from the 1988 excavations at Windmill Hill.

bone no	context	trench	find no	ditch	level	taxon	bone	part	cut marks, etc.
1491	523	E	12082	middle	primary	bos	navicular	fragment	cut mark
5902	524	E	12198	middle	primary	bos	metatarsal	proximal half	cut mark anteriorly and proximally
141	317	C	3968	outer	up secondary	bos	prox. phalanx	proximal	chopped diagonally
699	503	E	5745	middle	secondary	bos	dorsal vert.	dorsal arch	?cut through horiz?
1383	629	F	6384	inner	secondary	bos	lumbar vert.	damaged	cut marks
4577	225	B	16981	outer	secondary	bos	lumbar vert.	centrum and arch	cut mark, gnawed
571	503	E	5710	middle	secondary	bos	rib VI?	proximal	cut marks?
417	746	BB	7689		primary bank	bos	rib	proximal	?cut marks
3283	202	B	2503	outer	soil	bos	rib	proximal	cut marks on articular surface
1876	522	E	12008	middle	primary	large mammal	rib	section	proximal cut marks
557	227	B	23090	outer	primary	large mammal	rib	fragment	transverse cut mark
4755	308	C	10405	outer	primary	large mammal	rib	proximal	cut mark inside neck
5330	115	A	1688	outer	secondary	large mammal	rib	proximal	cut marks or ?only root erosion on neck
5337	115	A	1686	outer	secondary	large mammal	rib	damaged	cut marks or ?only root erosion on neck
138	317	C	3970	outer	up secondary	large mammal	rib	fragments	cut marks
1925	512	E	12206	middle	primary	large mammal	rib	section	cut marks
1876	522	E	12008	middle	primary	large mammal	rib	section	cut marks proximally
2077	610	F	6274	inner	primary?	pig	humerus	distal shaft	cut marks on shaft
1950	522	E	12118	middle	primary	pig	pelvis	ilium	cut marks
4103	214	B	16175	outer	up secondary	pig	femur	shaft	proximal cut marks
4608	229	B	23244	outer	primary	pig	rib I	proximal	multiple cut marks diagonally on neck
48	525	E	12316	middle	primary	pig	rib	proximal	cut marks - 4 on upper side nr articular surface
178	319	C	10593	outer	primary	sheep/goat	calcaneum	proximal	cut mark? posterior ly
1321	630	F	6439	inner	secondary	goat	scapula	distal	cut marks on neck
1400	629	F	6361	inner	secondary	dog	humerus	distal half	cut marks? on trochlea
853	202	B	9213	outer	soil	red deer	metatarsal	proximal	chopped off?
4261	206	B	16858	outer	secondary	roe deer	radius	nearly complete	proximal cut marks

Appendix 3.2: Bones (excluding antler) with cutmarks from the earlier excavations at Windmill Hill.

year excavation	bone no	period	ditch	level	taxon	bone	part	cutmarks etc.
1929	229	primary	MD XA	3b-4a	bos	skull	frontlet + occipital	cutmarks
1927	1355	primary	MD IVB	4	bos	horncore	base	cutmarks
1928	1073	primary	ID VII	3	bos	horncore	base	cutmarks?
1928	293	primary	ID VIII	3	bos	scapula	distal	cutmarks
1928	266	primary	MD VII	4	bos	humerus	distal	cutmarks
1928	284	primary	MD VII	4	bos	humerus	distal	cutmarks
1928	1315	primary	MD VII	5	bos	humerus	distal half	cutmark
?	873		?		bos	humerus	distal shaft	cutmarks
?	868		?		bos	radius	proximal	cutmarks
?	869		?		bos	radius	proximal	cutmarks
1928	902	primary	MD VIII	5	bos	metacarpal	proximal	cutmarks
1928	348	primary	MD VIII	5	bos	astragalus	complete	cutmarks
1928	351	primary	OD IB	5	bos	astragalus	complete	cutmarks
1928	361	primary	MD IB	4	bos	astragalus	complete	cutmarks
1928	1319	primary	MD VII	4	bos	calcaneum	damaged	cutmarks
?	889		?		bos	cervical vertebra III?	nearly complete	cutmarks
1929	876	primary	ID XIV	3	bos	lumbar vertebra	nearly complete	cutmarks
1929	913	primary	MD XIB	5	bos?	sacrum	fragment	cutmarks
1928	1489	primary	OD IC	4	bos?	sternebra		cutmarks
1929	1488	primary	ID XVB	3	large mammal	rib	fragment	cutmarks
1928	694	primary	MD IX	3	goat	radius	proximal	cutmarks
1927	82		MD IV	re-ex	sheep	radius	complete	cutmarks

12

Small Vertebrates

Amanda Rouse and Stephen Rowland

The Amphibia *(Amanda Rouse)*

Over 4,800 bones were identified as frog (*Ranus* sp.) or toad (*Bufo* sp.) (table 153). The vast majority of the bones were recovered from context 734, a dark soil with chalk within the pre-bank grave pit (707), at the same stratigraphic level as the skeleton. Smaller quantities of amphibian bones came from contexts 103, 104, 109 (Trench A), 202, 203, 216, and 225 (Trench B), all being secondary ditch fill contexts. In addition, a virtually intact toad skeleton was recovered from context 527 (Trench E), a primary fill; these bones are not included in the total above but are presented separately in table 154.

It was evident during excavation that there were significant concentrations of small animal bones within the grave pit, so samples of the soil were taken. Nonetheless, given that sieving and some degree of sorting had already taken place in order to extract small mammal bones, and that the amphibian bones recovered from the other contexts were 'chance' finds, the numbers of bones indicated in this report and the estimate of minimum numbers will be a considerable under-representation.

Identification

Identification was made using unpublished diagrams drawn and provided by Dr Terry O'Connor and reference material borrowed from the School of Pure and Applied Biology, Cardiff University.

The bone elements were divided into two groups; first, the major body parts (some 2,200 bones), which could be considered for fuller analysis: ilium, humerus, scapula, suprascapula, coracoid, tibio-fibula, radio-ulna, first and ninth vertebrae, urostyle, femur, maxilla, dentary, pterygoid, sphenethmoid, exoccipital, pro-otic, nasal, parasphenoid, and prontoparietal; and second, smaller or less distinct elements or categories of fragmented material (some 2,600 bones): vertebrae (not first or ninth), calcaneus, astragalus, metatarsals/metacarpals/phalanges, bones identified only as far as metatarsal/metacarpal/ calcaneus/astragalus, those identified as tibio-fibula/radio-ulna (distal), and those identified as 'other skull parts' and epiphyses.

Except where bone elements had suffered from severe fragmentation, distinguishing between *Ranus* sp. and *Bufo* sp. could be made confidently with the following: ilium, humerus, scapula, suprascapula, tibio-fibula, first vertebra, ninth vertebra, urostyle, femur and maxilla. Some distinction was attempted with the other elements in the first group of bones, but this was possible only when the specimens were complete and well-preserved, and they are described here only as frog/toad. Identification was made only as far as *Bufo* sp. and *Ranus* sp. It was not clear if there was more than one species in either group, though there was some metrical variability.

Preservation was generally good, especially in context 734. The bones from the fills in Trench A were not quite so well preserved, and a larger proportion could not be attributed with confidence to one of the two species groups. There seemed to be disproportionate survival between species group elements. For example, toad humeri and femora are consistently more abundant than frog, whilst frog scapulae and ninth vertebrae are more abundant than toad. Especially fragile are frog suprascapulae and will always be under-represented in the record. On the other hand, frog maxillae will be over-represented as even the tiniest fragment is easily recognisable and each has been counted.

Results

Almost 120 individuals are represented as a minimum number (based on the count of tibio-fibula). A ratio of approximately 43 percent frog and 57 percent toad is estimated, based on all the elements that could be distinguished. Within the grave context there was some spatial differentiation. A comparison can be made between sample '707/734 Bag A' and '707/734 No. 133' which were the

Table 153: Amphibian skeletal elements.

| | Trench | BB 707/ 734 Bag A | BB 707/ 740/734 | BB 707/ 734 18 | BB 707/ 734 30 | BB 707/ 734 44 | BB 707/ 734 47 | BB 707/ 734 118 | BB 707/ 734 133 | BB 734 (7412) | A 109 | A 104 | A 103 | B 202 | B 203 | B 216 | B 225 |
	Context																
Ilium	Frog, left	14	2	2	-	5	-	1	16	-	-	-	1	-	-	-	-
(whole/distal)	Frog, right	12	-	2	1	3	-	1	17	1	1	-	4	-	-	-	-
	Toad, left	5	-	2	2	1	-	-	25	2	1	-	1	-	-	-	1
	Toad, right	4	2	3	2	3	-	-	30	3	-	-	1	-	-	-	-
	F/T - L/R	3	-	2	-	2	-	-	4	1	3	-	2	-	-	-	-
Humerus	Frog, left	7	-	-	-	2	-	-	14	-	3	1	4	-	-	-	-
(whole/distal)	Frog, right	4	-	1	-	1	-	-	12	1	-	-	3	-	-	-	-
	Toad, left	12	2	5	1	5	-	-	30	-	-	-	5	1	-	-	1
	Toad, right	17	-	8	1	5	-	1	25	-	1	-	-	-	2	-	2
	F/T - L/R	6	-	-	-	8	-	-	-	-	-	-	6	-	-	-	-
Scapula	Frog, left	13	-	2	-	8	-	-	12	-	1	-	2	-	-	-	-
	Frog, right	12	1	6	-	8	1	1	15	-	1	-	5	-	-	-	-
	Toad, left	5	1	1	2	3	-	-	20	-	-	-	4	-	-	-	-
	Toad, right	3	1	4	1	2	1	-	22	-	-	-	3	-	-	-	1
	F/T - L/R	-	-	-	-	2	-	-	4	-	-	-	2	-	-	-	-
Suprascapula	Frog	1	1	-	-	1	-	-	-	-	-	-	-	-	-	-	-
	Toad	3	-	1	1	3	-	-	16	-	-	-	-	-	-	-	-
	Frog/Toad	1	-	3	-	-	-	-	6	-	-	-	6	-	-	-	-
Coracoid	Frog/Toad	38	2	7	-	22	2	-	42	-	-	-	6	-	-	-	-
Tibio-fibula	Frog	16	2	4	1	20	1	-	20	2	3	-	4	-	-	-	-
	Toad	14	3	13	2	5	-	-	25	1	1	-	13	-	1	2	4
	Frog/Toad	11	-	4	-	2	1	-	52	-	2	-	4	-	-	-	-
Radio-ulna	Frog/Toad	65	7	10	1	12	1	-	89	2	6	-	12	-	-	1	1
1st Vertebra	Frog	4	-	-	-	-	-	-	3	-	-	-	-	-	-	-	-
	Toad	-	-	-	2	2	-	1	8	-	-	-	-	-	-	-	-
9th Vertebra	Frog	5	-	1	-	12	-	-	10	-	-	-	3	-	-	-	-
	Toad	3	-	2	-	2	-	-	8	-	1	-	1	-	-	-	1
Vertebra	Frog/Toad	109	5	19	16	66	1	6	161	-	9	-	49	-	-	-	8
Urostyle	Frog	6	-	2	-	6	-	1	9	-	-	-	4	-	-	-	-
	Toad	7	1	3	2	2	-	-	16	1	-	-	5	-	-	-	-
	Frog/Toad	7	1	-	-	1	-	-	8	-	1	-	3	-	-	-	-
Femur	Frog	12	1	4	2	12	-	-	16	1	-	-	2	-	-	-	-
	Toad	6	1	3	3	5	-	1	60	-	-	-	4	-	1	-	2
	Frog/Toad	-	-	3	-	-	-	-	11	-	-	-	-	-	-	-	-
Maxilla	Frog	39	-	6	1	35	1	-	10	-	2	-	14	-	-	-	-
	Toad	10	2	-	1	4	-	2	31	1	1	-	9	-	-	-	-
Dentary	Frog/Toad	34	4	7	-	22	2	1	53	-	3	-	17	-	-	-	-
Pterygoid	Frog/Toad	12	1	-	2	13	2	-	16	-	-	-	8	-	-	-	-
Sphenethmoid	Frog/Toad	10	-	3	-	1	-	-	9	-	-	-	6	-	-	-	-
Exoccipital	Frog/Toad	19	1	2	2	21	-	-	25	-	2	-	6	-	-	-	-
Pro-otic	Frog/Toad	1	-	1	-	1	-	-	6	-	-	-	2	-	-	-	-
Nasal	Frog/Toad	5	1	-	-	4	-	-	8	-	-	-	8	-	-	-	-
Parasphenoid	Frog/Toad	8	-	-	1	2	-	-	17	-	-	-	2	-	-	-	-
Frontoparietal	Frog/Toad	10	2	3	2	1	1	-	24	-	2	-	10	-	-	-	-
Other skull parts	Frog/Toad	14	-	-	-	18	-	-	8	-	1	-	6	-	-	-	-
Calcan./Astrag.	Frog/Toad	54	1	8	6	10	7	2	36	-	1	-	8	-	-	-	2
M'tarsals/carpals	Frog/Toad	267	5	38	9	167	6	19	149	-	6	-	214	-	-	-	12
Calcan./Astrag./ M'tarsals/carpals	Frog/Toad	289	9	13	-	35	1	1	206	-	4	-	104	-	-	-	-
ulna	Frog/Toad	64	9	2	1	21	1	2	67	-	3	-	21	-	-	-	1
Ilium (centre)	Frog/Toad	6	-	1	-	1	-	-	12	-	-	-	2	-	-	-	1
Epiphyses	Frog/Toad	189	3	15	6	34	1	1	34	-	2	-	58	-	-	-	1

Table 154: Trench E, context 527, find no. 12371, discrete toad skeleton.

Ilium	left, right, 'centre'
Tibio-fibula	left, right
Radio-ulna	left, right
Femur	left, right
Humerus	left, right
Suprascapula	left, right
Scapula	left
Coracoid	
Urostyle	
Frontoparietal	left, right
Exoccipital	left, right
Pro-otic	right
Pterygoid	
Parasphenoid	
Maxilla	
Astragalus	left, right
Calcaneum	left, right
Metatarsals	
Metacarpals	
Phalanges	
Epiphyses	

two samples richest in amphibian material. 'Bag A' contained 57 percent attributed to frog and 43 percent to toad; 'No. 133' contained 34 percent frog and 66 percent toad.

Indications of environment

It is clear that both frogs and toads were present at the site in some abundance. Both groups breed in water during the spring but then migrate during the remainder of their annual cycle over considerable distances and may hibernate at some distance from suitable breeding habitats. Wooded areas are particularly attractive (Dr Trevor Beebee *pers. comm.*). M. Smith (1951) quotes a nineteenth-century account of a colony of toads travelling over two miles from their breeding site every year. More recent experiments show that both species groups will travel at least a kilometre from breeding habitats (M. Smith 1951; Savage 1961; Gittens *et al.* 1980). Pits and ditches may act as accidental pit-fall traps or they may be chosen as winter habitats. Both frogs and toads secrete themselves in holes or cavities in convenient places, and toads, in particular, are inclined to burrow into soft earth.

Death by natural causes (for example, a particularly hard winter), predator attack (birds of prey often kill Amphibia but take only their soft parts: Dr Trevor Beebee *pers. comm.*), an inability to escape from the grave pit or ditch (though toads are especially good climbers) or suffocation when the grave pit was filled in, are all possible reasons for entombment.

Although records of frogs and toads are quite rare in the published literature, they have been found in suitable archaeological contexts when they were sought and recognised; in fact they are liable to be found in all sorts of buried context, death occurring before or at the time of burial. Published examples include ditch fill contexts at Maiden Castle, Dorset (Evans and Rouse 1990), and Easton Down, Wiltshire (Whittle *et al.* 1993) and limestone cairn material at Wigber Low, Derbyshire (Maltby 1983).

It is impossible to arrive at an environmental interpretation of the site based on the amphibian material alone. However, shaded macro-environments and micro-habitats are favoured by both frogs and toads during their annual cycle of migration away from their breeding sites.

The small mammal remains from the pre-bank grave in Trench BB *(Stephen Rowland)*

The small mammal remains were collected from a deposit originating around, and contemporaneous with a complete human skeleton that had been placed in the steep-sided grave pit. This pit had acted as a trap into which many amphibians and some small mammals had fallen. That the material did not arise from owl pellets was indicated from the recovery of several long bones in articulation (Don Brothwell *pers. comm.*).

The nature and condition of the remains

Of the 191 fragments recorded, only 24 were of post-cranial origin. These had a dry and pitted appearance and seemed rather brittle due to the chalk environment of deposition. The few surviving mandibles were in a similar condition, with thin friable bone that flaked away from the teeth. Only one delicate maxilla and no skull fragments were found. The nature of the preservation would seem support the idea that the pit was left open and exposed to weathering for some time, possibly accompanied by some trampling, leaving only the more robust teeth relatively unscathed.

Identification

Teeth are the most diagnostic elements in species identification of small mammals. Although long bones have been recognised to species level through multivariate analyses (Graham and Saunders 1978), the small sample size here precludes such study.

All the teeth were examined under a low-magnification binocular microscope and identified tentatively from Hillson (1986) and then from the reference collection in the Environmental Archaeology Unit, York. Certain criteria were needed for the separation of the vole teeth which formed the majority of the assemblage, and in this case the upper third molar was used as it is distinctive between the two species *Microtus agrestis* and *Clethrionomys glareolus*. Such a selective sample has the disadvantage that the usable data set is greatly reduced. This is justifiable on two grounds. First, the other cheek teeth are not so immediately different between the two species as Corbet and Southern (1977) suggest. Secondly, presence or absence is as important as relative quantity.

Results

There were 167 teeth, of which only 17 could be considered diagnostic. Six were identified as mole (*Talpa europaea*), six as field vole (*Microtus agrestis*) and two as bank vole (*Clethrionomys glareolus*). There were an immature upper M^1 from a yellow-necked mouse (*Apodemus flavicollis*) and a very worn M_1 and M_2 from a mandible, again probably of *A. flavicollis*.

Indications of environment

Small mammals, particularly those that are non-commensal, are potentially useful as environmental indicators (cf. Evans and Rouse 1990; Rouse in Whittle *et al.* 1993). Most aspects of their ecology, behaviour and physiology are better understood than those of insects or molluscs. In comparison with the latter two phyla, there are relatively few species, most of which are identifiable from dentition. The conditions of preservation mean that they can be used to complement molluscan evidence in calcareous environments where insect and plant macro-fossil data would be sparse. Whilst the teeth should survive better than most bone in acidic environments, the small jaws would be exceedingly susceptible to chemical weathering, tiny teeth being extremely hard to recover when disassociated from their supportive tissue (Lyman 1994).

Most small mammals are not as discerning in their choice of temperature range, habitat or diet as in the case of stenotopic coleopterons, and are much more mobile in their quests for sustenance than could be expected of land snails. Environmental reconstruction of fine resolution cannot normally be attempted as relatively large margins of error have to be accounted for. The origin of the deposit is also vital when considering the individuals, as for instance assemblages of owl pellets could be regurgitated at a roost some distance from where the prey was caught, which in turn may be some way from where the small mammal normally forages or nests. Additionally, the larger and more mobile the creature, the further it would be expected to forage and therefore the less accurate the environmental indication.

The vole and mouse species identified here can live in similar conditions, mainly deciduous woodland, particularly in the case of *A. flavicollis* and to a lesser extent *C. glareolus*, which is tolerant of the rough ungrazed grassland preferred by *M. agrestis* (Corbet and Southern 1977). These three species prefer relatively dense and undisturbed cover. Moles could have been found in all these environments (Corbet and Southern 1977). A pattern of rough, dense grassland followed by scrub, then full woodland cover could be suggested radiating from the area of activity, based upon the increasing foraging ranges of *C. glareolus* and *A. flavicollis*, both of which can be extensive when compared to that of *M. agrestis*, which on average travels less than 27 m from its nest (Corbet and Southern 1977). *M. agrestis* is a poor climber and would be expected to die in a pit-trap, whereas both *C. glareolus* and *A. flavicollis* are described as agile climbers of trees (Corbet and Southern 1977), and their inclusion might relate to specific conditions in the base of the pit or an inability to scale the steep and unconsolidated sides.

A very rough seasonal indication can be found in the immature *A. flavicollis*. This species has a relatively restricted breeding season and such an individual is likely to derive from a summer litter (Corbet and Southern 1977). If the animal was active in late summer, this would coincide with a period of more adventurous movement out of woodlands observed in that season. The fact that the animal is immature might suggest that this movement was of relatively short range and that woodland was in close proximity to the pit-trap.

Acknowledgements

I would like to thank Don Brothwell and Keith Dobney for their assistance in the identifications, and Deborah Jacques for guiding me to the relevant reference collections.

13

Pottery

Lesley Zienkiewicz and Michael Hamilton

Introduction

The Windmill Hill ditches have produced a substantial Neolithic pottery assemblage. Some 20,000 sherds of pottery were recovered during the Keiller excavations, the majority Early Neolithic; 1165 Early Neolithic vessels were identified by their rims (Smith 1965a). Just under a thousand more Neolithic and Bronze Age sherds were recorded during the 1988 excavation, with perhaps some 43 Early Neolithic vessels, making a minimum of around 1200 vessels so far (figs 186–209, and tables 155–61 and 164–66).

Significant landmarks in the study of stylistic development, sequence and regional distribution of Neolithic pottery have been inspired by and formulated from the Windmill Hill assemblage. The importance of the collection was initially established by Piggott in his pioneering paper on the Neolithic pottery of the British Isles (1931), giving the first definition of the bi-partite division of Neolithic pottery into Windmill Hill and Peterborough Ware. Using the stratigraphy of the Windmill Hill ditches, Piggott proposed a universal typological sequence, or sequence dating as he referred to it, for Neolithic pottery. His simple numerical formula for Early Neolithic pottery (Piggott 1931, 83) indicated a gradual progression through time, from predominantly plain vessels (class A1), which occurred in the lowest layers of the ditches, to heavy-rimmed, often decorated vessels (class A2), which occurred at a slightly higher level. An hiatus of unspecified time separated these from Peterborough Ware. His sequence was no doubt a 'bulked' one, encompassing all three ditch circuits.

Piggott later refined his dual scheme for Early Neolithic pottery (1954), when he subdivided the developed, heavy-rimmed type of Early Neolithic pottery into the regional variants of Whitehawk, Abingdon and East Anglian. These three sub-styles were further developed by Smith in her PhD thesis (1956) (where she renamed the East Anglian style as Mildenhall).

The Windmill Hill assemblage was more fully published by Smith (1965a). On the whole, Smith accepted Piggott's observations on the stratification of the different pottery styles in the ditches, but with a few qualifications (Smith 1965a, 14). She pointed out that very little pottery of any kind had come from the ditch bottoms and, as a consequence, the perceived lack of 'developed' types from those levels had been afforded undue significance. Smith went on to point out that such pottery had occurred deep in the primary rubble, for example, from 7′ in Outer Ditch I. She was of the opinion that the lower (i.e. primary) levels of the inner and middle ditches had formed rapidly, although it was impossible to estimate a timescale and, thus, in so rapidly forming a silt a particular object had little relevance to any chronological scheme other than on a microscopic scale (Smith 1965a, 13–14). Smith considered that the pottery from the lower levels could be regarded as a single chronological unit (a statement which could be supported by her claims for evidence of conjoining sherds from different parts of the enclosure).

Questions for re-assessment

Piggott's formula of a unilinear typological progression for Neolithic pottery based on the stratigraphy of the Windmill Hill ditches, and Smith's notion of chronological uniformity, were based on schematic or generalising use of the site evidence. Detailed contextual study of the pottery, made possible by the information provided by the 1988 excavations and by re-examination of the Keiller and Smith archives, points the way to further assessment of the ceramic sequence. It also shows that earlier research did not do justice to the depositional patterning of different types of Early Neolithic pottery within the enclosure (Zienkiewicz 1996).

Piggott (1931) introduced the term 'Windmill Hill Ware' to describe the earlier of the two major groups of Neolithic pottery. Since then, it has been applied as a generic term for Early Neolithic pottery in southern

Britain; as a regional style of decorated pottery divided into sub-styles; and, to confuse matters further, Smith (1965a) applied the label to define a minor variant amongst the Keiller assemblage (summarised in Cleal 1992c). A recent generation of researchers, notably Cleal (1992c) and Herne (1988), has criticised this confused nomenclature.

Neolithic pottery studies over the last 60 or so years have been obsessed with labelling and classifying assemblages into regional style-zones. The premises within which we set about defining the styles and types of Early Neolithic pottery and the consequent mapping of geographical style-zones need to be addressed. Excavation in 1988 and the subsequent re-examination of the Keiller archive provide the opportunity to reassess what precisely is meant by the term 'Windmill Hill style', and alternative approaches to the regional style-zone construct can be suggested (Zienkiewicz 1996; cf. Cleal 1992c).

In terms of the development of Late Neolithic and Early Bronze Age ceramic studies Windmill Hill played a significant role. It was the stratigraphy of the ditches, where Peterborough Ware and Beaker occurred together in the upper silts, which Piggott (1931, 83) used in his landmark paper to argue a late date for Peterborough Ware. The apparent hiatus between Windmill Hill Ware and Peterborough Ware/Beaker in the ditch led to a notion that Peterborough Ware was 'in no sense a development from' the earlier pottery but had a 'different origin', thus in part giving rise to the whole Neolithic B hypothesis and an origin for Peterborough Wares in a Mesolithic tradition.

Though the defining of Peterborough Ware sub-styles and the final identification of origin essentially rested on

other sites than Windmill Hill (Piggott 1954; Smith 1956), nevertheless the new excavations by Smith, together with her publication of the Keiller material (1965a), did demonstrate that Ebbsfleet Ware predated the other two sub-styles (Mortlake and Fengate Ware) and predated Grooved Ware, Beaker and Early Bronze Age styles. She also noted that there was 'no stratigraphic evidence for the priority of Bell Beakers' over Long-Necked Beakers.

Given the importance of the Windmill Hill Peterborough Ware and Beaker pottery, in terms not only of research history, but also of the size of the assemblage and its context, it is surprising that so little discussion has been devoted to this material. Piggott described Windmill Hill as a Peterborough Ware habitation site, but without structures, but did not further elaborate what this might mean (Piggott 1954). The Beaker assemblage has received rather more attention but the overall conclusions were similar (e.g. Gibson 1982; Bamford 1982, 43). More recently most concern with the Late Neolithic and Beaker material on the site has shifted to possible 'ritual' implications of the pottery (e.g. Bradley 1984, 80; Thomas 1991, 175).

The assessment of the 1988 finds has provided an opportunity to re-examine the whole of the pottery archive and to publish the locations of the various styles both in terms of relative heights in the ditches and overall site distributions. The areas of particular importance are: the validity of the stratigraphic evidence used for the contemporaneity of various Late Neolithic and EBA pottery styles; the implication this has for the site and wider sequence of ceramic styles; and the explanation for the occurrence of the pottery on the site.

PART 1: EARLY NEOLITHIC INCLUDING EBBSFLEET

Lesley Zienkiewicz

Early Neolithic pottery from the 1988 excavations

The P numbers referring to the illustrated vessels (figs 186–92) start at 500 in order to avoid confusion with Smith's (1965a) published vessels. The P numbers for the previously unillustrated Ebbsfleet Ware vessels from the Keiller archive start at P324 to continue the sequence from the Smith (1965a) catalogue. Two sherds illustrated in 1965 are redrawn and these retain their Smith numbers.

There were approximately 795 Early Neolithic sherds (7.91 kg) of which a minimum of 43 vessels could be identified by their rims. 26 sherds (250 gm) were identified as belonging to the Ebbsfleet style, representing a minimum of two vessels. The Early Neolithic pottery came principally from primary contexts in the ditches, but also from secondary contexts and from the old land surface

beneath the outer bank. 45 percent and 37 percent of the assemblage came from the middle and outer ditches respectively, with 7 percent from the inner ditch; the remainder were from the bank cutting in Trench BB (figs 186–92; tables 155–61).

Fabrics: type and distribution

A simpler scheme for fabric discrimination than in Part Two of this report has been used (table 162; cf. table 170). Three main fabric groups were identified: flint (63 percent of sherds), shell (29 percent) and sand (8 percent). Amongst individual vessels, relative proportions of fabrics were very similarly represented: flint-tempered 56 percent, shell-tempered 37 percent and sand-tempered 7 percent. Two shell-tempered sherds had oolitic temper incorporated with the shell. There were no sherds of gabbroic pottery.

Table 155: Trench BB, sherds by style and context.

Sequence	Context	Early Neolithic	Ebbsfleet	GW 1	Bkr 7	EBA 1	EBA 3	EBA 6	LN/BA 1	BA/IA 1	Undef. 1	RB
Treeholllow	712	1	-	-	-	-	-	-	-	-	-	-
OLS	705/747	24/9	-	-	-	-	-	-	-	-	-	-
	741	13	-	-	-	-	-	-	-	-	-	-
	742	2	-	-	-	-	-	-	-	-	-	-
	Total	48	-	-	-	-	-	-	-	-	-	-
Posthole	710	1	-	-	-	-	-	-	-	-	-	-
Pit	714	1	-	-	-	-	-	-	-	-	-	-
	726	3	-	-	-	-	-	-	-	-	-	-
	Total	4	-	-	-	-	-	-	-	-	-	-
Grave	707/ 733/ 734/736/735	4	-	-	-	-	-	-	-	-	-	-
Primary Bank	764	13	-	-	-	-	-	-	-	-	-	-
Main Bank	703	7	-	-	-	-	-	-	-	-	-	-
	702	6	-	-	-	-	-	-	-	-	-	-
	Total	13	-	-	-	-	-	-	-	-	-	-
Tail of Bank	701	7	21	1	6	1	1	2	2	5	1	2
TOTAL		**91**	**21**	**1**	**6**	**1**	**1**	**2**	**2**	**5**	**1**	**2**

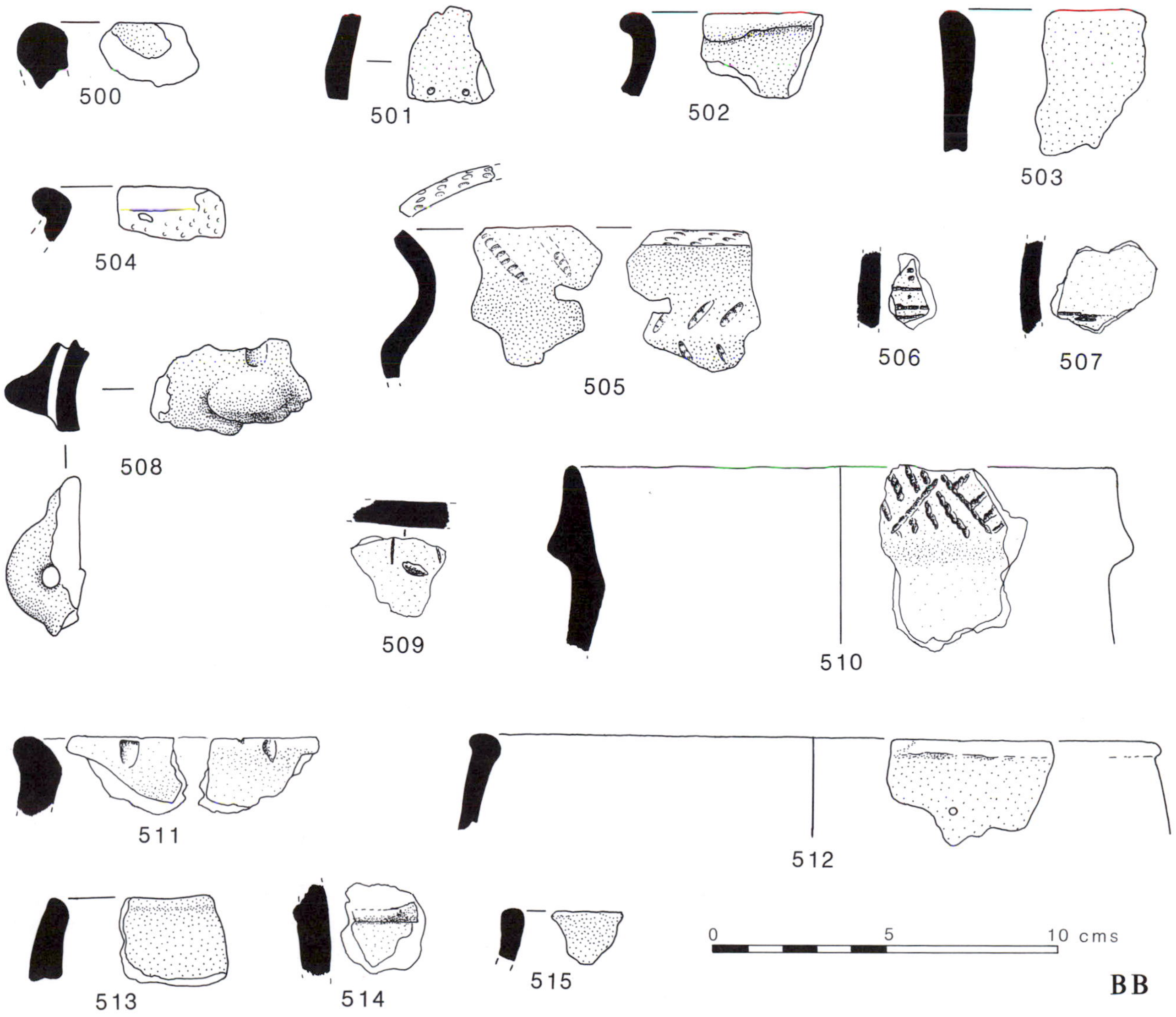

Fig. 186. Pottery from Trench BB.

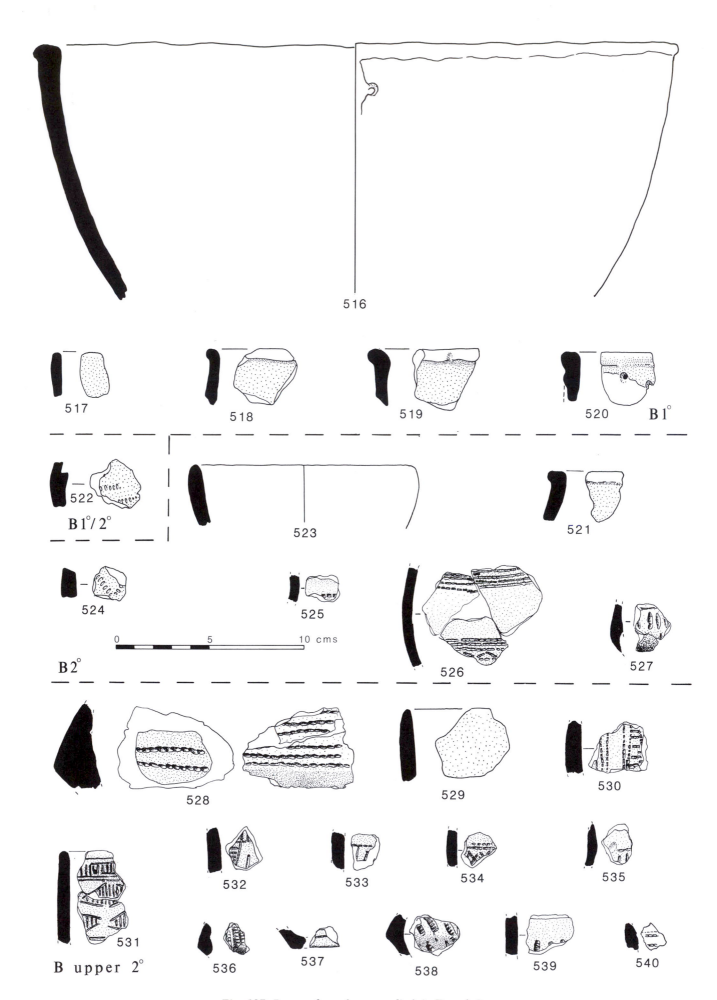

516

517 518 519 520 B 1°

522
B 1°/ 2°
523
521

524 525
B 2°
526 527

528 529 530

531
B upper 2°
532 533 534 535
536 537 538 539 540

0 5 10 cms

Fig. 187. Pottery from the outer ditch in Trench B.

Table 156: Trench B, sherds by style and context.

Style

Sequence	Context	Early Neo.	Ebbs-fleet	Bkr 1	Bkr 2	Bkr 3	Bkr 4	Bkr 5	Bkr 6	Bkr 15	?Bkr 1	Rus 1	Rus 2	Rus 5	Rus 6	LN/ EBA1	LN/ BA3	EBA 1	EBA 2	EBA 3	EBA 4	EBA 5	EBA 6	BA/ IA1	RB
Primary	228	66	-	-	-	-	-	-	-	-	-	-	-	-	-	-	-	-	-	-	-	-	-	-	-
	229	54	-	-	-	-	-	-	-	-	-	-	-	-	-	-	-	-	-	-	-	-	-	-	-
	210	11	1	-	-	-	-	-	-	-	-	-	-	-	-	-	-	-	-	-	-	-	-	-	-
	227	1	1	-	-	-	-	-	-	-	-	-	-	-	-	-	-	-	-	-	-	-	-	-	-
	Total	132	2	-	-	-	-	-	-	-	-	-	-	-	-	-	-	-	-	-	-	-	-	-	-
Secondary	207	2	-	-	-	-	-	-	-	-	-	-	-	-	-	-	-	-	-	-	-	-	-	-	-
	226	1	-	-	-	-	-	-	-	-	-	-	-	-	-	-	-	-	-	-	-	-	-	-	-
	225	1	-	-	-	-	-	-	-	-	-	-	-	-	-	-	-	-	-	-	-	-	-	-	-
	206	1	-	-	-	-	-	-	-	-	-	-	-	-	-	-	-	-	-	1	-	-	-	-	-
	213	-	-	-	-	-	-	-	-	-	-	-	-	-	-	-	-	-	-	-	-	-	-	-	-
	205	2	-	-	-	-	-	-	-	-	-	-	-	-	-	-	-	-	-	-	-	-	-	-	-
	204	2	-	-	-	-	-	-	-	-	1	-	-	-	-	-	-	-	-	2	-	-	-	-	-
	203	2	-	1	-	-	-	-	-	-	1	-	-	-	-	-	-	-	-	-	-	-	-	-	-
	Total	11	-	1	-	-	-	-	-	-	2	-	-	-	-	-	-	-	-	3	-	-	-	-	-
Upper Secondary	222	-	-	-	-	-	-	-	-	1	-	-	-	-	-	-	-	-	-	2	-	-	-	-	-
	220	-	-	-	3	-	-	-	-	-	-	-	-	-	-	-	-	-	-	-	-	-	-	-	-
	219	-	-	-	-	-	-	-	-	-	-	-	-	-	-	-	-	7	-	1	-	-	-	-	-
	216	1	-	-	?1	2	-	-	-	-	1	-	-	-	1	1	-	12	-	32	-	-	4	-	-
	214	1	-	-	-	-	-	-	-	-	-	-	-	-	-	-	-	2	1	8	-	-	-	-	-
	215	2	-	-	-	-	1	-	-	-	1	-	-	-	-	-	-	-	-	-	-	-	-	-	-
	211	-	-	-	-	-	-	-	1	-	-	-	-	-	-	-	-	1	-	-	-	-	-	-	-
	212	-	-	-	-	-	-	-	-	-	-	-	-	-	-	-	-	1	-	1	-	-	-	-	-
	Total	4	-	-	4	2	1	-	1	1	2	-	-	-	1	1	-	23	1	44	-	-	4	-	-
Soil	202	3	-	1	1	2	5	2	-	-	1	5	1	2	-	-	-	29	12	20	1	1	4	1	19
Tertiary	201	3	-	-	-	-	3	1	-	-	-	1	-	1	-	1	1	4	-	-	-	-	-	-	34
	200	-	-	-	-	-	-	-	-	-	-	-	-	-	-	-	-	-	-	-	-	-	-	-	2
	Total	3	-	-	-	-	3	1	-	-	-	1	-	1	-	1	1	4	-	-	-	-	-	-	36
	Unstrat.	-	-	1	-	-	-	-	-	1	-	-	-	-	-	-	-	-	-	-	-	-	-	-	-
TOTAL		**153**	**2**	**3**	**5**	**4**	**9**	**3**	**1**	**2**	**5**	**6**	**1**	**3**	**1**	**2**	**1**	**56**	**13**	**67**	**1**	**5**	**4**	**1**	**38**
	Backfill	3	4	-	1	-	-	-	-	-	-	-	-	-	-	-	-	2	-	-	-	-	-	-	-

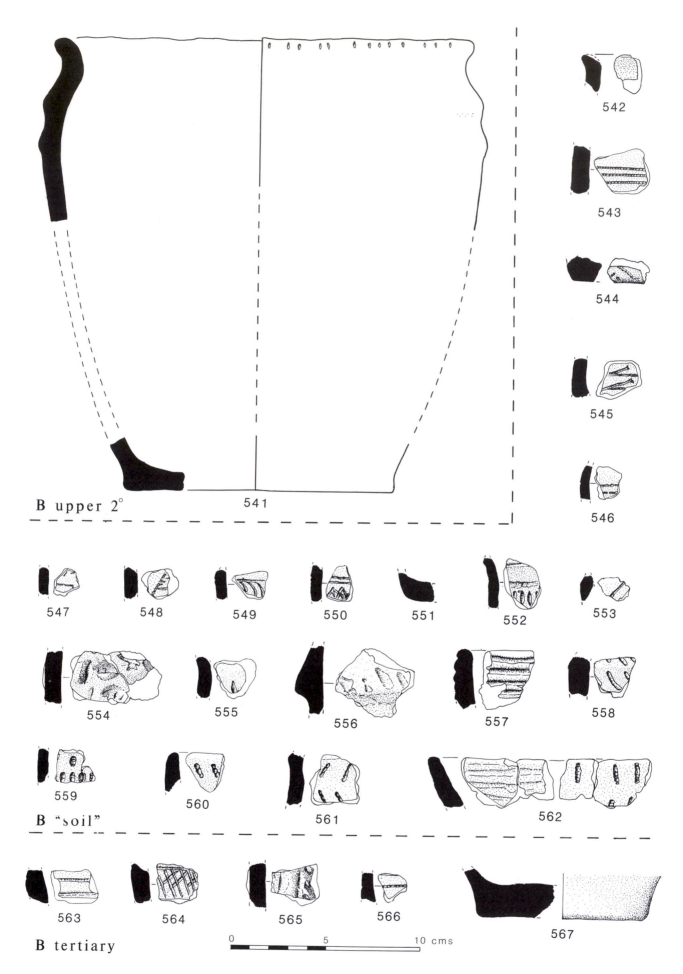

B upper 2°

541

542

543

544

545

546

547   548   549   550   551   552   553

554   555   556   557   558

559   560   561   562

B "soil"

B tertiary

563   564   565   566   567

0   5   10 cms

Fig. 188. Pottery from the outer ditch in Trench B.

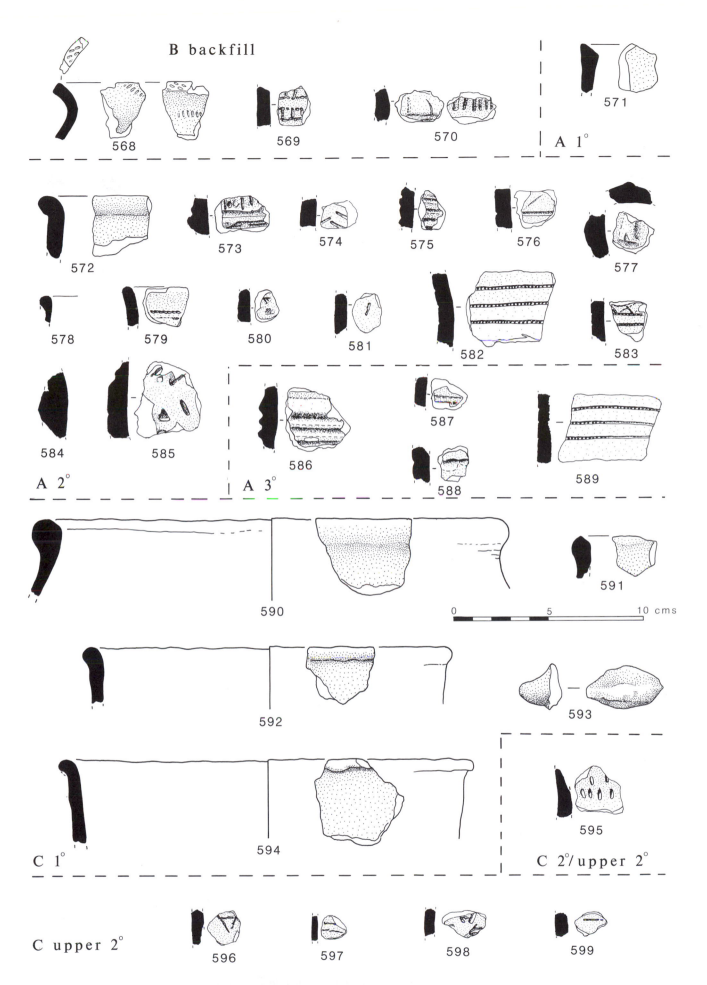

Fig. 189. Pottery from the outer ditch in Trenches B, A and C.

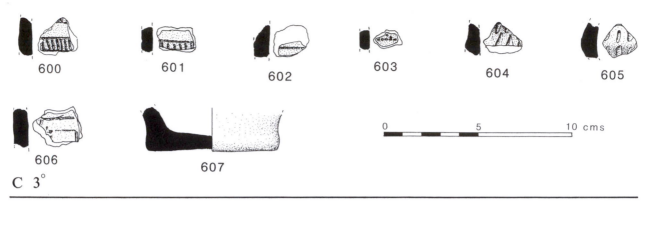

600   601   602   603   604   605

606   607

0   5   10 cms

C 3°

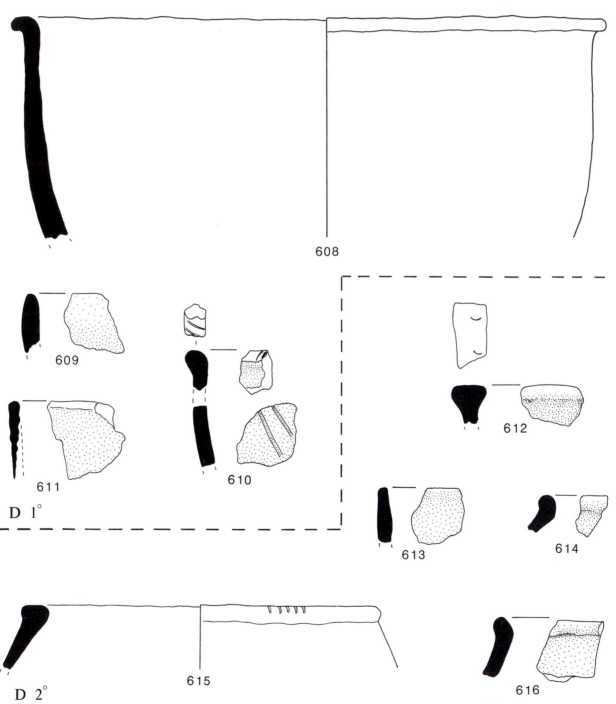

608

609

611   610

612

613   614

D 1°

D 2°   615   616

Fig. 190. Pottery from the outer ditch in Trench B, and the middle ditch in Trench D.

Table 157: Trench A, sherds by style and context.

Sequence	Context	Early Neolithic	Neo 1	Neo 2	GW 2	Bkr 8	Bkr 13	Rus 4	LN/EBA 2	LN/BA 2	BA/IA 6	M/LBA 1	RB
Primary	112	1	-	-	-	-	-	-	-	-	-	-	-
	109	3	-	-	-	-	-	-	-	-	-	-	-
	111	2	1	-	-	-	-	-	-	-	-	-	-
	115	3	1	-	-	-	-	-	-	-	-	-	-
	106	36	11	1	2	-	-	-	-	3	-	-	-
Secondary	110	1	-	-	-	-	-	-	-	-	-	-	-
	?108	15	-	-	-	-	-	-	-	-	-	-	-
	103	1	2	1	-	-	-	-	-	-	-	-	-
	104	9	3	-	5	7	3	7	2	-	-	-	1
	Total	70	18	2	7	7	3	7	2	3	-	-	1
	102	7	-	-	3	3	1	7	-	3	1	1	34
Tertiary	101	-	-	-	-	-	-	-	-	-	-	-	3
	100	-	-	-	-	-	-	-	-	-	-	-	1
	Total	-	-	-	3	3	1	7	-	3	1	1	38
TOTAL		**78**	**18**	**2**	**10**	**10**	**4**	**14**	**2**	**6**	**1**	**1**	**39**

Table 158: Trench C, sherds by style and context.

Sequence	Context	Early Neolithic	Bkr 10	Bkr 11	Bkr 12	Bkr 14	Bkr 16	?Bkr 2	EBA 1	BA/IA 4	BA/IA 6	RB
	324	1	-	-	-	-	-	-	-	-	-	-
	323	1	-	-	-	-	-	-	-	-	-	-
	315	5	-	-	-	-	-	-	-	-	-	-
	315/312	1	-	-	-	-	-	-	-	-	-	-
	312	1	-	-	-	-	-	-	-	-	-	-
	312/308	1	-	-	-	-	-	-	-	-	-	-
Primary	322	1	-	-	-	-	-	-	-	-	-	-
	308	25	-	-	-	-	-	-	-	-	-	-
	309	3	-	-	-	-	-	-	-	-	-	-
	307	1	-	-	-	-	-	-	-	-	-	-
	306	3	-	-	-	-	-	-	-	-	-	-
	319	3	-	-	-	-	-	-	-	-	-	-
	Total	46	-	-	-	-	-	-	-	-	-	-
	305	2	-	-	-	-	-	-	-	-	-	-
Secondary	304	-	-	-	-	-	-	*	-	-	-	-
	303	4	-	-	-	-	-	-	-	-	-	-
	Total	6	-	-	-	-	-	1*	-	-	-	-
Upper	316	1	1	-	1	1	-	*	4	-	-	-
Secondary	317	1	-	1	-	-	-	-	-	-	-	-
	Total	2	1	1	1	1	-	1*	4	-	-	-
	302	2	3	2	-	-	2	3	2	1	4	28
Tertiary	301	1	-	-	-	-	3	-	-	-	-	6
	Total	3	3	2	-	-	5	3	2	1	4	34
TOTAL		**57**	**4**	**3**	**1**	**1**	**5**	**4**	**6**	**1**	**4**	**34**
	Backfill	-	-	-	-	-	-	-	-	-	-	2

* - sherd from 304/316

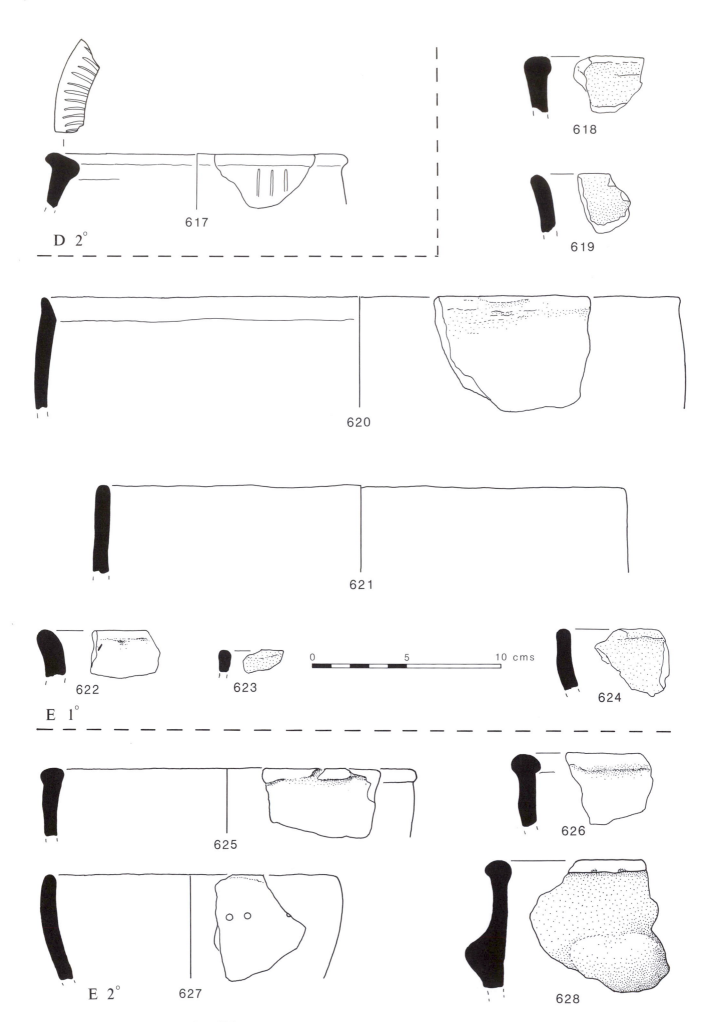

D 2°

617

618

619

620

621

622

623

0   5   10 cms

624

E 1°

625

626

627

628

E 2°

Fig. 191. Pottery from the middle ditch in Trenches D and E.

Table 159: Trench D, sherds by style and context.

| | | | | | Style | | | |
| | | Early | EBA | LN/BA | BA/IA | BA/IA | RB | Mod |
Sequence	Context	Neolithic	1	1	6	7		
	416	75	-	-	-	-	-	-
	417	3	-	-	-	-	-	-
Primary	415	5	-	-	-	-	-	-
	409	6	-	-	-	-	-	-
	Total	89	-	-	-	-	-	-
	411	13	-	-	-	-	-	-
	414	21	-	-	-	-	-	-
Secondary	413	crumbs	-	-	-	-	-	-
	406	-	-	-	1	-	-	-
	?403	-	-	-	-	-	1	-
	404	-	1	1	3	1	4	-
	Total	34	1	1	4	1	5	-
	402	-	-	-	-	-	1	-
Tertiary	401	1	-	-	1	1	5	1
	400	-	-	-	-	-	4	2
	Total	1	-	-	1	1	10	3
TOTAL		**124**	**1**	**1**	**5**	**2**	**15**	**3**

Table 160: Trench E, sherds by style and context.

| | | | | | | | | | Style | | | | | |
| | | Early | GW | GW | LN/BA | ?Bkr | Rus | EBA | EBA | BA/IA | BA/IA | BA/IA | BA/IA | RB |
Sequence	Context	Neolithic	3	4	1	3	3	1	2	4	5	6	7	
	514	1	-	-	-	-	-	-	-	-	-	-	-	-
	527	11	-	-	-	-	-	-	-	-	-	-	-	-
	512	1	-	-	-	-	-	-	-	-	-	-	-	-
	510	20	-	-	-	-	-	-	-	-	-	-	-	-
	510/508	3	-	-	-	-	-	-	-	-	-	-	-	-
	519	1	-	-	-	-	-	-	-	-	-	-	-	-
	520	2	-	-	-	-	-	-	-	-	-	-	-	-
	524	4	-	-	-	-	-	-	-	-	-	-	-	-
	523	1	-	-	-	-	-	-	-	-	-	-	-	-
Primary	506	3	-	-	-	-	-	-	-	-	-	-	-	-
	511	2	-	-	-	-	-	-	-	-	-	-	-	-
	509	7	-	-	-	-	-	-	-	-	-	-	-	-
	508	13	-	-	-	-	-	-	-	-	-	-	-	-
	518	9	-	-	-	-	-	-	-	-	-	-	-	-
	504	14	-	-	-	-	-	-	-	-	-	-	-	-
	525	90	-	-	-	-	-	-	-	-	-	-	-	-
	Total	182	-	-	-	-	-	-	-	-	-	-	-	-
	503	27	-	-	-	-	-	1	-	-	-	-	-	-
Secondary	502	7	3	1	1	-	-	1*	-	-	2**	-	-	-
	Total	34	3	1	1	-	-	2*	-	-	2**	-	-	-
Tertiary	501	4	2	11	20	2	1	1*	6	20	5**	2	2	10
TOTAL		**220**	**5**	**12**	**21**	**2**	**1**	**2**	**6**	**20**	**6***	**2**	**2**	**10**
	Backfill	-	-	-	-	1	-	-	-	3	2	2	-	4

* - This includes a sherd marked 501/502

** - A sherd from 501 conjoins with a sherd from 502

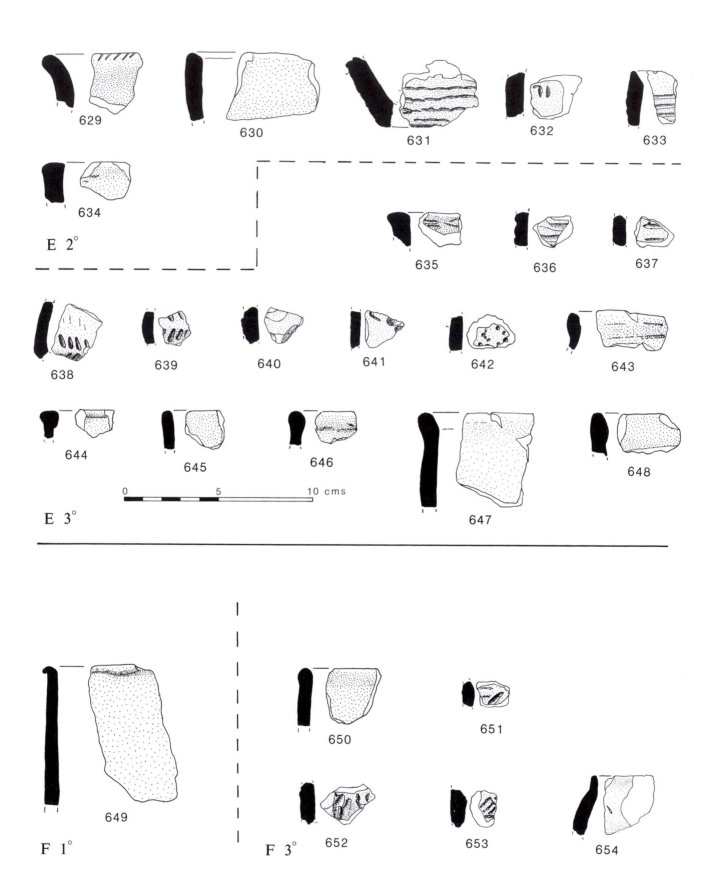

Fig. 192. Pottery from the middle ditch in Trench E and the inner ditch in Trench F.

Table 161: Trench F, sherds by style and context.

Sequence	Context	Early Neolithic	Bkr 9	Rus 1	LN/BA 1	EBA 1	EBA 2	BA/IA 4	BA/IA 7	RB
Primary	610	2	-	-	-	-	-	-	-	-
	630	4	-	-	-	-	-	-	-	-
	629	19	-	-	-	-	-	-	-	-
Secondary	628	7	-	-	-	-	-	-	-	-
	627	1	-	-	-	-	-	-	-	-
	604	4	-	-	-	-	-	-	-	-
	605	2	-	-	-	-	-	-	-	-
	Total	37	-	-	-	-	-	-	-	-
	602	-	2	1	1	3	4	2	-	7
Tertiary	601	-	-	-	-	-	2	-	1	1
	600	1	-	-	-	-	-	-	-	-
	Total	1	2	1	1	3	6	2	1	8
TOTAL		40	2	1	1	3	6	2	1	8
	Backfill	2	-	-	-	-	-	-	1	1

The crushed angular flint inclusions were occasionally as large as 5–7 mm, but were more often 2–3 mm or less. The density of flint also varied as did its distribution. In a relatively small number of cases, the flint was calcined. The flint-tempered sherds contained an admixture of sand, which also varied in terms of grain size, density and distribution. Flint-tempered pottery occurred in grey or dark brown colours.

Fossil shell-temper was also variable in size, frequency and distribution. Slivers of shell were occasionally up to 7–8 mm in length. Some sherds had abundant tiny particles of shell. Some sherds were densely packed with crushed shell. A large number of shell-tempered sherds were partially oxidised, with buff, brown and occasionally reddish surfaces.

A rather smaller group of sherds contained sand, either added or naturally occurring, as the principal recognisable constituent in the fabric. Very few sherds were sandy enough to be described as particularly coarse and granular, with the exception of P625, which also had a sparse addition of shell.

Only a very small number of sherds occurred in other fabrics. A few were a combination of shell- and flint-temper. Some sherds within all the main fabric groups contained small particles of chalk, perhaps accidentally incorporated. A few sherds contained a small amount of grog. Although more often associated with later Neolithic pottery, grog-temper appears to be a recurring if uncommon feature of earlier Neolithic wares, as noted by Smith (1965a, 46). Oolites were identified in only two sherds, occurring as a single grain in both cases. One of those was the lug sherd P593. (Oolitic pottery comprised only c. 0.4 percent of the Keiller assemblage, almost invariably incorporated with shell-temper.)

Fabric origin

Possible origins for the sources of fabrics were suggested by Smith (1965a) and Cornwall and Hodges (1964). Whilst the flint- and sand-tempered pottery was considered to have been manufactured from locally available resources, the shell and shell/oolitic wares were thought to have been imported from a distance of 20 miles away. However, a much closer source can now be postulated. Darvill has noted (1983) the proximity of the Corallian limestone, with its fossil shell and oolitic beds, to the site of Cherhill (9.5 km to the west and north-west of Cherhill and about 12 km from Windmill Hill). The great majority of the pottery at Windmill Hill may have been produced not far away.

Fabric distribution

The distribution (laterally or vertically) of sherds in the different fabrics varies across the 1988 trenches, but given the very limited size of the excavations these differences may not be significant (table 162). It is also clear that large numbers of sherds in some contexts were probably from single vessels, for example, shell-tempered sherds dominate Trench B but most seem to belong to P572. It is also possible that the high incidence of flint-tempered sherds in Trench A mostly belong to P572. The flint-tempered sherds in Trench E could be accounted by two vessels. A sizeable portion of the pottery from Trench D came from a shell-tempered vessel P608.

Table 162: Percentage of fabrics in the 1988 assemblage by trench.

Ditch	Flint	Shell	Sand
B	26	53	21
A	99	1	-
C	44	49	7
D	47	46	7
E	89	7	4
F	92	8	-

If the minimum number of vessels (as defined earlier) rather than the number of sherds is used, then a few variations may be noted. Though flint-tempered vessels represents 53 percent of vessels from the whole 1988 excavations, this increases for the middle ditch, where flint-tempered vessels represent two-thirds of the assemblage. In terms of sequence, shell-tempered vessels are a slight majority under the outer bank in Trench BB. There are no flint-tempered vessels from the small primary assemblage in outer ditch Trench C. However, as noted earlier the small size of the 1988 excavations limits the inferences to be drawn from these distributions and a more coherent picture emerges from the Keiller archive (see later).

Fabric and finish

Pottery in flint- and shell-tempered fabrics was variable in terms of finish. A number of vessels appeared to have been well-made. Amongst the flint-tempered group in particular were a number of hard and compact sherds with a smooth surface finish. Other examples were extremely coarse, with large and protruding flint grains (the result of abrasion in some cases). This variation applied equally to shell-tempered pottery. Both flint- and shell-tempered vessels of coarse and fine quality exhibited traces of burnishing. There are ethnographic examples of burnishing being carried out to enhance the efficiency of cooking pots and also to clog the surface pores. Burnishing need not necessarily be associated with the 'finer' component of any assemblage. As there is sooty encrustation on a large number of sherds, both plain and decorated, a variety of vessels appears to have been employed for cooking. There may have been a distinction between vessels employed in direct heating processes (in the flames) and indirect (over the flames), with coarser fabrics built for greater resistance to thermal shock.

Sherd condition

The condition of sherds has important implications for the understanding of discard and deposition at the enclosure. Whilst a small number of sherds were reasonably fresh, the bulk of the assemblage ranged from moderately to excessively worn sherds. Sherds from the old land surface of Trench BB were, as might be expected, extremely abraded. Most sherds in the assemblage were small. The majority were 2–4 cm (maximum length) on average. A smaller number measured as much as 5–6 cm, and in rarer instances, more. An exceptionally large rim sherd, P608, from the primary fill of Trench D, measured at maximum 20.5 cm. A significant number of flint-tempered sherds from the primary levels of Trench E were crushed to crumbs, incorporated with a spread of bone. Most individual vessels were represented by a very few sherds. In some cases a vessel was represented by rather more sherds, but still the majority of the vessel was missing. This, together with the overall character of sherd size and condition, supports an argument for the middening of material prior to disposal in the ditches.

The extent of sherd weathering appeared to bear little relation to fabric type. Shell-tempered sherds were typically softer than the hard, compact flint-tempered sherds, but the latter did not necessarily always survive in better condition. It is likely that weathering has reduced the recognition of burnishing and originally this may have been more common.

Vessel form and style

The analysis here uses the broad but distinctive division of simple and expanded rims, much as in Smith's report. Of the 43 individual vessels, 63 percent were simple, 37 percent expanded. The same division amongst the Keiller assemblage was 69:31 percent (table 163). Of the 1988 assemblage of vessels, 19 percent were decorated (Keiller: 17 percent).

Table 163: Percentage of rim types in the 1988 assemblage.

	Simple	Expanded
Plain	70	30
Decorated	38	62
All	63	37

Simple rims were more associated with plain vessels (70 percent simple, 30 percent expanded). Stylistically, simple rims could be subdivided into everted, upright and rolled types. Expanded rims comprised rolled, everted, T-shaped, internally projecting and bevelled. All those types can be found amongst Smith's table of rim styles (Smith 1965a, fig. 11). Her A and B groups represented simple types; C to F, expanded forms.

The type most often associated with both simple and expanded rims was rolled, comprising 42 percent of the 1988 rims. Upright rims accounted for 30 percent of simple rims and did not occur with the expanded type. Everted rims tended to occur with simple rims; only one was expanded.

Form could be distinguished for 13 vessels. The three categories of open, closed and neutral forms occurred in roughly equal quantities. All the open bowls (relatively uncommon amongst the Keiller assemblage) came from the outer ditch (Trenches B and A). All the neutral vessels, which comprised the largest group, came from the middle ditch cuttings.

The assemblage demonstrated little distinction generally in the relationship between rim-style or vessel form, and fabric. Whilst all but one of the closed vessels had rolled rims, a variety of rim-types occurred amongst the open and neutral forms. 58 percent of simple rims and 60 percent of expanded rims were flint-tempered, which equates roughly with the overall percentage of flint-tempered sherds for the excavations (63 percent). There are interesting patterns within the decorated pottery which is dealt with below.

Overall, the 1988 sample was too small for meaningful inferences about relationships between form, fabric and decoration. Two closed, one neutral and no open bowls were decorated. There was no evidence for carinated forms, although this may be due to insufficient survival of vessels to allow recognition of such.

In terms of vessel size (taken from the measurement of the outer mouth diameter) a range from 12 cm to 34 cm was present, reflecting the general range present in the larger Keiller assemblage. Most of the assemblage from Windmill Hill as a whole can be assigned to an intermediate size range, of c. 14–25 cm, perhaps a reflection of functional inter-changeability of vessels within that size range. There was no obvious relationship between size, fabric and form. Of the three vessels with mouth diameters of 30 cm or more, two were neutral, whilst one was open.

Five lug sherds, including both solid and perforated types, were recovered in 1988.

Decoration

19 percent of vessels were decorated, including the decorated body sherd P2. Of these, 62 percent had expanded, and 38 percent simple, rims. (P501 most likely had a simple rim, to judge from close parallels to vessels with similar pin-prick decoration published by Smith.) The relative occurrence of the two rim-styles amongst the decorated component was very similar to that in the Keiller assemblage (64:36 percent). The decorated vessels find good parallels with those published by Smith. All but two of the decorated sherds came from the middle circuit, where seven of a total of 22 vessels were decorated (32 percent). The two remaining vessels came from Trench BB.

The decorated group could be divided equally between shell- and flint-tempered vessels (four each). The flint-tempered sherds were equally divided between expanded and simple rims (two each), whereas there was a strong relationship between expanded rims and shell-tempered sherds (3 out of 4 vessels). The least frequent association amongst the decorated pottery was between shell-tempered vessels and simple rims.

The range of decorative motifs all find parallels amongst Smith's collection. In two cases rims were incised with narrow scored lines (P610 and 629). In three cases they were decorated with deeper grooves (P615, 617 and one unillustrated). Similar channelled decoration occurred on the upper part of a vessel body (unillustrated); in one instance where the rim was similarly decorated (P617), in another where the rim had been scored (P610). One expanded rim had very faint finger-nail impressions (P612). There were two examples of pin-prick decoration (including the body sherd, P501). There were no observable relationships between decorative motif, fabric and vessel style.

The decorated sherds were generally small and it was difficult to reconstruct original form. P512, P610, P625, P627 and probably P501 were uncarinated bowls. P629 could have been carinated. P612 was too fragmentary to

permit any judgement. Although there was no definite evidence for such, the two closed vessels, P615 and P617, could have been carinated, to judge from examples of similar vessels in Smith's figs 26 and 27 (Smith 1965a).

Context and vessel style

Outer bank and ditches (figs 186–90). With the exception of Trench BB, both expanded and simple rims occurred together in the same cutting. BB produced only vessels with simple rims, and Smith had also noted the absence of expanded rims in her excavations under the outer bank in cuttings IV–VI. P501 and P512 from BB were decorated, which contradicts Smith's findings that no decorated sherds came from under the outer bank (Smith 1965a, 58). Vessels with simple rims were in a slight majority (57 percent) in the outer circuit. That type was especially dominant in Trench B, both in primary and secondary layers. Two vessels with perforations came from Trench B (P516 and 520). One other vessel was probably a cup or small bowl (P517). Lugs occurred in outer Trenches B and C (as well as in middle ditch in Trench E).

There was no decorated pottery from any of the 1988 outer ditch cuttings (in contrast to the Keiller assemblage).

Middle ditches (figs 190–92). The middle ditch produced the most varied range of both plain and decorated vessels, 22 in all, almost half the total number of minimum vessels. The number of vessels was evenly divided between primary and secondary levels as a whole. Of the twelve simple rims (two decorated) from cuttings D and E, nine came from primary contexts. Simple rim-types were in a majority in the primary layers of both Trench E and D. Eight out of the ten expanded rims (seven decorated) came from secondary levels. Of the two which came from a primary context, one was decorated (P610), representing the only decorated vessel from a primary context.

In the secondary levels of Trench E, decorated vessels with both simple and expanded rims occurred together, whilst in Trench D only decorated vessels with expanded rims were found. All the decorated sherds from Trench D were associated with bone deposits. Trench D produced the largest collection, four in all, of decorated vessels from any one of the 1988 cuttings. Three decorated bowls came from Trench E.

Inner ditch (fig. 192). The assemblage from the smaller inner ditch in Trench F produced only plain pottery, almost half of which belonged to single vessel (P649). This was flint-tempered with a simple and very fine, rolled rim.

Context, sequence and deposition

Further details of context and other depositions (e.g. animal bone) are given in chapters 4, 11 and 17, but it is important and relatively rare to be able to consider the pottery directly in connection with other material.

Outer bank, Trench BB. 91 sherds (11 percent of the assemblage) came from Trench BB. Although most contexts produced a few sherds, 48 percent of the pottery was recovered from contexts associated with the old land surface. P501 and P503 came from a sealed context (741) beneath the bank.

Pottery consisted of very worn, mostly small scraps. All the rims were simple and decorated pottery also occurred. There was also a lug (P508). Apart from the absence of expanded rims, the pottery was no different to much of that recovered from the enclosure ditches. The decorated sherd, P512, came from re-deposited material, part of the primary bank make-up. The other decorated sherd, P501, was recovered from the old land surface. A few, mostly small, sherds of pottery were found in the grave (707), including a very worn rim, P500. Those sherds could possibly have tumbled into the grave if it had been left open for any length of time, which the presence of small mammal and amphibian bones indicates. A rim, P513, came from the tail of the bank (701), where there were also sherds of Ebbsfleet pottery, as well as Later Neolithic, Early and Late Bronze Age sherds and a Romano-British sherd. Other pottery, P502 and P504, came from the old land surface (741) and (705).

None of the sherds could be said with any certainty to have been recovered from the context where they were originally deposited. The condition of most sherds suggested that they had suffered exposure to the elements and to other post-depositional processes. In terms of style and fabric, the pottery was not at variance to the pottery from the enclosure ditches.

Outer ditch, Trench B. 20 percent (156 sherds) of the assemblage came from this trench, the largest of the cuttings. 85 percent of sherds came from the primary fill, with very little pottery of any type being recorded from secondary contexts. All the pottery was plain; two-thirds of the rims were simple, including the two rims from secondary and upper-secondary contexts. All the rim sherds, apart from those belonging to P516, came from five separate vessels, and few of the rim-sherds had any matching body sherds. Although less than half of P516 was represented (about 100 moderately worn sherds and small fragments), the sherds were found fairly close together (some with a bone deposit) although not in a coherent cluster. These sherds came from three contiguous layers, the majority from 229 and 228, with a small amount from 210, and probably represent a single act of deposition.

The illustrated sherds were all associated with a series of bone spreads which occurred in the lowest part of 228, the basal chalk rubble, and in 229, a layer of fragmented chalk. Another bone deposit occurred in the top part of 210, in 227, at the interface of the primary and secondary fill, which also produced a small worn Ebbsfleet sherd, P522. (Ebbsfleet sherds also occurred in the equivalent layer of Smith's adjacent cutting V, and probably belong to the same vessel.) The rarity of matching body sherds for most rims, and the absence of most of P516, suggest that the pottery from the primary fill was unlikely to have been disposed of immediately after breakage. The pottery was abraded, but not in all cases excessively.

A few Early Neolithic sherds came from secondary contexts, including P523. A small, weathered Ebbsfleet sherd, P524 (probably the same vessel as P522), came from a secondary context. There was a very small number (12) of residual early Neolithic sherds in the upper-secondary and tertiary levels.

Trench A. 10 percent (79 sherds) of the assemblage came from Trench A. In contrast to the other outer cuttings, a far greater quantity came from the secondary layers. Only 1 percent of the pottery came from the primary silts (P571), an excessively abraded rim-sherd from 112, immediately beneath a bone spread. The sherd may have lain around on the ground surface for some time prior to deposition in the ditch. Of the pottery from the secondary silts, 72 percent (53 sherds) belonged to a single vessel (P572). Both vessels from this cutting had expanded rims. All the pottery was plain.

The sherds belonging to P572 came from a series of contiguous layers, with the majority of sherds coming from two contexts: 106, a dark, humic lens within which was a concentration of charcoal-flecked and burnt bone fragments (110); and 108, a thin spread of brown soil. One of the rim-sherds came from a dump of cattle ribs in 115/111. Many of the sherds were comparatively fresh, although none was particularly large. In contrast to much of the pottery from the assemblage as a whole, these sherds may not have been exposed for any great length of time and could have been deposited not long after breakage.

Trench C. 7 percent (57 sherds) came from this cutting. Of those, 80 percent came from the primary fill, a similar picture to that of Trench B. A few sherds were recovered from the basal chalk rubble, which was overlain towards the inner part of the ditch by 315 which produced P591 and P594. P590 and P592 came from higher up the primary silts, in a localised, brown silty lens with some scattered animal bone (319). Only six sherds came from the secondary fill, where there was very little pottery of any type. Five Early Neolithic sherds came from the upper secondary and tertiary fills.

All the pottery was plain, and included an equal number of both simple and expanded rims. There appears to have been comparatively little deposition in the primary, but more in the secondary fill.

Middle ditch, Trench D. 18 percent (145 sherds) of the assemblage came from Trench D. Sherds from primary contexts were in the majority. Of the pottery from primary contexts, 43 percent came from a single vessel, P608. Much of the pottery in the primary fill consisted of comminuted fragments and crumbs. Very few body sherds could be matched with the rim-sherds. Both simple and expanded rims were present, with five out of the six expanded rims coming from secondary levels, whilst three of the four simple rims came from primary contexts. Decorated pottery occurred in both primary and secondary contexts, with three of the four examples coming from the latter. All the decorated vessels had expanded rims and occurred equally in both flint- and shell-tempered fabrics.

Plain and decorated sherds (P608 and P610) were recovered from the basal chalk rubble, 416, on the floor of the ditch. P608 consisted of a particularly large rim sherd (as well as numerous body sherds), measuring up to 20.5 cm, the largest sherd in the assemblage. 31 body sherds were also identified as belonging to P608. The outer surface of the large sherd was pock-marked, quite deeply in places, with a variety of seed and other vegetal impressions. P609 came from a discrete patch of dark soil and charcoal, 417, within the basal rubble, 416. Both P608 and P610 were closely associated with a spread of bone. Another vessel was represented by P611, from a little higher up in the primary fill, in 415.

Most of the sherds from the secondary fill came from closely associated layers, the majority from three contexts, 411, 408 and 406, a series of contiguous dark brown, humic silts. A decorated and a plain rim, P612 and P613, came from 411 which also contained two successive bone deposits which were adjacent to an interleaved bundle of ribs and other bones (414) together with much fragmented pottery. Other crushed pot sherds were associated with a concentrated dump of bone (413). The crushed pottery with spreads of bone recall a very similar picture from Trench E (below). Plain and decorated sherds, P614, P615, P616 and P617, came from the layers immediately above 411 (408, 406 and 404), layers of dark silt with scatters of bone and charcoal. All the decorated pottery was associated with deposits of bone.

A link between the primary and secondary fill was provided by a body sherd from low in the secondary silt (414), which was part of P609 from the base of the ditch (417). A single Early Neolithic sherd came from the tertiary fill.

A rather more intensive level of depositional activity could be recognised in Trench D. Pottery, much of it crushed, was associated with bone spreads and dumps and discrete localised patches of dark soil and charcoal, both in primary and secondary layers. There was no observable difference between primary and secondary activity, and deposition, whilst possibly episodic in character, may have been closely-spaced in terms of time.

Trench E. 27 percent of the assemblage (213 sherds) came from Trench E. 82 percent of sherds came from primary contexts, of which 60 percent belonged to two vessels, P621 and P622. Both plain and decorated pottery was recovered from this cutting, with all three decorated vessels coming from secondary contexts. Whilst all but one of the rims from the primary silts were simple, there was a more even balance between simple and expanded rim-styles in the secondary layers.

Three body sherds belonging to both P621 and P622 came from a secondary context, providing a link between the primary and secondary fill. Further links between primary and secondary levels was provided by P 618, which was represented by a rim-sherd from a primary context, 510 and a (non-joining) rim-sherd from a second-

ary context, 503. Furthermore, P628, which was represented by a rim-sherd from 503, was possibly part of the same vessel as P618. Some of the sherds, notably those from 525, a significant deposit of animal bone, were fresh, with sharp edges. Some were burnt. Most of the sherds from these vessels came from a single context, 525, with a smaller amount from 518.

Only a single sherd came from the lowest levels of the ditch (514). A few sherds occurred in the chalk runs and silt lenses at the inner side of the ditch and in the loose brown soil at the outer side. There were sherds of pottery associated with a bone spread in 527, which lay just above the base of the ditch. A small number of sherds were associated with a matrix of brown soil, flecks of charcoal, burnt chalk and a small concentration of bones (524). Overlying that group of material in 510 were rims from two vessels, P618 and P620 and, in the top of the layer (523) a large, concentrated spread of bone and a rim from P619. Generally only about half a dozen, mostly small (the largest being 6.5 cm), sherds occurred in contexts other than 525.

The majority of primary sherds came from the dark humic lens (525) which comprised a spread of bone and charcoal immediately overlying angular chalk rubble towards the outer side of the ditch. Sherds also came from 508, in the base of 525, with a significant deposit of bone, a little burnt chalk and many fragments of charcoal. Much of the pottery from 525 comprised small fragments and many crushed crumbs (altogether about 80 countable pieces) from which a single vessel represented by its rim could be recognised (P621). As noted above, many of these sherds and fragments were quite fresh, despite the small size of most of the material. Sherds belonging to P622 may also have been amongst this group. Sherds representing P624 came from an oval scoop of loose brown soil (504), which also produced a small concentration of large bone and several flint flakes. One fairly extensive bone spread (522) did not produce any pottery.

Pottery in the primary fill of Trench E was associated with a series of contiguous bone spreads and with deliberately cut scoops of humic soil containing bone and a little flint. Only one context (525) produced pottery in any reasonable quantity.

There was overall little pottery in the shallower secondary silts of the ditch. There were 34 sherds in all, mostly featureless scraps, but including the three decorated vessels, P625, P627 and P629. One other vessel had a lug attachment (P628). Most of the pottery came from a single context (503), a layer of dark humic silt with a scatter of bones. Only Early Neolithic pottery came from the secondary fill. Body sherds belonging to vessels from a primary context (525) were recovered from 503; and the base of 503 (528) was closely associated with 504 and 518 in the primary fill. 528 was a spread of bone and flint, and there was no pottery directly associated with it, although there were a few sherds higher in the secondary silt (502).

Inner ditch, Trench F. 7 percent of the assemblage (54 sherds) came from the small cutting in the inner circuit. Just under 70 percent of the pottery came from the secondary fill. The primary chalk fill was virtual sterile of finds; only two sherds of pottery were recovered, from the smaller chalk rubble and silt (610) on the inner side of the ditch. Only one vessel, P649, was represented. 44 percent of the pottery from the secondary contexts (628 and 629) also belonged to that vessel. (A small rim sherd from P649 was also recovered from the tertiary fill in 602.) Several of the sherds were comparatively large and quite fresh,

although most of the sherds from the secondary fill consisted of miscellaneous scraps. All the pottery from the trench was plain (Smith recovered some decorated sherds from her adjacent cutting XVII), and over 90 percent was flint-tempered.

The sherds belonging to P649 were recovered from a series of laterally or vertically adjacent deposits in the secondary fill: 604, 605, 630, 629 and 628. 630, 629 and 628 were bone deposits placed in the lower part of 604. 629 produced most of the sherds from P649. 628, a linear spread of dark soil with scattered, smaller bone, produced two

Table 164: The outer ditch assemblage from excavations by Kendall, Keiller and Smith by style and context.

	Total Sherds	Early Neolithic	Ebbsfleet	Mortlake	Fengate	Undia. PW	LN/EBA
Kendall's Excavation							
18"	?	?	-	-	-	-	-
2-3'	?	?	-	(P278)	-	-	-
6'	?	?(P198a)	-	-	-	-	-
Bottom at 6.3'	?	?(P227)	-	-	-	-	-
Outer Ditch I (max depth 8.7')							
Excavation	44	31	-	-	1(P352)	-	-
At 2.5'	10	-	-	-	-	-	-
At 3.2'	2	-	2(P333)	-	-	-	-
Re-excavation	30	-	-	1	-	-	-
Outer Ditch Ib(8.7')**							
Surface - 1'	101	**	-	2	3(P280; 353)	-	-
1 - 2'	51	**	-	-	1(P280)	-	-
2 - 3'	18	**	-	-	-	-	-
3 - 4'	36	**	-	-	-	-	-
4 - 5'	20	**	-	-	-	-	-
5 - 6'	37	**(P73)	-	-	-	-	-
6 - 7'	36	**(=P73)	-	-	-	-	-
7 - 8'	44	**(P224)	-	-	-	-	-
Outer Ditch Ic(8.7')**							
Surface - 1'	247	**	-	-	-	1	-
1 - 2'	34	**	9(P253)	-	1(P280)	-	1
2 - 3'	40	**(P56)	5(P253)	-	-	-	-
3 - 4'	43	**	-	-	-	-	-
4 - 5'	54	**(P84; P113)	-	-	-	-	-
5 - 6'	10	**	-	-	-	-	-
6 - Bottom	5	**	-	-	-	-	-
Outer Ditch II (9.6')							
Surface - 0.8'	211	13(P102)	-	-	-	1	37 + 4*(P368-9)
0.8 - 1.4'	191	20(P102)	-	-	3(P276)	-	26(P316)
1.4 - 2.3'	171	25(P102)	-	1(P348)	-	-	36(P315)
2.3 - 3.5'	89	64(P101; P102)	-	-	-	-	8
At 2.6'		-	-	-	-	-	-
3'		(P113)	-	-	-	-	-
3.5 - 5'		(P166)	-	-	-	-	-
3.5 - 6'	156	156 (P102)	-	-	-	-	-
6 '- Bottom (8.32')	28	28 (P102)	-	-	-	-	-
Causeway	1	0	-	-	-	-	-
Refill	17	10	-	-	-	-	1
Outer Ditch V (Smith)							
Layer 2	?	-	-	-	-	-	-
Layer 3	?	-	-	-	-	-	4(P272; 317)
Layer 4	3	-	-	-	-	-	-
Layer 5	6	-	6(P237)	-	-	-	-
Layer 6	8	8	-	-	-	-	-
Bottom of ditch	4	4	-	-	-	-	-
Bank VI (Smith)							
Excavation	c. 50	c.50	-	-	-	-	-

quite large, but non-joining rim sherds of P649. The related deposit, 627, produced a single sherd from another vessel.

The Keiller assemblage: a study of spatial patterning

Some 20,000 sherds, the majority Early Neolithic, were recovered by Keiller. A shortcoming of Smith's report (1965a) was that the majority of the illustrated vessels remained contextually anonymous. It has been possible to identify in the Alexander Keiller Museum the context of

133 out of the 236 Early Neolithic vessels illustrated by Smith. Fresh analysis of the assemblage suggests the differential distribution and patterning of particular types of pottery within the enclosure during possibly episodic sequences of activity. Sequence, stylistic variability and the contexts of deposition can be examined, using samples from provenanced drawings (133 vessels) in the Keiller archive. Tables 164–66 (cf. tables 1–44) list the segment and depth of all provenanced vessels, as well as sherd numbers. It is possible to suggest vertical and horizontal spatial patterning of vessels which could point to a

*Key: * LN/BA Material not seem by MAH; ** after mid-1927 the pottery archive is less detailed. One can probably assume that most of the pottery is Early Neolithic; ~ this indicates conflict between drawing of Smith 1965 and MAH; = similar to*

GW	BK	Grog/ Rus	EBA	BA	RB	Not Pot
-	?3	-	-	-	?	-
-	-	-	-	-	-	-
-	-	-	-	-	-	-
-	-	-	-	-	-	-
-	3	-	-	-	9	-
10(P314)	-	-	-	-	-	-
-	-	-	-	-	-	-
-	-	-	-	-	-	-
11(P279~; P361-2)	3	-	1(P371)	-	-	-
2(P284; P363)	2	-	-	-	-	-
6(284)	1	-	-	-	-	-
-	-	-	-	-	-	-
-	-	-	-	-	-	-
-	-	-	-	-	-	-
-	-	-	-	-	-	-
-	-	-	-	-	-	-
-	14(P300; P304)	-	?6	?1	-	-
1(P364)	6(P300)	-	-	-	?	-
-	?1	-	-	-	?	-
-	-	-	-	-	-	-
-	-	-	-	-	-	-
-	-	-	-	-	-	-
-	-	-	-	-	-	-
-	74 + 4*(P294; 305; 307)	26(P315)	-	4	45	3
1	69 + 6*	14(P298)	8(P273; P370; P372)	8	30	6
-	63 + 8*(P294; 303)	24(P315)	3(P373-4)	8*	3	-
-	8 + 1*	2	2	2	2	-
-	-	-	1(P320)	-	-	-
-	-	-	-	-	-	-
-	-	-	-	-	-	-
-	-	-	-	-	-	-
-	1	-	-	-	-	-
-	2	-	-	1	3	-
-	1	-	-	-	1	2
1(P289)	18	2	Many (P323; 275; 274~; P376-8)	-	-	-
-	-	-	-	-	-	-
-	-	-	-	-	-	-
-	-	-	-	-	-	-
-	-	-	-	-	-	-
-	-	-	-	-	-	-

Table 165: *The middle ditch pottery assemblage from excavations by Kendall, Keiller and Smith, by style and context. Key: * LN/BA Material not seen by MAH; ** after mid-1927 the pottery archive is less detailed. One can probably assume that most of the pottery is Early Neolithic; ~ this indicates conflict between drawing of Smith 1965a and MAH; = similar to; ~ list found in Alexander Keiller Museum; # - drawing differs from Gibson 1982, fig WH1.13.*

	Total Sherds	Early Neolithic	Ebbsfleet	Mortlake	Fengate	Undiagn. PW	?LN/EBA	GW	BK	RUS	BA	RB etc	Not Pot
Middle Ditch I (Max depth 5.8')													
Surface - 3.5'	62	47 (=P212); (P197)	-	2(P266; P341)	-	-	-	?5	3 + 2*	-	-	3	-
4.4'	-	-	-	-	-	-	-	-	-	-	-	-	-
3.5' to lowest foot of silt	86	86	-	-	-	-	-	-	-	-	-	-	-
Lowest foot of silt	30	30	-	-	-	-	-	-	-	-	-	-	-
Surface to lowest 1' of silt	31	31 (P42)	-	-	-	-	-	-	-	-	-	-	-
Surface - lowest 1' of silt/re-ex.	4	4	-	-	-	-	-	-	1	-	-	-	-
Re-excavation	33	-	-	-	-	-	-	-	-	-	-	-	-
Middle Ditch Ib(5.8')**													
Surface - 1'	179	-	-	-	-	5(P319)	-	-	-	-	-	-	-
1 - 2'	83	(P142)	-	-	-	7(P319)	-	-	-	-	-	-	-
2 - 3'	108	(P35)	-	-	-	-	-	-	-	-	-	-	-
3 - 4'	222	(P25: 85: 148: 152: 212)	-	-	-	-	-	-	-	-	-	-	-
4' - Bottom	38	-	-	-	-	-	-	-	4*	-	-	-	-
Layer not specified--	-	-	-	-	-	-	-	-	-	-	-	-	-
Middle Ditch I - II**													
Causeway	7	**	-	-	-	-	-	-	-	-	-	-	-
Middle Ditch II (7')													
Excavation	63	37	1(P254)	4(P222)	-	-	-	15(P283)	5	1	-	-	-
2.75'	-	-	-	1(P222)	-	-	-	-	-	-	-	-	-
2.8'	-	(P130)	-	-	-	-	-	-	-	-	-	-	-
Bottom	28	28 (P178)	-	-	-	-	-	-	-	-	-	-	-
Re-excavation	56	45(P184)	1	-	-	-	-	1(P355)	1	-	-	5	-
Middle Ditch IIb (7')													
Surface - 0.8'	158	110	7(P238; 252; 255; P328-9)	1(P342)	-	1 + 2*	3	2(P356)	14(P292)	-	-	17	-
0.8 - 1.4'	418	279	49(P238; 250; 252; 254-5; 246~; P330-1)	5(P343-4)	-	1	4(P367)	6(P285#; P357-8)	56(P292)	1	-	17	-
1.4 - 2.3'	505	331 (P38; P98; P196)	160(P238-9; 242; 250; 252; P254-5; 245~; P332)	-	-	7	1	-	3	-	-	3	-
2.3 - 3.5'	425	419 (P37; P70; P95)	4 (P250; 252; 254)	-	-	-	1	-	-	-	-	-	-
3.5 - 5'	305	304 (P37; P177)	1(P255)	-	-	-	-	-	-	-	-	-	-
4'	-	(P221)	-	-	-	-	-	-	-	-	-	-	-
4.4'	-	(P155)	-	-	-	-	-	-	-	-	-	-	-
Bottom (3.5 - 5')	17	17	-	-	-	-	-	-	-	-	-	-	-
5' - Bottom	43	43	-	-	-	-	-	-	-	-	-	-	-
Refill	56	45	5(P250)	-	-	1 + 2*	1*	-	-	-	-	-	-
Middle Ditch III (4.1')													
Surface - 3'	95	86	-	-	-	?3	-	-	2	-	-	4	-
3'	-	(P75)	-	-	-	-	-	-	-	-	-	-	-
3.5'	-	(P33)	-	-	-	-	-	-	-	-	-	-	-
3' to bottom	126	126 (P33; P61; P99; P105)	-	-	-	-	-	-	-	-	-	-	-
Re-excavation	51	46 (P178)	-	-	-	-	-	-	-	-	-	5	-
Middle Ditch III - IV													
Causeway	11	4	-	-	-	-	-	-	-	-	-	6	1
Middle Ditch IV (4.5')													
Surface - 1.5'	96	87 (P82; 141; 174)	-	-	-	-	-	-	-	-	-	9	-
3.3'	-	(P106)	-	-	-	-	-	-	-	-	-	-	-

Table 165 continued

	Total Sherds	Early Neolithic	Ebbsfleet	Mortlake	Fengate	Undiagn. PW	?LN/EBA	GW	BK	RUS	BA	RB etc	Not Pot
4.75'	-	(P69)											
Bottom foot	-	(P173)											
1.5' - bottom	172	170 (P76)										2	
Re-excavation	110	95							1			14	
Middle Ditch IVb (4.5')													
Surface - 0.8'	109	71 (P178)			2(P282~)							36	
0.8 - 1.4'	114	79 (P217)			16(P270)							17	2
1.4 - 2.3'	158	153 (P78; P120)			4(P282~)							1	
2.3 - 3.5'	68	68 (P39)											
3.5' - Bottom	36	36 (P45)											
Refill	35	27										8	
Middle Ditch V(4.0')**													
Surface - 0.8'	67	**											
0.8 - 1.4'	52	**											
1.4 - 2.3'	311	**(P151: 195)											
2.3 - 3.5'	83	**(P37)											
3.5' - Bottom	2	**											
Refill	3	**											
Middle Ditch VI(6')**													
Surface - 0.8'	40	**		=P318*									
0.8 - 1.4'	40	**											
1.4 - 2.3'	48	**(P147)											
2.3 - 3.5'	256	**											
3.5 - Bottom	104	**											
Refill	1	**											
Re-excavation	72	**											
Middle Ditch VII(5')**													
Surface - 1'	130	**(P168)	1 (P244)						9(P296)	2			9
1 - 2'	98	**(P125)	1	5(P345-6)			2						
2 - 3'	266	**(P34; 77: 152; 180; 192)		1		1							
3 - 4'	464	**(P47: 60: 174)											
4' - Bottom	212	**(P54: 97: 107)											
Middle Ditch VIII(3.5')**													
Surface - 1'	67	**	5(P251)			1			1				
1 - 2'	205	**	79(P251; P256)			10							
2 - 3'	136	**(=P212; P78)											
3' - Bottom	34	**(P78)							1*				
Layer not specified--						11							
Middle Ditch IX(4.8')**													
Surface - 1'	43	**							3				
1 - 2'	40	**											
2 - 3'	122	**(P214)											
3' - Bottom	103	**(P44; 226)											
Middle Ditch Xa(5.9')**													
Surface - 1'	152	**	1(P247)	1(P260~)	1(P271)								
1 - 2' (2a)	109	**(P172: 225)			15(P271)	1							
1 - 2' (2b)	104	**(P206)											

Table 165 continued

	Total Sherds	Early Neolithic	Ebbsfleet	Mortlake	Fengate	Undiagn. PW	?LN/ EBA	GW	BK	RUS	BA	RB etc	Not Pot
2 - 3' (3a)	152	**(P223)	-	-	-	-	-	-	-	-	-	-	-
2 - 3' (3b)	118	**(P161; 182; 223)	-	-	-	-	-	-	-	-	-	-	-
3 - 4' (4a)	22	**(P83)	-	-	-	-	-	-	-	-	-	-	-
3 - 4' (4b)	116	**(P83)	-	-	-	-	-	-	-	-	-	-	-
4 - 5'	31	**(P103)	-	-	-	-	-	-	-	-	-	-	-
Refill	9	**	-	-	-	-	-	-	-	-	-	-	-
Middle Ditch Xb(5.9')**													
Surface - 1'	99	**	-	-	-	-	-	1(P359)	?	-	-	-	-
1 - 2' (2a)	44	**(P83)	-	-	-	-	-	-	1	-	-	-	-
1 - 2' (2b)	42	**(P83; 150)	-	1 (P264)	-	-	-	-	?	-	-	?	-
2 - 3' (3a)	152	**(P150; P183)	-	-	-	-	-	-	-	-	-	-	-
2 - 3' (3b)	146	**(P43; P92; P145; P150)	-	-	-	-	-	-	-	-	-	-	-
3 - 4' (4a)	30	**(P92; P150)	-	-	-	-	-	-	-	-	-	-	-
3 - 4' (4b)	16	**(P31; P150)	-	-	-	-	-	-	-	-	-	-	-
4 - 5'	102	**(P36; P59)	-	-	-	-	-	-	-	-	-	-	-
5 - 6'	25	**	-	-	-	-	-	-	-	-	-	-	-
Refill	7	**	-	-	-	-	-	-	-	-	-	-	-
Middle Ditch X1a(5')**													
Surface - 1'	131	**	-	3(P374)	-	-	-	-	-	-	-	-	-
1 - 2' (2a)	80	**(P233)	-	4(P258)	-	-	-	1(P360)	3	-	-	1	-
1 - 2' (2b)	35	**(P233)	-	1(P258)	-	-	-	-	-	-	-	-	-
2 - 3' (3a)	116	**(P167; P198c)	-	-	-	-	-	-	-	-	-	-	-
2 - 3' (3b)	64	**	-	-	-	-	-	-	-	-	-	-	-
3 - 4'	25	**	-	-	-	-	-	-	-	-	-	-	-
4 - 5'	11	**	-	-	-	-	-	-	-	-	-	-	-
Refill	16	**	-	-	-	-	1	-	-	-	-	-	-
Middle Ditch X1b(5')**													
Surface - 1'	102	**	-	-	-	-	-	-	2	-	-	-	-
1 - 2' (2a)	114	**(P233)	-	-	-	-	-	-	-	-	-	-	-
1 - 2' (2b)	79	**(P233)	-	-	-	-	-	-	-	-	-	-	-
2 - 3' (3a)	273	**(P72; P188)	-	-	-	-	-	-	-	-	-	-	-
2 - 3' (3b)	234	**(P94; P132; P186; P228)	-	-	-	-	-	-	-	-	-	-	-
3 - 4' (4a)	120	**	-	-	-	-	-	-	-	-	-	-	-
3 - 4' (4b)	41	**	-	-	-	-	-	-	-	-	-	-	-
4 - 5'	27	**	-	-	-	-	-	-	-	-	-	-	-
Refill	37	**	-	-	-	-	-	-	-	-	-	-	-
Middle Ditch XII (Smith)													
Layer 2	90	Yes	-	-	-	-	?	?	?	?	?	6	-
Layer 3	1	1	-	-	-	-	-	-	-	-	-	-	-
Layer 4	6	6	-	-	-	-	-	-	-	-	-	-	-
Layer 5	14	14	-	-	-	-	-	-	-	-	-	-	-

*Table 166: The inner ditch pottery assemblage from excavations by Kendall, Keiller and Smith, by style and context. Key: * LN/BA Material not seen by MAH; ** after mid-1927 the pottery archive is less detailed. One can probably assume that most of the pottery is Early Neolithic; ~ this indicates conflict between drawing of Smith 1965a and MAH; = similar to.*

	Total Sherds	Early Neolithic	Ebbsfleet	Mortlake Ware	Fengate Ware	Undiagn. PW	?LN/ EBA	GW	BK	Grog & Rustic.	EBA	RB etc	?
Inner Ditch I (Max depth 3')													
1-1.5'	18	11	-	2(P269)	-	-	-	-	1*	-	-	4	-
1' - bottom, west side	28	25	-	-	-	-	-	-	-	-	-	3	-
1.5' - bottom	15	15(P15; 124)	-	-	-	-	-	-	-	-	-	-	-
2.1' bottom of black earth	10	9	1(P240)	-	-	-	-	-	-	-	-	-	-
Re-excavation	34	29	-	1	-	-	-	-	-	-	-	4	-
Inner Ditch I - II													
Surface - 0.8'	32	25	-	-	-	-	-	-	-	-	-	7	-
0.8 - 1.4'	125	96(P86; 124)	-	1(P334)	-	-	-	-	3	1	-	24	-
1.4 - 2.3'	168	168(P86; 169)	-	-	-	-	-	-	-	-	-	-	-
2.3' - Bottom	21	21(P86)	-	-	-	-	-	-	-	-	-	-	-
Refill	19	17	-	-	-	-	-	-	-	-	-	2	-
Inner Ditch II (5')													
Surface - 1.5'	25	15	-	5(P267)	-	-	-	-	1	-	-	3	1
1.5' - Bottom (2.2')	63	62(=P78; P86; 124)	-	-	-	-	-	-	-	-	-	1	-
Re-excavation	28	25	-	-	-	-	-	-	-	-	-	3	-
Inner Ditch IIb (5')													
Surface - 0.8'	13	13	-	-	-	-	-	-	-	-	-	-	-
0.8-1.4'	31	28	-	-	-	-	-	-	-	-	-	3	-
1.4 - 2.3'	81	81 (P54; 59; 86; 200; 210)	-	-	-	-	-	-	-	-	-	-	-
Inner Ditch III (3.5')													
0.5 - 1.5'	70	59 (P57)	-	1(P265)	-	-	-	-	1	-	-	9	-
0.5 - 2.5' causewayed end	36	34 (P57)	-	-	-	-	-	-	-	-	-	2	-
1.5' - bottom	39	39 (P57; 123)	-	-	-	-	-	-	-	-	-	-	-
Re-excavation	46	40	-	-	-	-	-	-	-	-	-	6	-
Inner Ditch IIIb (3.5')													
0.8 - 1.4'	53	51(P146)	-	-	-	-	-	-	-	-	-	1	1
1.4'		(P175)	-	-	-	-	-	-	-	-	-	-	-
1.4 - 2.3'	20	20 (P130; 187)	-	-	-	-	-	-	-	-	-	-	-
Inner Ditch IIIb - IVb													
Surface - 0.8'	66	39	-	?1	-	-	-	-	1	-	-	25	-
Inner Ditch IVb (3.4')													
0.8 - 1.4'	188	172 (P130; 146)	-	2(P261)	-	-	-	-	1*	-	-	13	-
1.4 - 2.3'	248	248(P1; 54-5; 175)	-	-	-	-	-	-	-	-	-	-	-
2.3' - Bottom	13	13 (P1; 128)	-	-	-	-	-	-	-	-	-	-	-
Inner Ditch IV (3.4')													
Surface - 1.3'	121	112	-	-	-	-	-	-	-	-	-	9	-
1.3' - bottom	19	19	-	-	-	-	-	-	-	-	-	-	-
Re-excavation	32	25	-	-	-	-	-	-	-	-	-	7	-
Inner Ditch IV-V													
Causeway	3	1	-	-	-	-	-	-	-	-	-	2	-
Inner Ditch V (4.4')													
Excavation	65	62	2(P324)	-	-	1	-	-	-	-	-	-	-
1.5'		(P143)	-	-	-	-	-	-	-	-	-	-	-
Re-excavation	98	89	-	-	-	-	-	-	-	-	-	9	-
Inner Ditch VI (3.3')													
Upper level	76	71	1(P325)	-	1(P277~)	-	-	-	-	-	-	3	-
1.3'		(P193)	-	-	-	-	-	-	-	-	-	-	-
Lower level	58	58	-	-	-	-	-	-	-	-	-	-	-
No depth recorded		(P71)	-	-	-	-	-	-	-	-	-	-	-
Inner Ditch VII (5.1')													
Surface - 0.8'	174	152 (P64)	-	-	?1(P351)	-	-	-	1*	2	-	18	-
0.8 - 1.4'	316	300(P18; 64; 129; 162; 179)	-	-	-	2	3(P319)	-	-	-	2	9	-
1.4 - 2.3'	270	265(P40; 50-1;64; 100; 107; 129; 135)	-	1(P262)	-	-	1 + 1*	-	-	-	-	2	-
2.3' - 3.5'	718	715(P32; 40; 53; 62; 64; 79; 67; 90; 97; 100; 107; 129; 179; 181; 216)	-	-	-	-	-	-	-	1	2*	-	-
3 - 3.5'	88	88 (P64; 97; 107)	-	-	-	-	-	-	-	-	-	-	-
3.5' - bottom	11	11(P159)	-	-	-	-	-	-	-	-	-	-	-
Bottom	3	3	-	-	-	-	-	-	-	-	-	-	-
Re-fill	37	36	-	-	-	1	-	-	-	-	-	-	-
Inner Ditch VIII(4')**													
Surface - 1'	258	**(P140;220)	1(=P244)	5(P335-6)	-	3	-	-	-	-	-	-	-
1 - 2'	261	**(P140; 160)	9(P326-7))	0(P318; P337-8	-	1	-	-	4	-	-	-	-
2 - 3'	80	**(P140)	-	-	-	-	-	-	-	-	-	-	-
3' - Bottom	12	**(P140)	-	-	-	-	-	-	-	-	-	-	-
Re-excavation	5	**	-	-	-	-	-	-	-	-	-	-	-

Continued over the page

Table 166 continued

	Total Sherds	Early Neolithic	Ebbsfleet	Mortlake Ware	Fengate Ware	Undiagn. PW	?LN/ EBA	GW	BK	Grog & Rustic.	EBA	RB etc	?
Inner Ditch IX**(2.')**													
Surface - 1'	109	**(P65)	-	1(P339)	-	-	1	-	1 + 1'	-	-	-	-
1 - 2'	47	**	-	-	-	-	-	-	-	1	-	-	-
2' - Bottom	4	**(P48; 66; 190)	-	-	-	-	-	-	-	-	-	-	-
Refill	12	**	-	-	-	-	-	-	-	-	-	-	-
Inner Ditch X**(2.2)**													
Surface - 1'	104	**	-	-	-	-	-	-	?1	-	-	-	-
1 - 2'	91	**	-	-	-	-	1	-	-	-	-	-	-
2' - Bottom	39	**	-	-	-	-	-	-	-	-	-	-	-
Refill	6	**	-	-	-	-	-	-	-	-	-	-	-
Inner Ditch XI**(2.3')**													
Surface - 1'	98	**(P176; 178)	-	-	-	-	-	-	-	-	-	-	-
1 - 2'	79	**(P176; 178)	-	-	-	-	-	-	-	-	-	-	-
2' - Bottom: Hearth I	17	**(P136; 178; 208)	-	-	-	-	-	-	-	-	-	-	-
Hearth II + IV	20	**	-	-	-	-	-	-	-	-	-	-	-
"Ditch"	53	**(P176)	-	-	-	-	-	-	-	-	-	-	-
Inner Ditch XII**(2.2')**													
Surface - 1'	104	**(P134)	-	-	-	1	-	-	-	-	-	-	-
1 - 2'	105	**(P119; 160)	-	-	-	1	-	-	-	-	-	-	-
2' - Bottom	61	**(P49; 136; 160; 198b)	-	-	-	-	-	-	-	-	-	-	-
Inner Ditch XIII**(4.2')**													
Surface - 1'	66	**	-	-	-	-	?2(P232)	-	-	-	-	-	-
1 - 2'	20	**	-	-	-	-	-	-	-	-	-	-	-
2 - 3'	86	**(P91)	-	-	-	-	-	-	-	-	-	-	-
3' - Bottom	17	**(P218)	-	-	-	-	-	-	-	-	-	-	-
Refill	4	**	-	-	-	-	-	-	-	-	-	-	-
Inner Ditch XIV**(3')**													
Surface - 1'	45	**	-	-	-	1	-	1*	-	-	-	-	-
1 - 2'	63	**	-	-	-	1	2(P232)	?1	-	-	-	?Yes	-
2 - Bottom	4	4	-	-	-	-	-	-	-	-	-	-	-
Refill	3	**	-	-	-	-	-	-	-	-	-	?Yes	-
Inner Ditch XVa**(6')**													
Surface - 1'	32	**	-	1(P257)	-	-	-	-	1	-	-	Yes	-
1 - 2'	67	**	3(P241)	-	-	1	1(P232)	-	(P29.	-	-	-	-
2' - Bottom	21	**	-	-	-	-	-	-	-	-	-	-	-
Refill	8	**	-	-	-	-	-	-	-	-	-	-	-
Inner Ditch XVb**(6')**													
Surface - 1'	41	**	-	1(P257)	-	-	-	-	(P29.	-	-	-	-
1 - 2'	161	**(P58; 68)	-	2(P257)	-	-	-	-	(P29.	-	-	-	-
2 - 3'	42	**	-	-	-	-	-	-	-	-	-	-	-
3 - 4'	20	**(P201; 207)	-	-	-	-	-	-	-	-	-	-	-
Refill	19	**	-	-	-	-	-	-	1	-	-	-	-
Inner Ditch XVI**(4.3')**													
Surface - 1'	67	**(P219)	-	-	-	-	-	-	-	-	-	-	-
1 - 2'	89	**	-	-	-	-	-	-	-	-	-	-	-
2 - 3'	97	**(P52; 63; 118)	-	5 (P257)	-	-	4(P232)	-	-	-	-	-	-
3 - 4'	51	**(P88)	-	-	-	-	-	-	-	-	-	-	-
4' - Bottom	1	**	-	-	-	-	-	-	-	-	-	-	-
Inner Ditch XVII (Smith)													
Layer 2			-	1(P340)	-	-	-	2	9	-	-	9	-
Layer 3	17		-	-	-	-	-	-	-	-	-	-	-
Layer 4	11		-	-	-	-	-	-	-	-	-	-	-
Layer 5	4		-	-	-	-	-	-	-	-	-	-	-

Table 167: Percentages of rim types and decoration in a samle of 1156 vessels from the Keiller assemblage.

	Simple rims	Expanded rims
Plain vessels	73	27
Decorated vessels	36	64
All	69	31

Table 168: Percentages of rim types and decoration by ditch circuit in a sample of 133 Early Neolithic vessels from the Keiller assemblage.

Ditch circuit	Simple rims	Expanded rims	Plain vessels	Decorated vessels
Outer	28	72	5	45
Middle	52	48	53	47
Inner	49	51	49	51
All	47	53	52	48

Table 169: Vertical distribution and percentages of traits in the three ditch circuits in a sample of 133 Early Neolithic vessels from the Keiller excavations.

Context	Simple rims	Decorated rims	Plain	Decorated
OD 6'-8'+	15	85	43	57
OD 3.5'-5'	17	83	67	33
MD 3'-5'	68	32	68	32
MD 2.3'-3.5'	33	67	67	33
MD 2'-3'	41	59	35	65
MD 0'-2'	40	60	28	72
ID 3'-5'	50	50	33	67
ID 2.3'-3.5'	67	33	67	33
ID 2'-3'	27	73	36	64
ID 0'-2'	50	50	50	50

functional demarcation of activity within the ditches, and possible selective deposition from a range of available vessel types.

An examination of the 133 vessel sample in terms of the relationship between rim-types and vessel style generally supported Smith's association of plain vessels with simple rims, and decorated vessels with expanded rims (table 167). Over two-thirds of the Keiller assemblage comprised plain vessels with simple rims. Although this dominance was reflected overall in the sample of 133 vessels, a contextual analysis demonstrated that a relatively higher proportion of vessels with expanded rims occurred in the outer ditch segments (table 168).

Vertical distributions. The dominance of vessels with expanded rims in the outer circuit (table 169) was observable from the lowest levels from which pottery was recorded, c. 8.5′–3.5′. The frequent occurrence of this vessel-style also explains the relatively large amount of decorated pottery; all the decorated vessels had expanded rims, as did nearly half of the plain vessels (a less often recurring combination: 13.5 percent of the 133 vessel sample.

The lower levels of the middle ditch were dominated by simple-rimmed, plain pottery, in distinct contrast to the outer circuit (table 169). Higher up the silting, the dominance of the plain over the decorated component remained

much the same, but there was an increased emphasis on expanded rim-styles. The sample from the inner ditch was rather smaller than those discussed already. The relative proportion of simple and expanded rims appeared to be equal. At an equivalent depth (3′–5′) in the middle ditch the inner ditch by contrast produced more decorated pottery relatively. At higher levels in both the middle and inner ditches, at 2′–3′, decorated and expanded-rimmed pottery was in the majority (table 169). The apparent change in emphasis from plain to decorated pottery in the middle ditch segments was most notable (35 percent plain: 65 percent decorated) compared to results for the lower levels of the silting. In the inner ditch at this level, there was a clear divergence between simple and decorated rims (27 percent simple:73 percent expanded). The emphasis on expanded/decorated styles in the middle ditch was carried on into the highest silting of the ditch segments, at 0′–2′, with an even balance between pottery styles prevailing in the inner ditch segments at this level.

There was a distinct contrast between the pottery in the lowest levels of the outer ditches, with its emphasis on decorated bowls with expanded rims, and the middle circuit, where plain bowls with simple rim-styles prevailed. Overall there was a greater range of vessel styles in both the inner and middle ditches. The quantity of pottery from the outer circuit was small in comparison to the other two

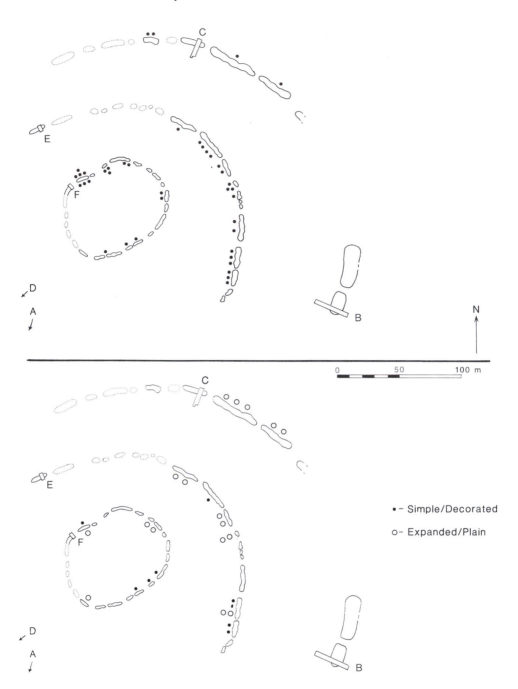

Fig. 193. Distribution of top: *plain, simple-rimmed vessels, and* below: *decorated, simple-rimmed and plain, expanded-rimmed vessels.*

circuits; so much so that samples were too small from the higher levels of the silting in the outer segments to be statistically meaningful. This in itself reinforces the difference between the outer and the other two circuits in that the level of depositional activity there was less intense.

Horizontal distributions. The same sample was used for plotting the horizontal patterning of pottery. The exception was lugs where all lugs from the Keiller and the 1988 assemblages were used. The inter-circuit analysis of pottery laterally across the enclosure reinforced some of the observations produced by the vertical study.

A number of different categories of pottery was looked at. Vessels which were plain, with simple rims, showed a fairly even distribution across the enclosure, apart from the outer ditch, where a relatively small number occurred (fig. 193). 73 decorated vessels were plotted (fig. 193) and were divided into carinated with expanded rims (66 percent), and uncarinated with simple rims (34 percent) (fig. 194). 51 percent of decorated vessels came from the middle, 37 percent from the inner, and 12 percent from the outer circuit. In the middle ditch, 54 percent were carinated; 46 percent uncarinated. in the inner, 74 percent were carinated; 26

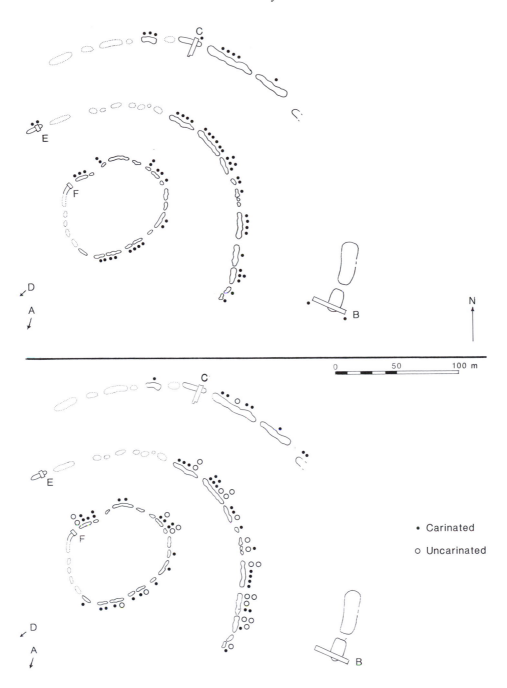

Fig. 194. Distribution of top: lugs, and below: decorated vessels, carinated and uncarinated.

percent uncarinated. Only one uncarinated vessel occurred in the outer circuit. Most middle ditch segments produced uncarinated decorated vessels, invariably occurring with the other type. In the inner circuit, the uncarinated type was more unevenly distributed, with the carinated vessels occurring without the other in a number of segments. The uncarinated vessels did not occur alone in any segment, whilst carinated vessels did feature without the other on a number of occasions. The outer circuit stood out for its paucity of uncarinated decorated pottery; the single example had an expanded rim.

A total of 61 lug fragments were recorded. As lugs came in pairs, the plot (fig. 194), does not represent individual vessels. Of the total, 51 percent came from the middle ditch, 34 percent from the inner, and 15 percent from the outer. 11 of the lugs (23 percent) were decorated, occurring in all three circuits, with just over half coming from the middle. One of the lowest recorded sherds of pottery from the enclosure was a lug from outer segment II, at 8.32′ (Smith 1965a, P102). The relatively large number of lugs from the middle and, to a lesser extent, the inner, ditch, might be explained by the spatial demarcation

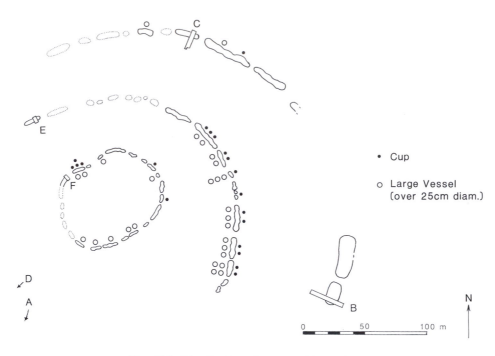

Fig. 195. Distribution of cups and large bowls.

of particular activity. Vessels with a handling device would be suitable for storage and cooking (lifting and suspending). Again, the outer circuit appeared to be different, with few plain bowls with simple rim-styles and a comparative lack of vessels with handles.

The occurrence of small vessels (mouth diameter of 12 cm or less) and those in the largest size-range of 25 cm or more was plotted (fig. 195). Presumably size of vessel was related to individual and communal use for the consumption of food and drink, with the smallest being used as individual eating and drinking vessels (as well, conceivably, as lids and scoops). Distribution of the smallest vessels was fairly even over the enclosure, apart from the outer ditch, where there was only one small bowl/cup. Just over half of the examples from the middle ditch were in the larger size category, and the same proportion was applicable to the inner ditch. The middle and inner area of the enclosure appears to be associated with more multi-purpose vessels, suitable for a range of practical functions, whereas the outer circuit might have been associated with a restricted repertoire of vessels which were preferred for more specialised activity.

Discussion: the 1988 and Keiller assemblages combined
Despite the obstacles of the Keiller recording system, there is compelling evidence for the differential deposition of a variety of vessels in the different ditch segments and circuits of the enclosure.

Investigation of the Keiller material yielded a picture of intensive depositional activity in the inner and middle circuits, in contrast to the relatively less densely filled outer ditch. The outer ditch, however, indicated that there

was a different depositional emphasis, not only in terms of process and intensity, but also in terms of the character of its pottery assemblage. The outer circuit assemblage was defined by decorated (and to a lesser extent plain) vessels with expanded rim-styles. All but one of its decorated bowls were carinated. It produced only a single small cup/bowl in the sample examined. Relatively fewer vessels possessed lugs. There were very few plain vessels with simple rims. More vessels were made in shell-tempered fabrics than the other types of fabric, which could be directly linked to the strong presence relatively of decorated, carinated bowls and those with expanded rims.

This information is generally supported and augmented by the 1988 results. Not only did pottery deposition vary at the inter-circuit level, but also within the different circuits to some extent. There was less deposition in the outer circuit as noted from the Keiller material. The primary fill of Trench B reflected generally the pattern of episodic or repeated deposition of bone with sherds of pottery. This was not the case, however, with Trenches A and C. In the former, the bulk of pottery came from the secondary fill (unlike Trenches B and C), but it was not associated with the deposition of significant quantities of bone. Most of the sherds did, however, occur with localised patches of dark, humic soil, as was the case in most excavated segments. There was a bone spread in the primary fill of Trench A but no pottery. In Trench C pottery was relatively sparsely represented, and there were no discrete deposits of pottery with bone. In all the outer cuttings, the majority of sherds could be assigned to a single vessel, and in terms of vessels numbers, the scale of deposition was low.

Depositional activity in the middle and inner circuits appeared to be more intense. Most of the pottery from the excavated segments was associated with a repeated pattern of bone spreads or dumps and patches of dark soil. This was a feature of primary and secondary silts in both circuits, although to a more limited extent in the secondary fill of the middle ditch in Trench E. The repetitive nature of this activity provided a strong link between primary and secondary contexts. If a sequence is to be discerned between the separate deposits in particular segments of the circuits, then it was likely to be on a micro-scale, perhaps all part of a single occasion or event, although any differences in time-scale between acts of deposition in the different circuits is more difficult to quantify.

Despite the more intensive nature of activity in the middle ditch cuttings, there was no striking evidence for the deposition of generally greater amounts of pottery, certainly in terms of individual vessels. The assemblages from the primary fill of both middle ditch cuttings were monopolised by a single vessel, as was the case with outer Trench B and the secondary fill of A. The assemblages from Trenches D and E were similar in that both produced a large amount of crushed sherds, integrated with bone spreads. It was almost as if broken sherds had been subjected to trampling prior to burial. A greater variety of pottery came from the middle ditch cuttings, with both plain and decorated vessels represented. In Trench D, and to a less marked extent Trench E, all the decorated pottery occurred with significant deposits of bone.

A similar picture of repeated depositions of plain pottery, bone and dark soil could be observed in inner Trench F, although, as with outer Trench A, there was a minimal amount of pottery from the primary silt. Pottery from a single vessel was associated with closely juxtaposed dumps and linear spreads of bone, and it seems probable that the series of deposits were part of a single phase of activity.

The generally weathered condition of the majority of sherds suggests that they had spent some time prior to deposition, possibly in middens alongside other discarded material. Middening was suggested also by the fact that although many of the sherds in the trenches could be seen to belong to very few and, in some cases, single, vessels, typically less than half the vessel could be seen to be represented. Some of the evidence for the recovery of parts of the same vessels from different parts of the enclosure (Smith 1965a, 14; for example, P 198a, b, c) is disputable (Zienkiewicz 1996). The argument has important implications for the dispersal and possible middening of broken vessels. If randomly dispersed and shattered pieces of pottery were eventually carefully deposited along with other categories of refuse, then it is possible that it was the act of deposition of vessels, rather than their particular contents, which may have been of greatest significance. Whilst it seems likely that acts of deposition could have taken place over a relatively condensed time-scale, it is difficult to understand the sequence of events prior to that;

between the use of various pots, the discard of broken pieces and their subsequent middening, and their eventual disposal in the ditches. If the act of deposition was invested with special significance, as the evidence for careful placing of animal bone would suggest, then it is possible that the middening of pots may have represented a liminal period, marking the time between the active use of pots and their ultimate disposal, and where they were divested of any association with their employment in earlier activities. Pots may have been deliberately smashed. Any previous meaning embodied in the vessel would have been dislocated during this process of transformation.

The evidence for the deposition of particular types of pottery in different parts of the enclosure, together with variation in the rate and intensity of deposition, can be explained by the spatial demarcation of activity within the enclosure, in terms of both character and scale. Pottery in the inner part of the enclosure was associated with abundant deposits in the ditches and the interior of the inner circuit. Pottery used and discarded there could have been connected with domestic pre-occupations, witnessed by the wider range of plain and decorated wares from the middle and inner ditches, and supported by the animal bone evidence (see chapters 4, 11 and 17).

There may have been more specialised activity on the periphery of the enclosure. The emphasis on decorated, carinated bowls and the less intense scale of depositional activity in the outer circuit can be linked with the idea of ritual or special activities taking place at the outer edge of the arena. There may have been an emphasis here on vessels for display and handling. It may have been important to employ visually more distinctive pottery styles at the periphery of the enclosure. The perimeter of the enclosure may well have been invested with an enhanced symbolic significance, representing a barrier to and a boundary with the everyday world without. Decorated, carinated bowls have not so far been recovered from the environs of Windmill Hill (Zienkiewicz 1996), which could suggest that their use was exclusive to activity taking place within the confines of the enclosure.

Windmill Hill was likely to have been an arena for a wide audience of participants and spectators and accordingly activity there may have been highly structured and formalised, which may have been reflected and played out in the deployment of certain material symbols, pottery amongst them. Rules for the use of pots and the conduct of activity in which they were involved could have applied no less for domestic pre-occupations than for more specialised ritual occasions, both of which the pottery would indicate went on in parallel at the enclosure. Both the practical and the symbolic dimensions of pottery could have been interwoven in a variety of roles at Windmill Hill; pottery could have been part of a dynamic inter-play between specialised ritual activity and other domestic roles.

A Windmill Hill style?

In the years since Piggott (1931) first used it, there has been much confusion in the use of the term 'Windmill Hill ware'. It has been used loosely and uncritically used to define a large-scale regional style of pottery in southern Britain, and a decorated style with or without sub-styles. Terms used to describe the pottery from the site of Windmill Hill itself draw heavily on imported stylistic labels, such as South-Western, Abingdon and Whitehawk, definitions which are firmly established in the archaeological literature (e.g. Smith 1974; Whittle 1977; Thomas 1991).

Adherence to geographical style-labels has had the unfortunate effect of obscuring formal variation and contextual difference, and inhibiting the examination of possible reasons behind diversity. Re-assessment of selected assemblages from sites in the south-west, south Dorset, the Stonehenge area and the Avebury area, shows that whilst there is a certain measure of coherence across this large area, there was nonetheless much contextual diversity in pottery use (Zienkiewicz 1996).

Given all their internal variety and distinctiveness, assemblages of pottery from sites in the Avebury area and from Windmill Hill itself do not sit easily within the traditional terms of reference. Rather than resorting to the comfortingly familiar style-zone concept, the Windmill Hill Early Neolithic assemblage can be evaluated as an independent stylistic entity, as individual rather than as a collection of disjointed elements imposed from type-site assemblages elsewhere.

Assemblages of Early Neolithic pottery such as those from Carn Brea, Hambledon, Maiden Castle and the Coneybury 'Anomaly' pit, as well as some smaller collections in areas to the south-west of Windmill Hill, each had distinctive stylistic characteristics and emphases (Zienkiewicz 1996). Whilst there are a number of stylistic traits in common, there is really no assemblage that could be considered 'typically' South-Western. However, these assemblages did a provide a major contrast to pottery from Windmill Hill and some of the sites in its environs, with their dominance of plain pottery with simple rim-styles, features which are regarded as the defining elements of the South-Western style of Early Neolithic pottery. Whilst there was variation between the different contexts, there was generally more in common amongst assemblages from sites in the south-west and from the Stonehenge area, than between either of those and the Avebury area.

The presence of the South-Western style in the early Neolithic assemblages of the Avebury area appears to rest principally on the occurrence of simple rims, particularly in association with plain pottery, and lugs. In the Cherhill pottery report, Smith was challenged by the absence of lugs, and the excess of carinated sherds, which made it difficult for her to accept the assemblage as typically South-Western (Evans and Smith 1983, 91). In some reports, a similar lack of conformity to the accepted norm usually requires the specialist to treat the assemblage as a 'variant' of the style. Elsewhere in Britain plain pottery with simple rims and lugs is part of the Early Neolithic repertoire. At Windmill Hill itself, a direct south-western connection appears to rest on the presence of two small gabbroic sherds (probably from a single vessel), some Cornish-style lugs (in local fabrics) and a Cornish stone axe. Whilst this represents a supra-regional connection with territory to the south-west, the significance of such links is impossible to quantify.

A striking feature of the assemblages from Windmill Hill and sites in the locality was the presence of decorated vessels (17 percent of the Windmill Hill assemblage; 16 percent of sites in the Avebury area), providing the greatest contrast to pottery from areas to the south-west. Vessels with expanded rim-styles also occurred in a number of assemblages. At the enclosure decoration could be closely correlated with carinated bowls with expanded rims and shell-tempered fabrics. Some assemblages were particularly individually distinctive, such as that from the large Neolithic pit beneath Bishops Canning round barrow G.61 (WANHM 1965), with its wide-mouthed, plain, carinated bowls; and Cherhill (Evans and Smith 1983), with its emphasis on plain, carinated vessels. At the intra-regional scale, certain differences could be observed between Windmill Hill and local assemblages. For example, at Windmill Hill, plain, carinated vessels were rare (only two published examples: Smith 1965a, fig. 19); in distinct contrast to the two sites just mentioned. Indeed, the wide-mouthed, carinated, vessels such as those from the Bishops Cannings pit, have been recovered from no other site in the area. Furthermore, the decorated, carinated bowls (typically shell-tempered) found at the enclosure have not been recovered from sites in the locality, where uncarinated forms with simple rims (more commonly flint-tempered) were more often decorated. The carinated type could have been for use exclusively at the enclosure.

The decorated, carinated bowls with expanded rims at Windmill Hill were likened by Smith (1965a) to either Abingdon or Whitehawk pottery. When the pottery from these sites is examined in detail, however, striking dissimilarities are evident. For example, although there was a strong connection between decoration and expanded rims, there were very few carinated bowls which were decorated at Abingdon. A common form at that site, amongst both the plain and decorated component, was a deep form with splayed walls, a type not occurring at all amongst the decorated pottery at Windmill Hill. Zoning, if not the techniques, of decoration was generally different at Abingdon. At Whitehawk, decorated bowls were typically open; at Windmill Hill there was only a single open bowl which was decorated. Whilst there may have been a common repertoire of techniques for decorating pottery, it may be more meaningful to understand individual assemblages on their own merits, where differences could have been guided by local selection and tradition and, furthermore, according to the various contexts of pottery use.

So much has attention been devoted to assigning pottery

to regional styles that this has tended to obscure the possibility that decorated pottery was part of a unitary phenomenon that included plain pottery as well. It need not necessarily be separated from associated plain wares in terms of the functional role which pottery was required to fulfil in particular contexts. Herne (1988, 12) noted the disagreements that often arise in the literature as to whether an assemblage should be classified as belonging to the Decorated style or not, where plain assemblages share formal characteristics in common with decorated pottery. One author demonstrated the confusion aptly with a reference to decorated plain bowl pottery (Holgate 1988). Both the plain and the decorated wares from Windmill Hill and surrounds represented a range of forms suitable for most functional needs, including the preparation and consumption of food. No doubt roles were shared between plain and decorated pottery, but with possibly differing emphasis in different contexts.

A context-based analysis of Early Neolithic pottery could help redress the balance of attention away from the regional models which have been developed from a few particularly large assemblages according to the type-site/culture construct. The Windmill Hill assemblage, the scale of which makes it difficult to compare it to neighbouring sites, was not 'typical' of the pottery from its locality. In fact, the term 'Windmill Hill style' may not really be applicable to any assemblages other than that from the site itself (Zienkiewicz 1996). Diversity of pottery between different sites needs to be understood perhaps in terms of the relationship between functional intent and context of use, as well as factors such as availability, choice, local preference and access to commodities.

Old boundaries and new frameworks

We also need to rethink our ideas of space and frames of operation, as an alternative to the old style-zone framework, which has been developed from arbitrarily imposed boundaries delimiting the influence of the type-site (see also Cleal 1992c). Differing scales and structures could be investigated, with ceramic strategy being looked at in terms of concepts of identity and integration, of the movement of people and social space, against an unstable Early Neolithic background. A more complex and fluid system of pottery manufacture and distribution may have operated, the mechanics of which will be less susceptible to investigation if we continue to employ the regional strait-jacket, which of necessity demands the assumption of internally consistent and coherent entities.

An alternative to geographically-determined classifications would be to approach Early Neolithic pottery as not only functional containers serving a variety of roles, but as a category which, along with other items of material culture, was also an integral part of a structure of social strategies and relationships, part of a framework for understanding the world. Differences (style) may have been intended to signify ethnic difference, or uniformity and integration, between social units. The ethnographic research of writers such as Hodder (1982) and Sterner (1989) has demonstrated that this is not necessarily a straightforward matter. Hodder found in his East African research that there was not a simple relationship between material culture boundaries, interaction and ethnicity. Sterner recorded that the Sirak Bulahay people of Cameroon did not use pottery principally to signal to groups from other villages; messages invested in the pots conveyed meanings in the first place to their users. The pottery from Windmill Hill did not mirror in all respects that from nearby sites. The deployment of different vessels at the enclosure there could have been an excluding and, at the same time, an including strategy, dependent on the category of people using it and its particular context of use. Differences might have been invested in pottery in a way that we are not able to detect simply from the analysis of formal variation. Meaning and even simple functional purpose could have been transformed according to context and users.

Models of mobility and sedentism for the Early Neolithic can also be used for understanding strategies of pottery use. The sedentary model would have pottery as part of a fixed lifestyle, where it would be potentially more important as a carrier of local or regional identity. Fixed style-zones, on the other hand, would be less compatible with a model of mobility. People would move in and out of different landscapes and locales, open to the influence of a wider range of pottery containers. Some of those elements might be transported in the mind to become absorbed into local ways of making pots, others rejected. Certainly the distribution of gabbroic pottery and other 'exotic' material items demonstrates that contact was taking place over large tracts of territory, the character and scale of which is difficult to assess. Long-range contact could have enhanced the need for group solidarity on occasion, with outsiders seen as potentially disruptive to the social order.

Instead of imposing our own structures on the archaeological record in order to provide a framework for our operations, we can perceive people as active agents who not only moved along with the project of their own daily lives, but who encountered others and who moved within and between the boundaries of different groups of individuals (Barrett 1994). Material culture, along with places and settings, may have acted as a guide and provided a structure for social interaction and for negotiating different locales. Pottery, whether being deployed in more mundane daily spaces or, at another scale, in a monumental framework such as Windmill Hill, was part of the conceptual ordering of the world.

The Ebbsfleet pottery

The 1988 assemblage

26 sherds (250 gm) were identified as belonging to the Ebbsfleet style of Neolithic pottery. A minimum of two vessels was represented. Ebbsfleet pottery comprised only 3 percent of the 1988 Neolithic assemblage.

Contexts

Outer bank, Trench BB (fig. 186, and table 155). A total of 21 sherds, including five rim fragments, came from the tail of the outer bank, and the Ebbsfleet sherds were associated with worn early and later Neolithic, Bronze Age and Romano-British sherds. Nine of the Ebbsfleet sherds, including four rim-sherds and a neck fragment, bore worn traces of impressed whipped-cord decoration. The Ebbsfleet sherds were almost all extremely weathered and small in size. The largest measured a maximum of 5 cm; on average, they ranged from 2.5–3.5 cm. All these sherds are considered to belong to a single vessel, P 505.

Outer ditch, Trench B (figs 187 and 189, and table 156). Two worn body sherds (there were no rim fragments) came from this cutting. P522 came from the interface of the primary and secondary silts (227) at roughly the same level as the Ebbsfleet sherds recovered by Smith from her adjacent cutting V (published as P237; Smith 1965a, fig. 31). P524 came from the secondary fill (225). A very worn rim, P568, (reconstructed from three very small rim fragments) was recovered from the backfill from Smith's excavation. All these sherds are likely to belong to a single vessel, and are conceivably part of Smith's P237.

Fabric

The fabrics of the two Ebbsfleet vessels were different, but both were generally composed of the same materials as those identified amongst the early Neolithic pottery. Smith also noted this point (Smith 1965a, 74). The sherds from Trench B and the backfill were of a very fine, sandy fabric with very sparse flint-temper, up to 3 mm, and some ferruginous grains. Surfaces were soapy in feel and micaceous in appearance, chocolate brown in colour, with an almost black core. The sherds from BB were moderately tempered with flint and shell, with slightly more of the former. Flint-temper occurred up to 4 mm; shell up to 6 mm. External surfaces were light brown/orange, with grey patches on some sherds where the surface had been insufficiently oxidised. Interior surfaces were very dark grey, occasionally light brown/orange, and the core dark grey. Wear was such that the temper had been exposed on both surfaces and the pitted condition of sherds was likely to be the result of water percolating down from the soil surface.

Style

The two vessels were very similar in terms of style. Both rims (P505 and P568) were everted with a squared-off lip, and both were decorated with oblique short lengths of whipped-cord. P505 (BB) was certainly carinated; the vessel represented by P522, P524 and P568 (Trench B), was likely also to have been. Both vessels have traces of internal decoration just beneath the rim. P505 was decorated externally with an impressed herringbone motif of whipped-cord maggots; only a lone segment of whipped-cord survived on the exterior of P568. Short lengths of

whipped-cord were discernible externally on P522 and P524 and on a number body sherds belonging to P505.

The vessel represented by P522, P524 and P568, from Trench B, was the same as that published by Smith as P237 (Smith 1965a, fig. 31). The sherds she recovered came from the lowest part of her level 4, the level above the lowest sediments in the ditch fill. This would be equivalent to context 227 where P522 was found. The other Ebbsfleet body sherd, P524, was recovered from some 63 cm higher up the fill. Both sherds could have filtered down from higher positions, possibly as a result of worm or mole action, for which there was some evidence in that trench.

Ebbsfleet pottery from the Keiller assemblage: context, distribution and sequence

The Ebbsfleet Ware in Trench B/V is clearly lower and nearer the primary fill than any other Ebbsfleet Ware recovered on Windmill Hill. In terms of the provenanced Ebbsfleet sherds from the Keiller archive, the majority came from the upper 2′ of the ditch fills (tables 164–6). For example, Smith noted that sherds from Middle Ditch II (which produced a third of the total of Ebbsfleet vessels, 15 bowls, from the Keiller excavations) were distributed from the top of the ditch down to about 3.5′ (Smith 1965a, 14). Of the 233 Ebbsfleet sherds recorded in the Keiller notebooks, 160 came from 1.4′–2.3′ and 56 from 0.8′–1.4′. Only six sherds amongst otherwise Early Neolithic pottery came from lower than 2.3′. 97 percent of the Ebbsfleet sherds came from 2.3′ and above. As far as other excavated ditch segments were concerned, Ebbsfleet pottery did not occur below 2′. 14 sherds described in the notebook as having whipped-cord decoration occurred down to 3′ in Outer Ditch Ic. As the maximum depth of the outer ditch at this point was 8.7′, the apparently low position of the Ebbsfleet pottery has to be seen in relation to the greater depth of this ditch. However, while most Ebbsfleet pottery clearly does not occur in the lower ditch fills, and has not been identified from contexts associated with the construction of the site, there is no reason to doubt the integrity of its provenance in Trench B/Outer Ditch V, in the absence of evidence for disturbance.

About 500 sherds (2.5 percent) of the Keiller assemblage) were termed 'Neo B' in the catalogues, meaning Peterborough Ware in later terminology. No distinction was made between individual facets of that tradition in the Keiller records. Roughly 350 sherds can be classified as Ebbsfleet. The Ebbsfleet sherds from Middle Ditch IIb alone represented almost half the amount of 'Neo B' pottery (published as Ps 238, 239, 242, 245, 246, 249, 250, 252, 254, 255: Smith 1965a, figs 31, 32). Smith (1965a, 73) arrived at a total of 41 Ebbsfleet vessels from the site. A thorough inspection of the Keiller archive by the authors of this chapter resulted in the minimal figure of 31 vessels (33 in total including the two from the 1988 excavations). The criteria employed (largely based on Smith 1956) were applied strictly to sherds (rim and body) with whipped-

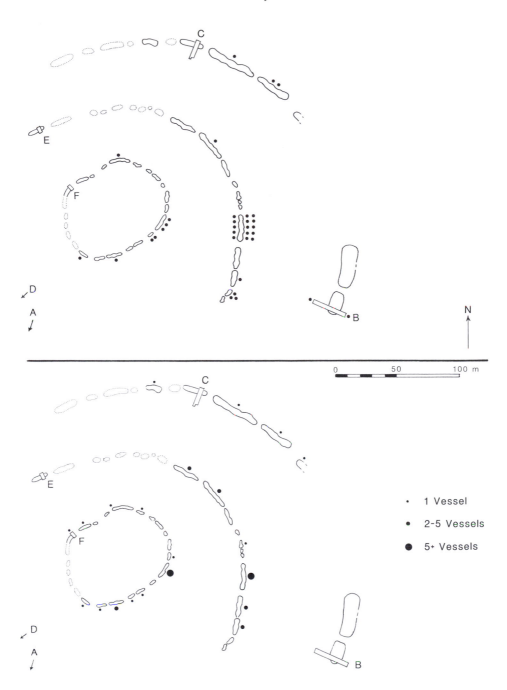

Fig. 196. Distribution of top: Ebbsfleet vessels, and below: Mortlake vessels

cord herringbone and maggot impressions, and in a few cases where there was a problem of distinguishing sherds from other pottery styles, classification was made on the basis of fabric identification. Plain sherds, and those with twisted-cord decoration, were discounted.

Fig. 196 gives the distribution of the 33 Ebbsfleet vessels, defined by rim and body sherds by the methods just described. Ebbsfleet vessels occurred in all three circuits, with more from the middle ditch. 61 percent came from the middle, 24 percent from the inner and 15 percent from the outer ditch. The Ebbsfleet sherds from Middle Ditch IIb represented 65 percent of the total of Ebbsfleet

sherds from the enclosure (229 of a total of at least 355). All the contexts which produced Ebbsfleet sherds also yielded early Neolithic decorated pottery, except Middle Ditch VIII. There was no observable association between the two styles of Neolithic pottery in terms of preferential distribution in the enclosure as was noted for the site at Staines. There, Ebbsfleet pottery coincided with Early Neolithic styles of decorated pottery, and formed a very restricted distribution, being found only in a short length of the outer ditch (Robertson-Mackay 1987, 53).

80 sherds in Middle Ditch VIII belonged to P 256 and 19 to P 251. A number in Inner Ditch VII were decorated

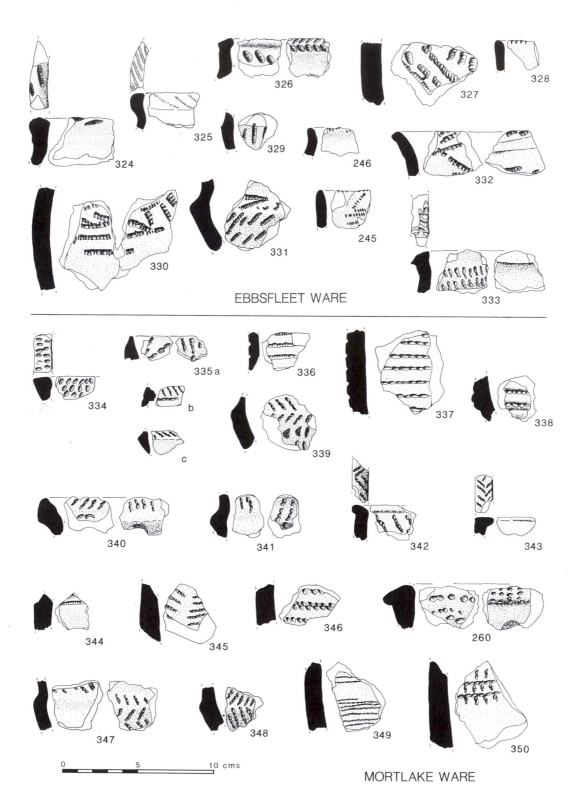

Fig. 197. *Previously unpublished Ebbsfleet* (top) *and Mortlake* (below) *sherds from the Keiller assemblage.*

with impressed whipped-cord, including a rim (unpublished). Two outer ditch segments yielded a small quantity of sherds; cutting I produced 28, cutting II, 16. Only Middle Ditch II and VIII, and Inner Ditch VIII, produced Ebbsfleet sherds in any quantity; other cuttings produced figures averaging between two and seven sherds.

A number of unpublished Ebbsfleet vessels are featured in fig. 197, (P324–333; these numbers follow on from Smith's published sequence), which also includes two re-drawn vessels originally published by Smith (1965a, P245 and P246).

Individual Ebbsfleet vessels were made up of a larger number of sherds on average than was the case for Early Neolithic vessels, which were typically represented by a small number of sherds. For example, P 256 was represented by 80 sherds. 15 vessels were reconstructed from the 233 sherds from Middle Ditch II, which represented on average about 16 sherds per vessel. This may be due to a difference in the manner of deposition of Ebbsfleet pottery. These sherds were not associated with dark soil and bone spreads, which characterised much of the Early Neolithic pottery. It is possible that Ebbsfleet pottery was not left to accumulate amongst other debris in middens or other deposits for any length of time, which in turn suggests that the nature of activity in which this type of pottery was deposited had a different emphasis and meaning.

That argument might find support from the fact that the distribution of Ebbsfleet pottery over the enclosure was quite different to that of the Early Neolithic pottery. Whilst acknowledging the discrepancy in terms of quantities between the Early Neolithic and Ebbsfleet pottery, fig. 196 clearly demonstrates the restricted distribution of the latter type. The plot shows that it occurred in roughly the same eastern sector of the enclosure. In contrast to the Early Neolithic pottery, Ebbsfleet pottery did not turn up in every excavated segment. The different manner of pottery deposition previously noted strongly suggests that the use and discard of Ebbsfleet pottery bore little relationship to activity connected with Early Neolithic vessels.

Ebbsfleet pottery may be associated with secondary activity on the site, based on the evidence for its occurrence higher up in the ditch silts. The evidence for the different character of its deposition and for its restricted distribution can be used to augment that suggestion. But, if secondary, it is another matter to try to define the time-scale for the activities connected with the deployment of the different types of pottery on the site. The nature of Keiller's recording makes it difficult to reconstruct the stratigraphic context of Ebbsfleet pottery in any detail. The wider dating of the Ebbsfleet style itself remains unclear, though there are certainly radiocarbon dates for the pottery style elsewhere which could suggest contemporaneity with the dates for the construction of the Windmill Hill monument (Hamilton 1995).

Ebbsfleet pottery in the local context

Ebbsfleet pottery is rather poorly represented in the local area although it has occurred on most of the sites that have produced Early Neolithic pottery. While numbers of recognisable vessels and sherds are low, the Ebbsfleet style has nevertheless been identified at a range of locations, quite widely dispersed in the area.

Six Ebbsfleet vessels were recorded from the secondary filling of the West Kennet long barrow (Piggott 1962a, fig. 11, P1–5, P8). Total numbers of Ebbsfleet sherds cannot be elucidated from either Piggott's report or the re-evaluation by Thomas and Whittle (1986). Whilst there is certainly no clear phasing to be seen in the secondary filling between the Ebbsfleet pottery and the sherds belonging to the Mortlake style, Ebbsfleet pottery did not occur with the primary burials.

Two Ebbsfleet vessels (a decorated rim and a decorated, carinated body sherd) were represented amongst a small collection of sherds of Peterborough pottery, including an Mortlake rim, from the nearby Millbarrow chambered tomb (Whittle 1994, fig. 17, P2, P3). The illustrated Ebbsfleet rim and body sherd were recovered from two of the chamber stone holes, contexts which were much disturbed, presumably during stone removal, and produced medieval and other finds. The fabric of the Ebbsfleet pottery was unlike that from Windmill Hill, including as it did a quartz component as well as the ubiquitous flint. At Windmill Hill, the fabrics of the Ebbsfleet pottery represented much the same range as that of the Early Neolithic pottery, if occasionally in different proportions.

At West Overton G.6b, Ebbsfleet sherds occurred along with other Neolithic sherds in and on the old land surface sealed by the barrow mound (Smith and Simpson 1966). Rims from three Ebbsfleet vessels were illustrated (fig. 7, nos 6, 7, and 8) and another was unillustrated. Total sherd numbers are not recorded.

Possible Ebbsfleet sherds occurred at Cherhill (Evans and Smith 1983). These, as well as sherds of Mortlake pottery, came from higher up in the ditch fill than the Early Neolithic pottery. P42, P47 and P49 were seen as having possible Ebbsfleet traits (Evans and Smith 1983, 87; fig. 24). Other illustrated sherds appear to be decorated with impressed whipped-cord.

Two large water-worn sherds from the upper part of an Ebbsfleet bowl, along with bones and horn cores of cattle, were found in 1833 during the removal of a mound, beside River's Bank to the west of Cherhill village (A. Smith 1885; Cunnington 1937). Smith gave the finds-spot as NG 02857035. Originally quite large, with a mouth diameter of c. 30 cm, the bowl was decorated internally with lines of oblique whipped-cord; externally there are traces of oblique whipped-cord, and there is a slight groove around the shoulder.

A sherd from the neck and shoulder of a bowl decorated with whipped-cord impressions, and four fragments of what was described as an Ebbsfleet/Mortlake bowl were recovered from the secondary fill of the ditch of the South Street long barrow (Ashbee *et al.* 1979, 272, fig. 30, nos 3 and 4). The rim form of no. 4, however, described as 'moderately developed', and the twisted cord decoration, may rather suggest the Mortlake tradition. Five sherds from four other bowls, one with 'indeterminate' impressed decoration, also occurred.

A few sherds with what appears to be whipped-cord decoration were reported from the Sanctuary (Cunnington 1931, plate VII). Of 14 otherwise Early Neolithic sherds examined in Devizes museum by myself, one sherd bore faint traces of whipped-cord decoration. The Early Neolithic and Peterborough sherds have been seen to represent residual material from the pre-monument phase (Pollard 1992, 219).

A few sherds of Ebbsfleet pottery were recovered, along with Early Neolithic and Grooved Ware sherds, from Beaker-period pits sealed by the Avebury G. 55 round barrow (Smith 1965b). Of a very fragmented assemblage, only one vessel seems likely to represent the Ebbsfleet style (Smith 1965b, fig. 5, no. 2).

An Ebbsfleet vessel is recorded from Gray's excavations under the south-east sector of the Avebury henge bank (Smith 1965a, fig. 76, P343). This was found on the old land surface along with sherds of Early Neolithic, Peterborough and Grooved Ware pottery. Three Ebbsfleet vessels came from the occupation site along the West Kennet Avenue (Smith 1965a, 233, fig. 79, P357, P361 and possibly P358). These were part of an assemblage of 600 sherds, mostly Peterborough.

With the Early Neolithic assemblage (largely plain, with carinated bowls) from the Neolithic pit beneath the Bishops Cannings round barrow G.61, whipped-cord impressions could be observed on the otherwise plain Vessel VI (Zienkiewicz 1996); these may have been accidental. Nine body sherds decorated with whipped-cord were found during Proudfoot's excavations at the site (although not from the Neolithic pit), and were reported as coming from 'Thurnam's excavation' (WAHNM 1965).

Ebbsfleet pottery, whilst not strongly represented in the area around Windmill Hill, is nevertheless present at a range of sites. Apart from Windmill Hill itself, it has been found at sites associated with mortuary structures, in Neolithic ditches (Cherhill), and on old ground surfaces sealed by Late Neolithic and Bronze Age monuments. Windmill Hill nevertheless offers the best insight in terms of stratification and sequence, and it is difficult to compare that site with any other in the area, the scale being so radically different. The pottery from the other local sites has nearly all come from disturbed and residual contexts, allowing little opportunity for determining sequence, all of which is very typical of this pottery style in southern Britain generally. It was certainly secondary to the burials at West Kennet; at Cherhill it was found in contexts overlying the Early Neolithic pottery.

With regard to 'potting recipes' (Cleal and Allen 1994, 69), generally the same range of fabric recipes appears to have been used for Early Neolithic and Ebbsfleet pottery at Windmill Hill. However, at Millbarrow the Ebbsfleet pottery was of a different fabric to those found at the enclosure. Perhaps the difference was site- rather than style-specific. This needs further investigation.

PART 2: LATE NEOLITHIC AND BRONZE AGE

Michael Hamilton

The 1988 assemblage

Fabrics and styles

All pottery has been defined by style (e.g. Beaker). Within each style, groups of sherds of shared characteristics are defined (e.g. Bkr5), by fabric, finish, sherd thickness, technique of decoration, and colour, which frequently could originate from one vessel. Because of the much greater variety of styles compared to the Early Neolithic assemblage, a more elaborate fabric analysis was used. Fabrics were determined by examination with a x20 microscope, and the percentage of inclusions estimated by eye. Many of the fabrics so determined are very similar; major groupings are summarised in table 170, and the full details have been deposited with the archive.

The range of styles

A wide range of Late Neolithic and Bronze Age pottery styles was found in the 1988 excavations: Grooved Ware, Beaker and possible Beaker, Rusticated Ware (here listed with Beaker), Early Bronze Age including Enlarged Food Vessels, Collared Urns and other vessels, including Late Neolithic/Bronze Age, Bronze Age/Iron Age and Middle/Late Bronze Age (figs 186–92 and 197–99). Unlike in Keiller's excavations there was no certain Mortlake or Fengate pottery (unless LN/BA1 can be seen as Fengate) (fig. 200).

With grog-tempered fabrics, it can be difficult to separate body sherds of Fengate Ware (perhaps also Mortlake Ware), Grooved Ware, Beaker, and Early Bronze Age wares. Even decorated or featured grog-tempered sherds can be difficult to classify (for example, see Longworth's (1984, no. 1650) re-classification of some of Smith's Fengate Ware (1965a, P273) as Collared Urn.) Even amongst the shell-tempered fabrics there is ambiguity. P279, illustrated by Smith as Fengate Ware, is shown here (fig. 208) as part of a Grooved Ware vertical

With quartz: 1; 21; 23; 28; 35

With grog: 2; 5; 6; 10; 11; 15; 16; 18; 29; 36

With grog and quartz: 3; 7; 8; 19; 32

With shell: 4; 24

With few inclusions: 9; 13

With quartz, grog and shell: 12; 22

With quartz and calcite: 14

With quartz and flint: 17; 26; 30; 33

With iron oxide and grog: 20

With flint, quartz and grog: 25; 34

With flint: 27; 31

cordon. As a result, this report resorts on occasion to using vague classifications such as 'Late Neolithic/Early Bronze Age'.

Style, contexts and groupings by vessel
?Neolithic

Two groups of sherds were identified as Neolithic by virtue of their position in the secondary fill of the outer ditch in Trench A (table 157). Neither seems Early Neolithic on the basis of fabric, and nothing similar is recorded in the primary fill.

Neo1 (fabric 19). Probably a single vessel (18 sherds).
Neo2 (fabric 21). Probably a single vessel (two sherds). One sherd has a possible deep impression.

Grooved Ware

Fabric. All the sherds contained some shell and this largely distinguishes them from the rest of the 1988 assemblage. Grog was a recurrent inclusion, though not in the amounts normal for Beaker or Early Bronze Age pottery.

Groupings, possibly by vessel. Further details are given below in the catalogue of illustrated sherds (see also fig. 208).

GW1 (fabric 29). Cordoned sherd (P514) from behind bank in Trench BB.
GW2 (fabric 12). Ten sherds from Trench A decorated with horizontal grooves, grooved herringbone, cordons, and some impressed decoration (P573–7; P586–7). Possibly these are from three very different vessels, one decorated with shallow grooves (like GW4), another with cordons, and a third with deep grooves which have displaced clay to give cordons on either side.
GW3 (fabric 24). Possibly one vessel (five sherds) from Trench E decorated with edge-to-edge fingernail impressions and horizontal rows of vertical fingernail impressions (P631–2).
GW4 (fabric 12). Probably one vessel (twelve sherds) from Trench E decorated with horizontal grooves (P633; P636–7). Four rim sherds of Longworth (1971a, fig. 20) form 21.

Classification. Grooved Ware is normally described in terms of the Longworth (1971a) sub-styles. While Longworth's catalogue of traits is very important, the sub-styles rest on relatively few characteristics and may obscure patterning in the data (Hamilton 1995). In any event most of the 1988 material does not easily fit into the usual sub-styles (fig. 198). Possibly P577 could be a vertical cordon and therefore of the Durrington Walls sub-style, as could P514.

Form. The only rim (P633) suggests a vessel which was slightly closed.

Decoration. The decoration below the horizontal cordon of P573 is paralleled in Pit 1, West Kennet Avenue (Smith 1965a, P365), Cherhill (Evans and Smith 1983, P75), and possibly at Burderop Down (Cleal 1992a, fig. 49.14).

P631 is paralleled in decoration, shape and fabric by P314 (but not P313), which Smith identified as 'Beaker and allied ware'. She identified the decorative technique (notes in Keiller Museum) as an imitation of twisted cord. However, similar decorated sherds at Durrington Walls (Longworth 1971a, P438–9), and Tye Field, Lawson, Essex (Smith 1985) were identified as Grooved Ware, and that interpretation is followed here.

The possible herringbone of P574 is paralleled by P287.

Horizontal grooves are the most frequent decorative technique, an observation also true for the Keiller/Smith material. Grooves can be relatively shallow (P633), or deep, displacing clay to produce ridges/cordons on either side (P586).

Beaker, including possible Beakers (?Bkr) and Rusticated Ware (Rus)

Fabric. The variation among the Beaker fabrics is generally small. Almost all contain grog with small amounts of sand and iron oxide. The only significant variations appear to be a few sherds with shell and a few with flint.

Groupings, possibly by vessel. All references to Beaker motifs, style, and groups use the descriptive terminology of Clarke (1970). The Roman numerals after motifs refer to particular forms of the motifs in Clarke, Appendix 1.4. Reference to 'Middle' or 'Late' relates to Case (1977). For Rusticated Ware, the division into non-plastic, plastic, and plastic zone is based on Bamford (1982, 60–66) (though it it is not claimed here that all Rusticated pottery is Beaker-related).

Bkr1 (fabric 1). Probably a single vessel (three sherds), partly from features in the upper secondary ditch fill in Trench B, with combed decoration, narrow chevron band (motif 7i), and broad undecorated bands (style b) (P526; P547). Possibly W/MR or European.
Bkr2 (fabric 5). Possibly a single vessel (six sherds), mostly from feature 219 in Trench B, with combed decoration of perhaps pendant triangles (P530; P532; P548: P569). Probably S1, S2, or S3.
Bkr3 (fabric 4). Probably two vessels (four sherds), from

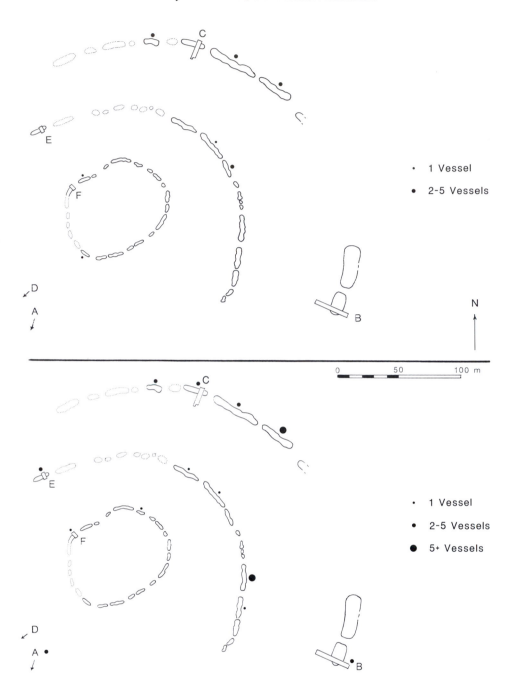

Fig. 198. Distribution of top: *Fengate vessels, and* below: *Grooved Ware vessels.*

Trench B, one represented by a rim sherd with an incised lozenge design (?motif 33), and the other by two combed sherds with a lattice motif (?motif 4) (P531; P534; P550–1). One other sherd could belong to either. The rim sherd comes from the S1, S2, or S3 Beaker group.

Bkr4 (fabric 6). Probably a single vessel (nine sherds), from Trench B, decorated with comb (P543–5; P563–4). One sherd has a lattice motif (?motif 4) and another a possible triangular motif above the base. The motifs are compatible with Middle Beaker.

Bkr5 (fabric 10). Probably a single vessel (three sherds),

from Trench B, all with horizontal combed lines (P546; P566). Possibly Middle Beaker.

Bkr6 (fabric 7). Single sherd, from Trench B, with a horizontal combed line, joined by oblique combed lines (P533).

Bkr7 (fabric 7). Six sherds, mostly with horizontal comb, probably from a single vessel, all found close together behind the bank in Trench BB (P506; P507). The large empty areas on these sherds are consistent with style b. Possibly Middle Beaker.

Bkr8 (fabric 18). Possibly a single vessel (ten sherds), from Trench A, with combed horizontal lines and

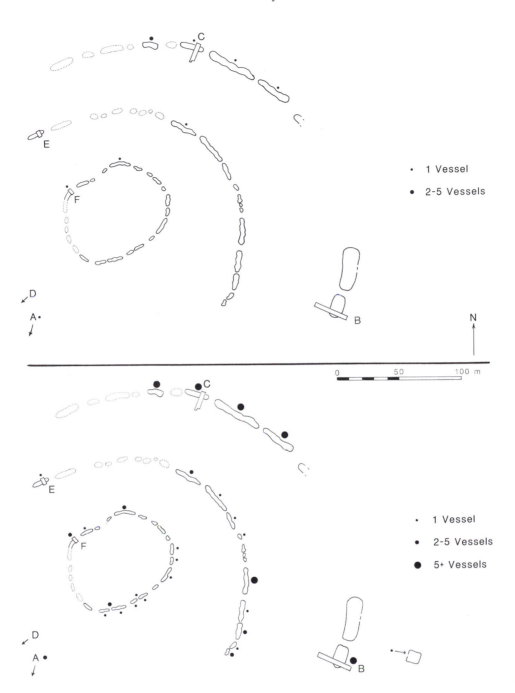

Fig. 199. Distribution of top: *cord-decorated Beakers, and* below: *Beakers.*

lattice (P582–3; P588). Possibly Middle Beaker.

Bkr9 (fabric 18). Probably a single vessel (two sherds), from Trench F, with combed triangular motif (P653). Combed triangles (away from the base-angle) seem more common on Late Beakers.

Bkr10 (fabric 18). Probably a single vessel (four sherds), from Trench C, decorated with combed triangular motif and motif 5 (P596; P600; P603). Possibly Late Beaker.

Bkr11 (fabric 5). Varying thickness and decoration suggest that these three sherds from Trench C could represent more than one vessel. Decorated with horizontal comb (continuous and intermittent) and possibly motif 2 (P599; P601–2).

Bkr12 (fabric 13). One sherd from Trench C decorated with incised opposing triangles or lozenges (P598). Incised decoration of this type seems more common on S4 Beakers.

Bkr13 (fabric 8). Possibly four sherds representing two vessels from Trench A. One vessel could be AOC, and the other has impressed decoration (P579–81).

Bkr14 (fabric 13). One sherd from AOC Beaker in Trench C (P597).

Bkr15 (fabric 20). Possibly a single vessel (two sherds)

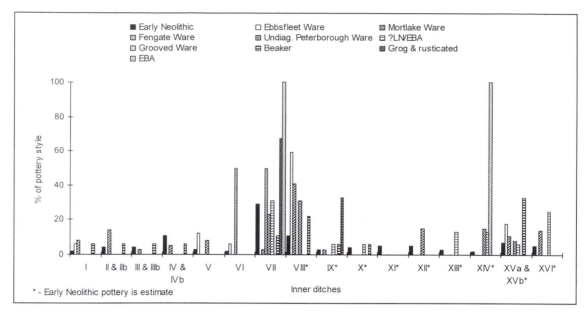

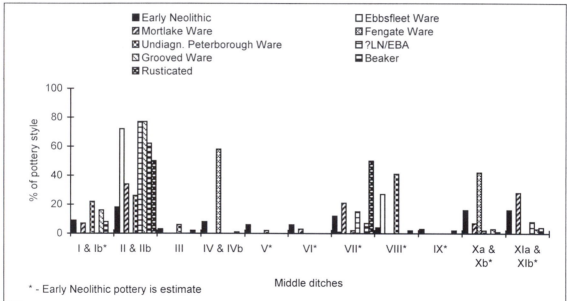

Fig. 200. Percentage representation of the various pottery styles across the inner and middle ditch segments.

decorated with horizontal comb (P525; P537). There is also a base-angle. These came from a feature in the upper secondary ditch fill in Trench B.

Bkr16 (fabric 22). Possibly a single vessel (five sherds). There is a base-angle and one sherd which is possibly decorated with comb (P606–7). All the sherds are abraded, which is consistent with their context (mostly 301) in Trench C.

?Bkr1 (fabric 18). Probably a single vessel (five sherds), from Trench B, decorated with thick horizontal twisted cord and vertical impressions (motif 5) (P527; P535: P552). Possibly European.

?Bkr2 (fabric 18). Four sherds from Trench C (and one

from Smith OD IV) probably from single vessel, mostly decorated with a wedge-shaped tool, or occasionally oval-shaped tool (P595; P604–5). The vessel of P604 may have had a cordon or carination. A combination of collar and wedge-shaped impressions does occur with Beaker (Clarke 1970, fig. 378).

?Bkr3 (fabric 10). Three sherds, at least two vessels, identified as possible Beaker because of the shared fabric, the sherd thickness, and the finish. All from Trench E.

Rus1 (fabric 2). Probably a single vessel from Trench B (six sherds), all profusely decorated with fingernail impressions (P554; P565). Decoration is plastic and

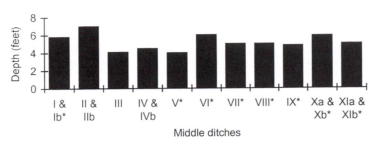

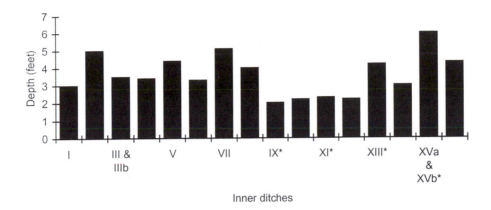

Fig. 201. Maximum depth of excavated segments of the middle and inner ditches.

probably zoned, possibly with an area of horizontal fingernails to one side of a vertical line of vertical fingernail impressions or a pinched-up cordon. A second vessel is represented by a sherd from Trench F (P652).

Rus2 (fabric 2). One sherd from Trench B decorated with a horizontal incised line, with closely spaced regular fingernail impressions below (P549).

Rus3 (fabric 32). One sherd from Trench E decorated with finger-impressions (?non-plastic) (P640).

Rus4 (fabric 15). 14 sherds from Trench A; only two have fingernail impressions, so it is possible that more than one vessel is represented (P584–5; P589). However, the carinated sherd P584 seems best paralleled in the collared Beaker sherds from Dean Bottom (Cleal 1992a, figs 47.3, 47.12) which have only sparse non-plastic fingernail impressions. The thinning of the sherd thickness in P585 cannot be matched at Dean Bottom.

Rus5 (fabric 5). One sherd from Trench B with a single fingernail impression (non-plastic) (P555); and 2 unillustrated sherds.

Rus6 (fabric 2). One unillustrated sherd with two fingernail impressions (non-plastic).

Form. The sherds are so small and the vessels so fragmentary that reconstruction of forms is difficult. P531 is a Long-necked Beaker. P579 is an everted rim sherd from a Bell Beaker, as is perhaps the gentle curving sherd of P582.

Decoration. There were small amounts of cord-decorated Beaker pottery from Trench A (Bkr13) and Trench C

(Bkr14), both presumably AOC Beakers. Trench B produced ?Bkr1, which has rather thicker cord than normal for Beaker pottery, and the combination of cord and vertical impressions as Clarke motif 5 (1970, Appendix 1.4) is unusual. It may be paralleled by a sherd from Avebury (Gray 1935, no. 163). Possibly both these vessels could be European Beaker.

Comb decoration was predominant (fig. 199), with some incisions and possible impressions. The most frequent design was simple horizontal comb, with or without empty zones. Lattice (Clarke motif 4) was the next most frequent, with a lesser emphasis on: bands of enclosed vertical or oblique lines (motif 2 or 5); various triangle motifs; and lozenge motifs (table 171).

Context. Some of the Beaker pottery in Trench B was associated with probable features (fig. 202). There were parts of three vessels, with three the maximum number of sherds per vessel. Three sherds conjoined though found in two features, 1.5 m apart (P526).

Most Beaker sherds did not come from recognisable features in the ditch. Plotting of the finds in Trench B suggests sherds from single vessels occurred in isolated little groups, though such sherds generally did not conjoin (fig. 203). 219, below and perhaps truncated by 216, contained parts of a long-necked Beaker (Bkr2), while an Enlarged Food Vessel (P541) was largely localised in 216. Directly above the contexts with the Beaker (Bkr1) were sherds of Early Bronze Age pottery in 202 and 201. In Trench A, Grooved Ware generally occurred lower than Beaker.

Table 171: Distribution by ditch circuit and segment of Beaker motifs (following Clarke 1970).

Key: Numbers relate to Clarke motifs; Roman numerals refer to the Clarke drawings;

1 - sherds only decorated with all over horizontal decoration; 1i - sherds decorated with horizontal lines in bands;

ab - immediately above base; * - conjoining sherds counted as 1; ** - only illustrated sherds of P295 included in sample;

/ - Number to right refers to possible examples of motif

Cutting	Examined sherds*	1*	1i**	2	3i	3ii	4	5	6i-iii	7	8	6/8 /18	9/28	13/19	17	27	28i	29	29 ab	31ii	32ii	33i	33iii-vi	? Triangle/lozenge	Not clear Complex	Unbounded Horiz. dec.
												Bounded														
Inner Ditch																										
I - II	3	-	2	1	-	-	-	-	-	-	-	-	-	-	-	-	-	-	-	-	-	-	-	-	-	-
II	1	-	-	1	-	-	-	-	-	-	-	-	-	-	-	-	-	-	-	-	-	-	-	-	-	-
III	1	-	1	-	-	-	-	-	-	-	-	-	-	-	-	-	-	-	-	-	-	-	-	-	-	-
III-IV	1	-	-	-	-	-	-	-	-	-	-	-	-	-	-	-	-	-	-	-	-	-	-	-	-	1
VII	1	-	-	-	-	-	-	-	-	-	-	-	-	-	-	-	-	-	-	-	-	-	-	-	-	1
VIII	4	-	4	-	-	-	-	-	-	-	-	-	-	-	-	-	-	-	-	-	-	-	-	-	-	-
IX	1	-	-	-	-	-	-	-	-	-	-	-	-	-	-	-	-	-	-	-	-	-	-	1	-	-
XVa	3	1	1	-	-	-	-	-	-	-	-	-	-	-	-	-	-	-	-	-	-	-	-	-	-	-
XVb	3	3	-	-	-	-	-	-	-	-	-	-	-	-	-	-	-	-	-	-	-	-	-	-	-	-
XVII+F	6	-	1	/1	-	-	-	-	-	-	-	-	-	/2	-	-	-	-	-	-	-	-	-	2	-	-
Middle Ditch																										
I	2	-	-	1	-	-	-	-	-	-	-	-	-	-	-	-	-	-	-	-	-	-	-	2	-	-
II	6	-	1	2	-	-	/1	/1	-	-	-	-	-	-	-	-	-	-	-	-	-	-	-	2	1	-
IIb	73	11	32	10/2	-	-	1	3	1	-	-	1	-	1	1	-	-	-	-	-	-	-	-	7	5	-
III	2	-	-	-	-	-	-	-	-	-	-	-	-	-	-	-	1	-	-	-	-	-	-	2	-	-
IV	1	-	-	/1	/1	-	-	-	-	-	-	-	-	-	-	-	-	-	-	-	-	-	-	-	-	-
VII	9	6	-	/1	-	1	-	-	-	-	-	-	-	-	-	-	-	-	-	-	-	-	-	-	-	-
VIII	1	1	-	-	-	-	-	-	-	-	-	-	-	-	-	-	-	-	-	-	-	-	-	-	-	-
IX	3	-	3	-	-	-	-	-	-	-	-	-	-	-	-	-	-	-	-	-	-	-	-	-	-	-
Xb	1	-	-	-	-	-	-	-	-	1	-	-	-	-	-	-	-	-	-	-	-	-	-	-	-	-
XIa	3	-	-	-	-	-	-	3	1	-	1	-	-	-	-	-	-	-	-	-	-	-	-	1	-	-
XIb	2	-	1	-	-	-	-	-	1	-	-	-	-	-	-	-	-	-	-	-	-	-	-	1	1	-
Outer Ditch																										
I	2	-	1	-	-	-	-	-	-	-	-	-	-	-	-	-	-	-	-	-	-	-	-	2	-	-
Ib	5	-	3	-	-	-	-	-	-	-	-	-	-	-	-	-	-	-	-	-	-	-	-	2	-	-
Ic	5	1	-	1	-	-	-	/2	-	-	1	-	-	-	-	1	-	-	-	-	-	-	-	1	-	-
II	187	14	8	5/5	-	-	4/16	6/20	2	-	-	-	5	4	-	/1	1	-	/1	1	5	1/1	-	85	1	15
IIIa	27**	4	5	/3	-	-	/1	/3	-	-	-	-	-	-	-	-	-	-	-	-	-	-	-	13	-	1
IIIb	8	-	-	/1	-	-	-	/3	-	-	-	-	-	-	-	-	-	-	-	-	-	-	-	2	-	2
IIIc	5	1	1	-	-	-	-	1	-	-	-	-	-	-	-	-	-	-	-	-	-	-	-	1	-	1
V+BB+B	35	3	10	/1	-	/1	/4	2/1	-	2	-	-	-	1	-	-	-	-	-	-	-	-	-	10	-	1
C	12	1	2	2/1	-	-	-	/1	-	-	-	-	-	-	-	-	-	-	-	-	-	-	-	2	-	4
A	4	-	3	-	/1	-	/1	-	-	-	-	-	-	-	-	-	-	-	-	-	-	-	-	-	-	-

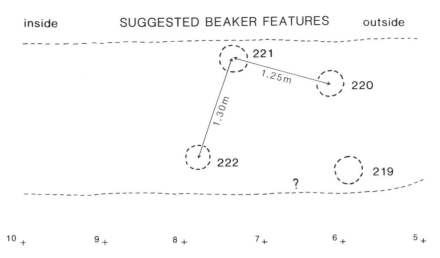

Fig. 202. *Schematic plan of suggested Beaker features in the outer ditch in Trench B.*

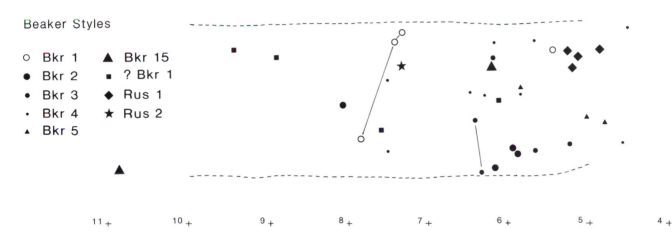

Fig. 203. *Distribution of Beaker styles in the outer ditch in Trench B.*

Early Bronze Age including Enlarged Food Vessel and Collared Urn

Fabric. All the Early Bronze Age pottery is grog-tempered.

Groupings, possibly by vessel

EBA1 (fabric 2). There are 58 sherds in this style from Trench B. Most sherds are plain. The decorated sherds have a range of technique used, mostly whipped cord, but also incision and twisted cord (P536; P538; P540; P553; P556; P558; P567; P570; P651). The range of decorative techniques, sherd thickness, and colour, suggests that at least four vessels are involved. Many of the sherds have a red/brown 'skin' which Smith saw as a Fengate trait (1957–58 excavation pottery archive in Keiller Museum; Smith 1956, 106). The same style is probably represented by sherds illustrated by Smith 1959, fig. 6.2; the lower half of the vessel in Smith 1965a, P323; P321; and P375.

Additional sherds probably of this style come from Trench BB (1 sherd); Trench C (6), Trench D (1), Trench E (2), and Trench F (3). A sherd from Trench F is decorated with whipped cord.

EBA2 (fabric 2). Possibly one or two vessels (13 sherds) from Trench B decorated mostly with whipped cord (P539; P559; P562). The rim sherd suggests an open vessel. There are three parallel shallow lines on the inside of the rim, possibly grooves or impressed decoration. Similar internal decoration can be paralleled on Grooved Ware, even with whipped cord (Marden: Longworth 1971b, P39), but there seem closer parallels on Collared Urns (e.g. Longworth 1984, nos 2030, 1025).

Trench E produced a probable single vessel (six sherds), decorated with whipped cord on either side of a carination (P638–9; P641).

EBA3 (fabric 3). 67 sherds from a single Enlarged Food Vessel mostly from a scoop (216) in Trench B. This has a single short everted rim with occasional oblique incised lines (P541). There are two horizontal ridges. The base is simple. A single rim sherd perhaps

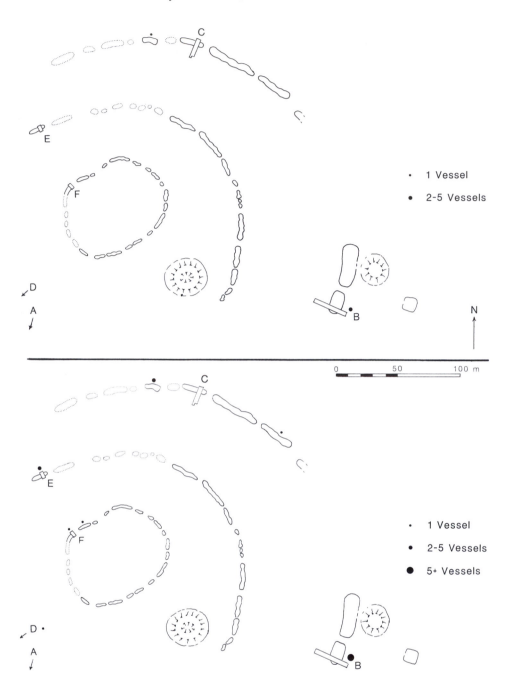

Fig. 204. Distribution of top: *Enlarged Food Vessels, and* below: *Collared Urns.*

representing a second vessel came from behind the bank in Trench BB (P511).

EBA4 (fabric 2). A single rim sherd from Trench B with four horizontal lines, either grooved or impressed, possibly with whipped cord (P557). This sherd looks similar to EBA2. There are parallels in Grooved Ware (Longworth 1971b, P38–9), but again numerous examples from Collared Urns (motif A: Longworth 1984, 10).

EBA5 (fabric 11). This Collared Urn is represented by a collar decorated with twisted cord (P528) and four body sherds. One body sherd may have a small finger-pinched cordon; another has a small ridge with possible decoration to one side. Not easy to separate from EBA3.

EBA6 (fabric 9). One Collared Urn is represented by a rim and collar decorated with twisted cord (P510), and a body sherd, from behind the bank in Trench BB. Another one is represented by a rim sherd from Trench B (P560), which conjoins with the upper part of P323 (Smith 1965a). (Smith's P323 mixes sherds of my EBA1 and EBA6.) A third vessel is represented in Trench B by a decorated body sherd (P561). There are two plain body sherds.

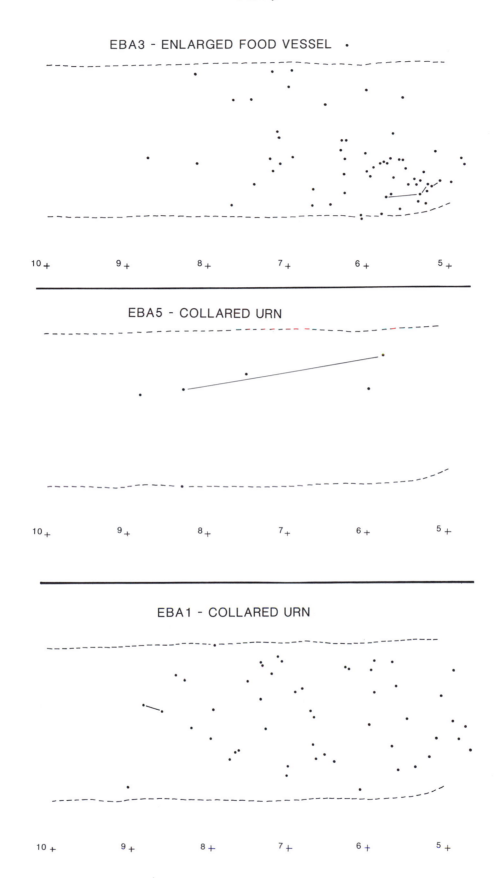

Fig. 205. Distributions in the outer ditch in Trench B of top: *EBA3 – Enlarged Food Vessel;* middle: *EBA5 – Collared Urn; and* below: *EBA1 – Collared Urn.*

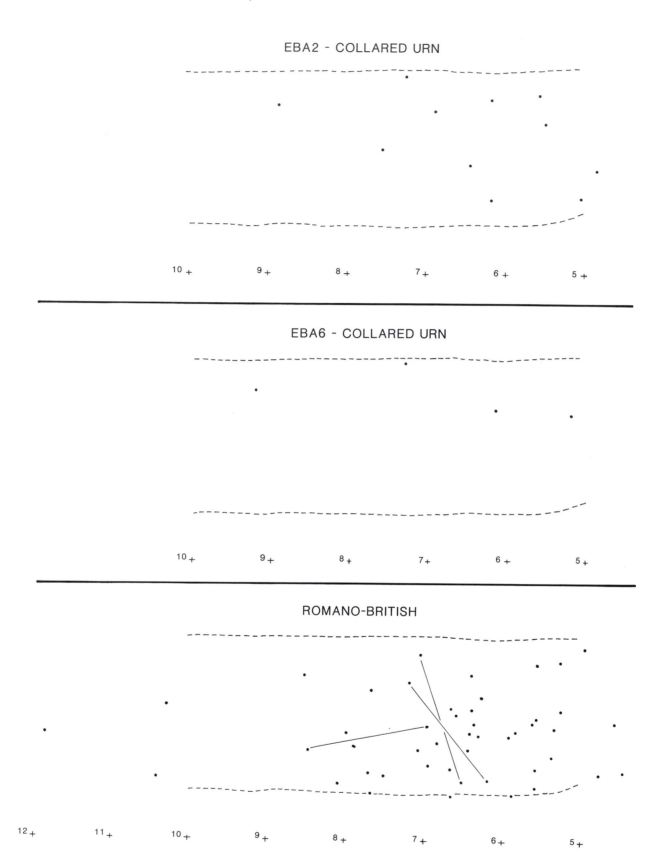

Fig. 206. *Distributions in the outer ditch in Trench B of* top: *EBA2 – Collared Urn;* middle: *EBA6 – Collared Urn;* and below: *Romano-British pottery.*

Enlarged Food Vessel

Form. Parts of two vessels were recovered from Trench B and BB, one from the ditch and one from behind the bank. The everted rim and rim-edge decoration of both, and the shoulder ridges of P541 are diagnostic of Wessex Food Vessels. If the internal decoration of P511 is deliberate then it mirrors a number of vessels from south Wiltshire (Amesbury G71: Christie 1967; Wilford G74: Stone 1938). The everted rims of the Windmill Hill vessels are not particularly pronounced and are best mirrored by that from Hemp Knoll (Robertson-Mackay 1980, P10). These rims seem better paralleled in the small Food Vessels from south Wiltshire (such as Annable and Simpson 1964, no. 493–5).

Sequence and context. P541 was represented by over 50 percent of its sherds, though the base and lower body were better represented than the shoulder ridges and rim. It had mostly been placed in a shallow scoop (context 216), though sherds were also found in a spread running to the north-west (fig. 205), and in Trench V. The deposition of the Enlarged Food Vessel, mostly in 216, may post-date the deposition of Bkr1 and Bkr2. The possible gap in the deposition of Beaker pottery created by 216 (except for pottery *in situ* in 219) may indicate that the deposition of EBA3 post-dates the deposition of the Beaker pottery. From near 216 came a Conygar Hill barbed and tanged arrowhead which is known for its Food Vessel associations (Green 1980). A copper/copper alloy awl of Thomas's type 2 (N. Thomas 1968) came from 201 above.

P511 came from behind the bank.

Collared Urn

Form. Using the Longworth (1984) scheme, P510 is Primary Series (internal moulding and simple rim). Many other sherds have features suggestive of the Primary Series: the whipped cord of P538; the internal decoration on the moulding of P528; the straight external collar surface of P556; and the simple rim and convex surface of 560, 557, and 562, the last two possibly also in whipped cord. Secondary Series urns are absent.

Context and sequence. The most notable feature of the Collared Urn sherds in Trench B (mostly EBA1, but also EBA2) was their even spread, suggesting a possible deposition after the digging of 216 and the deposition of the Enlarged Food Vessel (EBA3). Unlike EBA3 there was no strong focus for this activity, though sherds of EBA2, EBA5 and EBA6 did show a bias towards the inner part of the ditch.

Other styles and uncertain attributions: Late Neolithic/Early Bronze Age, and Late Neolithic/Bronze Age

Groupings, possibly by vessel

LN/EBA1 (fabric 16). A rim sherd, body sherd and other fragments from the same findspot in Trench B. Possibly the rim of a Beaker (P578).

LN/EBA2 (fabric 35). Two sherds from probably the same vessel. Superficially similar to EBA1 in appearance.

LN/BA1 (fabric 25). Two sherds from Trench BB (including part of base) (P509), one from D, one from F, and 21 (including two rims) from Trench E (P634–5). The presence of grog separates this style from the Later Bronze fabrics described in Gingell (1992). The two rim sherds differ slightly in fabric from the body sherds, and possibly belong to a different grouping, or reflect deliberate variation in tempering for different parts of the vessels (cf. Rice 1987, 121).

LN/BA2 (fabric 17). Six sherds from Trench A (106 and 102), of which one may be decorated, possibly with fingernail, and possibly in a herringbone pattern. Fabric and decoration have parallels in local Fengate Ware (West Kennet long barrow: Piggott 1962a, P13, P19–22). The three sherds from 102 may belong to a different vessel.

LN/BA3 (fabric 36). 1 sherd from Trench B.

Middle/Late Bronze Age

Groupings, possibly by vessel

M/LBA1 (fabric 14). Calcite-tempered pottery was recorded at Bishops Canning Down (Gingell 1992), but those detailed fabric descriptions do not match this sherd. However, no calcite is recorded from ceramics from other periods around Windmill Hill.

Bronze Age/Iron Age

Fabric. It is difficult to distinguish flint-tempered pottery of the Early Neolithic from that of the Bronze Age/Iron Age.

Groupings, possibly by vessel

BA/IA1 (fabric 34). Two rims from Trench B and Trench BB (P515; P542), and 4 unillustrated sherds from Trench BB. The sand-tempered sherds from Rockley Down (Gingell 1992, 93) offer a parallel, both in fabric and rim form.

BA/IA2 (fabric 33). This loose grouping contains more than five vessels (P642). These sherds (seven from Trench E and six from Trench F) are grouped together largely by fabric. There is only one rim, a simple upright form, very slightly everted (P650). Such a rim form occurs amongst Later Bronze Age pottery (for example, Tomalin 1992, fig. 64.23), but I have been unable to find one with the same fabric.

BA/IA3 (fabric 27). Seven sherds from Trench E may belong to one or two vessels. The main characteristic of this grouping is the tendency of flint temper to occur towards the exterior of the pottery, producing a rough exterior, whilst the interior is often quite smooth. Most sherds have red exteriors, and dark cores and interiors.

BA/IA4 (fabric 31). A loose grouping linked by similarity in fabric (23 sherds from Trench E (P644–6; P648); one from Trench C; two from Trench F), representing probably seven vessels at least. The rims consist of one expanded form, a T-shaped, a simple, and a flat-topped. There are parallels in form and fabric from Rockley Down (Gingell 1992).

BA/IA5 (fabric 26). Eight sherds from Trench E of which four are rims. The rim may have been tempered differently from the body (cf. Rice 1987, 121). These sherds look similar to BA/IA4. One rim is simple (unillustrated), another is possibly the same pot but has a slight bevel (P630), and the third is everted (P647). The fourth appears to have a low fillet below an everted rim (P643), paralleled in sherds from Burderop Down (Gingell 1992, fig. 72).

BA/IA6 (fabric 30). A distinct group of sherds from Trench A (one), Trench C (four), Trench D (five) and Trench E (four), probably from at least five vessels.

BA/IA7 (fabric 28). Dark sherds from Trench D (two), Trench E (two), and Trench F (two). The only illustrated sherd (P654) is an upright rim from a closed, possibly globular vessel.

Form. There is nothing in the plain pottery from Windmill Hill comparable to Deverel-Rimbury styles from Bishops Canning Down (Tomalin 1992), nor the fossil shell-tempered fabric which represents most of the sherds. The only sherds which are roughly similar in style would be the flat-topped rims of LN/BA1. However, the 'non-Deverel-Rimbury pottery' from Marlborough Downs sites (Cleal and Gingell 1992, 100) is a better parallel, including a possible rim with fillet (P644).

Undefined

Undef1 (fabric 23). Fabric may be the same as Bkr3.

Discussion

Sequence

Since all the Late Neolithic/Early Bronze Age pottery styles occur on Windmill Hill in ditch contexts which accumulated gradually, it was anticipated that the detailed sequence of Late Neolithic and other later styles might be resolved by stratigraphy. This approach mirrors the use of Windmill Hill by Piggott (1931), who observed that Peterborough Ware occurred in the upper ditch silt along-side Beaker pottery and later wares. The depth of Peterborough Ware in the ditch (Piggott 1931, 128) was seen as an indication of its lateness. Piggott believed that its appearance slightly pre-dated Beaker, but was mostly contemporary. Smith (1965a, 15) identified Ebbsfleet low in the secondary fill of OD V. However, she still observed that the 'more evolved forms of Peterborough Ware' (and Grooved Ware) did not occur below the level at which the first Beaker sherds appeared, and there was no strati-graphical priority for either Long-necked or Bell Beakers.

In the event the aim of using the stratigraphy of the ditches alone for establishing chronological precision has not been realised, because of the nature of the formation of ditch fills and because of the way that Keiller recorded the finds of pottery. Both processes are discussed fully above (chapters 3–4) and below (chapter 17). The previous use

of the upper fills to demonstrate contemporaneity of all Late Neolithic/Early Bronze Age pottery was flawed by the lack of a clear understanding about the rate and nature of secondary silting, the degree of post-depositional movement, and the possible presence of unidentified recuttings and features.

The most important evidence for the lack of useful stratigraphy in the upper silts is the proximity of Romano-British pottery to the Late Neolithic/EBA material. In the modern excavations of the middle and inner ditches there was no significant difference in depth of this material whereas outer ditch Trench C had an average of 10 cm difference and Trench B 30 cm difference between the LN/EBA and RB material. This lack of significant silting for 1500 years after the Early Bronze Age must have implications for the rate of silting during the Later Neolithic to Early Bronze Age. It is likely that the depth difference between LN/EBA ceramics deposited over many hundreds of years was slight and is therefore not useful in the identification of pottery sequence. This would explain the absence of clear separation between LN and EBA material (fig. 201). Note also that Piggott's evidence for contemporaneity of Peterborough Ware and Beaker rested on Keiller's spits, the arbitrary nature of which in terms of stratigraphy has already been discussed. These spits were also so deep that a single spit may well have encompassed the entire Late Neolithic/Early Bronze silting. This claim that there was little meaningful strati-graphy in the upper silts at Windmill Hill has important implications for other Early Neolithic chalkland ditches where contemporaneity of ceramic styles has been argued on the basis of depth in the upper silts. Nonetheless the 1988 results together with reconsideration of the Keiller/Smith material have enabled evaluation of the position of the individual styles in their site and regional contexts, to which we now turn.

Styles in their site and regional context
Peterborough Ware: Mortlake and Fengate

Windmill Hill is a major site for Peterborough Ware in north Wiltshire and played an important role in the creation of the sequence for Peterborough Ware sub-styles. Even though Peterborough Ware was identified in 1910 (R.A. Smith 1910) to be later classified by Piggott (1931) and Smith (1956), it remains poorly understood. The identification of three sub-styles for southern Britain and their relationships – Ebbsfleet, Mortlake and Fengate – rests on limited evidence (Smith 1956). The occurrence of most Peterborough Ware in secondary or derived contexts, usually with little associated material, has restricted discussion of function or role. However, the division of Peterborough Ware into three sub-styles is supported by the evidence from Windmill Hill. An early date for Ebbsfleet Ware is clear from its position just above the primary fill of the ditches. Mortlake and Fengate Ware probably only occurred in the upper fills. There are differences in how the sub-styles were deposited, both in terms of distribution and structure, which suggest that the existing division into sub-styles is real.

Mortlake Ware

This report uses the classification of Smith (1956) in its identification of Peterborough sub-styles and in most cases the defining element has been the rim. This differs from some modern identifications based on a more generalised notion of the sub-styles (Gibson 1995). It can be difficult to determine whether some sherds are Ebbsfleet or Mortlake Ware. In general this report classes flint-tempered sherds decorated with twisted cord as Mortlake Ware unless the shape was especially suggestive of Ebbsfleet Ware.

Dating. In MD IIb the large Ebbsfleet Ware assemblage occurred as low as the 3.5–5′ spit, and the majority of the material was in the 2.3–3.5′ spit, whereas Mortlake Ware did not appear until the 0.8–1.4′ spit. While this pattern is repeated in other trenches (ID I, ID XVa), there is an exception (MD VII). Overall, Ebbsfleet Ware clearly appears to precede Mortlake Ware on the site.

Nationally, radiocarbon dates indicate an earlier date for the first appearance of Mortlake Ware (Hamilton 1995). There is a case for the appearance of Mortlake Ware in the late fourth millennium BC, whereas the evidence for a continuation into the late third millennium is weak, resting mostly on radiocarbon samples poorly associated with pottery. The notion that Mortlake ware and Beaker pottery were contemporary is difficult to sustain. The issue will be pursued at greater length elsewhere.

Regional style. The style of the Windmill Hill Mortlake Ware appears catholic in comparison to other sites. All the rims from the West Kennet long barrow can be roughly described in terms of Smith (1956) forms M2a and M3a, and those from Cherhill mostly M2a and M1a, whereas at Windmill Hill there are forms M1a, M2a, M2b, M3a and perhaps M1b (depending on how P222 is identified), together with a large number of rims which do not easily fit with the Smith scheme. Examples of this are externally enlarged rims (P264; P342) which are a feature of Wiltshire Mortlake Ware (see Wilsford barrows: Smith 1991, P19; and unpublished pottery from outside Robin Hood's Ball: Julian Richards *pers. comm.*). The rim size and sherd thickness at Cherhill and West Kennet are all similar, whereas at Windmill Hill there is a wide range, from the very thick (P258; P260) down to the fine (P334; P342).

The Cherhill assemblage has mostly twisted cord herringbone or rows of oblique twisted cord. Whipped cord is used in a similar fashion. There is a tiny amount of horizontal twisted cord and one neck pit. At West Kennet twisted cord is used in a similar fashion, with one example of horizontal twisted cord (Piggott 1962a, P10). However, there is more use of bone impressions and perhaps finger impressions and incisions. (All the neck pits appear to come from Fengate Ware vessels.) At Windmill Hill designs using horizontal twisted cord are a major feature, as are neck pits. Bone impressions and finger impressions are rare.

Regional distribution. Mortlake Ware in north Wiltshire occurs mainly within 5 km of Windmill Hill. It is not represented on the neighbouring causewayed enclosures of Knap Hill, Rybury or Crofton, though the latter two have only seen limited investigation. Cherhill (Evans and Smith 1983) produced large quantities of Mortlake Ware in a secondary context in an Early Neolithic 'quarry', and in ditches interpreted as Early Bronze Age field boundaries. Of the 11 modern excavations on long barrows in north Wiltshire and south-west Oxfordshire, five have yielded Mortlake Ware (seven have Mortlake and/or Ebbsfleet Ware). Mortlake Ware occurred on many of the Late Neolithic monuments (such as the West Kennet palisade enclosures, the Sanctuary, the West Kennet Avenue, and perhaps Avebury). Of the 41 well recorded round barrow excavations in the same area probably only four produced Mortlake Ware (seven had Mortlake and/or Ebbsfleet Ware).

Fengate Ware

The defining characteristics of Fengate Ware are less exclusive than those of Ebbsfleet and Mortlake Ware. For example, two of the three typical rim-edge profiles illustrated by Smith (1956, 108, F2 and F3) also occur with Collared Urns (Longworth 1984, fig. 3).

While P270, P276, and P278 are clearly Fengate Ware because they have neck pits which were a rare Collared Urn feature (Longworth 1984, 21), the vast majority of vessels from Windmill Hill are less diagnostic. For the classification of sherds for tables 164–6 it was decided to include all the flint-tempered sherds with grooved and incised decoration as Fengate Ware. To this was added a small number of other sherds where the shape seemed more in keeping with Fengate Ware. Whereas most of the grog-tempered and twisted cord-decorated sherds were assumed to be Early Bronze Age unless there was a strong Fengate Ware parallel.

The most diagnostic Fengate Ware sherds are tempered either with flint and sand (P270), or with sand, shell, and grog (P276), while the sherds which are more doubtful are mostly grog-tempered (Smith 1985, P273–5).

Most certain Fengate Ware sherds are decorated with fingernail impressions, neck pits, and grooves/incisions. P278 may be Fengate Ware though the narrow heavy collar appears more in keeping with Mortlake Ware. This was the only rim with twisted cord. The absence of twisted cord is the major contrast with Mortlake Ware. The typical motif was herringbone (P277, P282, P352–3). P276 has a complex opposing triangular motif, as might P282c.

Twisted cord is also rare on local Fengate Ware sites (West Kennet long barrow: Piggott 1962a; West Overton G6a: Smith and Simpson 1964), where fingernail impressions, neck pits, grooves and herringbone motifs are most common.

Dating. The lowest spit to produce Fengate Ware is 1.4–2.3′ in MD IVb. With this exception all the other Fengate

Ware is recorded within 2' of the ditch top. In MD Xa P271 appears to be lower than two sherds of Mortlake and Ebbsfleet Ware, but it is possible that Fengate Ware was deposited into pits (see below).

The national dating for Fengate Ware has long depended on a single radiocarbon determination from a pit at Letchworth (Moss-Eccardt 1989) which suggested an Early Bronze Age date. Newer dates from Down Farm (Barrett, Bradley and Green 1991); Pit 1 in the West Kennet Avenue (Pitts and Whittle 1992); and now Manor Farm, Berkshire (Ian Kinnes *pers. comm.*) and Brynderwen, Powys (Gibson 1993), suggest a position nearer to the late fourth or early third millennium BC. The traditional link with Collared Urns (Longworth 1984) may no longer be valid.

Regional distribution. Two local long barrows have produced Fengate Ware, and only three round barrows. It was represented at the West Kennet occupation site (Smith 1965a), and from pits on Overton Hill (Smith and Simpson 1964) and at Yatesbury (A. Reynolds *pers. comm.*).

Grooved Ware

Given the small scale of the 1988 excavations, it may be significant that parts of five vessels (28 sherds) were recovered, whereas only 12 vessels ('twenty-odd' sherds; in fact about 100) were claimed for the Keiller/Smith excavations (Smith 1965a, 78). At least two of these vessels came from the Smith excavations.

Most Grooved Ware from Windmill Hill is not classically distinctive. There are a number of grog-tempered sherds, with simple rims and decorated with horizontal grooves. For example, the fabric of rim sherd P285 is not distinguishable from material identified as Early Bronze Age or Beaker, and indeed this sherd was illustrated by Gibson (1982, fig. WH1.13) as Beaker.

The majority of the Keiller/Smith Grooved Ware was similar to that from 1988, consisting of horizontal grooves and occasional horizontal cordons. The only exceptions amongst the illustrated vessels were P283, which had triangles filled with impressions, and P284 with a cordon on the bevel, which were classified as Clacton sub-style, and P287 which featured a grooved herringbone pattern. Base-angle P289 had an applied semi-circle, but further examination suggests it may be a rim, with the applied motif on the inside.

There is more variation to the Windmill Hill Grooved Ware than the published illustrations suggest. Diagonal and opposed grooves are used on one vessel (P282 re-drawn), which may be Grooved Ware, though the rim seems to be Fengate Ware, but it could belong to another vessel. The sherds when correctly orientated show diagonal and opposed grooves. Sherd P357 uses diagonal grooves and vertical cordons. Vertical cordons are also represented by the re-drawn P279.

Dating. Grooved Ware occurred no lower than 3' in the Keiller trenches. It tended to occur lower than Beaker. The relationship between it and Mortlake and Fengate

Ware was not clear, due to the rarity of the styles occurring together. The relationship of the various Grooved Ware sub-styles is also unclear. It may be significant that one Clacton vessel (P283) occurred on its own in MD II, whereas MD IIb produced several vessels, decorated with a mixture of fingernail impressions (P358), horizontal grooves (P356; P285 (re-drawn); P358), and at least one sherd with vertical cordons (P357). The other Clacton vessel (P284) came from OD Ib, with the majority of the sherds in the 2–3' spit, whereas the other Grooved Ware sherds, mostly from the uppermost spit, had possible vertical cordons (P279 redrawn) or vertical grooves (P363), and horizontal grooves and/or fingernail (P361–2).

Grooved Ware from henge monuments and of the Durrington Walls sub-style is well radiocarbon dated. A case can be made for a Wessex Grooved Ware sequence, in which open vessels, an absence of vertical cordons, and decoration in horizontal bands were early. These features occur on sites dated before 2500 BC, and as early as 3000 BC. Vertical cordons and vertical panels are better dated later than 2650 BC, with few reliable dates after 2200 BC (Hamilton 1995). I have set out the detailed arguments elswhere (Hamilton 1997).

Regional distribution. Grooved Ware is mostly distributed in the area around Avebury and Windmill Hill. Most of the assemblages are associated with Late Neolithic monuments. No Grooved Ware was recovered from the neighbouring causewayed enclosures at Rybury, Knap Hill or Crofton, and from only one long barrow, West Kennet. Pits containing Grooved Ware were discovered by chance at Blackpatch, (Annable 1977) and Burderop Down (Gingell 1992, 41), both well away from known Neolithic monuments. More local detail is set out elsewhere (Hamilton 1997).

Beaker

Only a small proportion of the Beaker pottery recovered by Keiller and Smith was published. In fact, as well as the simple motifs of Clarke's motif group 1 (1970, Appendix 1.4), there are also a large number of sherds probably belonging to Clarke motifs 29, 31, 32 and 33. In general the fabrics of the Keiller/Smith material are similar to those in the 1988 assemblage.

Dating. In the outer ditch excavated by Keiller Grooved Ware generally occurred lower than most of the Beaker pottery; a similar pattern is true for Mortlake and Fengate Ware.

The recent problems in dating Beaker pottery nationally are well known (Kinnes *et al.* 1991; Boast 1995; Case 1995). I have suggested elsewhere that the reliable time-span for Beakers may be as short as 2200 to 1900 BC (Hamilton 1995).

Regional patterns. The Beaker pottery assemblage from Windmill Hill is the largest such concentration in north Wiltshire. The other large assemblage is from a pit at Dean

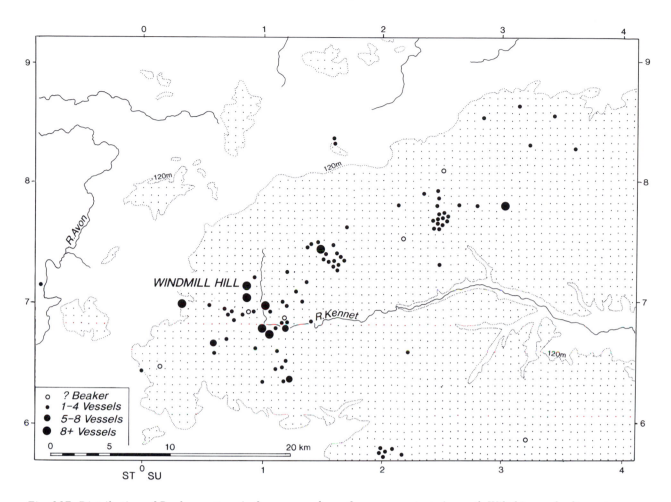

Fig. 207. Distribution of Beaker pottery in funerary and non-funerary contexts in north Wiltshire and adjacent areas.

Bottom (Gingell 1992). Beaker pottery was also recovered from the causewayed enclosure at Knap Hill.

Beaker pottery is widely distributed across north Wiltshire (fig. 207). Within this overall pattern, the distribution of cord-decorated Beaker is mainly in the area around Avebury.

The grave was not the ultimate destination for most Beakers (*contra* Thomas 1991, 102). The vast majority of excavated Beaker pottery has no association with human bone. The area shown on the map (fig. 207) has produced in excess of ninety findspots of Beaker, representing a minimum of 357 vessels. Only 25 vessels are directly associated with burials, with a 7 further arguable cases, which is about 9 percent. Many sherds have been recovered from barrows, but were from pre-barrow occupation, or were accidental inclusions.

Beaker pottery may have been very common. 50 percent of the more recently excavated round barrows in north Wiltshire have produced Beaker pottery, mostly incorporated in the mound building material. Two of the four Later Bronze Age sites on the Marlborough Downs excavated by Gingell (1992) produced Beaker pottery. There are a large number of surface finds by Meyrick and others, none of which represents systematic field-walking but the result of opportune finds (e.g. Swanton 1987). All this evidence suggests a contemporary landscape where Beaker pottery was deposited in abundance.

Early Bronze Age: Enlarged Food Vessels
P370 (Smith 1965a) is another vessel in this style, from OD II. There are a further five sherds possibly belonging to this vessel, including possible shoulder cordons/ridges. The majority of distinctive sherds for P370 came from OD II, spit 0.8–1.4'. The Keiller archive records other sherds from the 2.3–3.5' spit and Pit 63. P274 was classified by Smith as Fengate Ware, but could be redrawn with a everted rim (Smith 1965a, fig. 34). P511 and P274 do not have any body sherds. The more pronounced rims of these vessels are more typical of the Enlarged Food Vessels from south Wiltshire and Dorset (Forde-Johnston 1966). *Dating.* Enlarged Food Vessels are very poorly radiocarbon dated, with most of the dates being on charcoal and poorly associated with the pottery. The majority of dates overlap in the period 1950–1700 BC, though there are dates as early as 2300 BC, and there is some case for an end nearer 1750 or 1800 BC (Hamilton 1995).

Enlarged Food Vessels consistently post-date Beakers in barrows (Hamilton 1995), though the relationship with other Early Bronze Age pottery is less clear. Tomalin (1983; 1988) has argued that Food Vessels and Collared Urns were contemporary, but Collared Urns can still plausibly, on the available stratigraphic and radiocarbon evidence, be seen as a development of Everted Rim Food Vessels (Hamilton 1995).

Regional distribution. These vessels are rare in north Wiltshire and the counties immediately to the north, but more common in south Wiltshire and Dorset. Generally they occur with secondary burials, mostly cremations, in round barrows, where the primary internment is an inhumation, frequently associated with a Beaker. They are rare outside burials.

Collared Urns

Most of the Collared Urn sherds came from OD V, next to Trench B, or OD II. P323 and P373 probably belong to Longworth's Primary Series, whereas P320 and probably P374 are Secondary Series. P232 is difficult to identify though it does seem to possess a collar. The presence of abundant flint temper is unusual for Early Bronze Age fabrics in this area, as indeed is the presence of the perforated lug, which only occurs on three of the vessels collected by Longworth (1984).

Dating. Nationally, Collared Urns could appear as late as 1850 BC and could have waned by 1500 BC (Hamilton 1995).

Regional distribution. In north Wiltshire Collared Urns from burials are abundant (Annable and Simpson 1964). The only long barrow to produce Collared Urn was Beckhampton (Ashbee *et al.* 1979), but the presence of a later round barrow on top of the site may suggest a funerary origin. Though five north Wiltshire Late Neolithic sites have seen significant excavations there is only a single Collared Urn, that from Avebury (Gray 1935, no. 167).

Late Bronze Age/Iron Age
Distinguishing between Later Bronze Age/Iron Age and Early Neolithic pottery is difficult. The Early Neolithic pottery from layer 1 of Smith MD XIII seems similar to that identified as Bronze Age/Iron Age from neighbouring Trench E.

Deposition

Deposition in later phases at Windmill Hill has been discussed by several authors (e.g. Piggott 1954; Smith 1965a; Gibson 1982; Bradley 1984; Morton 1990; Thomas 1991). This section contributes to characterising such activity. It concentrates on the ceramic evidence for patterning within the site, using the Keiller material. There is further discussion in chapter 17.

Mortlake Ware

There was no major concentration of material in any single ditch segment, a contrast with the Ebbsfleet pottery. Only in ID VIII and MD II were there 10 or more sherds and more than five vessels represented (tables 165–66). All Mortlake Ware vessels are represented by very few sherds, none by more than six, again a contrast with the Ebbsfleet pottery. The style was better represented in the inner and middle ditches than in the outer ditch, though that had a smaller sample. Though there are no large concentrations, there is a higher incidence of sherds in ID VIII and MD II, and the area to the south of these. It is probable that activity involving Mortlake Ware was concentrated in this area and may have mostly consisted of surface deposition. The more restricted concentrations of Ebbsfleet Ware occur in the same area and this may have implications for continuity or contemporaneity.

In terms of later pottery there is a lack of correlation with Fengate Ware and it is possible this avoidance was deliberate. There are correlations between Mortlake Ware, and undiagnostic Peterborough Ware, rusticated pottery, and ?LN/EBA pottery, suggesting that some should be classified as Mortlake Ware (fig. 200). Some ditches produce Mortlake Ware and Grooved Ware, but there is no clear pattern. Mortlake Ware occurred frequently in the same segments as Beaker pottery, but the latter was ubiquitous. It is notable that the highest density of Mortlake Ware in the middle ditch (II/IIb) also corresponds with the highest densities of Grooved Ware and Beaker, though this is the deepest and one of the longest middle ditch segments (fig. 201). There is a concentration of Mortlake Ware and Beaker in inner ditch VIII which corresponds to a common axis with MDII and may suggest that entry to the site was by a long established route. There is no evidence of bias towards the possible entrance suggested by Smith (1965a, 5).

Mortlake Ware may have been principally deposited on ground surfaces. This was the case elsewhere in the region at Avebury and the West Kennet Avenue (Smith 1965a), Cherhill (Evans and Smith 1983) and probably in south Wiltshire (Hamilton 1995). No Keiller records suggest the presence of Mortlake (or indeed Ebbsfleet) pottery in ditch bone deposits, nor bias towards ditch terminals.

Fengate Ware

Unlike Mortlake Ware no ditch produced more than two vessels. In comparison to Mortlake Ware, some of the Fengate Ware vessels seem to be represented by relatively large numbers of sherds (tables 164–6); both P270 and P271 are represented by more than 10 sherds, and this may represent deposition into pits.

There appears to be a bias towards the north-east of the site, mostly in the outer but also the middle ditch (fig. 198). Due to the excavation bias it is not known if a similar high level of Fengate Ware is true for the whole outer ditch circuit, though it was notably absent from OD V/B and Trench A. This distribution is in marked contrast to that for Mortlake and Ebbsfleet Ware. There is some overlap with the distributions of Grooved Ware and cord-decorated Beaker (tables 164–6).

Locally, Peterborough Ware as a whole was absent from the three nearest causewayed enclosures. It has been found in the majority of the long barrows excavated in modern times, though, with one exception (West Kennet), the amounts were tiny. Larger quantities were recovered from Cherhill and the West Kennet Avenue, and it may be that Peterborough Ware was not so rare that its mere occurrence at Windmill Hill was of especial significance in itself. Surface deposition of Mortlake Ware, putatively in middens, may reflect settlement activity on sites such as Cherhill (Evans and Smith 1983), West Kennet Avenue (Smith 1965a), Downton (Rahtz 1962), Wilsford barrows (Smith 1991), North Kite (Richards 1990a, 184–92), and Winterslow Roman earthwork (Vatcher 1963). It is possible that depositions on Windmill Hill did not reflect symbolic continuity on the site but simply incidental reuse during settlement activity; this is discussed further in chapter 17.

Grooved Ware

A number of the Grooved Ware vessels were relatively well represented in terms of sherd numbers (P281, P283, P314). This may reflect deposition in pits within the ditches. Grooved Ware seems comparatively better represented in the 1988 and Smith trenches than the Keiller excavations. The deposition of Grooved Ware is too intermittent to reflect a coherent re-definition of the entire circuit (tables 164–66).

All Late Neolithic and Early Bronze Age material is comparatively rare in the inner ditch and therefore the absence of Grooved Ware from Trench F was not surprising. Keiller recovered some 60 sherds from the total excavation of three outer ditch segments, whereas 10 sherds (two vessels) were recovered from the 2 m-wide Trench A and two sherds (two vessels) from the combined 4 m-wide Trench B/V. Trench E produced two vessels (17 sherds), which compares with the roughly 30 sherds from Keiller's 11 completely excavated middle ditch segments. It is therefore possible that Grooved Ware was deposited more frequently to the south and north-west of the site and that the relatively small size of the Keiller assemblage reflects his excavation bias to the north-east and east (fig. 198). Two Grooved Ware pits were indeed found to the south of the enclosure in the 1993 season. The only exception to these patterns is Trench D, which may have been largely filled by the end of the Early Neolithic.

The occurrence of Grooved Ware in MD II/IIb coincided with high levels of Ebbsfleet and Mortlake Ware, Beaker and Rusticated Ware, and possible Late Neolithic/Early Bronze Age pottery (table 165). However, MDII/IIb was the largest and deepest middle ditch segment. In terms of overall site distribution, there is overlap with Fengate Ware and cord-decorated Beaker, with a bias towards the north-east.

Beaker

In Trench B some Beaker pottery was associated with features probably cut into the upper secondary ditch fill, and given the nature of the Keiller excavations and the difficulty of recognising these features, it is possible that other ditches had similar features. In OD II such activity was identified outside the ditch. However, even in Trench B the majority of the Beaker pottery was not in such features.

Though Beaker pottery is abundant, in general individual vessels are poorly represented by sherds. The Keiller archive up to mid-1927 deliberately set out to identify sherds from single vessels, but most vessels were represented by five sherds or less. In 1988 eight was the maximum number of sherds assigned to a single vessel. Most of the pottery is in good condition, with comparatively few very abraded sherds. The majority of Beaker was therefore probably deposited in the ditch when fresh.

Beaker pottery occurred across the site, but was unevenly distributed (fig. 199). In general the outer ditch is emphasised, especially the north-east quarter, though the amounts of pottery from the small excavations of Trench A and B/V could also suggest that concentrations occurred frequently around the outer ditch as a whole.

There does appear to be a relationship between the frequency of Beaker sherds and the size of the ditch. This is roughly matched by the Romano-British pottery, and possibly it reflects a common explanation for some of the distribution, relating to survival and the existence of suitable archaeological traps.

There is a marked bias for cord-decorated Beaker to have occurred towards the north of the site.

Clarke's motifs (1970, Appendix 1.4) were used to examine the Beaker distribution in detail (table 171). Sherds with just horizontal comb, or just horizontal comb and gaps (referred to in table 171 as 1i) represent the majority of finds from the middle (52 percent) and inner (54 percent) ditches, compared to only 17 percent of the 261 examined sherds from the outer ditch in the north-east quarter. Trench B/V is intermediate (37 percent) and Trench A has predominantly motif 1i. Triangles and lozenges, together with positively identified motifs of Group 3, 4, or 5, show a marked bias. Of the 187 examined sherds from OD II, 45 percent belong to these groups. A similar proportion is true for the other outer north-east ditches. However, of the 25 examined sherds from the inner ditch, only 16 percent belong to these groups. Similarly, of the 103 sherds from the middle ditches only 19 percent are possibly Group 3, 4, or 5. Trench B/V produced only 29 percent of sherds with triangle/lozenge motifs, and the small sample from A contains none. This suggests that the concentration of such motifs was localised in the north-east sector, though the proportion of triangles/lozenges from B/V is still higher than from the middle ditches.

This could suggest that the earliest Beaker activity,

represented by AOC material, was towards the north of the site, followed by Middle Beaker pottery in the centre and perhaps south, followed in turn by activity involving Late Beaker in the north-east. Trench B/V might reflect the spatial overlap between the Middle and Late activity.

The significance of Beaker material on the site is discussed further in chapter 17.

Early Bronze Age

Enlarged Food Vessels are difficult to recognise unless a rim or shoulder ridge is found. Given the small size of Trench B/V (a combined width of 4m) the recovery of three vessels, compared to one vessel from the rest of the site, does suggest a genuine localisation (fig. 204).

In Trench B, EBA3 (P541) was found close to a flint arrowhead and an awl, and a round barrow was only c. 30 m away. Could this have been part of a mortuary deposition? Further south in Wiltshire, at Shrewton G23 the urn and burial was found 'on the bare chalk' 6 m beyond a bowl barrow (Green and Rollo-Smith 1984). At Amesbury G71 (Christie 1967), a large proportion of an Enlarged Food Vessel was scattered in an arc across the top of a bell barrow; there was cremated bone from the same layer and it is possible that it reflects a disturbed burial spread during the re-modelling of the site.

The diagnostic sherds of Collared Urn were mostly located in Trench B/V with small assemblages from OD II, the Picket barrow, and Trench E (fig. 204). The total number of sherds in the combined 4 m wide cutting of B/V was several hundred, whereas there were less than 50 from the rest of the site. Furthermore this cutting contained an almost complete Collared Urn (P323). This concentration may be related to the round barrow cemetery within some 30 m.

Nationally, Longworth (1984, 76–8) identified a number of domestic and non-funerary contexts, but Burgess (1986,

341) suggested that Collared Urns were primarily connected with burial or ritual sites, including causewayed enclosures. However, the incidence of EBA material on causewayed enclosures is rare, and in Wessex is rare on Neolithic sites in general.

The Milton Lilbourne round barrow cemetery (Ashbee 1986), some 14 km south of Windmill Hill, produced over 500 sherds of pottery, mostly from the barrow mounds, the majority of which belonged to Collared Urns, representing at least 20 vessels. Human bone from the same contexts was very rare. Chemical analysis of residues from the inside of the sherds suggested a range of food-products. While none of this excludes a 'ritual' use, it could suggest a domestic midden accidentally or deliberately reused during the construction of the barrows.

Later Bronze Age/Iron Age

Discussion is limited here to the 1988 excavations, though limited examination of the Keiller/Smith archive suggests similar material was present. The relevant material comes principally from Trench E, with smaller amounts from D and F, and very little from the other trenches, suggesting a distribution mainly on the western side of the site. Generally its condition is good and fresh, but each vessel is represented by very few sherds.

Unlike on the Marlborough and Bishops Canning Downs there do not appear to be any Celtic fields across the top of Windmill Hill, though the earthwork survey shows features on the northern slope (probably of later date). Gingell (1992) argued that Celtic fields were Later Bronze Age in date. On the Overton and Fyfield Downs these field boundaries were retained by the Romans (Bowen and Fowler 1962). On Windmill Hill alongside the Bronze Age pottery there was much abraded Romano-British pottery suggestive of manuring and major arable activity, usually associated with fields.

CATALOGUE OF ILLUSTRATED SHERDS

Lesley Zienkiewicz and Michael Hamilton

The first number is the P no., followed by the Trench (letter), context and find number(s). Style is Early Neolithic unless otherwise stated.

500. BB 707 7272. Simple, rolled rim. Common shell-temper. Grey-brown surfaces and core. Worn. Traces of burnishing on inner rim edge. Rim is of heavy proportions but not made with addition of extra clay.

501. BB 741 7723. Body sherd. Hard, sandy fabric. Sparse small flint-temper. Dark grey surfaces and core. Worn. Pin-prick decoration.

502. BB 741 7632. Simple rolled rim. Laminar fabric; mostly tiny shell-temper, occasionally up to 4 mm. Brown-grey surfaces; orange-brown core. Very worn.

503. BB 741 7738. Simple, upright rim. Hard, well-made fabric; sparse flint-temper. Red-brown, smooth surfaces; grey core. Worn.

504. BB 705 7521. Simple, rolled rim. Fabric as P3; possibly part of same vessel (counted as a separate vessel for minimum number count). Very worn.

505. BB 705 7546. Ebbsfleet-style carinated vessel. Sparse shell-temper, up to 9mm; fairly common quartz, mainly tiny, occasionally up to 2mm. Originally dark brown-grey surfaces; dark grey core. Very worn.

506. BB 705 7591. Brown throughout. Bkr7. Three horizontal combed lines. Possible diagonal decoration.

507. BB 705 7628. Same as P506. Horizontal combed line.

508. BB 705 7919 Horizontally perforated lug. Hard fabric;

moderate calcined flint-temper. Dark grey surfaces and core. Fairly fresh.

509. BB 705 7446. Buff surface, dark surface and core. LN/BA1. Probably from base of pot. Possibly the marks on one surface (unclear if top or bottom) are from a burnt out seed-impression and some narrow organic material.

510. BB 705 7475. Reddish brown exterior, and dark core and interior. EBA6. Rim and collar sherd, with twisted cord in an filled triangles motif (Longworth 1984, 11, motif H).

511. BB 705 7555. Brown exterior, and dark core and interior. EBA3. Rim sherd with fingernail and possibly a bone impression. Possibly the same Enlarged Food Vessel as found in Trench B (P541), but as that lacks impressions, this probably represents a second vessel.

512. BB 703 7044. Simple rim; partly rolled, partly smoothed down, with a flat top. Abundant shell-temper. Dark to lighter brown surfaces, grey-brown core. Worn. Pin-prick decoration.

513. BB 701 7169. Simple, upright rim. Hard, well-made, laminar fabric; moderate flint-temper. Grey exterior; dark orange interior and core. Fairly fresh.

514. BB 701 7186. Buff throughout. GW1. Cordon, but orientation of sherd is uncertain.

515. BB 701 7207. Brown throughout. BA/IA1. Simple rim.

516. B 229 23250; 229 23218; 228 23351 (rim sherds). Simple, rolled rim of varying thickness. Hard, well-made fabric; sparse shell-temper, rare flint. Dark grey surfaces, lighter grey core, occasionally orange just below exterior surface. Fairly worn. Burnished. Traces of sooty residue on exterior and particularly on interior at base. Perforation immediately beneath rim; drilled after firing, possibly an attempt at repair. This vessel was represented by c. 100 sherds and countable fragments.

517. B 228 23303. Simple, slightly inturned rim. Hard, very fine fabric; no visible temper apart from fine quartz sand. Grey exterior, dark orange interior and core. Very worn. Possibly part of cup or small bowl.

518. B 228 23337. Simple, rolled rim. Granular, sandy fabric. Grey exterior, grey-brown interior and core. Worn.

519. B 210 23125. Internally expanded, rolled rim. Very hard, coarse fabric; common flint-temper, mainly less than 2 mm, occasionally up to 5 mm. Pale grey-brown surfaces, darker on exterior; light grey core. Fairly fresh.

520. B 229 23227. Simple, upright rim. Commonflint-temper, up to 3 mm. Grey-brown exterior, pale orange-brown interior and core. Very worn. One complete, and the remnant of a second, perforation, made before firing.

521. B 228 23306. Internally expanded, rolled rim. Laminar fabric; sparse flint-temper. Dark grey-brown surfaces and core. Worn.

522. B 227 23072. Ebbsfleet body sherd. Very fine fabric; slightly micaceous surfaces. A single flint grit of c.1 mm. Dark chocolate brown surfaces; very dark grey core. Worn. Whipped-cord impressions.

523. B 203 16771. Simple, upright rim. Moderateflint-temper, up to 4 mm but mainly 2 mm or less. Orange-brown surfaces and core. Worn. Sooty residue on exterior and rim.

524. B 225 16907. Ebbsfleet body sherd. Fine fabric, as for P522, but with two grains of flint of c.1 mm and a single sandstone grit. Very worn. Whipped-cord impressions. Probably part of the same vessel as P522.525. B 204 16310.

Brown exterior and interior, and dark core. Bkr15. Combed horizontal line. Same vessel as P537.

526. B 203 16675, 16799, 16783. Reddish-brown exterior, dark core, and brown interior. Bkr1. Horizontal combed lines and a narrow band of combed chevrons.

527. B 203 16652. Brown throughout. ?Bkr1. Curving sherd, with possible horizontal cord line and vertical impressions below.

528. B 216 16453, 16461. Brown exterior and interior, and dark core. EBA5. Sherd from base of collar, with six horizontal rows of twisted cord on the collar, and two horizontal rows on the interior.

529. B 215 9805. Simple, upright rim. Hard fabric; common flint-temper, mainly less than 2 mm. Grey exterior and core, lighter grey-brown interior. Very abraded.

530. B 219 16585. Brown exterior and interior, andorange-brown core. Bkr2. Combed decoration probably of elongated pendant triangles.

531. B 216 16534, 16535. Possibly dark exterior, core, and brown interior. Bkr3. Rim sherd with horizontal incised lines bordering short vertical lines. Below is a incised lozenge design.

532. B 219 16529. Orange-brown throughout. Probably the same vessel as P530. Probably pendant triangular motif, with other motifs, all produced with comb.

533. B 211 9665. Brown exterior and 50 percent of core, and dark remainder of core and interior. Bkr6. Horizontal combed line with oblique combed lines below.

534. B 216 16541. Orange-brown throughout. Bkr3. Two horizontal combed lines with start of combed lattice below.

535. B 214 16124. Buff-brown throughout. Same as P527. Horizontal probable cord with a horizontal row of vertical impressions below.

536. B 215 9858. Buff exterior, and dark core and interior. EBA1. Carinated sherd with oblique whipped cord on one side of the carination.

537. B 220 16895. Brown exterior, and dark core and interior. Base angle sherd with a horizontal combed line. Probably same vessel as P525.

538. B 214 9892. Probably the same vessel as P536. Oblique whipped cord on one side of a carination, with stab impressions on the other.

539. B 214 9953. Brown exterior and interior. Dark core. EBA2. Horizontal line of oblique whipped cord.

540. B 216 16537. Very abraded sherd. Dark throughout. Possibly EBA1. Two rows of fine twisted cord.

541. B various contexts: 202; 203; 211; 212; 214; 216; and 222. Large numbers of sherds. Mostly buff to reddish-brown exterior, dark core, and dark or brown interior. EBA3.

542. 202 9029. Orange-brown throughout. BA/IA1. Everted rim.

543. B 202 9305. Red-brown throughout. Bkr4. Three horizontal combed lines with undecorated areas on either side.

544. B 202 2907. Same as P543. Base-angle with triangular motif, possibly done with comb.

545. B 202 2719. Same as P543. Two horizontal combed lines. Oblique to these is two lines, technique uncertain, which appear to end in a spiky impression.

546. B 202 9273. Dark brown exterior and interior, and dark core. Bkr5. Two horizontal combed lines.

547. B 202 2585. Brown exterior and 50 percent of core, with dark remainder of core and interior. Possibly same as P526.

This could be decorated with an incised horizontal line, which changes direction, and continues diagonally, but this may be burnt out organic material.

548. B 202 2682. Brown throughout. Possibly same vessel asP530. Probably a triangular or lozenge motif, probably done with a comb.

549. B 202 9221. Reddish-brown throughout. Rus2. Horizontal incised line with closely spaced regular fingernails below.

550. B 202 9574. Brown exterior and interior, and centre of core is dark. Probably same vessel as P534. Two horizontal combed lines with combed lattice below.

551. B 202 2976. Brown throughout. Possibly belongs to same vessel as P531 or P534. Base-angle.

552. B 202 9352. Same as P527. Two horizontal probable cord lines with a horizontal row of vertical impressions.

553. B 202 2858. Buff throughout. EBA1. Carinated sherd with a diagonal incised line.

554. B 202 2954. Reddish exterior, extending slightly into core, and dark core and interior. Rus1. If the orientation of the drawing is correct, then the decoration is a vertical line of vertical fingernail impressions, with horizontal fingernail impressions to the right.

555. B 202 2446. Buff exterior and interior, and dark core. Rus5. Sherd has fingernail impression.

556. B 202 2563. Buff exterior, dark core, and brown interior. EBA1. Collared sherd, with oblique decoration on collar, but the sherd is too damaged to determine technique.

557. B 202 9550. Brown exterior, and dark core and interior. EBA4. Rim with four horizontal grooves (or perhaps impressions).

558. B 202 2558. Buff throughout. EBA1. Carinated sherd with oblique twisted cord on either side of the carination.

559. B 202 2845. Same as P539. Two horizontal rows of vertical short whipped cord.

560. B 202 2513. Reddish-brown exterior, dark core, and brown interior. EBA6. Rim sherd with a horizontal row of oblique twisted cord.

561. B 202 9234. Brown exterior and interior, and dark core. EBA6. Possibly the same vessel as P560. A sherd with a concavity (?), below a carination. In this concavity is a twisted cord herringbone.

562. B 202 9233, 9521. Possibly same as P539. Rim with two horizontal rows of oblique whipped cord below the rim. On the inside are three shallow horizontal grooves.

563. B 201 2210. Same as P543. Two horizontal combed lines.

564. B 201 2418. Same as P543. Horizontal combed line with lattice below. The lattice could be comb.

565. B 201 2382. Same as P554. If the orientation of the drawing is correct then the decoration consists of a possible pinched-up cordon with oblique fingernail impressions to the right.

566. B 201 2159. Same as P546. Single horizontal combed line.

567. B 201 2394. Buff throughout. EBA1. Base-angle.

568. B Backfill 2013–5. Ebbsfleet-style rim and part of neck. Fabric same as that for P 522 and P 524. A single visible flint grit of c. 3 mm. Very worn. Whipped-cord impressions on interior and exterior over rim. P 522, P 524 and P 568 are all probably from the same vessel and are likely to belong to Smith's P 237 (from cutting V).

569. B Backfill 2009. Brown exterior and interior, and dark core. Possibly same vessel as P530. Decorated with comb.

570. B Backfill 2013. Buff exterior, and dark core and interior.

EBA1. Exterior has oblique narrow whipped cord impression. On the interior is a possible horizontal twisted cord line, with possible fingernail impressions.

571. A 112 1664. Internally expanded, bevelled rim. Sandy fabric; rare shell-temper. Uniformly dark grey surfaces and core. Very worn.

572. A 115, 111 1698; 110 1661; 108 1669; 106 1636, 1498, 1599. Internally expanded, rolled rim. Six rim fragments from same vessel. Hard, compact, coarse fabric; moderate flint-temper, up to 4 mm but mainly 2 mm or less. Mottled dark grey to brown surfaces, dark orange-brown to light grey core. Traces of burnishing over rim. Not excessively worn.

573. A 106 1692. Brown exterior, and dark core and interior. GW2. Two horizontal grooved lines creating a possible cordon, above which is a line of vertical stab impressions.

574. A 106 1396. Brown exterior, and dark core and interior. GW2. Abraded but possibly has some sort of grooved herringbone pattern.

575. A 104 1384. Dark throughout. GW2. Three or four horizontal grooves.

576. A 104 1204. Brown exterior, and dark core and interior. GW2. Horizontal grooved line with a diagonal on one side.

577. A 104 1210. Brown exterior, and dark core and interior. GW2. Orientation of this sherd is not clear. Either it has a cordon or perhaps part of a applied semi-circular motif.

578. A 104 1302. Very abraded. Dark core. LN/EBA1. Simple rim.

579. A 104 1322. Reddish-brown throughout. Bkr13. Rim with one or two horizontal lines of fine twisted cord.

580. A 104 1333. Reddish-brown throughout. Bkr13. Twosemi-circular impressions, not unlike fingernail, except they contain oblique impressions at their base.

581. A 104 1225. Reddish-brown throughout. Bkr13. Abraded sherd. Oblique impression, possibly twisted cord.

582. A 104 1294. Brown exterior, and dark core and interior. Bkr8. Three horizontal lines of comb.

583. A 104 1348. Brown exterior and interior, and dark core. Probably the same as P582. Two horizontal combed lines with lattice above (possibly Clarke (1970) motif 4).

584. A 104 1219. Brown exterior, and dark core and interior. Rus4. Carinated sherd.

585. A 104 1239. Brown exterior and interior, and dark core. Rus4. Fingernail and possible bone impressions.

586. A 102 1078. Same as P575. Three horizontal grooves and a possible slight cordon.

587. A 102 1068. Buff exterior and core, and brown interior. GW2. Two or three possible horizontal grooved lines.

588. A 102 1092. Same as P582.

589. A 102 1146. Possibly the same as P585. End to end fingernail impressions.

590. C 319 10604. Externally expanded, rolled rim. Abundant, mainly tiny, shell-temper, occasionally between 3–5 mm. Dark brown exterior, dark grey-brown interior, grey core. Fairly fresh. Traces of sooty residue on exterior.

591. C 315 10616. Internally expanded, bevelled rim. 'Soapy' micaceous fabric; sparse grog-temper. Light grey-brown surfaces and core. Very worn.

592. C 319 10607. Simple, everted rim. Abundant, mainly tiny, shell-temper, occasionally up to 3–5 mm. Light brown exterior, grey interior and core. Worn.

593. C 308 10474. Solid horizontal lug. Abundant rounded

sandy grains, sparse flint- and shell-temper, including a single oolite. Pale orange exterior, dark grey core. Moderately worn.

594. C 315 10631. Simple, rolled rim. Common shell-temper, up to 7 mm. Grey-brown surfaces and core. Worn.

595. C 304/316 10062. Brown exterior, and dark interior and core. ?Bkr2. Horizontal rows of vertical stab impressions.

596. C 316 3663. Brown exterior, and dark core and interior. Bkr10. Pendant triangle or lozenge possibly done with comb.

597. C 316 3767. Buff exterior and interior, and dark core. Bkr14. Two horizontal lines of fine cord.

598. C 316 3815. Buff throughout. Bkr12. Incised decoration, probably representing the points of three triangles or lozenges.

599. C 317 3906. Buff throughout. Bkr11. A single intermittent horizontal combed line.

600. C 302 3248. Possibly same as P596. Horizontal combed line enclosing short oblique lines, with possibly this motif is repeated on the top of the sherd.

601. C 302 3472. Reddish exterior and interior, and buff core with dark centre. Bkr11. A combed horizontal line with vertical comb below.

602. C 302 3112. Reddish exterior, brown interior, and dark core. Bkr11. Possibly the same as P601. Horizontal combed line.

603. C 302 3557. Probably same as P596. Horizontal combed line with a diagonal combed line to one side.

604. C 303 3260. Probably same as P595. Sherd from close to thickened area of pot. Two horizontal rows of vertical stab impressions.

605. C 302 3522. Probably same as P595. Carinated sherd with horizontal rows of vertical stab impressions.

606. C 302 3518. Reddish-buff throughout. Bkr16. Horizontal possible combed lines. Others perhaps at right-angles and diagonal.

607. C 301 3033. Probably same as P606. Base-angle.

608. D 416 4323. Simple, rolled rim. Coarse, vesicular fabric; common shell-temper. Patchy dark grey, dark brown to pale orange, exterior; grey interior and core. Worn. Soot encrustation covers interior surface where not abraded, extending over and immediately beneath rim on exterior. Exterior pitted with sub-rectangular and sub-rounded, and some linear voids up to 1.3 cm, the remains of organic matter burnt out on firing. This was the largest single vessel in the assemblage, at 20.5 cm max. 31 body sherds, mostly small and worn, were part of this vessel.

609. D 417 4359. Simple, upright rim. Moderateflint-temper. Uniformly grey-brown surfaces and core. Worn.

610. D 416 4314. Decorated rim and body sherd from same vessel. Expanded, slightly rolled, rim. Hard fabric; common flint-temper. Very dark grey surfaces, lighter grey core. Worn. Burnished on exterior and interior. Narrow oblique incisions over rim; wider channelling on body sherd.

611. D 415 4268. Simple, upright rim. Fine, soft fabric; moderate flint-temper. Dark grey exterior, lighter grey-brown core. Interior completely worn away. Very worn.

612. D 411 4165. Expanded, T-shaped rim. Abundantshell-temper, sparse limestone particles. Patchy buff to dark grey exterior; dark grey interior, including wide rim lip, and core. Worn. Faint fingernail impressions on rim.

613. D 411 4215. Simple, upright rim. Common, mostly tiny, shell-temper. Grey-buff surfaces, grey core. Worn.

614. D 406 4119. Expanded, rolled rim. Moderateflint-temper. Grey surfaces and core. Worn.

615. D 408 4135. Expanded, rolled rim. Soft fabric; abundant shell-temper, occasionally up to 6 mm. Dark grey surfaces and core; orange-brown tint on rim. Worn. Extremely faint traces of vertical channelling on rim. Exterior possibly burnished, with a rippled effect, below rim.

616. D 406 4106. Expanded, everted rim. Moderatelyflint-tempered, 'soapy' fabric. Grey-brown exterior and core, light brown interior. Worn.

617. D 404 4032. Expanded, T-shaped rim. Sandy fabric; moderate small flint-temper, some calcined. Dark grey surfaces and core. Worn. Vertical, close-spaced channelling over rim. Wider, vertical channelling on body below rim.

618. E 510 12040. Expanded, internally projecting rim. Moderate flint-temper, some calcined. Uniformly dark grey surfaces and core. Worn and flakey. (P 628 possibly belongs to this vessel but was counted separately for the minimum vessel total).

619. E 523 12099. Simple, everted rim. Sandy fabric; sparse flint-temper. Brown exterior, dark grey interior and core. Worn. Smooth surfaces with traces of burnishing over rim.

620. E 510 12062. Simple, everted rim with steep internal bevel. Rim lip is sharply defined. Coarse fabric; common flint-temper, occasionally up to 5–7 mm. Patchy dark grey-brown exterior, dark grey interior, light grey core. Fairly fresh. Sooty encrustation on exterior.

621. E 525 12304. Simple, upright rim with flattened top. Hard, slightly micaceous, fabric; common flint-temper. Brown exterior, pale orange-brown interior and core. Fairly fresh. Distinctive smooth, silky finish. Sooty staining on exterior. c. 24 sherds and fragments were part of this vessel.

622. E 518 5914. Simple, everted rim. Moderateflint-temper, some up to 5 mm. Dark brown exterior, brown-grey interior and core. Fairly fresh. Smooth, silky finish. Traces of burnishing over rim.

623. E 518 12025. Simple, upright rim. Sandy clay; no visible added temper. Uniformly dark grey surfaces and core. Worn.

624. E 504 5972. Simple, upright rim. Flaky, laminar fabric; abundant shell-temper. Dark grey-brown surfaces and core. Very worn.

625. E 503 5893. Expanded, rolled rim. Granular, sandy fabric; sparse shell-temper. Light grey-brown surfaces and core; orange between surfaces and core. Deep wide-spaced oblique channelling over rim. Extremely worn.

626. E 503 5805. Expanded, almost T-shaped rim with internal ridge. Soft fabric; common shell-temper. Uniformly dark grey surfaces and core. Very worn.

627. E 503 5828. Simple, upright rim. Soft 'soapy' fabric; moderate flint-temper. Grey-brown exterior, buff interior, buff/light grey core. Worn. Sooty deposit on exterior. Two perforations, and a scar of a third, made before firing.

628. E 503 5818. Expanded rolled rim from vessel with solid lug. Hard, coarse fabric; moderate flint-temper. Uniformly dark grey surfaces and core; browner over lug. Worn.

629. E 503 5708. Simple, everted rim. Fine fabric; common flint-temper, occasionally up to 7 mm. Light brown-pale orange exterior, patchy light brown and dark grey interior, light grey-buff core. Very worn. Very faint traces of oblique incised lines over rim.

630. E 502 5695. Brown throughout. BA/IA5. Rim with slight bevel.
631. E 502 5694. Brown exterior, and dark core and interior. GW3. Base-angle with four rows of edge to edge fingernail impressions.
632. E 502 5702. Possibly same as P631. Buff exterior, and dark core and interior. Two fingernail impressions, possibly part of a row.
633. E 501,502 5616. Brown exterior, and dark core and interior. GW4. Rim with bevel and three horizontal grooved lines.
634. E 502 5689. Brown exterior and interior, and dark core. LN/BA1. Flat-topped rim.
635. E 501 5423. Abraded exterior and interior, probably originally brown, and dark core. Possibly the same as P634. Flat-topped rim.
636. E 501 5546. Probably same as P633. Two horizontal grooved lines.
637. E 501 5592. Probably same as P633. Two horizontal grooved lines.
638. E 501 5426. Brown throughout. EBA2. Carinated sherd with a horizontal row of oblique whipped cord on either side. Above may be a horizontal row of faint oblique incised lines.
639. E 501 5551. Same as P639. Two horizontal rows of oblique whipped cord.
640. E 501 5250. Red exterior, and dark core and interior.Rus3. One finger-impression and possibly two others.
641. E 501 5185. Brown exterior and interior, and dark core. EBA2. Orientation of sherd is not clear. Two possible impressions and perhaps a linear piece of decoration.
642. E 501 5095. Buff exterior, and dark core and interior. BA/IA2. Possible impressions.
643. E 501 5162, 502 5657. Brown exterior and interior, and dark core. BA/IA5. Everted rim. The right of this sherd has a prominent fillet (cf. Gingell 1992, 97).
644. E 501 5233. Dark throughout. BA/IA4. T-shaped rim.
645. E 501 5537. Dark throughout. BA/IA4. Simple rim.
646. E 501 5261. Dark throughout. BA/IA4. Simpleflat-topped rim.
647. 501 5600, 5518. Dark to brown exterior, and dark core and interior. BA/IA5. Everted rim.
648. 501 5093. Dark throughout. BA/IA4. Expanded rim.
649. F 628 6354 (unillustrated: 628 6352; 602 6155). Simple, rolled rim. Hard fabric; moderate flint-temper, one grain 7 mm. Mottled grey-brown exterior and core, dark grey interior. Worn exterior; interior smooth and fairly fresh.
650. F 601 6023. Dark brown throughout. BA/IA2. Slightly everted rim.
651. F 602 6159. Reddish-brown exterior, and dark interior and core. EBA1. Diagonal impressions with possible horizontal decoration to one side.
652. F 602 6151. Exterior destroyed. Interior and core is dark. Rus1. Fingernail impressions. The sherd has been drawn with stipple as if the exterior had survived.
653. F 602 6166. Reddish-brown exterior, and dark core. Interior destroyed. Bkr9. Combed squat pendant triangle.
654. F 601 6023. Dark throughout. BA/IA7. Upright rim from a closed vessel, apparently round bodied jar. The oblique line may be decoration or accident.

Catalogue of significant but previously unillustrated sherds

A number of previously unpublished sherds and few others freshly interpreted deserve illustration (figs 197 and 209). None of the Beaker is illustrated but instead is summarised in terms of Clarke (1970) motifs in table 171.

Ebbsfleet Ware

P324. Dark throughout. Flint and some sand. Whipped cord.
P325. Sherd not located; the drawing is a copy of one in the Alexander Keiller Museum. Keiller archive refers to flint temper.
P326. Dark throughout. Few inclusions, some sand and shell. Whipped cord.
P327. Brown exterior, and dark core and interior. Flint and sand. Whipped cord.
P328. Brown exterior and interior, and dark core. Flint and sand. Possible fingernail on rim. This could be same vessel as P246.
P329. Dark brown exterior and interior, and dark core. Shell. Whipped cord.
P246. Probably illustrated by Smith as P246 and probably same vessel as P328. Dark brown exterior and interior, and dark core. Flint and sand. Decoration on rim edge.
P330. Red exterior, dark interior, and dark brown core. Flint and sand. Whipped cord.
P331. Brown exterior, and dark interior and core. Flint and sand. Whipped cord.
P245. Probably illustrated by Smith as P245. Buff to red exterior and interior, and dark core. Flint and sand. Whipped cord.
P332. Dark exterior, red interior, and grey core. Flint and some sand. Whipped cord.
P333. Dark throughout. Flint. Tool is not clear.

Mortlake Ware

P334. Brown exterior and interior, and dark core. Flint and sand. ?Whipped cord.
P335. Dark throughout. Flint, sand and grog. Twisted cord.
P336. Dark throughout. Flint and some sand. Horizontal ?whipped cord. Smith (1956, 99) seems to imply that lines of continuous horizontal whipped cord is more characteristic of Mortlake.
P337. Purple exterior, and dark core. Flint and sand. Twisted cord.
P338. Dark throughout. Flint. Twisted cord.
P339. Dark throughout. Fabric not recorded. Twisted cord and possible fingernail.
P340. Brown exterior and interior, and dark core. Rare shell. Possible twisted cord.
P341. Brown exterior, and dark interior and core. Flint and sand. Twisted cord and possible impression.
P342. Dark throughout. Flint. Twisted cord.
P343. Dark throughout. Sarsen inclusions. Twisted cord
P344. Dark throughout. Grog. Twisted cord.
P345. Buff throughout. Dense oolites. Twisted cord.
P346. Orange brown exterior and part of core, and dark interior and most of core. Shell, sand and rare flint. Twisted cord.
P260. Dark throughout. Flint and sand. Bone impressions.
P347. Brown exterior and interior, and brown or dark core. Flint and sand. Twisted cord.
P348. Flint and sand. Twisted cord.

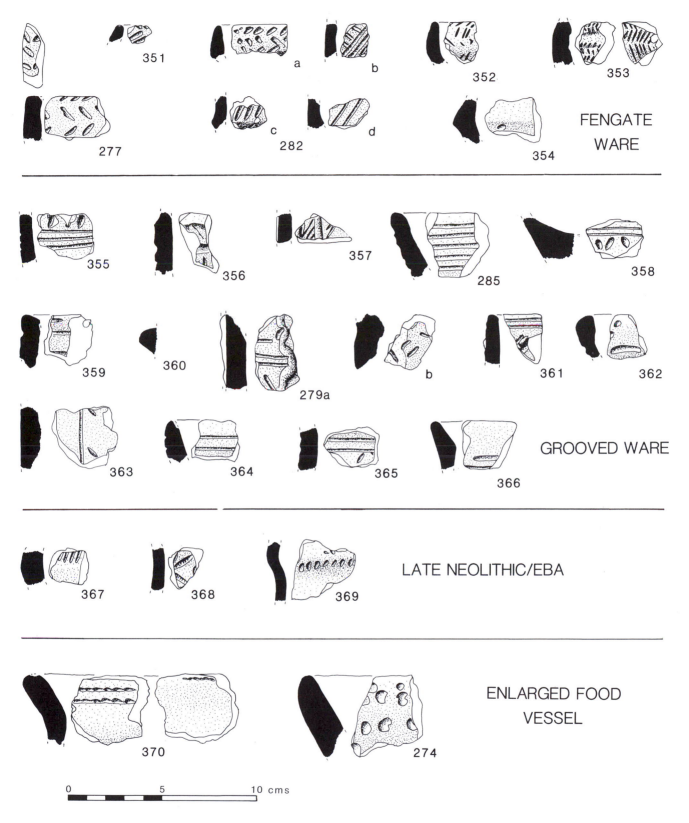

351
a
b
352
353
277
c
282
d
354

FENGATE
WARE

355
356
357
285
358

359
360
279a
b
361
362

363
364
365
366

GROOVED WARE

367
368
369

LATE NEOLITHIC/EBA

370
274

ENLARGED FOOD
VESSEL

0   5   10 cms

Fig. 208. *Previously unpublished sherds from the Keiller assemblage of* top: *Fengate Ware;* upper middle: *Grooved Ware;* lower middle: *Late Neolithic/EBA style; and* below: *Enlarged Food Vessel.*

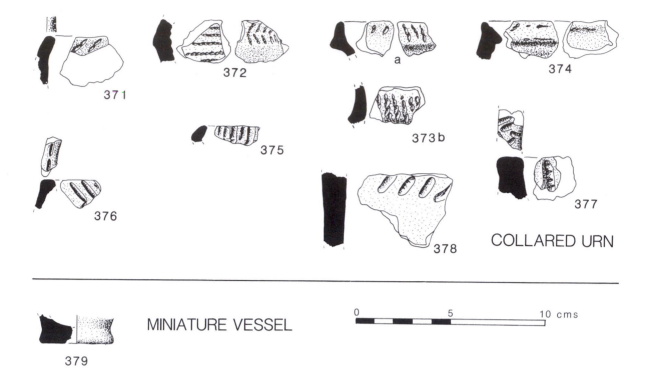

COLLARED URN

MINIATURE VESSEL

379

0   5   10 cms

Fig. 209. Previously unpublished sherds from the Keiller assemblage of top: *Collared Urn, and* below: *Miniature Vessel.*

P349. Dark throughout. Shell. Twisted cord.

P350. Grey exterior, and dark core and interior. Flint and some sand. Twisted cord.

Fengate Ware

P277. Dark or brown exterior, interior possibly red or destroyed, and dark core. ?Medium shell and ?sparse grog. This pot is included in the Fengate group because of the rarity of Grooved Ware with rim top decoration, and its slight resemblance to P13 from West Kennet (Piggott 1962a).

P351. Colour not recorded. Flint. This is included as Fengate because grooving seems to be regarded as a trait of that style at Windmill Hill (Smith 1965a, 78).

P282. Dark throughout. Grog. It is possible a second vessel is represented. Possibly the grooved sherds vessel could be Grooved Ware, and the rim sherd Fengate.

P352. Brown exterior and interior, and dark core. Grog and flint. Incisions. Counted as Fengate because of its resemblance to P353.

P353. Dark red throughout. Grog and sand. Deep incised lines. Regarded as Fengate, because: a) internal decoration is more common for Peterborough Ware than any other style; b) Smith does not mention any incised Mortlake; c) the shape would be unusual for a Collared Urn. A Fengate parallel for the decoration comes from West Kennet Long Barrow (Piggott 1962a, P13).

P354. Buff and dark exterior, grey core, and buff interior. Shell. Impression below collar. It is possible this is a Grooved Ware cordon.

Grooved Ware

P355. Brown exterior and interior, and dark core. Grog and sand. Grooved lines and fingernail.

P356. Dark throughout. Some grog and shell. Fingernail and grooves.

P357. Brown exterior and interior, and dark core. Grog. Vertical cordon and incised decoration.

P285 (top sherd of Smith group). Same as Gibson 1982, fig. WH1.13. Dark throughout. Grog. Grooves.

P358. Red exterior, dark interior, and brown core. Grog. Grooves and fingernail.

P359. Dark brown exterior, and dark interior and core. Possible grog. Impressed or grooved horizontal lines. Possible impression on bevel.

P360. Buff throughout. Shell. Cordon.

P279. Re-orientated. Orange exterior (extending 2 mm into core), and dark core and (occasionally brown) interior. Shell and sand. Grooves and cordons.

P361. Same as Gibson 1982, fig. WH1.10. Buff exterior and interior, and dark core. Grog. Grooves and rustication.

P362. Exterior destroyed, and dark core and interior. Some shell and grog. Orientation of sherd is not certain. ?Groove and impression.

P363. Orange exterior and half of core, and remainder dark. Shell. Grooves.

P364. Brown exterior and interior, and dark core. Some shell and grog. Grooves.

P365. Dark throughout. Grog. Groove and crow-foot rustication.

P366. Brown or dark exterior and interior, and dark core. Shell. ?Grooves.

?Late Neolithic/Early Bronze Age

P367. Dark brown exterior and interior, and dark core. Grog and some flint. ?Grooved decoration.

P368. Brown exterior, and dark core. Grog. Whipped cord.

P369. Brown exterior and interior, and dark core. Grog and sand. Bone impressions.

Enlarged Food Vessel

P370. Dark brown exterior, and dark core and interior. Grog. Twisted cord. Other sherds have possible shoulder ridges or cordons.

P274. Brown-red exterior and interior, and dark or brown core. Sparse grog, and occasional flint. Impression possibly with bone.

Collared Urn

P371. Mostly brown. Grog. Possible twisted cord.

P372. Pale brown exterior, and dark core and interior. Grog and some sand and iron oxide. Twisted cord. The pottery archive believes this and P273 to be the same vessel, but they have different fabrics. There are Fengate vessels which appear to be similar (West Kennet long barrow: Piggott 1962a, P24). However the arrangement seems more common on Collared Urns (Longworth 1984).

P373. Grey throughout. Grog. Twisted cord and impressions.

P374. Buff exterior (extending 2 mm into core), and dark core and interior. Grog, sand and some chalk. Twisted cord.

P375. Dark throughout. Grog. Possible whipped cord.

P376. Brown/yellow throughout. Rare quartz. Probably whipped cord.

P377. ?Brown exterior and interior, and dark core. Common grog, and rare quartz. Sketch is only approximate.

P378. Possibly the same as above. Dark throughout.

?Miniature Accessory Vessel

P379. Brown exterior, and dark core and interior. Grog.

14

Flint

Joshua Pollard

Introduction

The 1988 assemblage is formally described and discussed. It is then put in context by partial re-evaluation of the large lithic assemblage from the Keiller excavations and by consideration of other lithic assemblages from the region.

The 1988 assemblage

3393 worked flints were recovered in the 1988 excavations (figs 210–16, and tables 172–79). Of these 3044 came from the ditches and 349 from the old ground surface and bank in Trench BB. Quantities in the ditches varied. There were 288 pieces from the inner ditch in Trench F, 249 and 414 from the middle ditch in Trenches D and E respectively, and 247, 1294 and 552 from the outer ditch in Trenches A, B and C respectively. Quantities in primary levels were in all cases low in comparison to the prodigious quantities from the secondary and tertiary fills.

Raw material

Most of the assemblage is heavily patinated, but some less affected pieces suggest a basically dark flint. It is difficult to distinguish between the thick white patina claimed for old natural fractures and other patina, and it has therefore not been possible to replicate the figure, principally using this criterion, of up to 40 percent of weathered surface flint in the assemblage excavated by Keiller (Smith 1965a, 85). Cortex may be a better guide to general source. The colour and condition of the generally rather thin cortex vary, from white to brown, and from a little worn to very fresh. One or two pieces suggest small nodules little more than 5 cm long, but other nodules were clearly larger, and there are quartering flakes and roughly trimmed blocks up to 8 cm long. One cortical piece from the upper secondary layers in Trench A was tabular, with thin, smooth cortex. The general character of nodules suggests that much of the flint used on the site was quarried or otherwise acquired from good sources. Whether these were on nearby Middle

and especially Upper Chalk, as on the Marlborough Downs at Hackpen Hill and Liddington (Holgate 1988, 61; Passmore 1940), on clay-with-flints, as on the Marlborough Downs (Holgate 1988, 63) or in soliflucted chalk deposits in the region (Pitts 1983, 79), requires further detailed research, but it seems clear that such flint need not have come from far away. There are two flakes from the primary layer 512 in Trench E which have thin, worn, grey cortex, suggestive of an origin in river gravels; flint gravel is reported from the Kennet valley (Pitts 1983, 79). There are a few flakes, from upper levels, with obviously old flake surfaces, defined by gross differences in patination and abrasion. In Trench A, in 104 and 103 (and in 102, presumably derived from below), there are several cores and a number of flakes with very worn brown cortex and old, partly iron stained, flake surfaces. This appears to be surface flint, from the hill itself or nearby, perhaps from gravels at Whyr Farm, Winterbourne Bassett, to the north (Smith 1965a, 85). The axe fragments may be of a different flint. Although patinated white, they appear to be creamier in colour, some with cherty inclusions, and generally of a good quality.

Core reduction techniques

106 roughly quartered blocks without recognisable or regular platforms were recovered. A few were large, up to 8 cm in any one dimension, but the great majority were less than 5 cm. These were found in both primary and other levels. The 114 cores may be divided into those with one, two or three platforms, following Holgate (1988) (table 180, and figs 210–16). The majority had one platform, but significant numbers had two or more platforms. As the variety of two platform forms is so great, no attempt has been made to divide them according to the scheme presented by Clark (Clark *et al.* 1960, 216) and used by Smith (1965a, 87). There does not appear to be any stratigraphical difference between the different types, though it is notable that 59 percent of cores from primary

contexts exhibit narrow flake and blade scars against only 26.7 percent from secondary contexts. Platform abrasion, intended to remove ridges and overhangs, thus strengthening the striking platform, was commonly employed on cores from Earlier Neolithic contexts, being present on 45.5 percent of cores from these levels compared with only 13.5 percent from secondary contexts. Abrasion facets appear to have been mistaken for retouch by Smith, leading her to distinguish an erroneous category of core scrapers (Smith 1965a, 87). Formal platform preparation is otherwise only indicated by occasional flakes with faceted butts. Generally, the quality of flaking control on earlier cores was superior to that on later examples, with care being taken to flake along the length of a core and maintain consistent angles between platform and core face.

Core rejuvenation flakes were recognised. The majority were trimming flakes struck to renew the step-fractured face of a core. A few core tablets were also present (from Trenches A and B), as were a small number of flakes struck laterally in order to remove the top of the core face and edge of the platform where step-fracturing had made it unworkable. Indications of formal rejuvenation were not, however, particularly well represented (except from the old land surface under the bank in Trench BB), and clearly the preference was to exploit one platform as far as desired and then to begin another platform when required.

A few single-platform cores from tertiary layers have minimal platform preparation. There are flakes struck with a hard-hammer from primary, secondary and tertiary layers. Most of these appear to be larger flakes. Hard-hammer technique may have been most used in the early stages of nodule and core reduction, and during rejuvenation. (There were three small flint hammerstones from 202 in Trench B, not listed in the tables.) It is noticeable that the maximum dimension of most cores rarely exceeds 4 cm, and the last flaked face is usually less than 3.5 cm long. There are large numbers of small flakes less than 3 cm long in all layers. The purpose of this extended core reduction is not clear. Recognisable tool types are for the most part made on stouter or larger flakes. It may be that the role of small unretouched flakes for general purpose tasks was far greater than is usually recognised, and could suggest an economical use of flint throughout the occupation of the site.

Flakes struck from multi-platform discoidal and bi-conical cores, along with the discarded cores themselves, were present in all levels, though particular concentrations were noted in the secondary and tertiary layers of Trenches A and C. Gardiner (1987, 27) suggests that discoidal cores were employed for the production of single blanks to be modified into transverse arrowheads (examples of which came from Trenches A and C), though here they would also appear to have been used for unspecialised flake production. Similar cores can result through strategies of alternate flaking (P. Harding 1991, 79).

684 unbroken waste flakes from four separate areas (Trenches BB, B, D and E) were formally analysed in an attempt to identify both changes in lithic technology through time and the presence of different stages in core reduction within particular contexts (tables 181–85). Smith (1965a, 89) and Pitts (1978), among others, have recognised changes in flake form through the Neolithic, characterised as a move from the production of narrow flakes and blades to broad, squat flakes in the later part of the period. Holgate (1988, 59–61) has viewed this as a result of a decline in general knapping technique, with progressively poorer flaking control being manifest in the frequent presence of hard-hammer struck pieces, hinge fractures and an absence of formal core preparation within Later Neolithic assemblages.

Flake length and breadth were determined using the system described by Smith (1965a, 89). Platforms were also measured, from ventral to dorsal faces, and laterally; and the presence or absence of cortex was noted. Flake lengths varied from 11–70 mm, but in almost all contexts the majority were very short, with a peak incidence between 21–30 mm. Exceptions were in the primary and lower secondary contexts of the outer ditch (Trench B), which peaked at 31–40 mm (26 percent and 35 percent respectively), and the tertiary contexts of the middle ditch where the maximum number (37 percent) also lay between 31–40 mm. Flake breadths ranged from under 10 mm to 60 mm, the greatest number being in the range 11–20 mm. Again, the exceptions were in the primary and lower secondary contexts of Trench B, with flakes showing a peak incidence in the 21–30 mm range. In terms of breadth:length ratio, the majority of flakes from all contexts fell in the range 0.5:1.0–1.0:1.0. A significant proportion were truly blade-like (averaging 23 percent), with only a small number being squat. The primary contexts of Trench B were notable in that only 10 percent of flakes were blade-like.

Platform antero-posterior dimensions ranged between 1–9 mm, and laterally from 2.5–25 mm, most platforms being elongated laterally. Variation is apparent, with flake platforms from primary contexts in Trench B generally being larger than average, and those from upper secondary levels in this ditch and the primary levels of the middle ditch tending to be miniscule. The lateral dimensions of platforms showed a peak incidence between 5–10 mm. The primary contexts in Trench B again provided an exception with a peak at 10–15 mm. The percentage of cortical and non-cortical flakes was generally even, though there was some variation, with 62 percent of those from Trench BB being non-cortical, contrasting with only 37 percent from primary contexts in Trench B.

Although qualitative and quantitative differences are apparent, at first sight formal analysis of waste flakes would not suggest major technological differences through time. This is rather misleading since only Trench B presents a reasonably clear lithic sequence from Earlier Neolithic to Early Bronze Age (note that the tertiary fill includes a residual component). It is also appparent that different stages in core reduction are represented in different spatial and temporal locations, so overall comparison is not justified. In particular, the high percentage of large and cortical flakes from primary contexts in Trench B reflects core preparation, whereas flakes from Trench BB (largely non-cortical and occasionally squat in shape) include much debitage from core rejuvenation and maintenance activities. A subjective assessment of knapping techniques, which takes into account material from all the trenches, does suggest qualitative differences are discernible across time, as noted above in the case of cores. Debitage from the old land surface in Trench BB and from the lower ditch fills includes a significant component of narrow flakes and blades, with small butts, abraded platforms and dorsal flake scars that run parallel with the longitudinal flake axis. All imply competent flaking control. Contrast is provided by material from the uppermost ditch fills (particularly Trench B, 201), where irregular flakes with wide, plain platforms, frequent step-fracturing and prominent conchoidal features characteristic of hard-hammer flaking predominate. Such differences in reduction techniques are by no means exclusive, since crude, hard-hammer struck flakes are frequently present in the primary ditch fills, and blades from tertiary levels (though perhaps residual).

Utilised, bevelled and serrated flakes

As in the previous excavations all three types were present (Smith 1965a), but in low numbers. Bevelled flakes are characterised as pieces with fine, steep and blunting microflaking along one or more of the edges. Rather than reflecting deliberate retouch, this regular spalling could result through cutting or scraping of resilient materials such as bone or hard wood (Smith 1965a, 93). Denticulations on serrated flakes were made from the ventral surface, except on one flake from 627 in F, and were small and closely spaced (between 8–17 per 10 mm). Six serrated flakes were observed to have silica gloss which was limited to the very edges. All these types comprise stout flakes, often keeled, which were presumably selected for strength. Both flakes and blades, often with slightly concave edges, were employed.

Scrapers

Of the 75 scrapers, 62 were flake scrapers, 8 thumbnail scrapers and 5 were blade or narrow flake end scrapers (table 186, and figs 210–16). The flake scrapers were mostly made on stout flakes, some still with cortex. Butts were broad and many, including examples from primary levels and the old ground surface in Trench BB, had been struck using hard-hammer technique. Most had a rounded, steeply retouched working edge on the flake end. In two cases, from secondary layers in A and E, there was retouch on the side of the flake as well, and in two cases, from primary layers in B and D, retouch was only on the side of the flake. 2214 from 201 in B is exceptional in having been made on an oval flake with a faceted butt struck from a discoidal 'Levallois' core (fig. 211, 38).

Small thumbnail scrapers, 3 cm long or less and neatly flaked, were restricted to the secondary and tertiary layers of B and C (204; 203; 216; 211; 202; and 316) (fig. 213, 13; fig. 211, 11–12, 18–19, 23). All but one were on thick, hard-hammer struck flakes with plain platforms; the exception being made on an old and heavily patinated flake with the butt removed. Four of the eight examples had been subjected to some degree of burning. Larger scrapers with similar invasive retouch were recovered from layers 202 and 220 of Trench B (fig. 211, 20–21).

At the very top of Trench C (in 302, 301 and 300) there were four scrapers made by neat blunting retouch across the end of a stout blade or narrow flake (fig. 213, 26–29). A similar piece came from the Romano-British ploughsoil at the top of Trench F (602). This had been used or blunted, so that the edge was very steep and looks slightly pointed or peaked when viewed from the dorsal surface.

Knives

None of the 16 knives came from the primary levels of the ditches, though one came from the old ground surface in Trench BB (table 187). Seven had one edge retouched, seven had both edges retouched, and there were two plano-convex knives with extensive retouch. Of those with one edge, five had shallow invasive retouch typical of the 'Beaker' knives noted by Smith (1965a, 108). The retouched edge may have been the cutting edge, since 1412 from 104 in A had cortex on the other edge. The large knife from the old ground surface in BB (on a flake struck from a multi-platform core or axe) has steep, short retouch on one edge and utilisation and bevelling on the other (fig.

Table 172: The flint assemblage from the 1988 excavations at Windmill Hill.

Tr	Core	CRF	Blck	Flks	Serr	Bev	Util	Scr	Knvs	Axe	Ah	Various
BB	11	14	5	300	2	3	4	9	1	-	-	-
B	38	16	56	1124	2	4	1	30	11	1	2	9
A	12	1	10	205	3	3	-	8	2	-	1	2
C	15*	11	15	481	2	3	1	11	2	2	3	6
D	15	4	5	209	2	3	3	-	1	-	7	-
E	13	7	11	353	3	9	1	13	-	1	-	3
F	10	5	4	251	6	3	2	3	-	1	-	3
Tot.	114	50	106	2923	18	27	12	77	16	6	6	30

* one made from axe fragment

KEY: CRF, Core rejuvenation flake; Blck, Flaked block; Flks, Flakes; Serr, Serrated flakes; Bev, Bevelled; Util, Utilised; Scr, Scrapers; Knvs, Knives; Ah, Arrowheads

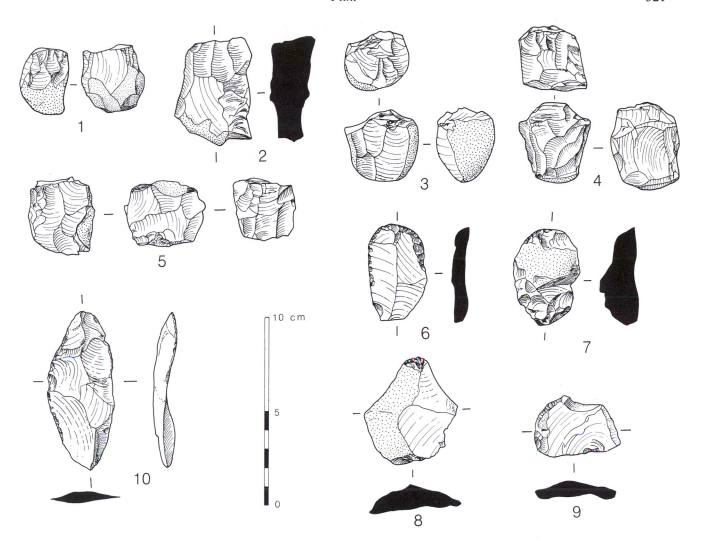

Fig. 210. Worked flints from the old ground surface and features beneath the outer bank in Trench BB. 1–2: one-platform cores (714, 705); 3–4: two-platform cores (705); 5: three-platform core (765); 6–8: end scrapers (707, 707, 755); 9: side scraper (705); 10: knife (705).

Table 173: The flint assemblage from Trench BB.

Ctxt	Core	CRF	Blck	Flks	Serr	Bev	Util	Scr	Knvs	Axe	Ah	Various
712	-	-	-	2	-	-	-	-	-	-	-	-
742	-	-	-	1	2	-	-	-	-	-	-	-
741	-	1	-	43	-	-	-	-	-	-	-	-
743	-	1	-	4	-	-	-	-	-	-	-	-
705	5	5	2	112	1	1	2	2	1	-	-	-
707	-	-	-	33	-	-	1	2	-	-	-	-
714	1	-	-	13	1	-	-	-	-	-	-	-
760	-	1	-	1	-	-	-	1	-	-	-	-
710	1	-	-	-	-	-	-	-	-	-	-	-
755	-	-	-	1	-	-	-	2	-	-	-	-
745	-	-	-	2	-	-	-	-	-	-	-	-
751	-	-	-	-	-	-	-	1	-	-	-	-
711	-	-	-	1	-	-	-	-	-	-	-	-
750	-	1	-	3	-	-	-	-	-	-	-	-
746	-	1	1	10	-	1	-	-	-	-	-	-
765	1	3	-	4	-	-	1	-	-	-	-	-
708	-	-	-	-	-	1	-	-	-	-	-	-
703	3	-	1	30	-	-	-	-	-	-	-	-
702	-	-	-	9	-	-	-	-	-	-	-	-
701	-	1	-	30	-	1	-	-	-	-	-	-
Tot.	11	14	5	300	2	3	4	9	1	-	-	-

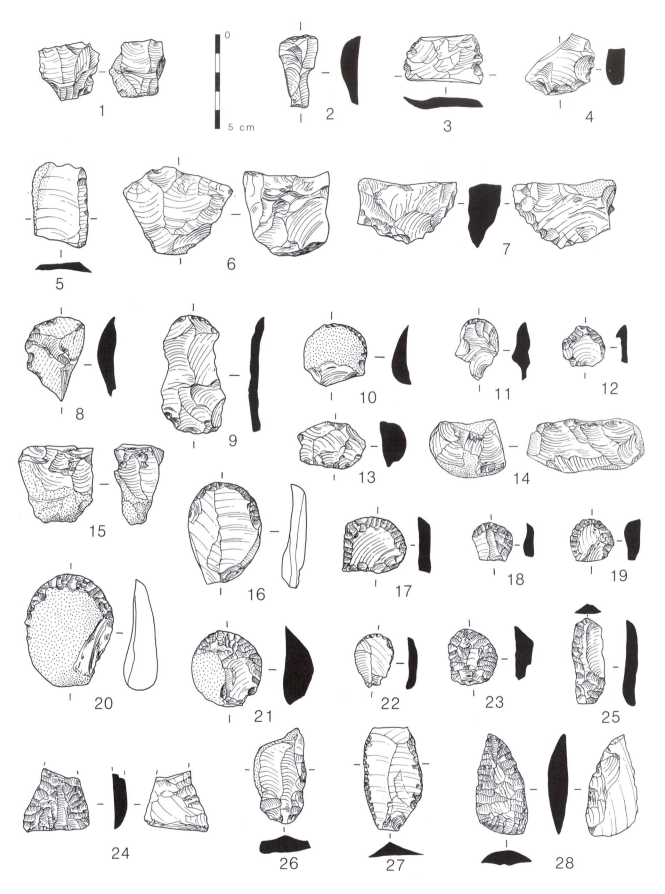

Fig. 211. Worked flints from the outer ditch in Trench B. 1–5: primary contexts; 6–13: secondary; 14–41: tertiary. 1: two-platform core (228); 2: end scraper (228); 3: side scraper (228); 4–5: irregularly retouched flakes (229); 6: one-platform core (213); 7: two-platform core (203); 8–10: end scrapers (225, 206, 204); 11–12: thumbnail scrapers (204, 203); 13: end scraper (203); 14–15: one-platform cores (216, 202); 16–17: end and side scrapers (220); 18–19: thumbnail scrapers (216, 211); 20–21: end scrapers (202); 22: end scraper (202); 23: thumbnail scraper (202); 24: plano-convex knife (216); 25–27: knives (216, 215, 214); 28: plano-convex knife (202);

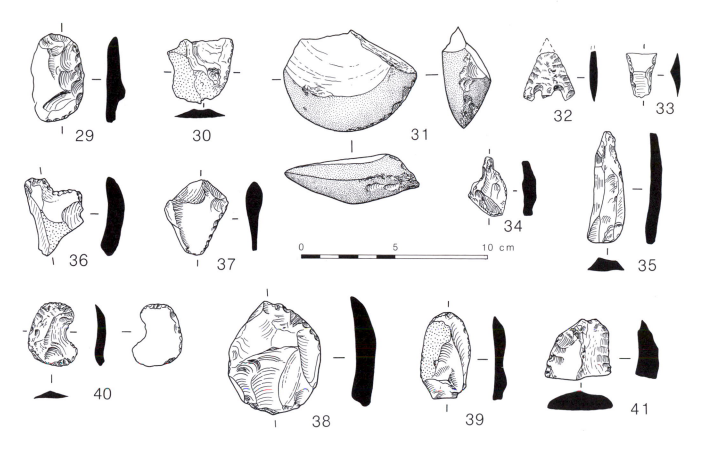

Fig. 211. Continued. 29–30: knives (202); 31: polished axe fragment (202); 32: barbed and tanged arrowhead of Conygar type (216); 33: petit tranchet derivative arrowhead (214); 34: awl (212); 35: awl/fabricator (202); 36: notched flake (202); 37: irregularly retouched flake (202); 38–39: end scrapers (201); 40–41: knives (201).

Table 174: The flint assemblage from Trench B.

Ctxt	Core	CRF	Blck	Flks	Serr	Bev	Util	Scr	Knvs	Axe	Ah	Various
228	6	2	4	13	-	-	-	2	-	-	-	-
229	-	-	2	7	1	-	-	-	-	-	-	2
210	1	-	1	15	-	-	-	-	-	-	-	-
227	-	-	-	12	-	-	-	-	-	-	-	-
207/8	-	1	-	6	-	-	1	-	-	-	-	-
225	-	-	-	8	1	-	-	1	-	-	-	-
224	1	-	-	-	-	-	-	-	-	-	-	-
223	1	-	-	-	-	-	-	-	-	-	-	-
206	-	-	-	8	-	-	-	1	-	-	-	-
213	1	-	-	2	-	-	-	-	-	-	-	-
205	-	-	-	4	-	-	-	-	-	-	-	-
204	-	-	-	7	-	-	-	2	-	-	-	-
203	1	1	1	32	-	-	-	3	-	-	-	-
222	-	-	-	1	-	-	-	-	-	-	-	-
221	-	-	-	1	-	-	-	-	-	-	-	-
220	1	-	-	8	-	-	-	2	-	-	-	-
219	-	-	-	12	-	-	-	-	-	-	-	-
217	-	-	-	10	-	-	-	-	-	-	-	-
216	1	-	7	87	-	3	-	2	2	-	1	-
215	4	-	2	39	-	-	-	-	1	-	-	1
214	2	2	6	80	-	1	-	1	1	-	1	-
211/2	-	-	1	13	-	-	-	1	-	-	-	1
202	12	6	26	503	-	-	-	13	5	1	-	3
201	7	4	6	256	-	-	-	2	2	-	-	2
Tot.	38	16	56	1124	2	4	1	30	11	1	2	9

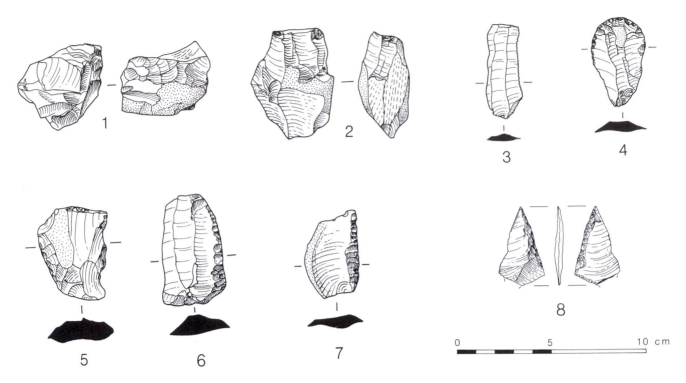

Fig. 212. Worked flints from the outer ditch in Trench A. 1: primary context ; 2–8: secondary contexts. 1: three-platform core(117); 2: two-platform core (104); 3: serrated flake(108); 4–5: end scrapers (104); 6–7: knives (103, 104); 8: petit tranchet derivative arrowhead (104).

Table 175: The flint assemblage from Trench A.

Ctxt	Core	CRF	Blck	Flks	Serr	Bev	Util	Scr	Knvs	Axe	Ah	Various
118	-	-	-	1	-	-	-	-	-	-	-	-
117	1	-	-	-	-	-	-	-	-	-	-	-
112	-	-	-	1	-	-	-	-	-	-	-	-
109	-	-	-	5	-	-	-	-	-	-	-	-
108	-	-	-	1	1	-	-	-	-	-	-	-
107	1	-	-	3	-	-	-	-	-	-	-	-
106	-	1	-	26	1	-	-	-	-	-	-	-
105	-	-	-	1	-	-	-	-	-	-	-	1
104	7	-	10	77	1	-	-	5	1	-	1	-
103	-	-	-	12	-	-	-	-	1	-	-	-
102	3	-	-	61	-	2	-	3	-	-	-	1
101	-	-	-	6	-	1	-	-	-	-	-	-
100	-	-	-	11	-	-	-	-	-	-	-	-
Tot.	12 1	10	205	3	3	-	8	2	-	1	2	

Table 176: The flint assemblage from Trench C.

Ctxt	Core	CRF	Blck	Flks	Serr	Bev	Util	Scr	Knvs	Axe	Ah	Various
324	-	-	-	1	-	-	-	-	-	-	-	-
322	-	1	-	-	-	-	-	-	-	-	-	-
312	-	-	-	10	-	-	-	-	-	-	-	-
314	-	-	-	1	-	-	-	-	-	-	-	-
311	1	-	-	4	-	-	-	-	-	-	-	-
308	1	-	1	14	-	-	-	-	-	1	-	-
319	2*	1	1	10	-	-	-	1	-	-	-	-
309	-	-	-	1	-	-	-	-	-	-	-	-
306	-	-	-	5	-	1	-	-	-	-	-	-
307	-	-	-	7	-	-	-	-	-	-	-	-
313	1	-	-	1	-	-	-	-	-	1	-	-
321	1	-	1	-	-	-	-	-	-	-	-	-
305	-	-	-	9	-	-	-	-	-	-	-	-
304	-	-	-	19	-	1	-	1	-	-	-	-
303	-	1	-	13	-	-	-	-	-	-	-	1
317	-	2	-	11	-	-	1	1	-	-	-	-
316	3	3	-	74	2	-	-	1	-	-	2	2
302	6	3	10	225	-	1	-	2	2	-	1	3
301	-	-	2	51	-	-	-	3	-	-	-	-
300	-	-	-	25	-	-	-	2	-	-	-	-
Tot.	15	11	15	481	2	3	1	11	2	2	3	6

* one made from axe fragment

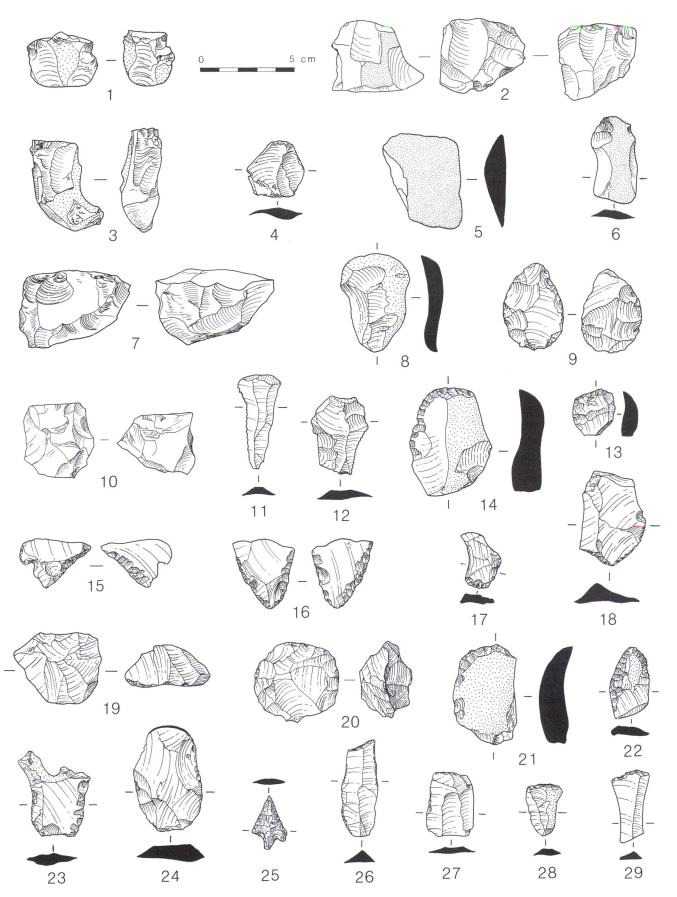

Fig. 213. Worked flints from the outer ditch in Trench C. 1–6: primary contexts; 7–18: secondary; 19–29: tertiary. 1: two-platform core (308); 2: three-platform core (319); 3: one-platform core (313); 4: end scraper (319); 5–6: polished axe fragments (308, 313); 7: one-platform core (321); 8: end scraper (304); 9: ovate (303); 10: three-platform core (316); 11–12: serrated flakes (316); 13: thumbnail scraper (316); 14: end scraper (317); 15–16: chisel arrowheads (316); 17: notched flake (316); 18; irregularly retouched flake (316); 19–20: two-platform cores (302); 21: end scraper (302); 22–23: knives (302); 24: end-polished knife (302); 25: barbed and tanged arrowhead of Sutton type (302); 26–29: straight end scrapers (301, 301, 300, 302).

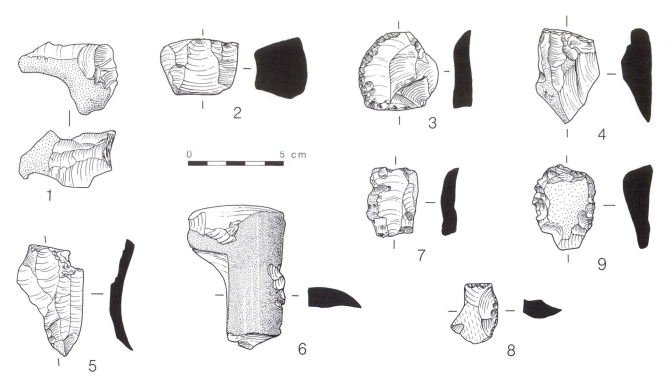

Fig. 214. Worked flints from the middle ditch in Trench D. 1–2: primary contexts; 3–8: secondary; 9: tertiary. 1: two-platform core (417); 2: one-platform core (415); 3: side scraper (409); 4: one-platform core (404); 5: core face rejuvenation flake (404); 6: polished axe fragment (406); 7: end-trimmed flake (404); 8: irregularly retouched flake (404); 9: end and side scraper (402).

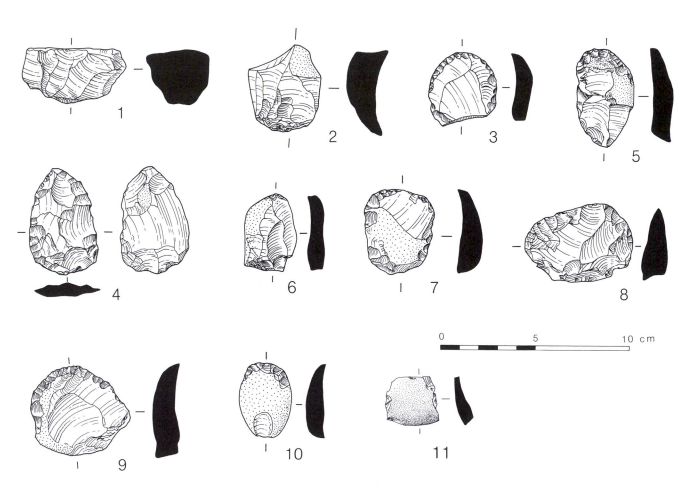

Fig. 215. Worked flints from the middle ditch in Trench E. 1–4: primary contexts: 5–8: secondary; 9–11: tertiary. 1: two-platform core (525); 2: core face rejuvenation flake (525); 3: end and side scraper (514); 4: ovate 9515); 5–10: end scrapers (509, 518, 516, 503, 502, 501); 11; polished axe fragment (501).

Table 177: The flint assemblage from Trench D.

Ctxt	Core	CRF	Blck	Flks	Serr	Bev	Util	Scr	Knvs	Axe	Ah	Various
409	-	-	-	-	-	-	-	1	-	-	-	-
416	-	-	-	10	-	-	-	-	-	-	-	-
417	1	-	-	4	-	-	-	-	-	-	-	-
415	2	-	1	8	-	1	-	-	-	-	-	-
411	2	1	2	17	-	-	1	-	-	-	-	-
414	1	1	-	2	-	-	-	-	-	-	-	-
413	1	-	-	3	-	-	-	-	-	-	-	-
408	-	-	-	10	-	-	1	-	-	-	-	-
406	-	1	-	35	-	1	1	-	-	1	-	-
404	1	1	1	29	-	-	-	-	-	-	-	2
403	1	-	1	-	-	-	-	-	-	-	-	-
402	-	-	-	37	-	-	-	1	-	-	-	3
401	5	-	-	33	-	-	-	-	-	-	-	2
400	1	-	-	21	-	-	-	1	-	-	-	-
Tot.	15	4	5	209	-	2	3	3	-	1	-	7

Table 178: The flint assemblage from Trench E.

Ctxt	Core	CRF	Blck	Flks	Serr	Bev	Util	Scr	Knvs	Axe	Ah	Various
527	-	-	-	5	-	1	-	-	-	-	-	-
514	-	-	-	3	-	-	-	1	-	-	-	-
515	-	-	-	4	-	-	-	-	-	-	-	1
512	-	-	-	4	-	-	-	-	-	-	-	-
510	2	1	2	10	-	2	-	-	-	-	-	-
511	-	-	-	3	-	-	-	-	-	-	-	-
525	1	1	-	7	-	-	-	-	-	-	-	-
508	1	-	-	6	-	-	-	-	-	-	-	-
524	-	-	-	3	-	-	-	-	-	-	-	-
507	-	-	-	1	-	-	-	-	-	-	-	-
509	-	-	-	10	-	-	-	1	-	-	-	-
520	2	-	-	2	-	-	-	-	-	-	-	-
518	1	-	-	14	-	1	-	1	-	-	-	-
519	1	-	-	2	-	1	-	-	-	-	-	-
523	-	-	1	1	-	-	-	-	-	-	-	-
506	-	-	-	22	-	-	1	1	-	-	-	-
504	2	1	1	11	-	-	-	1	-	-	-	-
503	-	-	-	18	-	-	-	1	-	-	-	-
516	-	-	-	4	-	-	-	1	-	-	-	-
517	-	-	-	1	-	-	-	-	-	-	-	-
502	-	2	2	27	-	1	-	2	-	-	-	-
501	3	2	5	162	2	3	-	3	-	1	-	2
500	-	-	-	33	1	-	-	1	-	-	-	-
Tot.	13	7	11	353	3	9	1	13	-	1	-	3

Table 179: The flint assemblage from Trench F.

Ctxt	Core	CRF	Blck	Flks	Serr	Bev	Util	Scr	Knvs	Axe	Ah	Various
610	-	-	-	3	-	-	-	-	-	-	-	-
630	-	-	-	1	-	-	-	-	-	-	-	1
629	-	1	-	10	-	-	-	-	-	-	-	-
628	-	-	-	12	-	-	-	1	-	-	-	-
627	-	-	-	10	1	2	1	-	-	-	-	2
604	4	1	1	41	2	1	1	-	-	1	-	-
626	-	-	-	1	-	-	-	-	-	-	-	-
605	-	-	2	13	-	-	-	-	-	-	-	-
602	4	2	1	90	2	-	-	1	-	-	-	-
601	2	1	-	70	1	-	-	1	-	-	-	-
Tot.	10	5	4	251	6	3	2	3	-	1	-	3

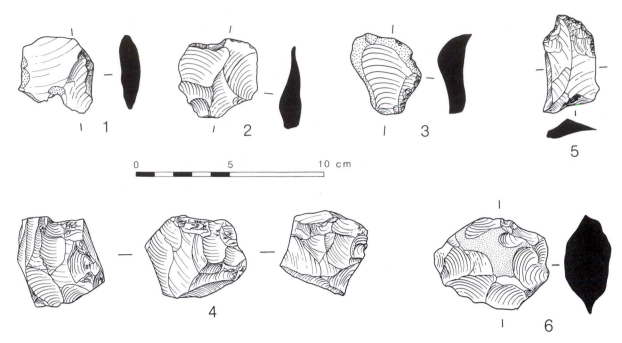

Fig. 216. Worked flints from the inner ditch in Trench F (all secondary contexts). 1: core platform rejuvenation flake (629); 2: bevelled flake (627/628); 3: irregularly retouched flake (627/628); 4: three-platform core (604); 5: end scraper (602); 6: polished axe fragment reused as core (604).

Table 180: The distribution of core types.

Trench	One platform			Two platform			Three platform	
	1°	2°	3°	1°	2°	3°	1°	2°
BB	4	-	-	5	-	-	2	-
B	5	20	7	2	4	1	-	-
A	-	8	2	-	-	1	1	-
C	3	1	-	1	1	6	1	2
D	2	5	4	1	1	2	-	-
E	6	-	2	4	-	1	-	-
F	-	2	5	-	1	1	-	1

Table 181: The platform width (antero-posterior) of a sample of 684 unretouched flakes. Values are expressed as percentages.

	0-2	2-4	4-6	6-8	8-10	10-12	12-14mm
BB	39.5	37	14	6.5	3	0	0
B primary	16	26	37	21	0	0	0
B lower secondary	6	48	32	10	3	0	0
B upper secondary	40	34	20	4.5	0.5	0	0
D+E primary	44	39	11	4	2	0	0
D+E secondary	32.5	44	14.5	6	1	0	1
D+E tertiary	30	39	21	6.5	2.5	1	1

Table 182: Percentages of cortical and non-cortical flakes within a sample of 684 unretouched pieces.

	Cortical	Non-cortical
BB	38.1	61.9
B primary	62.8	37.2
B lower secondary	51.1	48.9
B upper secondary	53.1	46.9
D+E primary	56.7	43.3
D+E secondary	46.9	53.1
D+E tertiary	57.2	42.8

Table 183: Length range of a sample of 684 unretouched flakes. Values are expressed as percentages.

	0-10	10-20	20-30	30-40	40-50	50-60	60-70	70-80	80-90	90-100mm
BB	0	22.5	39.5	23	9	4	1.5	0.5	0	0
B primary	0	10.5	21	26	21	16	5	0	0	0
B lower secondary	0	3.5	35	35	16	6.5	3	0	0	0
B upper secondary	2	21	31	25	17	4	0	1	0	0
D+E primary	0	15	46	26	11	2	0	0	0	0
D+E secondary	0	12.5	29.5	25.5	22	8.5	0	2	0	0
D+E tertiary	0	6	32	37	17	5.5	2	0	0	0.5

Table 184: Breadth range of a sample of 684 unretouched flakes. Values are expressed as percentages.

	0-10	10-20	20-30	30-40	40-50	50-60	60-70	70-80mm
BB	9	54	28.5	7	2.5	0	0	0
B primary	0	26	58	16	0	0	0	0
B lower secondary	6	39	39	13	3	0	0	0
B upper secondary	11	41	33	10	4	0.5	0	0
D+E primary	6.5	46	39	9	0	0	0	0
D+E secondary	5	51.5	31.5	6	3	1	0	1
D+E tertiary	2.5	46	32.5	15	2.5	1	0	0

Table 185: Breadth:length ratio of a sample of 684 unretouched flakes. Values are expressed as percentages.

	<0.5:1.0	0.5:1.0-1.0:1.0	1.0:1.0-1.5:1.0	>1.5:1.0
BB	26	65	6	2
B primary	11	79	11	0
B lower secondary	25	64	12	0
B upper secondary	24	60	13	3
D+E primary	17	67	13	2
D+E secondary	28	68	3	0
D+E tertiary	28	62	8	2

Table 186: The distribution of scraper types.

	Flake			Thumbnail		Blade end		
Trench	1°	2°	3°	2°	3°	1°	2°	3°
BB	8	-	-	-	-	1	-	-
B	2	19	2	7	-	-	-	-
A	-	5	3	-	-	-	-	-
C	1	2	3	-	1	-	1	3
D	1	-	2	-	-	-	-	-
E	5	4	4	-	-	-	-	-
F	-	1	1	-	-	-	-	1

Table 187: The distribution of knife types.

	One edge			Two edge		Plano-convex	
Trench	1°	2°	3°	2°	3°	2°	3°
BB	-	1	-	-	-	-	-
B	-	3	1	4	1	2	-
A	-	2	-	-	-	-	-
C	-	-	-	-	2	-	-

Table 188: The distribution of miscellaneous retouched pieces.

Type	1°	2°	3°
Ovate E C	-		
Bifacial piece	-	B	A
Awl	-	B	-
End-smoothed piece	-	B;C	-
Irregular retouch, one edge	B;B	A;C;D;D; F;F;F	B;B;C;C; D;D;D;D;D
Irregular retouch, two edges	-	-	E
End-trimmed flake	-	B	E
Notched flake	-	C	B

210, 10). The retouch here is therefore presumably backing. Another piece 9393 from 202 in B had bifacial retouch on one edge, also presumably backing (fig. 211, 29).

Five of the knives with two retouched edges have shallow, slightly irregular retouch. 2302 from 201 in B has one concave edge (fig. 211, 40). 2369 also from 201 has steep retouch on both edges. It is not clear which side in these cases constitutes the backing. 2626 from 202 in Trench B has flat trimming on its ventral edges as well as shallow retouch on both dorsal edges.

Only one of the two plano-convex knives (from 216 and 202 in B) is complete, but both were plainly triangular in shape (fig. 211, 24, 28). Both are made on the distal ends of large broken flakes and have neat, invasive retouch/pressure flaking covering much of the dorsal surfaces. There is some flat, thinning retouch on the ventral surfaces, mainly from one edge, which resulted from roughing-out. This is truncated by the more extensive retouch on the dorsal surfaces. The bases of the pieces are carefully fashioned, one straight across, the other slightly curving.

Axe fragments

There are seven fragments of polished axes made from flint which despite patination may be slightly creamier in colour than the rest of the assemblage. There are four flakes, from the primary layers 308 and 313 in C (fig. 213, 5–6), the secondary layer 406 in D (fig. 214, 6), and the tertiary ploughsoil 501 in E. A larger piece from the secondary layer 604 in F had been crudely flaked into disc form, perhaps as a simple two platform core (fig. 216, 6). Another substantial piece re-worked as a core came from 319 in C (fig. 213, 2). From the inner side of the ditch in B, at the base of 202 where it merged with the very top of the secondary silting, came a cutting edge, little used, with both faces preserved, but broken abruptly from the rest of the implement (fig. 211, 31). Battering occurs along the edge on one side where it was re-used as a hammerstone. None of the axe fragments re-fit, and the three pieces from primary levels in Trench C come from separate implements. In their original form, most of the axes appear to have been thick and heavy, and extensively ground.

Arrowheads

From 216 in B came a fine barbed and tanged arrowhead of Conygar Hill type d or e (Green 1980) (fig. 211, 32). The retouch is fine and the ends of the barbs are squared. The base of the piece is not convex in plan but the end of the tang is missing. Above it in 214 was a simple petit tranchet made from a blade segment (fig. 211, 33). In Trench C the sequence was reversed, though the uppermost piece was from a mixed layer. From 316 came one large chisel arrowhead, 3658, and another piece, 3892, which can be classified either as a chisel or perhaps as a simple oblique arrowhead of British type (fig. 213, 15–16). The latter has a prominent notch on one otherwise un-retouched edge. Above this in the Romano-British ploughsoil 302

was a small, simple barbed and tanged arrowhead of Sutton type b (perhaps subtype i), whose barbs are a little broken (fig. 213, 25). A second oblique arrowhead, with the tang broken, came from 104 in the upper secondary silts of A (fig. 212, 8). All three petit tranchet derivatives were produced by modification of flakes struck from multi-platform cores.

Various

Included in tables 172–79 under the heading 'various' for the sake of brevity are types both recurrent and irregular (table 188).

Ovates or laurel leaves. Both pieces are simply but neatly retouched by flat, invasive flaking. 12348 from 515 in E has minimal flaking on the ventral face, and was finished by more extensive retouch covering the dorsal surface (fig. 215, 4). The second example, from 303 in C, shows minimal flaking on both faces (fig. 213, 9).

Bifacial pieces. Both pieces are from the tertiary layers, and are simple, rather flat bifacially flaked discs (not illustrated).

Awl. This is a simple artefact, retouched on both edges of a stout trimming flake to form an elongated point at the distal end (fig. 211, 34).

End-polished or -smoothed pieces. 3388 from 302 in C is an oval 'Levallois' flake with minimal retouch on its distal end, which has then been polished or smoothed (fig. 213, 24). The flake appears to have been carefully struck using a soft hammer, although the butt is missing, probably having broken off during flaking. 2499 from 202 could be classed as a fabricator (fig. 211, 35). It is a thick narrow flake/blade retouched to form a rounded point at the distal end, which exhibits extensive wear or smoothing.

Flakes irregularly retouched on one edge. 18 flakes of various shapes and sizes were irregularly retouched on one edge only. These occur in all stages of the silting.

Flake irregularly retouched on both edges. As with many of the miscellaneous pieces, this came from the tertiary silting, in E.

End-trimmed flakes. Two flakes had irregular trimming on their ends, less neat than the end scrapers noted in the tertiary layers of C and F.

Notched flakes. Two stout flakes had notches retouched on their dorsal surfaces, one having an additional area of scraper-like retouch along one side (fig. 213, 17). 3564 from 316 in C was made on a broken flake, and 2472 from 202 in B on an old, patinated flake (fig. 211, 36).

Discussion of the 1988 assemblage

A primary assemblage can be defined from the 1988 excavations, from the old ground surface in BB and from the primary and secondary layers in D, E and F. All stages of the core reduction process are represented, and the reality of flintworking in and around the enclosure cannot be doubted. Good quality flint probably from sources on the Marlborough Downs was quartered and then struck from one-, two- and three-platform cores, which were regularly reduced to a small size. The only three-platform cores from primary layers are from A and C in the outer ditch, though there is one from a secondary context from F and two from the old ground surface in BB. Typically for an Earlier Neolithic assemblage (Holgate 1988, 59), core platforms were prepared and many flakes with narrow butts and diffuse bulbs of percussion were struck off by soft hammer. However, there are also hard-hammer flakes, and this technique may have been part of the earlier stages of core reduction and core rejuvenation. The overall range of tool types is considerable, with scrapers and cutting implements (knives, serrated and bevelled flakes) dominant. Stout flakes were used for bevelling and serration, and there are also some irregularly retouched flakes and utilised flakes. Flake scrapers were the dominant tool, mainly on the ends of broad, robust flakes. There was a large knife in BB, and an ovate or laurel leaf in Trench E. No leaf arrowheads occurred in this part of the 1988 sample. Polished axe fragments occurred in primary contexts in Trench C, secondary contexts in Trenches D and F, and the junction of the secondary silts and tertiary ploughsoil in Trench B.

Despite the quantity of material, flintworking does not appear to have taken place in the ditches themselves whilst the primary and secondary silts were forming. No knapping groups occurred; there is little refitting potential amongst flakes from single contexts; and debitage chips are largely absent, even from sieved samples. This would suggest that much if not all of the flint from these contexts represents the deliberate secondary deposition of material brought from elsewhere in the enclosure. It is difficult to establish if any selection took place prior to re-deposition in the ditches given the absence of reliable samples of contemporary lithics from surface contexts against which to compare. However, cores and blocks, and retouched pieces are seemingly over-represented from bone deposits, with a ratio of one core for every 10.3 flakes, and one retouched piece per 9.4 flakes from such, compared with averages of 1:26 and 1:16.3 respectively for the primary and secondary silts in general (tables 189 and 190). The ratios in table 189 for the old land surface in BB and those in the tertiary layers of A, B and C are rather similar, particularly if the ratio of cores to waste is examined. As at Cherhill, one local point of possible comparison (Evans and Smith 1983), retouched pieces outnumber cores. High numbers of flakes compared to cores also come from the uppermost levels of E, but almost exclusively from the later plough layer. The lesser proportions of flakes in other contexts could suggest preferential selection there of cores and tools. Although the difficulties are obvious, it is tempting to suggest that the character of activity in BB and in the uppermost layers of the outer ditch especially was rather different from that elsewhere on the site and in other phases. In Schiffer's terms (1976, 31–32), the material in BB might be seen as primary refuse, discarded at place of use. It has also been suggested that any occupation longer than seasonal is likely to involve significant redeposition (Holgate 1988, 104).

Secondary (and tertiary) layers undoubtedly include some residual material from the phase of activity contemporary with the primary layers in the ditch, but there are a number of indications that there is a genuine difference in the character of the flint assemblage in these respective

Table 189: Ratios of numbers of cores: waste: retouched pieces.

	TrBB	TrB	TrA	TrC	TrD	TrE	TrF
1°	11:324:14	7: 57: 4	1: 21: 0	5: 58: 4	3: 23:2	10:115:12	0: 3: 0
2°	-	24:1072:49	8:133:10	4:133:12	6:105:6	0: 54: 5	4: 97:11
3°	-	7: 266: 6	3: 79: 6	6:316:14	6: 91:7	3:206: 9	6:165: 4

Table 190: Flint in principal placed deposits defined by animal bones.

Trench	Context	Content
B	229	2 blocks, 8 flakes
	227	12 flakes
A	117	1 core
C	321	1 core, 1 block
	317	2 core rejuvenation flakes, 11 flakes, 1 utilised flake, 1 scraper
D	418	-
	414	1 core, 1 core rejuvenation flake, 2 flakes
	413	1 core, 3 flakes
E	527	5 flakes, 1 bevelled flake
	525	1 core, 1 core rejuvenation flake, 7 flakes
	523	1 block, 1 flake
	522	-
	518	1 core, 14 flakes, 1 bevelled flake, 1 scraper
F	630	3 flakes, 1 irregularly retouched flake
	629	1 core rejuvenation flake, 10 flakes
	628	12 flakes, 1 scraper
	627	10 flakes, 1 serrated flake, 2 bevelled flakes, 1 utilised flake

divisions in the 1988 excavations. Smith (1965a, 89) observed a tendency for flakes to become progressively broader and squatter with time, though it should be noted that her metrical analysis of waste from Windmill Hill compared material from the primary ditch fills with flakes from the Later Neolithic West Kennet 'occupation' site, and not from the uppper levels of the enclosure ditches themselves. This said, there is an apparent decline in the quality of core reduction techniques in Later Neolithic and Early Bronze Age levels, seen in the appearance of flake cores without abraded platforms, broad hard-hammer struck tertiary flakes, and less emphasis upon the standardised production of narrow flakes and blades. There is not, however, a wholesale decline in flintworking techniques and characterisation should not be too simplistic or exclusive, since tools made on flakes from prepared discoidal and 'Levallois' cores are present, such as the end-polished knife from 302 in C and the petit tranchet derivative arrowheads. Typically, with many of the later implements effort was placed on extensive (and often highly skilled) secondary modification of flake blanks through elaborate retouch, seen with thumbnail scrapers, plano-convex knives and barbed and tanged arrowheads. Poor quality flint, noted by Holgate as characteristic of the Later Neolithic (1988, 60), occurs only in the upper part of the secondary layers in Trench A.

Thumbnail scrapers first appear in the secondary layers in Trench B and in the upper secondary layers of Trench C. These are traditionally associated with Beakers (Smith 1965a, 107), though a broader Early Bronze Age currency may be applicable. Barbed and tanged, petit tranchet and chisel arrowheads also first appear in the upper secondary layers of Trench B and Trench C. Compatibly with the national pattern of associations, in C two transverse arrowheads occur below a Sutton b type barbed and tanged arrowhead in 302 (though this is possibly derived), though in B a barbed and tanged arrowhead of Conygar type occurs below a petit tranchet. The Conygar type has Food Vessel and Beaker associations, the Sutton type a broad range of Beaker and Earlier Bronze Age associations, and the petit tranchet a long currency in the third millennium BC. The chisel and oblique arrowheads are most closely associated with Grooved Ware ceramics (Wainwright and Longworth 1971, 257–59; Green 1980, 111, 114, 138–39; Riley 1990, 228). With the exception of the example in Trench BB, all the knives occur in secondary contexts, especially in the incipient soil layers, including the plano-convex knives from Trench B, which elsewhere have Collared Urn and Food Vessel associations (Clark 1932; Pierpoint 1980, 130–31). Both the Conygar arrowhead and plano-convex knife from 216 were in fact asociated with sherds from an Enlarged Food Vessel (see chapter 13). The perhaps unusual end scrapers in Trenches C and F are also from uppermost secondary layers, and most of the miscellaneous pieces are also from this context, especially in the outer ditch but also from Trench E in the middle ditch. It is noticeable that this presumably Later Neolithic material is concentrated in the outer ditch as opposed to the middle and inner circuits; and furthermore, that definable Beaker and Early Bronze Age types, such as thumbnail scrapers and plano-convex knives, were predominantly from the upper levels of Trench B, within the area of the presumably contemporary round barrow cemetery.

Flintworking may have taken place within the hollow of the outer ditch in Trench B during the Earlier Bronze Age. A sizeable assemblage of debitage chips (defined as pieces under 15 mm) was recovered by sieving from the soil layer 202. Such pieces are generally indicative of *in situ* working, since, unless inadvertently scooped up, their small size usually prevents them being moved from the place of knapping (Newcomer and Karlin 1987, 35). Around 15 percent of those from 202 may be defined as retouch chips, and include possible scraper rejuvenation chips and pieces produced by invasive retouch. Three flint hammerstones came from 202, and the axe fragment from the same context and macehead from 216 had been re-used as hammerstones.

The lithic assemblage from the Keiller excavations

The 1925–29 excavations produced an immensely rich lithic assemblage, much of it deriving from secure Neolithic contexts in the ditches of the enclosure, pits and varied features such as the Square Enclosure (Smith 1965a, 85–109). Because of the scale and compositional diversity of the assemblage, and the quality of its recording, characterisation of Earlier and Later Neolithic components was possible, and its study helped provide a framework for a wider understanding of southern English Neolithic flint industries in the pre- and immediate post-war years (Keiller 1934, 138; Piggott 1954, 75–80). Clark, for example, relied heavily on data from Windmill Hill in developing a classificatory scheme for transverse arrowheads (Clark 1934).

The definitive report on the Keiller lithics, which also incorporated material from the 1957–58 excavations, was published by Smith in 1965. By contemporary standards this was a thorough and very influential study, still much cited, providing something of a yardstick against which other Neolithic assemblages have been measured. The report was structured into studies of raw material types and sources, reduction techniques (involving metrical analysis) and typology. Distinctions were drawn between the primary assemblage, 'Secondary Neolithic' lithics, Beaker types and unattributable later components; in part following the cultural divisions proposed by Piggott (1954). From the perspective of the present, the weaknesses of the report can be seen to lie in the absence of any overall quantification and the dearth of contextual detail, other than the divisions between Earlier and Later Neolithic and Beaker components. A summary table was given for implements from primary contexts (Smith 1965a, 91), and quantification and basic contextual detail provided for selected artefact categories such as piercers, sickles, leaf arrowheads and axe fragments (Smith 1965a, 93–103). However, no formal listing was provided for implements from Later Neolithic contexts, and the figures given for debitage from primary levels are misleading since they comprise an ill-defined sample (Smith 1965a, 86–87). No definition of a 'primary level' was given, though presumably these are contexts which produced exclusively Earlier Neolithic pottery. Such criticism is comparatively minor, and the enormity of Smith's task in bringing the Windmill Hill material to publication should not be forgotten.

A thorough re-analysis of the Keiller and Smith lithic assemblage has not been possible. It has nonetheless been possible to quantify the assemblage, according both to context and artefact category (tables 191–92), and some observations, general and specific, are offered on selected aspects of the material (particularly relating to the Earlier Neolithic component). The tables have been compiled from original finds catalogues held in Avebury Museum, with supplementary information on discarded pieces (flakes, cores and blocks) deriving from lists produced apparently on-site by Alexander and Veronica Keiller. Further details have been taken from the published report (Smith 1965a). There are a number of minor discrepancies between the figures presented here and those given for selected artefact categories in the published analysis. Where such occur, Smith's figures should be taken as the more accurate, since the identifications given in the Keiller catalogues are occasionally erroneous. Implements listed in the Keiller catalogues as 'beaked' tools are taken to be

awls/piercers, but the category undoubtedly includes a few denticulated scrapers and crude cores, for example. Without a re-examination of every piece in the collection such minor errors of detail cannot be resolved, but the figures do at least offer an indication of the scale, variability and context of the assemblage.

In excess of 95,000 pieces of worked flint are recorded from the Keiller excavations, and over 1500 from those of Smith (details of lithic waste are not recorded in the finds catalogues for 1957–58, though the material exists in Avebury Museum). The Keiller figures are undoubtedly an under-representation of the numbers of worked flints originally present since the quantities of unretouched flakes, cores and flaked blocks are not recorded for all contexts, in particular being absent for OD II and the ditch of the Picket Barrow (Winterbourne Monkton 2). It was not regular practice during pre-war excavations to retain lithic debitage, or necessarily all retouched pieces – witness, for example, the recovery strategies at Maiden Castle (Edmonds and Bellamy 1991, 220) – and it is a credit to Keiller's systematic approach that from 1927 onwards accurate records were kept of debitage, with large samples of such being retained from the 1929 season. An informed estimate would suggest an original total of 100,000–110,000 pieces of worked flint from all excavated contexts. To this should be added around 200 unworked nodules.

Even taking into account the scale of the 1925–29 excavations, which involved the clearing of 365 m of ditch fill and a substantial area of the interior (chapter 3), the quantities of worked flint are prodigious; and if such

Table 191: Summary of worked flint from the excavations of 1925–37.

	Flks	Cores	Blks	1	2	3	4	5	6	7	8	9	10	11	12	13	14	15
I.Ditch	22968	1360	732	368	365	237	138	-	40	2	7	37	8	6	28	-	3	20
	87.3	*5.2*	*2.8*	*<*						*4.8*		*.*					*>*	
M.Ditch	32612	2072	1346	631	197	259	111	-	34	3	4	30	11	7	31	3	2	41
	87.2	*5.5*	*3.6*	*<*						*3.6*							*>*	
O.Ditch	10951	901	2002	507	62	99	72	-	40	6	3	16	15	9	12	-	-	27
	74.4	*6.1*	*13.6*	*<*						*5.9*							*>*	
Surface	12625	714	1695	173	6	66	56	1	12	2	3	16	3	-	7	-	2	13
	82.0	*4.6*	*11.0*	*<*						*2.3*							*>*	
S.E'work	613	115	35	17	-	4	4	-	2	-	-	-	-	-	-	-	-	4
	77.2	*14.5*	*4.4*	*<*						*3.9*							*>*	
P.Barrow	+	2+	+	195	31	45	16	2	8	10	1	5	6	1	5	-	-	5
Pits	665+	25+	+	11	22	6	4	-	-	1	-	2	1	-	2	-	-	1

KEY: 1. Scrapers; 2. Serrated flakes; 3. Utilized and retouched; 4. Knives and sickles; 5. Plano-convex knives; 6. Piercers/points; 7. Fabricators; 8. Laurel leaves; 9. Leaf arrowheads; 10. Transverse arrowheads; 11. Barbed and tanged arrowheads; 12. Axe fragments; 13. Adze fragments; 14. Miscellaneous heavy tools; 15. Hammerstones.

(Figures in italics are percentages.)

Table 192: Summary of worked flint from the excavations of 1957–58.

	Flks	Cores	Blks	1	2	3	4	5	6	7	8	9	10	11	12	13	14	15
I.D. XVII	+	6	-	11	24	31	2	-	4	-	-	1	1	1	2	-	-	-
M.D. XII	+	9	-	13	7	18	1	-	-	-	-	-	-	-	-	-	-	-
O.D. IV	+	3	-	4	6	14	1	-	-	-	1	-	1	-	1	-	-	-
O.D. V	+	13	-	17	10	57	2	-	12	1	2	2	-	1	4	-	-	5
O.B. IV	840+	22	49	17	30	14	1	-	1	-	1	3	-	-	2	-	-	1
O.B. V	}134	}12	}3	13	10	9	1	-	-	-	-	-	-	-	-	-	-	1
O.B. VI	}	}	}	15	5	9	3	-	2	1	-	-	-	-	-	-	-	-

numbers are representative then the whole enclosure may contain between a quarter to half a million pieces. Admittedly, the material represents the residue of 1500 years of intermittent activity, from the Earlier Neolithic to at least the Early Bronze Age, though a sizeable percentage (possibly as much as 60–70 percent) apparently relates to a relatively limited episode associated with the primary use of the enclosure. Few excavated Earlier Neolithic sites, whether enclosures or open settlements, but excluding extraction sites, have produced such densities of lithics, perhaps only Hurst Fen (Clark *et al.* 1960), Staines (Healey and Robertson-Mackay 1983; R. Robertson-Mackay 1987), Carn Brea (Mercer 1981a) and certainly Maiden Castle (Sharples 1991, 253) being comparable.

There is considerable variation in the representation of different artefact categories within individual features and between the major context divisions of the Keiller excavations. It is immediately apparent that not only does the density of worked flint vary between each of the ditch circuits – the inner, middle and outer ditches producing 181.0, 256.1 and 176.3 pieces per metre respectively (figures comparable with those from 1988) – but that the proportions of individual artefact categories differ significantly. The outer ditch produced a higher percentage of implements and retouched pieces (5.9 percent of the overall total) than the middle and inner circuits (3.6 percent and 4.8 percent), though the under-representation of debitage from OD II may have skewed the figures slightly. The most notable differences are to be seen in the relative proportions of serrated flakes and scrapers, with the former accounting for 29.0 percent of the implement assemblage from the inner ditch, yet only 14.4 percent and 7.1 percent in the middle and outer circuits. Conversely, 58.4 percent of retouched forms from the outer ditch were scrapers, contrasting with 46.3 percent and 29.2 percent in the middle and inner ditches. Patterning could be the product of myriad processes, including the spatial organisation of subsistence activities within the enclosure. However, it is argued elsewhere (chapter 17) that lithic deposition was subject to the same formal spatial structure as that seen with human and animal bone, during the Earlier Neolithic at least. Further discussion of intra-site patterning is offered in chapter 17.

A high percentage of irregular flaked blocks are recorded from the outer ditch (13.6 percent overall), largely a product of the abnormal numbers from layer 1 of OD III, where they made up 24.3 percent of the layer total. Large numbers of partially worked blocks could either be a product of nodule testing or poor flaking control, and might be seen as characteristic of a Later Bronze Age component to the assemblage (P. Harding 1992, 127).

The assemblages from the surface and the ditch of the Picket Barrow deserve some comment. The former derives almost exclusively from the interior of the inner enclosure. Over 15,000 pieces were recorded, much perhaps originating from surface middens (see chapters 3 and 17). Diagnostic Earlier Neolithic implements such as laurel leaves and leaf arrowheads are well represented, though later styles of arrowhead are scarcely present, there being only three transverse examples and no barbed and tanged. This gives the impression of a largely uncontaminated Earlier Neolithic assemblage. One surprising feature is the relative absence of serrated flakes, which account for only 1.7 percent of the implement assemblage. It is quite likely that edge damage resulting from ploughing could have obliterated fine serration on these pieces, though genuine scarcity is also a possibility. Quite considerable quantities of worked flint came from the upper (probably colluvial) silts of the Picket Barrow ditch during excavations in 1937 (Smith 1965a, 3). No figures are available for debitage, although the occurrence of 330 implements would, assuming they accounted for around 5 percent of the assemblage, suggest an original presence of between 6–7000 pieces of worked flint. This assemblage comprises a mixture of Neolithic and Early Bronze Age material, with a number of unusual and specialised types such as square and plano-convex knives, a high percentage of fabricators, and at least one polished-edge tool being present. Although from a derived context, the abundance of worked flint implies the former existence of substantial surface deposits between the inner and middle ditches of the enclosure, in this area of the monument at least. It is important to recognise that deposition was not restricted wholly to pits and the enclosure ditches.

Both the primary and Later Neolithic-Early Bronze Age components of the assemblage may be considered 'domestic' in character, in that a wide range of discarded implements are present, with flintworking seemingly being directed towards the production of serviceable flakes and finished implements for use on-site. Given the poor availability of raw material on the hilltop (Smith 1965a, 85), nodule testing and initial core preparation are unlikely to have been significant activities. A number of tools, principally axes, but also large flake knives (Smith 1965a, figs 42–43) and occasional arrowheads (Smith 1965a, 100), were almost certainly brought to the enclosure as finished implements.

Core reduction strategies of the Earlier Neolithic were largely directed towards the production of narrow flakes/blades, which were subsequently utilised unmodified or prepared by slight retouch. Both Edmonds (1987) and Bradley (1987) have commented on the efficiency of a narrow flake/blade technology in the context of a relatively mobile pattern of settlement, and argue that controlled and efficient reduction techniques can be understood as responses to the insecurity of procuring suitable raw materials. Other modes of flintworking were also employed. Scrapers produced on bi-polar split nodules are present from ID I and VII, and presumably reflect a specific technological response to the difficulties of working small flint nodules (as seen by the frequency of this technique in areas where small pebble flint was the only available source of material (Jacobi 1980, 177)).

In other instances the character of working was conditioned less by strategies of resource maximisation than by a desire to produce implements conforming to a readily identifiable stylistic form. Leaf arrowheads may have been preferentially produced on broad rather than narrow flake blanks (Saville 1981, 126), with investments of time and specialist skill being placed in their finishing through pressure-flaking. A number of large knives or sickles (cf. Smith 1965a, figs 42–43) show the specific utilisation of 'Levallois' style flakes with only minor secondary modification. These are of interest since corresponding large cores with indications of multi-directional flaking are not present on the site, and by implication the knives must have been brought from elsewhere, possibly along the same exchange routes as flint axes. Their value as both effective tools and as symbols, perhaps conveying associations relating to age, gender and specific work practices, may have been high. Furthermore, acknowledging that material culture is an active medium (Hodder 1982), and accepting that the enclosure may have served as a locale for the aggregation of dispersed communities, then it is also possible that synchronic variations in artefact style – seen for example in the range of leaf arrowhead styles present (Smith 1965a, fig. 45) and the occurrence of axes with both rounded and faceted sides (Smith 1965a, fig. 46) – could have been expressions of differing social identity.

A wide variety of tasks is indicated by the range of implements present, such as cutting, cereal processing, scraping/hide preparation, woodworking and hunting or conflict. However, a direct relationship between the presence of specific implements and the enactment of functionally related activities, actually within the enclosure, is difficult to establish. A number of serrated flakes and knives were interpreted by Smith as sickle flints (1965a, 97) because of the presence of edge gloss (following Curwen 1935; though see Bamford 1985, 77, and Saville 1981, 132, for the problems of certain identification). The pre-bank soil was much disturbed, perhaps by cultivation (chapters 6–7), and cereals may have been processed on the site (chapter 8), but there is no definite evidence for cereal cultivation in the wooded environs of the hilltop itself during the life of the enclosure. Likewise, axes and adzes need not signify tree-felling or woodworking within the site, nor need arrowheads imply hunting or human conflict (Dixon 1988; Saville 1981, 145–6) here. Processes of implement use, curation and deposition can be complex (Foley 1981; Binford 1983b, 262–68). Serviceable tools would not necessarily be left or discarded at the location where they were used, but may have been carried back to residential locations. Irreparable damage could result in an implement being discarded at the point of usage, though in the case of large core tools such as axes there would be a secondary value as a re-usable source of good quality flint. None of the flint axes from the enclosure are complete (Smith 1965a, 100), and many are represented by extensively re-worked fragments (personal inspection suggests that the minimum axe numbers given by Smith (1965a, 103) are gross under-estimates). It is even possible that a percentage were brought to the site in an already broken state as potential cores, or specifically for deposition. The placing of substantial, re-workable, fragments of axes in the primary ditch fills (for example from layer 5 of ID XVII (Smith 1965a, fig. 46, F116)) is a reminder that the value of such objects as a potential source of raw material often took second place to an ascribed symbolic role.

Analysis of the Keiller scraper collection

450 randomly selected scrapers were categorised according to the system devised for the Stonehenge Environs Project (Riley 1990, 225), in an attempt to identify any broad chronological trends in scraper style (fig. 217). 95 of those studied came from definable primary levels, 290 from upper ditch fills (representing a mixture of Earlier and Later Neolithic and Early Bronze Age implements) and 65 from surface contexts or unrecorded levels.

Riley's analysis suggested that single and double-ended scrapers produced on long flakes and blades, types with a length:breadth ratio of 1:1 and those on squat flakes (types 1, 2, 3 and 5) possessed good Earlier Neolithic associations; side and thumbnail scrapers (types 6 and 7) Beaker associations; with irregular, often denticulated, examples (type 9) being characteristic of the Later Bronze Age (Riley 1990, 226). The Windmill Hill study came to rather different conclusions. Excluding scrapers from uncertain contexts, the only significant differences in representation are to be seen in the proportions of types 5, 6, 7 and 8. Type 7 'thumbnail' scrapers may be considered to have good Beaker and Early Bronze Age associations; and, indeed, virtually all of those covered in the analysis came from the upper levels of OD II, which also yielded considerable quantities of Beaker pottery. The same context produced several invasively flaked type 4 scrapers; and it is really this characteristic mode of secondary working which is diagnostic. Types 5, 6 and 8 are demonstrably more frequent from primary than upper levels, accounting for 13.7, 9.5 and 9.5 percent respectively from the former contexts, against 7.9, 2.8 and 4.1 percent from the latter. Types 1 and 2 were too poorly represented to give meaningful results. Type 4 was evenly represented throughout.

Points of divergence from the Stonehenge Environs analysis are to be seen in the relative presence of scrapers of types 6 and 8, which in the Stonehenge region are considered to occur frequently in Later Neolithic and Bronze Age contexts (Richards 1990a, table 127). Diversity in the preference of scraper type on a regional or site level is a possibility, and it would be unwise without further study of other excavated assemblages to use the results of both analyses to propose broad trends. Only invasively flaked thumbnail scrapers appear chronologically and culturally diagnostic.

Later Neolithic scrapers tend in general to be thinner than those of the Earlier Neolithic (Smith 1965a, 95; Wainwright and Longworth 1971, 168; P. Harding 1990, 222), and in this respect a distinction could be made

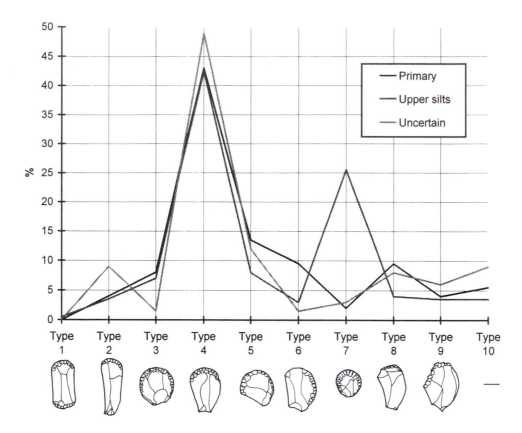

Fig. 217. Types of scraper (following Riley 1990) in a sample of 450 scrapers from the Keiller assemblage.

between early and heavy-duty tools, and later and lighter implements. Whether this reflects changes in the mode of usage, or in productive technology and the conceptualisation of how scrapers, along with any other artefact, should conform to a changing cultural idealised 'norm' is open to investigation. Thumbnail scrapers provide one instance where rigid standardisation in form can be observed, and in which the act of production, expressing a specialized technological knowledge, should not necessarily be separated in importance from function and style (Edmonds and Thomas 1987, 195–96).

The Earlier Neolithic assemblage in context

Excavated Earlier Neolithic flint assemblages from the Avebury area are few in number. There were very few struck flints in the Earlier Neolithic pits outside the enclosure excavated in 1993. Much of the very large assemblage recovered from the surface of the slope south of the enclosure may in fact belong to the Later Neolithic, on the basis of investigations in 1993 (Alasdair Whittle *pers. comm.*). The enclosures at Knap Hill (Connah 1965) and Rybury (WANHM 1964) provide comparable contexts, but excavation at both has been limited in scale and only those at the former site have been published. Of the 2759 pieces of worked flint recovered during the 1961 excavations at Knap Hill, 5.3 percent were utilised or retouched, diagnostic implements being represented by

only 12 scrapers and five serrated flakes (Connah 1965, 14–15), suggesting more emphasis upon the utilisation of unmodified pieces than is seen at Windmill Hill. This scenario is repeated at the anomalous Earlier Neolithic site at Cherhill (Evans and Smith 1983). Leaf arrowheads were present, but standardised implements were otherwise poorly represented (Pitts 1983, 83). One notable feature is the adoption of alternate flaking, seen in the presence of bifacially worked discoidal cores (Evans and Smith 1983, fig. 20, 66–68).

An extensive assemblage from five Earlier Neolithic pits sealed by a Beaker round barrow on Hemp Knoll provides closer comparison with that from the primary levels at Windmill Hill, setting aside the obvious contrasts in scale. Serrated flakes accounted for 23.1 percent of the implement assemblage; scrapers, piercers, a large blunted-back knife, axe fragment, and numerous utilised and retouched flakes also being present (Robertson-Mackay 1980, 129–35). The presence of a wide variety of utilised and retouched pieces, which made up a massive 23.9 percent of the assemblage total, suggests an essentially domestic character. By contrast, groups of knapping debris from under the mound of the South Street long barrow (Ashbee *et al.* 1979, 270–71) and from the primary ditch fills of the Easton Down long barrow (Whittle *et al.* 1993; Pollard 1993b) are indicative of core preparation and reduction with serviceable pieces being removed for utilisation elsewhere.

These comparisons underline the heterogeneous character of Earlier Neolithic lithic assemblages in the region. Indeed, this variation has been noted for sites of the period as a whole (Healey and Robertson-Mackay 1983). There is often superficial similarity, in that standardised working techniques and implement types – such as serrated flakes, leaf arrowheads, laurel leaves and blunted-back knives – have a wide currency, but there is also marked variation in the occurrence and relative proportions of different tool forms (Healey and Robertson-Mackay 1983, 20–24). To explain such compositional variability simply as the result of differential raw material availability and corresponding technological responses (Healey and Robertson-Mackay 1983, 24) seems highly reductionist. Whilst the presence or absence of a good material source within the immediate environs of a site would obviously influence the extent to which activities such as nodule testing and core preparation were significant, the representation of various other functional tasks, the ability of groups or individuals to acquire goods and resources, and the specific social context of technology (Pfaffenberger 1988) will all serve to shape the character of an assemblage. To this should be added the selective effects of depositional practices (see chapter 17).

Later assemblages are also briefly discussed in chapter 17.

Acknowledgements
Alasdair Whittle undertook the initial analysis of the 1988 assemblage, and Maggie Hunt and Doris Probert provided sterling help with the metrical analyses.

15

Other Finds

Joshua Pollard and Alasdair Whittle

with a contribution by Michael Hamilton

Stone other than flint

1988 finds

There were only seven stone artifacts from the 1988 excavations (fig. 216).

Macehead

16437 from 216 in Trench B (fig. 218, 1) is a broken shafthole macehead, which can probably be included in Roe's type Ovoid B or C (Roe 1968). The diameter of the slightly waisted shafthole is only 2 cm. The piece is made of fine-grained sandstone. The surviving surface has been extensively ground and polished. There are traces of battering on the original end of the implement apparently made after it had broken, suggesting a secondary use as a hammerstone.

Quern, rubbers and pounders

23243 from the placed deposit 229 at the bottom of the outer ditch in Trench B is a substantial fragment of sarsen quern, slightly dished on top and with clear signs of abrasion and wear (fig. 218, 2).

9726 from 216 in Trench B (fig. 218, 3), 12201 from 508 in Trench E and 7386 from the upper fill of the grave 707 in Trench BB (fig. 218, 4) are sarsen rubbers, each fashioned from a larger piece by flaking to a size comfortably fitting the hand. 9726 and 7386 have a flat or very slightly convex face worn by abrasion, but the wear on 12201 is concentrated at the angle between the sarsen cortex and a broken face.

16647 from 324 in Trench C (fig. 218, 5) and 1488 from 105 in Trench A are sarsen pounders with curved edges formed by repeated blows, concentrated on two parts on the former piece and on one on the latter.

In addition there were 167 fragments of stone, predominantly sarsen with other sandstone as well. There were 34 from Trench A (mainly from the secondary silting), 94 from Trench B (of which 89 were from the tertiary silting), four from Trench C, five from Trench D,

21 from Trench E (mainly from 504 and 501), seven from Trench F, and two from Trench BB. Most of these were small, though some were bigger than a fist. One or two were recognisable pebbles, but the majority were much broken, many by burning.

Discussion

The macehead fragment is the sixth shafthole implement to come from Windmill Hill, excluding a stage III battle-axe from an unlocated round barrow (Stone and Wallis 1951, fig. 8, 295). A perforated quartzite pebble was found on the surface of the hill in 1884 (Smith 1965a, 124; Roe 1979, fig. 14f), and four implements were recovered by Keiller during excavations in 1925–9 and 1937. Of the latter, there were two perforated sarsen pebbles from a presumably derived context in the ditch of the 'Picket Barrow' (Winterbourne Monkton 2), a dolerite shafthole adze fragment from layer 2 of OD IIIA, and a broken Ovoid B 'Maesmore' macehead of Group VII stone from the secondary silts of ID VII (Smith 1965a, fig. 51, S9–12). None of these implements are intact, the macehead from the 1988 excavations having been re-used as a hammerstone, and all could be curated pieces, collected from existing middens or brought from elsewhere for re-working or re-use.

The macehead from 216 in B was associated with Early Bronze Age flintwork and Food Vessel sherds. The shafthole adze from OD IIIA came from the same spit as numerous Beaker sherds, and the Maesmore macehead from a level that produced Later Neolithic pottery. All accord with the Later Neolithic-Early Bronze Age date range suggested by Smith (1979, 15–6) and Roe (1968; 1979, 30). Ovoid maceheads, and particularly those of the Maesmore group, may have more specific associations with late Peterborough and Grooved Wares, such as those from Skara Brae (Smith 1979, 15), Rinyo, Cam in Gloucestershire, and Stonehenge (Roe 1968, 153; Montague and Gardiner, in Cleal *et al.* 1995, 394). The superb example from the main tomb at Knowth is decorated using motifs

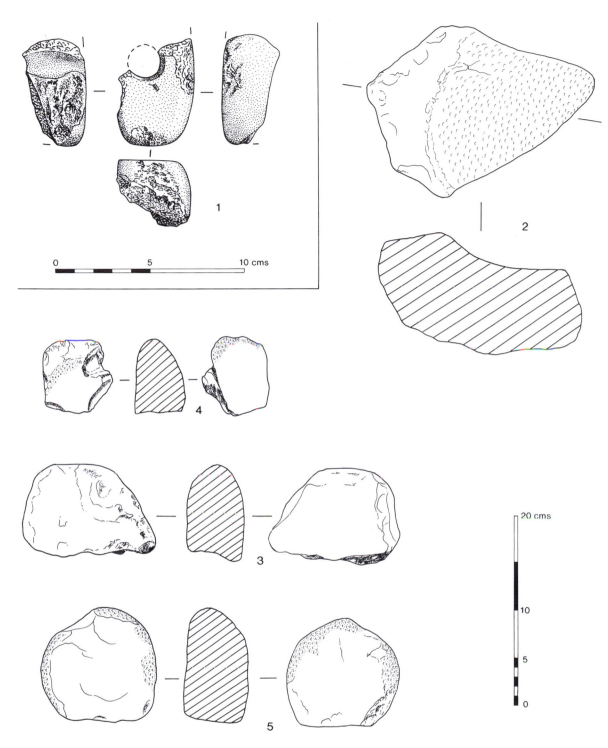

Fig. 218. Worked stone. 1: shafthole macehead, Trench B, upper secondary; 2: part of sarsen quern, Trench B, primary; 3–4: sarsen rubbers, Trench B, upper secondary, and Trench BB, old land surface; 5: sarsen pounder, Trench C, primary.

from Boyne Passage Grave Art (Eogan 1983), which is considered to have links through elements of portable material culture with the Grooved Ware complex (Wainwright and Longworth 1971, 246; Cleal 1991a, 143–44). The two Ovoid maceheads from Windmill Hill may thus represent pieces already several centuries old at the time of their final deposition.

Imported stone, especially axes

The concentration of shafthole implements from Windmill Hill is matched by that of foreign stone artifacts in general (Smith 1965a, 20–21). There were perhaps as many as 22 complete and fragmentary Grouped stone implements from the Keiller excavations, along with parts of slate and tuff axes, and a range of non-local stones, some of which were utilised as hammerstones, hones, rubbers and so forth (Smith 1965a, 110–20) (tables 193–94). There were no imported stone axes or fragments from the 1988 excavations; flint axe fragments have been described in chapter 14.

Eight of the Grouped stone axes came from Lake District sources (VI and XI), seven from south-west Wales (VIII and XIII), four from north Wales (VII), with two Cornish axes (I and IIa) and one of Group XX from the Charnwood Forest also being present (table 193).

The majority of foreign stone axes from the Keiller excavations came from the upper levels of the ditches, with only two flakes from a Group VI axe and one of Group XI having been found in secure primary contexts (Smith 1965a, 111). A Group VIII axe flake from 1.5–2 ft. in MD XIB may also come late in the primary phase. This pattern may also hold true for other causewayed enclosures, where non-flint axes belong to late stages in their development (Bradley and Edmonds 1993, 177). Because of the coarse character of the original recording of material

from the upper fills, specific artifactual and cultural associations are not definable, though a number of the imported axe fragments came from layers that produced Grooved Ware and Beaker sherds.

The ubiquity of imported stone axes from the enclosure led to suggestions that the site was involved in long distance exchange (Stone and Wallis 1951, 133), or that it served as a high status settlement (Bradley 1984, 28–35). While the presence of imported axes may indicate consumption, the fact that these implements stayed on the enclosure does not support the view that exchange was articulated through the site (Bradley 1984, 29; Bradley and Edmonds 1993, 51). The fragmentary nature of the axes, and particularly the large number of flakes present (table 193), implies their utilisation and reworking on site. In the case of the complete Group IIa axe from OD IIIA and the broken, but reconstructable, Group VI axe from ID VIII and ID XVI deliberate, formal deposition may be inferred.

In addition to the ground and polished implements there

Table 193: Ground and polished implements from the Keiller excavations.

Context	Description	Material	Ser. no.
OD II, 1.4-2.3	Fragment	Slate	6
OD IIIa, 1.5	Half a macehead	Dolerite	34
OD IIIa, 1.5	Complete axe	IIa	35
OD IIIa, 2-2.5	4 axe fragments	I	36
OD IIIa, 3-4	Flake (poss. from ? pebble)	Micaceous quartzite	-
MD XIa, top-1	Fragment, from ? axe	VII	1000
MD XIa, 1-2	Axe cutting adge	XX	32
MD XIb, 1.5-2	Flake from ? axe	VIII	33
MD Xa, 1-2	Fragment (poss. from rubber)	Limestone	28
MD Xa, 2-2.5	Flake	Quartzite	29
MD Xb, 2-3	Flake	Chert	30
MD IV, re-excav	Flake	VI	10
MD IVb, top-0.8	Chip from ? axe	VII	9
MD III, top-2	Flake, but no polish	VI	996
MD VI, top-0.8	Core made from axe	VIII	11
MD IIb, 3.5-5 (nearly on base)	Flake from ? axe	XI	8
MD Ib, 2-2.5	Misc. artefact fragment	XIII	12
ID VII, 1.4-1.9	Macehead fragment	VII	1
ID VII, 1.7	Axe (upper third missing)}	VI	2
ID XVI, top-1	Axe butt }	VI	25
ID XVI, top-1	? Pebble fragment	Slate	26
ID XVI, 1-2	Chip from ? axe	Tuff	27
ID XIV, top-1	Fragment of ? axe	Spotted slate	23
ID XI, 2-base	2 flakes, probably from same axe	VI	21, 22
ID IX, top-1	Flake	XI	19
ID interior, SE sector, III-IV Pit 3	Chip from ? axe	VI	38
ID interior, NE sector, V-VI	Chip from ? axe	VIII	39
ID interior, NE sector IX-X	Axe fragment used as hammerstone	VII	41
ID interior, NE sector, XI-XII	Fragment of ? axe	Slate	42
Picket barrow, cutting 2, NE sector, layer 1	Fragment	VIII	142
ditto	Fragment	XI	141
ditto	Axe reshaped as adze	VIII	139
Found in 1982 among unwashed flakes	Flake from axe	VIII	1797

Table 194: Other stone foreign to the site from the Keiller excavations.

Context	Description and Material
OD II, 0.8-1.4	Piece of ferruginous grit
ditto	Piece of lower greensand
OD II, 1.4-2.3	2 pieces of ferruginous sandstone
OD II, 0.6	Polishing stone of silicified sandstone
OD II, 1.4-2.3	Honing stone of micaceous sandstone
ditto	Grooved piece of lower greensand
OD IIIa, 4-5	Piece of Stonesfield slate
OD IIIc, 1.8	Piece of Stonesfield slate
OD Ic, top-1	Hammerstone of lower greensand
OD Ic, 1-2	Shaped piece of glauconitic sandstone
OD I, re-excav	Piece of lower greensand
ditto	Hammerstone of lower greensand
ditto	Piece of lower greensand
ditto	Piece of Corallian sandstone
MD XIa, 1-1.5	Slab of fine-grained calcareous grit
ditto	Piece of micaceous sandstone
MD VI, top-0.8	Piece of lower greensand
MD VI, 1.4-2.3	3 pieces of limestone
MD V, top-0.8	2 pieces of lower greensand
MD IIb, top-0.8	Piece of lower greensand
ditto	5 pieces of ferruginous grit
MD IIb, 0.8-1.4	Piece of lower greensand
MD IIb, 3.5-5	Piece of lower greensand
MD Ib, layer 3b	Slab of limestone
MD I, re-excav	Piece of lower greensand
MD VII, 1-2	Calcite crystals from limestone pebble
MD VIII, top-1	Fragment of honing stone of lower greensand
MD IX, top-1	Calcite crystals from limestone pebble
ID VII, 1.4-2.3	Hammerstone of Bunter Beds ferruginated grit
ID XVI, top-1	Piece of silicified sandstone
ID XIV, 1-2	Piece of Portland Beds siliceous rock
ID XIII, 2-3	Piece of Stonesfield slate
ID IX, 1-2	Piece of micaceous sandstone
ID V, re-excav	Piece of lower greensand
ID I/II, 1.4-2.3	Pebble of micaceous schist
ditto	Sandstone pebble with flake removed
ID II re-excav	3 pieces of lower greensand
ID interior, NE sector, VII-VIII	Piece of silicified sandstone
ditto	Piece of Portland Beds siliceous rock
Square Earthwork Surface and ditch	21 pieces of oolitic limestone

is a sizeable assemblage of worked and unworked imported stone from the site (table 194: Smith 1965a, 110–120). Much of this again comes from upper levels in the ditches or from surface finds, and may well relate to Late Neolithic-Early Bronze Age activity on the hill. A comparable assemblage of foreign stone came from similarly late contexts in the ditches of the nearby Horslip long barrow (Ashbee *et al.* 1979, 223–24).

Various pieces of foreign sedimentary rock, along with a few pieces of schist and quartzite, were recovered from primary ditch fills (Smith 1965a, 110–20). Of particular significance, though unfortunately not from an undoubted Early Neolithic context, are several fragments of oolitic limestone from the surface and ditch of the Square Earth-

work. This rock hardly occurs elsewhere on the site (Smith 1965a, 118). Its intentional incorporation in the structure of funerary monuments in the region, most notably the West Kennet long barrow (Piggott 1962a, 58), lends support to an Early Neolithic date for this earthwork and its function as a form of mortuary enclosure (Smith 1965a, 33). Oolitic limestone evidently held special associations, both with a particular architectural tradition represented by Cotswold-Severn tombs, and perhaps by extension with qualities associated with human bone and ancestral vitality (cf. Taçon 1991).

Domestic tasks: querns, rubbers and pounders

Sarsen saddle querns (complete and fragmentary), rubbers and pounders have been recovered in some quantity from the enclosure, most (including examples from 1988) from primary contexts (Smith 1965a, 121). Their presence may provide more concrete evidence of the scale of cereal processing on the site than the charred plant remains (chapter 8). Querns in particular are durable artifacts with a potentially long use-life. Precise numbers of querns and rubbing stones are difficult to quantify; at an estimated guess maybe over 50 querns (when complete rather than fragmentary) and 70 rubbing stones have come from all three campaigns of excavation at Windmill Hill. Much smaller quantities came from contemporary occupation sites at Hemp Knoll (Robertson-Mackay 1980, 137) and Cherhill (Evans and Smith 1983, 99–101), though the scale of these sites, and their excavation, was considerably more limited. As a yardstick against which to measure ubiquity, the short-lived (probably of a few years' duration), single unit occupation from beneath the Hazleton North long cairn produced fragments from perhaps two querns (Saville 1990, 178).

It is striking that sarsen quern stones and rubbers are so difficult to find in the landscape, as evidenced by the absence of such from the programme of fieldwalking on the southern slopes of the hill in 1993. They are, however, a frequent component of Early Neolithic pit deposits, as well as occurring in ditches at Windmill Hill, Cherhill and the Horslip long barrow. Two rubbers came from a pit excavated outside the enclosure in 1993, and two unfinished querns from Pit 1 on Hemp Knoll (Robertson-Mackay 1980, 137), for instance. As obvious symbols of domestic production and nurture, and perhaps intimately linked to prescribed female roles (Haaland 1997), querns and rubbing stones appear as a common component of placed deposit-ions during the period (see chapter 17), and this may be skewing their representation in surface deposits.

Antler

Combs

Two fragments of comb were found in the 1988 excavations, both from the inner ditch in Trench F, in bone deposit 627/628 (fig. 219, 1–2). They fit well within the range of

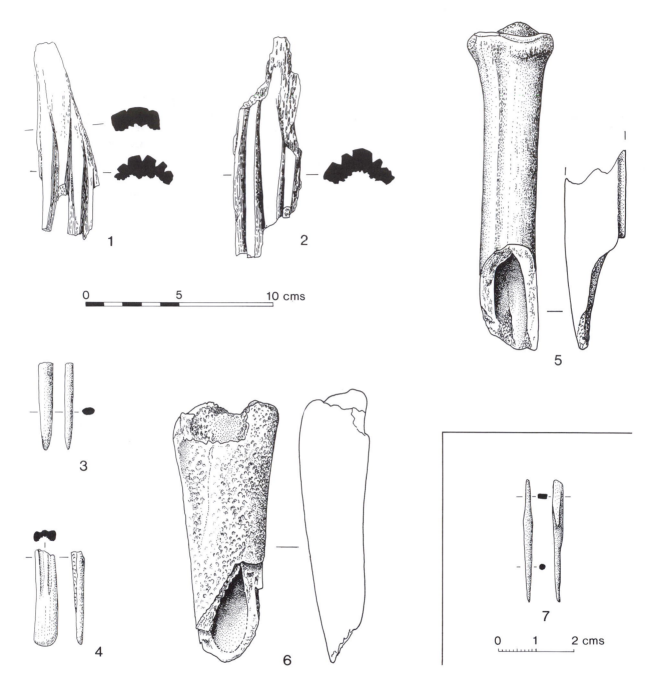

Fig. 219. 1–2: fragments of antler combs, Trench F (627/628); 3: bone pin, Trench BB, old land surface; 4: bone gouge or spatula, Trench B (202); 5–6: ? bone gouges, Trench F (630) and Trench A (102); 7: awl possibly of bronze, Trench B (201).

antler combs already described by Smith (1965a) from the Keiller excavations, though their surfaces are very smooth and look at first sight like bone. That account makes it clear that although there were quite frequent finds of pieces of antler, antler tools of any form were comparatively rare in the ditches of the enclosure. Piggott (1954, 83) had already drawn attention to this tool category, nearly always made from antler, and suggested by analogy a use for dehairing animal skins. If this is accepted, the selection of antler, from wild red deer, to process the skins of domestic animals becomes significant (Niall Sharples *pers. comm.*).

Symbolic implications of this kind are further considered in chapters 17 and 18.

Bone

Pin
One small shaped bone pin came from the surface of the pre-bank soil in Trench BB (fig. 219, 3).

Small gouge or spatula
One small gouge or spatula, with a flattened end, came

from the soil 202 above the secondary fill of the outer ditch in Trench B (fig. 219, 4).

? Gouges

Two examples of possibly deliberately split and shaped gouges on cattle limb-bones were found, one from deposit 630 in the inner ditch in Trench F and the other from the tertiary fill of the outer ditch in Trench A (fig. 219, 5–6). Four similar items came from the Keiller excavations (Smith 1965a).

Bronze? *(Michael Hamilton)*

Awl (fig. 219, 7)

The awl was found immediately under the turf in Trench B. The awl is 32 mm long, with a maximum width of 3 mm. The tang is 12 mm long and represents 38 percent of the total length. The tang appears to be produced by hammering and then grinding or filing to reduce its width. No chemical analysis has been done, but the object appears to be bronze.

This belongs to Group 2B of N. Thomas (1968), characterised as single ended awls with tang, the tangs generally less than 50 percent of length, and filed or ground to produce a tang width equal or less than the maximum width of the awl. Awls of this type have abundant associations with later Early Bronze Age finds (especially Collared Urns, but also Miniature Accessory Vessels, developed bronze daggers, Food Vessels, and so on), but none appear to be associated with Beaker pottery. Similar awls occur in the Middle Bronze Age (Mercer 1981b, 74–75) and may be under-represented in the later Bronze Age by a change in depositional practice (Needham 1986). However, most of the awls cited by Needham are much larger and/or thicker than the Windmill Hill example, which looks much closer to EBA grave-good material (Annable and Simpson 1964).

Bronze awls are most commonly recovered from burials, and after pottery are probably the most common LN/EBA grave-good. They are very rare from EBA non-funerary contexts. Given that Trench B was close to three round barrows, it is possible that the deposition of the awl, like the destruction of two whole EBA pots (P541 and P323) in Trench B, was associated with funerary rites. However, the act of deposition was not associated with human bone, and parallel behaviour is difficult to find. In Wiltshire the only EBA awl which appears to have a non-funerary context is an awl from Stonehenge (Lawson 1995, 430) from the eastern terminal of the main north-east entrance. Given the rarity of such items outside burials, the location of this Stonehenge awl may be significant, especially as the Windmill Hill awl was also close to a still visible ditch terminal.

16

Human Remains

Don Brothwell

with a contribution by Michael Wysocki

The bone of the human skeletal remains sent for study was generally strong, but vertebrae and ribs were not so well preserved.

Adult male burial under the outer bank, Trench BB

When examined *in situ*, this inhumation (chapter 4) at first appeared to be an articulated skeleton. However, as the bones were more fully exposed, it became clear that the body was not totally undisturbed. In normal articulation were the skull, vertebrae, ribs, both humeri, scapulae, pelvis and left leg. The bones of both feet were also still in reasonable position in relation to one another. The right forearm and both hands appear to be disturbed, as well as the right leg below the thigh. Disturbed bones of special note are:

1. The right radius has been rotated perhaps through 80° to the elbow joint and is placed across the left humerus shaft (and extends towards the pit side);
2. The right fibula appears to be rotated and has dropped down into the pelvic basin;
3. The right tibia has been displaced up the body and appears to be superimposed over the left forearm (and rotated);
4. The right femur has slipped down and away from the pelvis (acetabulum) and has rotated laterally about 90°.

An explanation for the disturbed body is suggested by the large number of amphibian bones at the base of the grave (chapters 4 and 12). These suggest that the pit was dug, the body placed in it and then left exposed until the body was well rotted. This pit then acted as a trap, so that over a period of at least months, amphibians (and a few small mammals) fell into the hole and died there. The larger disturbed bones are unlikely to have moved because of later small mammal burrowing, and it seems far more likely that they were pulled about by a dog or fox while the

pit was open. There are no carnivore tooth marks on any bone to confirm this point of view.

Some amphibian bones were clearly in articulation, which strongly supports the view that they dropped into the pit when alive, and are not the result of decomposed pellets from predatory birds.

Biological detail

The skeleton represented a male individual, probably between 35 and 45 years (on dental evidence). The skull, pelvic fragments and long bones suggest a physique which was probably more robust than the average Neolithic male. Associated stature is also greater, being probably between 171.5 and 173.3 cm. This is over 3 cm taller than the English Neolithic average of 168.5 cm (Brothwell 1973). The skull was severely crushed, but was reconstructed to a considerable degree. However, some post-mortem distortion occurs in parts. The dentition was:

$$\underline{8\ 7\ 6\ 5\ 4\ 3\ \not{2}\ 1\ \ 1\ 2\ 3\ 4\ 5\ 6\ 7\ 8}$$
$$8\ 7\ 6\ 5\ 4\ 3\ 2\ 1\ \ 1\ 2\ 3\ 4\ 5\ 6\ 7\ 8$$

Possibly $\not{2}$ was lost after death; otherwise, there is no evidence of caries, abscesses or tooth loss. There is mild alveolar recession and mild calculus formation on most teeth. An unusual feature is the heavy wear on the upper incisors, suggesting that they may have been used for some technical purpose. There were three wormian bones, but no sagittal, coronal, inca, parietal notch or pterionic bones. There was no metopism and no oral tori. Orbital cribra were absent, but there was mild surface pitting on the posterior parietals and upper occipital.

There are six well defined pachionian impressions on the endocranial surface (possibly related to age and an increasing blood pressure). The left maxilla, near the nasal aperture, has a small amount of additional bone, which may be traumatic in origin.

Cranial measurements (in mm) which are probably fairly accurate are:

Max. length (L)	207?
Max. breadth (B)	139?
Basi-bregmatic Ht (H')	149?
Frontal chord (S'1)	121
Parietal chord (S'2)	132
Occipital chord (S'3)	108?
Basi-nasal length (LB)	113?
Upper facial height (G'H)	80?
Upper facial breadth (GB)	95
Nasal height (NH')	60.5
Nasal breadth (NB)	26.8
Orbital breadth (O'1)	35.0.

Although cranial length and breadth measurements may have been slightly influenced by distortion, we are clearly dealing with a typical long, narrow-headed individual (cephalic index = 67).

The post-cranial skeleton consisted of numerous fragments of what was clearly a complete skeleton originally. Bone collapse was especially severe in the region of the vertebrae, ribs and pelvis. Conservation was undertaken to a limited degree, and specifically to recover osteometric or pathological data.

Measurements of the post-cranial skeleton (in mm) were restricted to the long bones as follows:

Femur (Rt.)	Max. length (FeL1)	457
	Antero-posterior diameter (FeD1)	24.0
	Transverse diameter (FeD2)	33.2
	Platymeric index	72.3
Tibia (Lt)	Max. length (TiL1)	388
	Antero-posterior diameter (TiD1)	38.4
	Transverse diameter (TiD2)	19.8
	Platycnemic index	51.6

The femur shaft was thus severely platymeric, and the tibia was extremely platycnemic, again characteristic of prehistoric peoples.

Palaeopathology

The post-cranial skeleton displays various pathology. Owing to considerable damage and crushing to parts of the post-cranial skeleton, the extent of vertebral arthropathies was somewhat obscured. There was, however, clear evidence of severe osteoarthritic changes at four cervicals.

The right clavicle is noticeably shortened and clearly this is the result of an old fracture, which is well healed.

At the distal ends of both ulnae there are slight osteoarthritic changes to the margins of the joints. Both humeri show evidence of what may have been minor trauma long before death. In the right humerus, towards the base of the bicipital groove, is an extra prominence of bone (? minor tear injury). The left humerus displays a smooth distal notch in the articular surface, on the trochlea, but near to the capitulum. This could well indicate a fracture of the distal epiphysis in early childhood.

While the right femur appears to be normal, the left femur head displays eburnation and irregular new bone. There is also an associated reaction extending along the femur neck (additional, irregular bone). This appears to indicate a fairly advanced state of hip arthritis, probably but not certainly associated with significant hip pain.

Both tibiae display fine striations along the shaft, with faint vascular channels just visible.

In the feet, the third right metatarsal has a noticeably swollen shaft with local irregularity. This could be the result of old trauma, but not so long before death. The tuberosity of the right navicular bone displays some irregularity and remodelling, and on the right calcaneum the area for the insertion of the tendo calcaneus is noticeably spicular. These changes to the right foot may all indicate stress and some degree of old trauma.

In the left foot (talus), the lower articular surface for the calcaneum displays an osteochondritic lesion, which again suggests trauma in the past. Overall, some of the pathology may well be age-related, but the changes probably associated with trauma probably indicate an episode of stress in childhood, as well as one not so long before death.

Outer ditch, Trench A, child cranium 1710 in bone group 117

This contained the collapsed and scattered cranium of a child (chapter 4). There were at least 20 large pieces and numerous small fragments to attempt to reconstruct. Only the brain box could be assembled, the face remaining in many pieces. The mandible was not found associated with the cranium. Eight milk teeth were present (4 m, 2 pm, 2 inc), and the crowns of six permanent teeth (2 m, 2 pm, 1 c and one medial inc). The state of development of these crowns suggests an age of about three years. The deciduous and permanent crowns are in good condition and show no evidence of hypoplasia. The deciduous molars remain surprisingly unworn.

The cranial vault displays an open metopic suture and probably a number of wormian bones occurred on the lambdoid suture. No other non-metric traits were visible. Slight cribra orbitalia occurs as a relatively thin band. The endocranial surface was without pathology.

Detail

Fragment 12. Left half of frontal, damaged near nasal bones. Metopic suture still present. No pathology. Skull noticeably thin (3.5 mm in thickest region), and the frontal is small relative to the adult size.

Fragment 11. Most of the left temporal, broken into four pieces. These articulate together. It was from a child with very small mastoid development. No evidence of pathology.

Fragment 15. Fragment of skull, possibly right frontal near the nasal bones. Thickness c. 2.7 mm (avoiding inner medial ridge).

Fragment 25. Numerous teeth and fragments of bone. Parts of the left and right maxilla, including part of the palate. Also part of the right molar. There are 16 teeth, consisting of four milk molars, two milk incisors and two milk canines. The adult teeth are two upper medial crowns, two molar crowns and two premolar crowns. Also within the left maxilla, there is a canine crown and premolar crown. In the permanent molar and medial incisor there are hypoplastic lines and defects extending down these crowns. The age from the degree of dental development is between three and four years. There is a minor notched defect in the occlusal margin of the medial incisor.

Fragment 2. Two skull fragments, the major piece being the right parietal and a small piece of left parietal near bregma. No pathology. Maximum thickness = 3.7 mm.

Fragment 7. Large piece of left parietal with part of the sagittal and coronal suture present. A part of fragment 2 fits this bone.

Fragment 6. Most of the right frontal of a child, judging from the skull thickness (c. 3.2 mm). This piece fits fragments 12 and 15. Within the orbit there is very slight cribra orbitalia.

Fragment 23. Small fragment of parietal with deep meningeal impressions, and a small area of ? coronal suture.

Fragment 5. Part of a left molar.

Fragment 21. Right greater wing of the sphenoid.

Fragment 9. Lower posterior part of a left parietal, with part of the lambdoid suture.

Fragment 19. Most of an occipital of a thin skull, with much of the lambdoid suture.

Fragment 17. Thin parietal fragment. 3.6 mm, probably the left side at the lambdoid suture.

Fragment 10. Fragment of parietal with suture to the temporal.

Fragment 4. ?Front of a child's parietal with coronal suture and small area of sagittal suture.

Fragment 22. Right, front lower area of the parietal. Thin skull of child.

Inner ditch, Trench F, immature femur 6422 inserted into *Bos* humerus in bone deposit 630 (*Michael Wysocki*)

The fragment was found inserted into the medullar cavity of a *Bos* distal humerus (see fig. 161, chapter 11) and identified as human by Caroline Grigson. Precise identification was undertaken with reference to the collection of immature human skeletal remains held at the Anatomy Unit, School of Molecular and Medical Biosciences, Cardiff University.

The bone is a human immature distal left femoral diaphysis and metaphysis. On the basis of size, the estimated age category is older child (c. 5–7 years).

The anterio-posterior diameter at the diaphyseal margin is rather larger than one would normally expect to find in

a bone at this stage of development and the lateral supracondylar line forms a notably sharp border. The metaphyseal architecture is also unusual, presenting a shallow concavity instead of the grooved convex configuration usually observed.

Bone surface modifications are limited to a few random scratch or cut-like marks, possibly the result of animal trampling or natural attritional processes. The bone shows no macroscopically visible indications of weathering.

Other remains

Pre-bank surface, Trench BB
7741, 741. Lower canine with hypoplastic enamel.
7673, 741. Probably human. Distal shaft fragment. Tibia.
7813, 741. Possibly a small fragment of immature occipital.
7848, 747. An upper second molar of an adult.

Outer ditch, Trench B, secondary fill
16896, 206. Small shaft fragment. Distal ulna.
16715, 203. Probably a small fragment of an adult parietal bone.
16721, 203. Distal shaft fragment. Tibia.

Outer ditch, Trench B, upper secondary fill
9563, 202. Ten shaft fragments, one being identified as a proximal ulna of a robust male (Right side).

Inner ditch, Trench F, secondary fill
6285, 604. Fragment of parietal. Adult.

Conclusion

The principal human remains consist of much of one individual, a mature male with Neolithic cranial affinities, but taller and more robust than average. There is also a series of skeletal fragments. In all, it seems likely that there is a minimum of six individuals represented, two probably male and two children under five years of age, with another child slightly older.

The pre-bank burial in Trench B provides important evidence of corpse exposure. In terms of the pathology displayed, the complete individual had serious arthritis in his hip. Today, such a condition would not commonly occur in an individual of his relatively young age (and eventually would lead to hip replacement surgery). Because there is evidence of trauma in the skeleton, it may be questioned whether there had been mechanical stress to the hip in the past, which had resulted in the premature arthropathy.

17

Interpretations

Alasdair Whittle, Joshua Pollard and Caroline Grigson

with contributions by Michael Hamilton and Joanna Brück

The setting and early settlement

All lines of evidence point to the continued existence of woodland as the dominant vegetation of the region in the Earlier Neolithic period. This mantle may have been, by analogy with elsewhere, a little affected by the activities of Mesolithic people, but it has been argued that in fact this area of the Chalk (and many others like it in Wessex) may have been comparatively little used in the Mesolithic, principally for short-stay hunting forays (Whittle 1990). The course of the Kennet valley may have provided some variation in vegetation cover (Evans *et al.* 1993), and there could also have been natural clearings (Brown 1997).

The recurrent situation in the Earlier Neolithic seems to have been of small, mostly short-lived man-made clearances, alongside natural clearings (cf. Brown 1997), creating an unstable and fluid mosaic of woodland and small areas of more open or cleared ground. Long barrows and chambered tombs seem to have been sited on patches of ground which had remained open for a while, and could have gradually created, as they were successively built, a permanent frame, a series of fixed points, in the landscape. Given that the enclosure at Windmill Hill is later within the Earlier Neolithic than the first long barrows and chambered tombs (Whittle 1993), the enclosure represents an enhancement of this process. The very size of the enclosure and the whiteness of its freshly dug ditches and such banks or spoil dumps as it had, would have made it stand out from some perspectives, but its visual effect as a monument would have been principally from close range, and some at least of its significance may have been drawn from its woodland setting.

Such a woodland setting could hardly conceal knowledge of the site. Windmill Hill stands out physically in the local topography, as described in chapter 2. It is highly visible not only from the surrounding higher Chalk to its south and east, but also from the Lower Chalk plateau to the north. Figures 11–12 attempt to convey something of this striking position, admittedly in a now very open environment.

Other causewayed enclosures in the area also commanded striking views. Rybury and Knap Hill overlook the Vale of Pewsey. (The status of Crofton in the Vale has been debated in chapter 2.) Though both are in prominent places, neither has quite such an obvious position as Windmill Hill for the observer looking from any direction. As far as is known at present, there are no causewayed enclosures along the north scarp of Salisbury Plain, that is along the south side of the Vale of Pewsey, nor on the Lower Chalk plateau to the north of Windmill Hill, nor in the Vale of Swindon further north still. On a wider scale, and for a variety of reasons, Windmill Hill stood out.

The settlement evidence from the area as a whole provides a further, if uncertain, insight into the context of the enclosure. This is not the place to review all the evidence, but a number of points can be stressed. It is hard to date the available evidence of lithic scatters and parts of occupations to phases within the Earlier Neolithic: in the terms of Whittle (1993), to Phases A–C. This immediately implies that it is hard to see any progressive increase in the number of sites with time, or to distinguish the very earliest occupations. The character of the pre-enclosure occupation at Windmill Hill can be matched elsewhere, including in the features immediately outside the enclosure (Whittle *et al.* forthcoming).

Occupation evidence largely consists of lithic scatters on the one hand, and pits and other features normally discovered under later monuments. There has been little systematic survey in the area; to the collecting of Kendall, Keiller and Passmore can be added more recent work by Holgate (1987; 1988) and the National Trust (Ros Cleal *pers. comm.*). Earlier Neolithic scatters, such as they can be distinguished, are widespread. Their density can be low, as on the higher chalk around the Easton Down long barrow (Dennis 1993). Many of the larger assemblages are multi-period, and the bulk of that from Windmill Hill itself may be of Later Neolithic date. Also of Later Neolithic date seem to be some of the larger assemblages on lower ground (Holgate 1987). The foul sewer line from

Avebury past Silbury Hill to East Kennet village, however, passed through no major flint concentration, nor indeed any other sign of Neolithic occupation (Powell *et al.* 1996). What, if anything, lies under flint scatters has barely been tested in the area; at Windmill Hill, fairly extensive geophysical survey with allied sample excavation found only one small cluster of Earlier Neolithic pits (Whittle *et al.* forthcoming).

Apparently small clusters of pits preserved under later monuments have often been commented upon (e.g. R. Smith 1984; Whittle 1990; 1993; Thomas 1984; 1991). Examples include Hemp Knoll (Robertson-Mackay 1980), Avebury G55 (Smith 1965b), Overton Hill (Smith and Simpson 1964), Roughridge (WANHM 1965), Millbarrow (Whittle 1994) and Horslip (Ashbee *et al.* 1979). There were fence lines, ard marks and other possible remains of cultivation variously under the South Street and Beck-hampton longbarrows (Ashbee *et al.* 1979). The less numerous open sites include pits on Waden Hill (N. Thomas 1956) and the irregular ditches or quarries at Cherhill (Evans and Smith 1983). All in all, this is not an impressive tally. Is it the tip of the iceberg or does it more or less fairly indicate a low-level occupation density, the destructive effects of later landuse notwithstanding ? The answer remains elusive, but the lack of results from both the foul sewer line (Powell *et al.* 1996) and the valley investigations of the 1980s (Evans *et al.* 1993) may suggest lower rather than higher densities overall. The pits that have been investigated regularly have selected and carefully deposited contents (Thomas 1991; Pollard 1993a), which, it has been suggested, had to do with the comings and goings of an at least partly mobile population (Whittle 1990, 107). The general style of Earlier Neolithic flint working is also compatible with this characterisation (see chapter 14). There is no other structure to match the possible one under the outer bank at the enclosure itself (see chapter 4 and below, fig. 220; Darvill 1996).

In all, the evidence as it presently exists may suggest a scattered, mobile population, perhaps part of a much wider pattern or system, living in an environment dominated more by woodland than by the fluctuating clearings and clearances within it (cf. Edwards 1993). If the gradually increasing density of shrines and ossuaries in the area is any guide, this was one of the most intensively used or frequented parts of the wider region, and the relative paucity of evidence from the immediate area under discussion is therefore an important index of the wider situation. How far people ranged in a given season, year or lifetime is quite unclear. Given that there was mobility, similar patterns of movement can be suggested for adjacent areas, on Salisbury Plain to the south and in the Upper Thames to the north (see Richards 1990a; Barclay *et al.* 1996; Hey 1997). The Windmill Hill enclosure was therefore probably built in a world of low population, tethered mobility or short-term sedentism, woodland, cattle keeping and limited cultivation (see below, and chapters 8 and 11), and episodic contact between social groups. The enclosure itself represents by far and away the largest accumulation of residues and materials for many miles around.

Subsistence

The evidence for the subsistence economy set out in chapters 8 and 11, supported also by the environmental evidence in chapters 6, 7, 9, 10 and 12, suggests overall that the people who used the enclosure on Windmill Hill utilised a range of domesticated and wild animals and plants in a mainly wooded setting, which had a mosaic of shifting clearings and clearances. This bald summary raises classic questions of the balance of resources, of the scale of their use, of the residential patterns which went with their exploitation, and of the context and goals of production. The brief discussion here will concentrate on the site evidence, with some reference to regional and wider evidence.

Balance of resources

There seems no reliable method of determining from site residues themselves what was the balance of resources. The superficial impression is that animals dominated the scene, and it is clear that within the animal spectrum it was domestic cattle that were the predominant concern at the enclosure.

It may be dangerous to underplay the role of cereal cultivation, and chapter 8 has drawn attention to variations elsewhere in the abundance of charred cereal remains. In total, however, evidence from elsewhere may well also suggest a limited role for cereal cultivation. The extent of clearances was limited, cereal pollen (a poor disperser anyway) is not abundant in the pollen record (Edwards 1993), and new stable isotopic evidence suggests either meat-dominated diets or mixed diets but not so far plant-dominated ones (M. Richards 1998; and *pers. comm.*). Insect evidence, for example from Runnymede in the lower Thames, suggests that cattle were of importance right from the start of the Neolithic, even before substantial opening of the woodland canopy (Robinson 1991).

It is possible that this and other enclosures present a selective view of what was important in the sphere of subsistence, promoting the importance of domesticates and especially cattle (Grigson 1981b; 1982a; 1984; Thomas 1996a); the Coneybury Anomaly with its range of wild as well as domesticated animals (Richards 1990a) is often quoted in support of this view. The local evidence certainly suggests a varied representation and perhaps therefore balance of species. Cattle are predominant in the faunal assemblages from the Earlier Neolithic occupation at Hemp Knoll (Grigson 1980), and the same is true in primary contexts at the nearby Horslip long barrow (Ashbee *et al.* 1979), and at Cherhill (Grigson 1983). However, sheep/goats are more frequent amongst the material from under the South Street long barrow (Ashbee *et al.* 1979) and, along with pig, from pits on Roughridge Hill (Pollard

1993a; Edwina Proudfoot *pers. comm.*). Deer remains (principally antler with some bone) were also present at several of these sites. Further afield, the occupation at Runnymede is notable for the dominance there of cattle bone (Serjeantson 1991; 1996). An alternative model that people celebrated or displayed the main elements of their subsistence economy at causewayed enclosures, rather than distorted and selected elements of it, could be posited, but the evidence outlined above makes the issue far from clear. It is perhaps best to think of subsistence practices and the balance of resources as being contextually specific: different economies for different occasions, rather than a single monolithic 'economy'. For the authors of this chapter at least, this is likely to have been a mixed economy, but one dominated by domesticated animals, especially cattle.

Isotopic analysis is now under way on human bone from Windmill Hill (M. Richards *pers. comm.*), which may help to throw further light on these issues.

What have become clearer from the analyses presented in chapter 11 are the main ways in which different animals were used, at least as represented in the site samples. The overall pattern of older cows, young pigs and older sheep/goats, may give important insights into other issues, including that of patterns of residence (and see below).

Scale

The question of the balance of resources spills over into the next, that of scale. Again, residues in themselves can hardly provide reliable answers, though the superficial impression is of limited cereal cultivation and of a lot of animals. There are comparatively few remains from cereal processing, though pots have cereal impressions (Dennell 1976), which could allow the possibility of already processed remains having been brought in from wide areas roundabout. Neither pottery nor pits in general suggest the extensive storage of cereals, though no analysis has yet been undertaken of pot residues and of course cereals could have been stored in other ways. There is local evidence for both fencing and ploughing, at the South Street long barrow nearby (Ashbee *et al.* 1979), but fencing is compatible with small clearances (cf. Whittle *et al.* 1993) and it is not certain that the South Street ard marks represent prolonged activity. Further evidence of cereal production may come from finds of querns and other processing equipment (though querns need not indicate the processing of cultivated plant foods). There are relatively large numbers from Windmill Hill (see chapter 15), and there are querns at local sites such as Cherhill (Evans and Smith 1983, 99–101).

Chapter 11 drew attention to the occasional but conspicuous non-consumption of slaughtered animals, and it is worth stressing the possible numbers of animals represented in the deposits of all three ditch circuits, assuming numbers of deposits to have been roughly equal around them. The total must run into thousands, but this was the sum of repeated acts of deposition, itself in many cases perhaps following curation or storage of bone, played out over a period of perhaps generations. No one deposit seems to display the abundance of animals apparently represented in Later Neolithic contexts, for example of cattle above the Irthlingborough Beaker burial in the Nene valley (Davis and Payne 1993) or of pig in the construction phase of the West Kennet palisade enclosures locally (Whittle 1997a). This could suggest a 'household' scale of cattle keeping (cf. Bogucki 1993). There are minimum requirements for viable herd size, but beyond that we understand little about the extent to which cattle herds could have been built up. Presumably there were different spatial and temporal rhythms in the animal economy. Pigs could have fed on pannage within the woods. The dominance of young pigs strongly suggests their use for meat, so pork could have been a regular if minor component of the diet. Sheep and goats may have been concentrated in clearances and clearings under supervision, while cattle could have been herded over shorter and longer distances through woodland. The presence of wild cattle and large red deer also confirms the existence of large tracts of woodland.

Residential patterns

Residential patterns in the Earlier Neolithic could have encompassed a spectrum of mobilities and short-term sedentism (Whittle 1997b). There may have been much movement, though in patterned and repetitive ways, over seasonal, annual and lifetime scales. There is evidence from a new study of human remains that some people had extremely active lives, perhaps to do with ranging mobility, and there is some evidence for gender differences (Whittle and Wysocki 1998). Some of the mobility in Earlier Neolithic subsistence and occupation patterns may have been encouraged by the importance given to cattle, but tethers may also have existed in the form of cultivated plots, sheep and goats, and perhaps pigs. Speculatively, there may have been much diversity, not only perhaps from region to region but also over a generational or lifetime scale. In special places like causewayed enclosures, it was perhaps important to celebrate what was of enduring importance, which brings us back to cattle once again.

The context and goals of production

It seems likely that the subsistence economy was highly successful. People could draw on a wide range of resources, which should have buffered them against prolonged shortage or worse, though human bones and teeth from the Neolithic in general do show some evidence of periodic shortages in the form of Harris lines and enamel hypoplasia (Whittle and Wysocki 1998). Keeping animals and growing and gathering plants was more than a matter of physical survival. It was, rather, the fabric of social existence, one of the key means of social participation and interaction. The ability to provide food and drink, especially meat, seems to have been central, and we can only guess at the range of other transactions carried out through the medium of live animals. Large herds could have been fostered, but there seem to have been mechanisms for the dispersal or sharing of slaughtered animals through participatory ceremonialism at enclosures and elsewhere. This does not seem to have been a system of exclusive accumulation. Production was for use in social interaction. We go on later in this chapter and in the last to explore these questions of use from other angles.

Activity sealed by the outer bank of the enclosure

The date of sealing

It has been easy to assume that the pre-bank evidence of the outer circuit at Windmill Hill represents the pre-enclosure horizon, with the premise that the three circuits of the enclosure were laid out as a unitary plan. Support for this hypothesis is provided by the radiocarbon dates from the old land surface, BM-73 from Smith's excavations and OxA-2406 from 1988; as set out in chapter 5, the pre-bank horizon can constitute a first phase of activity on the hill as a whole.

This simple model of the development of the site, however, needs to be challenged. The evidence for unitary layout is equivocal, as discussed again below, and there are other, later radiocarbon dates from contexts sealed by the outer bank in Trench BB, OxA-2403 and OxA-2404 from the grave, and OxA-2405 from the old land surface itself. As set out in chapter 5, these dates may in themselves relate to later phases of site development (though OxA-2405 has to be seen as intrusive, which can find no support from field observation), but they can also point to another possibility, that activity continued in the area eventually sealed by the outer bank while other parts of the enclosure were being created and first used. It cannot automatically be assumed that the bone in the primary fill of the outer ditch which was the sample for BM-2669 was exactly contemporary with ditch construction and not older; the bone comes from a placed and possibly therefore reworked deposit (see further below).

Two other features lend support to this alternative model. First, rather weakly, there was Ebbsfleet pottery from the area of the inner tail of the outer bank in Trench BB (as well as above the primary fill of the outer ditch in the adjacent Trench B), which, given that this is not the earliest style of Early Neolithic pottery, could indicate continued activity in this area. Secondly, the environmental evidence, especially for the buried soil itself and its molluscan fauna (chapters 6 and 7), strongly suggests a very long sequence of activity, the end of which could also overlap with the beginning of other parts of the enclosure.

BM-73 was based on a charcoal sample; this might be an 'old-wood' determination. OxA-2406 came from the old land surface below the primary bank described in chapter 4, and although only it is a single determination, may be a clue to the process of the layout of the outer circuit. Its sample came from under the line of the primary bank, which could indicate that at an early stage of the enclosure, represented by the inner and middle circuits, the outer circuit was marked at most by a very slight earthwork. There is obviously no way of telling whether such an earthwork was accompanied by a ditch, or was continuous. The primary bank was made of three banded layers of chalk and soil (fig. 71), in turn suggesting not only careful construction but perhaps again some period of time. A soil was also noted over the primary bank, and perhaps even over the suggested rear inner bank (see chapter 4, contexts 746, 763), which if reliable would tend to support the notion of some time-depth to the history of the outer circuit.

There are no further soil-lines within the outer bank to suggest a further phase of construction, but there was a difference between the zones 703 and 702. Either this reflects an uninterrupted constructional sequence in which progressively larger blocks were prised from the ditch and placed at the back of the bank, or it shows separate episodes of enlargement using ditch scourings and further ditch excavation. The presence of bands of grey puddled silt within the bank might support the idea of episodes, since it is difficult to see how these could be part of material which had essentially been quarried straight from the ditch and dumped without significant delay. The grave, 707, lay under the material of 702, and it is therefore not *absolutely* certain that it was covered by the bank from the outset, though this is likely.

The potentially long-drawn out process recalls the claim that monuments in general were rarely actually finished, but rather represent a series of ongoing or unfinished projects (C. Evans 1988a; Barrett 1994, 13–15).

The duration of pre-bank activity

The molluscan evidence suggests a long history of use before eventual bank construction (chapter 7). In view of evidence elsewhere in the country, it cannot automatically be excluded that some of the supposed clearance and disturbance goes back into the Mesolithic period, but there is no artifactual support for such a dating here. Not all the postholes were seen from the surface of the buried soil (e.g. 760, 718, 745, 751), and a majority of the artefacts recovered were also not on the actual surface. The grave (cut through the old land surface) may have been open for a period of time before its eventual filling. There can be little precision in the timescale, but there is enough evidence to argue in general for a longer rather than a shorter span of use within the Earlier Neolithic period and before construction of the bank.

Pre-bank activity

A wide range of activity is documented. Clearance and cultivation were suggested by soil, molluscan and charcoal evidence. Animal carcasses (or parts) were butchered and consumed. Plants including cereals were processed and probably consumed, and charcoals may suggest the presence of fires, although there was only one charcoal concentration. Pottery is represented only by sherds, but a wide range of flint-working processes is evident; there were small concentrations of material, which could represent primary refuse.

Structures and sequence. Postholes show the former presence of some kind of structure or structures. The small area excavated limits interpretation. The straight line formed by 709, 710, 711, and 713, and the right angle formed by 751 and 745 (and by 718 and 760) suggest that there may have been a coherent structure. The postholes are within an area about 7 by 3 m, and it is not impossible that this is part of a building, but it is hardly possible to suggest its true alignment. In Outer Bank VI to the north there is a further line of postholes (Smith 1965a, 26–27 and fig. 8, A–E). Posthole E lies some 14 m from the 709–713 line, and is approximately on the line of 710, 751 and 745. This could suggest a structure with a north-south alignment of its long axis, and of a size within that seen in other British and Irish timber structures (fig. 220; see also Darvill 1996, fig. 6.5).

It was suggested that postholes A–E in Outer Bank VI and a hearth were earlier than pits 44–47 (Smith 1965a,

27–28), and this matches the possibility that 707 and 714 could be later than the postholes in Trench B, because they were more immediately visible after the bank had been dismantled in the 1988 excavation. Whether or not a regular structure is in question, there could be a sequence from postholes to pits and deposition in pits and re-used postholes (as suggested by 709 noted above).

Grave. There are two grounds for suggesting that the body in the grave may have been exposed before being covered over. First, the displacement of some of the bones is difficult to explain by disarticulation of the skeleton, as the spinal column was clearly intact on deposition, as were the hands and feet. Displacement suggests rather that the body was exposed to disturbance from scavengers or simply to the effects of decomposition. It might be possible to explain the splaying of the femurs by the knees having been originally set upright, with the feet bound together. Secondly, the concentration of small rodents and amphibians is unusual. Rodents may have been attracted to an open grave, and both categories could have simply fallen into the trap represented by an open grave. Amphibians can be seen on high, relatively dry downland today.

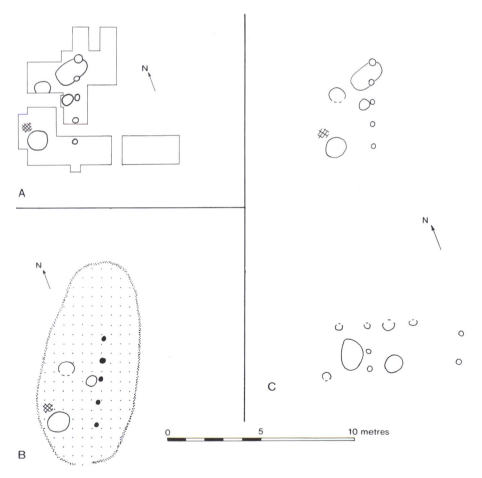

Fig. 220. *Postholes and pits from the pre-bank soil under the outer bank. A: features excavated in Outer Bank VI in 1957–58; B: the same features interpreted by Darvill 1996 as a house; C: features in both Outer Bank VI and Outer Bank V/ Trench BB.*

Primary burial and exposure have long been predicted from the contents of long barrows and chambered tombs. The presence of pit 45 in Outer Bank VI is also relevant. This large sub-rectangular pit was of similar size to 707, and of similar orientation. Its sides and base had been clay lined and its fill was brown clay and angular chalk rubble. Is it possible that this pit was some part of the practice reflected more clearly in 707?

This place was therefore in use for a long period of time before the outer bank was constructed. It seems that it must have been in use for longer than the history of the inner and middle circuits. It may have been visited along paths (cf. Barrett 1994; Tilley 1994) and it was used for a wide range of activities. Just as there was a likely cycle of clearance, disturbance and regeneration, so there may have been a shift from structures and consumption to burial and deposition. Practically all the elements and practices found in the ditches of the enclosure as a whole can be found already in the pre-bank soil (which, to repeat, does not necessarily predate the whole of the enclosure), though not in the same formations and concentrations. Perhaps the evidence as a whole can be seen as a gradual consecration of a special place, culminating in first the definition of the inner and middle circuits and finally the construction of the outer circuit.

Other pre-enclosure activity

Earlier Neolithic pits were found and excavated by Keiller elsewhere across the hilltop (Smith 1965a, 22–24, 29–33). Many could relate to episodes of pre-enclosure activity. A concentrated scatter of 32 occurred within the area of ID VIII–X, several being cut by the inner ditch. Twelve contained small quantities of bone, flint and pottery; combinations not unlike those found in the deposits in the inner ditch, though in real terms the quantities of material were low (Smith 1965a, 22–24). Although they have no direct stratigraphic relationship with the enclosure, a further 19 pits might also be ascribed to a pre-earthwork phase. Two pits (36 and 37) occurred between the inner and middle ditches, five (38–41) between the middle and outer, and 12 within the area of the Square Enclosure. Large quantities of material, looking very much like placed deposits and including items of worked chalk and sarsen, came from 36, 37, 41 and 42. Another Earlier Neolithic pit cluster, with placed deposits of sarsen rubbers and flint knives, was excavated to the south-east of the Square Enclosure in 1993.

The pit depositions themselves could represent special activities (Thomas 1991, 76), perhaps tied to events surrounding the ending of occupation events (Pollard 1999). Elsewhere, seen locally at Hemp Knoll (Robertson-Mackay 1980), pit clusters of this kind are closely associated with occupation. The precise chronology of those at Windmill Hill is uncertain, and they may pre-date the earthwork by a long or short interval. Some may even be contemporary with the enclosure. They need not all relate

to a single occupation event, but rather represent the cumulative record of several short-lived episodes of settlement. It is tempting to link this history of occupation, along with the record of other activities witnessed under the outer bank, to the decision to build the enclosure here. Earlier activity may have created a place redolent in associations that were drawn upon in the construction of the enclosure (cf. chapter 18).

Sequence

The simplest hypothesis is that all three circuits of the enclosure were laid out at one time as part of a single unified design. Sherds, recovered by Keiller, supposedly from the same vessel, were used to support the idea that all three circuits were open at the same time, or at least some segments in all three circuits. In particular, sherds from one vessel, P 198, were found near the base of one segment of the outer ditch and near the base of one segment of the inner ditch, and about halfway down one segment of the middle ditch. There were also similar links between outer and middle ditch segments, and between middle and inner ditch segments (Smith 1965a, 14). Within the imprecision of the method, the radiocarbon dates from primary contexts in all three circuits seem to show no appreciable differences in age.

There are, however, arguments against this view, apart from those already discussed in connection with the date of the sealing of the pre-bank soil. None of the sherds in question actually conjoin, and none are therefore incontrovertibly from the same individual vessel; in a large assemblage such as this, repetition of comparatively simple rim form and decoration would not be surprising. None of the sherds is wholly fresh, and any or all of them might therefore have been deposited elsewhere before final deposition in a particular ditch segment.

There is a different pattern to the finds from the different circuits as seen in the 1988 cuttings. Plain Early Neolithic pottery was in use throughout the filling of the middle and inner ditches, and in the primary fill of the outer circuit, but in the case of Trench B there were weathered sherds of Ebbsfleet pottery at the base of the secondary fill. In the upper secondary fills of Trench B and Trench A there were Later Neolithic wares. It may not simply be a case of wider ditches filling right up more slowly than narrower ones, but of a genuine chronological development. The outer circuit could be secondary to the middle and inner circuits, having been added still within the currency of Windmill Hill pottery.

The radiocarbon dates are imprecise. They offer a minimum age range of some two hundred years for the primary use of the enclosure, but realistically this range must have have been greater, providing plenty of time for a succession of circuit constructions, which the radiocarbon method is not precise enough to distinguish. As already described, each circuit has a distinctive layout and character, and each circuit might have had its own individual sequence or history. In the inner and middle circuits in particular, there might have been a succession from smaller pits to larger segments. The molluscan analysis suggests that secondary woodland took longer to close in again in the area of the middle and inner ditches than in the area of the outer ditch, which could imply that the middle and inner ditches had been open for a longer period. As noted in part above (chapters 3–4) and discussed further below here, there are significant differences in the character of depositions between the circuits of the enclosure. Once again, there is a tendency for the outer ditch to be distinguishable from the middle and inner ditches (and the interior within the inner ditch).

Excavations at other causewayed enclosures have shown at least three kinds of sequence. First, at Maiden Castle, Dorset (Sharples 1991), it is likely that the two circuits were laid out at the same time, but after an interval the outer ditch was largely backfilled and the nature of activity and deposition in the inner ditch changed. Something similar may have occurred at Abingdon, Oxfordshire (Avery 1982; Bradley 1986). Secondly, the single circuit at Haddenham, Cambridgeshire (C. Evans 1988b), may have been defined and redefined several times by recutting and enlargement of pits and segments. Thirdly, at Crickley Hill replacement was shown of two interrupted ditch circuits by a single, more continuous circuit (Dixon 1988), and at Hambledon Hill the existing Stepleton enclosure was incorporated into later outwork ditches (Mercer 1988).

From analogy, therefore, there is no reason why redefinition, replacement or addition of circuits cannot be entertained for Windmill Hill. The best model for the Windmill Hill sequence might be that a primary enclosure was laid out consisting of the inner and middle ditches, which were added to after a short interval by the rather different outer circuit; a miniature primary bank may have been laid out whilst activity continued in its area, which was later replaced by the substantial earthwork of the outer circuit.

Banks and layout

The distinctive layout of the enclosure has been stressed in chapter 2. The existence of a bank inside the outer ditch in Trench BB is matched in Trenches A and C not only by a surface heave in the appropriate position but also by a markedly asymmetrical fill in both primary and secondary fillings. Asymmetry can also be seen in the outer ditch in Trench B, in the section on the interface of Outer Ditch V/ Trench B. The silting in the south section of Trench B is more symmetrical, but here the section is much closer to the ditch terminal, a position which has affected the filling. The silting of the ditches in the middle and inner circuits is strikingly different, and gives no clear sign of the former existence of inner (or indeed outer) banks. There are no surface indications of such, although it is possible that these could have been removed by Romano-British cultivation which seems to have extended over the whole hill.

It may therefore be simplest to suppose that there were no formal banks in the middle and inner circuits. Perhaps one may envisage instead irregular spoil heaps, perhaps on each side of the ditch.

The filling of the ditches

In all the 1988 cuttings the major factor in the filling of the ditches appears to have been the natural processes of weathering, in both the primary and the secondary silting. There were only minor episodes of recutting, as at the top of the secondary silting in Trench B, or the small scoops within the primary fill of Trench E. There may have been some scouring of the primary fill in Trench B. Likewise there was only limited dumping, as in the secondary fill of Trench A, and perhaps in the primary fills of Trench D and Trench E. Much of the weathered material appears to have come from the ditch sides and surrounding turf and topsoil. The restriction of the Romano-British ploughsoil to the area of the ditch in Trenches A, C, D, E and probably F suggests that the original chalk surface was higher than the modern one. The situation in Trench B where the Neolithic land surface is preserved under the bank shows that the loss in height may not have been great, but it was enough, together with a weathering back of the ditch sides and tops, to account for the quantities of chalk rubble observed in the ditches.

Taking into account also the descriptions in chapter 3, it is clear that the majority of ditch segments silted up by natural processes (fig. 221). Recutting seems to be rather rare in the Windmill Hill ditches. There may have been limited recutting in ID X, and in Trench E and in MD IV. It is possible that the whole of Trench V/B in the outer ditch was scoured out, because of the paucity of typical primary chalk rubble, but this interpretation is uncertain.

There are more instances of limited or partial backfilling (fig. 221). Some minor asymmetries in the fill of the outer ditch may be due simply to slope or the presence of the outer bank within it, or both: such as in the primary fill in Trench V/B, Trench IV/C, Trench A, OD I, and in the secondary fill of OD III. Possible instances of backfilling have been noted in: ID XV secondary fill, ID XIII, ID III and ID II; and in Trench D, Trench E, part of MD XI, part of MD X, part of MD I, MD III secondary fill, MD VI secondary fill, and MD II. Backfilling may also be possible in OD III and OD I.

It is likely that primary chalk fill formed rapidly, judging by the behaviour of the Overton Down experimental earthwork and from other observations (Bell 1990; Bell *et al.* 1996). There is more primary chalk rubble in the Windmill Hill ditches than has accumulated in the Overton Down experimental earthwork so far, and the general setting of the two, including climate, is likely to have been rather different. The timescale may have been longer at Windmill Hill, but it is possible that in the case of most of the ditches this was little more than a couple of generations. One exception suggested by the radiocarbon

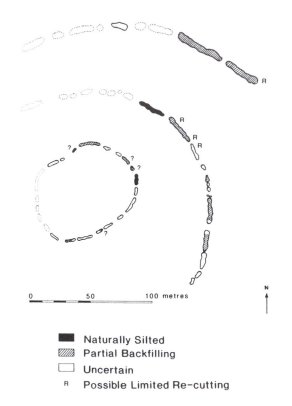

0   50   100 metres   N

■ Naturally Silted
▨ Partial Backfilling
▢ Uncertain
ᴿ Possible Limited Re-cutting

Fig. 221. Summary representation of major ditch silting and fill patterns as recorded for the 1925–29 excavations.

evidence is the inner ditch in Trench F, where there is an apparent interval between the primary and the low secondary fills. Most parts of the enclosure circuits, however, appear to have been left to fill in by themselves, a process which is likely to have taken place rather rapidly. There is evidence for human intervention, but that appears to have hastened rather than prolonged the process of infill.

The nature of the upper secondary fill, especially in the outer ditch in Trench B, is discussed below.

Activities at the enclosure in the primary phase of its use

Much of the rest of this chapter is concerned with trying to assess the processes and meanings of the various acts of deposition that characterise so much of the primary history of the enclosure. What we can observe, however imperfectly, is not an enclosure in action but the cumulative patterns created by successive depositions of varying character (and by other post-depositional transformations). Clearly, however, many different kinds of activities went on at, or were in some form or other represented at the enclosure, and it is important at this stage briefly to spell these out. In the next chapter we consider the possible significance of these activities in the arena of the enclosure.

The layout of the enclosure and the history of the infill

of the ditches are to do with the monumental, probably successive definition of a special area, place or arena, in a locale with a long and remembered history which was itself perhaps already distinctive. The people who built and used the enclosure cleared woodland, burnt fires, prepared the ground and grew and consumed cereals. They also used wild plants and hunted and consumed woodland animals, principally red deer and wild cattle (aurochs). They kept domestic cattle, pigs, sheep and goats, and they had dogs, which seem to have had licence to roam freely in all parts of the enclosure. Animals were butchered and consumed, either at the site or elsewhere or both. Dead infants were interred in the ditches of the enclosure, and the partial remains of children and adults were also placed in the ditches. People worked and used flint on a considerable scale, and they also used bone and antler tools and pottery. Whole vessels do not occur and it is unclear whether pots were made at the site. Presumably they were used at the site for the preparation or serving of food and drink, but both sherds and animal bones can also suggest the storage or middening of material, either on the site or elsewhere, before its eventual deposition. On-site middening is also suggested by the patterns of flint distribution within the inner circuit. As well as digging ditches, people also dug pits (not all necessarily in a pre-enclosure phase) and used some of them for depositing things in. People used querns, rubbing stones and pounders, and their equipment included flint and stone axes. Many of those originated far away from north Wiltshire. Some of the pottery was also non-local (though perhaps rather less than suggested by earlier studies), and the further implication is that both animals and people at the enclosure may not all have been long-term or permanent residents of the immediate area.

The enclosure created or reinforced a special place. It commanded the presence of people, perhaps in very varying numbers and at varying intervals; it is unclear whether we should talk in terms of 'occupation' at the enclosure in its primary phase. These people seem to have been principally concerned, apart from the definition of the arena of the enclosure, with the consumption of animals in feasts and other contexts and with the deposition of their remains. But they also dealt with virtually all other dimensions of the early Neolithic way of life that are accessible through the archaeological record: the landscape, relations with the natural world, subsistence, the dead, the past in general, social relationships among and between both close and more distant groups, eating, feasting, the temporary storage of used food remains and cultural materials, procurement of raw materials, and exchange. Small wonder that an earlier generation of research used Windmill Hill as the type-site for the early Neolithic way of life (e.g. Piggott 1954). But *why* is so much represented at *this* kind of site and in *this* place? We now have to consider in detail both how the varied materials were treated and deposited (in the rest of this chapter), and what wider meanings might be attributed to materials, activities, and depositions (in the final chapter).

Deposition

The Keiller, Smith and 1988 excavations produced a considerable range and quantity of artifactual and faunal material (already outlined by Smith (1965a), and in chapters 3, 11–16 above). As the 1988 excavations demonstrated, bone, pottery and flint, along with occasional items of worked stone and bone tools, were present in primary and secondary contexts of all three ditch circuits. The presence of such material on the site and in its particular contexts within the ditches demands explanation, of the mechanisms by which it entered the ditches, the kinds of activities that lay behind its generation, and the intended consequences of its deposition. The range of possible activities responsible for the generation of this material, including both occupation and more specialised action, will be discussed in detail later. First, consideration needs to be given to the mechanisms by which so much material entered the ditches, since this itself has a wider bearing on any interpretations that can be placed upon the monument.

The range of depositional possibilities

Artefacts and faunal remains could have worked their way into the ditches through a variety of processes: by accident, through casual disposal, patterned disposal routines, or intentionally 'structured' deposition. Accidental incorporation would presume the existence of ditch-side sources, such as artefact-strewn occupation surfaces and/or middens. The site was certainly not clean, and material from any pre-enclosure occupation (Smith 1965a, 22–33) would still have been present across parts of the hill during the construction and primary use of the monument. Surface middens may also have been a feature of the enclosure during its primary phase. Re-analysis of the Keiller archive suggests that spreads of worked flint, perhaps the residues of erstwhile middens (see also chapter 8), occurred within the interior of the inner circuit, at least across the area stripped in 1929 (fig. 65). Furthermore, the character and composition of a number of bone groups from the enclosure are in accord with their primary derivation from a midden source. If these had been located close to the ditch sides then primary erosion of the ditch edges (Bell *et al.* 1996) would have led to small fragments of bone, occasional pot sherds and pieces of worked flint working their way into these features. Intensive activity by people and animals would also result in the piecemeal re-incorporation of material into ditch contexts through processes of erosion and scavenging.

The great mass of bone and artefacts does, however, indicate that accidental incorporation alone cannot account for the range of depositional processes associated with the material from the ditches. We would still follow Smith's conviction (1965a, 7) that:

> Although an occasional sherd, flint, or fragment of bone may have strayed in from the edges, there is no doubt whatever that the mass of this material was deliberately thrown or placed in the hollows.

Recognising intentionality – a degree of considered human agency – in depositional practice is not, of course, enough in itself. Fuller characterisation is vital in order to define the degree of significance that should be placed upon deposition as a practice. Intentional deposition could include casual dumping and patterned disposal routines, as well as more directed, intentionally 'structured' incorporation, consciously bound up in the establishment and negotiation of specific symbolic values.

In the case of casual dumping, little consideration would be invested in the end-product of the practice of disposal, the deposits themselves. Disposal would have served no end beyond the maintenance of activity areas through the clearing of harmful or obstructive refuse. In such a situation little concern would be given to the format of deposition, nor to the mixing of constituent types of refuse; and the location of deposits might reflect considerations of convenience alone. The demonstration of such activity would carry with it the assumption that the material being deposited was categorised as undifferentiated 'rubbish', a material category whose universality has been questioned (Moore 1982). As we shall try to demonstrate below, casual discard is an unlikely mechanism for the incorporation of bone and other materials within the Windmill Hill ditches since pattern, spatial arrangement and repeated formats are discernible in the deposits. The carefully observed 1988 deposits showed how rare it was for deposits to be strewn *down* the sides or scattered *along* the centre of the ditches (see chapter 4), which might be the case if material had been carelessly thrown in and then subjected to gravity, erosion and scavenging. So too in the ditches excavated by Keiller, one of the most striking features of the primary fills was the occurrence of *discrete* groups of animal bone along the length of a number of the ditch segments (Smith 1965a, pl. Va) (e.g. figs 57–64).

Refuse accumulating under the conditions of domestic routine, through the relatively unthinking and sub-conscious process of daily production and maintenance activities, can be expected to incorporate a degree of spatial and compositional structure. Such a result develops in part from the physical preconditions of action – that refuse-generating activities, such as butchery and flint knapping, will take place within specific spatial and temporal locales – and from the constraints of the physical environment and the human body. Patterned disposal routines are probably therefore the general norm, and may be seen to operate at a series of levels from the hearth (Binford 1983a; 1983b) to the settlement (Clarke 1972) and the wider landscape (Foley 1981). The particular format of such patterned disposal is, however, constructed through the routine reproduction of specific sets of cultural values, and as such is an outcome of the contingent symbolic order that constitutes culture. Deposition is therefore as culturally specific a form of practice as burial or speech.

Hodder's (1982) and Moore's (1982; 1986) often cited ethnoarchaeological studies of the Nuba and Marakwet in

East Africa have shown how specific gender relations and concomitant categories of purity and association are instrumental in the organisation of refuse disposal. Moore's study of the Marakwet drew attention to the fact that rubbish is not a fixed universal category. The Marakwet have different types of refuse (ash, dung and chaff) that are conceptually and semantically different, being bound into gender relations and ideas of opposing male and female forms of fertility. Fears of pollution result in the separation of these different types of refuse, making them potentially powerful material categories that can be intentionally draw upon and employed as a part of gender-specific power strategies (Moore 1982). Much the same process was noted by Hodder among the Mesakin and Moro. In an archaeological situation, the resulting patterning in the distribution and association of different material categories might appear distinctly odd, if not 'ritualistic', simply because it would fail to fit our norms of what constitutes practical behaviour. One context for the interpretation of the deposits from Windmill Hill is that they result from such patterned disposal routines, and that any sense of peculiarity in their format is simply a reflection of the cultural 'difference' presented by the values of Neolithic society.

Deposition is therefore a meaningful form of action, in so much as it is implicated in the creation and reproduction of the symbolic categories that constitute culture. Whilst often a routine and largely unconsidered form of action, there is evidence that depositional practices occasionally took on a more central social role in the process of ascribing or negotiating meaning and reference in relation to people, places and activities (e.g. Hill 1995; Thomas 1991, 56–78). Acts of so-called 'structured deposition' have been recognised in a variety of Neolithic contexts, from pits (Case 1973), to funerary monuments (Thomas and Whittle 1986; Thomas 1991, 68–70), enclosures (Thomas 1991, 65–68) and henges (Richards and Thomas 1984; Pollard 1995). 'Structured' deposits have been defined on the basis of evidence for selection and compositional and spatial patterning in their make-up which cannot be explained through recourse to functional criteria. There is a problem here, in that deciding on what constitutes the 'functional' or 'non-functional' involves the imposition of *our* norms upon the archaeological record, and not those of the past. The exercise of interpreting deposition therefore needs contextualisation in relation to other (different) realms of value.

The term 'structured deposition' is, of course, insufficiently precise, since structure will also exist within deposits that have formed through normal disposal routines, as well as through special acts. Furthermore, the definition of what is or is not a 'structured deposit' remains largely undefined, and the contexts and intended outcomes of such actions may well have been very varied. Richards and Thomas (1984) in their re-analysis of Durrington Walls, and more recently Hill (1995) in dealing with deposits in the ditches and pits of Iron Age settlements, have argued that 'structured deposition' should be categorised as a form

of ritual practice, or at least be seen as the material correlate of ritual action. Formal categorisation of the wide range of special depositional practices encountered in the archaeological record may well be inappropriate, and it is probably best to circumvent the problem of defining what constitutes ritual practice, and how it might be recognised archaeologically (cf. Renfrew 1985; Garwood *et al.* 1991). Rather, if we recognise deposition as a meaningful form of social practice (Thomas 1991, 56–57), enacted in a variety of contexts, by a range of practitioners, at different scales, with different degrees of intentionality, and different motives, then we should accept the wide range of intended outcomes that were potentially embedded within it (cf. Needham and Spence 1997). When dealing with a potential continuum of practices, some routinised and largely unconsidered, others overtly self-conscious, a strict categorisation ('typology') of deposition becomes an interpretive hindrance.

How best then should the deposits in the Windmill Hill ditches be interpreted? The focus here is on analysing both pattern and process: on looking for degrees of intentionality in terms of selections of material, recurrent associations, and evidence for placement on the one hand, and the sources of the material present and the transformations it underwent prior to deposition on the other. Following others (e.g. Thomas 1991; Edmonds 1993), we regard the deposits as being actively involved (whether intended or not) in the process of creating meaning, helping to sustain and transform the values embodied within the construction and use of the enclosure, and those of the wider social world of local Neolithic communities. However, we do not regard the deposits simply or only as a kind of material culture 'text', nor as a sign system with encoded meanings that acted as a form of non-verbal symbolic communication (e.g. Hodder 1988; 1989; Tilley 1989), nor would we see deposition as a passive playing out of underlying symbolic rules. A valuable interpretive direction can be sought from recent calls to break down the dichotomy frequently set up between subject and object, resulting from an awareness of the embedded, inextricable relationships that exist between people and the material world (Tilley 1996; Thomas 1996a). Through their involvement in social life and the processes of metaphor and metonymy that guide dealings with the world, objects (and by extension the assemblages of material that form deposits) may be seen to hold many of the qualities considered inherently human. Objects (and deposits) can possess biographies (Kopytoff 1986), times of being or temporalities, a complex involvement in the creation of personal identity (Strathern 1988), physical qualities analogous to those of animate beings, and even a degree of social agency (Boast 1997).

Depositional practices in other Neolithic contexts
Further interpretational context for the deposits in the ditches at Windmill Hill is provided by similar acts of intentional deposition in contemporary enclosures, funerary

monuments and pits. These have been described in detail elsewhere (Thomas 1991, 56–78; Pollard 1993a) and will only be briefly covered here. Suffice it to say that deposits from Windmill Hill share points of comparison with those from other enclosures within and beyond Wessex, as well as contemporary long barrows and pits. Enclosure ditches are associated with a great diversity of depositional practices, which include placed bone groups, deposits of pottery, flint and organic materials, disarticulated human bone, and occasional animal and human (predominantly infant) burials (Pryor 1988a; 1988b; Mercer 1988; Thorpe 1984). A more restricted range of deposits is characteristic of pits and long barrows; pits often being backfilled with combinations of midden material, linked perhaps to the abandonment of occupation sites (Pollard 1993a). In addition to their role in the complex depositional treatment of human remains, barrows were also the locations for the intentional incorporation of deposits of cattle bone (frequently skulls, partial carcasses, and sometimes hides), as well as antler, flint debitage and carved chalk. Although enacted within different contexts, common themes may link all these depositional practices. It will be argued below that dominant themes may have revolved around ideas of renewal and concerns for mediating points of physical and spiritual transition and transformation.

Interpreting deposition

Kinds of deposition

Analysis of the carefully recorded deposits from the 1988 excavations (chapter 4) and of the records and finds from the Keiller excavations (chapter 3) provides a wealth of information about the composition, sequence and frequency of deposits, about sources and transformations of material, and about contrasts between ditch segments and circuits.

The deposition of animal bone was the major feature in the ditches excavated in 1988. The deposits clearly varied in terms of scale, composition and form, and working characterisations of these are given in chapters 4 and 11, the former based on bone deposit morphology and the latter on the condition and type of bone contained within them. Morphologically, three broad categories of deposit can be identified: individual bones and scatters; spreads; and groups. Scatters include two or more bones, with no particular orientation, and as much on the sides of the fill in question as in the centre (e.g. 207 and 208 in Trench B). These are relatively infrequent. More typical are spreads and groups; usually located in the centre of the silting and, in the case of spreads, with individual bones sometimes oriented along the line of the ditch segment in question (e.g. 525). Some have more bone, constituting in some cases discrete groups as opposed to spreads. These deposits were more frequent in the inner and middle circuits, and particularly good sequences of such occur in the primary and lower secondary fills of Trenches D and F. Bone groups of this kind, generally well defined and around a metre in diameter, were frequently encountered during the Keiller excavations. The distribution of those from the inner circuit segments of 1928–9 is shown in fig. 53. In this instance, the scale of the Keiller excavations allows an appreciation of the orderly manner in which bone groups had been placed at any one level, care evidently being taken to avoid overlapping. Groups within ID XI to XIV illustrate this particularly clearly (figs 57–63).

The evidence suggests the careful and deliberate placing of the groups and perhaps spreads as well, set against a background of limited incidental incorporation of bone, sherds, flint and other materials. Whilst there are occasional references in the Keiller notebooks to bones in spreads and groups being 'mixed-up' (ID XI, layer 3), or in 'clutters' and 'jumbles' (ID X, layers 2 and 3), the detail of the 1988 excavations often hints at arrangement. Most obvious are instances such as the human infant and cattle skull deposit in 117 of Trench A (outer ditch), the vertically set horncore from Trench E 524 (middle ditch), and the human child femur inserted in an ox humerus from Trench F 630 (inner ditch), where careful juxtaposition must be inferred (fig. 161). The impression is reinforced by the tightly confined arrangement of some groups, which could even indicate the use of organic containers (e.g. Trench C, 321, outer ditch). 414 and 413 in Trench D (middle ditch), and 115 in Trench A, included medium sized and large mammal ribs that may have been originally tied up in bundles (a similar deposit is recorded from the enclosure at Etton (Pryor 1988b, 114)). Mention can also be made of the placing of pig and sheep/goat bones around the periphery of a cattle bone deposit in 525 of Trench E, and the similar position of worked flint and sherds around the rib bundle in 413 of Trench D.

Further instances of careful arrangement come from the Keiller excavations. For example, a substantial portion of a goat skull (frontal and horncores) was found on top of bone group 1 of ID XII, and an ox skull on top of group 3; other skull fragments and horncores being rare in these groups. Group 3 of ID XII also contained a series of nested sherds, which could not have been casually thrown into the ditch. Other instances of apparently intentional arrangement will be described later. In general, it is clear that similar phenomena were found in the parts of the enclosure ditch opened by Keiller and in those opened in 1988.

The physical format of the 1988 deposits is not the only clue to their formation. Analysis of the animal bone presented in chapter 11 suggests that degrees of intentionality in deposition might be discerned on the basis of bone size, condition and states of articulation. Again, three broad 'sets' of deposit can be defined: so-called 'deliberate placements', 'less formalised deposits' and those of 'intermediate type'. Here 'deliberate placements' are defined as containing large bone fragments, and frequently several parts from one individual animal (e.g. 321). Bones are sometimes found in articulation, suggesting deposition as joints of meat. Such deposits are more frequent from the primary and lower secondary fills, that is from Earlier

Neolithic contexts, than the upper ditch silts. 'Less formal-ised deposits' include a smooth distribution of fragment sizes, though heavily skewed towards smaller pieces. These deposits are frequent in the upper fills of the ditch, such as 501 in Trench E and the tertiary levels of Trench F, where post-depositional weathering might in fact have distorted their original form.

The categories of deposit given in chapters 4 and 11 simply provide working characterisations of the hetero-geneous collection of deposits encountered in 1988, and should not in themselves be taken to imply particular degrees of intentionality in deposition. That there is little repeated correspondence between the morphology and content of individual deposits, with 'deliberate place-ments' including groups, spreads and scatters, for example, indicates that the use of a formal typology or pre-determ-ined range of criteria for deposit definition (and therefore interpretation) may be inappropriate. However, the use of such categories does serve to illustrate the varied sources and histories of material and the range of ways in which it was gathered and deposited. At the very least, when taken together the details of their morphology and composition strongly suggest that many bone deposits were deliberat-ely, if not always carefully, placed in the ditches.

We would argue that most of the material from Earlier Neolithic levels was deposited with some formality rather than casually discarded. This is further brought out by an examination of the kinds of material deposited and their pre-depositional and depositional treatment.

Kinds of material and their treatment

Animal bone forms the principal component of the deposits, though the full range of material from Earlier Neolithic contexts is diverse: pottery, worked flint, worked sarsen, foreign stone, worked chalk, worked bone and antler, and human bone. The material probably derived from a number of sources both within and beyond Windmill Hill; much of the bone, pottery and worked flint perhaps coming from deposits present inside or immediate to the enclosure. The human bone, and 'specialised' objects such as worked chalk, could have been drawn from further afield. It has been claimed that local chambered tombs such as West Kennet may have provided a source for the human bone in the Windmill Hill ditches (Smith 1965a, 137), a possibility that might be given further credibility by the near-identical dates obtained from both these sites (Whittle 1993, table 1). Other sources remain possible, and the burial under the bank in Trench BB shows *in situ* excarnation on the hill either during the pre-enclosure phase or overlapping with the first phase of the enclosure. Pieces of human bone may have been circulating widely between different contexts anyway, and the recent claims for the long-term curation of cattle mandibles found at Stonehenge I (Cleal *et al.* 1995, 479) suggest that selected animal bone may have had a similar pre-depositional history.

Most of the bone from the 1988 deposits is broken and fully processed, down to the fracturing of long bones and

skulls (see chapter 11). Pottery is represented by sherds rather than whole pots, and the flint implements include broken and used pieces. The condition of this material illustrates a series of transformations prior to deposition. In certain cases this was minimal, as with the intact animal burials from OD III and MD X, and the freshly butchered animals from 210 in Trench B and 321 in Trench C (both outer ditch). A number of other partial animal skeletons, predominantly of cattle, were noted during the 1925–29 excavations and are described in chapter 11 and below (fig. 185). Other deposits comprise assemblages of articu-lated and disarticulated bone (e.g. 416 and 418 in Trench D, and 525 in Trench E, both middle ditch), which could imply the selection of material, some old and some new, from several sources. In many instances, however, the time span between the initial discard of bone, sherds and flint and their final deposition in the ditches could have been prolonged. There is good reason to argue for the culling of materials for ditch deposits from surface middens (or something of this kind). This rests partly on the processed character of the bone and the weathered condition of some of the pottery, which does not give the appearance of primary refuse. Likewise, the worked flint from the bone groups and spreads has little refitting potential, and so cannot be regarded as *in situ* or rapidly re-deposited knapping debris. In several deposits excavated during 1988 localised concentrations of dark, charcoal-flecked soil occurred around the bones (i.e. 418, 527 and 524 in the middle ditch, and 629, 630, 628 and 627 in the inner). This seems to be particular to deposits from the inner and, to a lesser extent, middle ditches. It was also recorded by Keiller, being a consistent feature of the bone groups from the inner circuit excavated in 1929. Such a matrix would be consistent with an occupation or midden soil. Evidently, the range of sources from which the components of individual deposits were drawn was diverse, and many materials may have undergone complex life-cycles before final deposition in the ditches.

The detailed descriptions of the deposits excavated in 1988 provide a hint of the complexity of treatment afforded to materials during their deposition in the ditches. The varied kinds of bone deposit encountered during 1988 have been briefly outlined above, but these do not exhaust the full range of deposits from the enclosure ditches, for which reference must also be made to the Keiller excava-tions. Valuable information gained from the notebooks, finds catalogues and photographs of 1925–29 has allowed the reconstruction of general depositional patterns, in addition to providing detail on a number of apparently non-random associations between artifactual material and faunal and human remains (see also Pollard 1993a). These serve to illustrate the ubiquity of placed deposits in the enclosure ditches. In the following section, data from the 1988 and Keiller excavations are used to define the range of different deposit types belonging to the Earlier Neolithic use of the enclosure. For ease of description, this is done according to individual categories of finds (animal bone, human bone, pottery and so forth). Numerous associations and contextual links exist between different materials, and these are described where appropriate below. More general comments on the spatial distribution of deposits, and timescales and contexts of deposition are offered later on in the chapter.

Animal bone

Animal bone is the most common find from all three campaigns of excavation. The overwhelming majority belong to the four principal domestic species, cattle, pig, sheep and goat, with dog also being present. In some of the bone spreads and groups from 1988 there is a small amount of bone from wild animals (wild cattle, wild boar, red deer, roe deer, fox, cat, polecat, possibly otter and bird) and there are occasional fragments of red and roe deer antler. Cat, fox, badger and hare (some perhaps intrusive) are recorded from Earlier Neolithic contexts excavated by Keiller (Jope 1965, 143). The poor representation of wild species is a consistent feature of faunal assemblages of the period (Grigson 1981b; 1982d; Thomas 1991, 21), and may be taken to indicate either a low degree of exploitation, or complex forms of depositional treatment which led to their remains being regularly excluded from domestic and ceremonial contexts. Explanation ultimately depends upon our view of the position of domestic and wild foodstuffs within the Neolithic economy, an issue still debated (Entwistle and Grant 1989; Legge 1989; Thomas 1991, 19–25). Whatever view is favoured, there is a sense that wild species were regarded as different to domesticates, holding a distinct position within Neolithic social ecologies. The debate surrounding the role of wild species brings to attention the importance of animals as a symbolic resource, as well as an economic one. The way that domestic and wild animals were thought of, classified and brought into human social life can be expected to have had an effect on the way that their remains were treated in deposition (Richards and Thomas 1984, 204).

Analysis of the 1988 deposits shows how rare it is for bone spreads and groups to be wholly dominated by the remains of single species. Whilst cattle bone is often numerically dominant, it is accompanied by the remains of pig and sheep/goat with such frequency that it almost seems as though a conscious decision was made to include representative elements of all three species within single deposits (for detail, see chapter 11). Likewise, the small numbers of sherds and pieces of worked flint found in association might equally be token inclusions. Bones of dog and of the rarer wild species as well as pieces of red deer antler might represent intentional additions, accidental inclusions, or a mixture of both.

Whilst token inclusion remains a possibility, there is more compelling evidence for the selection and preferential treatment of particular species and skeletal elements. It has been argued that specialised depositional treatment was afforded to cattle remains in contemporary funerary contexts (Ashbee 1984, 74–77; Kinnes 1992, 110; Thomas 1991, 24–25). Locally, there are the cattle skulls found under and in the mound of the Beckhampton Road long barrow (Ashbee *et al.* 1979, 247), whilst further to the south, on Salisbury Plain, finds of cattle skulls and foot bones in the mounds of several long barrows are convincingly interpreted as deliberate deposits of hides (Grigson 1966). Here, metaphorical connections were perhaps being drawn between the transformation of cattle through butchery and consumption and the transformation of the human corpse in mortuary ritual. Patterns of association and placing suggest that cattle remains were equally subject to special depositional treatment at Windmill Hill, the clearest expression of this being seen with skulls and horncores. Skulls might be seen as emblematic of the animal as a whole, or as the part of the animal within which vital essences were perceived to reside. The patchy data from the Keiller excavations suggest that cattle skulls are proportionately more frequent in the middle circuit than the inner or outer circuits. In 12 out of 13 instances where the specific context of skulls is reconstructable (table 195), they occurred against causeways, and always with other cattle bones. Deliberate placing can be inferred in most instances, both through positioning and sets of

Table 195: Contexts and associations of cattle skulls.

Context	Position in ditch	Associations (Cattle bone	Other bone)
Tr. A, 117	Inverted. ditch terminal	horncores and other bone	human infant cranium
Tr. D, 418	Ditch terminal	various	pig, red deer (antler), human skull frags
MD IB, 1.4b	Upright, ditch terminal	skull frags	yes (no details)
MD VI, 1.5	?	articulated group?	?
MD VIII, 1.4	Upright, ditch terminal	horncore	-
MD XA, 1.4a	Ditch terminal	horncores	dog skeleton nearby
MD XB, base	Ditch terminal	articulated group	-
MD XIA, 1.3a	?	?	
MD XIA, 1.4b	Minor terminal	horncores	-
ID II, 1.4	Ditch terminal	horncores	-
ID XII, 1.2	Upright, centre of ditch	various	pig, sheep/goat
ID XVI, 1.3a	Upright, ditch terminal	articulated group	sheep/goat
ID XVII, base	Ditch terminal	horncore	-

associations. In layer 3 of ID XVI and layer 4 of MD IB crania had been placed upright (fig. 39), within bone groups, facing the adjoining causeways. Skull and horn-core associations are frequent. A substantial portion of cranium from the east terminal of ID II was found with three horncores, one being of *Bos primigenius*. Three cattle skulls and two odd horncores from the south end of MD XA were found close to the skeleton of a dog. Other associations between skulls and horncores occurred in the base of ID XVII, layer 4 of MD VIII, layer 4 of MD XIA, and 117 of Trench A.

Other associations of cattle horncores can be noted. A sarsen pounder from the primary fill of ID VIII was ringed by three horncores. Although not particularly rich in bone, this ditch produced the greatest number of horncores from any of the inner ditch segments. Horncores were also found with the skeleton of a puppy in the north terminal of MD XB, and with a leaf arrowhead in the secondary fill of the south half of the same ditch. We can also note the upright placing of a horncore in 524 of Trench E in the middle ditch.

Although most bone entered the ditches in a disarticulated and broken state, indicative of full processing, finds of articulated bone and even entire animal skeletons do occur (fig. 185). Significantly, most of the articulated bone is of cattle. Eight contexts from the 1988 excavations produced articulated bone, seven of these consisting of small collections of cattle ankle, wrist and foot bones and/or strings of vertebrae (117 in Trench A; 317 and 321 in C; 413 and 418 in D; 525 in E; and 630 in F). Articulated groups are also recorded from the Keiller excavations. Most of these come from Earlier Neolithic levels in the middle and outer ditches. A few contexts in the inner ditch had articulated bone. In layer 2 of ID IX and layer 3 of ID XII these were simply paired vertebrae. Two more substantial deposits of ox bones were in the top of the primary fill of ID XVI, a segment flanking the main causeway through the inner circuit. The first abutted the south-west terminal and included an articulated hind leg (pelvis, femur, tibia and astragalus) with a skull placed on top (Smith 1965a, pl. Vb). The second, in the north-west part of the segment, comprised radii, ulnae and several vertebrae. There were at least five major groups of articulated cattle bones in the primary fills of the middle circuit, in layer 3a and layer 5 of MD VII (trunk and limb bones), and from the base of MD VI, MD XB, and MD IV. Two groups of bones from the base of MD VI may have come from the same animal; one being a vertebral column resting on a lower jaw in association with two scapulae (Smith 1965a, pl. Vc), and the second a string of vertebrae to the south of this. Photographs in the Keiller archive show an intact vertebral column from MD XB associated with a mass of cattle bones and a number of worked flints, and there is a reference in a letter from Keiller to V.G. Childe (6.3.28) to a complete ox skeleton from the primary layers of MD IV or IVB. It is not known whether the latter was intact or butchered.

Three articulated lumbar vertebrae of an ox were found in layer 6 of OD IIC, and the feet, ankle, wrist and tail bones of a small beast were found in layers 6 and 7 in OD IB. The representation of bones in the latter suggests a hide: an interpretation placed on similar collections of cattle bone found over the chamber areas of contemporary long mounds on Salisbury Plain (Grigson 1966). This may not have been the only animal skin deposited. A collection of cat remains, consisting of bones of the feet and tail and a few teeth, probably all from the same individual, were found together in layer 5 of MD XIB, apparently in association with several dog bones. Other possible deposits of articulated bone can be inferred from surviving collections of animal bone, and are shown in fig. 185.

Perhaps a reflection of their special (or ambiguous) position as animals whose domestic status was not created purely on the basis of being a food resource (cf. Larsson 1990), dogs were afforded distinct depositional treatment. Several whole dog burials were found in the enclosure, and among the disarticulated bones from the 1988 excavations there is a dominance of skull, legs and feet. The same may be true of the assemblages from the Keiller excavations. At least two intact dog burials were noted in the primary fills of MD X, and a third, perhaps semi-articulated, dog burial was found in layer 4 of MD IX. In MD X an adult dog skeleton lay amongst a concentration of charcoal, cattle bones and knapping debris adjacent to the southern terminal, and the bones of a puppy had been placed against the northern terminal. There were also collections of disarticulated dog bone close to the base in MD XI, one comprising a skull, jaw and a few longbones, the other with a lump of sarsen on top. There is a reference in a notebook to an 'immense amount' of dog bones in layer 3 of MD IB, with charcoal and cattle bones. If not eaten, and therefore not subjected to the same breakage and treatment as the bones of food animals, then the depositional representation and degree of articulation of dog bones would differ from those of the other domesticates. Some dogs may of course have been eaten, and casual disposal of the bodies of pet, hunting, guard or herding dogs is a possible explanation. Dog remains are not confined to any one ditch circuit, though skeletons and groups of dog bone are more frequent in the middle ditch than elsewhere. Collections of disarticulated bones deposited as single events might even imply prior exposure and reburial, in much the same way as happened with human remains. Formal burial of pet dogs, accompanied by grief and even eulogy, is recorded in the anthropological literature (e.g. Serpell 1996, 65–66), and there is evidence for analogous mortuary treatment of dogs and people in certain late Mesolithic contexts (Larsson 1990).

There are references in the Keiller notebooks to dog coprolites amongst some of the bone groups in the inner ditch and they may well have been present in the other ditches as well. It is possible that they were selected, deliberately or inadvertently, for deposition along with the bones, but a more prosaic and more likely explanation is that dogs defecated within the ditches. The fact that the coprolites survived at all implies that the dogs had a calcium-rich diet (Stallibrass 1990, 156), presumably from the ingestion of many of the numerous animal bones within the ditches. Some of the surviving bones do indeed have gnaw marks which can be attributed to dogs (see tables 97–102), and the presence of long bones reduced to cylinders by the removal of the epiphyses at either end is also almost certainly a sign of depredation by dogs (Binford 1978). Indeed it should be noted that dogs may have been responsible not only for reducing the total numbers of animal bones in the ditches, but also of damaging others and even of converting some erstwhile complete or nearly complete skeletons to a semi-complete state.

Other animal burials have been recorded, though these are extremely infrequent deposits and seem to have been limited to the outer circuit. Two entire burials were found in primary levels in OD IIIC (layer 5) and OD IIIB (layer 3), of a pig (fig. 176) and a young goat (fig. 178) respectively. Both lay against the inner side of the ditch, the goat in a crouched position, and each was covered by chalk rubble and silt raked down from the bank. Several fragments of human bone occurred in the silt around the pig burial, and the skeleton of an infant was within 5 m of the goat. A collection of bones from a neonatal pig from 210 in Trench B could represent a further complete burial. As with OD III, a human infant burial had been placed nearby (layer 4 of OD V), suggesting that individual animal burials were frequently part of more extensive arrangements involving the deposition of human remains.

Three key points emerge from the analysis of the animal bone. First, there is the range of pre-depositional and depositional processes to which bone was subjected, with remains entering the ditches in varied states of completeness and articulation. Whilst articulated deposits and full burials are obvious formal deposits, we should be wary of assuming that broken and disarticulated bone simply represents 'rubbish' given the evidence for selection, arrangement and the particular treatment afforded to some remains (for example horncores). The evidence from Stonehenge I illustrates how individual bones could be subject to long-term curation as trophies or relics (Cleal *et al.* 1995, 479), and there is no reason why similar processes may not have gone on at Windmill Hill. The very act of transformation through butchery and weathering may itself have been important and arguably imbued animal remains with particular values and symbolic qualities (see chapter 18).

Secondly, the treatment given to animal remains in deposition varied according to species. Cattle and dogs were afforded special status, with cattle skulls frequently being placed in a prime position against causeways. Bones of wild species are notably rare, and this might be as much a product of exclusion from deposition as a lack of their exploitation. It is tempting to see hierarchical relationships or at least classificatory differences between species in this, an archaeological reflection of Neolithic folk taxonomies (cf. Thorpe 1984). Thirdly, there are associations between animal bone and human remains in some deposits. These will be considered next.

Human bone

34 finds of disarticulated human bone were recorded from the 1925–29 and 1957–58 excavations (fig. 222; information from catalogues in Avebury Museum), and 11 from 1988. In addition there were two burials of young children

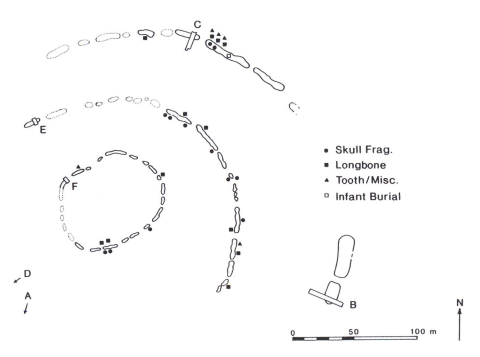

Fig. 222. *Distribution of human bone in the primary ditch fills as recorded for the 1925–29 excavations.*

from the outer circuit. All the human bone came from Earlier Neolithic contexts, with the exception of a second upper molar from layer 1 of OD IIIC. Skull and long bone fragments predominate, the only exception being a single vertebra from OD IIIC. Weathering implies that some bone may already have been old by the time it entered the ditches (Smith 1965a, 137), potentially following lengthy periods of storage and/or circulation. Other pieces, such as an infant skull still with mandible from MD XI, were probably fresh if not partially fleshed at the time of deposition. The same is obviously true of the two infant burials (from the bottom of OD III and from 3 feet down in OD V: Smith 1965a, 9). A potent symbol, there is little reason to doubt that most, if not all, of the human bone was intentionally deposited. Finds of human bone are regularly encountered in enclosures in Britain and on the Continent (Andersen 1997, 307–9). The presence of disarticulated bone is taken as indicative of secondary burial and the circulation of human remains, bound into beliefs in the potency of ancestral relics (Thomas 1991, 112; following Bloch and Parry 1982, and Huntingdon and Metcalf 1979, amongst others). Suggestions have been made that excarnation was practised at some enclosures (Drewett 1977; Mercer 1988), and extended rites can certainly be suggested on the basis of the burial in the pre-bank phase in Trench BB at Windmill Hill.

Six contexts from the 1988 excavations (excluding the pre-enclosure phase) produced human bone. Most of the this comprised small fragments of longbones, or teeth. Two finds are of particular significance. From 117 in Trench A there is the exceptional arrangement of an infant cranium nested within an ox frontlet; and in 630 in Trench F a broken infant human femur was inserted into the shaft of an ox humerus (fig. 161). Apart from 117 and 630, these finds were not in association with large or significant deposits of animal bone. The four finds from the pre-bank soil in Trench BB were also scattered and small.

The human bone from Trenches A, B and F came from sections of ditch adjacent to terminals, and from information in the Keiller records this may be a recurrent position for such finds. A quantity of the human bone recovered during 1925–29 came from ditch segments flanking major causeways, for example a fibula from ID XI, a skull fragment from ID V, the lower and upper mandible of an infant from MD III, and a femur from MD II. Human bones were placed against ditch terminals in ID I, MD XI and OD III.

Most of the human bone from the Keiller excavations is recorded as seemingly isolated finds. There were, however, several associations with animal bone and other human bone. There were notable groups in the west half of ID I, MD XIB, and OD IIIC. In ID I, an adult distal humerus was found in the primary fill of the west terminal amongst an assortment of material including a large fragment of sarsen, cattle vertebrae, a sheep/goat astragalus and a portion of pig's skull. There was an adult human ulna to the east of this group. A substantial portion of infant cranium and a temporal bone from a second, older

individual were found in the centre of the ditch, associated with two scapulae (one of pig, the other of a red deer or ox). In MD XIB, the entire cranium and lower mandible of a 6–7 year old child was found amongst a mass of dog bones. There was also a fragment of adolescent occipital.

Eight pieces were found in the north-west terminal of OD III (OD IIIC), in two clusters, at least three individuals being represented. The occipital of an adult and a substantial portion of an adolescent cranium (temporal and occipital) were placed within a metre of each other against the terminal. The other cluster consisted of a femur, humerus, adult cervical vertebrae and an adult canine, and was about 5 m to the south-east of the skull fragments, though still within the area of the ditch terminal pit. The bone was, however, distributed through about a metre of chalk rubble, implying several episodes of deposition. From around and just below the tooth, there was a quantity of burnt bone, presumably a human or animal cremation, with some antler fragments and a pig rib. Just above the tooth there was the pig burial described above. The skeleton of a 2–3 year old child was found on the solid chalk base of OD III at its shallowest point, in the middle of the segment. A second infant inhumation came from the top of the primary fill (layer 4) of OD V in 1957–58. Both lay on their right sides with heads to the east, and had been covered with backfilled silt or chalk (Smith 1965a, 136).

One of the most striking patterns to emerge is the parallel treatment sometimes afforded to human and animal bone within individual bone groups and ditch segments. It would appear that comparable human and animal skeletal elements, or bones in a similar state of disarticulation and damage, were regularly selected and placed together. Thus, the infant cranium from 117 in Trench A was placed adjacent to the frontlet of a young cow, and an intact infant burial in OD III occurred at a similar level and within a few metres of the intact skeletons of a pig and goat. A combination of piglet skeleton and infant burial may have existed in Trench B/OD V; in 630 in Trench F a broken human femur was found inserted into a broken ox humerus (fig. 161); and a broken infant mandible occurred alongside an ox skull fragment in 414 in Trench D.

There seems to be an equality between human and animal remains in these deposits. Domestic animals were unlikely to have been invested with precisely the same rights and qualities as people. They were after all eaten. The equivalent treatment of animal remains could have been a metaphor for the staged treatment of human remains in mortuary rituals: a symbolic play on the processes by which people underwent conversion from fleshed corpse to dry bones, in much the same way as animals were butchered, consumed and reduced to bone. Indeed, cattle remains have a close connection with mortuary deposits during the period (Thorpe 1984, 51), even, in the case of the Beckhampton Road long barrow, apparently taking the place of human remains (Ashbee *et al.* 1979, 247).

Material other than bone

Although animal and human bone forms the principal component of the deposits, and is frequently present in selected combinations and arrangements, other material was also subject to careful deposition. The impression is of a constant 'play' of materials, with some sense of repetition in format, content and arrangement, but with also many seemingly *ad hoc* deliberate combinations. Many of these deposits were referred to in chapter 3, and the following section provides further detail of and cross-reference to some of these.

Worked flint

Concentrations of flint-knapping debris were extremely rare, though associated groups of tools were found. Small assemblages of debitage and tools were recovered from other collections of material in the inner and middle ditches (fig. 223). Some might have been inadvertent inclusions, but others may have been deliberately represented. There are other instances where flint artefacts were probably deposited in their own right. There was a 'cache' of 11 serrated flakes in layer 2 of ID IVB. Two knives, a pair of retouched flakes and a serrated flake were found with 16

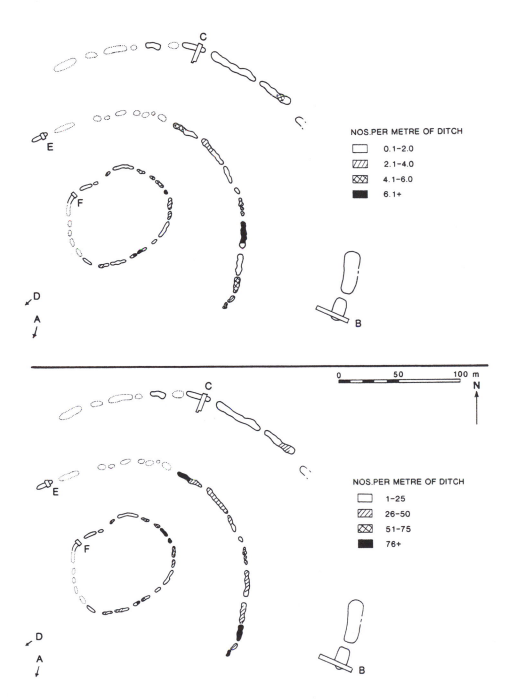

Fig. 223. Densities as recorded in the primary ditch fills for the 1925–29 excavations of top: *flint implements, and* below: *flint waste.*

flakes and a core in layer 4 of MD VII. Four retouched flakes from layer 3 of OD IC were in exclusive association with 10 flakes, 13 cores and four unworked fragments of flint. In two spots in the primary fill of MD IIB, small assemblages of tools and debitage were found mixed with sherds (along with a bone awl and a piece of sarsen in one group).

Worked flint did regularly occur in association with bone groups and spreads, though most of the lithics were distributed throughout the ditch fills. This in itself could be indicative of different depositional and pre-depositional histories, and of attitudes towards flint as a material category. Quantities of flints in placed deposits defined principally by the character of animal bone are low (table 190). The greatest number of flakes in any one deposit is 12, in 227 in Trench B and 628 in F, and there are never more than one or two retouched pieces. For comparison, there are 33 flakes, one utilised flake and two scrapers from the grave 707 in BB, and one core, 12 flakes, and one serrated flake from the pit 714 in BB. In this respect the small assemblages of debitage and tools recovered from bone spreads might be viewed as inadvertent inclusions. Alternatively, they may have been deliberately represented as token additions. Cores, flaked blocks and retouched pieces occur in greater frequency in the bone groups and spreads than from the silting in general (see chapter 14), which might imply some selection. There is, however, no indication of selection of particular tool types.

The catalogues and notebooks of the Keiller finds provide more definite evidence of selected flint deposits. Concentrations of flint knapping debris were rare, though associated groups of tools ('caches') were found. There was a collection of 11 serrated flakes in layer 2 of ID IVB. Two knives, a pair of retouched flakes and a serrated flake were found with 16 flakes and a core in layer 4 of MD VII. Four retouched flakes from layer 3 of OD IC were in exclusive association with 10 flakes, 13 cores and four unworked fragments of flint. The presence of implements indicates that none of these are likely to be knapping clusters, such as those from contemporary long barrow ditches (e.g. Easton Down: Whittle *et al.* 1993, 208–10).

The significant quantities of material in the plough layer at the top of each ditch examined in 1988 should also be noted (102, 201, 302, 402, 501 and 602; with corresponding figures from the Keiller excavations as set out in the tables of chapter 3). These might reflect continued deposition in the ditches later in the history of the site (see also below), which was then disturbed by the plough. They may also reflect the plough dragging in material scattered round about, as also observed at South Street long barrow in the Later Neolithic (Ashbee *et al.* 1979). This might argue for a more general domestic use of Windmill Hill than otherwise argued here, with activity not solely restricted to the ditches.

Pottery

There were small collections of sherds from placed deposits, much of it showing signs of wear and probably from having been deposited previously elsewhere. Again, these could be token representations. A few larger portions of plain vessels were recovered from the primary fills of Trenches B and D. Details are provided in chapter 13. Occasional sherd arrangements are implied by details in the Keiller notebooks. One vessel (or part of it) was found inverted in the area above a deposit of human and animal bone in MD XI. Mirroring the situation in Trench D, large portions of pottery were encountered against terminals in sections of the Middle Ditch (MD X, VI and VII). The description of a nested group of sherds in ID XII sounds reminiscent of the deposits within the broadly contemporary Coneybury Anomaly pit near Stonehenge (Richards 1990a, 42).

Sarsen

Large quantities of sarsen were brought to the enclosure and subsequently worked into a variety of implements primarily used in food production tasks (querns, rubbers, pounders and miscellaneous artefacts such as discs) (Smith 1965a, 120–4) (fig. 224). From the 1988 excavations there is a substantial quern fragment from a bone spread in 229 at the base of Trench B, and a rubber from the fill of the pre-enclosure grave 707 (see chapter 15). Intentionally deposited assemblages of worked and unworked sarsen were noted from the primary fills of several ditch segments dug by Keiller. Two discrete groups of sarsen fragments were recovered from the base of ID XII. Four sarsen implements occurred in an area of charcoal-rich soil, in association with worked flint and a chalk cup, in the top of the primary fill in OD IIIA. A collection of sarsen pounders and hammerstones and unworked fragments came from the primary fill of MD XIA. Centrally in layer 6 of OD IB there was an entire quern, with a perfectly fitting rubbing stone in contact with it (Smith 1965a, pl. XVIIIc). Another entire quern came from the base of ID XIV, apparently in association with a splinter-and-groove worked antler. Another antler association is with three quern fragments found close together near the base of MD IB. Finally, there were two large quern fragments from the primary rubble of MD X, separate from other material and placed in the middle of the ditch.

A good number of the quern fragments (including that from 229) and large unworked blocks of sarsen came from on or near the base of the ditches, or low in the primary fills, indicating deposition immediately following enclosure construction. There is consequently a possibility that they were curated from pre-enclosure occupation sources, and might have been deposited as initial dedications. Such offerings could have drawn upon a body of existing practices and meanings given the occurrence of placed deposits of rubbers, pounders and quern fragments in pits 36, 42 and 43 of the pre-enclosure phase. Similar deposits of sarsen implements are known from other Earlier Neolithic pits in the region. A placed deposit of two rubbers came from a pit excavated outside the enclosure in 1993,

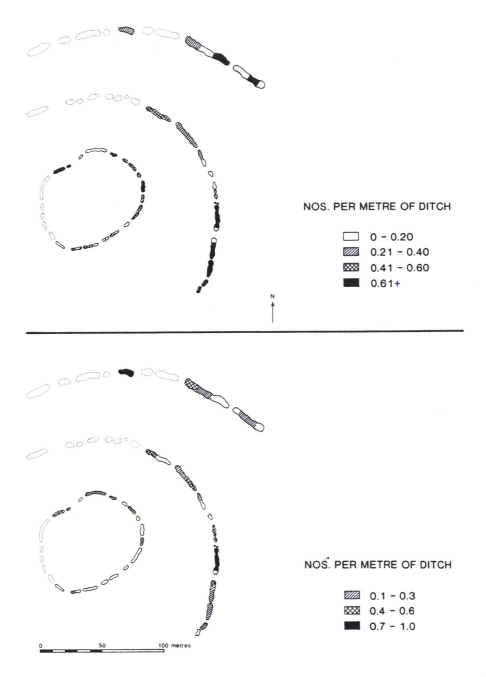

NOS. PER METRE OF DITCH

☐ 0 – 0.20
▨ 0.21 – 0.40
▧ 0.41 – 0.60
■ 0.61+

N

NOS. PER METRE OF DITCH

▨ 0.1 – 0.3
▧ 0.4 – 0.6
■ 0.7 – 1.0

0   50   100 metres

Fig. 224. Densities as recorded for the 1925–29 excavations of top: *worked sarsen, and* below: *antler from the primary fills.*

and further afield there is the deposit of two quern rough-outs from Pit 1 at Hemp Knoll (Robertson-Mackay 1980, 137).

Antler, worked bone and carved chalk
All three categories were most frequent in the primary fill of the middle circuit, and comparatively infrequent in the inner circuit (figs 224–26).

Antler picks and rakes (construction tools commonly deposited in the ditches of Neolithic monuments) were few, but there were several antler and bone combs, pieces of manufacturing debris, pins and awls (Smith 1965a, 125–

29). Antler generally occurred as single finds, but was occasionally mixed with animal bone (for example in 227, 228, 210, 207, 208, 104 and 418; and ID XII, ID XVI, MD II, MD IXB and MD XA of the Keiller excavations). In addition to the associations with sarsen querns mentioned above, there are other deposits of interest. A tine was found alongside a chalk ball and an incised chalk piece from the primary fill (layer 4) of MD VI; an intact red deer frontlet was in the same layer a metre to the south. An antler comb from the west terminal of OD III was found near two substantial pieces of human skull; and in MD II an unusual antler haft (Smith 1965a, 127) occurred with an ox radius

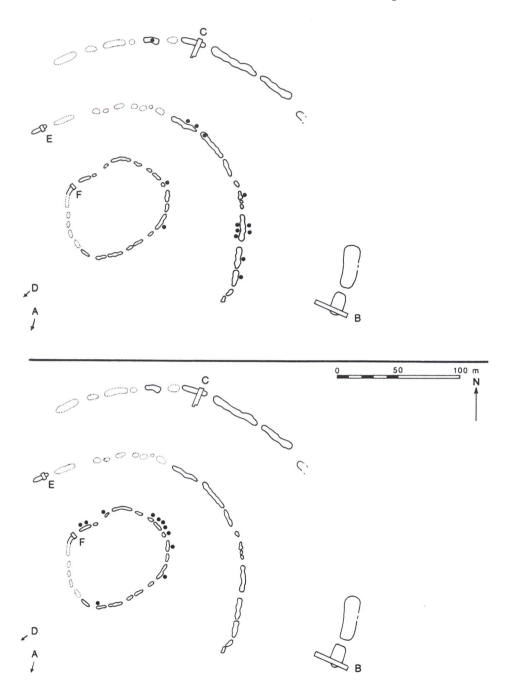

Fig. 225. Distribution as recorded in the primary ditch fills for the 1925–29 excavations of top: *worked bone, and* below: *leaf arrowheads.*

and a pig jaw. With a single exception, all the roe antler from primary contexts in the outer ditch came from layers 4 and 5 of OD II, but it was also found in various contexts in the inner and middle ditches. A notable collection of worked antler and bone, including two fragments of comb and a gouge, came from 629 and 630 in Trench F.

Worked bone may be under-represented from the enclosure ditches, perhaps only infrequently being selected for deposition. For comparison, the secondary filling of the chambers at the West Kennet long barrow produced an assemblage of worked bone comparable in quantity to that

from all levels at Windmill Hill (Piggott 1962a, 49–50).

There is a variety of carved chalk objects from Earlier Neolithic contexts at Windmill Hill, some representational such as phalli and two possible 'figurines', along with non-representational objects such as balls, cups and incised and perforated pieces (Smith 1965a, 130–34). It is difficult to avoid the obvious fertility symbolism of some of these, especially in light of the occurrence of objects within the same areas of the enclosure which are identifiable as male (phalli and perhaps balls) and potentially female (cups). The six carved chalk cups have a very restricted distribution.

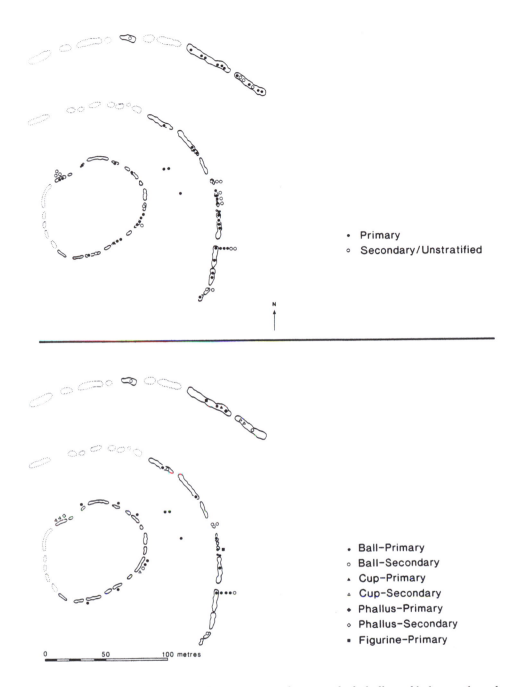

Primary
Secondary/Unstratified

N

Ball–Primary
Ball–Secondary
Cup–Primary
Cup–Secondary
Phallus–Primary
Phallus–Secondary
Figurine–Primary

0   50   100 metres

Fig. 226. Distribution as recorded for the 1925–29 excavations of top: *worked chalk, and* below: *selected worked chalk.*

Two were unstratified from the backfill of ID VII, though in fresh condition, suggesting 'they lay fairly deep' in the silting (Smith 1965a, 130). Three came from adjoining terminals in OD IC and OD IIIA, though at different levels in the fill. The two chalk phalli with known contexts also came from ID VII and OD IIIA. There were no carved chalk cups from the middle circuit, though this had the greatest number of other worked chalk pieces. An unusual assemblage from ID IV and IVB (perhaps from the top of the primary fill) included a perforated pendant, an engraved piece and a carved ball.

Timescales and spatial distributions

Timescales

The sheer quantity of material from the ditches implies quite intense depositional activity following on immediately from the construction of the enclosure. Within individual circuits and ditch segments the timescales of deposition are nonetheless varied. In the outer ditch, successive spreads of bone in apparently rapid succession were a feature of the primary and lower secondary fills of Trench B, though were comparatively infrequent in A and C. The massive scale of this circuit may have meant that deposits were thinly spread around, or focused in particular areas. Trenches D and E of the middle ditch produced numerous bone groups from the primary and lower secondary fills also incorporated in relatively rapid succession, those in the primary rubble perhaps separated by intervals of a year or two at most. The Keiller records suggest a similar pattern in the middle and inner ditches, with numerous bone deposits incorporated in relatively rapid succession following immediately on from the digging of the ditch. The inner ditch (Trench F) included closely superimposed bone groups from the lower secondary fills, though little deposition appears to have taken place in this particular part of the ditch whilst the primary fills were forming. Elsewhere in the inner circuit there were deposits of sarsen and bone from on or just above the base of the ditch (e.g. ID XI and ID XII), with more intensive deposition corresponding with the upper primary and lower secondary fills (as in Trench F and other segments on the northern side such as ID VII, ID XVI and ID XV).

Even with the detail from the 1988 excavations it is not possible to say whether deposits were made on a regular and recurrent basis (for example, annually), though those from Trenches D and E might be read as such. The picture is more of intense 'bursts' of activity in particular segments and areas of the enclosure, with the focus of deposition perhaps changing episodically. This is perhaps illustrated most clearly, albeit towards the end of the Earlier Neolithic use of enclosure, by the restricted distribution of Ebbsfleet pottery around MD II and the south-eastern part of the inner ditch (fig. 196). It may also be picked up by the substantial scale of deposition in the lower secondary fills on the northern side of the inner enclosure, an area where, in contrast to other parts of the circuit, there was comparatively little depositional activity during the formation of the primary fills.

Some deposits could have entered in single self-contained acts, while in others we may be witnessing the laying down of several separate deposits within the same segment at the same time. This certainly seems to be the case at other enclosures where the excavation of entire segments, or large portions of them, allows precise horizontal and vertical relationships to be established. The complex arrangements of wood, pottery, human and animal bone along single horizons in the ditches at Etton (Pryor 1988a; 1988b) provide one case in point, and the simultaneous placement of human skulls along the base of the Main Enclosure ditch at Hambledon Hill another (Mercer 1988, 95). Similar horizons of deposition may be discernible at Windmill Hill thanks to Keiller's technique of clearing whole segments at a time. The lines of bone groups exposed along the lengths of ID XI to XIV appear to have gone in simultaneously, or at least over a very short interval to judge from available photographs (cf. Smith 1965a, pl. V). The complex arrangements of cattle bones, dog bones and other material in the primary fills of MD X and XI could be further examples of concurrent deposits. We should perhaps see deposition as episodic, working within many different timescales, but with occasional major events akin to acts of renewal or reinstatement of the enclosure.

Individual segment histories

Whilst the character of successive depositions could vary within the same ditch section, seen for instance in the outer ditch in 228 and 210 in Trench B (the latter included much articulated animal bone), and 117 and following deposits in Trench A, the details of the bone groups from the 1988 excavations show that later deposits frequently mimicked earlier ones in both form and content. In effect, there is a style or grammar to certain depositions which was repeated during later episodes. This in itself implies memory of the form of earlier deposits, perhaps the culling of material from the same source amongst many, and perhaps even the involvement of the same practitioner or practitioners in successive acts of deposition in particular parts of the enclosure. A good illustration is provided by the form and composition of the deposits in Trench D. Cattle skull fragments were included in several contexts (416, 418, 414 and 413), perhaps 'commemorating' or marking the initial deposition of an intact ox cranium from near the base of the ditch. Furthermore, human bone was present in two contexts, and there were similar tightly interleaved bundles of medium-sized mammal rib from the successive deposits 414 and 413.

The idea of particular styles and grammars of depositions can be extended further to the level of ditch segments as a whole. Whilst recurrent formats are discernible, such as the placing of bone groups along the centre of ditches, and the consistent occurrence of selected material against causeways, it is apparent that separate ditch segments could have had individual styles and histories of deposition. A good example of such variation, in this case between adjacent segments, can be seen with OD I and III. OD III included not only entire burials of animals and an infant, but also several deposits of disarticulated human bone. OD I contained no human bone, but did produce unique deposits such as a probable ox hide and a sarsen quern with a fitting rubbing stone.

At a coarser level, quantities of worked flint, pottery and other materials can be seen to vary markedly between adjoining segments. This does not necessarily imply there is a lack of pattern in terms of the location of deposits around the enclosure circuits, as will be shown below. It might mean, following an earlier argument advanced to explain the segmentary form of causewayed enclosure ditches (Startin and Bradley 1981, 293), that individual kin, family, household or other social groups had responsibility for depositions in particular parts of the circuit. Alternatively, the character of deposition in individual segments may have been prescribed by specific sets of meanings ascribed to different areas of the monument, or by contingent readings and remembrance of former deposits, and a wish to do what seemed appropriate in respect of earlier acts of deposition in the same location, with variation occurring through a kind of divergent evolution produced through partial rememberings and reworkings (cf. Barth 1987).

Recurrent contexts

Across the site as a whole, there are significant variations in the occurrence of different kinds of artefact and deposit. As well as the intentional placing of individual deposits, the contexts of depositions across the site strongly suggest that the use of the ditches was patterned. The 1920s excavations were imperfectly recorded. Much detail must have been lost from the areas of Keiller's investigations, and recent excavations at other causewayed enclosures, for example at Etton, Cambridgeshire (Pryor 1987; 1988a; 1988b), have shown that near-total excavation may be essential for spatial variation in activity fully to be understood. Nonetheless, the results from the first excavations at Windmill Hill that do survive in the archive can legitimately be used in conjunction with the evidence from the later excavations to investigate patterns of deposition across a broad swathe of the site. In this way, the Windmill Hill enclosure can better, if still far from perfectly, be understood as an arena of special activity.

Patterning occurs at several levels, from specific occurrences within parts of ditch segments (described above), to a focus upon major causeways and particular sections of ditch, and to variation in the scale and kinds of deposit in each of the three ditch circuits. This patterning is of course the cumulative result of numerous individual depositional events, and need not be seen as the product of any original, prescribed 'grand scheme'. There probably were commonly recognised ways of doing things, which extended to agreed notions of the kinds of deposition deemed suitable for particular parts of the site. The form of the enclosure would itself have carried meanings, related to boundedness and realms of the sacred, and perhaps including a sense of enclosure hierarchy between the outer, middle and inner ditches. Different kinds of depositional practice could have reaffirmed or respected such meanings, though their precise format may be seen as a kind of *bricolage*, 'the reworking of the available resources by those with a competent and inventive understanding of particular orders of spatial practice' (Barrett 1994, 24). As indicated above, later depositions could be strongly influenced by memory of earlier events and a desire to mimic or reinstate. Contingency, novelty and invention might also have had a role, transforming and bringing into being new meanings and spatial orders (cf. Thomas 1996b, chapter 7).

Deposits at major causeways

The detail of the Keiller record shows that ditch segments flanking major causeways, such as ID VII on the west side of the main entrance into the inner enclosure, and MD II on the north side of a major causeway through the middle circuit, became chosen locations for unusual or large-scale depositions. The two segments of ID VII produced the largest single concentration of early Neolithic pottery from the site, 95 vessels in total (Smith 1965a, 5). There were also flint tools, worked sarsen and worked chalk pieces in quantity. The majority of the finds derived from a dark, humic and charcoal-rich soil overlying the primary fill. Both the character of the fill and the quantity of finds suggest that it was back-filled with midden material immediately after the primary fill had accumulated. This event could correspond with the deposition of substantial bone groups, including articulated joints, on top of the primary rubble in ID XVI, on the east side of the causeway in question.

Some of the opposing segments flanking major causeways have markedly different assemblages. For example, while ID VII had around 120 sherds per metre of primary fill, the opposing segments ID XV and XVI produced an average of only 14 sherds per metre. ID VII produced five pieces of worked chalk (two from the primary fill and three unstratified); there was one chalk ball from ID XVI and one incised piece from the refill of ID XV. MD IIB produced nearly twice the density of pottery and over five times the density of flint tools compared with MD IB (46.6 and 28.8 sherds, and 6.5 and 1.2 implements per metre respectively). There were five bone pins or awls from the primary fill of MD II and IIB, the largest such assemblage from one context, but only one chalk ball. Low in the primary fill of the north terminal of MD I there were four chalk balls, the largest assemblage from a single context. Another unstratified example from this segment might belong with the group. There was one bone pin only from MD I. Flint-tempered sherds were predominant in MD II, and there were 15 Ebbsfleet sherds from the top of the primary and from the secondary fill (Smith 1965a, 73–74). Shell-tempered sherds were predominant in MD I, and there was no Ebbsfleet pottery.

In both instances it was the right-hand segment, as the enclosure was entered, which produced the greater quantity of material. That pattern is repeated in ID X and XI, on either side of a substantial causeway on the east side of the inner enclosure. This asymmetry appears intentional. It is also a recognised feature of depositional practices in Later Neolithic enclosures (Pollard 1995, 143; Thomas 1996b, 212), and perhaps has a relationship to recurrent asymmetries noted in the construction of contemporary 'tombs' (Hodder 1994, 75), including deposits in opposing flanking ditches of Wessex long barrows (Pollard 1993a, chapter 4.4). Such asymmetries may be an extension of principles of bodily classification and symbolism, sidedness carrying sets of associations linked to different realms of social and cosmological order and processes of transformation (cf. Hertz 1960: and Shanks and Tilley 1982, and Tilley 1996, 221–41, for discussion in relation to the Scandinavian Early Neolithic). We might consider the possibility of left- and right-hand sidedness having had structural associations with particular gender categories, auspiciousness and inauspiciousness, order and anti-order, and even states of being (worlds of the living and that of ancestors). In the case of the opposed collections of bone pins and chalk balls from MD I and II, pins might have a particular connection with the female and chalk balls with the male, or, respectively, worldly existence and sacred realms.

Circuit patterns

Each of the three ditch circuits possessed its own depositional character. In Trenches D, E and F of the middle and inner ditches, the emphasis is on repeated depositions, often in the same spot, either in the primary silting or at the base of the secondary silting, or in both zones. In the outer ditch in Trenches A and C the extent of deposition in such positions was more limited, though there were three episodes of deposition in the primary fill of Trench B. For all their size there was little deposition in the secondary fill of the outer ditch cuttings, and by contrast with the middle and inner ditches, there was renewed activity in the upper secondary fills of Trenches B and C. While the spread 317 in Trench C mirrors earlier depositions, the activity in the upper secondary fill of Trench B was novel.

Whilst accepting its limitations, analysis of the distribution of material from the Keiller excavations shows quite marked differences in the kinds and quantity of deposits entering each of the three circuits during the primary use of the enclosure. The results of the 1925–29 work are here used simply because the large scale of Keiller's excavations provides a more sizeable sample (and therefore more reliable, since it is not susceptible to localised variation) than that from 1988.

Bone deposits can be considered first. It has been shown that bone groups were more frequent in the inner and middle ditches than the outer. Most of the bone from these had been fully processed (it was disarticulated and broken), but there were several major groups of articulated bone, mostly of cattle, and at least six entire skeletons in the primary fills. Taking the 1925–29 excavations alone, there were only 2.7 such occurrences of articulated bone per 100 m of inner circuit, but 14.4 and 8.4 per 100 m of the middle and outer circuits, illustrating a distinct rise in frequency from the inner to outer ditches. A similar pattern can be seen with finds of human bone, which were also more concentrated in the outer than the middle and inner circuits (13.9, 9.5 and 4.8 occurrences per 100 m respectively). The representation of different skeletal elements does remain fairly even across all the circuits, though it is notable that both infant burials (the only articulated human remains from the enclosure) came from sections of the outer circuit (OD IIIB and OD V).

The same kind of inter-circuit variation can be seen with other materials, such as worked flint, pottery and sarsen. In the primary fills of the ditches excavated in 1928–9, there is a gradual decline in the density of flint tools and waste (measured as an average per metre of primary ditch fill) from the inner to the outer circuit (cf. Smith 1965a, 9) (table 196). By contrast, tools form a slightly higher percentage of the assemblage from the outer

Table 196: Densities (per 100 m of the fill) of pottery, and worked sarsen, bone, antler and chalk from Earlier Neolithic contexts.

Circuit	Pottery (sherds)	Worked sarsen	Worked bone	Worked antler	Worked chalk
Outer	1340	31.0	1.2	22.8	12.0
Middle	4040	58.0	7.5	33.6	13.7
Inner	2890	40.0	1.4	8.3	5.5

circuit (9.1 percent) compared with the middle (5.1 percent) and inner circuits (7.8 percent). In more detail, scrapers account for 16.6 percent of the tool assemblage from the inner circuit, 30.3 percent in the middle circuit and 36.3 percent in the outer circuit. A similar rise in frequency can be seen with axe fragments, which comprise 1.8 percent, 2.4 percent and 6.5 percent of the tool assemblages from the inner to middle and outer circuits. Conversely, denticulated flakes and knives comprise 49.1 percent of the inner circuit tool assemblage, 37.1 percent in the middle circuit, and 33.3 percent in the outer circuit. Leaf arrowheads were absent from primary contexts in the middle and outer circuits, but eight examples came from the primary fills of the 1928–9 inner ditch segments (fig. 225). Chi-squared tests show such variations to be statistically significant (Pollard 1993a, appendix 1).

Pottery, worked sarsen, worked bone and carved chalk possess a different distributional pattern, being most frequent in the middle circuit (chapter 13 and figs 224–26). Compositional variability is also evident in the pottery and sarsen assemblages from each circuit. There are marked differences in the styles of pottery vessels being deposited in different parts of the enclosure. This has been dealt with in detail above (chapter 13) where it was observed that decorated vessels were most frequently encountered in the middle circuit. Plain vessels with heavy expanded rims and decorated carinated vessels were proportionately more common in the outer, as were vessels in shell-tempered fabrics. Whilst the frequency of sarsen quern fragments and hammerstones remains relatively constant, there were more pounders in the outer circuit than in the inner and middle (42.9 percent: 35.5 percent: 20.8 percent), and fewer rubbing stones in the inner and outer than the middle (8.9 percent: 12.5 percent: 25.0 percent).

Taken at a very general level, it can be seen that more unusual and/or specialised deposits were more frequent in the outer and, to a lesser extent, middle ditches than in the inner ditch. Whereas human bone and full or partial animal burials occurred with frequency in the outer and middle circuits, the inner ditch was characterised by a greater quantity of fully processed bone and worked flint, materials that are typically associated with routine maintenance and consumption. Although not intentionally chosen for practices of intentional deposition, similar inter-circuit variations in the representation of plant remains can also be identified (see chapter 8), with the assemblage from the inner ditch being notable for the exclusive presence of domestic plants. The patterns of distribution are marked and clearly illustrate a complex spatial organisation of depositional, and perhaps routine, activity based around the concentric form of the enclosure.

Outline of a pattern and process

Deposition is the most archaeologically visible feature of the primary use of the enclosure. The deposits are marked by the very varied range of materials employed, some of which were generated on the hill (much of the bone, pottery and lithics for example), while others were brought in from further afield. Animal bone was a major feature; and like many of the materials had frequently undergone transformation through middening before being redeposited in the ditches. An analogy can be made with the contemporary treatment of human remains, undergoing prior stages of primary burial or exposure before final deposition. Transformation, and with it an alteration of the qualities considered inherent in the material, was evidently important. Certain objects (human bone in particular) may have been in circulation for some time, carrying with them long biographies and associations with other peoples and places which were drawn upon in deposition. The mixing of materials in depositions was perhaps used to create complex symbolic statements, and draw together disparate realms of social life and existence. Whilst depositions were sometimes localised events, major horizons of deposition are tentatively identified, perhaps marking points in time when people came together. The scale, regularity and focus of deposition varied across the enclosure, and over time as symbolic traditions were continually reworked.

The location of deposits was structured. Patterning within individual segments can be recognised. With certain categories of material, for example cattle skulls, an emphasis on deposition against ditch terminals can be seen. Within each circuit, there was considerable variation in the density and range of material from individual segments. There was little relation between the size or depth of a segment and the quantity of material contained within it. Segments flanking major causeways were emphasised, both by the increased scale of deposition and by the inclusion of unusual deposits (for example, articulated cattle bone groups in ID XVI, and worked chalk and bone in MD I and MD II). An intentional asymmetry in depositional practice between opposing segments flanking major causeways can also be demonstrated, and is perhaps related to symbolic classifications of the body, gender or states of being.

During the formation of the primary and lower secondary fills each circuit seems to have had its own depositional character. Substantial groups of disarticulated animal bone, mixed with other material, were a striking feature of the inner and the middle circuits. Conversely, human bone and major groups of articulated animal bone were more

Table 197: Principal features of deposits from each circuit.

> **Outer**
> Articulated animal bone groups (including entire burials of pig and goat), human bone including infant burials; decorated pottery vessels with carinations and plain with heavy rims; flint tools more frequent by percentage; scrapers and axe fragments more common here than elsewhere; unworked antler more frequent.
>
> **Middle**
> Articulated groups of cattle bone; dog bone groups; pottery includes large percentage of uncarinated decorated vessels; high densities of pottery generally; worked sarsen, worked bone and antler, and carved chalk more frequent here than elsewhere.
>
> **Inner**
> Large scale deposition of groups of fully processed bone in dark soil; articulated bone groups rare; high density of flint; denticulated flakes and knives proportionately more frequent. Middening in the interior?

frequent in the middle and outer circuits, as were entire animal and human infant burials. Deposits of dog bone and sizeable groups of articulated cattle bone were a particular feature of the middle circuit. Amongst the lithic assemblages, there were more tools associated with light-duty cutting (denticulated flakes and knives) in the inner circuit, whereas flint scrapers and axe fragments were more frequent from the middle and outer. Different styles of pottery also had marked distributions. A summary of the major characteristics of deposits in each of the circuits is given in table 197. The patterning is the end-product of a long process of deposition, but does seem to embody commonly held notions about appropriate actions in relation to particular parts of the monument. The periphery of the enclosure was seemingly associated with more marginal or socially dangerous realms, whereas the interior perhaps had closer associations with more central aspects of life including consumption, sharing and the enactment of routine tasks (see fig. 227). In part, such patterning may relate to the spatial demarcation of functional tasks, though these were presumably themselves reproducing a symbolic order that was further emphasised through deposition. Here, space was being given meaning not through any abstracted plan, but through repeated practice (Barrett 1994, 18–19).

Drawing upon these and other themes, further interpretation of depositional practices during the Earlier Neolithic use of the enclosure will be given in the final chapter.

The Later Neolithic and Early Bronze Age use of the enclosure

The arguments for and against gradual deposition of the upper secondary fill of the outer ditch in Trench B have been set out briefly in chapter 4. They deserve fuller treatment here, and behind this is the issue of how the enclosure was used in its later history in the Late Neolithic/

Early Bronze Age. Both issues remain open, though the arguments for continued recognition of the significance of the enclosure ditches are tempting.

The wider issue has been much discussed. Piggott (1954) included Windmill Hill amongst his Peterborough culture 'habitation sites', but noted that it was not associated with any structures. Smith (1965a, 20) argued that the quantity of animal bone in the Late Neolithic layer of OD V 'may hint at the continuance for a time of earlier customs'. It was suggested that Beakers may have been manufactured on the site (Smith 1965a, 84). In general, Smith had little to say about Late Neolithic/Early Bronze Age activity. The Urn fragments were seen as 'likely to be connected with the construction of the Bronze Age round barrows on the site' (Smith 1965a, 82). Gibson (1982, 2) stated that the Beaker pottery from causewayed enclosures was 'ostensibly domestic debris', but 'this could represent dumping as part of some ritual'. Bradley (1984, 80) argued that Wessex Beakers had a special role and that this was reflected by the 'usually high proportion of finely decorated vessels' found on causewayed enclosures; Beakers (especially early Beakers) were deliberately being placed in causewayed enclosure ditches in a conscious emphasis on tradition. 'Communities were using traditional sites as a way of establishing their own position.' This was repeated by Thomas (1991, 175), specifically for Windmill Hill and AOC Beakers: 'the deposition of Beaker material on a variety of earlier sites nonetheless indicates that all links with the past had not been broken, even if the central authority had collapsed'. Thomas also (1991, 38) saw Peterborough Ware and Beaker pottery as being deposited on some causewayed enclosures to invoke their continuing 'significance' and as a 'contradistinction' to the contemporary practice associated with Grooved Ware. Finally, Morton (1990, 303), in discussing Windmill Hill, argued that 'some change in 'ritual practice' took place in the Late Neolithic/Early Bronze Age period, whereby the focus for pottery depositions shifted from the inner to outer ditches'.

The nature of the upper secondary fill in the outer ditch in Trench B: the case for gradual deposition
(Michael Hamilton)

The more detailed argument here rests on two claims: that there is nationally a ceramic sequence in the Late Neolithic to Early Bronze Age from Beaker to Food Vessel to Collared Urn (Hamilton 1995), and that such a sequence can be seen in the three-dimensionally recorded finds from Trench B.

Beaker (fig. 203). The lowest Beaker sherds were three conjoining sherds of style Bkr1 and two sherds of style Bkr15. These were c. 0.5 m below the horizon of the main Beaker/Early Bronze Age material. The sherd breaks were old and one of the conjoining sherds was separated from the others by a horizontal distance of 1.3 m. 0.5 m seems an excessive amount of silting between the deposition of

Beaker pottery in an upper silt and it is probable that these lowest Beaker sherds came from features cut into the upper silt. One sherd was identified to a feature (220) provisionally identified as an animal burrow. The location of two of the conjoining sherds would roughly correspond to feature 211. A sherd of Bkr15 came from the extreme west of the trench in context 204 and again its depth suggests that it derived from a feature. If, say, animal burrows were to explain the fortuitous burial of three conjoining sherds in two different locations it is strange that they have left them well enough preserved to conjoin. Bkr1 and Bkr15 are very disproportionately represented amongst these lowest sherds.

There is some regularity in the location of these proposed features (fig. 202). They correspond with three of the four corners of a square (1.3 by 1.3 m). The hypothetical fourth corner would be on the very edge of the excavated area. No postpipes were identified in excavation, but it is unlikely such features would survive worm action in a secondary silt. Posts 1.3 m apart would make a small structure. Alternatively, the features could be pits. Such an arrangement was recorded under Avebury G55 (Smith 1965b), where they were interpreted as pits for storage, and it was argued that one pit had an organic inner liner. A similar arrangement of pits was recorded by Keiller next to OD II (Smith 1965a, 29–30). These pits were associated with charcoal. The spacing of the OD II pits and some of those from Avebury G55 would be comparable to those from Trench B.

Another probable pit was context 219. It contained mostly Southern Beaker (Clarke 1970), whereas the context above (216) contained an Enlarged Food Vessel. Only one Food Vessel sherd came from 219, and this was 6 cm above the Beaker sherds. There are additional Southern Beaker sherds from 216, but it is significant that these came from lower down than virtually all the Food Vessel sherds. There was a marked distribution of Southern Beaker sherds for the area of 219, which either reflects that they were still *in situ* in a broad shallow feature almost entirely destroyed by 216, or that they all came from 219 and were dislodged during the digging of 216.

The sequence of the putative Beaker pits cannot be determined directly by stratigraphy. Bkr1 and Bkr15 have simple comb decoration and could be 'Middle' Beakers (Case 1977), whereas pit 219 and the surrounding area produced 'Late' Beaker sherds. Recent radiocarbon dates have put the Case sequence in doubt (Kinnes *et al.* 1991), but it still remains the sequence best supported by relative chronology on burial sites.

Apart from these pits, there is a distribution of Beaker sherds in the Beaker/Early Bronze Age layer which runs right across the upper secondary fill. These are mainly Beaker styles (Bkr4; Bkr5) and related ceramics (?Bkr1; Rus1; Rus2; Rus5) which are not represented in the putative pits. Several Beaker sherds of these styles lie almost directly above the supposed 'Middle' Beaker features. This could suggest that all or part of this distribution of Beaker sherds took place after the digging of those pits. The relationship of feature 219 to the Beaker distribution was destroyed by the digging of 216.

There were two clusters of sherds against the eastern edge of the ditch (Rus1 and Bkr5), whereas sherds of other styles, from the main part of the ditch, seem more broadly distributed. Possibly sherds by the eastern edge were protected, whereas there was a process in the main part of the ditch which scattered the sherds.

Enlarged Food Vessel (fig. 205). If those Beaker sherds in supposed features are excluded from the overall distribution (fig. 203), and if the Southern Beaker sherds are likely to be derived from feature 219, then there is a marked gap in the distribution around 219, in which the distribution of the Enlarged Food Vessel sherds (fig. 205) is concentrated. One explanation for this is that originally the whole trench had a distribution of Beaker sherds, but when feature 216 was dug this displaced the sherds close to surface and created the hole in the Beaker distribution.

Into feature 216 was placed a large percentage of an Enlarged Food Vessel (P541). The distribution of sherds from this vessel extends also in a north-westerly direction. One possibility is that the violence of P42's destruction explains its distribution. This would also explain the presence of sherds from this vessel in Smith's adjacent cutting.

In section, the distribution of Food Vessel sherds may suggest hollows, rises and a generally uneven surface.

Collared Urns (figs 205–6). EBA1 appears to represent three or more Collared Urn vessels. The distribution of these sherds ignores the presence of 216 and is fairly evenly distributed across the whole trench, which would be consistent with their post-dating the digging of that feature. This is supported by their general occurrence at a higher level than the Food Vessel sherds. Unlike with the Beakers or Food Vessel there was no clear sign of any features.

EBA6 was comparatively sparsely represented, and therefore its non-occurrence in the area of 216 may not be significant. However, one of these sherds belongs to a substantially complete Collared Urn recovered from Smith's Trench V (1965a, P323). It is significant that while Smith recovered most of the vessel in her 2 m cutting, very little occurred in the next 2 m. This suggests a very discrete deposition. The deposition of a large part of an Urn in Trench V has marked echoes of the deposition of the Enlarged Food Vessel in 216. The area produced a Conygar arrowhead and a copper/copper alloy awl.

Romano-British pottery (fig. 206). The distribution of Romano-British pottery in the trench appears even and does not avoid feature 216. The conjoining of sherds separated by 2 m suggests disturbance of the upper silts. This movement seems mainly north-south. The main concentration of RB pottery is roughly 30 cm above that of the EBA. The very slow speed of this silting (30 cm for 1500 years) has implications for the speed of silting during the Later Neolithic and Early Bronze Age. The occasional mixture of EBA and RB sherds may reflect animal or human disturbance.

Secondary use of causewayed enclosures in the region and beyond: Peterborough Ware, Beaker pottery and round barrows (*M. Hamilton*)

The presence of Peterborough pottery at other enclosures is rather varied and often slight. 15 of 34 excavated sites have produced Peterborough Ware, though only Windmill Hill and Combe Hill (of the published sites) have yielded more than 50 sherds. Many excavations have been on a small scale, but even some of the larger excavations have produced nothing (Orsett, Trundle, Crickley Hill), or very little (Abingdon, Hambledon Hill).

Neither does the location of Peterborough pottery appear to have any recurring significance. At Maiden Castle Peterborough Ware occurred in most of the inner ditch cuttings (Cleal 1991b), though its presence in the bank barrow ditches may suggest a general concern with the interior. The outer ditches were also largely backfilled and this may explain the absence of pottery. The inner spiral was preferred at Briar Hill (Bamford 1985). At Staines the evidence was all from the outer ditches, though all but one vessel came from the north-east quadrant (Robertson-Mackay 1987). Whitehawk had intermittent finds from the middle two ditches (Curwen 1934; 1936). On most sites it is difficult to fit deposition into simple patterns tied to ditch circuits, and it is easier to see the distributions as reflecting nucleated occupation of specific areas. Most sites can be reduced to one or two hypothetical areas of deposition which in most cases ignore the presence of ditches, which merely act as incidental depositories for pottery spreads which later land-use has destroyed outside the ditches. Therefore at Windmill Hill there was one spread of Mortlake Ware across the inner and middle ditches in the centre of the site. At Hambledon Hill it occurred at the Stepleton enclosure. At Maiden Castle there was possibly one deposition area to the west and centre, and another to the east. At Staines there was a single large deposition to the north-east.

Another indication of the special nature of such sites would be evidence of remodelling. At Maiden Castle there was a hollow in the upper fill of one of the ditch cuttings (Sharples 1991, 56–57) which could be 'redefinition' of the enclosure or a domestic structure. At Haddenham 'minor' recutting of some ditch circuits was associated with Mortlake/Ebbsfleet Ware (C. Evans 1988b, 144), and possibly a remodelling of a palisade. At Briar Hill (Bamford 1985) a pit containing Peterborough Ware was cut into the upper ditch fill, but the distribution of other Late Neolithic pits could suggest that this was accidental. At Etton the almost completely silted ditches were used for the deposition of Fengate pottery (Ian Kinnes *pers. comm.*).

Focus on monuments as monuments may have prevented

recognition that the Peterborough Ware depositions on causewayed enclosures are not atypical of Middle Neolithic activity in general (Hamilton 1995). Nucleated deposits occur on a number of unenclosed sites across southern Britain, such as the West Kennet Avenue (Smith 1965a), Downton (Rahtz 1962), Winterslow Roman Earthwork (Vatcher 1963), and many other sites. Superficially the nature of these deposits appears little different from similar nucleated deposits on causewayed enclosures. This raises two possibilities. Activity at causewayed enclosures could be part of a wider continuum of special activity, which is, due to recovery bias, very under-represented in the archae-ological record. Alternatively, nucleated Peterborough Ware deposits may reflect 'everyday' activity, and their occurrence on sites with earlier enclosure activity is largely a matter of chance.

Nationally the evidence for Grooved Ware on cause-wayed enclosures is sparse (Orsett; Maiden Castle; Briar Hill; Windmill Hill). Thomas (1991, 38) has drawn attention to the variation in the way Peterborough Ware is used on causewayed enclosures and 'in contradistinction to the contemporary practices associated with Grooved Ware'. In the light of recent dates the extent to which they were contemporary is questionable. However, beyond this, if one examines just the Fengate sub-style, which most scholarship still accepts as the latest style to develop, then their distributions are remarkably similar. Fengate is only recorded on four sites, only one of which may not produce Grooved Ware (Etton), unlike the three other sites (Maiden Castle, Briar Hill, and Windmill Hill). This link between the occurrence of these styles may suggest a social con-nection or perhaps one should re-examine the individuality of the two styles. More importantly it may suggest that some of the claims of dichotomy between Grooved Ware and Peterborough Ware are only valid if the latter is viewed as a monolithic unit. If one also addresses my suggestions about chronology (Hamilton 1995), then it is possible that the rarity of Grooved Ware (and Fengate) from causewayed enclosures does not reflect an active exclusion, but a gradual decline of interest in these sites during the Late Neolithic.

The nature of Grooved Ware deposition is difficult to interpret. Nationally the occurrence of Grooved Ware on causewayed enclosures is sparse. Such ceramics (especially the Clacton sub-style) are frequently interpreted as ritual, though the use of structured deposition may occur inside settlement sites, rather than be special activity limited to monuments. Overall there is too little evidence to decide if the appearance of Grooved Ware relates to settlement activity or involves special activity associated with the causewayed enclosure.

Finds of Beaker not directly accompanying a burial can be interpreted as the relic of settlement evidence (Cleal 1992b; Smith 1965b). However, some writers (Bradley 1984, 78, 80–81; Thomas 1991, 38, 172, 175) have made claims for ritual use of Beaker pottery on causewayed enclosures, in order to emphasise ritual traditions. The main argument of Bradley and Thomas was simply the presence of Beaker pottery on a site of significance in the Early Neolithic. However, of the 34 enclosure sites in southern Britain which have seen excavation, only 12 have produced Beaker pottery, with seven producing more than five sherds; only four have produced more than 100 sherds. In Dorset and East Sussex two of the three excavated sites in each area produced Beaker pottery; in Wiltshire only two out of six sites produced Beaker pottery. One of the arguments used by Bradley (1984, tables 4.2–3) was that Early Beaker (in the sense of Case 1977) represented 43 percent of the Beaker styles from causewayed enclosures in Wessex, which is out of proportion with its frequency on other sites. However, this figure can no longer be sustained and a re-examination of the Wessex material suggests that Early Beaker only represents 11 percent of Beaker styles at Wessex causewayed enclosures, much more in line with its usual frequency.

There is no evidence for Beaker constructional activity at any enclosure, with the possible exception of the ditches at Hambledon Hill which had a layer of flint (Mercer 1980). Neither is it possible to identify a systematic re-defining of ditch circuits by pottery depositions. Maiden Castle (Cleal 1991b) may have Beaker pottery around most of the perimeter, but even there Beaker pottery was also recorded inside and outside the enclosure in the bank barrow ditches, with the suggestion that the western side of the enclosure was most favoured. Most sites have a pattern of depositions which favour particular areas and which largely ignore the ditch circuits (Hambledon Hill, Whitehawk, Briar Hill). Neither is it possible to identify a bias on multiple-ditched sites for the location of finds, with Maiden Castle favouring the inner ditch, Whitehawk the middle, and Windmill and Briar Hill the outer. The pattern at Hambledon Hill cannot be broken down into such simple terms, unless like Windmill Hill there were multiple occupations, each favouring a different part of the site. In conclusion, there is not a consistent national or regional pattern for which areas of the enclosures received depositions. Indeed the patterns make more sense, not in terms of the Early Neolithic ditches, but as isolated areas of occupation and deposition.

It may be more appropriate to look instead at the range of 'non-funerary' Beaker pottery from elsewhere in the landscape. Easton Down excavated by Stone (1931; 1933; 1935) produced in excess of 300 sherds from rabbit disturbances and excavation of 'houses'. Though the excavations records are very poor, the finds do seem to reflect discrete clusters, possibly conforming to divisions within Beaker style. The large area of deposition is comparable to the spread of Beaker pottery across Wind-mill Hill. Snail Down (Nicholas Thomas *pers. comm.*) has a similar spread of pottery, this time sealed by a round barrow cemetery. Both sites could reflect settlement activity, as could numerous other finds of Beaker pottery without strong evidence for burials. Additional weight for this interpretation is provided by the identification of such scatters at Windmill Hill and Maiden Castle with woodland clearance and cultivation. Similar activity with Beaker pottery has been identified on long barrows (Evans 1990).

It is generally assumed that the majority of round barrows in northern Wiltshire belong to the Early Bronze Age. There are four major concentrations of barrows in Wessex, and Windmill Hill lies on the northern edge of one of these (Fleming 1971; Woodward and Woodward 1996). On Windmill Hill itself the main group of barrows forms a slightly dog-legged linear cemetery, which is roughly at right angles to the valley of the Winterbourne. This arrangement is well paralleled in nearby barrow groups. The siting of barrows seems to relate to visibility from the valley bottom, and in this regard the Windmill Hill cemetery is no different. Neither is the number of barrows particularly exceptional, being matched in numbers by the Fox Covert Group (*c.* SU0768), Overton Hill Group (*c.* SU1168), and a linear group of ploughed out barrows north of Beckhampton (*c.* SU0969). Neither are the Windmill Hill barrows especially large, nor is there a unusual high incidence of Grinsell's fancy barrows. None of the barrows have produced a 'rich' burial, though the excavation record for the hill is very patchy. The only notable grave-good is a possible jet bead from Avebury G46b, and a Grape cup and battle-axe, but the context of the later finds (burial rite and barrow) is unknown (Grinsell 1957, 200).

The Enlarged Food Vessel from Trench B (P541) and the Collared Urn from Smith Trench V (P323) appear to represent the deliberate deposition of complete pots into the ditch. It is difficult to find parallels for this practice outside burial rites, a resemblance made stronger by the presence of the bronze awl, a common grave-good. The absence of similar activity in the rest of the excavated part of the site suggests that it was location on the line of barrows on the hill that was of crucial importance in these depositions, rather than the causewayed enclosure ditch itself.

Once again, it is possible to argue for a break in tradition after the primary phase of use of the enclosure.

The nature of the upper secondary fill in the outer ditch, Trench B: the case for more rapid deposition and continued significance of the enclosure
(Joanna Brück)

A study of Early Bronze Age depositional practice can provide an insight into the kinds of activities that were carried out at the enclosure during this period. Data on the size and degree of abrasion of sherds, and on the fragmentation and depositional histories of particular vessels may help to distinguish between *in situ* activities, middening and special deposits. The repertoire of Early Bronze Age pottery derives largely from the secondary and tertiary ditch silts. The assemblage includes Beakers, Collared Urns, rusticated vessels, at least one Food Vessel and a variety of undiagnostic Late Neolithic /Early Bronze Age ceramics.

Hamilton's study of the pottery indicates that approximately 45 individual vessels are represented. Most of these are extremely fragmentary. Excluding the single Food Vessel from Trench B, for which approximately 75 sherds were present, vessels are represented by an average of 5 sherds. Edge and surface abrasion was examined for all of those sherds stratified below the Romano-British and later ploughsoils. The majority of these (90 percent) have partly or extremely abraded edges. In contrast, 67 percent of the sherds have well preserved surfaces (tables 198–99). Abrasion to the edges of sherds is generally indicative of weathering. Surface preservation, on the other hand, is closely linked to mechanical attrition as well as weathering; processes such as trampling by humans and animals affect the surfaces of sherds to a greater degree than their edges (Last 1995, chapter 5). The lack of surface abrasion suggests that sherds were not exposed to much trampling before they were deposited in the ditches. The high degree of edge abrasion, on the other hand, may be explained in one of two ways. Either sherds were exposed to weathering *prior* to dumping, or they were deposited in a matrix which formed slowly in a relatively unsheltered location. By the Late Neolithic/Early Bronze Age, the ditches of the causewayed enclosure had largely filled. Natural processes of silting would therefore have progressed at a slow rate, providing conditions not conducive to the preservation of friable

Table 198: Windmill Hill: edge abrasion of sherds (complete assemblage).

	Stage 1	Stage 2	Stage 3
Percentage	10	29	61
No. of sherds	23	64	136

Edge abrasion scale:

1. Lightly abraded pottery. Edges fairly sharp and unrounded. Clay particles and pieces of temper visible in broken sections are also mostly unrounded. Edges do not have the fresh colour of recently broken pottery.
2. Abraded pottery. Some rounding of the edges. Many of the clay particles and pieces of temper visible in broken sections are rounded. Colour of broken sections indicates a high degree of patination.
3. Very abraded pottery. Edges very rounded. Separate clay particles and pieces of temper not visible in broken sections.

Table 199: Windmill Hill: surface preservation of sherds (complete assemblage).

	Stage 1	Stage 2	Stage 3
Percentage	67	7	26
No. of sherds	149	15	59

1. Little or no surface abrasion. Surfaces well preserved across entire sherd on both sides.
2. Some surface abrasion. Parts of one or both surfaces lost. Indications of chemical leaching or root disturbance may be present.
3. Much surface abrasion. All of one or both surfaces lost.

ceramic material; one might therefore favour the latter possibility. However, as will be argued below, most of the sherds in question derive from contexts that do not seem to have formed under natural conditions and that appear to have accumulated over a relatively short period. Furthermore, the fragmentary nature of individual vessels suggests that sherds were subjected to processes of attrition and dispersal prior to dumping. This indicates that some time lapsed between breakage and final deposition and that the high degree of edge abrasion is largely due to weathering during this intervening period. It also suggests that the majority of the later pottery from the ditches was dumped away from its location of primary use.

Almost two thirds of the Early Bronze Age ceramics were recovered from Trench B during the 1988 excavations (table 200). This pottery was mainly found in the series of dark midden-like layers which form the upper secondary fill. The lowest sherds, mostly Beaker and Food Vessel (style EBA3), appear to have been deposited in several scoops or features (216, 219, 222 and possibly 220) cut into the top of the lower secondary silts. A few further sherds were found in contexts 203 and 204, the uppermost layers of the lower secondary ditch fill. These

may derive from features. Above scoops 216, 219, 222 and 220, a chalk surface, 214, had been laid (215 is a possible extension of this towards the centre of the ditch). Over this, several further dark deposits (211 and 212) formed and at the top of the upper secondary fill, a thick black soil developed (202), containing large quantities of pottery (table 200), animal bone and flint.

There is some indication that these layers formed quickly. Sherds from a single vessel are frequently distributed throughout several layers. For example, a sherd of style ?Bkr1 from context 202 conjoins another from 215, while sherds of Bkr2, which seem to derive from a single vessel, were found at both the top and bottom of the upper secondary fill (contexts 219 and 202). Either this results from post-depositional disturbance or it is the product of several separate depositional events, each of which involved sherds from the same vessel. Although it is undoubtedly the case that some post-depositional disturbance took place (for example animal burrowing), it is unlikely that the distribution of sherds from a single vessel can be uniquely attributed to this. For example, three sherds of Bkr1 appear to have been deposited in features cut into the top of the lower secondary silts (context 203). A fourth Bkr1 sherd

Table 200: Trench B, Windmill Hill: number of sherds of different styles per context (note: contexts ordered by stratigraphical height).

Context	Bkr 1	Bkr 2	Bkr 3	Bkr 4	Bkr 5	Bkr 6	Bkr 15	?Bkr 1	Rus 1	Rus 2	Rus 5	Rus 6	EBA 1	EBA 2	EBA 3	EBA 4	EBA 5	EBA 6	LN/EBA 2
202	1	1	2	5	2	-	-	2	5	1	1	-	28	12	21	1	1	4	-
211	-	-	-	-	-	1	-	-	-	-	-	-	1	-	-	-	-	-	-
212	-	-	-	-	-	-	-	-	-	-	-	-	3	-	1	-	-	-	-
213	-	-	-	-	-	-	-	-	-	-	-	-	-	-	1	-	-	-	-
214	-	-	-	1	-	-	-	-	-	-	-	-	12	1	8	-	-	-	1
215	-	-	-	-	-	-	-	1	-	-	-	-	3	-	-	-	-	-	-
216	-	1	3	-	-	-	-	-	-	-	-	1	6	-	36	1	5	-	-
219	-	3	-	-	-	-	-	-	-	-	-	-	-	-	1	-	-	-	-
220	-	-	-	-	-	-	1	-	-	-	-	-	-	-	-	-	-	-	-
222	-	-	-	-	-	-	-	-	-	-	-	-	-	-	2	-	-	-	-
204	-	-	-	-	-	-	1	-	-	-	-	-	-	-	-	-	-	-	-
203	3	-	-	-	-	-	-	1	-	-	-	-	-	-	3	-	-	-	-

Table 201: Trench B, Windmill Hill: number of sherds (style 'EBA 1')

	4mm	5mm	6mm	7mm	8mm	9mm	10mm	Unknown
Context 202	3	5	6	3	2	0	2	7
Context 211	0	0	1	0	0	0	0	0
Context 212	0	3	0	0	0	0	0	0
Context 214	0	0	3	4	0	0	0	5
Context 215	1	2	0	0	0	0	0	0
Context 216	0	2	1	2	0	0	0	1

was found in context 202, over half a metre higher than the others and roughly two metres to the west of these. The edges of this sherd were unabraded unlike those from the lower features. If the sherd had been disturbed from a feature at the base of the upper secondary fill, one would expect it to show more abrasion than those found in their original depositional context.

A similar argument can be made for other vessels. A possible Collared Urn (EBA5) is represented by six sherds, five of which were recovered from context 216 and the sixth from context 202; again, the latter is much less abraded than those from 216, suggesting that it is not derived from this context. Over half of the sherds from the 2–4 Collared Urns represented by style EBA1 were recovered from context 202. One might suggest that all sherds of this style were originally deposited in this layer and that those found in lower contexts were displaced through post-depositional disturbance. If the latter do indeed derive from a source in 202, then one might expect a high degree of similarity between sherd assemblages in each context. This does not appear to be the case, however. Sherds from layer 202 vary in thickness from 4–10 mm, indicating the presence of more than one vessel (table 201). In contrast, the range of sherd thicknesses within each context below 202 is much smaller, suggesting that individual contexts contain sherds from only one vessel. If the sherds in the lower deposits were derived from 202, one would expect a greater range of sherd thicknesses to occur. EBA1 sherds in lower contexts such as 216 and 214 are therefore probably the result of depositional episodes prior to the formation of 202.

The above examples demonstrate that the same sources of refuse appear to have been in use throughout the period during which the upper secondary ditch fill was forming. This suggests that the time lapse between depositional events was probably one of years rather than decades or centuries and that the top layer of the upper secondary fill may not have formed very much later than the lower levels. If so, this has implications for the relative chronology of different styles of pottery, supporting arguments (e.g. Bradley 1984, 70–73) for some degree of contemporaneity between Beakers, Food Vessels and Collared Urns.

Context 202 deserves further comment as it differs somewhat from the deposits below it (table 200). It is the most compositionally diverse of the contexts, containing 15 different styles of Early Bronze Age pottery (as identified by Hamilton) and parts of at least 18 vessels. In contrast, other contexts produced an average of 2–3 styles. This diversity can in part be explained by the size of the ceramic assemblage in 202 (87 sherds), as well as by the thickness and extent of this context. However, it also suggests that the pottery in 202 may have derived from many different sources in contrast to the more homogeneous assemblages in other contexts. Equally important is the observation that the sherds from 202 are the least abraded of the entire assemblage, which one would not expect if this context had formed gradually *in situ* (table 202). Context 202 contains

Table 202: Trench B, Windmill Hill: edge abrasion of sherds by context (only those contexts containing more than 10 sherds have been included because there is a high likelihood that patterning in contexts containing small numbers of sherds is the result of chance factors alone).

	Stage 1 (%)	Stage 2 (%)	Stage 3 (%)	Total no. of sherds
202	19	28	53	87
214	0	13	87	23
216	7	23	70	53

sherds from vessels which were broken before it began to accumulate (in other words, it contains sherds from the same vessels as those in contexts stratified below it). Some of these are less abraded than sherds from the same vessels that were dumped during earlier depositional events. This suggests that at least some of the sherds in context 202 were protected from the elements prior to their deposition in the ditch; an intermediate context such as a surface midden is a possibility. The relatively good condition of the sherds and the presence of so many different styles of pottery may therefore indicate that 202 did not accumulate gradually *in situ* but rather comprises redeposited material from a midden which formed elsewhere. Although we know all too little about the formation of Late Neolithic/Early Bronze Age midden deposits, the act of redepositing midden material in the ditch of the earlier monument may indicate that the causewayed enclosure was still recognised as a significant place.

The depositional histories of different types of pottery recovered during the 1988 excavations appear to vary. The Beaker and rusticated vessels tend to be more fragmentary (an average of three and five sherds per vessel respectively) than the possible Collared Urns for which an average of 10 sherds per vessel are present. This suggests that the Beaker ceramics were exposed to processes which would lead to their dispersal and that more time may have elapsed between breakage and deposition of these vessels than was the case for Collared Urns. In complete contrast, the single Food Vessel recovered from the 1988 excavations was represented by approximately 75 sherds. Approximately half of these had been deposited in a scoop (216) which may have been dug specifically for this purpose. The presence of a large portion of a single Food Vessel suggests that this was deposited soon after the pot was broken.

Contrary to expectations, the Beaker ceramics tend to show slightly less edge abrasion and have markedly better surface preservation than sherds of any other style. The edges and surfaces of the Food Vessel sherds, on the other hand, are more abraded than either the Beaker or Collared Urn sherds (tables 203–4). It is possible that the Beaker pottery was deposited in an intermediate context, such as a surface midden, prior to final deposition in the ditches; this may account for its well-preserved but fragmentary condition. The highly abraded nature of the Food Vessel sherds is more difficult to explain, and implies that these were subjected to more weathering and trampling than the

Table 203: Windmill Hill: edge abrasion of sherds by style.

	Stage 1 (%)	Stage 2 (%)	Stage 3 (%)	Total no. of sherds
Beakers	15	33	52	61
Collared urns	9	31	60	81
Food vessel	9	24	67	75

Table 204: Windmill Hill: surface preservation of sherds by style.

	Stage 1 (%)	Stage 2 (%)	Stage 3 (%)	Total no. of sherds
Beakers	84	8	8	61
Collared urns	68	7	25	81
Food vessel	52	5	43	75

other ceramics. This is surprising, given the suggestion that the Food Vessel was deposited soon after breakage. One possible explanation is that this attrition occurred *in situ* in context 216; perhaps the scoop in which the pot was deposited was left open for some time, before the layers above it formed. The degree of abrasion to edges and surfaces varies from sherd to sherd. If the proposal of *in situ* attrition is correct, one might expect sherds deposited higher up within the fill of scoop 216 to have been exposed to more weathering and/or trampling than those deposited in the lower fill of the feature. This does not seem to be the case. Context 216 is roughly 20 cm deep, yet the more eroded sherds were distributed evenly throughout the fill of the feature. This implies that the Food Vessel sherds were subjected to attritional processes prior to deposition. If so, the variation in degree of wear between sherds is interesting. Certain parts of the vessel may have undergone quite different pre-depositional histories to others; in other words, sherds may have became dispersed after breakage and then gathered together again for deposition in 216. More likely, perhaps, is the possibility that the broken Food Vessel was deposited in a surface midden prior to dumping in the ditch. Sherds closer to the surface of a midden would decay quicker than those within its core. If so, then it seems all the more remarkable that such a large portion of this vessel was redeposited in the ditch, and the presence of a number of relatively unabraded sherds implies that these were not simply collected from the surface of the midden but may have been dug out of its core. This suggests that the vessel may have been deliberately selected for redeposition in the ditch of the earlier monument. Its position within a pit, which was perhaps specially dug to receive it, corroborates this suggestion. It thus seems possible that this vessel formed part of a special deposit.

Turning to the flint assemblage, it is often assumed that artefacts which are broken or show evidence of use are unlikely to have been included as components of special deposits and may be categorised as refuse. Although this is a problematic assumption, the prevalence and distribu-

tion of worn flint artefacts might be a possible means of distinguishing different types of depositional activity. The upper secondary fill of Trench B produced the largest assemblage of Late Neolithic/Early Bronze Age flintwork from the 1988 excavations; all the retouched pieces from these contexts were examined for evidence of use-wear. 87 percent (35 out of 40) of these displayed use-wear. The five unworn artefacts comprise a scraper from context 202, a bevelled flake from 216, a retouched bifacial piece from 215 and a knife and petit tranchet derivative arrowhead from context 214. Unfortunately, the very small number of unworn objects makes it difficult to assess the likelihood that these represent a series of distinct special deposits and it may simply be that they were accidentally included in refuse deposits, or not used for sufficiently long to acquire macroscopic traces of use.

The percentage of retouched to unretouched pieces may also be informative: this is generally in the region of 4 percent. Contexts 220, 211/212 and 216 produced more retouched artefacts, however (18 percent, or 2 out of 11; 12 percent, or 2 out of 16; and 8 percent, or 8 out of 103 respectively). The small numbers of finds in 220 and 211/212 makes these results less convincing; chance alone may be at work. The relatively high proportion of retouched pieces in context 216 is suggestive, however, especially when it is recalled that this is the scoop into which most of the Food Vessel was deposited. It may be significant that the retouched artefacts in this context include one of two plano-convex knives and the only barbed-and-tanged arrowhead recovered from Trench B; both of these types of finely retouched object are found in contemporary grave assemblages, and if these items were indeed deliberately selected for deposition along with the Food Vessel in context 216, then it may be that some of the same symbolism was being employed.

The question of whether the Late Neolithic/Early Bronze Age deposits focus on the ditch segments is of direct relevance to whether this later activity can be linked to the presence of the Early Neolithic enclosure. Clearly, the concentration of later ceramics in the ditches of the earlier monument may be the result of differential preservation. Flint artefacts are more widely distributed, however, and it seems possible that there were once more extensive midden deposits across the top of the hill. This suggests that depositional activities may not have focused on the causewayed enclosure itself, weakening arguments for its continued importance during the Early Bronze Age.

Comparison of the flint assemblages from ditches and surfaces, however, may prove instructive. There is some evidence to suggest that the composition of the flint assemblage from surfaces and ditches may have been comparable. For example, the deposition of finely retouched implements does not seem to have been focused on the ditches. Smith (1965a, 107) records that almost as many small scale-flaked scrapers were collected from the surface of the enclosure as from the ditch sections during her own and Keiller's excavations. Pollard's recent re-examination (1993a) of the Smith and Keiller archives suggests some similar trends. Of the five classic plano-convex knives from the site, two were found in the Picket Barrow ditch (in silts probably derived from the surrounding land surface) and another example came from a surface context inside the inner circuit. Ten fabricators out of approximately 24 were collected from the Picket Barrow ditch (probably derived surface contexts), while another two were found on the surface of the inner enclosure.

Nonetheless, this does not conclusively prove that the presence of the causewayed enclosure was unimportant. A comparison with Early Neolithic depositional activity may be informative. We know that the ditches were a focus for special deposits during the Early Neolithic, yet fine Early Neolithic flintwork is not solely found in these contexts. For example, Smith (1965a, 99) notes that of the 25 laurel leaves found during the early excavations, eight were from surface contexts. The distribution of leaf-shaped arrowheads is likewise interesting (Smith 1965a, 100); 25 out of 132 of these came from the surface. This indicates that Early Neolithic depositional practice did not always centre on the ditches, even though these were clearly important. In other words, the presence of similar Late Neolithic/Early Bronze Age finds in both surface and ditch contexts does not mean that the causewayed enclosure itself was insignificant.

Furthermore, a few strands of evidence do hint that the ditches themselves may have been recognised as important. For example, 26 of the 30 or more barbed and tanged arrowheads found at the site were recovered from the ditch contexts. Although many similar artefacts were found in surface contexts, almost half of the thumbnail scrapers and most of the scale-flaked knives recovered during Smith's and Keiller's excavations were found in OD II (approximately 67 and 14 examples respectively). This suggests that particular ditch segments may have attracted considerable attention. Unfortunately, the lack of surface excavation in this area makes it difficult to demonstrate conclusively that OD II itself was a genuine focus of deposition, and for the moment we must conclude that it is equally possible that this concentration represents no more than the presence of a task-specific area in the north-eastern part of the site. Finally, distributional patterning across the site may hint that ditches and surfaces were being differentiated, implying that the presence of the causewayed enclosure was recognised. There are no barbed and tanged arrowheads in the inner enclosure whereas seven examples were found in the inner ditches; this creates a contrast between ditch and surface contexts. A single plano-convex knife was recovered from the surface of the inner enclosure; two further examples were found between the middle and inner ditch circuits in a context probably derived from the surface (layer 1 of the Picket Barrow ditch silts). These finds contrast with the two plano-convex knives from the outer circuit which were found in the ditch of the causewayed enclosure itself.

As for the overall spatial distribution of different classes of artefact, the Late Neolithic/Early Bronze Age ceramics were largely concentrated in the outer ditch segments. Two particular foci of activity can be identified. Collared Urn and Food Vessel sherds have mostly been found in the region of the Early Bronze Age barrows. The Beaker and rusticated wares, on the other hand, were distributed towards the north and north-west of the site, suggesting that not all of the Early Bronze Age activity on the hill can be related to the presence of the barrows. How these two foci relate chronologically is difficult to say. It is possible that the pottery assemblage recovered from the north and north-west of the site represents an earlier phase than that found in the area of the barrow cemetery. On the other hand, the two foci may be broadly contemporary, the difference in ceramic repertoire relating more closely to differences in the kinds of activities carried out. The distribution of Grooved Ware is similar to that of the Beaker sherds; Mortlake and Fengate pottery, on the other hand, concentrates in the middle and inner ditches. The Late Neolithic/Early Bronze Age flint assemblage also shows differential distribution across the site. The location of thumbnail scrapers and scale-flaked knives from ditch contexts mirrors that of the Early Bronze Age ceramics. Evidence for flint-knapping is also largely concentrated in the same parts of the site. Many cores and quartered flint blocks were recovered from the upper secondary and tertiary layers of Trench B. Some other flint artefact types seem also to show quite restricted distributions. For example, 10 of the 24 fabricators were recovered from the Picket Barrow ditch. However, other categories of artefact, including barbed and tanged arrowheads, awls and piercers were distributed more evenly across the site, suggesting that the differentiation of space occurred on several different levels according to the activities being carried out.

The distribution of artefacts across the site therefore suggests some differentiation and categorisation of space. Obviously, this could have occurred whether or not people were aware of the presence of the earlier monument. Without good comparative data from surface deposits at the site, it is difficult to say whether the ditch segments were themselves used as a means of creating and sustaining this organisation of space. However, the possibility that ditches and surfaces were being differentiated does bolster the argument that the divisions of space created by the Early Neolithic enclosure were being drawn on to create new discourses.

All told, there is little firm evidence to suggest that the causewayed enclosure continued to act as a focus of ritual activity during the Late Neolithic/Early Bronze Age. The finds assemblage from Trench B can best be described as the product of refuse disposal activities. The pottery appears to have been deposited away from its location of primary use, and at least some of the sherds may have been initially dumped in a surface midden prior to their final deposition in the ditch segments. Only the Food Vessel and perhaps some of its associated flint artefacts stand out as something different, although the status of these finds as placed deposits rather than as refuse is by no means conclusive. Indeed, even if this is a special deposit, such finds are frequent components of Bronze Age middens (e.g. Needham 1991) and its presence may not relate to the earlier monument.

Although there is little obvious evidence for ritual activity, the identification of 'refuse' should not lead to underestimation of the significance of the site during later use. What we might consider to be categories of refuse frequently form part of special deposits during the Bronze Age: witness the careful positioning of sherds of pottery in many contemporary burials, as well as the frequency of broken bronze objects in hoards. In the case of Windmill Hill, the presence of a layer of redeposited midden material (context 202) across the top of the upper secondary fill in Trench B is difficult to explain in practical terms. Indeed, the symbolic significance of midden material during the Neolithic and Bronze Age has often been stressed (e.g. Needham and Sørensen 1988; Thomas 1991; Pollard 1993a; Brück 1995) and one might argue that the reposition of this layer was in itself a symbolic action, imparting particular connotations to this location. It is not difficult to imagine that midden material might bring to mind such themes as transformation (the breaking down/recycling of material), marginality (refuse as dirty or 'other') and fertility (the use of midden material as manure) (see Brück 1995). Stretching the argument somewhat further, one might suggest that Windmill Hill was considered an appropriate place for middening activities *precisely because* of the presence of the earlier enclosure. The kinds of themes that were played out at the monument during the Early Neolithic could have made their way into local oral histories, sustaining yet transforming the meanings attached to Windmill Hill right into the Early Bronze Age.

The Later Neolithic and Early Bronze Age use of the enclosure: concluding comments

Although the monument shows no evidence of subsequent modification during the Later Neolithic and Beaker phases (contrasting with the lengthy sequence of re-working at enclosures such as Hambledon Hill (Mercer 1988)), it would have remained a prominent feature. We can speculate that it maintained a significance in the landscape, perhaps as a named or commonly recognised place. The outer ditch and bank constituted a sizeable earthwork that could not have been easily ignored, and whose significance was unlikely to have been lost on Later Neolithic communities who were themselves engaged in constructing earthwork, stone and timber enclosures (Whittle 1997a). It is visible from Later Neolithic monuments in the area, it can be seen from the interior of the Avebury henge and from the summit of Silbury Hill, and is 'framed' by part of the West Kennet Avenue as it approaches Avebury.

Activity of this period can be documented from the south slope of the hill outside the causewayed enclosure.

Whilst continued significance might be claimed on the basis of the physical recognisability of the site, any understanding of later activity should begin by taking account of the material recovered during excavation. The analyses presented above of the deposits in the upper secondary fills of Trench B clearly indicate the varied range of interpretations that can be placed on the later activity at the enclosure. Part of the problem is that interpretation is hindered by the poor survival of these later deposits. It is also complicated by the fact that activity and meanings probably changed over the third and early second millennia BC, and the significance that the enclosure may have held during the Early Bronze Age, when the round barrow cemetery was established on the hill, was probably rather different to that during the Later Neolithic.

Continuity of activity and significance from the Earlier Neolithic to the Early Bronze Age can certainly be ruled out; though there are instances of seemingly carefully deposited bone groups, such as that in Trench C of the outer ditch, which date to the early third millennium BC. Here we may need to stand back from the detail. Regardless of how it entered the ditches and any degree of intentional symbolism that this may have held, much of the later material from the enclosure was probably generated through occupation events. The range of pottery, worked stone, flint implements and debitage would accord well with this. However, we must not fall into a trap of functionalist logic in which the identification of Later Neolithic and Bronze Age settlement is equated with a lapse of sanctity, whereas the only proof of continued significance is seen to reside in the identification of continued 'ritual' practice. After all, the primary use of the enclosure might have included occupation by people at least some of the time. The significance of occupation should not be underplayed. Factors other than simple resource availability were important in decisions which prehistoric communities made about how to occupy the landscape, and the associations that a place may have held seem at times to have played a key role in the choice to settle there (Pollard 1999; in press). To judge from the ceramic and lithic record (chapters 13 and 14) Windmill Hill witnessed repeated, though probably not continuous, activity from the fourth to the early second millennium BC. This in itself is something rather exceptional in the local record (perhaps only matched on Overton Hill). It is evidence that people were repeatedly drawn back to the hill, probably because of the associations the enclosure continued to hold. It is probably not going too far to suggest that the monument established a tradition of gathering and shared value that was periodically invoked by occupation. In this way repeated occupation at the enclosure can best be understood as one way in which the past was respected, remembered and continually brought to the fore.

18

The Harmony of Symbols: Wider Meanings

Alasdair Whittle and Joshua Pollard

Kinds of meaning

At the Windmill Hill enclosure people celebrated fundamental, shared aspects of their way of life, in a created space which facilitated participation. The enclosure was, in that sense, a harmony of symbols. Its wider meanings, however, were probably many, and perhaps endless. This final chapter attempts to review some of the potential range of wider meanings, without claiming to understand or to have grasped them all. The aim here is deliberately to focus on the evidence from this one monument, with some reference to the local context, but without much discussion of the wider worlds to which it belonged.

Windmill Hill was a monumental creation. The people involved in its planning and construction, and their descendants or successors, continued to come to it to carry out various activities, not least depositing animal bone and other items in the ditches of the enclosure. There must therefore have been a direct kind of significance for the site, one that might have been on the one hand directly felt and on the other taken for granted in the process of participation. The bringing together of people at intervals, in smaller or larger groups, has long been recognised as important (e.g. Piggott 1954; Smith 1965a), and this can be emphasised in the light of the local and regional settlement evidence noted in the previous chapter. As well as serving social needs among a scattered population, such periodic comings together could also have had very specific reasons, which we explore again towards the end of this chapter.

Windmill Hill and the activities represented at it also stood for many things. The distinction has often been made between metaphor and metonymy, between arbitrarily associated symbol and part standing for the whole (e.g. E. Leach 1976; Moore 1986; Hodder 1988; Tilley 1996; 1999). The enclosure may be thought of as a complex set of both metaphoric and metonymic meanings. Some aspects of the site may have acted in both ways, although it is also possible that metaphor and metonym were on occasion in some sense opposed; the distinction has been made between the very different kinds of thought which they may represent (e.g. Lakoff and Johnson 1980; Lakoff 1987). Whether or not such a distinction can be applied to the Neolithic, it is likely that different meanings were ascribed by different people. We have already resisted the notion of the enclosure as a kind of set text, or as a set of encoded, fixed messages, though we will go on to suggest that there are recurrent patterns to the use of the different parts of the enclosure. Meanings were created, remembered, re-worked, perhaps contested, and kept alive but also altered by repetition.

The enclosure therefore might have had one set of direct meanings: it was *that* place at *that* time where *those* people built and gathered. It might have been involved with very specific kinds of rites. Some or much of what was done there might not have been thought about consciously, being perhaps experienced 'affectively' (cf. Bloch 1995c; Roscoe 1995), or may not have been thought about separately from the routines of everyday life; in the general absence of other occupation or settlement evidence from the region, such comparisons are notoriously difficult. However, particular things that were built or dug, or were eaten or otherwise consumed, middened, stored and deposited, may also have stood metonymically for larger wholes, and metaphorically for larger ideas. The activities at the enclosure may also have stood metonymically and metaphorically for other dimensions of Neolithic life. And the site as a whole may have stood for, in the sense of being one arena where they were played out, experienced and commemorated, a set of ideas and values fundamental to the people involved.

It is difficult to keep these categories of meaning separate, and our argument here is that it is not in the end profitable to try.

Times

The Windmill Hill enclosure is imbued with references to the past. The general form of the enclosure can plausibly

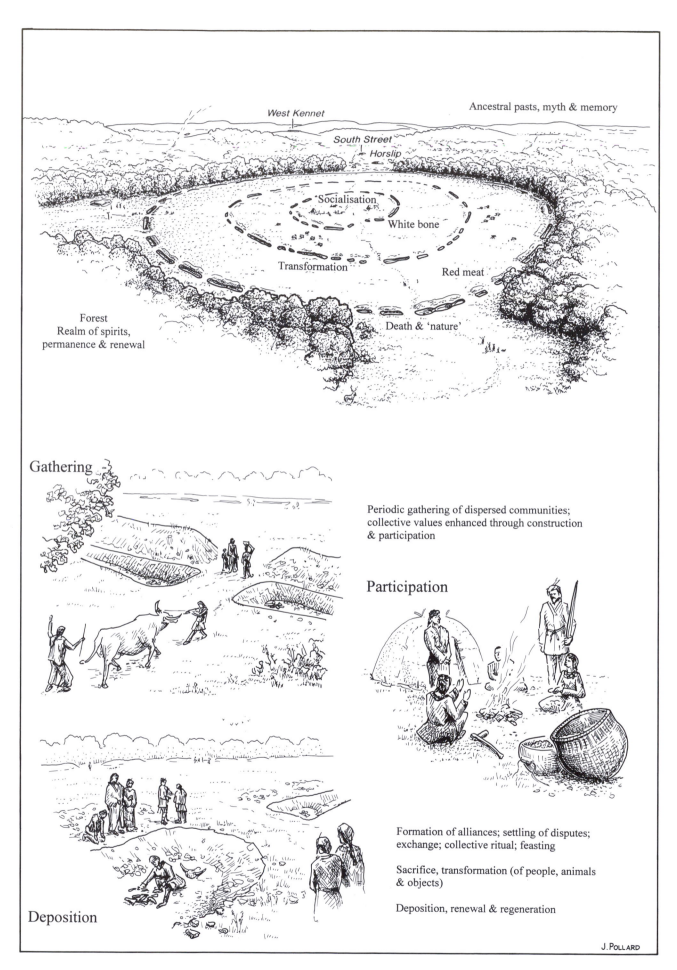

Labels within the figure:

West Kennet

Ancestral pasts, myth & memory

South Street

Horslip

'Socialisation'

White bone

Transformation

Red meat

Forest
Realm of spirits,
permanence & renewal

Death & 'nature'

Gathering

Periodic gathering of dispersed communities;
collective values enhanced through construction
& participation

Participation

Formation of alliances; settling of disputes;
exchange; collective ritual; feasting

Sacrifice, transformation (of people, animals
& objects)

Deposition, renewal & regeneration

Deposition

J. POLLARD

*Fig. 227. Simplified interpretation of the setting, major activities and possible meanings of the enclosure.
Drawing by Joshua Pollard.*

be seen as in some way evoking and drawing upon memory of earlier enclosures in continental Europe, going back through the Rössen, *Stichbandkeramik* and Lengyel traditions of the fifth millennium BC to the *Linienbandkeramik* or LBK culture of the later sixth millennium BC (see Whittle 1996; Jeunesse 1996; Andersen 1997). The idea of ditched enclosure may have begun as some kind of formalisation of shared or communal space between LBK longhouses (Bradley 1996), and *Stichbandkeramik* and Lengyel enclosures enhanced the formal distinctions between inside and outside, and between ritual and mundane. How such a tradition was maintained and transmitted is quite another matter, though the issue is important, not least because neither Windmill Hill nor other southern British causewayed enclosures belong obviously to the very beginning of the British Neolithic sequence. Not only was the form of site a kind of distant or ancient memory, but that remembrance (cf. Connerton 1989) had its own special time for appropriate enactment or re-enactment.

Other possibilities should also be considered, such as of referring the general form of enclosures to the layout of camps or other occupations, to the general form of clearances, and to activities such as practical enclosures around plots (e.g. C. Evans 1988a, 93; Pryor 1988a). The idea that enclosures such as Windmill Hill re-worked and monumentalised the fact of woodland clearing and clearance is particularly attractive, and a sense of time need not be detached from this domain (fig. 227). In a southern British context, however, this representation does not adequately explain the widespread distribution of similar interrupted ditched enclosures in western Europe as a whole in the fourth millennium BC. It has been plausibly suggested that, just as long barrows played on a memory of vanished timber longhouses, so British and other enclosures evoked an 'ideal community of the past', 'mythical settlement', and 'a fusion of history and myth' (Bradley 1998, 49, 68, 81–82). A sense of deep time was fundamental.

The act of creating the enclosure was part of an already established though hardly fixed tradition of using the hill, for various activities which may have been changed through time to an eventual emphasis on deposition and the dead. The act of enclosure itself may have taken time, not only in the suggested succession from inner and middle circuits to the addition of the outer, but in the laying out and digging of individual circuits. The use of the enclosure involved repetition, harking back to the past, often with imperfect memory of what had gone before, and renewal. Unlike some other causewayed enclosures (Smith 1971; Edmonds 1993), the ditches of Windmill Hill seem to have been recut only occasionally; instead it has been suggested above that bone and other deposits often marked a reinstatement of the major boundaries and divisions within the enclosure. The difficulties encountered in trying rigidly to define or categorise the bone deposits, discussed at length in chapters 11 and 17, underline the imperfections of memory and the scope for invention.

In addition, things deposited had their own histories and associations (cf. Lucas 1997). Some bones, charred plant remains in ash and sherds may have been put straight into the ditches as metonyms of meals, feasts or other gatherings. Much may have been first stored or middened on the site or elsewhere, and the significance of subsequent selection and deposition then drew in part on a sense of the past. The timescales of such use must have been very varied. But through such depositions, the enclosure as a whole became a metaphor for time, within which we might specify the unbroken link between past and present, and the cyclicity of time. In this perspective, it is perhaps no accident that such a site should have emerged after several generations of Neolithic life.

The rhythms of enclosure use, whether regular, episodic or erratic, created another sense of time. Against this are to be set the times of individual occupations from which people came. Their transitory nature must have contrasted with the sense of permanence embodied in the earthworks of the enclosure.

Place

The place of Windmill Hill may have first achieved significance as an intersection of paths, a vantage point, or as a feature to look at. It seems not to have had significance in the Mesolithic. It does not appear to have particular advantages as a locus for occupation, residence or subsistence routines (and does appear to have disadvantages including a lack of water). It began to acquire significance in a landscape in which looking out and looking at were important (cf. Tilley 1994). Windmill Hill offered views in all directions, including over the sites of long barrows and chambered tombs (several at least of which were older than the enclosure), and it can be seen widely from the locality. Though the more rather than less wooded setting may have partly concealed the site, or the details of the site from any distance, the place chosen was perhaps one of the most visible, though not necessarily the most prominent, in the whole region.

The significance of the site undoubtedly rested on more than just its visibility. Pre-enclosure activity, some of which can be characterised as occupation, some of it to do with mortuary ritual and perhaps ancestral veneration, marked the hill as 'a place' a generation or more before. As the tradition of the enclosure grew, it became not just a pre-eminent place, but one with considerable quantities of material and therefore history stored in it. Gatherings continued to take place at it, probably with greater frequency and in larger numbers than at other local enclosures like Knap Hill or Rybury; each gathering presumably helped to enhance the special character of the place, since people kept on returning to it. At one level, it may have been regarded metonymically as an especially significant part of the seasonal, annual and lifetime occupation or settlement ranges of those who used it, and at another level it may have come to stand metaphorically for their existence as a whole: always there, rooted in one place, not permanently occupied but open to access in the appropriate conditions and at the right times. And perhaps the idea of the enclosure travelled widely in people's minds.

Building and setting

The building and use of the enclosure could have set up other metaphoric and metonymic meanings.

As often observed (e.g. Fleming 1973; Startin and Bradley 1981, 293), segmentation of the ditches can be seen to stand for the participation of smaller social groups within the larger body or community involved in the construction of the site. The ditch segment is a metonym of independence and autonomy within a wider community, and the layout of the whole is a metaphor for participation and intense social interaction. The layout of the ditches served to demarcate space within the arena of the enclosure. It may also have served to create a sense of inclusion and exclusion. The boundaries of such an enclosure were permeable, with multiple points of access through the notional perimeters of the site.

The circular form of the enclosure could have stood or come to stand as a metaphor for ideas of cyclical return and symbolic renewal (cf. Eliade 1965). Its circularity contrasts with the linear format of contemporary barrows; monuments that embodied ideas of process and directed transition, to judge from mortuary practices concerned with the wholesale transformation of the human body.

The scale of the Windmill Hill enclosure also represents what has been called 'a monumental intervention in nature' (Hodder 1990, 260). It might be seen as standing for control over nature and the wild, but there may also have been much ambiguity in such a relationship. It may well be a modern construct rigidly to separate nature and culture (e.g. Ingold 1996), and any distinction between the two categories may anyway be relational rather than opposed. The enclosure was in a wooded or scrub setting (admittedly altered), and its users in their daily lives drew upon the natural surroundings and resources including animals, which probably moved widely through woodland from season to season and from year to year. Rather than merely a symbol of control, the enclosure might better be regarded as a symbol of concern for the relationship between people and their natural surroundings.

The enclosure's position within woodland may be significant in itself. Many contemporary enclosures were constructed in similar ecological settings (Evans *et al.* 1988), contrasting with that of funerary monuments, frequently sited in clearings or on their edges (Whittle *et al.* 1993). It has been argued that the socially dangerous nature of activities carried out at enclosures (exchange, deposition and dealings with the dead) explains their position in woodland, away from areas of contemporary settlement (Sharples 1991; Thomas 1991, 35). Such an interpretation may reflect our own values regarding marginality and

landscape rather than those of Neolithic communities. We should seek in addition to ask what woodland *meant* to those who constructed and used the enclosure.

The process of living within a heavily wooded landscape, its encounter, and movement within it, cannot be reduced to the status of a passive 'ecological backdrop'. As an all-pervasive feature, forest or woodland must have held a central position within the concerns, myths, classifications and values of these communities, as something to live within and think through. Perhaps we should think in terms of a Neolithic woodland ontology and ethos, such as is evident in ethnographic accounts of shifting cultivators (for example the wild and independent values of Finnish backwoods settlers in Midland America (Jordan and Kaups 1989)). Admittedly, the ethnographic record illustrates very varied attitudes to forest. As examples, the Dogon perception of the bush as the source of knowledge, power and life, 'the *fons et origo* of everything that makes life possible' (van Beck and Banga 1992, 67), can be contrasted with more complacent or antagonistic attitudes to forest described as existing amongst the Zafimaniry of Madagascar (Bloch 1995a). The perception of forest and bush is often one of ambiguity, in that it can be understood as harbouring sources of both danger (real and symbolic) and beneficial potency (Croll and Parkin 1992, 18; cf. Morris 1995, on rural Malawi).

We might see woodland or forest in the Earlier Neolithic as having associations with durability, life essences, and the immutable realm of ancestors and various other spiritual powers. (We also offer below further reflections on the connection of woodland to issues of gender; and see also chapter 8.) This might be witnessed in the cultural use of constituent elements of woodland, particularly timber. In part following Bloch (1995b), the use of massive timber in contemporary mortuary monuments (cf. Kinnes 1992) can be suggested to have been tied to its qualities of durability and fertility, metaphoric analogy perhaps being drawn between it and the 'hard' ancestral bones (another source of fertility) which the wooden chambers of these monuments enclosed. The distinction may be one between the transient nature of human worldly existence associated with clearings and temporary occupations, and the more permanent realm of ancestors and other spirits seen as residing within a life-giving, if potentially dangerous, woodland. The setting of Windmill Hill drew together, mediated and celebrated these intertwined realms of existence.

Gathering, feasting and depositing

People came to the enclosure probably at varying intervals and in varying numbers. They brought with them a very wide range of things, from pots and axes (or the remains of these) to live animals and perhaps old bones. It is hard to think of a dimension of the Earlier Neolithic way of life in the region which is not made present at the enclosure, in strong contrast to the much more specialised and restricted presences at ancestral shrines and ossuaries (long barrows and chambered tombs). The enclosure therefore can be seen as a kind of presentation or representation of social existence, and of its practical routines and recurrent subsistence concerns; it is in part to do with the routine materiality of Neolithic existence, and with the keeping of cattle. It is unlikely, however, that it actually maps or mirrors the daily ethnography of Neolithic life. The materials and symbols chosen for presentation were media through which central images, concepts and values were played out. An enclosure of this kind helps to create the way of life and value system as much as it reflects it. The site can be seen as in part a symbol of success, of subsistence prowess, in which there may well have been an element of competition and emulation. The display of abundance may also have expressed concerns about the risk of failure.

The enclosure was also to do with food and drink. Windmill Hill was a place where things were consumed, and where already consumed things (some perhaps long stored) were deposited and referred to. The bones of animals, sherds of pots and ash deposits containing charred plant food remains seem to stand metonymically for meals and feasts, for eating and drinking. Plants, especially cereals, may have stood for new ways of doing things, underlining distinctions between wild and tame and representing a cycle of growth, death and regeneration. Parts of stone and flint axes (though these are not a prominent feature of the primary phase of the site) may stand for exchange and alliance. All of these in turn perhaps stand for broader concepts of sharing, hospitality, generosity and sacrifice.

We have already hinted that the treatment of animal bone mimics or echoes that of human bone in ancestral shrines and ossuaries. Animal bone itself may have stood as a metaphor for human existence, though the association can hardly be considered arbitrary. Neolithic people were closely bound up with their animals and probably moved with them through their lives. It is likely that both the birth and death of each animal would have been observed and noted, just as would be the case for each human. The consumption, storage and careful placing, as well as the deliberate mixing, of animal bone may have acted as a metaphor for the life cycle.

It is possible that people drew symbolically on other features of cattle in choosing to present them so prominently in the enclosure: their size, strength and independence, allied to their potential malleability; their mobility; their fertility (cf. Tilley 1996); and the abundance of meat which the sacrifice of even one life would have provided (and see below). For all the density of bone around the enclosure circuits, there is an impression that particular deposits draw on only a few animals at a time. There is nothing like the potential slaughter perhaps represented in the Later Neolithic deposits of pig at the West Kennet palisade enclosures (Whittle 1997a) or the Beaker horizon deposit of cattle remains at the Irthlingborough barrow (Davis and Payne 1993).

One analogy offers suggestive (though incomplete) echoes of the varied roles and valuations potentially placed upon cattle. Among the Himba of Namibia, cattle in one category are of little symbolic importance, though they are necessary for ritual and for the generation of wealth. Cattle of the opposing category have great symbolic value, by contrast, but are not often used for ritual or political gain. The difference is to do with concepts of time. 'Cattle relationships symbolizing aspects of a perceived stable, timeless, encompassing reality are symbolically superior to cattle relationships reflecting the temporal, unstable and encompassed aspects of human life' (Crandall 1998, 102). The argument in the analysis of Windmill Hill has obviously been rather simpler. In what ways could we look for variation among Neolithic cattle roles in the future? The occasional presence of cattle remains in direct association with the human dead, or with shrines and ossuaries, may provide one potential insight. It could be significant that the pre-bank burial in Trench BB was *not* associated with cattle. Locally at Beckhampton Road long barrow there were three axially placed cattle skulls on the surface beneath the long mound, an association repeated also at Fussell's Lodge long barrow further south, though different in detail (Ashbee *et al.* 1979; Ashbee 1966). The link in the Neolithic context, compared to that of the Himba, might be with body part. The interest in the human skull evident in both the placings at and probable removals from shrines and ossuaries may find some sort of equivalence in significance given to the cattle skull. Prominent examples from the 1988 excavations again include deposit 117 in the outer ditch in Trench A, and the primary deposits in the middle ditch in Trench D.

The human dead made present at the enclosure may likewise have had varied meanings. Child or infant burials may have stood for ideas of renewal or rebirth. The partial remains of adults, and sometimes also of children, may be referred to the wider pattern of the treatment of the dead, which in part involved long processes of transformation and circulation (e.g. Thomas and Whittle 1986; Thomas 1991; Whittle 1991; Lucas 1997). Such material as a whole may also have stood in general not only for the past but for the ancestors and the idea of ancestry as part of the ordered nature of the Neolithic cosmos. But while this theme is certainly visible at the enclosure (in the 1988 excavations most strikingly perhaps in the deposit 117 in the outer ditch in Trench A), it is far from overwhelming. The contrast may be instructive. At the enclosure the dominant emphasis was on life.

Central concepts

So far, we have dealt with varied meanings of different kinds. There has been no attempt to keep such meanings rigidly apart, but the account has been in part a linear one. The recurrences and overlaps now need to be emphasised. It has been suggested that many people do not think in a linear or mapped fashion, but around a series of connected nodes of consciousness, which are sometimes kept separate, and sometimes not, and which are not necessarily continuously contemplated in a conscious fashion (Bloch 1992a). This is a useful concept for thinking about the recurrences and overlaps in the symbolic schemes which were worked through at Windmill Hill, especially if it also avoids any idea of set text or fixed code.

The recurrent central concepts or 'base metaphors' are those of inclusion, transition, transformation, sociality, domesticity or domesticness, relationships with the natural world and especially with animals, the life cycle and its renewal through time. These are recurrent because they can be treated both metonymically and metaphorically and because they can be seen in more than one kind of representation.

Inclusion can be argued from the circular layout of the site, from the permeable boundaries of the site, and from the combinations and range of materials and things deposited in the ditches of the site. Transition is a feature of the layout of the site, of the potential movement through particular points of access and past emphasised features including the terminals of ditch segments. It is also potentially a major feature of the symbolic layering of the site, both as a whole seen from the outside as separate from daily life and within the enclosure. There was movement between different realms, between the spheres of the living and the dead, the socialised and unsocialised, the present and past, and the cultural and the natural. Transformation is everywhere: again in the layout of the site and its physical construction, in the creation of place, in the treatment of materials and residues including animal bone, especially in the play between red meat and white bone, and in their eventual depositions around the ditches. And many of the transformations are to do with inclusion.

Deposition was a constant though endlessly varying process of mediating with the world of spirits and powers (earthly and otherwise), and of bringing it into being. Much of the material entering the ditches had undergone various states of transformation before deposition. This transformation took a number of forms. Much of the bone was fully processed, broken, and had probably been sitting in middens or surface refuse spreads for some time prior to incorporation in the ditches. Other bone groups included parts of freshly butchered carcasses, though these are infrequent and largely limited to the middle and outer ditches. Pottery was almost invariably broken, and flint comprised debitage and utilised tools. Such transformations were important in their own right, ascribing an additional or 'collective' meaning to the individual constituents of the deposits, and could be regarded also as a re-working of the transient and mutable conditions of everyday existence (Pollard forthcoming).

The key to understanding the significance of these processes, and by extension the place of the deposits in the general scheme of things, is perhaps provided by the deliberate mimicking of treatment given to human and animal remains in some deposits (e.g. 117 in Trench A and

the primary levels of OD III). The idea of animal remains undergoing an equivalent, or comparable, process to that of human remains following death was perhaps being deliberately stressed. It is even possible to envisage the transformation and subsequent deposition of animal remains as a kind of three-stage ritual process; slaughter and butchery being equivalent to acts of separation, transformation through middening to a liminal stage, and final deposition to a process of reincorporation and resocialisation (cf. van Gennep 1960; and see further below). Seen in such light, the treatment of animal remains was little different in terms of the technology of process to that accorded human remains. Following ethnographic analogy with societies practising secondary burial, it is generally recognised that Earlier Neolithic mortuary ritual involved a complex process intended to transform the polluting and socially dangerous (fleshed) remains of the dead into a material form (dry bones) in which an essence of ancestral power and fertility was perceived to reside (van Gennep 1960). The source of fertility that human bone was perhaps seen to hold could have been considered critical in the whole process of social and human reproduction (Bloch and Parry 1982). Is it not possible that such beliefs held a more general currency, encompassing other elements of the natural and material world ? Again, we should recognise the historical specificity of the categorical distinctions we make between object (inanimate) and subject (animate, sentient) and the human world and that of animals. The accordance of proper treatment to animal remains, and even artefacts, may have been considered essential to maintain their continued reproduction.

Sociality is played out through the layout of the site and the conditions of its construction, through the patterns of exchange more or less evident in the origins of pottery and stone axes, and through the repetition of meals, feasts and gatherings. Domesticity or perhaps better 'domesticness' is made present by the range of materials used, by the incorporation of things like rubbers, querns and pounders, flint cores and waste, antler and bone tools, chalk objects, and charcoal-rich soil deposits containing plant remains, as well as of more common objects such as animal bones and sherds. Users of the site undoubtedly made use of wild plants and animals, but neither is emphasised, whereas domestic things and domesticated resources are. Within this orientation, the central relationship or the central concern is with animals. Does this on this occasion 'reflect' and celebrate the major emphasis of a new economy, or does it not rather through its very emphasis show a far from settled situation (cf. Thomas 1991, 28) ? If the latter, may the situation not betray an overwhelming and continuing need to come to terms with the domestication of animals, to assuage guilt perhaps over the probably changed relationship with animals compared to earlier hunter-gatherer existence (cf. Eliade 1960), and to honour animals as partners in a shared universe at the same time as consuming them (cf. Whittle 1996)?

Finally, it is the concerns of life and the life cycle rather than of death which are presented, worked and celebrated at the enclosure. There is an overwhelming sense of activity, admittedly at intervals, of people and animals coming, doing things, engaging with each other. Memories behind the site, and the histories of things used and deposited, drew the past into the present, and offered the cyclicity of time for contemplation.

The enclosure as map

There is variation in the presence and frequency of many aspects of deposition. Excavations at other enclosures such as Hambledon Hill and Etton have also shown variation across their space (Mercer 1988; Pryor 1987; 1988b). A tentative schema can be suggested for Windmill Hill, drawing on such variation (compare the earlier, rather more rigid, version in Whittle and Pollard 1998).

The pre-enclosure activity perhaps provided a sort of 'pre-text' for the enclosure, the enclosure from this perspective coming to be a formalisation of an already existing set of meanings and practices. Even the grading of space implied by the ditches and their different deposits may already have existed before its construction. The inner ditch cuts pits filled with material not dissimilar to the deposits in that ditch (mixtures of bone, flint, pottery and so forth), whereas the outer bank seals evidence of more overtly marginal and dangerous practices (dealings with death in the case of the pre-bank burial), again echoed in the unusual deposits later placed around the outer circuit of the enclosure.

The outer circuit presents the major boundary between outside and inside. It has the deepest and broadest ditch segments, and the only certain evidence for a bank (whether interrupted or continuous). The outer circuit can, however, hardly be seen as a barrier, and anyway runs off the higher ground on the west side of the hill (see chapter 2). In the outer ditch, the relative emphasis in deposition (see especially chapters 3, 4, and 17) is on articulated animal bone and on human remains, including those of infants. The densities of material are lower than in the other circuits, as though to some extent the symbolism of the outer circuit was sufficient largely to speak for itself. In the middle and inner ditches, the segments are shallower and narrower, the inner ones more so than the middle. While articulated bone groups occur in the middle circuit, there is a greater emphasis on worked and transformed bone, with also the most prominent and frequent bone deposits (see again chapter 17). It is possible that the area within or adjacent to the inner ditch was the locale for middens containing among other things animal bone, pottery and charcoal. There are more sherds and worked flints in the middle and inner ditches than in the outer.

It is as though a rather different set of concerns were being expressed in the outer circuit: with nature or the natural surroundings, with the dead, ancestors and the past, with animals in their own right and in relationship with people, and perhaps with the unsocialised or not fully socialised. If the surrounding woodland can be accepted as a realm of spirits, potential danger and ambiguity, it was perhaps no accident that remains of the dead were more frequently encountered in the outer circuit, closest to the woodland edges. In the middle and inner circuits, the principal concerns being expressed may have been domesticity or 'domesticness', socialisation, and the sphere of the living including their use of animals in meals, feasts and rituals.

If this can be accepted, there is an evident set of transitions as the participant approaches, enters and traverses the spaces of the enclosure. Visiting the heart of the enclosure involves a kind of Neolithic socialisation: leaving the natural surroundings to enter a constructed arena, and then passing from and through time past to the spheres of the living in the present, with its intense participatory ceremonialism which in turn drew on histories of gatherings and material things.

The difficulty with such a model is that it may present too static a view of what must have been a whole succession of events, happening at intervals, perhaps irregular. Perhaps it does not take adequate account, at least for the early history of the enclosure, of the possibility that the outer circuit began later than the middle and inner ones. It may presuppose too map-like a view of the enclosure, and perhaps more seriously a prescribed set of rules for what went where. Despite these difficulties it is still plausible that there was a general sense of appropriate action in agreed places. This may not have been determined from the outset, and could itself have been the outcome of a long, active and inventive tradition of use. The depositional pattern was perhaps something achieved by repeated practice, depending on remembrance of past practice (cf. Barth 1987; Connerton 1989), improvisation and innovation, rather than predetermined in detail. The differences are at least as important as the linking patterns. That 'complicated relationship between tradition and invention' (Bradley 1998, 73) is evident not only in the diversity of practice from enclosure to enclosure, but within individual enclosures as well.

Participants and audiences

Another weakness of the spatial map offered above is that it takes participants and audiences for granted. We have said almost nothing so far about the identity, composition, residence, numbers and gender of users of the enclosure, apart from some references to age. There is no way of knowing how many people built the enclosure. Either rather small groups working their way through the construction of segment after segment or an altogether larger and quicker affair can be considered. Nor does the number of constructors in itself reveal their normal place or sphere of residence.

We have said little about the size of audiences for any one gathering or act of deposition. Individual depositions detailed in chapters 3 and 4 (see also 11 and 17) might suggest small audiences, but it would also be possible for surprisingly large numbers of people directly to witness activity in individual ditch segments, from tens to low hundreds in the case of larger segments.

We are able to say that the primary use of the enclosure must have encompassed at least a few generations. Our intuition is that this span was matched by a breadth of involvement at any one time, engaging a lot of people from far and wide both in the construction (or constructions) of the enclosure and in its use. Our initial supposition is that distinction was made between participants only on the basis of age, with only the young separated as not fully socialised (but still with an important symbolic role). The danger of circular argument is obvious, but the lack of obvious or overt distinction between male and female could be taken as a further sign of the inclusivity of the enclosure.

We have talked a lot about people, but have not found specific clues to gender. What if – to be simplistic – such an enclosure were fundamentally female space, opposed say to a male concern with descent and ancestry expressed at shrines and other monuments, or if the inner space of the enclosure were a female domain separated from an outer, male sphere? In either case, interpretation would be radically and fundamentally altered. It is possible that a much more sensitive reading of the evidence is needed. There may be more clues than evident at first sight. If axes and arrowheads could normally be to do with male identity (Edmonds and Thomas 1987), and pottery perhaps to do with female identity (cf. Haaland 1997), the recurrence of sherds of pottery and the relative rarity of both axes and arrowheads at the enclosure become significant. It has also been suggested above (chapter 8) that plant processing could have been a female domain. Who might have dealt with other activities and concerns, with animals, the shedding of their blood and their butchery, cooking meat and handling bones, for example, and why should we regard these as organised on lines of gender?

One way into this problem may be to combine presences, absences (cf. Hodder 1986) and analogies, though of course such attempts at gender ascription may be little more than an evocation of 'essentialist' views of what males and females did in the past (cf. Gilchrist 1991). There are other Neolithic contexts, including locally, where there is a much more overt concern with gender, for example in the placing of human remains within the chambers of the West Kennet long barrow (Thomas and Whittle 1986; Thomas 1991). There is an overt concern at Windmill Hill with the human young and generally, as argued on the basis of the cattle bones, with fertility. In some situations, not only is woodland potentially dangerous, as discussed above, but women and men have different roles in it. Clearance and cultivation can be seen as social performances within a cycle of history (M. Leach 1992; cf. J. Moore 1997). Men and women may have been involved in varying ways in these cycles: by analogy with the Mende of Sierra Leone, men clearing in the short term, herding, and hunting, and women tending and consolidating over a longer term (M. Leach 1992, 87; cf. Hurcombe 1997). In rural Malawi, men as affines, woodland, wild animals and the spirits of the dead are associated at one level, in some sort of opposition to consanguineal women in the villages, but men were also directly involved with clearance and cultivation (Morris 1995). There was potentially much to negotiate in the Neolithic context. Enclosures set in clearances may have reproduced or played out a version of what went on in actual clearances. Did in a sense men bring meat to women, while women provided continuity, both roles and attendant tensions being submerged in the ritual acceptance of fusion? Did the social experimentation with the novelty of cultivation and other new subsistence practices (see chapters 8, 11 and 17) reach some sort of point of tension by the later part of the Earlier Neolithic, as new roles were in the process of becoming more fixed? The 'ideal community of the past' discussed above might also after all have been in some ways an ideal version of the present.

Special roles?: contestation, rites of passage and sacrifice

The Windmill Hill enclosure was a special arena, to which people returned time and time again, over a comparatively short timescale, and the acts performed there presumably had a powerful effect. We have suggested many general spheres of concern, and multiple possible meanings of different kinds. We have discussed possible numbers, identities and genders of participants. At its most general level of significance, the activity at the enclosure seems to be to do with commemoration, the establishment of place, the cyclicity of time, and inclusion or inclusivity, perhaps something akin to the *communitas* seen to be generated through ritual participation (Turner 1969).

These are all still very general explanations. Could there be a more specific characterisation of what took place at the enclosure? At least three possibilities (not necessarily mutually exclusive) can be considered: contestation and competition through 'tournaments of value', rites of passage, and sacrifice.

Going on all those elements which seem to emphasise inclusion, and drawing on the notion of ritual *communitas*, the argument so far has been for a 'harmony of symbols'. Others may wish to contest this. Feasts, for example, are often associated with competition and wasteful consumption (Hayden and Gargett 1990; Hayden 1995; Sherratt 1991). There may have been rivalry in the many activities represented at the enclosure (apart from possible gender tensions), and the enclosure itself could be seen at a broader spatial scale as a claim by particular groups to regional pre-eminence. This could be seen as part of the establishment of 'dominant locales', the acquisition of 'a pivotal position in the negotiation of contemporary power relations' (Edmonds 1993, 126 and 131). One of the ways in which this is achieved might be through 'tournaments of value' (Edmonds 1993; Appadurai 1986). These are episodic, non-routine events, open to those in power and a focus of status competition between them. 'What is at issue in such tournaments is not just status, rank, fame or the reputations of actors, but the disposition of the central tokens of value in the society in question' (Appadurai 1986, 21, and quoted in Edmonds 1993).

It is perhaps naive to expect that everything within the enclosure was done in perfect harmony, but one of the most telling arguments against such a model of contestation is the lack of identifiable change through time. Deposits can be quite varied, as emphasised many times above, but there is no impression of progressive emulation of successive deposits, no increase in the range or quantities of material deposited. Using such a model demands the *a priori* assumption of positions of power and of differentiations in rank and status, which find no separate support in the evidence. Rather, the challenge may be to attempt to capture the 'complexity and fluidity' of shifting and dynamic local traditions (Edmonds 1998, 252), 'the ways in which ranking or renown shifts back and forth from year to year and from generation to generation', and 'the ongoing reproduction of various forms of affiliation which is absolutely funda-mental amongst relatively small, dispersed communities' (Mark Edmonds *pers. comm.*). But in this guise, a possible specific explanation of the enclosure tends to slip back into a more general one of concern with central social themes and negotiations, which the discussion so far has already covered.

'Rites of passage are rituals which mark the passing of one stage of life and entry into another', for example birth, initiation and death (Barnard and Spencer 1996). Three rites or phases are often distinguished (starting from van Gennep 1960): of separation, liminality and incorporation or re-aggregation. Such rites of passage may serve to negate the normal rules of society and its hierarchy and to 'emphasise the bonds between people which enable society to exist', which have also been subsumed in the concept of *communitas* (Barnard and Spencer 1996, 490; Turner 1969). Could the activities represented at Windmill Hill be of this character, as already hinted above?

There are some grounds for supposing so. The setting of the enclosure might be seen to imply separation, and the probable middening of feast and other remains (though it need not universally apply to all deposits) could also imply controlled separation from daily life. The layout of the enclosure could invoke liminality, a passing into and through different times and conceptual (as well as physical) spaces. Liminality often involves reversals of normal roles, which could help to explain the lack of clear clues to gender and age in the enclosure. The nature of deposits and the act of deposition itself could suggest incorporation and aggregation. This might give a useful gloss on the claims made earlier in this chapter for a general concern with cyclicity and time. It may give some further insight into a possible conceptual link between communal ritual as progressive process and human life as unfolding process. It may serve to make us think about

connections between spatially and temporally separated sets of rituals (cf. E. Leach 1976), such as life celebrations at enclosures and treatments of death at shrines and ossuaries.

Rites of passage and liminality introduce another possibility: a mythic dimension. Initiations are to do with acquiring knowledge of how the world is thought to work and how it came into being, knowledge that may only be passed on to selected people at selected times. Myth is important as a way in which people learn and tell stories about origins. There are two sorts of view of the role of myth. The dominant anthropological model has been that of myth as charter, as a retrospective justification of the *status quo*. The alternative is to challenge the view that reality precedes language, and to see myth as potentially subversive, as an endlessly open way of telling and re-telling the world into existence (Weiner 1996). We have so far treated the inferred meals and feasts that lie behind the varying depositions at Windmill Hill as if they were straightforward social encounters, their residues being subsequently reworked in conceptually important ways and standing for a series of ideas in the symbolic schemes of the users. What if meals, feasts and depositions were them-selves to do with mythic realms, varying re-enactments of the ancestors' first meal in some story of origin, for example, or instruction to the initiates of what happened in that first time? This would link with that other sense of the past brought to the enclosure by memory of its descent from an ideal past community.

We have argued above that there was a dominant emphasis at Windmill Hill on life and the life cycle, but in contradiction the use of the enclosure involved the killing and subsequent consumption of many animals. The num-bers killed over the generations of the primary use of the site must have run into thousands, though obviously such calculations should be hedged with caution and reservation (see chapter 11). Apart from the event (or events) of construction and the symbolism of the enclosure layout, the killing of animals and the consumption of their meat could be seen not only as *the* dominant features of the enclosure in use, but also *the* dominant feature commem-orated in deposition. The explanations canvassed above have tended to refer to 'standings for', to possible symbolic meanings. There is a danger that the significance of animals in themselves and of their killing, and therefore also of the meaning of their consumption through feasting, may be overlooked. This brings us to the use of animals as sacrifice (a theme which we pursue in greater depth elsewhere). Can celebration of life and the practice of sacrifice be reconciled?

Many anthropological (and other) studies have been made of sacrifice (Bloch 1992b; T. Gibson 1996). A dominant early model was of obligating the gods by giving gifts through sacrifice (Bloch 1992b, 28). Then came an important model, propounded by Hubert and Mauss and followed and refined by Evans-Pritchard (1956), of sacri-fice as communication, of establishing contact with the divine to obtain forgiveness of sins or to end unwanted contact with the supernatural; such rites of sacralisation involved crossing between the sacred and the profane (Bloch 1992b, 28). This in turn was criticised on the grounds that such a distinction between sacred and profane is not universal, and that the emphasis on personal guilt and redemption is too redolent of Christian belief; Nuer sacrifice for example can be seen as an attempt to restore cosmic order when that has been threatened or breached (Heusch 1985; T. Gibson 1996). One other alternative is to see sacrifice as a kind of 'rebounding violence', a conquest and consumption of animals and their vitality, enabling people to both transcend their daily lives and achieve transformation and yet retain their place in the normal scheme of things (Bloch 1992b, 5). In specific cases, the role of sacrifice may be to cure or to avert troubles, especially disease, as among the Dinka (Bloch 1992b, 31; Lienhardt 1961).

The further important insight is to reflect on what makes animals suitable for such a role (Bloch 1992b; T. Gibson 1996; Tilley 1996). Animals, especially cattle as already noted above, have strength, vitality, fertility and sexuality. Their herd behaviour perhaps generated a sense of natural social order, and their movements through woodland and other physical environments must have influenced and constrained, as well as have been guided by, the movement of people. Animals were part of the same world, and probably bound much closer to people conceptually and emotionally (cf. Tilley 1996, 184) than plants including cereals. They were a possible way of thinking about the world. At the same time, animals are different. They cannot speak and they can be guided and controlled. The Neolithic worldview may have been in part a complex combination of ambivalent partnerships and relationships made possible by domestication, which demanded to be made sense of. Animals were on the boundary between human and non-human worlds, offering complex possibilities of classification and communication. '...one might almost say that animal sacrifice is to the husbandry of domesticated animals as animal totemism is to the hunting of wild animals' (T. Gibson 1996, 499). New evidence from the LBK might add another dimension. To the discovery of a mass grave at Talheim, into which men, women and children had been dumped after being beaten about the head (Wahl and König 1987), can now be added other evidence of killings, with bodies either abandoned or carefully deposited in the ditches of LBK enclosures, at Asparn-Schletz and Herxheim (Windl 1996; Teschler-Nicola 1996; Häusser 1998). Could memory of the past have included remembrance of old killings, and could the killing of animals have come to be a substitute for or expiation of the killing of people?

Thinking about animals and their killing and consumption, in relation to the deposition of their remains, may open important new insights. It may generate a sense of the values and beliefs shaping Neolithic social relationships, and it may suggest a sense of complex conceptual oppositions and overlaps within such beliefs and values, between human and non-human (both divine and animal), permanence and movement, sharing and exploitation, partnership and guilt, action and speech, the present and memory. The list is a long one, and could be longer still. Perhaps we are beginning to retreat from the possible specific explanation that Windmill Hill was mainly to do with sacrifice as a form of negotiation with the divine in order to participate in the immortal. We offer no final conclusion, but are reluctant to close the list of possibilities.

Wider worlds

It has been customary at this point to compare the site and area in question with others near and far, but this is not attempted here. It has been done in various ways many times (e.g. Burgess *et al.* 1988; Thomas 1991; Edmonds 1993; Whittle 1996; Andersen 1997; J. Harding 1998; Barber *et al.* 1999). On the other hand, while final reports exist for some sites (e.g. Abingdon: Avery 1982; Staines: Robertson-Mackay 1987; Maiden Castle: Sharples 1991), at the time of writing these are still in preparation or in press for several others, including Crickley Hill, Hambledon Hill, Etton and Haddenham (cf. Dixon 1988; Mercer 1988; Pryor 1988b; 1999; C. Evans 1988b).

This report is already long enough. For the future there will be two tasks, to expand the amount of evidence, region by region, for early Neolithic activity other than represented at enclosures and other monuments, thus to broaden our sense of context (see here chapter 17), and to examine in detail the ways in which a shared general style of enclosure was compatible with very diverse use of the space thus created. It is unlikely that any other enclosure was or could have been quite like Windmill Hill.

Bibliography

Albarella, U. and Payne, S. (n.d.). *The pigs from Durrington Walls: a Neolithic database*. Unpublished ms, Environmental Archaeology Unit, University of Birmingham.

Albarella, U. and Serjeantson, D. forthcoming. A passion for pork: butchery and cooking at the British Neolithic site of Durrington Walls. In P. Miracle (ed.), *Consuming passions and patterns of consumption*. Cambridge: MacDonald Institute.

Allen, H. 1973. The Bagundji of the Darling Basin: cereal gatherers in an uncertain environment. *World Archaeology* 5, 309–19.

Allen, M. J. 1988. Archaeological and environmental aspects of colluviation in south-east England. In W. Groenman-van Waateringe and M. Robinson (eds), *Man-made soils*, 67–92. Oxford: British Archaeological Reports.

Allen, M. J. 1994. *The landuse history of the southern English chalklands with an evaluation of the Beaker period using environmental data: colluvial deposits as environmental and cultural indicators*. Unpublished PhD thesis, University of Southampton.

Ambers, J., Matthews, K. and Bowman, S. 1987. British Museum natural radiocarbon measurements 20. *Radiocarbon* 29, 177–96.

Ambers, J., Matthews, K. and Bowman, S. 1989. British Museum natural radiocarbon measurements XXI. *Radiocarbon* 31, 15–32.

Andersen, N.H. 1997. *The Sarup enclosures*. Moesgaard: Jutland Archaeological Society.

Annable, F. K. 1977. Pewsey, Blacknall field. *Archaeological excavations 1976*, 69. London: Department of the Environment.

Annable, F. K. and Simpson, D. D. A. 1964. *Guide catalogue to the Neolithic and Bronze Age collections in Devizes Museum*. Devizes: Wiltshire Archaeological and Natural History Society.

Appadurai, A. 1986. Introduction: commodities and the politics of value. In A. Appadurai (ed.), *The social life of things: commodities in cultural perspective*, 3–63. Cambridge: Cambridge University Press.

ApSimon, A. 1985. The Bronze Age pottery. In A. F. Taylor and P. J. Woodward, 'A Bronze Age barrow cemetery and associated settlement at Roxton, Bedfordshire'. *Archaeological Journal* 142, 117–20.

Armitage, P. L. and Clutton-Brock, J. 1976. A system for classification and description of the horncores of cattle from archaeological sites. *Journal of Archaeological Science* 3, 329–48.

Armour-Chelu, M. and Clutton-Brock J. 1985. Notes on the evidence for the use of draught animals at Etton. *Antiquaries Journal* 65, 297–302.

Armour-Chelu, M. 1992. *Vertebrate resource exploitation, ecology and taphonomy in Neolithic Britain, with special reference to the sites of the Links of Noltland, Etton and Maiden Castle*. Unpublished PhD thesis, Institute of Archaeology, London University.

Ashbee, P. 1966. The Fussell's Lodge long barrow excavations 1957. *Archaeologia* 100, 1–80.

Ashbee, P. 1984. *The earthen long barrow in Britain* (second edition). Norwich: Geo Books.

Ashbee, P. 1986. The excavation of Milton Lilbourne barrows 1–5. *Wiltshire Archaeological and Natural History Magazine* 80, 23–96.

Ashbee, P., Smith, I.F. and Evans, J.G. 1979. Excavation of three long barrows near Avebury, Wiltshire. *Proceedings of the Prehistoric Society* 45, 207–300.

Atkinson, R.J.C. 1953. *Field archaeology* (second edition). London: Methuen.

Atkinson, R.J.C., Piggott, S. and Saunders, N. K. 1951. *Excavations at Dorchester, Oxon*. Oxford: Ashmolean Museum.

Avery, B. W. 1990. *Soils of the British Isles*. Wallingford: CAB.

Avery, B. W. and Bascomb, C. L. 1974. *Soil Survey laboratory methods*. Harpendon: Soil Survey.

Avery M. 1982. The Neolithic causewayed enclosure, Abingdon. In H.J. Case and A.W.R. Whittle (eds), *Settlement patterns in the Oxford region: excavations at Abingdon causewayed enclosure and other sites*, 10–50. London: Council for British Archaeology.

Babel, U. 1975. Micromorphology of soil organic matter. In J. E. Giesking (ed.), *Soil components. Volume 1: organic components*, 369–473. New York: Springer.

Bal, L. 1982. *Zoological ripening of soils*. Wageningen: Pudoc Agricultural Research Reports.

Bakels, C. 1988. Hekelingen, a Neolithic site in the swamps of the Maas estuary. In U. Körbe Grohne, *Der prähistorische Mensch und seine Umwelt*, 112–34. Stuttgart: Theiss.

Bamford, H. M. 1982. *Beaker domestic sites on the fen edge of East Anglia*. East Anglian Archaeology 6.

Bamford, H. M. 1985. *Briar Hill excavation 1974–1987*. Northampton: Northampton Development Corporation.

Barber, M., Dyer, C. and Oswald, A. 1999. *The Neolithic causewayed enclosures of England*. London: RCHME.

Barclay, A., Bradley, R., Hey, G. and Lambrick, G. 1996. The earlier prehistory of the Oxford region in the light of recent research. *Oxoniensia* 61, 1–20.

Barclay, G. 1997. The Neolithic. In K.J. Edwards and I.A.B. Ralston (eds), *Scotland: environment and archaeology, 8000 BC–AD 1000*, 127–309. London: John Wiley and Sons.

Barker, C. 1985. The long mounds of the Avebury area. *Wiltshire Archaeological and Natural History Magazine* 79, 7–38.

Barker, G. 1983. The animal bones from Isbister. In J.W. Hedges (ed.), *Isbister: a chambered tomb in Orkney*, 133–50. Oxford: British Archaeological Reports.

Barker, H. and Mackey, J. 1961. British Museum natural radiocarbon measurements III. *Radiocarbon* 3, 39–45.

Barnard, A. and Spencer, J. 1996. Rites of passage. In A. Barnard and J. Spencer (eds), *Encyclopedia of social and cultural anthropology*, 489–90. London: Routledge.

Barrett, J. C. 1980. The pottery of the Later Bronze Age in lowland England. *Proceedings of the Prehistoric Society* 46, 297–319.

Barrett, J.C. 1994. *Fragments from antiquity*. Oxford: Blackwell.

Barrett, J. C., Bradley, R. and Green, M. 1991.*Landscape, monuments and society: the prehistory of Cranborne Chase*. Cambridge: Cambridge University Press.

Barrett, J. C., Bradley, R. and Hall, M. (eds) 1991. *Papers on the prehistoric archaeology of Cranborne Chase*. Oxford: Oxbow.

Barth, F. 1987. *Cosmologies in the making*. Cambridge: Cambridge University Press.

Bedwin, O. 1984. The excavation of a small hilltop enclosure on Court Hill, Singleton, West Sussex, 1982. *Sussex Archaeological Collections* 122, 13–22.

Becze-Déak, J., Langohr, R. and Verrechia, E.P. 1997. Small-scale secondary $CaCO_3$ accumulations in selected sections of the European loess belt: morphological forms and potential for palaeoenvironmental reconstruction. *Geoderma* 76, 221–52.

Bell, M.G. 1990. Sedimentation rates in the primary fills of chalk cut features. In M. Robinson (ed.), *Experiment and reconstruction in environmental archaeology*, 237–48. Oxford: Oxbow.

Bell, M., Fowler, P.J. and Hillson, S.W. (eds) 1996. *The experimental earthwork project, 1960–1992*. York: Council for British Archaeology.

Bender, B. 1978. Gatherer-hunter to farmer: a social perspective. *World Archaeology* 10, 204–22.

Berry, J. 1929. Belas Knap long barrow, Gloucestershire, report on the excavation of 1929. *Transactions of the Bristol and Gloucestershire Archaeological Society* 61, 294.

Binford, L.R. 1978. *Nunamiut ethnoarchaeology*. New York: Academic Press.

Binford, L.R. 1983a. *In pursuit of the past: decoding the archaeological record*. London: Thames and Hudson.

Binford, L. 1983b. *Working at archaeology*. New York: Academic Press.

Binford, L.R. and Bertram, J.B. 1977. Bone frequencies – and attritional processes. In L.R. Binford (ed.), *For theory building in archaeology*, 77–153. London: Academic Press.

Bloch, M. 1992a. What goes without saying: the conceptualization of Zafimaniry society. In A. Kuper (ed.), *Conceptualizing society*, 127–46. London: Routledge.

Bloch, M. 1992b. *Prey into hunter: the politics of religious experience*. Cambridge: Cambridge University Press.

Bloch, M. 1995a. People into places: Zafimaniry concepts of clarity. In E. Hirsch and M. O'Hanlon (eds), *The anthropology of landscape: perspectives on place and space*, 63–77. Oxford: Oxford University Press.

Bloch, M. 1995b. The resurrection of the house amongst the Zafimaniry of Madagascar. In J. Carsten and S. Hugh-Jones (eds), *About the house: Lévi-Strauss and beyond*, 69–83. Cambridge: Cambridge University Press.

Bloch, M. 1995c. Questions not to ask of Malagasy carvings. In I. Hodder, M. Shanks, A. Alexandri, V. Buchli, J. Carmen, J. Last and G. Lucas (eds), *Interpreting archaeology: finding meaning in the past*, 212–15. London: Routledge.

Bloch, M. and Parry, J. 1982. Introduction: death and the regeneration of life. In M. Bloch and J. Parry (eds), *Death and the regeneration of life*, 1–44. Cambridge: Cambridge University Press.

Boast, R. 1995. Fine pots, pure pots, Beaker pots. In I. Kinnes and G. Varndell (eds), *'Unbaked urns of rudely shape': essays on British and Irish pottery for Ian Longworth*, 69–80. Oxford: Oxbow.

Boast, R. 1997. A small company of actors: a critique of style. *Journal of Material Culture* 2, 173–98.

Boessneck, J. 1958. *Zur Entwicklung vor- und frühgeschichtliche Haus- und Wildtier Bayerns im Rahmen der gleichzeitigen Tierwelt Mitteleuropas*. Studien an vor- und frühgeschichtlichen Tierresten Bayerns. Munich: Institut für Palaeoanatomie, Domestikationsforschung und Geschichte der Tiermedizin der Universität München.

Boessneck, J. 1969. Osteological differences between sheep (*Ovis aries* Linné) and goats (*Capra hircus* Linné). In D. Brothwell and E.S. Higgs (eds), *Science in archaeology* (second edition), 331–58. London: Thames and Hudson.

Bogucki, P 1993. Animal traction and household economies in Neolithic Europe. *Antiquity* 67, 492–503.

Bökönyi, S. 1977. *Animal remains from the Kermanshah Valley, Iran*. Oxford: British Archaeological Reports.

Bowden, M. 1991. *Pitt Rivers*. Cambridge: Cambridge University Press.

Bowen, H. C. and Fowler, P. J. 1962. The archaeology of Fyfield and Overton Downs, Wilts (interim report). *Wiltshire Archaeological and Natural History Magazine* 58, 98–115.

Bowman, S. 1990. *Radiocarbon dating*. London: British Museum Press.

Bradley, R. 1984. *The social foundations of prehistoric Britain*. London: Longman.

Bradley, R. 1986. A reinterpretation of Abingdon causewayed enclosure. *Oxoniensia* 50/52, 183–87.

Bradley, R. 1987. Flint technology and the character of Neolithic settlement. In A.G. Brown and M.R. Edmonds (eds), *Lithic analysis and later British prehistory*, 181–86. Oxford: British Archaeological Reports.

Bradley, R. 1996. Long houses, long mounds and Neolithic enclosures. *Journal of Material Culture* 1, 239–56.

Bradley, R. 1998. *The significance of monuments: on the shaping of human experience in Neolithic and Bronze Age Europe*. London: Routledge.

Bradley, R. and Edmonds, M. 1993. *Interpreting the axe trade*. Cambridge: Cambridge University Press.

Bradley, R. and Ellison, A. 1974. *Rams Hill: a Bronze Age defended enclosure and its landscape*. Oxford: British Archaeological Reports.

Bradley, R. and Holgate, R. 1984. The Neolithic sequence in the Upper Thames valley. In R. Bradley and J. Gardiner (eds), *Neolithic studies*, 107–34. Oxford: British Archaeological Reports.

Brain, C. K. 1967. Hottentot food remains and their bearing on the interpretation of fossil bone assemblages. *Scientific Papers of the Namib Desert Research Institute* 32, 1–11.

Bronk, C. R. and Hedges, R. E. M. 1989. Use of the CO_2 source in radiocarbon dating by AMS. *Radiocarbon* 31, 298–304.

Bronk, C. R. and Hedges, R. E. M. 1990. A gaseous ion source for routine AMS radiocarbon dating. *Nuclear Instruments and Methods* B52, 322–26.

Bronk Ramsey, C. 1995. Radiocarbon calibration and the

analysis of stratigraphy: the OxCal program. *Radiocarbon* 37, 425–30.

Brothwell, D.R. 1973. The human biology of the Neolithic population of Britain. In I. Schwidetzky (ed.) *Die Anfänge des Neolithikums vom Orient bis Nordeuropa*, 280–99. Köln: Böhlau.

Brown, T. 1997. Clearances and clearings: deforestation in Mesolithic/Neolithic Britain. *Oxford Journal of Archaeology* 16, 133–46.

Brück, J. 1995. A place for the dead: the role of humans in Late Bronze Age Britain. *Proceedings of the Prehistoric Society* 61, 245–77.

Buitenhuis, H. 1985. Preliminary report on the faunal remains of Hayaz Hüyük from the 1979–1983 seasons. *Anatolica* 12, 61–74.

Bullock, P., Fedoroff, N., Jongerius, A. , Stoops, G. J. and Tursina, T. 1985. *Handbook for soil thin section description.* Wolverhampton: Waine Research Publishers.

Burgess, C. 1986. 'Urnes of no small variety': Collared Urns reviewed. *Proceedings of the Prehistoric Society* 52, 339–51.

Burgess, C., Topping, P., Mordant C. and Maddison M. (eds), 1988. *Enclosures and defences in the Neolithic of western Europe.* Oxford: British Archaeological Reports.

Burleigh, R. 1986. Radiocarbon dates for human and animal bones from the Mendip caves. *Proceedings of the University of Bristol Spelaeological Society* 17, 267–74.

Burleigh, R., Clutton-Brock, J., Felder, P.J. and Sieveking, G. de G. 1977. A further consideration of Neolithic dogs with special reference to a skeleton from Grime's Graves (Norfolk) England. *Journal of Archaeological Science* 1, 353–66.

Campbell, A. T. 1995. *Getting to know Waiwai: an Amazonian ethnography.* London: Routledge.

Carter, P.L. and Higgs, E.S. 1979. The animal remains [Beckhampton Road]. In P. Ashbee, I.F. Smith and J.G. Evans, 'Excavation of three long barrows, near Avebury, Wiltshire'. *Proceedings of the Prehistoric Society* 45, 248–50.

Carter, S. P. 1990. The stratification and taphonomy of shells in calcareous soils: implications for land snail analysis in archaeology. *Journal of Archaeological Science* 17, 495–507.

Case, H.J. 1973. A ritual site in north-east Ireland. In G. Daniel and P. Kjaerum (eds), *Megalithic graves and ritual*, 173–96. Kobenhavn: Jutland Archaeological Society.

Case, H. J. 1977. The Beaker culture in Britain and Ireland. In R. Mercer (ed.), *Beakers in Britain and Ireland*, 71–101. Oxford: British Archaeological Reports.

Case, H.J. 1995. Beakers: loosening a stereotype. In I. Kinnes and G. Varndell (eds), *'Unbaked urns of rudely shape': essays on British and Irish pottery for Ian Longworth*, 55–67. Oxford: Oxbow.

Case, H.J. and Whittle, A.W.R. (eds) 1982. *Settlement patterns in the Oxford region: excavations at Abingdon causewayed enclosure and other sites.* London: Council for British Archaeology.

Chapman, J. 1997. Changing gender relations in the later prehistory of Eastern Hungary. In J. Moore and E. Scott (eds), *Invisible people and processes: writing gender and childhood into European archaeology*, 131–49. Leicester: Leicester University Press.

Christie, P. M. 1967. A barrow cemetery of the second millennium BC in Wiltshire, England: excavation of a round barrow, Amesbury G71 on Earl's Farm Down, Wiltshire. *Proceedings of the Prehistoric Society* 33, 336–66.

Clark, A. J. 1996. *Seeing beneath the soil* (second edition). London: Batsford.

Clark, G. and Yi, S. 1983. Niche-width variation in Cantabrian archaeofaunas: a diachronic study. In J. Clutton-Brock and C. Grigson (eds), *Animals and archaeology: 1. Hunters and their prey*, 183–208. Oxford: British Archaeological Reports.

Clark, J.G.D. 1932. The date of the plano-convex flint knife in England and Wales. *Antiquaries Journal* 12, 158–62.

Clark, J.G.D. 1934. Derivative forms of the petit tranchet in Britain. *Archaeological Journal* 91, 32–58.

Clark, J.G.D., Higgs, E.S. and Longworth, I.H. 1960. Excavations at the Neolithic site at Hurst Fen, Mildenhall, Suffolk, 1954, 1957 and 1958. *Proceedings of the Prehistoric Society* 26, 202–45.

Clark, K.M. 1996. Neolithic dogs: a reappraisal based on evidence from the remains of a large canid deposited in a ritual feature. *International Journal of Osteoarchaeology* 6, 211–19.

Clarke, D. L. 1970. *Beaker pottery of Great Britain and Ireland.* Cambridge: Cambridge University Press.

Clarke, D.L. 1972. A provisional model of an Iron Age society and its settlement system. In D.L. Clarke (ed.), *Models in archaeology*, 801–69. London: Methuen.

Cleal, R. 1991a. Cranborne Chase – the earlier prehistoric pottery. In J. C. Barrett, R. Bradley, and M. Hall, *Papers on the prehistoric archaeology of Cranborne Chase*, 134–200. Oxford: Oxbow.

Cleal, R. 1991b. Earlier prehistoric pottery. In N. M. Sharples, *Maiden Castle: excavation and field survey 1985–6*, 171–85, fiche M9, A1–E4. London: English Heritage.

Cleal, R. 1992a. The Neolithic and Beaker pottery. In C. Gingell, *The Marlborough Downs: a Later Bronze Age landscape and its origins*, 61–71. Devizes: Wiltshire Archaeological and Natural History Society.

Cleal, R. 1992b. Summary. In C. Gingell, *The Marlborough Downs: a Later Bronze Age landscape and its origins*, 151–53. Devizes: Wiltshire Archaeological and Natural History Society.

Cleal, R. 1992c. Significant form: ceramic styles in the Earlier Neolithic of southern England. In N. Sharples and A. Sheridan (eds), *Vessels for the ancestors*, 286–304. Edinburgh: Edinburgh University Press.

Cleal, R.M.J. and Allen, M.E. 1994. Investigation of tree-damaged barrows on King Barrow Ridge and Luxenborough Plantation, Amesbury. *Wiltshire Archaeological and Natural History Magazine* 87, 54–84.

Cleal, R., Cooper, J. and Williams, D. 1994. Shells and sherds: identification of inclusions in Grooved Ware, with associated radiocarbon dates, from Amesbury, Wiltshire. *Proceedings of the Prehistoric Society* 60, 445–48.

Cleal, R. and Gingell, C. 1992. Discussion. In C. Gingell, *The Marlborough Downs: a Later Bronze Age landscape and its origins*, 99–103. Devizes: Wiltshire Archaeological and Natural History Society.

Cleal, R.M.J., Walker, K.E. and Montague, R. 1995. *Stonehenge in its landscape: twentieth-century excavations.* London: English Heritage.

Clutton-Brock, J. 1981. *Domesticated animals from early times.* London: Heinemann and British Museum (Natural History).

Clutton-Brock, J. 1984. *Neolithic antler picks from Grimes Graves, Norfolk and Durrington Walls, Wiltshire. A biometrical analysis.* London: British Museum (Natural History).

Clutton-Brock, J. 1986. New dates for old animals: the reindeer, the aurochs, and the wild horse in prehistoric Britain. *Archaeozoologia Mélanges*, 111–17.

Clutton-Brock, J. 1992. *Horse power.* London: Natural History Museum Publications.

Clutton-Brock, J. and Burleigh, R. 1991a. The mandible of a Mesolithic horse from Seamer Carr, Yorkshire, England. In R.H. Meadow and H-P. Uerpmann (eds), *Equids in the Ancient World*, 238–41. Beihefte zum Tübinger Atlas des Vorderen Orients. Reihe A (Naturwissenschaften), 19/2. Wiesbaden: Reichert.

Clutton-Brock, J. and Burleigh, R. 1991b. The skull of a Neolithic horse from Grime's Graves, Norfolk, England. In R.H. Meadow and H-P. Uerpmann (eds), *Equids in the Ancient World*, 242–49. Beihefte zum Tübinger Atlas des Vorderen Orients. Reihe A (Naturwissenschaften), 19/2. Wiesbaden: Reichert.

Colt Hoare, W. 1819. *The ancient history of North Wiltshire.* London: Lackington, Hughes, Harding, Mavor and Jones.

Conkey, M. W. and Gero, J. M. 1991. Tensions, pluralities, and engendering archaeology: an introduction to women in prehistory. In J. M. Gero and M. W. Conkey (eds), *Engendering archaeology: women and prehistory*, 3–30. Oxford: Blackwell.

Connah, G. 1965. Excavations at Knap Hill, Alton Priors, 1961. *Wiltshire Archaeological and Natural History Magazine* 60, 1–23.

Connerton, P. 1989. *How societies remember.* Cambridge: Cambridge University Press.

Corbet, G.B. and Southern, H.N.(eds) 1977. *The handbook of British mammals* (second edition). Oxford: Blackwell Scientific.

Cornwall, I. W. 1958. *Soils for archaeologists.* London: Phoenix House.

Cornwall, I. W. 1966. Appendix IV. In P. Ashbee, 'The Fussell's Lodge long barrow excavation 1957'. *Archaeologia* 100, 74.

Cornwall, I. and Hodges, H.W.M. 1964. Thin sections of British Neolithic pottery: Windmill Hill – a test site. *Bulletin of the Institute of Archaeology, London*, 4, 29–33.1

Courty, M. A., Goldberg, P. and Macphail, R. I. 1989. *Soils and micromorphology in archaeology.* Cambridge: Cambridge University Press.

Couture, M.D., Ricks, M.F. and Housley, L. 1986. Foraging behaviour of a contemporary Northern Great Basin population. *Journal of Great Basin Anthropology* 8, 150–60.

Crabtree, K. 1990. Experimental earthworks in the United Kingdom. In D. Robinson (ed.), *Experimentation and reconstruction in environmental archaeology*, 225–35. Oxford: Oxbow.

Crabtree, K. 1996. Pollen analysis, old land surface. In M. Bell, P.J.Fowler and S.W.Hillson, *The experimental earthwork project, 1960–1992*, 129–31. York: Council for British Archaeology.

Crandall, D.P. 1998. The role of time in Himba valuations of cattle. *Journal of the Royal Anthropological Institute* 4, 101–14.

Crawford, O.G.S. 1927. Windmill Hill, Wiltshire. *Antiquity* 1, 104–5.

Crawford, O.G.S. 1953. *Archaeology in the field.* London: Dent.

Crawford, O.G.S. 1955. *Said and done: the autobiography of an archaeologist.* London: Weidenfeld and Nicolson.

Croll, E. and Parkin, D. 1992. Cultural understandings of the environment. In E. Croll and D. Parkin (eds), *Bush base: forest farm. Culture, environment and development*, 11–36. London: Routledge.

Crowther, J., Macphail, R. I. and Cruise, G. M. 1996. Short-term, post-burial change in a humic rendzina soil, Overton Down Experimental Earthwork, Wiltshire, England. *Geoarchaeology* 11, 95–117.

Cruise, G. 1993. Soil Pollen. In A. Whittle, A. J. Rouse and J. G. Evans, 'A Neolithic downland monument in its environment: excavations at the Easton Down long barrow, Bishops Cannings, north Wiltshire'. *Proceedings of the Prehistoric Society* 59, 219–21.

Cruise, G. M. and Macphail, R. I. forthcoming. Microstratigraphical signatures of experimental rural occupation deposits and archaeological sites. In D. Shotliff and N. Shepherd (eds), *Interpreting stratigraphy.* York: University of York.

Cunnington, M.E. 1912. Knap Hill Camp. *Wiltshire Archaeological and Natural History Magazine* 37, 42–65.

Cunnington, M. E. 1931. The 'Sanctuary' on Overton Hill, near Avebury. *Wiltshire Archaeological and Natural History Magazine* 45, 300–35.

Cunnington, M. E. 1937. Horns of Urus said to have been found in a barrow at Cherhill. *Wiltshire Archaeological and Natural History Magazine* 47, 583–86.

Curwen, E. C. 1934. Excavations in Whitehawk Neolithic camp, Brighton, 1932–3. *Antiquaries Journal* 14, 99–133.

Curwen, E.C. 1935. Agriculture and the flint sickle in Palestine. *Antiquity* 9, 62–66.

Curwen, E. C. 1936. Excavations in Whitehawk camp, Brighton: third season, 1935. *Sussex Archaeological Collections* 77, 60–92.

Darvill, T. 1983. The petrology of the Neolithic pottery from Cherhill. In J.G. Evans and I.F. Smith, 'Excavations at Cherhill, North Wiltshire, 1967'. *Proceedings of the Prehistoric Society* 49, 92–98.

Darvill, T. 1987. *Prehistoric Britain.* London: Batsford.

Darvill, T. 1996. Neolithic buildings in England, Wales and the Isle of Man. In T. Darvill and J. Thomas (eds), *Neolithic houses in northwest Europe and beyond*, 77–111. Oxford: Oxbow.

Davis, S. 1987. *The archaeology of animals.* London: Batsford.

Davis, S. 1992. *A rapid method for recording information about mammal bones from archaeological sites.* Ancient Monument Laboratory Reports 19/92. London: English Heritage.

Davis, S. J. M. 1982. Climatic change and the advent of domestication: the succession of ruminant artiodactyls in the late Pleistocene-Holocene in the Israel region. *Paléorient* 8, 5–15.

Davis, S. and Payne, S. 1993. A barrow full of cattle skulls. *Antiquity* 67, 12–22.

Degerbøl, M. 1963. Prehistoric cattle in Denmark and adjacent areas. In A.E. Mourant and F.E. Zeuner (eds), *Man and cattle*, 68–79. London: Royal Anthropological Institute Occasional Paper 18.

Degerbøl, M. and Fredskild, B. 1970. The urus (*Bos primigenius* Bojanus) and neolithic domesticated cattle (*Bos taurus domesticus* Linné) in Denmark. *Det Kongelige Danske Videnskabernes Selskab Biologiske Skrifter* 17, 1–177.

Dennell, R. 1976. Prehistoric crop cultivation in southern England: a reconsideration. *Antiquaries Journal* 56, 11–23.

Dennis, I. 1993. Test pits. In A. Whittle, A.J. Rouse and J.G. Evans, 'A Neolithic downland monument in its environment: excavations at the Easton Down long barrow, Bishops Cannings, north Wiltshire'. *Proceedings of the Prehistoric Society* 59, 206.

Dimbleby, G.W. 1965. Post-glacial changes in soil profiles. *Proceedings of the Royal Society* B, 161, 355–62.

Dimbleby, G.W. 1997. Pollen. In A. Whittle, *Sacred mound, holy rings. Silbury Hill and the West Kennet palisade enclosures: a Later Neolithic complex in north Wiltshire*, 29–32. Oxford: Oxbow.

Dimbleby, G. W. and Evans, J. G. 1974. Pollen and landsnail analysis of calcareous soils. *Journal of Archaeological Science* 2, 179–86.

Dixon, P. 1988. The Neolithic settlements on Crickley Hill. In C. Burgess, P. Topping, C. Mordant and M. Maddison (eds), *Enclosures and defences in the Neolithic of western Europe*, 75–88. Oxford: British Archaeological Reports.

Drewett, P. 1977. The excavation of a Neolithic causewayed enclosure at Offham Hill, East Sussex. *Proceedings of the Prehistoric Society* 42, 201–41.

Driesch, A. von den, 1976. *A guide to the measurement of animal bones from archaeological sites*. Peabody Museum Bulletin 1.

Driesch, A. von den and Boessneck, J. 1974. Kritische Anmerkungen zur Widerristhöhenberechtung aus Längenmassen vor- und frühgeschichtlicher Tierknochen. *Säugetierkundliche Mitteilungen* 22,325–48.

Driesch, A. von den and Boessneck, J. 1978. The significance of measuring animal bones. In R.H. Meadow and M. Zeder (eds), *Approaches to faunal analysis in the Middle East*, 25–39. Peabody Museum Bulletin 2.

Ducos, P. 1968. *L'origine des animaux domestiques en Palestine*. Bordeaux: Publications de Préhistoire de l'Université de Bordeaux 6.

Ducos, P. 1978. 'Domestication' defined and methodological approaches to its recognition in faunal assemblages. In R.H. Meadow and M. Zeder (eds), *Approaches to faunal analysis in the Middle East*, 53–56. Peabody Museum Bulletin 2.

Ducos, P. 1983. La contribution de l'archéozoologie à l'éstimation des quantités de nourriture: évaluation du nombre d'individus. In J. Clutton-Brock and C. Grigson (eds), *Animals and archaeology: 3. Early herders and their flocks*, 13–23. Oxford: British Archaeological Reports.

Dunn, C.J. 1988. The barrows of east-central Powys. *Archaeologia Cambrensis* 137, 27–42.

Edlin, H.L. 1948. *Forestry and woodland life* (second edition). London: Batsford.

Edlin, H. L. 1953. *The forester's handbook*. London: Thames and Hudson.

Edlin, H.L. 1956. *Trees, woods and man*. London: Collins.

Edmonds, M.R. 1987. Rocks and risk: problems with lithic procurement strategies. In A.G. Brown and M.R. Edmonds (eds), *Lithic analysis and later British prehistory*, 155–80. Oxford: British Archaeological Reports.

Edmonds, M. 1993. Interpreting causewayed enclosures in the past and present. In C. Tilley (ed.), *Interpretative archaeology*, 99–142. Oxford: Berg.

Edmonds, M. 1998. Sermons in stone: identity, value, and stone tools in Later Neolithic Britain. In M. Edmonds and C. Richards (eds), *Understanding the Neolithic of north-western Europe*, 248–76. Glasgow: Cruithne Press.

Edmonds, M. and Bellamy, P. 1991. The flaked stone. In N. M. Sharples, *Maiden Castle: excavations and field survey 1985–6*, 214–29. London: English Heritage.

Edmonds, M. and Thomas, J. 1987. The Archers: an everyday story of country folk. In A.G. Brown and M.R. Edmonds (eds), *Lithic analysis and later British prehistory*, 187–99. Oxford: British Archaeological Reports.

Edwards, A. and Horne, M. 1997. Animal bone. In A. Whittle, *Sacred mound, holy rings. Silbury Hill and the West Kennet palisade enclosures: a Later Neolithic complex in north Wiltshire*, 117–29. Oxford: Oxbow.

Edwards, K.J. 1993. Models of mid-Holocene forest farming for north-west Europe. In F.M. Chambers (ed.), *Climate change and human impact on the landscape*, 133–45. London: Chapman and Hall.

Eliade, M. 1960. *Myths, dreams and mysteries*. London: Collins.

Eliade, M. 1965. *The myth of the eternal return*. Princeton: Princeton University Press.

Entwistle, R. and Grant, A. 1989. The evidence for cereal cultivation and animal husbandry in the southern British Neolithic and Bronze Age. In A. Milles, D. Williams and D. Gardner (eds), *The beginnings of agriculture*, 203–15. Oxford: British Archaeological Reports.

Eogan, G. 1983. A flint macehead at Knowth, Co. Meath. *Antiquity* 57, 45–46.

Evans, C. 1988a. Acts of enclosure: a consideration of concentrically-organised causewayed enclosures. In J. C. Barrett and I. A. Kinnes (eds), *The archaeology of context in the Neolithic and Bronze Age: recent trends*, 85–96. University of Sheffield: Department of Archaeology and Prehistory.

Evans, C. 1988b. Excavations at Haddenham, Cambridgeshire: a 'planned' enclosure and its regional affinities. In C. Burgess, P. Topping, C. Mordant and M. Maddison (eds), *Enclosures and defences in the Neolithic of western Europe*, 127–48. Oxford: British Archaeological Reports.

Evans, C. 1989. Archaeology and modern times: Bersu's Woodbury 1938 and 1939. *Antiquity* 63, 436–50.

Evans, J. 1872. *Ancient stone implements, weapons, and ornaments of Great Britain*. London: Longmans, Green, Reader and Dyer.

Evans, J. 1986. The identification of residues on sherds of pottery. In P. Ashbee, 'The excavation of Milton Lilbourne barrows 1–5'. *Wiltshire Archaeological and Natural History Magazine* 80, 91–92.

Evans, J. G. 1971. Habitat changes on the calcareous soils of Britain: the impact of Neolithic man. In D. D. A. Simpson (ed.), *Economy and settlement in Neolithic and Early Bronze Age Britain and Europe*, 27–73. Leicester: Leicester University Press.

Evans, J.G. 1972. *Land snails in archaeology*. London: Seminar Press.

Evans, J.G. 1975. *The environment of early man in the British Isles*. London: Elek.

Evans, J.G. 1990. Notes on some Late Neolithic and Bronze Age events in long barrow ditches in southern and eastern England. *Proceedings of the Prehistoric Society* 56, 111–16.

Evans, J.G. 1991. The environment. In N. M. Sharples, *Maiden Castle: excavations and field survey 1985–6*, 250–3. London: English Heritage.

Evans, J.G. and Jones, H. 1973. Subfossil and modern landsnail faunas from rock-rubble habitats. *Cepaea* 28, 103–29.

Evans, J.G., Limbrey, S., Máté, I. and Mount, R.J. 1988. Environmental change and land-use history in a Wiltshire river valley in the last 14000 years. In J.C. Barrett and I. Kinnes (eds), *The archaeology of context in the Neolithic and Bronze Age: recent trends*, 104–12. Sheffield: Department of Archaeology and Prehistory, University of Sheffield.

Evans, J.G., Limbrey, S., Máté, I. and Mount, R. 1993. An environmental history of the upper Kennet valley, Wiltshire, for the last 10,000 years. *Proceedings of the Prehistoric Society* 59, 139–95.

Evans, J.G., Pitts, M.W. and Williams, D. 1985. An excavation at Avebury, Wiltshire, 1982. *Proceedings of the Prehistoric Society* 51, 305–10.

Evans, J. G. and Rouse, A. J. 1990. Small vertebrate and molluscan analysis from the same site. *Circaea* 8, 75–84.

Evans, J. G., Rouse, A. J. and Sharples, N. M. 1988. The landscape setting of causewayed camps: recent work on the Maiden Castle enclosure. In J. C. Barrett and I. A. Kinnes (eds), *The archaeology of context in the Neolithic and Bronze Age: recent trends*, 73–84. Sheffield: Department of Archaeology and Prehistory, University of Sheffield.

Evans, J. G. and Smith, I. F. 1983. Excavations at Cherhill, North Wiltshire, 1967. *Proceedings of the Prehistoric Society* 49, 43–117.

Evans-Pritchard, E.E. 1956. *Nuer religion*. Oxford: Clarendon Press.

Fairbairn, A. S. 1993. Charred plant remains. In A. Whittle, A. J. Rouse and J. G. Evans, 'A Neolithic downland monument in its environment: excavations at the Easton down long barrow, Bishops Cannings, north Wiltshire'. *Proceedings of the Prehistoric Society* 59, 221.

Fairweather, A. D. and Ralston, I. B. M. 1993. The Neolithic timber hall at Balbridie, Grampian Region, Scotland: the building, the date, the plant macrofossils. *Antiquity* 67, 313–23.

Field, N. H., Matthews, C. L. and Smith, I. F. 1964. New Neolithic sites in Dorset and Bedfordshire with a note on the distribution of Neolithic storage-pits in Britain. *Proceedings of the Prehistoric Society* 30, 352–81.

Fishpool, M. 1992. *Investigation of the responses of land snails and Carabid beetles to vegetation boundaries, with reference to the interpretation of subfossil assemblages*. Unpublished PhD thesis, University of Wales Cardiff.

Flannery, K.V. 1983. Early pig domestication in the fertile crescent a retrospective look. In L.S. Braidwood (ed.), *The hilly flanks: essays on the prehistory of southwestern Asia*, 163–87. Studies in Oriental Civilization 36. Chicago: University of Chicago.

Fleming, A. 1971. Territorial patterns in Bronze Age Wessex. *Proceedings of the Prehistoric Society* 37, 138–66.

Fleming, A. 1973. Tombs for the living. *Man* 8, 177–93.

Foley, R. 1981. A model of regional archaeological structure. *Proceedings of the Prehistoric Society* 47, 1–17.

Forde-Johnston, J. 1966. The Dudsbury Barrow and vessels with shoulder grooves in Dorset and Wiltshire. *Proceedings of the Dorset Natural History and Archaeology Society* 87, 126–41.

Fowler, P.J. and Evans, J. G. 1967. Plough marks, lynchets and early fields. *Antiquity* 41, 289–91.

Fraser, F.C. and King, J.E. 1954. Faunal remains. In J.D.G. Clark, *Star Carr*, 70–95. Cambridge: Cambridge University Press.

Gardiner, J. 1987. The occupation, 3500–1000 bc. In B. Cunliffe, *Hengistbury Head, Dorset: 1, The prehistoric and Roman settlement, 3500 BC-AD 50*, 22–60. Oxford: Oxford University Committee for Archaeology.

Garwood, P., Jennings, D., Skeates, R. and Toms, J. 1991. Preface. In P. Garwood, D. Jennings, R. Skeates and J. Toms (eds), *Sacred and profane*, v-x. Oxford: Oxford University Committee for Archaeology.

Gautier, A. 1984. How do I count you, let me count the ways? Problems of archaeozoological quantification. In C. Grigson and J. Clutton-Brock (eds), *Animals and archaeology: 4. Husbandry in Europe*, 237–251. Oxford: British Archaeological Reports.

Gebhardt, A. 1990. *Evolution du paleopaysage agricole dans le Nord-Ouest de la France: apport de la micromorphologie*. Unpublished thesis, University of Rennes 1.

Gebhardt, A. 1992. Micromorphological analysis of soil structural modifications caused by different cultivation implements. In P. C. Anderson (ed.), *Préhistoire de l'agriculture: nouvelles approches experimentales et ethnographiques*, 373–92. Paris: Centre Nationale de la Recherche Scientifique.

Gebhardt, A. 1993. Micromorphological evidence of soil deterioration since the mid-Holocene at archaeological sites in Brittany, France. *The Holocene* 3, 331–41.

Gibson, A. M. 1982. *Beaker domestic sites: a study of the domestic pottery of the late third and early second millennia B.C. in the British Isles*. Oxford: British Archaeological Reports.

Gibson, A. 1993. Radiocarbon date for a Fengate sherd from Brynderwen, Llandyssil, Powys. *Archaeology in Wales* 33, 34–35.

Gibson, A. 1995. First impressions: a review of Peterborough Ware in Wales. In I. Kinnes and G. Varndell (eds), *'Unbaked urns of rudely shape': essays on British and Irish pottery for Ian Longworth*, 23–39. Oxford: Oxbow.

Gibson, T. 1996. Sacrifice. In A. Barnard and J. Spencer (eds), *Encyclopedia of social and cultural anthropology*, 497–99. London: Routledge.

Gilchrist, R. 1991. Women's archaeology? Political feminism, gender theory, and historical revision. *Antiquity* 65, 495–501.

Gingell, C. 1992. *The Marlborough Downs: a Later Bronze Age landscape and its origins*. Devizes: Wiltshire Archaeological and Natural History Society.

Gittens, S.P., Parker, A.G. and Slater, F.M. 1980. Population characteristics of the common toad (*Bufo bufo*) visiting a breeding site in mid Wales. *Journal of Animal Ecology* 49, 161–73.

Goldberg, P. and Whitbread, I. 1993. Micromorphological studies of Bedouin tent floors. In P. Goldberg, D.T. Nash and M.D. Petraglia (eds), *Formation processes in archaeological context*, 165–88. Madison: Prehistory Press.

Graham, I. and Saunders, A. 1978. A multivariate statistical analysis of small mammal bones. In D.R. Brothwell, K.D. Thomas and J. Clutton-Brock (eds), *Research problems in zooarchaeology*, 59–68. London: Institute of Archaeology.

Grant, A. 1982. The use of tooth wear as a guide to the age of domestic animals – a brief explanation. In B. Wilson, C. Grigson and S. Payne (eds), *Ageing and sexing animal bones from archaeological sites*, 91–108. Oxford: British Archaeological Reports.

Gray, H.St.G. 1935. The Avebury excavations, 1902–1922. *Archaeologia* 84, 99–162.

Green, C. and Rollo-Smith, S. 1984. The excavation of eighteen round barrows near Shrewton, Wiltshire. *Proceedings of the Prehistoric Society* 50, 255–318.

Green, H. S. 1980. *The flint arrowheads of the British Isles.* Oxford: British Archaeological Reports.

Grieve, M. 1931. *A modern herbal.* London: Cape.

Grigson, C. 1965. Faunal remains: measurements of bones, horncores, antlers and teeth. In I.F. Smith, *Windmill Hill and Avebury*, 145–67. Oxford: Clarendon Press.

Grigson, C. 1966. The animal remains from Fussell's Lodge long barrow (including a possible ox-hide burial, with discussion on the presence of the horse in Neolithic Britain). In P. Ashbee, 'The Fussell's Lodge long barrow excavations 1957'. *Archaeologia* 100, 63–73.

Grigson, C. 1969. The uses and limitations of differences in absolute size in the distinctions between the bones of aurochs (*Bos primigenius*) and domestic cattle (*Bos taurus*). In P. Ucko and G.W. Dimbleby (eds), *The domestication and exploitation of plants and animals*, 277–94. London: Duckworth.

Grigson, C. 1978a. The craniology and relationships of four species of *Bos*. IV. The relationship between *Bos primigenius* Boj. and *Bos taurus* L. and its implications for the phylogeny of the domestic breeds. *Journal of Archaeological Science* 5, 123–52.

Grigson, C. 1978b. The late glacial and early flandrian ungulates of England and Wales – an interim review. In S. Limbrey and J.G. Evans (eds*), The effect of man on the landscape: the lowland zone*, 46–56. London: Council for British Archaeology.

Grigson, C. 1980. The animal bones. In M. E. Robertson-MacKay, 'A head and hooves burial beneath a round barrow, with other Neolithic and Bronze Age sites, on Hemp Knoll, near Avebury, Wiltshire'. *Proceedings of the Prehistoric Society* 46, 161–71.

Grigson, C. 1981a. The Mesolithic fauna. In I.G. Simmons and M.J. Tooley (eds), *The environment in British prehistory*, 110–24. London: Duckworth.

Grigson, C. 1981b. The Neolithic fauna. In I.G. Simmons and M.J. Tooley (eds), *The environment in British prehistory*, 191–99. London: Duckworth.

Grigson, C. 1982a. Sexing Neolithic cattle skulls and horncores. In B. Wilson, C. Grigson and S. Payne (eds*), Ageing and sexing animal bones from archaeological sites*, 24–35. Oxford: British Archaeological Reports.

Grigson, C. 1982b. Sex and age determination of bones and teeth of domestic cattle: a review of the literature. In B. Wilson, C. Grigson and S. Payne (eds*), Ageing and sexing animal bones from archaeological sites*, 7–23. Oxford: British Archaeological Reports.

Grigson, C. 1982c. Cattle in prehistoric Britain. *Ark* 9, 47–49.

Grigson, C. 1982d. Porridge and pannage: pig husbandry in Neolithic England. In S. Limbrey and M. Bell (eds*), Archaeological aspects of woodland ecology*, 297–314. Oxford: British Archaeological Reports.

Grigson, C. 1983. Mesolithic and Neolithic animal bones. In J. G. Evans and I. F. Smith, 'Excavations at Cherhill, North Wiltshire, 1967'. *Proceedings of the Prehistoric Society* 49, 64–72.

Grigson, C. 1984. The domestic animals of the earlier Neolithic in Britain. In G. Nobis (ed.), *Die Anfänge de Neolitikums vom Orient bis Nordeuropa. IX. Der Beginn der Haustierhaltung in der 'Alten Welt'*, 205–20. Köln: Bohlau.

Grigson, C. 1989. Size and sex – morphometric evidence for the domestication of cattle in the Near East. In A. Milles, D. Williams and N. Gardner (eds), *The beginnings of agriculture*, 77–109. Oxford: British Archaeological Reports.

Grigson, C. 1995. Plough and pasture in the early economy of the southern Levant. In T.E. Levy (ed.), *The archaeology of society in the Holy Land*, 245–68 and 573–76. Leicester: Leicester University Press.

Grigson, C. forthcoming. Animal husbandry in the Late Neolithic and Chalcolithic at Arjoune – the secondary products revolution revisited. In P. J. Parr (ed.), *Excavations at Arjoune, Syria.*

Grigson, C., Higgs, E.S. and Greenwood, W. 1987. Animal bone. In R. Robertson-MacKay, 'The Neolithic causewayed enclosure at Staines, Surrey: excavations 1961–63'. *Proceedings of the Prehistoric Society* 53, microfiche 73.

Grime, J. P., Hodgson, J. G. and Hunt, R. 1988. *Comparative plant ecology.* London: Unwin Hyman.

Grinsell, L.V. 1957. Archaeological gazetteer. In R.B. Pugh and E. Crittall (eds), *Victoria County History of Wiltshire* 1(2), 21–279. Oxford: Oxford University Press.

Guilbert, G. 1996. Findern is dead, long live Potlock – the story of a cursus on the Trent gravels. *Past* 24, 10–12.

Gulliksen, S. and Scott, M. 1995. Report of the TIRI workshop. *Radiocarbon* 37, 820–21.

Haaland, R. 1997. Emergence of sedentism: new ways of living, new ways of symbolizing. *Antiquity* 71, 374–85.

Hamilton, M. A. 1995. *The Latest Neolithic and Early Bronze Age pottery of Southern Britain.* Unpublished PhD thesis, University of Wales Cardiff.

Hamilton, M. A. 1997. Pottery. In A. Whittle, *Sacred mound, holy rings. Silbury Hill and the West Kennet palisade enclosures: a Later Neolithic complex in north Wiltshire*, 93–117. Oxford: Oxbow.

Hanf, M. 1983. *The arable weeds of Europe: with their seedlings and seeds.* Hadleigh, Suffolk: BASF.

Harcourt, R.A. 1971. The animal bones. In G.J. Wainwright and I.H. Longworth, *Durrington Walls: excavations 1966–1968*, 338–50. London: Society of Antiquaries.

Harcourt, R.A. 1974. The dog in prehistoric and early historic Britain. *Journal of Archaeological Science* 1, 151–75.

Harding, J. 1998. An architecture of meaning: the causewayed enclosures and henges of lowland England. In M. Edmonds and C. Richards (eds), *Understanding the Neolithic of northwestern Europe*, 204–30. Glasgow: Cruithne Press.

Harding, P. 1990. The comparative analysis of four stratified flint assemblages and a knapping cluster. In J. Richards, *The Stonehenge environs survey*, 213–25. London: English Heritage.

Harding, P. 1991. The worked stone. In P. Woodward, *The South Dorset Ridgeway: survey and excavations 1977–84*, 73–87. Dorchester: Dorset Natural History and Archaeological Society.

Harding, P. 1992. The flint. In C. Gingell, *The Marlborough Downs: a Later Bronze Age landscape and its origins*, 123–

33. Devizes: Wiltshire Archaeological and Natural History Society.

Hastorf, C. 1991. Gender, space and food in prehistory. In J. M. Gero and M. W. Conkey (eds), *Engendering archaeology: women in prehistory*, 132–59. Oxford: Blackwell.

Hather, J. G. 1993. *An archaeobotanical guide to root and tuber identification. Volume 1: Europe and the Near East*. Oxford: Oxbow.

Häusser, A. (ed.) 1998. *Krieg oder Frieden ? Herxheim vor 7000 Jahren*. Herxheim: Landesamt für Denkmalplfege.

Hayden, B. 1995. Pathways to power: principles for creating socioeconomic inequalities. In T.D. Price and G. Feinman (eds), *The foundations of social inequality*, 15–86. New York: Plenum Press.

Hayden, B. and Gargett, R. 1990. Big man, big heart ? A Mesoamerican view of the emergence of complex society. *Ancient Mesoamerica* 1, 3–20.

Healey, E. and Robertson-Mackay, R. 1983. The lithic industries from Staines causewayed enclosure and their relation to the other earlier Neolithic industries in southern Britain. *Lithics* 4, 1–27.

Hedges, J. and Buckley, D. 1981. *Springfield cursus and the cursus problem*. Chelmsford: Essex County Council.

Hedges, R. E. M. 1989. The radiocarbon dating of bone. *Applied Geochemistry* 4, 249–55.

Hedges, R. E. M., Housley, R. A., Bronk, C. R. and van Klinken, G. J. 1990. Radiocarbon dates from the AMS system: datelist 11. *Archaeometry* 32, 211–37.

Hedges, R. E. M., Humm, M. J., Foremen, J., van Klinken, G. J. and Bronk, C. R. 1992. Developments in sample combustion to carbon dioxide, and the Oxford AMS carbon dioxide ion source system. *Radiocarbon* 34, 306–11.

Hedges, R. E. M., Law, I. A., Bronk, C. R. and Housley, R. A. 1989. The Oxford accelerator mass spectrometry facility: technical developments in routine dating. *Archaeometry* 31, 99–113.

Helbaek, H. 1952. Early crops in southern England. *Proceedings of the Prehistoric Society* 12, 194–233.

Herne, A. 1988. A time and a place for the Grimston bowl. In J. Barrett and I. Kinnes (eds), *The archaeology of context in the Neolithic and Early Bronze Age: recent trends*, 9–29. Sheffield: University of Sheffield, Department of Archaeology and Prehistory.

Hertz, R. 1960. *Death and the right hand*. Aberdeen: Cohen and West.

Hesse, B. 1978. *Evidence for husbandry from the Early Neolithic site of Ganj Dareh in western Iran*. Ann Arbor, Michigan and London: University Microfilms International.

Hesse, B. 1982. Slaughter patterns and domestication: the beginnings of pastoralism in western Iran. *Man* 17, 403–17.

Heusch, L. de 1985. *Sacrifice in Africa*. Manchester: Manchester University Press.

Hey, G. 1997. Neolithic settlement at Yarnton, Oxfordshire. In P. Topping (ed.), *Neolithic landscapes*, 99–111. Oxford: Oxbow.

Higham, C.F.W. and Higgs, E.S. 1979. The fauna [Horslip Road]. In P. Ashbee, I.F. Smith and J.G. Evans, 'Excavation of three long barrows, near Avebury, Wiltshire'. *Proceedings of the Prehistoric Society* 45, 225–28.

Hill, J.D. 1995. *Ritual and rubbish in the Iron Age of Wessex*. Oxford: British Archaeological Reports.

Hillman, G. C. 1981. Reconstructing crop husbandry practices from charred remains of crops. In R. Mercer (ed.), *Farming practice in British prehistory*, 123–62. Edinburgh: Edinburgh University Press.

Hillson, S. 1986. *Teeth*. Cambridge: Cambridge University Press.

Hodder, I. 1982. *Symbols in action*. Cambridge: Cambridge University Press.

Hodder, I. 1986. *Reading the past*. Cambridge: Cambridge University Press.

Hodder, I. 1988. Material culture texts and social change: a theoretical discussion and some archaeological examples. *Proceedings of the Prehistoric Society* 54, 67–75.

Hodder, I. 1989. This is not an article about material culture as text. *Journal of Anthropological Archaeology* 8, 250–69.

Hodder, I. 1990. *The domestication of Europe*. Oxford: Blackwell.

Hodder, I. 1991. *Reading the past: current approaches to interpretation in archaeology* (second edition). Cambridge: Cambridge University Press.

Hodder, I. 1992. The Haddenham causewayed enclosure – a hermeneutic circle. In I. Hodder, *Theory and practice in archaeology*, 213–40. London: Routledge.

Hodder, I. 1994. Architecture and meaning: the example of Neolithic houses and tombs. In M. Parker Pearson and C. Richards (eds), *Architecture and order: approaches to social space*, 73–86. London: Routledge.

Hodder, I. 1997. The gender screen. In J. Moore and E. Scott (eds), *Invisible people and processes: writing gender and childhood into European archaeology*, 75–78. Leicester: Leicester University Press.

Hodgson, J. M., Catt, J. and Weir, A. H. 1967. The origin and development of Clay-with-Flints and associated soil horizons on the South Downs. *Journal of Soil Science* 18, 85–102.

Holgate, R. 1987. Neolithic settlement patterns at Avebury, Wiltshire. *Antiquity* 61, 259–63.

Holgate, R. 1988. *Neolithic settlement of the Thames basin*. Oxford: British Archaeological Reports.

Hubbard, R. N. L. B. and Clapham, A. 1992. Quantifying macroscopic plant remains. *Review of Palaeobotany and Palynology* 73, 117–32.

Hurcombe, L. 1997. A viable past in the pictorial present ? In J. Moore and E. Scott (eds), *Invisible people and processes: writing gender and childhood into European archaeology*, 15–24. London: Leicester University Press.

Huntingdon, R. and Metcalf, P. 1979. *Celebrations of death*. Cambridge: Cambridge University Press.

Ingold, T. 1996. Hunting and gathering as ways of perceiving the environment. In R. Ellen and K. Fukui (eds), *Redefining nature*, 117–55. Oxford: Berg.

Jackson, J.W. 1936. Report on the animal remains. In C.D. Drew and S. Piggott, 'The excavation of the long barrow 163a on Thickthorn Down, Dorset'. *Proceedings of the Prehistoric Society* 2, 93–94.

Jacobi, R. 1980. The early Holocene settlement of Wales. In J.A. Taylor (ed.), *Culture and environment in prehistoric Wales*, 131–206. Oxford: British Archaeological Reports.

Jacomet, S. 1987. *Prähistorische Getreidefunde*. Basel: Botanisches Institut der Universität, Abteilung Pflanzensystematik und Geobotanik.

Jeunesse, C. 1996. Les enceintes à fossés interrompus du Néolithique danubien ancien et moyen et leurs relations avec le Néolithique récent. *Archäologisches Korrespondenzblatt* 26, 251–61.

Jewell, P. 1963. Cattle from British archaeological sites. In A.E. Mourant and F.E. Zeuner (eds), *Man and cattle*, 80–91. London: Royal Anthropological Institute Occasional Paper 18.

Jones, M. 1980. Carbonised cereals from Grooved Ware contexts. *Proceedings of the Prehistoric Society* 46, 61–63.

Jones, M. and Nye, S. 1984. A quantitative analysis of crop debris. In B. Cunliffe, *Danebury: an Iron Age hillfort in Hampshire*, 439–47. London: Council for British Archaeology.

Jope, M. 1965. Faunal remains: frequencies and ages of species. In I.F. Smith, *Windmill Hill and Avebury*, 142–45. Oxford: Clarendon Press.

Jordan, T.G. and Kaups, M. 1989. *The American backwoods frontier: an ethnic and ecological interpretation*. Baltimore: John Hopkins University Press.

Keiller, A. 1934. Excavation at Windmill Hill. *Proceedings of the First International Congress of Prehistoric and Proto-historic Sciences*, 135–8. London: International Congress of Prehistoric and Protohistoric Sciences.

Keiller, A. and Piggott, S. 1938. Excavation of an untouched chamber in the Lanhill long barrow. *Proceedings of the Prehistoric Society* 4, 122–50.

Keiller, A. and Piggott, S. 1939. Badshot long barrow. In *A survey of the prehistory of the Farnham district*, 133–49. Surrey Archaeological Society.

Kendall, H.G.O. 1914. Flint implements from the surface near Avebury: their classification and dates. *Proceedings of the Society of Antiquaries of London* (second series) 26, 73–85.

Kendall, H.G.O. 1919. Windmill Hill, Avebury and Grimes Graves: cores and choppers. *Proceedings of the Prehistoric Society of East Anglia* 3, 104–8, 192–99.

Kendall, H.G.O. 1922. Scraper-core industries of north Wilts. *Proceedings of the Prehistoric Society of East Anglia* 3, 515–41.

Kent, S. 1992. The current forager controversy: real versus ideal views of hunter-gatherers. *Man* 27, 45–70.

Kinnes, I. 1992. *Non-megalithic long barrows and allied structures in the British Neolithic*. London: British Museum Publications.

Kinnes, I., Gibson, A., Ambers, J., Bowman, S., Leese, M. and Boast, R. 1991. Radiocarbon dating and British Beakers: the British Museum programme. *Scottish Archaeological Review* 8, 35–68.

Kopytoff, I. 1986. The cultural biography of things: commoditization as process. In A. Appadurai (ed.), *The social life of things*, 64–91. Cambridge: Cambridge University Press.

Kreutzer, L.A. 1992. Bison and deer bone mineral densities: comparisons and implications for the interpretation of archaeological faunas. *Journal of Archaeological Science* 19, 271–94.

Lakoff, G. 1987. *Women, fire and dangerous things*. Chicago: University of Chicago Press.

Lakoff, G. and Johnson, M. 1980. *Metaphors we live by*. Chicago: University of Chicago Press.

Lanting, J. N. and van der Waals, J. D. 1972. British Beakers as seen from the Continent. *Helinium* 12, 20–46.

Larsson, L. 1990. Dogs in fraction – symbols in action. In P. M. Vermeersch and P. van Peer (eds), *Contributions to the Mesolithic in Europe*, 153–60. Leuven: Leuven University Press.

Law, I.A. and Hedges, R.E.M. 1989. A semi-automated bone pretreatment system and the pretreatment of older and contaminated samples. *Radiocarbon* 31, 247–53.

Lawson, A.J. 1995. The copper alloy bead and awl. In R.M.J. Cleal, K.E. Walker and R. Montague, *Stonehenge in its landscape: twentieth-century excavations*, 430. London: English Heritage.

Leach, E. 1976. *Culture and communication: the logic by which symbols are connected*. Cambridge: Cambridge University Press.

Leach, M. 1992. Women's crops in women's spaces: gender relations in Mende rice farming. In E. Croll and D. Parkin (eds), *Bush base: forest farm. Culture, environment and development*, 76–96. London: Routledge.

Legge, A.J. 1981. Aspects of cattle husbandry. In R. Mercer (ed.), *Farming practice in British prehistory*, 169–181. Edinburgh: Edinburgh University Press.

Legge, A. J. 1989. Milking the evidence: a reply to Entwhistle and Grant. In A. Milles, D. Williams and D. Gardner (eds), *The beginnings of agriculture*, 217–42. Oxford: British Archaeological Reports.

Legge, A.J. and Rowley-Conwy, P. 1988. *Star Carr re-visited: a re-analysis of the large mammals*. London: Centre for Extra-Mural Studies.

Lesick, K. S. 1997. Re-engendering gender: some theoretical and methodological concerns on a burgeoning archaeological pursuit. In J. Moore and E. Scott (eds), *Invisible people and processes: writing gender and childhood into European archaeology*, 31–41. London: Leicester University Press.

Levitan, B. 1990. The non-human vertebrate remains. In A. Saville, *Hazleton North: the excavation of a Neolithic long cairn of the Cotswold-Severn group*, 199–214. London: English Heritage.

Levitan, B.M. and Smart, P.L. 1989. Charterhouse Warren Farm swallet, Mendip, radiocarbon dating evidence. *Proceedings of the University of Bristol Spelaeological Society* 18, 390–94.

Lienhardt, G. 1961. *Divinity and experience: the religion of the Dinka*. Oxford: Oxford University Press.

Limbrey, S. 1975. *Soil science and archaeology*. London: Academic Press.

Lobb, S. 1995. Excavation at Crofton causewayed enclosure. *Wiltshire Archaeological and Natural History Magazine* 88, 18–25.

Locock, M., Currie, C.K. and Gray, S. 1992. Chemical changes in buried animal bone: data from a postmedieval assemblage. *International Journal of Osteoarchaeology* 2, 292–304.

Long, A., Wilson, A.T., Ernst, R.D., Gore, B.H. and Hare, P.E. 1989. AMS dating of bones at Arizona. *Radiocarbon* 31, 231–38.

Longworth, I. H. 1971a. The Neolithic pottery. In G. J. Wainwright and I.H. Longworth, *Durrington Walls: excavations 1966–1968*, 48–155. London: Society of Antiquaries.

Longworth, I. H. 1971b. The pottery. In G. J. Wainwright, 'The excavation of a Late Neolithic enclosure at Marden, Wiltshire'. *Antiquaries Journal* 51, 197–215.

Longworth, I. H. 1979. The Neolithic and Bronze Age pottery. In G. J. Wainwright, *Mount Pleasant, Dorset: excavations 1970–1971*, 75–124. London: Society of Antiquaries.

Longworth, I. H. 1984. *Collared Urns of the Bronze Age in Great Britain and Ireland*. Cambridge: Cambridge University Press.

Lucas, G. M. 1997. Of death and debt. A history of the body in Neolithic and Early Bronze Age Yorkshire. *Journal of European Archaeology* 4, 99–118.

Lyman, R. L. 1994. *Vertebrate taphonomy*. Cambridge: Cambridge University Press.

Macphail, R. I. 1986. *Soil report on Hazleton long cairn, Gloucestershire*. London: English Heritage Ancient Monuments Laboratory Report.

Macphail, R. I. 1987. A review of soil science in archaeology in England. In H.C.M. Keeley (ed.), *Environmental archaeology: a regional review. Volume II*, 332–79. London: English Heritage.

Macphail, R. I. 1990. The soils. In A. Saville, *Hazleton North: the excavation of a Neolithic long cairn of the Cotswold-Severn group*, 223–6. London: English Heritage.

Macphail, R. I. 1991. The archaeological soils and sediments. In N.M. Sharples, *Maiden Castle: excavations and field survey 1985–6*, 106–18. London: English Heritage.

Macphail, R.I. 1993. Soil micromorphology. In A. Whittle, A.J. Rouse and J. G. Evans, 'A Neolithic downland monument in its environment: excavations at the Easton Down long barrow, Bishops Cannings, north Wiltshire'. *Proceedings of the Prehistoric Society* 59, 218–19.

Macphail. R.I. 1994. Micromorphological analysis of soils and sediments. In A. Whittle, 'Excavations at Millbarrow chambered tomb, Winterbourne Monkton, north Wiltshire'. *Wiltshire Archaeological and Natural History Magazine* 87, 32–34.

Macphail, R. I. 1995. Soils. In G. J. Wainwright and S. M. Davies, *Balksbury Camp, Hampshire: excavations 1973 and 1981*, 100–14. London: English Heritage.

Macphail, R. I. 1996. *Potterne: soils and microstratigraphy; a soil micromorphological and microchemical approach*. Unpublished report for Wessex Archaeology, Salisbury.

Macphail, R. I. and Cruise, G. M. 1996. Soil micromorphology. In M. G. Bell, P. J. Fowler and S. W. Hillson (eds), *The experimental earthwork project, 1960–1992*, 95–107. London: Council for British Archaeology.

Macphail, R. I. and Goldberg, P. 1990. The micromorphology of tree subsoil hollows: their significance to soil science and archaeology. In L. A. Douglas (ed.), *Soil micromorphology: a basic and applied science*, 431–40. Amsterdam: Elsevier.

Macphail, R. I. and Goldberg, P, 1995, Recent advances in micromorphological interpretations of soils and sediments from archaeological sites. In A. J. Barham and R. I. Macphail (eds), *Archaeological sediments and soils: analysis, interpretation and management*, 1–24e. London: Institute of Archaeology.

Magurran, A.E. 1988. *Ecological diversity and its measurement*. London: Croom Helm.

Malone, C. 1989. *English Heritage book of Avebury*. London: Batsford/English Heritage.

Maltby, M. 1983. The animal bones. In J. Collis (ed.), *Wigber Low, Derbyshire: a Bronze Age and Anglian burial site in the White Peak*, 47–49. Sheffield: Department of Archaeology and Prehistory, University of Sheffield.

Maltby, M. 1990. Animal bones. In J. Richards, *The Stonehenge environs project*, 57–61. London: English Heritage.

Mercer, R. 1980. *Hambledon Hill*. Edinburgh: Edinburgh University Press.

Mercer, R. 1981a. Excavations at Carn Brea, Illogan, Cornwall, 1970–1973: a Neolithic fortified complex of the third millennium bc. *Cornish Archaeology* 20.

Mercer, R.J. 1981b. *Grimes Graves, Norfolk: excavations 1971–72, volume 1*. London: Department of Environment.

Mercer, R. 1988. Hambledon Hill, Dorset, England. In C. Burgess, P. Topping, C. Mordant and M. Maddison (eds), *Enclosures and defences in the Neolithic of western Europe*, 89–106. Oxford: British Archaeological Reports.

Merewether, J. 1851. Diary of the examination of barrows and other earthworks in the neighbourhood of Silbury Hill and Avebury, Wilts, in July and August 1849. *Proceedings of the Annual Meeting of the Archaeological Institute of Great Britain and Ireland, held at Salisbury, July 1849*, 82–107.

Miles, A.E.W. and Grigson, C. 1990. *Colyer's variations and diseases of the teeth of animals*. Cambridge: Cambridge University Press.

Moffett, L. 1991. Pignut tubers from a Bronze Age cremation at Barrow Hills, Oxfordshire, and the importance of vegetable tubers in the prehistoric period. *Journal of Archaeological Science* 18, 187–91.

Moffett, L., Robinson, M. and Straker, V. 1989. Cereals, fruits and nuts: charred plant remains from Neolithic sites in England and Wales and the Neolithic economy. In A. Milles, D. Williams and D. Gardner (eds), *The beginnings of agriculture*, 243–61. Oxford: British Archaeological Reports.

Molleson, T. 1994. The eloquent bones from Abu Hureyra. *Scientific American* 271, 60–65.

Mook, W. G. 1986. Business meeting: recommendations/resolutions adopted by the Twelfth International Radiocarbon Conference. *Radiocarbon* 28, 799.

Moore, H.L. 1982. The interpretation of spatial patterning in settlement residues. In I. Hodder (ed.), *Symbolic and structural archaeology*, 74–79. Cambridge: Cambridge University Press.

Moore, H. 1986. *Space, text and gender: an anthropological study of the Marakwet of Kenya*. Cambridge: Cambridge University Press.

Moore, J. 1997. The infernal cycle of fire ecology. In P. Topping (ed.), *Neolithic landscapes*, 33–40. Oxford: Oxbow.

Moore, J. and Scott, E. (eds) 1997. *Invisible people and processes: writing gender and childhood into European archaeology*. London: Leicester University Press.

Morel, P. 1987. The fragmentation of bone material, a definable mathematical process. *Archaeozoologia* 1, 53–55.

Morris, B. 1995. Woodland and village: reflections on the 'animal estate' in rural Malawi. *Journal of the Royal Anthropological Institute* 1, 301–15.

Morton, A. E. W. 1990. *Beakers and pre-existing monuments: aspects of ritual in Neolithic and Bronze Age Britain*. Unpublished PhD thesis, University of Edinburgh.

Moss-Eccardt, J. 1989. Archaeological investigations in the Letchworth area. *Proceedings of the Cambridge Antiquarian Society* 77, 35–104.

Murray, L. 1999. *A zest for life: the story of Alexander Keiller*. Swindon: Morven Books.

Murphy, C. P. 1986. *Thin section preparation of soils and sediments*. Berkhamsted: A B Academic Publishers.

Murphy, P. 1988. Carbonised Neolithic plant remains from The Stumble, an intertidal site in the Blackwater Estuary, Essex, England. *Circaea* 6, 21–38.

Needham, S.P. 1986. Late Bronze Age artefacts. In I.M. Stead and V. Rigby, *Baldock: the excavation of a Roman and pre-Roman settlement, 1968–72*, 141–43. Britannia Monograph 7.

Needham, S. and Sørensen, M.L.S. 1988. Runnymede refuse tip: a consideration of midden deposits and their formation. In J. C. Barrett and I. A. Kinnes (eds), *The archaeology of context in the Neolithic and Bronze Age: recent trends*, 113–26. Sheffield: University of Sheffield, Department of Archaeology and Prehistory.

Needham, S. and Spence, T. 1997. Refuse and the formation of middens. *Antiquity* 71, 77–90.

Newcomer, M., and Karlin, C. 1987. Flint chips from Pincevent. In G. de Sieveking and M. Newcomer (eds), *The human uses of flint and chert*, 33–36. Cambridge: Cambridge University Press.

Nobis, G. 1954. Zur Kenntnis der ur- und frühgeschichtlichen Rinder Nord- und Mitteldeutschlands. *Zeitschrift für Tierzüchtung und Züchtungsbiologie* 63, 155–94.

Odum, E. P. 1983. *Basic ecology.* London: Holt-Saunders International Editions.

Passmore, A. D. 1940. Flint mines at Liddington. *Wiltshire Archaeological and Natural History Magazine* 49, 118–19.

Payne, S. and Bull, G. 1988. Components of variation in measurements of pig bones and teeth, and the use of measurements to distinguish wild from domestic pig remains. *Archaeozoologia* 2, 27–66.

Pearson, G. W., Pilcher, J. R., Baillie, M. G. L., Corbett, D. M. and Qua, F. 1986. High-precision 14C measurements of Irish oaks to show the natural 14C variations from AD 1840–5210 BC. *Radiocarbon* 28, 911–34.

Pfaffenberger, B. 1988. Fetished objects and humanised nature: towards an anthropology of technology. *Man* 23, 236–52.

Pierpoint, S. 1980. *Social patterns in Yorkshire prehistory.* Oxford: British Archaeological Reports.

Piggott, C. M. 1942. Five Late Bronze Age enclosures in north Wiltshire. *Proceedings of the Prehistoric Society* 8, 48–61.

Piggott, S. 1931. The Neolithic pottery of the British Isles. *Archaeological Journal* 88, 67–158.

Piggott, S. 1954. *The Neolithic cultures of the British Isles.* Cambridge: Cambridge University Press.

Piggott, S. 1962a. *The West Kennet long barrow: excavations 1955–56.* London: Her Majesty's Stationery Office.

Piggott, S. 1962b. Heads and hooves. *Antiquity* 36, 110–18.

Piggott, S. 1965. Alexander Keiller: 1889–1955. In I.F. Smith, *Windmill Hill and Avebury*, xix-xxii. Oxford: Clarendon Press.

Piggott, S. 1983. Archaeological retrospect. *Antiquity* 57, 28–37.

Piggott, S. 1985. *William Stukeley: an eighteenth-century antiquary* (revised edition). London: Thames and Hudson.

Pitts, M. W. 1978. On the shape of waste flakes as an index of technological change in lithic industries. *Journal of Archaeological Science* 5, 17–38.

Pitts, M. 1983. Procurement and use of flint and chert. In J. G. Evans and I. F. Smith, 'Excavations at Cherhill, North Wiltshire, 1967'. *Proceedings of the Prehistoric Society* 49, 72–84.

Pitts, M. and Whittle, A. 1992. The development and date of Avebury. *Proceedings of the Prehistoric Society* 58, 203–12.

Pollard, J. 1992. The Sanctuary, Overton Hill, Wiltshire: a re-examination. *Proceedings of the Prehistoric Society* 58, 213–26.

Pollard, J. 1993a. *Traditions of deposition in Neolithic Wessex.* Unpublished PhD thesis, University of Wales Cardiff.

Pollard, J. 1993b. Flint. In A. Whittle, A.J. Rouse and J.G. Evans, 'A Neolithic downland monument in its environment: excavations at the Easton Down long barrow, Bishops Cannings, north Wiltshire'. *Proceedings of the Prehistoric Society* 59, 208–10.

Pollard, J. 1995. Inscribing space: formal deposition at the Later Neolithic monument of Woodhenge, Wiltshire. *Proceedings of the Prehistoric Society* 61, 137–56.

Pollard, J. 1999. 'These places have their moments': thoughts on settlement practices in the British Neolithic. In J. Brück and M. Goodman (eds), *People, place and tradition: new dimensions in settlement archaeology*, 76–93. London: UCL Press.

Pollard, J. in press. Prehistoric settlement and non-settlement in two southern Cambridgeshire river valleys: the lithic dimension and interpretive dilemmas. In P. Bradley (ed.), *Locating and evaluating lithic scatters.* Oxford: Lithic Society Occasional Publication.

Pollard, J. forthcoming. Neolithic occupation practices and social ecologies from Rinyo to Clacton. In A. Ritchie (ed.), *Neolithic Orkney in its European context.*

Polunin, O. 1976. *Trees and bushes of Europe.* London: Oxford University Press.

Powell, A.B., Allen, M.J. and Barnes, I. 1996. *Archaeology in the Avebury area, Wiltshire: recent investigations along the line of the Kennet valley foul sewer pipeline, 1993.* Salisbury: Wessex Archaeology.

Pryor, F 1987. Etton 1986: Neolithic metamorphoses. *Antiquity* 61, 78–80.

Pryor, F. 1988a. Earlier Neolithic organised landscapes and ceremonial in lowland Britain. In J. C. Barrett and I. A. Kinnes (eds), *The archaeology of context in the Neolithic and Bronze Age: recent trends*, 63–72. Sheffield: University of Sheffield, Department of Archaeology and Prehistory.

Pryor, F. 1988b. Etton, near Maxey, Cambridgeshire: a causewayed enclosure on the fen-edge. In C. Burgess, P. Topping, C. Mordant and M. Maddison (eds), *Enclosures and defences in the Neolithic of western Europe*, 107–26. Oxford: British Archaeological Reports.

Pryor, F. 1999. *Etton: Excavations at a Neolithic causewayed enclosure near Maxey, Cambridge, 1982–7.* London: English Heritage.

Rackham, O. 1993. *Trees and woodland in the British landscape* (revised edition). London: Weidenfeld and Nicolson.

Rahtz, P. A. 1962. Neolithic and Beaker sites at Downton, near Salisbury, Wiltshire. *Wiltshire Archaeological and Natural History Magazine* 58, 116–41.

RCHME forthcoming. *The archaeology of a Wessex landscape: south Wiltshire.*

Renfrew, C. 1985. *The archaeology of cult.* London: Thames and Hudson.

Reynolds, P.J. 1979. *Iron Age farm: the Butser experiment.* London: British Museum Publications.

Rice, P. M. 1987. *Pottery analysis.* Chicago: Chicago University Press.

Richards, C. and Thomas, J. 1984. Ritual activity and structured deposition in Later Neolithic Wessex. In R. Bradley and J. Gardiner (eds), *Neolithic studies*, 189–218. Oxford: British Archaeological Reports.

Richards, J. 1990a. *The Stonehenge environs project.* London: English Heritage.

Richards, J. 1990b. Death and the past environment: the results of work on barrows on the Berkshire Downs. *Berkshire Archaeological Journal* 73, 1–42.

Richards, M. 1998. Bone stable isotope analysis: reconstructing the diet of humans. In A. Whittle and M. Wysocki, 'Parc le Breos Cwm transepted long cairn, Gower, West Glamorgan: date, contents, and context'. *Proceedings of the Prehistoric Society* 64, 165–66.

Riley, H. 1990. The scraper assemblages and petit tranchet derivative arrowheads. In J. Richards, *The Stonehenge environs project*, 225–28. London: English Heritage.

Robertson-Mackay, M.E. 1980. A 'head and hooves' burial beneath a round barrow, with other Neolithic and Bronze Age sites, on Hemp Knoll, near Avebury, Wiltshire. *Proceedings of the Prehistoric Society* 46, 123–76.

Robertson-Mackay, R. 1987. The Neolithic causewayed enclosure at Staines, Surrey: excavations 1961–63. *Proceedings of the Prehistoric Society* 53, 23–128.

Robinson, M. 1991. The Neolithic and late Bronze Age insect assemblages. In S. Needham, *Excavation and salvage at Runnymede Bridge, 1978*, 277–326. London: British Museum.

Rodwell, J.S. (ed.) 1991. *British plant communities. Volume 1: woodlands and scrub*. Cambridge: Cambridge University Press.

Roe, F. 1968. Stone mace-heads and the latest Neolithic cultures of the British Isles. In J.M.Coles and D.D.A.Simpson (eds), *Studies in Ancient Europe*, 145–72. Leicester: Leicester University Press.

Roe, F. 1979. Typology of stone implements with shaftholes. In T.H.McK. Clough and W.A.Cummins (eds), *Stone axe studies*, 23–48. London: Council for British Archaeology.

Roscoe, P.B. 1995. Of power and menace: Sepik art as an affecting presence. *Journal of the Royal Anthropological Institute* 1, 1–22.

Rozanski, K., Stichler, W., Godfiantini, R., Scott, E. M., Beukens, R. P., Kroner, B. and van der Plicht, J. 1992. The IAEA ^{14}C intercomparison exercise 1990. *Radiocarbon* 34, 506–19.

Ryder, M.L. 1983. *Sheep and man*. London: Duckworth.

Savage, R.M. 1961. *The ecology and life history of the common frog*. London: Pitman.

Saville, A. 1981. Flint and chert. In R. Mercer, 'Excavations at Carn Brea, Illogan, Cornwall, 1970–1973: a Neolithic fortified complex of the third millennium bc'. *Cornish Archaeology* 20, 101–52.

Saville, A. 1990. *Hazleton North: the excavation of a Neolithic long cairn of the Cotswold-Severn Group*. London: English Heritage.

Schiffer, M. 1976. *Behavioural archaeology*. London: Academic Press.

Sell, P.D. 1994. *Ranunculus ficaria* L. *sensu lato*. *Watsonia* 20, 41–50.

Serjeantson, D. 1991. 'Rid grasse of bones': a taphonomic study of the bones from midden deposits at the Neolithic and Bronze Age site of Runnymede, Surrey, England. *International Journal of Osteoarchaeology* 1, 73–89.

Serjeantson, D. 1996. The animal bones. In S. Needham and T. Spence, *Runnymede Bridge research excavations, Volume 2. Refuse and disposal at Area 16 East, Runnymede*, 194–223. London: British Museum.

Serjeantson, D. forthcoming. Chapter IV. Neolithic and Early Bronze Age. In D. Serjeantson (ed.), *A review of archaeological animal bone studies in southern Britain*.

Serpell, J. 1996. *In the company of animals: a study of human-animal relationships*. Cambridge: Cambridge University Press.

Shanks, M. and Tilley, C. 1982. Ideology, symbolic power and ritual communication: a reinterpretation of Neolithic mortuary practices. In I. Hodder (ed.), *Symbolic and structural archaeology*, 129–54. Cambridge: Cambridge University Press.

Shanks, M. and Tilley, C. 1987. *Re-constructing archaeology: theory and practice* (second edition). London: Routledge.

Sharples, N.M. 1991. *Maiden Castle: excavation and field survey 1985–6*. London: English Heritage.

Sherratt, A.G. 1991. Sacred and profane substances: the ritual use of narcotics in later Neolithic Europe. In P. Garwood, D. Jennings, R. Skeates and J. Toms (eds), *Sacred and profane*, 50–64. Oxford: Oxford University Committee for Archaeology.

Silver, I.A. 1963. The ageing of domestic animals. In D. Brothwell and E.S. Higgs (eds), *Science in archaeology*, 250–68. London: Thames and Hudson.

Smith, A.C. 1885. *Guide to the British and Roman antiquities of the North Wiltshire downs in a hundred square miles round Abury* (second edition). Devizes: Wiltshire Archaeological and Natural History Society.

Smith, I.F. 1956. *The decorative art of Neolithic ceramics in South-eastern England and its relations*. Unpublished PhD thesis, London University.

Smith, I.F. 1958. The 1957–8 excavations at Windmill Hill. *Antiquity* 32, 268–69.

Smith, I.F. 1959. Excavations at Windmill Hill, Avebury, Wilts, 1957–8. *Wiltshire Archaeological and Natural History Magazine* 57, 149–62.

Smith, I.F. 1965a. *Windmill Hill and Avebury: excavations by Alexander Keiller 1925–1939*. Oxford: Clarendon Press.

Smith, I.F. 1965b. Excavation of a bell barrow, Avebury G55, *Wiltshire Archaeological and Natural History Magazine* 60, 24–47.

Smith, I.F. 1971. Causewayed enclosures. In D.D.A. Simpson (ed.), *Economy and settlement in Neolithic and Early Bronze Age Britain and Europe*, 89–112. Leicester: Leicester University Press.

Smith, I.F. 1974. The Neolithic. In C. Renfrew (ed.), *British prehistory: a new outline*, 100–36. London: Duckworth.

Smith, I.F. 1979. The chronology of British stone implements. In T.H.McK. Clough and W.A.Cummins (eds), *Stone axe studies*, 13–22. London: Council for British Archaeology.

Smith, I.F. 1985. The pottery. In S. J. Shennan, F. Healy and I. F. Smith, 'The excavation of a ring-ditch at Tye Field, Lawford, Essex'. *Archaeological Journal* 142, 165–77.

Smith, I.F. 1991. Round barrows Wilsford cum Lake G51–G54: excavations by Ernest Greenfield in 1958. *Wiltshire Archaeological and Natural History Magazine* 84, 11–39.

Smith, I.F. and Simpson, D.D.A. 1964. Excavation of three Roman tombs and a prehistoric pit on Overton Hill. *Wiltshire Archaeological and Natural History Magazine* 59, 68–85.

Smith, I.F. and Simpson, D.D.A. 1966. Excavation of a round barrow on Overton Hill, North Wiltshire. *Proceedings of the Prehistoric Society* 32, 122–55.

Smith, M. 1951. *The British amphibians and reptiles*. London: Collins.

Smith, R. 1984. The ecology of Neolithic farming systems as exemplified by the Avebury region of Wiltshire. *Proceedings of the Prehistoric Society* 50, 99–120.

Smith, R.A. 1910. The development of Neolithic pottery. *Archaeologia* 62, 340–52.

Southwood, T.R.E. 1978. *Ecological methods* (second edition). London: Chapman and Hall.

Sparks, B.W. 1965. Mollusca. In G. Connah, 'Excavations at Knap Hill, Alton Priors, 1961'. *Wiltshire Archaeological and Natural History Magazine* 60, 19–20.

Speth, J.D. 1983. *Bison kills and bone counts*. London and Chicago: Chicago University Press.

Stace, C. 1991. *New flora of the British Isles*. Cambridge: Cambridge University Press.

Stace, C. 1997. *New flora of the British Isles* (second edition). Cambridge: Cambridge University Press.

Stallibrass, S. 1990. Canid damage to animal bones: two current lines of research. In D. Robinson (ed.), *Experimentation and reconstruction in environmental archaeology*, 151–65. Oxford: Oxbow.

Startin, W. and Bradley, R. 1981. Some notes on work organisation and society in prehistoric Wessex. In C. Ruggles and A. Whittle (eds), *Astronomy and society in Britain during the period 4000–1500 BC*, 289–96. Oxford: British Archaeological Reports.

Sterner, J. 1989. Who is signalling whom ? Ceramic style, ethnicity and taphonomy among the Sirak Bulahay. *Antiquity* 63, 451–59.

Stone, J.F.S. 1931. A settlement site of the beaker period on Easton Down. *Wiltshire Archaeological and Natural History Magazine* 45, 366–72.

Stone, J.F.S. 1933. Excavations at Easton Down, Winterslow. *Wiltshire Archaeological and Natural History Magazine* 46, 225–42.

Stone, J.F.S. 1934. Three Peterborough Ware dwelling pits and a doubly-stockaded EIA ditch at Winterbourne Dauntsey. *Wiltshire Archaeological and Natural History Magazine* 46, 445–53.

Stone, J.F.S. 1935. Excavations at Easton Down, Winterslow, 1933–4. *Wiltshire Archaeological and Natural History Magazine* 47, 68–80.

Stone, J.F.S. 1938. An Early Bronze Age grave in the Fargo Plantation, near Stonehenge. *Wiltshire Archaeological and Natural History Magazine* 48, 357–70.

Stone, J.F.S. and Wallis, F.W. 1951. Third report of the Sub-Committee of the South-Western group of Museums and Art Galleries on the petrological identification of stone implements. *Proceedings of the Prehistoric Society* 17, 99–158.

Strathern, M. 1988. *The gender of the gift*. Berkeley: University of California Press.

Stuiver, M. 1983. International agreements and the use of the new oxalic standard. *Radiocarbon* 25, 793–95.

Stuiver, M. and Pearson, G.W. 1986. High-precision calibration of the radiocarbon time scale, AD 1950–500 BC. *Radiocarbon* 28, 805–38.

Stuiver, M. and Polach, H.A. 1977. Discussion: reporting of ^{14}C data. *Radiocarbon* 19, 355–63.

Stukeley, W. 1743. *Abury, a temple of the British Druids*. London.

Swanton, G.R. 1987. The Owen Meyrick collection. *Wiltshire Archaeological and Natural History Magazine* 81, 7–18.

Taçon, P.S. 1991. The power of stone: symbolic aspects of stone use and tool development in western Arnhem Land, Australia. *Antiquity* 65, 192–207.

Teicherdt, M. 1975. Osteometrische Untersuchungen zur Berechnung der Widerristhöhe bei Schafen. In A. Clason (ed.), *Archaeozoological studies*, 51–69. Amsterdam: Elsevier.

Teschler-Nicola, M. 1998. Anthropologische Spurensicherung – Die traumatischen und postmortalen Veränderungen an den linearbandkeramischen Skelettresten von Asparn/Schletz. In *Rätsel um Gewalt und Tod vor 7,000 Jahren: eine Spurensicherung*, 47–64. Asparn a.d.Zaya: Museum für Urgeschichte.

Thomas, J. 1984. A tale of two polities. In R. Bradley and J. Gardiner (eds), *Neolithic studies*, 161–76. Oxford: British Archaeological Reports.

Thomas, J. 1990. Silent running: the evils of environmental archaeology. *Scottish Archaeological Review* 7, 2–7.

Thomas, J. 1991. *Rethinking the Neolithic*. Cambridge: Cambridge University Press.

Thomas, J. 1993. Discourse, totalisation and the Neolithic. In C. Tilley (ed.), *Interpretative archaeology*, 357–94. Oxford: Berg.

Thomas, J. 1996a. The cultural context of the first use of domesticates in central and north-west Europe. In D.R. Harris (ed.), *The origins and spread of agriculture and pastoralism in Eurasia*, 310–22. London: University College, London.

Thomas, J. 1996b. *Time, culture and identity*. London: Routledge.

Thomas, J. and Whittle, A. 1986. Anatomy of a tomb: West Kennet revisited. *Oxford Journal of Archaeology* 5, 129–56.

Thomas, N. 1956. A Neolithic pit on Waden Hill. *Wiltshire Archaeological Magazine* 56, 167–71.

Thomas, N. 1968. Note on the Carrickinab awl. In A.E.P. Collins and E.E. Evans, 'A cist burial at Carrickinab, Co. Down', *Ulster Journal of Archaeology* 31, 23–24.

Thorpe, I.J. 1984. Ritual, power and ideology: a reconstruction of Earlier Neolithic rituals in Wessex. In R. Bradley and J. Gardiner (eds), *Neolithic studies*, 41–60. Oxford: British Archaeological Reports.

Tilley, C. 1989. Interpreting material culture. In I. Hodder (ed.), *The meaning of things*, 185–94. London: Unwin Hyman.

Tilley, C. 1994. *A phenomenology of landscape*. Oxford: Berg.

Tilley, C. 1996. *An ethnography of the Neolithic*. Cambridge: Cambridge University Press.

Tilley, C. 1999. *Metaphor and material culture*. Oxford: Blackwell.

Tomalin, D. J. 1983. *British Biconical Urns: their character and chronology and their relationship with indigenous Early Bronze Age ceramics*. Unpublished PhD thesis, University of Southampton.

Tomalin, D. J. 1988. Armorican vases à anses and their occurrence in southern Britain. *Proceedings of the Prehistoric Society* 54, 203–21.

Tomalin, D. 1992. The Deverel-Rimbury and Late Biconical Urn domestic ceramic assemblage from Bishop Canning Down. In C. Gingell, *The Marlborough Downs: a Later Bronze Age landscape and its origins*, 61–71. Devizes: Wiltshire Archaeological and Natural History Society.

Tooley, M.J., Rackham, D.J. and Simmons. 1982. A red deer (*Cervus elaphus* L.) skeleton from Seamer Carrs, Cleveland, England: provenance of the skeleton and palaeoecology of the site. *Journal of Archaeological Science* 9, 365–76.

Turner, V. 1969. *The ritual process*. Harmondsworth: Penguin.

Ucko, P.J., Hunter, M., Clark, A.J. and David, A. 1991. *Avebury reconsidered: from the 1660s to the 1990s*. London: Unwin Hyman.

Uerpmann, H-P. 1979. *Probleme der Neolithisierung des Mittelmeeraums*. Wiesbaden: Reichert.

van Beck, W.E.A. and Banga, P.M. 1992. The Dogon and their trees. In E. Croll and D. Parkin (eds), *Bush base: forest farm. Culture, environment and development*, 57–75. London: Routledge.

van Gennep, A. 1960. *The rites of passage*. London: Routledge and Kegan Paul.

van Zeist, W. 1984. Lists of names of wild and cultivated cereals. *Bulletin on Sumerian Agriculture* 1, 8–15.

Vatcher, F. de M. 1963. The excavation of the Roman earthwork at Winterslow, Wiltshire. *Antiquaries Journal* 42, 197–213.

Vigne, J-D. and Marinval-Vigne, M-C. 1983. Methode pour la mise en evidence de la consommation du petit gibier. In J. Clutton-Brock and C. Grigson (eds) *Animals and archaeology: 1. Hunters and their prey*, 239–42. Oxford: British Archaeological Reports.

Wahl, J. and König, G. 1987. Anthropologisch-traumatische Untersuchung der menschlichen Skelettreste aus dem bandkeramischen Massengrab bei Talheim, Kreis Heilbronn. *Fundberichte Baden-Württemberg* 12, 65–186.

Wainwright, G. J. 1971. The excavation of a Late Neolithic enclosure at Marden, Wiltshire. *Antiquaries Journal* 51, 197–215.

Wainwright, G. J. 1979. *Mount Pleasant, Dorset: excavations 1970–1971*. London: Society of Antiquaries.

Wainwright, G. J. and Longworth, I.H. 1971. *Durrington Walls: excavations 1966–1968*. London: Society of Antiquaries.

WANHM 1964. Excavation and fieldwork in Wiltshire 1963. *Wiltshire Archaeological and Natural History Magazine* 59, 184–90.

WANHM 1965. Excavation and fieldwork in Wiltshire 1964. *Wiltshire Archaeological and Natural History Magazine* 60, 132–39.

Watson, D.M.S. 1931. The animal bones from Skara Brae. In V.G. Childe, *Skara Brae: a Pictish village in Orkney*, 198–204. London: Kegan Paul, Trench and Tubner.

Watson, J.P.N. 1979. The estimation of the relative frequencies of mammalian species: Khirokitia 1972. *Journal of Archaeological Science* 6, 127–37.

Weiner, J. 1996. Myth and mythology. In A. Barnard and J. Spencer (eds), *Encyclopaedia of social and cultural anthropology*, 386–89. London: Routledge.

Whittle, A. 1977. *The Earlier Neolithic of southern England and its continental background*. Oxford: British Archaeological Reports.

Whittle, A. 1990. A model for the Mesolithic-Neolithic transition in the upper Kennet valley, north Wiltshire. *Proceedings of the Prehistoric Society* 56, 101–10.

Whittle, A. 1991. Wayland's Smithy, Oxfordshire: excavations at the Neolithic tomb in 1962–3 by R.J.C Atkinson and S. Piggott. *Proceedings of the Prehistoric Society* 57(2), 61–101.

Whittle, A. 1993. The Neolithic of the Avebury area: sequence, environment, settlement and monuments. *Oxford Journal of Archaeology* 12, 29–53.

Whittle, A. 1994. Excavations at Millbarrow chambered tomb, Winterbourne Monkton, north Wiltshire. *Wiltshire Archaeological and Natural History Magazine* 87, 1–53.

Whittle, A. 1996. *Europe in the Neolithic: the creation of new worlds*. Cambridge: Cambridge University Press.

Whittle, A. 1997a. *Sacred mound, holy rings. Silbury Hill and the West Kennet palisade enclosures: a Later Neolithic complex in north Wiltshire*. Oxford: Oxbow.

Whittle, A. 1997b. Moving on and moving around: Neolithic settlement mobility. In P. Topping (ed.), *Neolithic landscapes*, 15–22. Oxford: Oxbow.

Whittle, A., Davies, J., Dennis, I., Fairbairn, A. and Hamilton, M. A. forthcoming. Neolithic activity and occupation outside Windmill Hill causewayed enclosure, Wiltshire: survey and excavation 1993. *Wiltshire Archaeological and Natural History Magazine*.

Whittle, A., Rouse, A.J. and Evans, J. G. 1993. A Neolithic downland monument in its environment: excavations at the Easton Down long barrow, Bishops Cannings, north Wiltshire. *Proceedings of the Prehistoric Society* 59, 197–239.

Whittle, A. and Pollard, J. 1998. Windmill Hill causewayed enclosure: the harmony of symbols. In M. Edmonds and C. Richards (eds), *Understanding the Neolithic of northwestern Europe*, 231–47. Glasgow: Cruithne Press.

Whittle, A. and Wysocki, M. 1998. Parc le Breos Cwm transepted long cairn, Gower, West Glamorgan: date, contents, and context. *Proceedings of the Prehistoric Society* 64, 139–82.

Wijngaarden-Bakker, L.H. van. 1974. The animal remains from the Beaker settlement at Newgrange, Co. Meath: first report. *Proceedings of the Royal Irish Academy* 74, section C, 313–83.

Wijngaarden-Bakker, L.H. van. 1986. The animal remains from the Beaker settlement at Newgrange, Co. Meath: final report. *Proceedings of the Royal Irish Academy* 86, section C, 18–111.

Windl, H. 1996. Archäologie einer Katastrophe und deren Vorgeschichte. In *Rätsel um Gewalt und Tod vor 7,000 Jahren: eine Spurensicherung*, 7–29. Asparn a.d.Zaya: Museum für Urgeschichte.

Woodward, A.B. and Woodward, P.J. 1996. The topography of some barrow cemeteries in Bronze Age Wessex. *Proceedings of the Prehistoric Society* 62, 275–91.

Zienkiewicz, L. 1996. *Early Neolithic pottery from Windmill Hill causewayed enclosure and the Avebury area: style, sequence, context and deposition*. Unpublished PhD thesis, University of Wales Cardiff.